CW00765691

PUBLISHER'S COMMENTARY

Copyright and 'fair use'

(Continued from rear cover)

**Dave McClure
(Liverpool 1962)**

When I first reviewed the author's work with the consideration of publishing it, I was struck by the fact that it was a historically significant and extremely important document. However, I was also concerned. The reason for my concern was that I suspected it possibly included 'copyrighted' material and/or images.

My concern lay with the sources that had provided the material. Almost all of it came from the personal memorabilia collections and scrapbooks of the various groups and individuals that were featured in the book. Unfortunately, like most family photo albums, there was little or no data identifying who, what, when and where the material originated from. Consequently, I quickly arrived at the conclusion that researching ownership of 500 plus images and random 'scrapbook clippings' so that the appropriate credits could be established, would be a huge and probably impossible task.

I also concluded that even if we attempted to validate the owners, it would take more than a lifetime of digging and communicating, as most of the material was 45 years old (or older) and many of the images were obviously snapshots taken by friends, family, 'roadies' or other non-professionals. Some were publicity photos obviously taken by professional photographers, some of whom were no longer in business and may have been commissioned, and paid for their services, by the groups. The real problem arose with the remaining images, how could we ever track down the owners of those images and, the answer was obvious, we likely could not.

Consequently, we are aware that this publication may unknowingly contain some material or images that may be subject to copyright. While every effort has been made to trace copyright holders of the material and images used in this book, we apologize for any omissions of the appropriate accreditation. However, as this is a digital publication, we can either apply the appropriate credit or withdraw the item immediately, upon notification of such. Even though the material or image may be subject to copyright, their use is very likely covered under section 107 of the US Copyright Act under the 'fair use' doctrine which allows limited use of copyrighted material without requiring permission from the rights holders as long as their inclusion adds significance and/or the material is the object of discussion within the story.

Finally, we ask that any copyright holders be commiserate to the intention of this book. It is meant to be a tribute to the individuals and the groups who contributed to what is possibly the most significant revolution in musical history in the 20th century and they deserve to have their story told. Therefore, we humbly request your unconditional approval for the unintentional use of any copyrighted material contained herein.

Dave McClure (info@VelocePress.com)

MUSICIAN'S FOREWORD

It was at a 'Beatles Convention' held in the Adelphi Hotel, Liverpool that Manfred fittingly asked me to write a foreword for his book. As we sat in the restaurant and I leafed through the manuscript, even I, a hardened Merseybeat veteran, was surprised at the details and the facts regarding many of the groups listed within. Some of the more obscure groups I had forgotten about and I found many of the rare photographs fascinating. I know Manfred has taken many years to compile, research and obtain the many photos used in this book, a feat of endurance and tenacity. The 1960's era is now many years past, memories fade, faces, facts and photographs are lost and dissipated with the passing of time, and I feel that this book will be the last of its kind, making it a permanent and fitting record and tribute to all the unknown and famous groups of a golden age, never to be forgotten.

Rock on always,

Johnny Guitar

(Rory Storm & the Hurricanes)

Johnny 'Guitar' Byrne sadly died on 18th August 1999.

A great guy and a real gentlemen who is much missed by everyone.

MANFRED KUHLMANN - THE LIVERPOOL- BIELEFELD CONNECTION

Manfred Kuhlmann´s hometown of Bielefeld sported a Star-Club subsidiary where all the Hamburg and Liverpool stars loved to play. Roy Orbison found his wife here. Manfred was born in the suburb of Schildesche on July 2nd 1952, and got the Beat bug forever, as he recalls vividly: "As a 13-year-old, I managed to sneak into the local Star-Club. The first act I saw there was Earl Royce & The Olympics". Other venues where young Kuhlman used to hang out were the 'Eisenhuette', and from 1967 onwards the 'Jaguar Club' in nearby Herford, where he was especially impressed by the Small Faces.

But for Manfred, the real joy still lay in the club´s Liverpool sounds – his new champions were The Searchers! Other Merseybeat favourites became Ian & the Zodiacs, the Remo Four and Denny Seyton & the Sabres. That same year, Kuhlmann won a Deejay competition, having become a regular disc jockey at the communication centre 'HOT' in Bielefeld. Later, he deejayed in various renowned clubs in his area. So how did the beat fan and record spinner become a legendary promoter?

In 1974, Manfred drove a truck when he saw a Searcher's poster on a roadside billboard – Mike Pender & Co. had been booked into the 'Riverside-Club' in Detmold. He went – and was hooked: The Searchers sounded better than on record! Soon, he negotiated a reasonable fee, and persuaded fans to sign IOU's for him – in case of an attendance disaster. No sweat: The Searchers rocked Bielefeld in September 1975, the fans raised the roof. Sold out – punters were turned away! The 'HOT' was to see more great concerts featuring Gerry & the Pacemakers, Ian & the Zodiacs, Billy J. Kramer & The Dakotas, The Merseybeats, The Undertakers as well as The Swinging Blue Jeans and the Pete Best Band. Kuhlmann also established a long tradition of 'Oldie Nights', and for those he managed to hire the famous concert venue Oetkerhalle. Here, The Tremeloes, Dave Dee Dozy Beaky Mick & Tich, The Troggs and The Hollies played to packed houses. So did US stars he brought over: Del Shannon, Percy Sledge, a moody but magnificent Wilson Pickett, the Mamas & Papas and Johnny & The Hurricanes.

Still, the challenge for Manfred lay in conquering Liverpool. Lee Curtis, who had found his way from Hamburg down to Bielefeld, invited our boy over: "If you´re ever round Liverpool way Manfred, you can kip at my brother´s!" At Easter 1987 Kuhlmann boarded a Boeing and stayed at Joe Flammery´s, starting a series of visits to the Scouse scene. Dreams came true – like meeting the Beatles motivator Bob Wooler, spotting an ad for Karl Terry & The Cruisers in the 'Liverpool Echo', or visiting the Old Cavern club. Karl Terry & The Cruisers hit a spot in Manfred´s beat sensitivity and were often invited to play Germany, including Bielefeld, and in 1994 he produced their only long player in Bielefeld. By then, Manfred had his own label, Merseyside Records, including a 'Beat Revival' with 11 local bands.

In 1990, after 15 years of managing bands, booking international stars, working as Radio-DJ, running his record label, and juggling turntables, Manfred Kuhlmann decided to put a lid on it all. A farewell gig for Merseyside Concerts, apart from local musos Barry & The Back Beats and the Thunderbirds, also starred Karl Terry & The Cruisers, The Undertakers and Beryl Marsden. But requests never stopped – and so for five more years Manfred got bands to Germany two or three times per season.

In 1995, he finally got hitched – marrying his beloved Chérie, but still took up old habits: managing the Rock 'n´ Roll matadors, The Rock-Ateers, starting the 'Beat City' movement for more concerts by the big names in Beat, and re-establishing the 'Liverpool Club' in Buende, also founding today's very successful 'Beat Club´66' in 2004.

Manfred Kuhlmann remains a local treasure, and of course he is the symbol of the Liverpool-Bielefeld connection. The book you are holding in your hands now? It´s the Liverpool Bible!

Uli Twelker

(Good Times magazine)

AUTHOR'S FOREWORD

**Manfred Kuhlmann and
"The Sound With The Pound"**

This book is the revised edition of my first book, "The Sound With The Pound", which is not available anymore.

I have to admit that I'm really proud of it, as I never expected it to generate such interest.

You may wonder why the first edition has been revised so soon, only two years after its publication.

The answer is very simple: Once "The Sound With The Pound" was on the market as the first real anthology of Merseybeat groups, many people contacted me to correct small errors or to provide me with a lot of additional information about their groups.

Sometimes it was only some small fact which led to a new connection and to a whole story appearing in a different light. I had to research some of the original stories using only old newspaper articles and various other bits and pieces of information, as I was unable to contact any of the members directly. The new contacts resulting from the publication of the original edition gave me a lot of very interesting details I hadn't known before.

But the new facts that came to light were not always positive and so I had to remove two stories from this edition of this book (the Blue Chips and the Mersey Four) as I had originally been supplied with incorrect information about their record releases.

I am delighted for all the groups featured here as they are finally getting what they deserve for pioneering the European Rock scene and for its immense musical influence around the globe: Worldwide recognition!

As for me, neither my motive nor my attitude has changed since I wrote the original book and I consider it best to leave my original foreword as it was:

"Well, it's done. After more than ten years I have finished a book which has been overdue for at least the same length of time. You may ask why I've written a book about a scene and bands which are almost forgotten today, but the question really answers itself. It shouldn't happen that the pioneering groups that opened the doors for pop music in Europe in the early Sixties are one day forgotten. The bands mentioned in this book were the basis on which groups like the 'Beatles', the 'Searchers' or 'Gerry & the Pacemakers' built their success, and which, in the end, led to the worldwide breakthrough of the Merseybeat, later simply called Beat music.

That's reason enough to keep their history alive in words and to pay them long overdue attention, even 50 years and more after it all started in Liverpool on the River Mersey. It's very difficult to find good information about this interesting and very important Merseybeat scene, although there are some books which are really good supplements to this one, namely, Let's Go Down The Cavern and Twist and Shout, both written by popular Liverpool DJ Spencer Leigh, as well as The Best Of Cellars by Phil Thompson, a book that tells the history of the Cavern.

This book is the first extensive biography of the Merseyside music scene. In addition to the bands that achieved worldwide stardom, it also includes those groups that were only locally or nationally successful.

It is certainly somewhat unfair that not every group from this era is named. They were all important in some way and they all had a role to play, but because there were so many it is simply impossible to feature them all. To balance this unfairness a bit, I have compiled some line-up and band name lists that I came across while researching the featured individual band stories, sometimes including short versions of the stories of other groups they were connected with. In spite of the fact that the material is more than interesting, this biography required an awful lot of work and the research brought me my first grey hair! I have only written about Liverpool groups who released a record, made test recordings or demos (on acetate) which might be released one day, as well as the ones that had huge importance in the development of the Merseybeat. The complete discographies up to 1970 are featured for all these group stories. These are based on the British market and are completed with different foreign releases.

While I was searching for information, I met some musicians of that era who expected me to change or manipulate history with this book. I did not want to do this because reality is not changeable by including a lot of mistakes and lies. The purpose of this book is to present history as it really was and so I researched as exactly as possible, just to take the bands out of the anonymity of Merseybeat and to take the musicians out of the anonymity of the band names. This biography will probably contain some mistakes, but after all, I am convinced that one cannot write such a book without accepting that risk.

I have written this book for all the people who are interested in the material as well as for all the musicians who were part of that unique era. Many of them gave me great help in completing the project. I want to specifically name Bob Wooler, the former disc jockey, compere and programme manager of the famous Cavern Club, whose importance on the scene was always underrated, even if he was sometimes accurately named as Mr. Merseybeat, the Baron of Beat or Mr. Big Beat. There are lots of groups that owe their careers to him and I personally owe him a lot more than mere thanks for all the information, interesting leads and contacts with lots of people who were involved in the scene. Words cannot describe his enormous help and kindness.

Bob Wooler sadly died in 2002, before he could finish the promised foreword to my book, which he often referred to as the 'Merseybeat Bible' in various letters to me. Because of his hugely important role in developing the Liverpool Beat scene, and in as much as one person, he was as important as lots of the groups featured here, he should never be forgotten and that is why this book is dedicated to him whom I proudly called my friend."

Manfred Kuhlmann

Bielefeld/Schildesche

Germany, Autumn 2007

(updated in Autumn 2011)

ACKNOWLEDGEMENTS

Firstly I would like to thank my wife, **Nelly**, who everyone knows as **Chérie**, for her understanding and support while I was working on this book. Not forgetting her patience in accepting the enormous telephone bills and the travel costs for my numerous trips to Liverpool.

Many thanks also to my friends **Armin Grants, Karl-Heinz 'Charly' Decker, Alfred Hebing, Holger Roggemann, Gerry Nolan, Dave Forshaw, Karl Terry, John Wishart, Alan Stratton, Brian Jones, Phil Eaves** from Preston, **Dave Lodge** and **Gina Hazlehurst** for their great help. Without them the realisation of this book would not have been possible.

Also very special thanks to all the musicians who helped me with information about their groups and gave me photographs that had never been seen before. I simply cannot name them all as there were hundreds I have spoken to over the years, but I can confirm that the contact and time I spent with them was a great pleasure for me.

Not forgetting my editor, **Dave McClure**, for being so kind, interested, patient and helpful in every respect. I was always carried away by his enthusiasm . . .

PUBLISHER'S ACKNOWLEDGEMENT

In my 'Publisher's Commentary' introduction to this book, I expressed considerable concern regarding the possibility of unknowingly including copyrighted images in this publication.

Many of the images supplied by the various groups had no identification attributed to them but it was fairly obvious that a number of them came from the pages of the **'Mersey Beat'** newspaper. This resulted in communications with **Bill Harry** (creator and owner of **'Mersey Beat'**) regarding the identification of any **'Mersey Beat'** copyright images and a willingness on Manfred's part to exclude them from the book. However, Bill was gracious enough to grant permission for the use of those images and I cannot thank him enough for his cooperation. Therefore, as you page through this book don't forget to thank another pioneer of the 'Mersey Sound" as, without **Bill Harry** and **'Mersey Beat',** many of these images would have never existed.

Thank you Bill ~ **Dave McClure & Manfred Kuhlmann**

THE SOUND WITH THE POUND

When a new sound was born at the beginning of the Sixties in dozens of cellars in Liverpool, no one could foresee that this movement would cause a musical revolution which has not been equalled since the birth of Rock 'n' Roll. It is no accident that the harbour and industrial city of Liverpool, at the mouth of the River Mersey on the Irish Sea, was the starting point of a musical style known first as Merseybeat and later as Beat, which was the most significant development in the history of European pop music. **Mike Evans**, born Liverpudlian and sax player with the **Clayton Squares** wrote about this in the foreword to the book 'Beat in Liverpool' (**Jürgen Seuss**, 1965):

"The city in its character has lots in common with the New Orleans of the turn of the century. The prosperity of the harbour, grown with the profit of cotton and slavery in the cosmopolitan tradition for the life in Liverpool has the same dominating role as at that time for the birthplace of Jazz."

It is said that the sailors who brought the first American Rock 'n' Roll and Rhythm & Blues records into the city were the originators of this musical revolution but that seems to be the romantic version. Most probably it was the American servicemen serving at the huge American Air Force base in Burtonwood that brought Rock 'n' Roll into Liverpool. Whichever it was, within months an idea had developed into a boom which was to influence the youth around the world.

Liverpool Skiffle groups, which had existed in huge numbers at the end of the Fifties, took on the American sound and gave it their own individual touch. Most of these groups changed their names and started to play this kind of music.

THE IRON DOOR CLUB

THURSDAY, April 23rd
THE REV. BLACK & THE ROCKING VICARS
SONNY WEBB & THE CASCADES

FRIDAY, April 24th
TONY D & THE SHAKEOUTS
THE VALKYRIES
LEE PAUL & THE BOYS

SATURDAY, April 25th
THE BLACKWELLS
THE PILGRIMS
THE CYMERONS

SUNDAY, April 26th
THE EXCHECKERS
THE PATHFINDERS
THE GRIMBLES

TUESDAY, April 28th
MIKE CADILLAC & THE PLAYBOYS
THE CASCADES

So the **Mars Bars** became **Gerry & the Pacemakers**, the **Raving Texans** evolved into **Rory Storm & the Hurricanes**, the **Quarrymen** initially changed their name to the **Silver Beatles** and then shortened it to the **Beatles**, the **Bluegenes** became the **Swinging Blue Jeans**, and so on and so on.

New clubs called 'Jive Halls' opened everywhere, or changed their programme from Jazz, Swing or Skiffle to Rock 'n' Roll and Beat, where these groups performed for very little money. Their fee for one evening at that time was around three to four English pounds.

The best known clubs in Liverpool were the Cavern, the Iron Door, the Blue Angel, the Casbah, the Peppermint Lounge, the Sink, the Downbeat, the Grafton Ballroom and Hope Hall. Outside the city centre there were ballrooms, church rooms and public halls such as the Litherland Town Hall, the Aintree Institute, the Orrell Park Ballroom, the Wilson Hall in Garston, the Majestic Ballroom in Birkenhead, the Tower Ballroom in New Brighton or the Jive Hive in Crosby.

— MERSEYSCENE PROMOTIONS —
present
'21' BEAT SPECTACULAR
at the GRAFTON BALLROOM
West Derby Road
on FRIDAY 13th. MAY, 1966

21 FANTASTIC GROUPS
The Dennisons, Hideaways, Dark Ages, Fix, Aztecs, Georgies Germs, Kop, Solomons Mines, Jigsaw, Calderstones, Runaways, Heatwave, Dions, Keez, Kringin Nabs, Proffits, Lonely, Crescendos, Roadrunners Do-Does, Outrage

Star Comperes—BILLY BUTTLER plus SACREMENTO FRED
DANCING IN THE GOLDEN CAGES
The Go! Go! Kittens

7. p.m. to 12. 30 a.m.   Admission 6/-   LICENCED BARS

Ticket for the Grafton

THE CAVERN

THE BIG TUESDAY SHOW, 30th JUNE
THE REDCAPS
THE ROAD RUNNERS
THE MARKFOUR
THE PILGRIMS
THE VIKINGS

Members: 3/-   Visitors: 4/-   7.30 p.m. start

MATHEW ST., LIVERPOOL

The Kirkbys at The Cavern

Every day new, talented and hopeful groups were formed and at the climax of Merseybeat. There must have been somewhere between 700 to 800 groups in and around Liverpool. There was **King Size Taylor & the Dominoes**, who claimed to have been the first Liverpool Rock 'n' Roll band, and **Cass & the Cassanovas**, who always quarrelled with them for that title. Or were, in the end, the **Black Cats** the first, or even **Gus & the Thundercaps**?

Above left:

    The Original Dominoes

Above right:

    Cass & The Cassanovas

Lower right:

    Gus Travis & The Thundercaps

In addition, there were **Rory Storm & the Hurricanes**, without doubt one of the local heroes in Liverpool; the **Chants**, the first Liverpool vocal group consisting entirely of coloured singers; **Derry & the Seniors**, the first Liverpool group that played in Germany (Kaiserkeller, Hamburg) and also the first Liverpool group that had a record released - under the name **Howie Casey & the Seniors**.

The Chants at The Cavern

Bob Evans & the Five Shillings, who a little later evolved into the legendary **Undertakers**; The **Bobby Bell Rockers** that became **Steve Bennett & the Syndicate**, the first Liverpool band to go to London in search of national stardom; **Johnny Rocco & the Jets**, **Cliff Roberts' Rockers**, **Karl Terry & the Cruisers** and **Johnny Tempest & the Tornadoes**, who all, without exception, played only Rock 'n' Roll.

Then there was **Tommy & the Metronomes**, the **Strangers**, the **Travellers**, **Danny & the Asteroids**, **Mark Peters & the Cyclones**, **Gene Day & the Jango-Beats**, **Carl Vincent & the Counts**, **Vince & the Volcanoes**, **Dee Young & the Pontiacs**, **Duke Duval's Rockers**, **Vinny & the Dukes**, **Rikki & the Red Streaks** and **Ogi & the Flintstones**, just to name a few of the typical pioneering groups.

Johnny Tempest & The Tornadoes

Rikki & The Red Streaks

Dee Young & The Pontiacs

Most of them were already popular and successful in Liverpool, while others came up with the **Beatles**, but not because of them.

It should be pointed out that the **Beatles** were a product of the Merseybeat and not the other way round!

The **Beatles** recorded for the first time in their own right in October 1962, if the German recordings with **Tony Sheridan** were not considered. "Love Me Do" climbed up the charts to No. 17 in December of the same year. In March 1963, **Gerry & the Pacemakers** had the first chart-topper to come out of Liverpool with "How Do You Do It", and from that moment on the international Merseybeat breakthrough was huge and unstoppable.

The next No. 1 hit came from the **Beatles** with their third release "From Me To You", followed by the **Searchers** with "Sweets For My Sweet", **Billy J. Kramer & the Dakotas** with "Bad To Me" (all No. 1 hits), the **Fourmost** with "Hello Little Girl" (No. 9), the **Swinging Blue Jeans** with "Hippy Hippy Shake" (No. 2), the **Merseybeats** with "I think Of You" (No. 5), **Cilla Black** with "Anyone Who Had A Heart" (No. 1), and so on. In the meantime, the **Searchers**, **Gerry & the Pacemakers** and of course the **Beatles** had more hits.

The Searchers

As a result of this success, promoters from all over the world became interested in booking groups from Liverpool, just the mention of 'from Liverpool' was a mark of quality at that time. So the problem arose that Liverpool promoters were suddenly faced with a shortfall of established local groups for their events, because these groups were being booked nationally or even internationally.

This of course was the big chance for new and lesser known Liverpool groups to step into the spotlight and also for groups from other cities such as Manchester (**Pete MacLaine & the Dakotas**, **Wayne Fontana & the Jets** and **Don Curtis & the Coasters**), Birmingham (**Gerry Levene & the Avengers**, the **Brumbeats** and the **Fortunes**), Stoke (the **Marauders**) or cities in the vicinity of Liverpool, including Southport, Chester, Crewe, Widnes, St. Helens, Wigan and Preston.

Most of them became a steady part of Liverpool's Merseybeat scene and that is why they are also included in this book - with the exception of the groups from Manchester and Birmingham, as in these cities individual and interesting band-scenes had grown.

Early chart success was brought to Liverpool by **Russ Hamilton** ("Rainbow" - 1957), the Rock 'n' Roll singer **Michael Cox** ("Angela Jones" - 1960) and the singer **Chris Morris** from the Birkenhead group the **Firecrests** who, under the name of **Lance Fortune**, had a top 10 hit with "Be Mine" in 1960 and who later continued to sing with **Dave Lee & the Staggerlees**.

Michael Cox

Lance Fortune at The Cavern

Johnny Gentle & George Harrison

Johnny Gentle was another Liverpool singer from the early days who should be mentioned here. He is mainly known for the fact that he was backed by the **Beatles** on certain dates, although he recorded four singles and an EP in his own right for Philips in 1959 and 1960. His final single "My Tears Will Turn To Laughter" was released under the name of **Darren Young** on Parlophone in 1963.

Undoubtedly the most important Liverpool artist of the early days was **Ronald Wycherley,** who achieved international fame under the name of **Billy Fury**. As he was part of the British Rock 'n' Roll scene (his individual story is not related in this book) he should be considered here along with some information about his impressive career. In his successful years, **Billy Fury** was backed by the **Four Kestrels**, the **Blue Flames**, the **Tornadoes** and by the **Gamblers** from Newcastle (who also recorded in their own right) but surprisingly never by a Liverpool group.

Billy Fury

Billy Fury was one of the outstanding personalities in British show business . It is not only because he had a string of hits, including "Maybe Tomorrow", "Jealousy" and "Halfway To Paradise" among others, that he is still remembered and admired in England these days, especially in his hometown of Liverpool; he was also a very nice and likeable guy who did not change after becoming successful. His records mostly were Rock ballads in the American High-school style.

From February 1959 until February 1983 his records were in the charts for a total of 281 weeks, and one must take into account that he took a recording break from September 1966 until September 1982. He never had a real chart topper, but his best placement was at No. 2 with "Jealousy" in 1961. Up to August 1966 he had 26 Top-40 hits, including 11 Top-10 hits. This is a record of success which deserves deep respect and which made him the most successful Decca artist of all time.

He was the real pioneer of Liverpool's successful and popular music scene, but sadly died much too young on 28th January 1983, having been ill for many years with a hole in his heart.

THE THREE BELLS

Others, who were not part of the Merseybeat revolution but part of Liverpool's more than interesting recording scene of the Sixties are the all girl groups **Vernon's Girls** ("Lover Please"), the **Three Bells** (Carol, Sue and Jean Bell – "Softly In The Night"), who also appeared at the Star-Club in Hamburg and later became the **Satin Bells**, the **Ladybirds** ("I Wanna Fly"), the **Bowbells** (with **Nola York** – "Not To Be Taken") and the **Breakaways** ("He's A Rebel"), who also sang backing vocals for other artists' records. The **Spinners** ("Dirty Old Town"), who for a long time were England's most popular folk group, as well as the country bands **Blue Mountain Boys** ("Drop Me Gently"), who were an offshoot of the very popular **Hank Walters & the Dusty Road Ramblers**, who also cut a nice album in the early Seventies on the 'Liverpool Sound' label, **Phil Brady & the Ranchers** (later also **Phil Brady & the Ranch Set**), who as the **Ranchers** released their first single on the newly founded 'Cavern Sound' label ("An American Sailor At The Cavern"), the **Kentuckians** ("Pop a Top"),

Hank Walters

who also recorded an album, the **Foggy Mountain Ramblers** ("Lovin' Lady's Man") and of course the legendary **Hillsiders**, who are featured in this book in the continuation of the story of **Sonny Webb & the Cascades**.

FAB! FAB! FAB!

NEW YEAR'S EVE BEAT CRUISE

ABOARD THE 'ROYAL IRIS'

DOWN THE MERSEY

8-30 p.m. from Liverpool Landing Stage
(Coaches leave from Manchester at 7 p.m.)

Non-stop dancing until 2-30 p.m. to

The Black Velvets

THE INFORMERS and

THREE DOTS AND A DASH others

REFRESHMENTS ● LICENSED BAR

HURRY! HURRY! HURRY! **15/-**

GET YOUR TICKETS NOW FROM

SIVEWRIGHT, BACON & CO.

SHIP CANAL HOUSE, KING STREET, MANCHESTER,
9 TITHEBARN STREET, LIVERPOOL
8 CAMBRIDGE STREET, ELLESMERE PORT,
or at LEWIS'S MANCHESTER OR LIVERPOOL TICKET
BUREAU

Comedy groups were the **Scaffold** ("Thank U Very Much") and the **Liverpool Scene** ("Baby").

Most of Liverpool's recording Beat groups only had one or two hits or releases, and then they disappeared from the international scene. Maybe this was the reason why lots of superficial critics state that there was not much quality in the Merseysound. This is definitely not true and, in all honesty, there are no differences in the quality of earlier or later popular sounds, only that the idea was better.

When you listen to their records today and consider the unfavourable circumstances that they were recorded under, it is impossible to claim that this sound or these bands were of poor musical quality, or that all groups sounded the same. Such a statement could only be made by people who do not have the correct knowledge and do not give too much thought to what they are saying, writing or pilfering from other people.

For example, the two **John Schroeder** produced albums 'This Is Merseybeat Vol. 1' and 'Vol. 2' were recorded at the Rialto Ballroom and the featured bands went on stage as they would for a normal live performance. It was recorded on a one-track machine and in one take without any chance to repeat the parts which did not work out too well.

Bearing this in mind, these records are just fantastic!

These days, bands record in special fully-mechanized recording studios on a 24-track machine with lots of special effects and overdubs. However, it is not necessary to defend this music and the musicians against some poor critics, who seem to have severe learning problems.

Regardless, everyone can judge for themselves by just listening to these records.

The most significant feature of the Merseysound was doubtless the feeling and the atmosphere which was around that music and spread by it. Never before was a generation on the international scene united and influenced by music as at that time. Screaming crowds of young people and fans who tried very hard to climb onto stages to get any little piece of their idols as a talisman or memento were a common occurrence. Compared with today it was more of a natural enthusiasm than manipulated mass-hysteria. Youth fashion was copied from their idols - pointed shoes (Cuban heels), drainpipe trousers, frilled shirts and shoelace ties.

Girls did their hair in the Farah Diba look, piled up like haystacks, and their stiletto heels left imprints behind in the wooden floors which can sometimes still be admired today.

The boys' Beatle haircuts were the cause of the biggest trouble in lots of 'honourable' families.

In front of the live clubs, hundreds and thousands of people queued up and fought for the last tickets. Fainting fits during the live performances were the order of the day, because everything was so wild and exciting - and the air sometimes so bad.

Motion pictures were made which documented the music and atmosphere for all time. These included 'Ferry Cross The Mersey' with **Gerry & the Pacemakers**, **Earl Royce & the Olympics**, the **Black Knights**, the **Fourmost**, the **Blackwells**, the **Koobas** and **Cilla Black**, or the **Beatles** films 'A Hard Day's Night' and 'Help'.

Another interesting aspect of the scene are the early live recordings such as the album 'At The Cavern' with the **Big Three**, **Beryl Marsden**, the **Dennisons** and **Lee Curtis & the All Stars** (all from Liverpool), the

The Big Three

The Dennisons
— Decca Records

Kennedy Street Enterprises Ltd.
Kennedy House,
14 Piccadilly, Manchester 1.
CENtral 5423

Fortunes (from Birmingham), the **Marauders** (from Stoke), **Dave Berry & the Cruisers** (from Sheffield), **Heinz** and **Bern Elliott & the Fenmen** (from Essex).

There was also the album 'Liverpool Today' with Liverpool groups including **Earl Preston's Realms**, the **Michael Allen Group** and the **Richmond**. The live

Michael Allen

recordings from the 'Iron Door' of **Freddie Starr & the Starr Boys** (This Is Liverpool Beat) and the **Excheckers** under the name of the **Liverpool Beats** (This Is Liverpool), as well as some German recordings of the **Swinging Blue Jeans** (Live at the 'Cascade' in Cologne) or the **Searchers**, **King Size Taylor & the Dominoes** and the **Roadrunners** (Live at the 'Star Club' in Hamburg).

A brilliant overall view of Liverpool's early Beat scene is given by the above mentioned Oriole albums 'This Is Merseybeat Vol. 1' and 'Vol. 2' with groups such as **Earl Preston & the TTs**, **Faron's Flamingos**, **Rory Storm & the Hurricanes**, the **Del Renas**, **Derry Wilkie & the Pressmen**, the **Nomads**, **Sonny Webb & the Cascades**, **Mark Peters & the Silhouettes**, the **Merseybeats** and **Ian & the Zodiacs** - all groups of the so-called 'pre-Beatles era'.

Faron's Flamingos

Mark Peters & The Silhouettes

Another important milestone in the development of Liverpool's Beat scene was the music paper 'Mersey Beat', edited by **Bill Harry**, which in the early years reported exclusively on the local groups, clubs and events. Not as popular but very interesting was another Beat paper called 'Combo', which was also published at the same time on Merseyside by **Matt D'Arcy** .

Bill Harry

The Combo 'team"

The most successful manager of this time without a doubt was **Brian Epstein**, despite the fact that the Merseybeat was built up by lots of managers and promoters including **Brian Kelly**, **Allan Williams**, **Dave Forshaw**, **Jim McIver** and **Doug Martin** (Ivamar Promotions), **Jim Ireland**, **Ralph Webster**, **Ted Knibbs**, **George Blood**, **Jim Turner**, **Sam Leach**, **Gordon Brown** and most of all **Bob Wooler**, just to name some of the important ones.

Above: Brian Kelly

Right: Dave Forshaw (left) with The Merseybeats

DAVID FORSHAW ENTERPRISES
6 DALEY PLACE   BOOTLE 20   AINTREE 9654
SOLE MANAGEMENT FOR—
RICKY GLEASON AND THE TOPSPOTS
J.J. AND THE HI-LITES * THE CASUALS
THE LEE EDDIE 5 * THE PREMIERS
THE FOUR MUSKETEERS
ADAM & THE SINNERS * THE DIAMONDS
FROM MYSELF AND ALL GROUPS UNDER MY MANAGEMENT WE
WOULD LIKE TO WISH EVERYBODY 'ALL THE BEST' FOR THE
COMING SEASON.

Brian Epstein became the most popular manager of all after he had taken over the management of the **Beatles**, **Gerry & the Pacemakers**, **Billy J. Kramer & the Dakotas**, **Tommy Quickly & the Remo Four**, the **Fourmost** and **Cilla Black**. Without him, only the **Searchers**, **Swinging Blue Jeans**, **Merseybeats**, **Escorts**, **Mojos**, **Lee Curtis & the All Stars**, **Beryl Marsden**, **King Size Taylor & the Dominoes**, **Ian & the Zodiacs**, **Denny Seyton & the Sabres** and the **Undertakers** made an international breakthrough from the Liverpool scene. But it would be wrong to call **Brian Epstein** the 'father of Merseybeat' because that accolade without a doubt belongs to **Bob Wooler**, who backed nearly every group in both word and deed, and who was something like the good spirit of the whole scene long before Brian Epstein appeared. For some, he suggested their names (**Merseybeats** and **Four Mosts**, etc.), for some he suggested the right songs for record releases ("Hippy Hippy Shake" by the **Swinging Blue Jeans**), and for others he helped to get recording contracts (**Masterminds**) or important gigs at the Cavern and other major venues, and concerts. He helped to build up an image for numerous bands. For some he wrote songs such as "Sidetracked" for **Phil Brady & the Ranchers** - a great song, or "I know" for **Billy J. Kramer**, or he took over their direct management, such as the **Clayton Squares**.

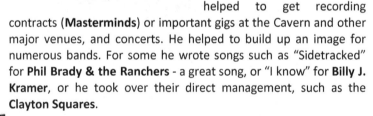

Bob Wooler

Brian Epstein

His contribution to the history of Liverpool's Merseybeat is immense and worth a special book alone. Without him, the Beat scene would not have been the same!

Compared to him, **Brian Epstein** was more a businessman who knew how to make a profit out of the local talent. This is not meant negatively, as it was also a very important part of achieving a breakthrough. In 1967 he, allegedly, committed suicide with sleeping pills, but this is not proven even today and lots of insiders of that time talk about a terrible accident in relation to this.

However, Merseybeat was already as good as dead in 1966. Not least to blame for this deterioration was the plague of talent seekers who descended upon Liverpool like a swarm of insects during the successful times and tempted all the more or less talented musicians away.

Also not too advantageous was the superior, dominating role of the **Beatles** as trendsetters. Because, from a certain time on, every group that came out of Liverpool was expected to be like them, which the groups could not be and, let's face it, the majority of them did not want to be.

Merseybeat was probably the last naturally grown music scene in Europe. Later, more or less everything was manipulated by the music industry before it could strengthen itself. Merseybeat was in many respects phenomenal. As well as the musical idealism, a lot of the famous Scouse sense of humour and a special kind

of closeness to Liverpool can be found in it, which is also shown in lots of the bands' names. Although there was no Liverpool group that included 'Liverpool' in its name, if the German releases of the **Pressmen** as **Liverpool Triumphs** and the **Excheckers** as **Liverpool Beats** are not taken into account, a hint of the River Mersey can often be found in group names such as the **Merseybeats** (later the **Merseys**), the **Mersey Four** or **Mersey Five**, the **Mersey Monsters**, the **Mersey Bluebeats**, **Mike & the Merseymen**, the **Mersey Blues Preachers** or the **Mersey Gonks**.

At this point the **Liverbirds** should not be forgotten.

The Mersey Blues Preachers

Right: The Liverbirds at the Star-Club (Hamburg)

Imagination and the above mentioned humour can be found in names such as, **Johnny Apollo & the Spartans, Gerry Bach & the Beathovens, Pete Picasso & the Rock Sculptors, Roy Satan & the Devils, Rip**

Roy Satan

Van Winkle & the Rip-It-Ups, Eddie Falcon & the Vampires, Dino & the Wild Fires, Dave & the Devil Horde, Al Quentin & the Rock Pounders, Johnny Anger & the Wild Ones or **Johnny Autumn & the Fall Guys**. Whatever might be thought about these names today, you get the feeling they were chosen with lots of love and imagination, which was characteristic of the scene at that time.

Well, what has happened to the previously well-known and sometimes very successful bands and their individual members ?

Some of them remained in the business, still playing in groups, working as session or studio musicians, some went solo or became disc-jockeys and producers, and so on.

Others switched to related parts of show business like entertainment, comedy or film. Here, to name a few, are especially big TV stars such as, **Faith Brown** (formerly the **Carrolls**), **Freddie Starr** (formerly with the **Midnighters**), plus **Lewis Collins** (of the **Mojos**), **Vince Earl** (in the Sixties with the **Zeros** and the **Talismen**) and **Ozzie Yue** (of the **Hideaways**). But detailed information about all this can be found in the individual group stories featured in this book.

Some groups still work as professionals, even if they all have had personnel changes over the years; for example, the **Searchers**, the **Merseybeats**, the **Pete Best Band, Gerry & the Pacemakers, Karl Terry & the Cruisers,** the **Undertakers** and also until 2010, the **Swinging Blue Jeans**.

Karl Terry & The Cruisers - 1978

These groups are still appearing in the clubs of England, mainly in the North, but some of them also tour on the European continent, in the United States and in Australia.

Every now and then they release records, but chart success is very rare. In 1978, **Karl Terry & the Cruisers** and **Faron's Flamingos** were featured on the revival compilation 'Mersey Survivors', together with other Liverpool groups including the **Dimensions**, the **Pawns**, the **Renegades**, **Groups Inc.** and the **Gibson James Band**, but these were more recording sessions than steady line-ups. The introduction on this record is spoken by **Bob Wooler**, as it was on some other samplers from the Sixties.

The 'MerseyCats' organisation is a very important part of Liverpool's Beat scene these days. It was formed in 1989 and has a lot of the original Merseybeat musicians as members. The 'MerseyCats' members promote concerts and other events for charity reasons only. Through 'MerseyCats', lots of groups and musicians came back onto the scene. The same is valid for the 'MerseyCats' offshoots such as 'New Brighton Rock', still going as the 'Cheshire Cats', 'Mersey Rats' or the 'Merseyside Rock 'n' Roll Society'.

Some of the re-formed groups split up again for various reasons for example, **Denny Seyton & the Sabres, Johnny Guitar & his Hurricanes,** the **Kansas City Five** and **Faron's Flamingos**.

Johnny Guitar & his Hurricanes

Some others still perform fairly regularly, such as the **Del Renas**, the **Dominoes**, the **Mojos**, the **Four Originals**, **Cliff Roberts' Rockers** and the **Black Knights**. With only a few exceptions, these groups do not play the normal circuit, but appear mainly for the various 'Merseybeat' charity functions. A fantastic idea which is greatly appreciated by real Beat fans and, of course, by those who benefit from it.

In spite of all this activity, it is obvious that this formerly so successful and exciting Merseysound has lost its meaning for the public at large... Sadly!

But lots of Beat fans can still be found worldwide who are interested in the Sixties bands from Liverpool still active on the scene. Sometimes these fans travel hundreds or even thousands of miles to see their former idols live again. They come from the USA, Japan, Australia or all over the European continent. For them it is a real adventure to see and hear the stars of their youth performing again and to dance to the old and fondly remembered hits. Of course, this is a kind of nostalgia and a rooting in memories, but is this so bad and so hard to understand? Those days in the unique Sixties were great and exciting, not only for the fans but, despite unfavourable circumstances, also for the bands that today are still playing their music - **MERSEYBEAT!!**

The Merseybeats - circa 2008

THE ADDICTS

In the very beginning they were **Rocky Stone & the Pebbles** from Widnes in Lancashire.

They were one of the pioneering Rock 'n' Roll groups from an area close to Liverpool that became quite popular locally.

Unfortunately, the original line-up is not known and it is also not known if there were some personnel changes when this group changed its name into the **Cadillacs,** sometime around 1962.

It was probably one year later, that the **Cadillacs** broke up totally and **Steve Duggan** and **Paul Nash** teamed up with other local musicians under the name of the **Addicts**, that from the very beginning consisted of:

Geoff Keeley	**(voc/rg)**
Steve Duggan	**(lg/voc)**
Paul Nash	**(bg/voc)**
Dennis Keeley	**(dr)**

The Addicts - L to R: Geoff Keeley, Steve Duggan, Paul Nash & Dennis Keeley

As can be concluded from their surnames, **Geoff Keeley** and **Dennis Keeley** were related to each other. They were cousins and both had previously played with **Geoff Stacey & the Wanderers**, where **Geoff Keeley** had used the stage name **Geoff Stacey**. The drummer, **Dennis Keeley** had previously played with the **Electrons**, which was a forerunner-group of **Geoff Stacey & the Wanderers.** The **Wanderers** were also very successful on the local scene, as well as in Liverpool. At one time they had even backed the popular coloured Liverpool singer **Derry Wilkie**.

But back to the **Addicts** who were a real beat group with their sound and their classic four-piece line-up. With their 'new sound', they became one of the busiest groups in the area and very soon had a large following. It is hard to understand that, in spite of this, they did not appear too often in downtown Liverpool and its popular clubs.

The Addicts

The Addicts

Paul Nash left the group and apparently disappeared from the scene. His replacement was **Denny O'Neill**, a former member of the **Deltics** Skiffle group, the **Electrons** and **Geoff Stacey & the Wanderers**.

Nothing is known about any particular management or agency for the **Addicts** and so, it is quite surprising that they were signed to Decca in 1963.

In the following year, they had their first record out with the **Geoff Keeley** original, "That's My Girl" coupled with "Here She Comes", which most likely was also an original number.

The record received good reviews from some of the music paper critics and opened the door for the **Addicts** to play the national circuit as professionals, but in the end the record did not sell well enough to get into the charts.

Although the quartet kept themselves busy gigging throughout England they still didn't play the Liverpool venues very often. Their only documented 'Cavern' appearance was in November 1964.

The **Addicts** were not given a second chance by Decca and no other recording contract was signed elsewhere, but they managed to make a living out of their music until they broke up around 1967/1968.

It is not known what happened to **Steve Duggan** after that, but **Geoff Keeley** and **Dennis 'Snowy' Keeley** became members of the **Michael Henri Group** in the late 60s, but then also disappeared from the scene.

Denny O'Neill later formed a cabaret-trio with his wife and guitarist/singer **Graham Garner**, who also was a Sixties-member of the **Wanderers**. They are still playing the local clubs today.

So, what's left of the **Addicts** besides a legendary name in their hometown of Widnes, is a nice beat record, worth looking out for . . . .

Discography :

That's My Girl / Here She Comes   UK- Decca F.11902 / 1964

ALBY & THE SORRALS

In 1960, **Albert Ellis** was singing with a vocal/guitar group which, in the beginning, probably did not even have a name, at a church club in Dingle.

In 1961, when this group was to play at a dance, a drummer was needed and so Alby asked a colleague from work to help out.

They apparently went down well as the group was asked to play a number of local club dances, which was very soon followed by some personnel changes.

The guitarist and the bass guitarist joined from the **Cadillacs**, whose drummer, **Trevor Morais** had left the **Cadillacs** to join **Robin & the Ravens**, who a little later became **Faron's Flamingos**. After that he played in other famous groups, including **Rory Storm & the Hurricanes**, Manchester's **Ian Crawford & the Bommerangs** and the **Peddlers**.

But back to that group from the church club, which was now in need of a name, and the musicians decided to become the **Sorrals** – in the following line-up with:

Alby Ellis	**(voc)**
Keith Draper	**(lg/voc)**
Brian Cox	**(rg)**
Dave Foley	**(bg/voc)**
Maurice Daniels	**(dr)**

It seems **Brian Cox**, in addition to **Alby Ellis**, was the only remaining member of the original vocal/guitar line-up and **Maurice Daniels** was of course the drummer who helped out for one gig, but then stayed with the group.

ALBY
and the
SORRALS

HUN 2809

Top: Dave Foley, Maurice Daniels & Pete Dobson
Middle: Keith Draper & Brian Cox - Front: Alby Ellis

Keith Draper and **Dave Foley** were both former members of the **Cadillacs**, who most probably were connected to **Eddie & the Cadillacs**, one of the very first Rock groups to appear at the 'Cavern' in late 1959.

The **Sorrals** very soon also appeared at the 'Cavern', as well as at the other usual venues in the city centre of Liverpool. But, when they took up a residency at Barnabus Hall in Penny Lane, their name was changed to **Alby & the Sorrals**. In early 1962, they were joined by sax player, **Pete Dobson** as an additional member, who came from the **Black Cats**.

Alby & the Sorrals at the Majestic Ballroom – Birkenhead 1962
L to R: Dave Foley, Keith Draper, Pete Dobson & Brian Cox

In late 1962, this line-up was recorded at the Brooklands Dance School by a mobile recording unit, which most probably was from Welsby Sound, Rainhill. The result was an interesting acetate with **Del Shannon**'s smash hit "Runaway", the **Bobby Vee** success "Someday" and the two instrumentals "Chariot Rock" and "Golden Earrings".

This acetate was also meant to be a Christmas present for the members of their fan club, but due to technical problems it was not released until early 1963.

In the middle of 1963, the existence of **Alby & the Sorrals** started to shake, when **Keith Draper, Brian Cox** and **Dave Foley** left to form the **Nocturnes**, together with **Dave Wilcox**, the singer from the **Young Ones**.

The three remaining members of **Alby & the Sorrals** then recruited two new members **Rodney Long** (lg) from **Gerry Bach & the Beathovens** and **Frank Smith** (bg).

Alby & the Sorrals at The Cavern - December 1963
L to R: Frank Smith , Maurice Daniels, Alby Ellis, Brian Johnson & Rod Long

This new line-up went into the Kensington studio of **Percy Phillips** and recorded the **Maurice Daniels** original "Why" and a very interesting version of "Please don't touch", which shortly before had been a successful release by **Johnny Kidd & the Pirates**.

It was most probably also at these sessions that the **Brian Cox** original "Foolin'" was recorded, which remained on the reel-to-reel tape and was not featured on the acetate.

Unfortunately, this really good acetate did not lead to a contract with a recording company and this fact could have been the reason for **Pete Dobson** leaving in January 1964.

He joined a local dance band and was replaced by **Brian Johnson** as rhythm guitarist, who came from the **Blue Country Boys**.

This line-up of **Alby & the Sorrals** continued successfully on the scene until the middle of 1964, when **Rod Long** left to join the **Young Ones**.

Alby Ellis apparently quit the music business, but is thought to have returned to it a bit later, singing with various groups. Unfortunately, what happened to **Frank Smith** is not known. **Brian Johnson**, who had also appeared with **Rodney Long** as a duo under the name of the **Two Tunes** during the time they both played with **Alby & the Sorrals,** joined the Merchant Navy for about 18 months. When he returned to Liverpool, he got back into the C&W scene, becoming a member of the **Country Cousins**, which, by the way, included **Tony Goldby**, formerly of **Tony Goldby & the Goldminers** and the **Premiers**.

Brian Johnson then became a member of the **Mo Silver Band**, played with **Sylvia Lee & the Clover**, a group called **Palomino** and after a spell as a compere at a club in Garston, he became a member of the very successful Liverpool Country group the **Kentuckians**.

He then formed a trio - the **Three Tunes** and later moved to Brighton, where he is still living.

Maurice Daniels continued on the music scene and did a few gigs with other groups including **Denny Seyton & the Sabres** and **Danny Havoc & the Ventures**, before he also joined the **Young Ones**, who changed their name into the **Coins** a little later – in the following line-up with:

Ricky Coburn	**(voc/rg)**
Rod Long	**(lg)**
George Varcas	**(bg/voc)**
Maurice Daniels	**(dr)**

The **Coins** kept very busy on the local scene, but in 1964, **Rod Long** left the music business to get married.

He was replaced by **Pete Corcoran**, who had previously played with the **Pilgrims**.

Pete Corcoran only stayed for a couple of months. He was replaced by a guitarist called **George**, whose surname is not known, but he had formerly played with a Country & Western group and it turned out that he was not the right guitarist for the kind of music that the **Coins** played, so he did not stay with them for too long.

His place in the **Coins** was taken by **John O'Reilly**, who remained with them until they finally broke up in 1966, when **Ricky Coburn** emigrated to Australia, where he is still living today.

The Coins - L to R: Ricky Coburn, Pete Corcoran, George Varcas & Maurice Daniels

As far as it is known, the **Coins** did not record anything and after the split, the musicians disappeared from the scene – with the exception of **Maurice Daniels**, who from 1968 into the Seventies was a member of **Gerry De Ville & the City Kings** and after that he played with the resident group at the 'Sportsman' in Wigan called **Total Sound**. In 1975, he joined the cabaret group **Patchwork Dream**, returned to **Gerry De Ville & the City Kings** in 1976 and later was a member of **Sandlewood**.

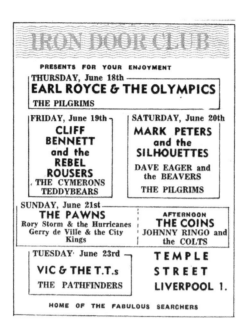

Discography :

Alby & the Sorrals

Runaway / Someday / Golden Earrings / Chariot Rock   UK- Welsby Sound acetate-ep/ 1963

Why / Please don't touch   UK- Kensington acetate/ 1963

(Besides these recordings it is known that the original **"Foolin'"** was recorded on a reel-to-reel in 1963)

STEVE ALDO & THE CHALLENGERS

This group was formed in Liverpool in the very early Sixties under the name of the **Cossacks**, initially they failed to make any progress on the scene.

In August 1962, their name was changed to the **Challengers** and a little later the band became the backing group for the singing brother and sister duo, **Thomas** and **Patricia Quigley**.

Tommy (Quickly) Quigley & The Challengers

This connection lasted until July 1963 when **Thomas Quigley** became **Tommy Quickly** and teamed up with the Remo Four.

Tommy Quickly & the Remo Four were managed by **Brian Epstein** and released a string of records, but only their great version of "Wild Side Of Life" became a chart success. That, however, is a different story that can be followed under the **Remo Four** in this book.

Pat Quigley continued on as a solo act for a short time then disappeared from the scene.

The **Challengers** then amalgamated with the coloured singer **Steve Aldo**, whose real name is **Edward Bedford**.

Steve Aldo & the Challengers, as they were named then, became very popular in the following line-up with:

Steve Aldo

Steve Aldo	(voc)
Bob Gilmore	(lg)
Pete Wilson	(rg)
Ray Anderson	(bg)
John Bedson	(dr)

John Bedson had formerly played with the **Four Clefs** and the short-lived **Roadrunners (II)**. He was the replacement for their original drummer, **Ian Bailey**, who left the **Challengers** to join the **Mafia Group**.

In the archives, **Ray Anderson** is sometimes identified as **Ray Dawson** and it is hard to determine what, in the end, was his real name. However, it can be taken for sure that they are one and the same person.

Steve Aldo & the Challengers were booked to appear at the Star Club in Hamburg in 1963, where they went down well. One of their live performances was recorded for an album which, unfortunately, was not released. During their stay in Hamburg, **Steve Aldo** fell out with some of the other group members and left the **Challengers**, who returned to Liverpool without him.

The **Challengers** then continued on as a four piece and, once again, played the Star Club in Hamburg. At that time, the vocals were shared by all the band members. After that, the group had some other vocalists, one of them was **Norby Del Rosa**, who had come from the recently disbanded **Mafia.**

It is also said that the original drummer, **Ian Bailey** possibly returned to the group.

TO ALL OUR GOOD FRIENDS AND FANS ON MERSEYSIDE AND IN GERMANY, OUR SINCEREST BEST WISHES FOR CHRISTMAS AND THE NEW YEAR

JOHN ★ ROB ★ PETE ★ RAY & FRED

The **CHALLENGERS**

STA 6068

The **Challengers** disbanded totally after **John Bedson** and **Bob Gilmore** left in March 1964 to join the **Harlems**, who were at that time the backing group for the very popular vocal group, the **Chants**. After that, both were members of the **Myths** before they disappeared from the scene.

Norby Del Rosa went on to sing with the **Calderstones**. Unfortunately, it is not known what happened to the other members after the split because the press at that time did not pay too much attention to the group, although it certainly was a very good one.

After **Steve Aldo** separated from the group in 1963, he remained in Hamburg and joined **King Size Taylor & the Dominoes** as an additional vocalist. He was also recorded for Polydor with this group by **Paul Murphy**, who incidentally, was a former member of the **Raving Texans** from Liverpool, a predecessor of **Rory Storm & the Hurricanes**.

While **Steve Aldo** was with **King Size Taylor & the Dominoes** they recorded an album for Polydor which, in the end, also remained unreleased, but some of the recorded songs later appeared on different compilation albums under the name **Boots Wellington & his Rubber Band**.

When **Steve Aldo** returned to Liverpool, he joined the **Nocturns** for a short spell and then became a member of the **Griff Parry Five**, who released the single "Can I Get A Witness" under the name **Steve Aldo**. This group later evolved into the **Steve Aldo Quintet**.

After that, **Steve Aldo** recorded one more great single with "Everybody Has To Cry", but on this single he was backed by studio musicians. It certainly was not the **Challengers** who backed him on that recording, as is so often stated.

Steve Aldo later became a member of the **Fyx**, the **In Crowd** and finally was backed by the **Fairies** for a time before he quit show business.

Discography :

The **Challengers** never released a record, but **Steve Aldo & the Challengers** were recorded at a live performance in 1963 at the Star Club in Hamburg for an album which, unfortunately, was never released.

For recordings of **Steve Aldo**, please see the stories of the **Griff Parry Five** and **King Size Taylor & the Dominoes**.

DAVE ALLEN & THE EXOTICS

Reconstructing the story of this group was very difficult, as it was hard to determine their place of origin – it could have been Wigan, Leigh or Liverpool. In the end it was all of them, plus Chester.

Dave Allen's real name is **Allan Parkinson**. He hailed from Leigh and started to play with the **Martinis**. After that he was a member of the legendary **Beat Boys** from Wigan. When he left that group in 1964, he, with other members of the **Beat Boys**, formed the Rhythm & Blues group, the **Rats**.

Under the management of **John Jenkins** from Liverpool, they recorded two singles and became a steady part of the Merseybeat scene with lots of appearances at all the major venues.

When **John Jenkins** returned from a holiday in Spain sometime in 1965, he had an interesting contract in his luggage which guaranteed the group 3 weeks work in the sunny South, but he found the **Rats** had split up during his absence. So he offered this contract to band leader **Allan Parkinson**, who already had adopted the stage name **Dave Allen** and who then looked for a new backing group to fulfil this contract.

In the end, he amalgamated with the **Exotics** from Chester, but their drummer, **Dave Fellows**, for some reason did not want to go to Spain so he was replaced by Liverpudlian, **Ian Broad** from **Rory Storm & the Hurricanes**, who had formerly played in other Liverpool groups including the **Five Stars**, **Gus Travis & the Midnighters** and the group which evolved from them, **Freddie Starr & the Midnighters**, as well as with the **Seniors** and the London based group **Heinz & the Wild Boys**.

So in 1965 **Dave Allen & the Exotics** went down to Spain with the following line-up:

Dave Allen	**(voc/g/harp)**
Ray Faulkner	**(lg/voc)**
Robert J. Hopkins	**(org/voc)**
Malcolm Rattrey	**(bg)**
Ian Broad	**(dr)**

Ray Faulkner had previously appeared on the scene as a member of the **Syndicate** from Widnes and **Vic Takes Four**.

Dave Allen & the Exotics went down a bomb in Spain and were immediately signed by Spanish Hispavox.

A really great EP was released on that established label.

Besides the two **Robert Hopkins** originals, "The Monkey" and "She Walks", it also included the **Chuck Berry** classic, "Sweet Little Rock 'n' Roller", and a Spanish version of the **Kinks** success, "A Well Respected Man", done as "Un hombre respectable".

The record apparently sold very well and from this EP a single with "The Monkey" and "Sweet Little Rock 'n' Roller" was coupled out for the Italian market later in the year, where it was released on the Derby label. This resulted in **Dave Allen & the Exotics** going to Italy where they became very popular. On a holiday trip back to Liverpool, **Ian Broad** left and later emigrated to the U.S.A., where he is still living in Hollywood.

He was replaced by the original **Exotics** drummer, **Dave Fellows,** and the group went back to Italy for a long residency but soon, for promotional reasons, changed their name to **Dave Allen & the Bigs**.

In 1967, **Dave Allen** left the group and continued as a solo singer in Italy under the name of **Al Torino**.

The group also remained in Italy and continued as the **Bigs**, adding two sax players and becoming something of a 'showband'.

When **Ray Faulkner** left to live in Spain, it was **Al Torino**, a.k.a. **Dave Allen**, who arranged for his old mate **Malcolm Grundy** from the **Beat Boys** and the **Rats** to take over as lead guitarist in the group, who continued to play successfully in Italy, but nothing is known of any further records.

Al Torino also took part in the famous 'Knokke' Beatfestival in the Netherlands. Around this time he was signed to the Decca label and the single "Inside, Outside, Upside Down" was released.

His A&R man for this record was none other than Liverpudlian, **Wayne Bickerton**, who amongst others, had formerly played with the **Pete Best Four**. After that release, **Al Torino** changed his name to **Guy Challenger**, returned to England and continued in the music business. He later emigrated to Spain and formed the Jazz group **East Coast Jazz**, which included **Ray Faulkner** again. When they disbanded, **Allan Parkinson**, under his real name again, continued to play as a solo artist in Spanish clubs, but he also took part in two **Beat Boys** reunion concerts in Wigan and Leigh in 2001 and 2002.

Discography :

Dave Allen & the Exotics - EP

- Un Hombre Respectable / Sweet Little Rock 'n' Roller /	ES- Hispavox HH 17-354 / 1965
The Monkey / She Walks	
The Monkey / Sweet Little Rock 'n' Roller	I – Derby DB 5144 / 1965

Al Torino – solo :

Inside, Outside, Upside Down / Can't Nobody Love You	UK – Decca F 12767 / 1968

THE MICHAEL ALLEN GROUP

This group came from the Birkenhead area on the west side of the river Mersey, or as the real Liverpudlians like to say, 'from over the water'.

They were formed as the **Abstracts** and their singer **Michael Allen Mulloy** was only 15 years old when the group started gigging in 1963. They played a sort of Rhythm & Blues and rehearsed in the basement of the lead guitarist's home in Woodside.

The **Abstracts** very soon became popular on the local scene and also started to play the venues in Liverpool's city centre - in the following line-up with:

Mike Mulloy	**(voc)**
John Thompson	**(lg)**
Dave Stanton	**(rg/lg)**
Gordon Didsbury	**(bg)**
Alan Westcot	**(dr)**

It seems it was the first group for all the musicians and in consideration of that, their success was really notable. They had a large following on both sides of the river Mersey and were regularly booked at the Cavern.

Therefore it is quite surprising that in late 1964 the group changed its name to **Mike Mulloy & the Mountwoods**, but this was only temporary for a few performances.

At one of these performances they were recorded and a little later the songs, "Spectatin' The Blues" and "Parchment Farm", were cut on a highly interesting acetate at Marble Arch in London. This acetate shows **Mike Mulloy** to be a good singer with great feeling for the Blues and this was also recognized by **Bob Wooler**, who took the group under his wing. It was probably his idea to change the group's name again – this time to the **Michael Allen Group**.

By that time **Dave Stanton** had left the group and joined the **Prowlers**, another great R&B group from the Wirral. He was replaced by a certain **'Jimmy'**, whose surname is not known.

John Thompson also left and disappeared from the scene and the group was joined by their former roadie, **Peter Bays** (org/p) and the sax-player **Derek Marl**.

It was probably this line-up of the **Michael Allen Group** that, in addition to **Earl Preston's Realms** and the **Richmond Group**, were featured on the second compilation from the Cavern, which was released on the Ember label with the title 'Liverpool Today – Live At The Cavern' in 1965.

On this interesting, but not live recorded album, the **Michael Allen Group** played the songs "Evenin", "Telegram", "I Can't Stand It" and "Trains And Boats And Planes".

The first three of these songs make it especially clear that the group had not really changed its musical style and was still a fine Rhythm & Blues band. In his spoken introduction on that record, **Bob Wooler** named them as one of the 'new wave Liverpool attractions'.

Unfortunately, the **Michael Allen Group**, although managed by the 'Cavern Artists Ltd.', never had any success on the national scene, but today they are still remembered as one of the better Liverpool Rhythm & Blues groups. It was probably towards the end of 1965 that the group disbanded totally. After that it is only known that **Derek Marl** occasionally appeared with the **Secrets** but without being a steady member. He then joined the **Times** who played in their own right but were also the backing group for the **Signs**.

In 1967 **Derek Marl** joined the **Almost Blues** and in the Seventies he was a member of the successful recording group **Champagne**.

All the other musicians of the **Michael Allen Group** disappeared from the scene – with the exception of **Mike Mulloy**, who followed Bob Wooler's advice and teamed up with the **Press Gang**, a group that was formed at Liverpool University and consisted of **James Trimmer** (g/voc), **Colin Jordan** (g), **John Rotherham** (p), **Ernie Hankin** (bg) and **David Mason** (dr).

This group did not really take part in the Merseybeat scene but played at universities all over the UK.

John Rotherham was a great piano player but his secret love was Jazz music. So he parted from the **Press Gang** and, together with **John Allcock** (bg) and **Barry Davenport** (dr), formed the **John Rotherham Trio**, which was also joined by **Mike Mulloy**, who sang with them at various Jazz festivals. This line-up later evolved into the seven-piece Rhythm & Blues band, **Gravy Train,** and continued on the scene for quite some time.

Mike Mulloy quit the band scene, went down to London and became a singing actor. As such, he appeared in the musical 'Hair' and in 1978 sang the part of Judas in 'Jesus Christ Superstar', both with enormous success. After that he regularly appeared on TV in the famous 'Benny Hill Show' over a period of eight years. Today he is still living in London but is no longer active in show business. He still sings from time to time, but just for fun .

Discography :

as **Mike Mulloy & the Mountwoods** :

Parchment Farm / Spectatin' the Blues	**UK Recorded Sound Studios acetate / 1964**

as **The Michael Allen Group** :

"Telegram"	on 'Liverpool Today - Live At The Cavern'	UK- Ember NR 5028 / 1965
"Evenin' "	on 'Liverpool Toady - Live At The Cavern'	UK- Ember NR 5028 / 1965
"I Can't Stand It"	on 'Liverpool Today - Live At The Cavern'	UK- Ember NR 5028 / 1965
"Trains And Boats And Planes"	on 'Liverpool Today - Live At The Cavern'	UK- Ember NR 5028 / 1965

THE ALMOST BLUES

In early 1964 **Alan Peters**, **Mike Haralambos** and **John Beasley** formed one of the best Liverpool Rhythm & Blues outfits. Within a short time the **Almost Blues** established themselves as one of the city's leading groups with this sound which, unfortunately, was still underrated at that time.

The very first line-up of the group only lasted until March 1964 and then the **Almost Blues** were joined by **Eddie Williams**, who came from the **Clayton Squares**. Under the name of **'Jerkin' George Paul** he took over the lead vocals, while former lead singer **Alan Peters** continued in the group as a trumpet player.

Additionally, the pianist named **'Bernie'** and the drummer, whose name was **'John'**, had left the group, which, from that time on, appeared in the following line-up:

Eddie Williams	**(voc)**
Mike Haralambos	**(g/voc)**
John Beasley	**(bg/voc)**
Alan Peters	**(voc/tr)**
John Weston	**(tr)**
Ray Fowlis	**(sax)**
Ronnie Wilson	**(dr)**

They were also joined on background vocals by two girls named **Angela** and **Lena**, who called themselves the **Bluesettes**. This was not only an unusual but also a very interesting line-up, and it was really good, as can be heard on their great Unicord acetate with the songs "Jerk" and "Just Won't Do Right" which, unfortunately, were never released on vinyl. The song "Jerk", by the way, was an original by the group, written by **Eddie Williams**.

When the **Bluesettes** left, the **Almost Blues** were joined by **Angela Williams** (the sister of the lead vocalist) as an additional singer. But this line-up only lasted until August 1965 and then **Eddie Williams** and his sister left and disappeared from the scene.

Colin Areety came in as their new lead singer and with this line-up, the **Almost Blues** recorded the songs "Who Is Going To Pick Up The Pieces", "Midnight Hour", "Try Me" and "Papa's Got A Brand New Bag" for EMI, which were not released.

In February 1966, the group went back into the Abbey Road Studios again for EMI and recorded the song "Tell Daddy", once again it was not released. But the connection with EMI continued and in the end this led to the departure of **Colin Areety** because there were disagreements about their musical style for further recordings. EMI wanted the **Almost Blues** to record "Cupid", which a little later became a big hit for **Johnny Nash**, but **Colin Areety** did not want to sing it and so he left to join the **Dennisons**. After that he became a member of the **Fyx** and then joined the **In Crowd**, before he appeared with the **Michael Henri Group**.

Colin Areety then started a solo career and in 1972 and 1973. He had record releases with "Poco Joe", "I Don't Want To Be Right" and "Holy Cow" on Deram, all great records, especially "Holy Cow", but none of them had any major success. He was active as a singer on the scene until he sadly died in 2007.

In 1968, the **Almost Blues** were joined by **Tommy Brown**, who had formerly sung with the **Valentinos**. At that time, founder member **Mike Haralambos** also left and was replaced by **Billy Faulkner**, a former member of the **Syndicate** from Widnes and **Vic Takes Four**.

Two sax players named **Pete Harvey** and **Tommy Husky** joined the group as additional members.

Tommy Husky, a former member of the **Dee-Jays**, the **Nashpool** and **Earl Preston's Realms**, only stayed for a short time and then left to join the **Detours**. Later, he became very successful on the British Rockabilly scene and recorded a solo album in the Nineties.

He was replaced in the **Almost Blues** by **Navo Nield**, while **John Rathbone** came in as the new drummer for the departing **Ronnie Wilson**. **John 'Jay' Rathbone**, sometimes also named **John Foskett**, was a former member of the **Masterminds**.

But that was still not the end of the personnel changes in the **Almost Blues** and the next to leave was **Billy Faulkner**, who was replaced by **John Hodgson**, who came from **Georgie's Germs**. Then **Graham Hetherington**, a new trumpet player, came in from the **Doug Barry Sound** for the departing **John Weston**. In 1969 **John Rathbone**, was replaced by **Barry 'Basher' Robinson**, the former drummer of the **Heartbeats**, **Excerts** and **Georgie's Germs**.

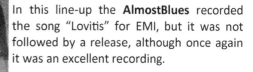

In this line-up the **AlmostBlues** recorded the song "Lovitis" for EMI, but it was not followed by a release, although once again it was an excellent recording.

Then **Tommy Brown** left and **Alan Peters** switched back to lead vocals. The departing **Ray Fowlis**, **Pete Harvey**, **Navo Nield** and **Graham Heatherington** were only replaced by two sax players **Graham Robertson** and **Derek Marl**, and so the group became a six-piece again, while it had been something like a small Rhythm & Blues orchestra previously. **Derek Marl** was a former member of the **Michael Allen Group**, the **Secrets** and the **Times**.

If all the steady changes in the line-up were taken into account, it is not really surprising that the **Almost Blues** never made a national breakthrough and probably disbanded totally in 1969.

Of the former members **'Jay' Rathbone** later played with **Karl Terry & the Cruisers** and **Derek Marl** was a member of **Champagne**.

Alan Peters joined **Liverpool Scene** before forming his own band **Tryptych**, which only existed for a short time. He then became a member of the internationally successful band **Supercharge**, before he again formed his own group with the unusual name of **29th & Dearborn**, who released one single and then disbanded. Then he played with the **Opposition** and the **Love Ponies** before he formed **Lawnmower** which became quite a successful live act in the clubs of Liverpool and its surrounding areas.

Discography :

The **Almost Blues** never had a record released but recorded the very good and interesting acetate

Jerk / Just Won't Do Right   UK – Unicord acetate / 1965

Other line-ups of the group from 1965 until 1969 recorded the following songs in the Abbey Road Studios for EMI : **"Who Is Going To Pick Up The Pieces"**, **"Midnight Hour"**, **"Try Me"**, **"Papa's Got A Brand New Bag"**, **"Tell Daddy"** and **"Lovitis"**, but for mysterious reasons none of these songs were ever released on vinyl.

THE AVENGERS

When in early 1964, the **Travellers** from Birkenhead (not the similarly named group of **Johnny Saint**) disbanded, their two guitarists, **Mike Rudd** (real name **Michael Rudzinski**) and **Billy Knaggs** formed the **Avengers** together with **Dave Pritchard** (bg) and **Robert Dennis** (dr).

Soon after, **Denny Jeffcoate** joined as the new bass guitarist. He came from a local group, the **Young Ones**, who did not have any connections to the recording group of the same name. In addition, **Pete Smith** joined as lead vocalist and made the group a quintet, but he did not stay for too long.

When also **Robert Dennis** went on to join the **Night Walkers**, still in 1964, the **Avengers** consisted of:

Jim Byers	**(voc)**
Billy Knaggs	**(lg)**
Mike Rudd	**(rg/voc)**
Denny Jeffcoate	**(bg)**
Les Hall	**(dr)**

After the **Avengers** had achieved some popularity on the scene, the Liverpool singer and songwriter, **Ron Anderson** offered the group one of his songs. So it was probably in late 1964 that the **Avengers,** together with **Ron Anderson,** went into the studio and recorded an acetate of "Any Day Now" on the Unicord label.

This was a great bluesy number, which was sung by **Ron Anderson** himself, coupled with a really interesting version of the **Johnny Kidd & the Pirates** success, "Shakin' All Over", sung by **Jim Byers**.

The London-based record producer, **Cyril Stapleton** got hold of this acetate and wanted to record the **Avengers** with "Any Day Now" for PYE, but this, of course, meant that the musicians had to become professionals, which the majority did not want.

These disagreements led to **Jim Byers** and **Les Hall** leaving and they were replaced by **Derek Peckham** from the **Renegades** on drums and a singer called **'Mitch'**, whose surname is not known.

Around that time, the group's name was changed into the **New Avengers**.

The group continued to be successful on the scene, now playing a sort of heavy Rhythm & Blues.

When **Denny Jeffcoate** also left, **Mike Rudd** took over the bass guitar and **Billy Knaggs** was temporarily replaced by **Pete Jones** on lead guitar. **Pete Jones** had formerly played with the **Crosbys**, the **Renegades** and **Groups Inc.**

The changes in the line-up continued and when **'Mitch'** and **Derek Peckham** left, the **New Avengers** continued as a trio with **Billy Knaggs** (lg), **Mike Rudd** (bg) and **Derek Cashin** (dr).

Mike Rudd was now sharing the vocals with the new drummer, but this also did not last for too long and the group broke up when **Mike Rudd** was offered the place as bass-guitarist in **Johnny Kidd & the Pirates** and went down to London to join this legendary, internationally successful group.

Billy Knaggs disappeared from the scene and **Derek Cashin** later joined the **Steve Alan Set**, that at that time changed their name to **Paper Chase**. After that, he played with the **New Merseybeats**, who also recorded under the name of **Crane**, and then he became a member of **Liverpool Express**, who had various international hits through the Seventies.

But this is not the end of the story, when **Johnny Kidd** disbanded the **Pirates** and decided to go solo, **Mike Rudd** returned to Liverpool and re-formed the **Avengers** together with his old mates **Billy Knaggs** and **Les Hall**.

This trio played all the main venues in and around Liverpool, as well as in North Wales, where they became very popular.

Then one day **Mike Rudd** received a telephone-call from **Johnny Kidd**, who was seeking a group again, Mike suggested the **Avengers** to him.

Johnny Kidd came up to Wallasey, rehearsed with the trio in the garage of Mike's father and then in 1965 the **Avengers** became **Johnny Kidd & the Pirates**.

For almost a year, the group toured all over England, had an appearance at the 'Star Club' in Hamburg and also recorded in a studio in Baker Street in London.

Of that session, the songs "The Fool", "Let's Talk About Us" and an alternative version of "Please Don't Touch" are known. None of these recordings were ever released.

With **Johnny Kidd** still living in London, it became quite exhausting for the Wallasey group, so in 1966 their ways parted again.

The **Avengers** continued playing the local circuit, but also kept in touch with **Johnny Kidd**, until he sadly died in a car-crash not too long after he split from the group.

Mike Rudd was so upset about his death that he decided to quit playing and sold his guitar and amplifier. That was the definite end of the **Avengers** in 1966.

It is not known what happened to **Billy Knaggs** and **Les Hall** after that, but **Mike Rudd** returned to the scene in the Seventies as a member of the **Dees**, then he had a short spell with the **New Dennisons** and today he plays bass guitar with **Karl Terry & the Cruisers**.

Discography :

The Avengers :

Any day now / Shakin' all over   **UK – Unicord acetate / 1964**

Unreleased tracks as **Johnny Kidd & the Pirates** :

The fool / Let's talk about us / Please don't touch - and probably some more recorded in London in late 1965.

THE BEAT BOYS

It can be debated here whether this group was more part of the Merseyside or the Manchester scene. They hailed from Wigan in Lancashire, which is a little closer to Liverpool, but they obviously appeared regularly on both scenes, later maybe more often in Manchester when **Jack Abadie**, who owned the 'Twisted Wheel' became their manager and, of course, the **Beat Boys** appeared there very often.

However, let's start at the beginning and that was the Wigan Skiffle/Rock 'n' Roll group the **Dominoes**, most probably formed in 1957. This group, amongst its members, included a certain **Clive Powell** on piano and vocals, who left in late 1959 and found international stardom as **Georgie Fame**.

The line-up of the group kept changing and in 1960, the **Dominoes** leader **Ronnie Carr**, together with the remaining members **Kenny Fillingham** and **Eric Eastham**, formed the **Beat Boys**.

After drummer **Eric Eastham** had left, the group consisted of:

Allan Parkinson	(voc/g/harp)
Kenny Fillingham	(lg)
Malcolm Grundy	(rg)
Ronnie Carr	(bg/voc)
Ronnie Simms	(dr)

Allan Parkinson was a former member of the **Martinis**.

The **Beat-Boys** soon became very popular on the scene but that did not stop **Kenny Fillingham** from leaving to join **Vince Taylor & the Playboys** in 1962, with whom he probably went to France.

Gerry Kenny, who also came from the **Martinis**, replaced him but he also left within a very short time. **Malcolm Grundy** then took over as lead guitarist and **Geoff Bibby** joined as their new rhythm guitarist.

This line-up was signed to Decca and **Joe Meek** produced their first single, "Third Time Lucky" which was coupled with the **Ronnie Carr** original, "That's My Plan". A great record that sold very well but, in the end, failed to make the charts.

In 1964, **Micky Most** produced another **Ronnie Carr** original with them for Decca, "A Little Lovin'" and also the song, "I'm Just A Rolling Stone", but for mysterious reasons they were not released. This was probably the reason that **Allan Parkinson** and **Malcolm Grundy** left the **Beat Boys**.

They teamed up with former member, **Gerry Kenny** to form the **Rats**, but that is another story in this book. **Allan Parkinson** later changed his name to **Dave Allen** and fronted **Dave Allen & the Exotics**, but this again can be found in another story. **Malcolm Grundy** also joined that group when it continued as the **Bigs** after **Dave Allen** left them while they were playing in Italy.

Back to the **Beat Boys**, who were joined by the returning **Kenny Fillingham** on lead guitar, while **Geoff Bibby** was replaced by a keyboard player, **George Twist**.

For a short time they continued as the **Beat Boys** but then they started to work for **Don Arden** and became more of a backing group for American Blues singers such as, **Memphis Slim**, **Screaming Jay Hawkins** and **Champion Jack Dupree** on their UK tours.

For that reason and because they found out that there was another recording group of the same name, the **Beat Boys** became the **Blues Set**.

In 1966, the group was tired of the continuous touring and returned to both their old name and to Wigan, where they became the resident band at the 'Sportsman' club.

But this was only for one more year and then **Ronnie Simms** left to join the **Martinis** and **George Twist** became a member of the **Sportsmen**.

Ronnie Carr and **Kenny Fillingham** joined the **New City Showband** in 1967 and after that their ways also separated, although they all remained in the music business.

A 2001 **Beat Boys** reunion at the 'Monaco Ballroom' in Wigan saw the Sixties' members **Allan Parkinson** (voc/harp), **Ronnie Carr** (voc/bg), **Eric Eastham** (dr) and **Ronnie Simms** (perc) together on stage again.

THE BEAT BOYS decca records

Discography :

Third Time Lucky / That's My Plan   **UK - Decca F. 11730 / 1963**

Unreleased tracks:

In 1964, **Micky Most** recorded the songs, **"A Little Lovin' "** and **"I'm Just A Rolling Stone"** with the **Beat Boys** for Decca, but they did not come out on record.

THE BEATLES

The story of what later became the most popular and successful Beat band in the world can be traced back to 1956.

At that time, **John Lennon** (voc/g) together with **Pete Shotton** (wb) and the other schoolmates **Nigel Whalley** (t-bass), **Ivan Vaughan** (bg), **Rod Davis** (bj), **Eric Griffiths** (g) and **Colin Hanton** (dr) formed the Skiffle group the **Quarrymen**. This name was chosen because all members were pupils of Quarry Bank High School in Liverpool.

In the same year, **Nigel Whalley** concentrated on managing the group and he was replaced by **Len Garry**, who joined as a second bass guitarist. Shortly after this, **Pete Shotton** and **Eric Griffiths** also left and were replaced by **Paul McCartney** and **George Harrison**, who both played guitar.

George Harrison was a former member of the **Rebels**, where he had played together with his brother **Peter Harrison**.

In 1958, this line-up probably recorded the demo, "In Spite Of All The Danger" on acetate, which was coupled with "That'll Be The Day". A little later **Len Garry** and **Rod Davis** left the group, which soon changed its name to **Johnny & the Moondogs**. After **Colin Hanton** and **Ivan Vaughan** had also left, **John Lennon**, **George Harrison** and **Paul McCartney** continued as a trio under various names, one of them being the **Rainbows**. Around this time, **John Lennon** and **Paul McCartney** also appeared as a duo under the name the **Nurk Twins**, while **George Harrison** sometimes played with the **Les Stuart Quartet**.

In 1959, **Johnny & the Moondogs**, who had no steady drummer at this point, consisted of **John Lennon** (voc/rg), **George Harrison** (lg/voc), **Paul McCartney** (voc/g) and **Ken Brown** (bg). **Ken Brown** was a former member of the **Les Stuart Quartet**, where he had met **George Harrison** who persuaded him to join **Johnny & the Moondogs**. Still in that same year, **Ken Brown** left to join the **Blackjacks** and was replaced by **Stuart Sutcliffe**, who couldn't really play the bass guitar but was a good friend of **John Lennon**. Then, in 1960, **Tommy Moore** joined them on drums and the band changed their name to the **Silver Beatles**. This line-up did not last and in early 1961, **Tommy Moore** left because of trouble with his girlfriend. For a short time, **Norman Chapman** played the drums but then went on to play with the **In Crowd** and was replaced by **Pete Best**, who had formerly played with the **Blackjacks**. It is said to have been the suggestion of **Brian 'Cass' Cassar** (later known as **Casey Jones**) to shorten the group's name to the **Beatles**, which was accepted by the musicians.

Accordingly, the first line-up that appeared under the name the **Beatles** consisted of:

John Lennon	(voc/rg)
George Harrison	(lg/voc)
Paul McCartney	(voc/g)
Stuart Sutcliffe	(bg)
Pete Best	(dr)

Initially, **Mona Best**, the drummer's mother, looked after the interests of the band until their management was taken over by **Alan Williams**.

A little later, the **Beatles** went to Hamburg for the first time, where they were booked to play the 'Indra', which later became the 'Hit-Club'.

After **Derry & the Seniors** and **Rory Storm & the Hurricanes**, the **Beatles** were the third Liverpool group to appear in Hamburg. **Howie Casey**, at that time with **Derry & the Seniors**, was not happy with the **Beatles**

The Original Beatles
L to R: Stuart Sutcliffe, Paul McCartney (on piano), George Harrison, Pete Best & John Lennon

coming over as he feared that they were not good enough and would possibly spoil the chances of more Liverpool groups going to Hamburg. Of course his doubts were exaggerated, but it is also true that the **Beatles** didn't have great musical quality at that time, a fact that can be heard very clearly on the early live tapes. **Derry & the Seniors** were certainly more professional, but in spite of this, it was the **Beatles** who started the Beat avalanche rolling over there.

In 1961, Bert Kaempfert signed them as the backing group for an album with **Tony Sheridan** on Polydor, for which the group's name was changed to the **Beat Brothers**. This name was also given to other musicians that backed **Tony Sheridan** on later releases. To avoid confusion, the **Beat Brothers** (not the **Beatles**) also recorded some instrumental singles in their own right with a dominant saxophone sound.

So, it is not true that the **Beatles** were identical to the **Beat Brothers** in general.

The single "My Bonnie" was taken from the above album, which led to **Brian Epstein** becoming aware of them and taking over the band's management.

After their return to Liverpool, the **Beatles** stage outfit, stage show and, of course, their musical transition into a really hard Rock 'n' Roll group caused a sensation on their hometown's scene.

With the support of producer, **George Martin**, **Brian Epstein** managed to obtain a recording contract with EMI, after Decca had turned them down.

Stu Sutcliffe had meanwhile parted from the group to study in Hamburg, where he died of a brain haemorrhage in 1962.

In August 1962, **Pete Best** was replaced by **Ringo Starr**, whose real name is **Richard Starkey** and who had previously played with the **Eddie Clayton Group**, the **Darktown Skiffle Group** and the **Raving Texans** which had become **Rory Storm & the Hurricanes**.

It was not that **Pete Best** wanted to leave, but he was sacked by the other members for mysterious reasons. It is more likely that it wasn't the 'others' but probably just one member, still active, and the obvious reason was jealousy. This change is and will always be one of the most controversial points in the **Beatles'** history, but it is definitely untrue when it is stated that **Ringo Starr** was a better drummer, or that **George Martin** was responsible for that change. But this is not the right place to go into it and therefore the advice for people who are interested in knowing the truth about it, is that they better ask a real insider of that time and scene. The advice for **Beatles'** fans is that it's better not to do it.

Pete Best joined **Lee Curtis & the All Stars** who later became the **Pete Best Four**- another story in this book.

The **Beatles** in this new line-up had their biggest success with records that included "Love Me Do", "Please, Please Me", "From Me To You", "She Loves You", "I Want To Hold Your Hand", "A Hard Day's Night", "I Feel Fine", "Ticket To Ride", "Help", "We Can Work It Out" and many others, which all became worldwide hits. Most of their records were Lennon/McCartney compositions and this team also wrote very successfully for other Beat stars of that time including **Billy J. Kramer & the Dakotas**, the **Fourmost**, the **Applejacks**, **Peter & Gordon**, **Cilla Black** and **Tommy Quickly**.

Their motion-pictures, 'A Hard Day's Night' and 'Help' became bestsellers, although they lacked any sensible storyline.

As it seems, their incredible, but at this point their deserved success, went to their heads and although they already were the most successful group, they wanted to be different to all the other groups. With a few exceptions such as "Hey Jude", "Yesterday", "Lady Madonna" and "Let It Be", this resulted in many trashy records being released. Songs like "Yellow submarine", "I'm The Walrus", "Ob-La-Di Ob-La-Da" and others would have brought an end to the careers of any other group, but the **Beatles** had enough fans unwilling to be critical and so they were the only group who could afford such escapades.

Their songs had also lost the drive that once had carried all before them. Typical examples of this are songs like "Michelle" or "Girl", which were no more than second or even third class lightweight pop songs. But of course they sold well and became big hits, although from the Rock 'n' Roll point of view the **Beatles** had taken a step backwards.

It is also quite hard to understand why 'Sgt. Pepper' is always claimed to be their best album, as some of their earlier ones were a lot better. As to the enormous influence that this album apparently had on popular music at large, it has to be pointed out that these kinds of musical experiments were not new at all as many American groups had done similar things years before.

In 1970, the **Beatles** disbanded, not having performed live together for quite some time. All of the members started solo careers, which were more (**John Lennon** and **Paul McCartney**) or less (**Ringo Starr**) successful.

The always underrated **George Harrison** also released some very good records and had some hits over the years. However, he gained real recognition for the first time in the Eighties, when he had his best time musically which ended up in a great project called the **Travelling Wilburys**.

On the 8th of December 1980, **John Lennon** was shot by a mentally disturbed fan in the hall of the Dakota building in New York and **George Harrison** died on the 29th of November 2001 of a cancerous brain tumour.

Single-Discography :

As the **Beatles** have made so many records that were released all over the world in many variations and there were already complete books written about it, it is sensible to cut their discography down to the English market plus the early German solo recordings and of course the ones with **Tony Sheridan**.

Love Me Do / P.S. I Love You	UK- Parlophone R 4949 / 1962
Please Please Me / Ask Me Why	UK- Parlophone R 4983 / 1963
From Me To You / Thank You Girl	UK- Parlophone R 5015 / 1963
She Loves You / I'll Get You	UK- Parlophone R 5055 / 1963
I Want To Hold Your Hand / This Boy	UK- Parlophone R 5084 / 1963
Can't Buy Me Love / You Can't Do That	UK- Parlophone R 5114 / 1964
A Hard Day's Night / Things We Said Today	UK- Parlophone R 5160 / 1964
I Feel Fine / She's A Woman	UK- Parlophone R 5200 / 1964
Ticket To Ride / Yes It Is	UK- Parlophone R 5265 / 1965
Help / I'm Down	UK- Parlophone R 5305 / 1965
We Can Work It Out / Day Tripper	UK- Parlophone R 5389 / 1965
Paperback Writer / Rain	UK- Parlophone R 5452 / 1966
Eleanor Rigby / Yellow Submarine	UK- Parlophone R 5493 / 1966
Strawberry Fields Forever / Penny Lane	UK- Parlophone R 5570 / 1967
All You Need Is Love / Baby, You're A Rich Man	UK- Parlophone R 5620 / 1967
Hello Goodbye / I Am The Walrus	UK- Parlophone R 5655 / 1967
Lady Madonna / The Inner Light	UK- Parlophone R 5675 / 1968
Hey Jude / Revolution	UK- Parlophone R 5722 / 1968
Get back / Don't Let Me Down	UK- Parlophone R 5777 / 1969
The Ballad Of John & Yoko / Old Brown Shoe	UK- Parlophone R 5786 / 1969
Something / Come Together	UK- Parlophone R 5814 / 1969
Let It Be / You Know My Name	UK- Parlophone R 5833 / 1970

(please note, that from "Get Back" onwards, all singles displayed the 'Apple' label)

Different German releases :

Cry For A Shadow / Why	G- Polydor 52275 / 1964
Ain't She Sweet / Take Out Some Insurance On Me Baby	G- Polydor 52317 / 1964
*Komm Gib Mir Deine Hand / Sie Liebt Dich	G- Odeon O 22671 / 1964

(*please note that these were the German versions of "I Want To Hold Your Hand" and "She Loves You")

EP discography :

THE BEATLES' HITS   UK- Parlophone GEP 8880 / 1963

- From Me To You / Thank You Girl / Please Please Me / Love Me Do

TWIST AND SHOUT   UK- Parlophone GEP 8882 / 1963

- Twist And Shout / A Taste Of Honey / Do You Want To Know A Secret / There's A Place

THE BEATLES (No.1)   UK- Parlophone GEP 8883 / 1963

- I Saw Her Standing There / Misery / Anna / Chains

ALL MY LOVING   UK-Parlophone GEP 8891 / 1964

All My Loving / Ask Me Why / Money / P.S. I Love You

LONG TALL SALLY   UK- Parlophone GEP 8913 / 1964

Long Tall Sally / I Call Your Name / Slow Down / Matchbox

A HARD DAY'S NIGHT - Extracts from the film   UK- Parlophone GEP 8920 / 1964

I Should Have Known Better / If I Fell / Tell Me Why / And I Love Her

A HARD DAY'S NIGHT - Extracts from the album   UK- Parlophone GEP 8924 / 1964

- Any Time At All / I'll Cry Instead / Things We Said Today / When I Get Home

BEATLES FOR SALE   UK- Parlophone GEP 8931 / 1965

- No Reply / I'm A Loser / Rock 'n' Roll Music / Eight Days A Week

BEATLES FOR SALE (No.2)   UK- Parlophone GEP 8938 / 1965

- I'll Follow The Sun / Baby's In Black / Words Of Love / I Don't Want To Spoil The Party

THE BEATLES' MILLION SELLERS   UK- Parlophone GEP 8946 / 1965

- She Loves You / I Want To Hold Your Hand / Can't Buy Me Love / I Feel Fine

YESTERDAY   UK- Parlophone GEP 8948 / 1966

- Yesterday / Act Naturally / You Like Me Too Much / It's Only Love

NOWHERE MAN UK- Parlophone GEP 8952 / 1966

- Nowhere Man / Drive My Car / Michelle / You Won't See Me

MAGICAL MYSTERY TOUR UK- Parlophone MMT 1 / 1967

- Magical Mystery Tour / Your Mother Should Know / I Am The Walrus / The Fool On The Hill / Flying / Blue Jay Way

LP discography :

PLEASE PLEASE ME UK - Parlophone PMC 1202 / 1963

- I Saw Her Standing There / Misery / Anna / Chains / Boys / Ask Me Why / Please Please Me / Love Me Do / P.S. I Love You / Baby It's You / Do You Want To Know A Secret / A Taste Of Honey / There's A Place / Twist And Shout

WITH THE BEATLES UK - Parlophone PMC 1206 / 1963

- It Won't Be Long / All I've Got To Do / All My Loving / Don't Bother Me / Little Child / Till There Was You / Please Mr. Postman / Roll Over Beethoven / Hold Me Tight / You Really Got A Hold On Me / I Wanna Be Your Man / Devil In Her Heart / Not A Second Time / Money

A HARD DAY'S NIGHT UK - Parlophone PMC 1230 / 1964

- A Hard Day's Night / I Should Have Known Better / If I Fell / I'm Happy Just To Dance With You / And I Love Her / Tell Me Why / Can't Buy Me Love / Any Time At All / I'll Cry Instead / Things We Said Today / When I Get Home / You Can't Do That / I'll Be Back

BEATLES FOR SALE UK - Parlophone PMC 1240 / 1964

- No Reply / I'm A Loser / Baby's In Black / Rock 'n' Roll Music / I'll Follow The Sun / Mr. Moonlight / Kansas City / Hey - Hey - Hey - Hey / Eight Days A Week / Words Of Love / Honey Don't / Every Little Thing / I Don't Want To Spoil The Party / What You're Doing / Everybody's Trying To Be My Baby

HELP! UK - Parlophone PMC 1255 / 1965

- Help / The Night Before / You've Got To Hide Your Love Away / I Need You / Another Girl / You're Going To Lose That Girl / Ticket To Ride / Act Naturally / It's Only Love / You Like Me Too Much / Tell Me What You See / I've Just Seen A Face / Yesterday / Dizzy Miss Lizzy

RUBBER SOUL UK - Parlophone PMC 1267 / 1965

- Drive My Car / Norwegian Wood / You Won't See Me / Nowhere Man / Think For Yourself / The Word / Michelle / What Goes On / Girl / I'm Looking Through You / In My Life / Wait / If I Needed Someone / Run For Your Life

REVOLVER
UK - Parlophone PMC 7009 / 1966

- Taxman / Eleanor Rigby / I'm Only Sleeping / Love You To / Here, There And Everywhere / Yellow Submarine / She Said She Said / Good Day Sunshine / And Your Bird Can Sing / For No One / Doctor Robert / I Want To Tell You / Got To Get You Into My Life / Tomorrow Never Knows

A COLLECTION OF BEATLES OLDIES
UK - Parlophone PMC 7016 / 1966

- She Loves You / From Me To You / We Can Work It Out / Help / Michelle / Yesterday / I Feel Fine / Yellow Submarine / Can't Buy Me Love / Bad Boy / Day Tripper / A Hard Day's Night / Ticket To Ride / Paperback Writer / Eleanor Rigby / I Want To Hold Your Hand

SGT. PEPPER'S LONELY HEARTS CLUB BAND
UK - Parlophone PMC 7027 / 1967

- Sgt. Pepper's Lonely Hearts Club Band / With A Little Help From My Friend / Lucy In The Sky With Diamonds / Getting Better / Fixing A Hole / She's Leaving Home / Being For The Benefit Of Mr. Kite / Within You, Without You / When I'm Sixty-Four / Lovely Rita / Good Morning Good Morning / Sgt. Pepper's Lonely Hearts Club Band / A Day In The Life

THE BEATLES
UK- Parlophone PMC 7067 + 7068 / 1968

- Back In The USSR / Dear Prudence / Glass onion / Ob-La-Di, Ob-La-Da / Wild Honey Pie / The Continuing Story Of Bungalow Bill / While My Guitar Gently Weeps / Happiness Is A Warm Gun / Martha My Dear / I'm So Tired / Blackbird / Piggies / Rocky Raccoon / Don't Pass Me By / Why Don't We Do It In The Road / I Will / Julia / Birthday / Yer Blues / Mother Nature's Son / Everybody's Got Something To Hide Except Me And My Monkey / Sexy Sadie / Helter Skelter / Long, Long, Long / Revolution / Honey Pie / Savoy Truffle / Cry, Baby, Cry / Revolution / Good night

YELLOW SUBMARINE
UK - Parlophone PMC 7070 / 1969

- Yellow Submarine / Only A Northern Song / All Together Now / Hey Bulldog / It's All Too Much / All You Need Is Love - plus seven soundtrack instrumentals by the George Martin Orchestra

ABBEY ROAD
UK-Apple (Parlophone) PCS 7088 / 1969

- Come Together / Something / Maxwell's Silver Hammer / Oh Darling / Octopus's Garden / I Want You / Here Comes The Sun / Because / You Never Give Me Your Money / Sun King / Mean Mr. Mustard / Polythene Pam / She Came In Through The Bathroom Window / Golden Slumbers / Carry That Weight / The End / Her Majesty

LET IT BE
UK-Apple (Parlophone) PCS 7096 / 1970

- Two Of Us / Dig A Pony / Across The Universe / I, Me, Mine / Dig It / Let It Be / Maggie May / I've Got A Feeling / The One After 909 / The Long And Winding Road / For You Blue / Get back

Releases with **Tony Sheridan** :

<u>Singles:</u>

My Bonnie / The Saints	**G - Polydor 24673 / 1961**
Why / Cry For A Shadow	**G - Polydor 52275 / 1964**
Ain't She Sweet / Take Out Some Insurance On Me Baby	**G - Polydor 52317 / 1964**
Skinny Minny / Sweet Georgia Brown	**G - Polydor 52324 / 1964**

(please note that "Cry For A Shadow" and "Ain't She Sweet" were recorded by the Beatles without Tony Sheridan)

<u>EPs:</u>

YA YA   **G - Polydor 21485 / 1961**

- Ya Ya (Pt. 1) / Ya Ya (Pt. 2) / Sweet Georgia Brown / Skinny Minny

MY BONNIE   **G - Polydor 21610 / 1964**

- My Bonnie / Why / The Saints / Cry for a shadow

plus some tracks accompanying **Tony Sheridan** on his first three albums **'My Bonnie'** (G-Polydor237112 / 1962) **'The Beatles First'** (G-Polydor Hi-Fi 46432 / 1964) and **'Meet the Beat'** (G-Polydor J 74557/ 1965), which were put out on a single and an EP (see above).

BERNIE & THE BUZZ BAND

This Liverpool Soul group was formed in 1967 in the Toxteth area by singer, **Bernie Wenton**, who had formerly sung with the **Sobells** and the **Triumphs**.

At this time, Liverpool's Merseybeat was no longer dominating the British music scene, and Beat music was changing into Rock on one hand and into Mainstream pop on the other.

But **Bernie Wenton** didn't want to take either of these directions, so he decided on Soul music when he formed **Bernie & the Buzz Band**, which included the following musicians:

Bernie Wenton	(voc)
Neil Ford	(lg)
Jan Schetheer	(bg)
Jeff Edmondson	(org)
Andy O'Hagan	(sax)
Dave O'Hagan	(sax)
Geoff Howard	(tr)
Jimmy Turner	(dr)

Neil Ford was a former member of the **Vaaveros** and **Johnny Ringo & the Colts**, while **Jeff Edmondson** had previously played with the **Calderstones**.

Andy O'Hagan and **Dave O'Hagan** both came from the **Times**, who were the backing group for the **Signs**, prior to this, **Andy O'Hagan** had played with the **Dions**, formerly known as **Roy & the Dions**. All the others were also experienced musicians, but it is not known in which groups they had played previously.

As well as at the Liverpool venues, **Bernie & the Buzz Band** frequently played in London, where **Noel Walker** became aware of them. He was working as a producer for the Decca sub label 'Deram' at that time and managed to get the group signed to that recording company. This was in early 1968 and a little later he produced their first single.

The A-side was "Don't Knock It", coupled with the **Sam & Dave** classic "When Something Is Wrong With My Baby". This outstanding record sold quite well, but did not get near the charts.

Dave O'Hagan, **Andy O'Hagan**, **Geoff Howard** and **Jeff Edmondson** left the group and **Alby Donnelly** (sax/fl) and **Nick Roman** (latin perc) joined. **Alby Donnelly** had formerly played with the **Plainsmen**, the **Terry Hines Sextet** and the **Clayton Squares**.

With this line-up, the group recorded "The House That Jack Built" (not to be confused with **Alan Price's** hit success) and a version of "Funky Broadway" for their next single. For unknown reasons it was never released, although "The House That Jack Built" was released a little later on the Decca label with "Midnight Confessions" by the **Pete Kelly Solution** from Southport on the B-side.

**Bernie Wenton with brothers Willie and Bobby
and the Shufflers Sound**

This record was also not too successful and **Bernie & the Buzz Band** split up in late 1968 or early 1969.

Alby Donnelly went to Germany and found stardom with his group **Supercharge**, while **Neil Ford** remained in the music business as a session guitarist and **Bernie Wenton**, together with his brothers **Willie** and **Bobby Wenton** (both also vocalists), amalgamated with a group called **Shuffler's Sound**. Following these changes, the group changed their name to **Shuffler's Sound featuring the Buzz Brothers**.

Besides **Bernie**, **Willie** and **Bobby Wenton** (all voc), the line-up consisted of **Silver Chantry** (g), **Billy Good** (bg), **Ivor Alli** (org), **Mike Kearns** (sax) and **Alan Seff** (dr).

Silver Chantry later was replaced by **Willie Osu** on guitar, and then the band changed its name (probably to **Black Magic**) and became a real Rock band, but by that time the Wenton brothers had already parted from them.

After that group split, **Mike Kearns** played with **Karl Terry & the Cruisers** and then joined **Gaz & the Groovers,** who also went to Germany where they changed their name to **Juke** and became a successful live-act for years. Sadly, **Mike Kearns** committed suicide in 1992.

Billy Good later played with the newly formed and very short-lived **Lee Curtis & the All Stars** and then joined the **Undertakers**, under the leadership of **Geoff Nugent**. He is still a member of that group and is also gigging as a solo performer in Liverpool clubs these days.

Bernie Wenton teamed up with **Alby Donnelly** in a band (was it already **Supercharge**?) and later, together with his brother **Willie Wenton**, sang backing vocals in **Chris Rea's** band.

Bernie Wenton also appeared quite often as an actor on British television until he sadly died in 2007.

All the other members of **Shuffler's Sound** disappeared from the scene.

Discography:

| Don't Knock It / When Something Is Wrong With My Baby | UK-Deram DM 181 / 1968 |
| The House That Jack Built / Pete Kelly's Solution: Midnight Confessions | UK-Decca 22829 / 1968 |

THE PETE BEST FOUR

The career of drummer and band leader **Peter Best** started in the late Fifties in Liverpool, when he was a member of a trio called **The Blackjacks**. In 1960 he replaced the departing **Tommy Moore** in the **Silver Beatles**, who a little later shortened their name to the **Beatles** and went to Hamburg.

Pete Best All Stars

When **Pete Best** was sacked from that band, for (not really) mysterious reasons, he joined **Lee Curtis & the All Stars,** who in the same month were voted second to the **Beatles** in the 'Mersey Beat' newspaper popularity poll. **Pete Best** remained with the group when **Lee Curtis** went to Germany with another backing band.

He then took over the leadership and their initial appearances were made as **Pete Best & the Original All Stars**.

Because **Lee Curtis'** new backing group also used the name of the **All Stars**, the **Original All Stars** changed their name into the **Pete Best Four**. Then lead guitarist, **Frank Bowen** left and was replaced by **Tommy McGuirk**, a former member of **Gene Day & the Django-Beats** and the **Aarons**.

As a result of these changes the **Pete Best Four** from then on appeared with the following line-up:

Tony Waddington	(g/voc)
Tommy McGuirk	(g/voc)
Wayne Bickerton	(bg/voc)
Pete Best	(dr/voc)

Tony Waddington was also a former member of **Gene Day & the Django-Beats** that later evolved into the **Comets**. He had also played with **Steve Bennett & the Syndicate**.

Wayne Bickerton had formerly played with the **Bobby Bell Rockers** and **Steve Bennett & the Syndicate**.

In 1964, the **Pete Best Four** were signed by Decca and soon after had their first single released with the **Tony Waddington/Wayne Bickerton** original "Why Did I Fall In Love With You", which was coupled with a good version of the **Eddie Hodges** success "I'm Gonna Knock On Your Door".

Pete Best Four

Tony Waddington and **Wayne Bickerton** later proved to be very talented songwriters. Unfortunately, this single took them nowhere.

The **Pete Best Four** toured Germany and besides the 'Star Club' in Hamburg, also played at the opening concert of the 'Star Club' in Bielefeld. Around the same time there was a single released under **Pete Best's** name in the USA with the songs "Kansas City" and "Boys", but this did not have any impact either.

Maybe because of their lack of success, the **Pete Best Four** disbanded in early 1965 after they had recorded some more of their own material, which was only released later.

Tommy McGuirk wanted to form a new group with **Denny Alexander**, whom he had played with in the **Aarons**, but that did not work out and **Tommy McGuirk** disappeared from the scene for some time, but later on he was a member of the **Everglades**.

Pete Best, **Tony Waddington** and **Wayne Bickerton** re-formed the group as the **Pete Best Combo** in the same year, together with two sax players, **Billy Burton** and **Trevor Baker**.

Billy Burton, sometimes also known as **Bill Wesley**, was a former member of the **Cyclones**.

Pete Best Combo

In this line-up the **Pete Best Combo** recorded the song "Last Night" for the European market but it was not released.

The independent US producer, **Bob Gallo** became interested in the group and got them to go to the United States where he recorded the band using the name **Peter Best** and, for the album, he chose the title 'Best of The Beatles'.

The album was released on the Savage label in 1965 and included the song, "Last Night" and, with the exception of "Shimmy Like My Sister Kate", "Casting My Spell" and "Some Other Guy", only featured songs by **Tony Waddington** and **Wayne Bickerton**. It could have been a really nice album had it been mixed and produced better. In any case, it was not successful but, today it is a very rare and expensive collector's item. A further **Peter Best** single was released in the USA with the songs, "If You Can't Get Her" and "The Way I Feel About You" on the Happening label in 1965 but, once again, it wasn't a great success and so did not help the group at all.

The **Pete Best Combo** returned to Liverpool where it then broke up. **Trevor Baker** disappeared from the scene and **Billy Burton** initially played with the **Denims** and later with **Karl Terry & the Cruisers** before he emigrated to South Africa. Sometime in the Nineties, he returned to Liverpool and played again with **Karl Terry**, as well as with various other groups on the scene.

For a short time, the **Pete Best Combo** was re-formed as a trio with **Pete Best**, **Tony Waddington** and **Wayne Bickerton**, but finally broke up again without having recorded any more songs.

Tony Waddington and **Wayne Bickerton** continued as a song-writing and producing duo and, as well as hits for the **Flirtations**, they also wrote all the early material for the **Rubettes**, including their million selling "Sugar Baby Love".

In addition, **Wayne Bickerton** was a member of the great group, **World of Oz**, who recorded a fantastic album and had hits with songs such as "The Muffin Man" and "King Croesus" in the late Sixties.

Pete Best quit show business and went back to a normal day job, but around 1967/68 there was a single released by **Peter Best** on the Australian Columbia label with the title "Want You".

Now, it is hard to say if it was **Peter Best** from Liverpool or just another singer with the same name, but there is at least the possibility that this was a solo record by the former **Beatles** drummer and that is why it is mentioned here. This **David Mackay** production was zapped up a bit with an orchestral sound, but its rhythm was still Beat.

It might be of interest to collectors to know that in 1982, an album was released in the USA on the 'Phoenix 10' label with the title 'The Beatle That Time Forgot', which featured previously unissued Sixties recordings from the **Pete Best Combo**.

However, **Pete Best** continued to work as the assistant manager of the 'Job Centre' in Liverpool and in 1988 he appeared on stage again for the first time, on the bill at the annual 'Merseybeatle Convention' in Liverpool. It was announced as a concert by the **Pete Best Band**, but this group only came together for this one performance and, besides members of **Liverpool Express** (**Billy Kinsley**, etc.), included his younger brother **Roag Best** as second drummer, who normally played with **Watt 4**.

It was an impressive performance and a lot of people later agreed that it was more than sad that this line-up did not stay together for further concerts.

In 1989, **Pete Best** sat in with the **Merseybeats** at a 'MerseyCats' charity concert for their original drummer **John Banks**, who had died in 1988. Besides him, the line-up consisted of the Sixties original members, **Tony Crane**, **Billy Kinsley** and **Aaron Williams**. He obviously enjoyed playing again, even if not with a steady band and on a regular basis. This line-up of the **Merseybeats** including **Pete Best** played some more concerts but only for the 'MerseyCats' organisation. In 1990, **Pete Best** recorded the single "Heaven/Fool In Love" together with **Billy Kinsley** which was released as **Kinsley & Best** on the English Prestige Label.

Shortly after, **Pete Best** and his brother **Roag** formed a new **Pete Best Band** who, with frequently changing line-ups, toured sporadically including the United States, Canada, Japan and Germany.

Besides the two brothers, since 2002 the group has included the two guitarists **Phil Melia** (ex **Mojo Filter**) and **Tony Flynn** (ex **Crowded House**), as well as bassist **Paul Parry** (formerly with the **Thunderboots**, the **Pretenders** and the **Georgie Fame** band). This is a really great line-up with all the members sharing the vocals.

<u>Single discography :</u>

as **The Pete Best Four** :

Why Did I Fall In Love With You / I'm Gonna Knock On Your Door	UK - Decca F. 11929 / 1964

Different US releases :

as **Peter Best** :

Kansas City / Boys	US-Cameo Parkway C 391 / 1964
I'll Try Anyway / I Wanna Be There	US- Original Beatles Drummer Best 800 / 1964

as **Peter Best** (Best Of The Beatles) :

Don't Play With Me / If You Can't Get Her	US- Happening 405 / 1964
If You Can't Get Her / The Way I Feel About You	US- Happening HA 1117 / 1965
I Can't Do Without You / Key To My Heart	US- Mr. Maestro 711 / 1965
Casting My Spell / I'm Blue	US- Mr. Maestro 712 / 1965

From that period in the late Eighties, a series of singles were released on the Collectables label. The last two were coupled with songs that **Pete Best** had recorded together with the **Beatles** for Polydor in Germany.

They are:

I'll Try Anyway / I Don't Know Why I Do	US- Collectables 1516 / 1987
She's Not The Only Girl In Town / More Than I Need Myself	US- Collectables 1517 / 1987
I'll Have Everything Too / I'm Checking Out Now Baby	US- Collectables 1518 / 1987
How'd You Get To Know Her Name / If You Can't Get Her	US- Collectables 1519 / 1987
Rock 'n' Roll Music / Cry For A Shadow	US- Collectables 1520 / 1988
I'll try anyway / Why	US- Collectables 1524 / 1988

Peter Best <u>solo</u> :

Want You / Carousel Of Love	AUS-Columbia DO 5039 / 1967

(There are doubts, that this record is by the **Pete Best** from this story - see text)

<u>Unissued tracks:</u>

In 1964, the **Pete Best Four** recorded the song, **"Last night"** as a follow-up single for Decca, but this was not released. The song was later included on the US album of the **Pete Best Combo,** but most probably not the original version.

as **Peter Best** :

BEST OF THE BEATLES   US - Savage BM - 72 / 1965

- Last Night / Why Did You Leave Me Baby / Shimmy Like My Sister Kate / I Need Your Lovin' / Nobody But You / I Can't Do Without You / Casting My Spell / Wait And See / Some Other Guy / I'm Blue / She's Alright / Keys To My Heart

Besides this, in 1965, US producer **Bob Gallo** recorded some more songs with the **Pete Best Combo**, which were not released at that time, but in 1982 under the name of **The Pete Best Band** the following albums were released:

REBIRTH US   PB Records 44 / 1981

- I Can't Do Without You / Off The Hook / She's Alright / I Need Your Lovin' / Why Did You Leave Me Baby / Shimmy Like My Sister Kate / I Wanna Be There / Everybody / Pete's Theme / Keys To My Heart

THE BEATLE THAT TIME FORGOT US   Phoenix10 PHX 340 / 1982

- I'll Try Anyway / I Don't Know Why I Do / She's Not The Only Girl In Town / More Than I Need Myself / I'll Have Everything Too / I'm Checking Out Now Baby / How'd You Get To Know Her Name / If You Can't Get Her / Rock 'n' Roll Music

THE BIG THREE

This Liverpool trio originated from the group, **Cass & the Cassanovas** after **Brian 'Cass' Cassar** had left them. **Brian 'Cass' Cassar** later became famous under the name of **Casey Jones** in Germany, where he had big hits with "Jack The Ripper", "Don't Ha Ha" and "Yockomo". His story can be followed under **Cass & the Cassanovas** in this book.

The **Big Three** soon earned the reputation of being a 'band's band', much admired by other musicians, due to their very good, but also very hard, Beat interpretations. But of course they were also loved by the public at large, a fact that is proven by their regularly high placing in the 'Mersey Beat's' popularity polls. The trio had a very high musical quality and originally consisted of:

Adrian Barber	(lg/voc)
Johnny 'Gus' Gustafson	(voc/bg)
Johnny 'Hutch' Hutchinson	(dr/voc)

Their amplifiers, which were constructed by **Adrian Barber** were of such interest to other bands, that he left the group to concentrate on building these so-called 'coffins'. His replacement in the **Big Three** was the great and imaginative guitarist, **Brian 'Griff' Griffiths**, who came from the recently disbanded **Howie Casey & the Seniors**, originally known as **Derry & the Seniors**.

The Big Three

The group was signed to Decca and with their first release, "Some Other Guy", the **Big Three** became the third Liverpool group to enter the British charts when the record climbed up to No. 39 in 1963. But apart from this, "By The Way" (No. 24) and their outstanding live EP 'The Big Three Live At The Cavern' (No. 6) became the group's only other chart successes.

Unfortunately, a number of very fine recordings such as "I'm With You/Peanut Butter" and "If You Ever Change Your Mind/ Gotta Keep Her Under Hand" were only known by some fans, insiders and specialists, although they are real mementos of the better part of Merseybeat history. But, it is also true to say that the **Big Three** were far better live than in the studio and just like **Rory Storm & the Hurricanes**, their exciting live sound was never captured on their records.

In 1964, **Johnny Gustafson** and **Brian Griffiths** left to form a trio under the name the **Seniors**, together with drummer **Ian Broad**, who had formerly played with the **Five Stars**, **Gus Travis & the Midnighters** and **Freddie Starr & the Midnighters**. But the **Seniors** were short-lived and broke up after their German tour, also in 1964.

Johnny Gustafson joined the **Merseybeats** and **Brian Griffiths** was one of the founding members of the **Griff Parry Five** before they both met up again in the **Johnny Gus Set**.

Their replacements in the **Big Three** in 1964 were **Billy 'Faron' Ruffley** and **Paddy Chambers**, who both came from the recently disbanded **Faron's Flamingos**.

They then became a four-piece with the arrival of **Paul Pilnick**, who had formerly played with **Vince & the Volcanoes** and **Lee Curtis & the All Stars**.

'**Faron**' later emigrated to France where he was a member of **Blue Suede**, but in the Seventies returned to Liverpool. His story can be followed under **Faron's Flamingos**.

Paddy Chambers also left the **Big Three** in 1965 to join the **Eyes**. He later played with **Paddy, Klaus & Gibson** and the **Escorts**, before he became a member of **Big John's Rock 'n' Roll Circus**, **Sinbad** and **Paddy Chambers & the Java Jive**.

He was replaced by **John 'Brad' Bradley** (bg) and **Howie Casey** (sax), while **Paul Pilnick** took over on lead guitar. Both new members of the **Big Three** (they kept the name, although they were a four-piece) came from the just disbanded **Krewkats**, who originally hailed from Birmingham, the hometown of the new bass guitarist.

Howie Casey, of course, was the former leader of **Howie Casey & the Seniors** and prior to joining the **Big Three** he had played with various Merseybeat groups, including **King Size Taylor & the Dominoes**.

But this line-up only lasted until July 1965 when the first major **Big Three** split occurred. At this time they had no recording contract and only played gigs on Merseyside.

Howie Casey had a short spell with the **Griff Parry Five**, while **John Bradley** joined the **Jam Buttees**, but very soon they both teamed up again to re-form the **Krew** - another story in this book.

Paul Pilnick went to Hamburg, where he joined **Lee Curtis & the All Stars** again, and after that he was a member of groups such as, **Stealer's Wheel**, **Badger**, **Sinbad**, and **Jake**.

The only remaining original member, **Johnny Hutchinson** joined the **Spidermen**, but in September 1965, he re-formed the **Big Three** with the two Southport musicians, **Ray Marshal** (bg/voc), formerly with the **Mersey Four**, and **Barry Womersley** (g/voc), a former member of the **Diplomats** and **Rhythm & Blues Inc.**. This was a very good line-up, but they only gigged in and around the Liverpool area.

It is not known exactly when the final line-up of the **Big Three** disbanded again, but it was probably in 1966. **Ray Marshall** went back to Southport where he remained in the music business.

Barry Womersley became a member of the **Clayton Squares**, but only for a short time and then he joined **Jasmin T**, who recorded a great version of "Some Other Guy" in 1969. In the mid-Seventies he played with **Inner Sleeve**, and in 1977 had a solo single out before he disappeared from the scene for years and then re-formed his old group **Rhythm & Blues Inc.**, which still appears on the scene sporadically.

For a short time **Johnny Hutchinson** played with the **Calderstones** and after that was a member of **Paul Craig & the Theme**. In 1967 he quit show business and never returned to it.

In 1973, both former members, **Johnny Gustafson** and **Brian Griffiths** re-formed the **Big Three** together with **Nigel Olson** (why not **Johnny Hutchinson**?), the former drummer with the **Spencer Davis Group** and **Elton John's** backing group.

But the new **Big Three** only recorded the album, 'Resurrection' in 1973, from which an EP with the songs "Let It Rock", "Some Other Guy" and "If You Gotta Make A Fool Of Somebody" were coupled out. The first two numbers were also released as a single for the German market. On this album, which was more Rock than Beat, the three musicians were supported by **Peter Robinson** (p), **Les Thatcher** (bj), **Henry Lowther** (horns), **Mick Grabham** (g) and **John Smith** (tuba).

After that release, the name of the **Big Three** disappeared from the scene with the only exception being a concert for 'MerseyCats' in 1991, but this was a session and did not include **Johnny Hutchinson** or **Johnny Gustafson**.

In 1966, **Johnny Gustafson** and **John Banks** of the **Merseybeats** teamed up as a duo under the name of **Johnny & John**. From there they both joined the **Quotations**. After that, **Johnny Gustafson** went on to play with **Quartermass**, **Hard Stuff** and **Roxy Music** in the late 60's and 70's. From 1975 until 1978 he occasionally appeared with the **Ian Gillan Band**, he later played with **Rowdy**, the **Rock Band** and after that, he was a member of the **Pirates**.

Brian Griffiths emigrated to **Canada** where he still lives, but he no longer plays guitar.

For collectors it might be interesting to know that in the mid-Eighties, an album was released on the Edsel label which featured the complete **Big Three** Sixties material.

Discography :

Some Other Guy / Let True Love Begin	**UK - Decca F.11614 / 1963**
By The Way / Cavern Stomp	**UK - Decca F.11689 / 1963**
I'm With You / Peanut Butter	**UK - Decca F.11752 / 1963**
If You Ever Change Your Mind / Gotta Keep Her Under Hand	**UK - Decca F.11927 / 1964**

EP

THE BIG THREE LIVE AT THE CAVERN	**UK-Decca DFE 8553 / 1964**

- **What'd I Say / Don't Start Running Away / Zip-A-Dee-Doo-Dah / Reelin' And Rockin'**

Songs on compilation albums :

"Bring It On Home To Me" (Live)	on **'At The Cavern'**	**UK- Decca LK 4597 / 1963**

Unreleased tracks :

The original **Cass & the Cassanovas** backed **Johnny Gentle** on his demo **"After The Laughter Came Tears"**, which was recorded during a Scotland tour in 1960.

CILLA BLACK

Liverpool born **Priscilla White** started her singing career in the early Sixties when she appeared with various bands on stage at the 'Cavern', where she was working as a cloakroom girl.

She performed with **Rory Storm & the Hurricanes**, the **Big Three** as well as some others. When **Brian Epstein** first became aware of her, he took over her management and led her along the same successful route that the **Beatles** had taken previously - a recording contract with EMI with **George Martin** as the producer.

Her first record was the **Paul McCartney** song "Love Of The Loved, which climbed up the charts to No. 35 by the end of 1963. The follow-up, "Anyone Who Had A Heart", a **Dionne Warwick** original written by **Burt Bacharach** and **Hal David**, became her first chart topper in February 1964.

This was the opener for a string of Top 10 positions by 1966 – "You're My World" (No. 1), "It's For You" (No. 7), "You've Lost That Loving Feeling" (No. 2), "Love's Just A Broken Heart" (No. 5), "Alfie" (No. 9) and "Don't Answer Me" (No. 6). She also had two Top 20 hits with "I've Been Wrong Before" (No. 17) and "A Fool Am I" (No. 13).

Cilla Black also appeared in the Gerry & the Pacemakers film, 'Ferry cross the Mersey', where she sang the song, "Is It Love". This was featured on the UK release of the soundtrack album, as well as on the B-side of her chart success, "You've Lost That Loving Feeling". Though doubtless a big success, Cilla Black was never a real Beat singer in the style of the great Beryl Marsden.

Cilla had quite a thin voice and her records were not very exciting, not even the Lennon/McCartney compositions. But her chart success continued until 1971, and included further Top 10 records such as "Step Inside Love" (No. 8 in 1968), probably her best record was "Surround Yourself With Sorrow" (No. 3 in 1969), "Conversations" (No. 7 in 1969) and "Something Tells Me" (No. 3 in1971).

After the Beatles, she was the most successful recording act out of Brian Epstein's stable.

Because she was already more of a family entertainer in the Sixties, it is not too surprising that she later became a TV star with her own shows, which are still quite popular in England.

Discography:

Love Of The Loved / Shy Of Love	UK- Parlophone R 5065 / 1963
Anyone Who Had A Heart / Just For You	UK- Parlophone R 5101 / 1964
You're My World / Suffer Now I Must	UK- Parlophone R 5133 / 1964
It's For You / He Won't Ask Me	UK- Parlophone R 5162 / 1964
You've Lost That Loving Feeling / Is It Love	UK- Parlophone R 5225 / 1965
I've Been Wrong Before / I Don't Want To Know	UK- Parlophone R 5296 / 1965
Love's Just A Broken Heart / Yesterday	UK- Parlophone R 5395 / 1966
Alfie / Night Time Is Here	UK- Parlophone R 5427 / 1966
Don't Answer Me / The Right One Is Left	UK- Parlophone R 5463 / 1966
A Fool Am I / For No One	UK- Parlophone R 5515 / 1966
What Good Am I / Over My Head	UK- Parlophone R 5608 / 1967
I Only Live To Love You / From Now On	UK- Parlophone R 5652 / 1967
Step Inside Love / I Couldn't Take My Eyes Off You	UK- Parlophone R 5674 / 1968
Where Is Tomorrow / Work Is A Four Letter Word	UK- Parlophone R 5706 / 1968
Surround Yourself With Sorrow / London Bridge	UK- Parlophone R 5759 / 1969
Conversation / Liverpool lullaby	UK- Parlophone R 5785 / 1969
If I Thought You'd Ever Change Your Mind / It Feels So Good	UK- Parlophone R 5820 / 1969
Child Of Me / That's Why I Love	UK- Parlophone R 5879 / 1970

EP discography:

ANYONE WHO HAD A HEART   UK- Parlophone GEP 8901 / 1964

- Anyone Who Had A Heart / Just For You / Love Of The Loved / Shy Of Love

IT'S FOR YOU   UK- Parlophone GEP 8916 / 1964

- It's For You / He Won't Ask Me / You're My World / Suffer Now I Must

CILLA'S HITS   UK- Parlophone GEP 8954 / 1966

- Don't Answer Me / The Right One Is Left / Alfie / Night Time Is Here

TIME FOR CILLA   UK- Parlophone GEP 8967 / 1967

- Abyssinian Secret / Trees And Loneliness / There I Go / Time

Different French EP:

LOVE'S JUST A BROKEN HEART   F- Odeon MEO 114 / 1966

- Alfie / Love's Just A Broken Heart / Yesterday / Night Time Is Here

LP discography:

CILLA   UK- Parlophone PMC 1243 / 1965

- Going Out Of My Head / Every Little Bit Hurts / Baby It's You / Dancing In The Street / Come To Me / Ole Man River / One Little Voice / I'm Not Alone Anymore / What'cha Gonna Do 'bout It / Love Letters / This Empty Place / You'd Be So Nice To Come Home To

CILLA SINGS A RAINBOW   UK- Parlophone PCS 7004 / 1966

- Love's Just A Broken Heart / Lover's Concerto / Make It Easy On Yourself / One Two Three / There's No Place To Hide / When I Fall In Love / Yesterday / Sing A Rainbow / Baby I'm Yours / The Real Thing / Everything I Touch Turns To Tears / In A Woman's Eyes / My Love Come Home

SHER-OO   UK- Parlophone PCS 7041 / 1968

- What The World Needs Now Is Love / Suddenly You Love Me / This Is The First Time / Follow The Path Of The Stars / Misty Roses / Take Me In Your Arms And Love Me / Yo Yo / Something's Gotten Hold Of My Heart / Step Inside Love / A Man And A Woman / I Couldn't Take My Eyes Off You / Follow Me

STEP INSIDE LOVE   UK- EMI (MFP) SPR 90019 / 1968

- same as 'Sher-oo'

BEST OF CILLA   UK- Parlophone PCS 7065 / 1968

- Love Of The Loved / Anyone Who Had A Heart / You're My World / You've Lost That Lovin' Feelin' / Love's Just A Broken Heart / Alfie / I Only Live To Love You / What Good Am I / Step Inside Love / Where Is Tomorrow / Sing A Rainbow / It's For You / Yesterday / Goin' Out Of My Head

SURROUND YOURSELF WITH CILLA   UK- Parlophone PCS 7079 / 1969

- Aquarius / Without Him / Only Forever Will Do / You'll Never Get To Heaven / Forget Him / It'll Never Happen Again / Think Of Me / I Am A Woman / Words / Red Rubber Ball / Liverpool Lullaby / Surround Yourself With Sorrow

YOU'RE MY WORLD (12 Big Hits)   UK- Regal Starline SRS 5044 / 1970

- You're My World / If I Thought You'd Ever Change Your Mind / Conversations / Liverpool Lullaby / Surround Yourself With Sorrow / Make It Easy On Yourself / What The World Needs Now Is Love / Don't Answer Me / When I Fall In Love / Every Little Bit Hurts / A Lover's Concerto / Take Me In Your Arms And Love Me

SWEET INSPIRATION   UK- Parlophone PCS 7103 / 1970

- Sweet Inspiration / Put A Little Love in Your Heart / The April Fools (from film of same name) / I Can't Go on Living Without You / From Both Sides Now / Across the Universe / Black Paper Roses / Mysterious People / Dear Madame / Oh Pleasure Man / Little Pleasure Acre / For Once in My Life / Rule Britannia

Different US album:

IS IT LOVE   US - Capitol ST 2308 / 1966

- Is It Love / I'm Not Alone Anymore / You've Lost That Lovin' Feelin' / Going Out Of My Head / Watcha Gonna Do / You'd Be So Nice To Come Home / Love Letters / Ole Man River / Love Is Like A Heatwave / This Empty Place / Anyone Who Had A Heart

Songs on compilation albums:

Is It Love on 'Ferry cross the Mersey'   UK- Columbia SX 1693 / 1963

THE BLACK CATS

This band is sometimes named Liverpool's first Rock 'n' Roll group, and it was certainly one of the very important pioneering groups of the Merseybeat era.

Formed in early 1955, the group played Skiffle music and appeared regularly at the 'Merryfield', initially as the **Black Cats Skiffle Group** and then as **Benny & the Black Cats**.

With their electric lead and rhythm guitars, they were one of the first guitar-dominated bands on Merseyside. The **Black Cats** at that time consisted of:

Benny Page	(voc/bg)
Peter Rice	(lg)
Jimmy Lynch	(rg)
Dave Stead	(dr)

In 1957, still as a Skiffle group, they played the 'Cavern' for the first time, together with **Lonnie Donegan**. A little later their sound changed to Rock 'n' Roll and, with **Gerry Stewart**, they added a sax player to the line-up.

The **Black Cats** appeared regularly at the legendary 'Jive Hive' in Crosby, and when they played the 'Cavern' for the second time in 1958, not only had their music changed but also their line-up, as **Dave Stead** had left to join the **In Crowd** and been replaced on drums by **Mal Thory**.

The **Black Cats** became the resident band at the 'Holyoake Hall'. In addition, they were probably the first Liverpool group to have a TV appearance, even if not playing a main role. They were shown performing in a film made by English Electric in July 1961.

A little later, **Jimmy Lynch** left and was replaced by **Alan Stratton**. Shortly after that, **Pete Rice** also left and **Jimmy Lynch** returned to the group as lead guitarist, but he soon left again to join the **Dimensions**. His replacement was **Dave Moore**, who had formerly played with the **Bobby Bell Rockers** and **Steve Bennett & the Syndicate**.

Gerry Stewart also left to join the **In Crowd** and after that became a member of **the Mastersounds,** that evolved into the **Bluesville Bats**, which then became the **Faces**. After the **Faces,** he joined the Jazz-scene and later emigrated to Canada, where he still lives in Ontario and publishes the magazine, 'Britannia'.

The new sax player with the **Black Cats** was **Peter Dobson**.

It seems that all these changes within a very short time led to the group splitting up in 1962.

Benny Page became a compere at a Skelmersdale club before he joined the navy and later performed for the British Forces in Gibraltar with his **Gibraltar Delta Rhythm & Blues Band**.

Peter Dobson joined **Alby & the Sorrals**, while **Mal Thory** became the new drummer for **Johnny Templer & the Hi-Cats**.

Alan Stratton joined the **Kansas City Five,** who for a while also backed singer, **Freddie Fowell**, who later became very famous under the name **Freddie Starr**. After that, **Alan Stratton** played with **Johnny Marlowe & the Whip-Chords**, the **Fables** and the **Chesterfields**. In the Nineties, he was a member of **Karl Terry & the Cruisers**.

In 1963, the Black Cats were re-formed by former members, **Peter Rice** and **Dave Stead**, together with **Billy Morris** (voc), **Alan Ashton** (rg) and **Tony Riley** (bg).

This group continued quite successfully on the scene and it is an interesting fact that the **Black Cats** also played at **Gerry Marsden's** wedding, which shows how popular and appreciated the group was at that time.

Despite their success, the **Black Cats** disbanded totally in 1966 and **Peter Rice** together with **Billy Morris** formed the nationally popular Country band, the **Saddlers**, while **Alan Ashton** and **Tony Riley** disappeared from the scene.

Dave Stead later appeared in a group called **Just Us**, where he met up again with former members of the **In Crowd**.

When this group disbanded, **Dave Stead** moved to Scotland, while **Billy Morris** emigrated to Australia after the **Saddlers** split.

Peter Rice played in various local groups until 1982 and in 1989 became a member of the 'MerseyCats' organisation and arranged for the **Black Cats** to appear one more time in the original line-up for a show at the 'Grafton Ballroom'.

Later on, he occasionally appeared with the re-formed **Kansas City Five** at various 'MerseyCats' concerts.

The Black Cats

THE BLACKHAWKS

This real Rock 'n' Roll group was formed in 1958 in the Seaforth area of Liverpool and, accordingly, has to be counted as one of the pioneer groups of the Merseybeat scene.

With one exception, it was the first group for all of the members and the **Blackhawks**, as they were named from the very beginning, consisted of the following musicians:

Cliff Webb	(voc)
Ken Shalliker	(lg)
George Watson	(rg)
Bernie Holloway	(bg/voc)
Ray Kavanagh	(dr)

George Watson was the only one with some experience in the music business, as he had formerly played with the **Sinners** and the **Dominoes**, soon to become **King Size Taylor & the Dominoes**.

Within a short time, the **Blackhawks** became quite popular locally and played the usual dance circuit, including the Litherland Town Hall, St. Luke's Hall, the 'Iron Door', Blair Hall, etc.

It was probably in late 1960 or early 1961 that the group went into the studio of **P. F. Phillips** in Kensington and cut a complete album on acetate, which among others included the songs, "Move It", "I Don't Want No Other Baby But You", "Wild Cat" and "Way Down Yonder In New Orleans".

An interesting piece of history but of course, at that time, it did not help move the **Blackhawks'** career along.

Probably the first to be replaced was **Ray Kavanagh**, whose place was taken by **Rod Hughes** and when **Cliff Webb** left, the new singer became **Jeff Price**.

It is not known if the new members had played or sung in other groups previously.

At the end of 1961, **Ken Shalliker** left and joined **King Size Taylor & the Dominoes**. As a member of that line-up he also went to Hamburg with them.

He did not stay with them for too long and went on to play with **Deke Rivers & the Big Sound**, one of the very first Manchester groups that appeared regularly in the Merseybeat scene.

Ken Shalliker then returned to Liverpool and formed a Country group, called the **Foggy Mountain Ramblers**, with whom he recorded the Unicord single "Lovin' Lady's Man", which was also written by **Ken Shalliker**.

After he had left the **Blackhawks**, the group continued on the scene for a while with **George Watson** taking over on lead guitar, but they disbanded totally in 1963.

None of the members appeared again after the group had disbanded, so it could be concluded that they all quit the music business.

Discography :

Little Queenie / Move It / Whole Lotta Shakin' Goin' On /

Johnny B. Goode / I Don't Want No Other Baby But You /

Bad Boy / Wild Cat / Way Down Yonder In New Orleans   UK- Kensington acetate-album / 1961

The Foggy Mountain Ramblers (featuring **Ken Shalliker**) :

Lovin' Lady's Man / Tomorrow   UK- Unicord UP 664 / 1964

THE BLACK KNIGHTS

This trio was formed in Liverpool in 1962 and were indistinguishable from most of the other groups, although they were musically good and had a 'rough' sound that was admired at that time.

They were a semi-professional group and well established on the scene because of their numerous appearances in Liverpool and the surrounding areas.

In the early days, **Cliff 'Taffy' Jones** was the drummer for the group, but he left to join the **Tempos** and after that nothing was heard of him again.

In 1963, the line-up of the **Black Knights** consisted of:

Bill Kenny	(voc/bg)
Kenny Griffiths	(g/voc)
Alan Schroeder	(dr/voc)

THE BLACK KNIGHTS
SOLE MANAGER   TELEPHONE
N. HURST   LAR 5574

Bill Kenny was a former member of the **Classics** from Liverpool and **Kenny Griffiths** had also played with them for a short time, while drummer **Alan Schroeder** came from **Cliff Roberts' Rockers**, one of the important pioneer groups of the Liverpool scene (they also have a story in this book).

In 1964, the **Black Knights** were paid the attention they deserved when they were chosen to appear in the film 'Ferry Cross The Mersey'.

They were featured with their own composition, "I Gotta Woman", which can also be found on the US release of the soundtrack album. This song was also released as a single on the Columbia label, and it was coupled with another original track by the group - a really great number with a strong Rhythm & Blues influence called "Angel Of Love", which probably would have been better as the A-side.

In retrospect, this single makes it clear that the **Black Knights** were underrated at the time.

An Interesting fact is that at the recording sessions, another great **Bill Kenny** original was recorded called "That feeling", which, unfortunately, remained unreleased at that time. However, in 2010, it was included on a CD (EMI 6944462), which was a re-release of the original album soundtrack plus additional bonus tracks.

In Summer 1965, the **Black Knights** went to Hamburg for a six-week engagement at the 'Star Club'.

After their return, a disillusioned **Alan Schroeder** left the group. He was 22 and did not want to play for 'teenies' any more. But he continued in the music scene as a freelancing drummer for the **Dave Forshaw** agency and, at some point, joined another band called **Admiral Street**, but only for a few months.

It is not known whether the **Black Knights** tried to continue with another drummer or if they broke up right away. What is certain is that they did not stay together for too long afterwards.

Bill Kenny and **Kenny Griffiths** apparently quit show business, as they did not appear in another group again. Of **Bill Kenny** it is known that he later moved to Swansea and became a member of the internationally successful **Morriston Phoenix Choir.**

Sadly, **Kenny Griffiths** died of cancer at the end of 2003.

Alan Schroeder returned to the group scene at the beginning of the Nineties via the 'MerseyCats' organisation as a member of **Johnny Sandon & the Specials.** When **Johnny Sandon** left, they continued as the **Mersey Specials** but split up totally in 1995. After that, **Alan Schroeder** re-formed the **Black Knights** with other musicians, mainly Merseybeat veterans from the Sixties, who still play quite regularly but mainly for 'MerseyCats' or one of the related organisations.

Discography :

I Gotta Woman / Angel Of Love   **UK - Columbia DV 7443 / 1964**

Unreleased tracks :

At the sessions for 'Ferry cross the Mersey' , the **Black Knights** also recorded the **Bill Kenny** original **"That Feeling"**, that was included as a bonus-track on a re-release of the soundtrack-album in 2010 (see text).

Songs on compilation-albums :

| **I Gotta Woman** | on **'Ferry Cross The Mersey'** | **US-United Artists UAS 6387 / 1964** |
| **I Gotta Woman** | on **'Liverpool Hop'** | **G - Columbia SMC 83983 / 1964** |

THE BLACKWELLS

This band was formed in St. Helens in 1962. As a distinguishing mark, all the members bleached their hair blonde, earning them the nickname of the 'Blonde Bombshells'.

Of course this little trick was good for publicity and won many female fans' hearts. Thus, they quickly became very popular on the scene and so the musicians were able to turn professional.

At that time, the **Blackwells** consisted of the following musicians:

Alby Cook	(voc/rg)
Tex McDermott	(lg/voc)
Dave Trimmell	(bg/voc)
Roy Little	(dr)

Dave Trimmell, who was the only one with naturally blonde hair, and **Roy Little** were former members of an amateur group named the **Ravens**, which may have had connections to **Faron's Flamingos'** predecessors.

In 1964, the **Blackwells** were chosen to take part in the **Gerry & the Pacemakers** musical film 'Ferry Cross The Mersey' which, of course, helped their popularity.

Their song in that film, "Why Don't You Love Me" was a great Beat tune in the typical Mersey Sound and was featured on the US release of the soundtrack album.

Columbia released the song on single, coupled with "All I Want Is Your Love", which had the same quality as the A-side. Unfortunately, It had no great success and so it was their first and last recording at the same time.

In January 1965, **Alby Cook**, whose real name was **Alby Gornall**, left the group and joined the **Vogue** from St. Helens. But he only stayed with them for a short time and then disappeared from the scene. He was replaced in the **Blackwells** by **Jimmy McManus**, a former member of **Bob Evans & the Five Shillings**, the **Vegas Five**, the **Undertakers** and the **Renegades** from Liverpool.

In May 1965, **Roy Little** is said to have joined the **Flower Pot Men**, but this is doubtful as at this time, the **Ivy League**, led by **John Carter** and **Ken Lewis**, still existed and they only became the **Flower Pot Men** later on. Of course, it's always possible there was another group with the same name around at that time that might have been a predecessor of that later group.

To add to the confusion, there was a drummer called **Little** in a later line-up of the **Flower Pot Men**, but this was **Carlo Little**, who hailed from the London scene.

However, the departure of **Roy Little** probably led to the **Blackwells** splitting up, as after that nothing more was heard of the group, nor of the individual musicians.

The only exception was **Tex McDermott**, who later appeared again on the scene as a studio musician. What remains of the **Blackwells** is a good name and a very good and interesting record, worth seeking out.

Discography :

Why Don't You Love Me / All I Want Is Your Love		**UK - Columbia DB 7442 / 1964**

Songs on compilation albums :

Why Don't You Love Me	on 'Ferry Cross The Mersey'	**US-United Artists UAS 6387 / 1964**
Why Don't You Love Me	on 'Liverpool Hop'	**G - Columbia SMC 83983 / 1964**

BILLY BUTLER & THE TUXEDOS

This group was originally formed in 1959 in Liverpool as a vocal/guitar trio under the name, **Terry & the Tuxedos**, by **Les 'Terry' Williams**, **Alan Crowley** and **Johnny O'Brian**.

Terry & The Tuxedos

A little later, **Dennis Swale** joined as bass guitarist, but the group disbanded in the early Sixties.

Dennis Swale joined the **Croupiers** and later played with various Merseybeat groups.

Alan Crowley, together with singer **Billy Butler,** formed a new group called the **Cherrypickers**. Unfortunately, the original line-up is not known, but **Les Williams** and **Johnny O'Brian** later replaced those members that left the group.

As the original line-up of **Terry & the Tuxedos** was back together again, the new group changed its name to **Billy Butler & the Tuxedos** and the line-up consisted of:

Billy Butler	(voc)
Les Williams	(lg/voc)
John O'Brian	(rg)
Alan Crowley	(bg)
Ronnie Myers	(dr)

Previously, **Billy Butler** had appeared sporadically as a guest vocalist with the **Merseybeats**, as well as with other Liverpool groups but never became a steady member in any of them.

In February 1963, **Billy Butler** recorded the single "I Reckon You", with songstress, **Polly Perkins** who sang the B-side alone, but this record did not sell too well.

The Tuxedos, for unknown reasons, were not featured on this single.

The Merseybeats with Billy Butler (centre)

Billy Butler & the Tuxedos never had a major breakthrough, but they did have a large following on Merseyside and did very well on the music scene until **Billy Butler** left in December 1964. He became a successful disc-jockey at various Liverpool venues (amongst them the 'Cavern') and then with 'Radio Merseyside', where he still has his very popular 'Billy Butler Show'.

After **Billy Butler** left the **Tuxedos,** the group split up.

Les Williams joined **Group One** for a short time and then became a member of the **Four Dimensions**, also named **Tiffany's Dimensions**, who later recorded as the **Dimensions**.

Until the early Nineties, **Les Williams** was with the cabaret trio, **Pendulum**, a very busy act on the Liverpool circuit. Later he was a member of the re-formed **Mojos** and he currently plays with the **Black Knights**, who mainly perform for the 'MerseyCats' organisation.

Of the others, only **Alan Crowley** appeared again on the scene, but more as a songwriter than as a musician. As such, he wrote "You Don't Have To Whisper", the B-side of the **Dimensions** single "Tears On My Pillow" and with **Billy Kinsley** of the **Merseybeats,** he co-wrote the songs, "Is It Love" and "I Hope You're Happy", both of which were released on singles by the **Merseys** in 1967 and 1968 respectively.

In 1970 the former **Cryin' Shames** vocalist, **Charlie Crane** recorded the **Alan Crowley** number, "Come Day, Go Day Man" on a single. His biggest success as songwriter was in 1989 when a complete album was released which, without exception, consisted of numbers written by **Alan Crowley** and **Frank O'Connor**, a Sixties-member of the **Hideaways** and **Confucius**.

The album, titled 'The Class Of '64' on the Holly label, besides Alan and Frank, featured various well-known Merseybeat musicians such as **Tony Crane** and **Billy Kinsley** (Merseybeats), **Mike Pender** (Searchers), **Kenny Parry** (Liverpool Express), **Ozzie Yue** (Hideaways), as well as **Johnny O'Brian** and **Billy Butler**.

Thus, three of the original members of **Billy Butler & the Tuxedos** recorded together for the first time. It's an interesting album which clearly shows the song-writing talent of **Alan Crowley** and **Frank O'Connor**.

From 1971 until 1974, **Alan Crowley** and **Frank O'Connor** performed as the cabaret duo, **Two's Company**.

In 1992, **Billy Butler & the Tuxedos** made one more appearance at a 'MerseyCats' event, but this of course, was an exception.

Alan Crowley sadly died in January 2013.

Discography :

'Billy Butler & Polly Perkins':

I Reckon You / The Girls Are At It Again   UK- Decca F.11583 / 1963

Billy Butler & the Tuxedos never released a record and nothing is known about demos or test recordings.

Billy Butler, **Alan Crowley** and **Johnny O'Brian** recorded together for the first time in 1989 on the album 'Class Of '64'. Interestingly, **Billy Butler** released a single on the 'Radio Merseyside' label in 1975, on which he was backed by **Kenny Johnson & Northwind**. The songs, "There Will Never Be Anyone Else But You" and "Little Helpers" were recorded at a live performance.

THEM CALDERSTONES

This group was formed as a four-piece in Liverpool in early 1964 and they accepted a suggestion, made by **Bob Wooler**, to call themselves the **Calderstones**, after the well known stone-monument close to their home base of Norris Green .

In their original line-up they consisted of **Peter Maxwell** (voc/lg), **Phil Inksip** (rg/voc), **Jimmy Ikonomides** (bg) and **Alan Moss** (dr).

Jimmy Ikonomides came from the just disbanded **Mafia Group** and before him, for a short time in the very beginning, it's probable that there was another bass guitarist by the name of **Harvey.** Unfortunately, his surname is not known.

The **Calderstones** soon became a busy band on the Merseybeat scene, playing a sort of Beat and Rhythm & Blues.

In July 1964, **Phil Inksip** and **Alan Moss** left to form the **Cordelles** together with **Doug Hatfield** (lg) and **Norman Bellis** (bg) from the **Inbeats**. After that **Alan Moss** was a member of the **Elektrons** (who were originally named the **Elektones**).

The remaining two **Calderstones** were joined by **Joe Kneen** (rg) and **Charlie Gallagher** (dr) from the just disbanded **Bumblies**, as well as the organist, **Phil Robert**.

This line-up did not stay together for too long and, in January 1965, all three new members left to re-form the **Bumblies** under the name of the **Cryin' Shames**, but that is another story in this book.

Tommy Maguire at the Witch's Cauldron

The **Calderstones** became a four-piece again with the arrival of singer **Norby Del Rosa**, a former member of the **Mafia Group** and the **Challengers**, and the drummer **Tommy Maguire**, who formerly had played with **Mark Anthony & the Alpha-Beats** that evolved into the **Mystery Four**.

In April 1965 when **Jimmy Ikonomides** left to join the **Kruzads,** it was **Norman Bellis** from the above mentioned **Cordelles**, who took over on bass guitar.

Then the only remaining original member, **Pete Maxwell** together with **Tommy Maguire** left to join the **Inmates**, which of course was the end of the **Calderstones** at that time.

Pete Maxwell sadly died a little later in a motorbike-accident.

After the **Inmates, Tommy Maguire** played with the **T-Squares**, which evolved from the **Clayton Squares**. He also played with the **Cryin' Shames**, the **Fruit Eating Bears** and **Karl Terry & the Cruisers**.

Norby Del Rosa disappeared from the scene, while the new bass-guitarist, **Norman Bellis** found new members with whom he continued as **Them Calderstones** in the following line-up:

Tom Evans	(voc/lg)
Jeffrey Edmondson	(org/voc)
Norman Bellis	(bg/voc)
Billy Geeleher	(dr)

Tom Evans had formerly played together with **Norman Bellis** in the **Inbeats**, while **Billy Geeleher** came from the **Modes**. Unfortunately, the former group of **Jeff Edmondson** is not known.

Them Calderstones

In late 1965, the **Calderstones** recorded a Unicord acetate as a demo with the songs, "Don't You Believe It" and "What'cha Gonna Do About It", which proved them to be an excellent group.

At the end of that year, **Charlie McBain**, who hired out sound equipment to bands and clubs (including the early 'Cavern'), took over the group's management. Thus, he had very good contacts with the scene's promoters, which of course was advantageous for the band.

In early 1966, **Johnny Hutchinson** of the **Big Three** replaced **Billy Geeleher** for a few months on drums but he then joined **Paul Craig & the Theme** and **Billy Geeleher** returned to the **Calderstones**.

Prior to leaving, **Johnny Hutchinson** had used his connections with Decca to arrange a recording session for the **Calderstones**.

They recorded the song, "Children And Flowers" as a demo. This was a nice melodic song and very well recorded. It was intended to be released on a compilation album, unfortunately this did not happen.

So, the **Calderstones** didn't achieve the national breakthrough they hoped for and this might have been a reason for the group disbanding in 1967.

Tom Evans became a founding member of the **Iveys**, who later became **Badfinger**, and found international stardom with great hit records like "Come And Get It", "Day After Day" and the fantastic "Baby Blue". Sadly, he committed suicide in November 1983.

Jeff Edmondson joined **Bernie & the Buzz Band**, led by **Bernie Wenton** and played a sort of **Temptations/ Drifters** style of music. After that he disappeared from the scene.

Billy Geeleher became a member of **Curiosity Shoppe** and **Norman Bellis** joined the **Seftons**, who changed their name to the **Perishers** and went down to London.

In 1969, **Norman Bellis** emigrated to the USA, where he played sessions with well-known artists such as the **Temptations**, **Jr. Walker & the All Stars** and the **Walker Brothers**.

After nine months, he returned to London and re-formed the **Perishers** under the name of **Worth**. After that he played for a short time with the band **Rusty Harness**.

Worth recorded for CBS and later changed their name to **Tiger** and became a real 'Hard Rock' band. When this group split, **Norman Bellis** returned to Liverpool and in the Seventies was possibly a member of **Perfumed Garden**, which was not the CAM recording-group of the same name.

After that he remained in the music business as a producer and ran his own recording studio in Devonshire.

Discography :

Don't You Believe Me / What'cha Gonna Do About It	**UK - Unicord-acetate / 1965**
Children And Flowers / Children And Flowers	**UK - Decca - demo (acetate) / 1966**

CAROL & THE MEMORIES

The beginning of this group's story is a little bit intricate, but it seems the **Five Aces** were formed in Aintree sometime during 1963-1964, although it is also possible that there was a connection between them and **Nick Olsen & the Aces**, that in late 1960 appeared at the 'Cavern'.

However, the **Five Aces** only played local gigs until they were signed to a Burnley-based agency, who offered the group a chance to play the US military bases in France. Sometime at the end of 1964, they travelled to Europe to entertain the American servicemen. They went down quite well and were invited to tour the US airbases in Germany, but only on the condition that they included a girl singer in their line-up. This most probably led to their original singer (**Nick Olsen**?) leaving in 1965 and the then unknown **Carol Whitfield** was introduced to them as a new vocalist and accordingly, the group went to Germany in the following line-up with:

Carol Whitfield	(voc)
Jimmy Chadwick	(lg/voc)
Steven Harvey	(rg/voc)
Kenny Harvey	(bg/voc)
Billy Bryden	(dr)

In Germany they played mainly in the Darmstadt and Aschaffenburg areas, close to Frankfurt.

As the group went down well with their new girl singer, they stayed together after their return to Liverpool.

Very soon, their Burnley management got CBS interested in signing the group, but the record company insisted on a name change because of an American group with the name **Four Aces**.

CBS initially suggested **Margaret & the Memories**, but as **Carol Whitfield** insisted on her real name being used, in the end the group became **Carol & the Memories**.

In 1966, they went to London and recorded the single, "Tears On My Pillow" – a great song that they did a good job on. The B-side, "Crying My Eyes Out" was written by **Johnny Stewart** who was a member of the **Kingston Trio**.

CBS wanted publicity for the group and the record and tried to create a story about a love affair between **Carol Whitfield** and **Scott Engel** of the **Walker Brothers**. Both did in fact meet once at a dinner CBS arranged for them in London and, of course, the press were also invited.

The only problem was that the two main protagonists didn't like each other very much and so only one major article was published in a London newspaper and that was the end of that story.

Nothing is known about the sales figures of the record but it apparently didn't become a big seller, as it was not followed by any further releases.

Carol presenting her single to the Lord Mayor

Carol & the Memories returned to Liverpool where they then played all the major clubs such as, the 'Cavern', the 'Iron Door' and the 'Mardi Gras'. They also appeared in the Manchester area.

In 1967, the management took **Carol Whitfield** out of the group as they wanted her to become a solo act on the cabaret circuit.

Barbara Curney became the new 'Carol' with the group for a few gigs, but this apparently did not work out too well and so the group continued without a girl-singer as the **Memories** on the Merseyside scene but did not make any headway. Sometime in 1967, they became the backing-group for the popular Manchester all girl vocal-group, the **Dollies**. This connection likely lasted for some time but after that, nothing more was heard of the **Memories** or the individual members.

Carol Whitfield tried to go solo after separating from the group but she did not like it and very soon joined a Country & Western band from Ellesmere Port called the **Renos**, with whom she sang for two years. In 1969, she joined the **Image**, where she met her future husband, **Jeff Loftus**. She formed the group, **Carousel** with him in the mid-Seventies and finally, both became members of a group called **Miller's Bridge**.

Today she sometimes appears at 'MerseyCats' events, where she proves she is still a great singer. She, along with her husband, also put another group together, originally called the **Smoky Joe Band,** but occasionally they also appear as **Carol & the Memories** again.

Discography :

Tears On My Pillow / Crying My Eyes Out   CBS 202 086 / 1966

THE CARROLLS

This is the story of a group that was obviously more a part of Liverpool's cabaret circuit than of the real Merseybeat scene, but there is a special reason for including them here.

Irene Carroll started to sing in the early Sixties and it could have been her, when on the 4th November 1960, a group with the name of **Irene & the Santa Fe's** had an appearance at the 'Cavern'.

After winning a contest, she became the resident singer at the 'Rialto Ballroom' for a time. She was backed at the 'Rialto' by a local group during her performances, which could have been the **Tall Boys**, as around that time there was a group appearing as **Irene & the Tall Boys**, who later continued with a certain **Jenny Ellison** as their vocalist under the name of **Jenny & the Tall Boys**.

Up to this point, the connections with these groups are just suppositions, although it is known for a fact that **Irene Carroll,** for some time, appeared with the **Invaders**, better known on the scene as **Liam & the Invaders**.

In late 1964 or early 1965, **Irene Carroll** formed a duo with her younger brother, **Michael Carroll**, who was most probably the musician of the same name who was a member of the **Stormers** until 1964, who also backed girl singer, **Jacki Martin,** for a time.

A little later, their two other brothers joined forces with them so the **Carrolls** were born in a line-up with:

Irene Carroll	**(voc)**
Michael Carroll	**(voc/g)**
Ronnie Carroll	**(voc/g)**
Leslie Carroll	**(vac/g)**

As all four members obviously concentrated on singing, they of course needed a backing group, at least a bass-guitarist and a drummer for their live appearances.

Nothing is definitely known about the group, but it is a possibility that **Len Wady** was on bass guitar, who later played a big role in **Irene Carroll's** life.

After playing on the scene for a while, the **Carrolls** were signed to Polydor and, in 1965, their first single with "Give Me Time" was released – with the wrong spelling of 'Carolls' on the label.

This record, although not too successful, was followed by "Surrender your love" as their second single, which also did not have any chart success.

Surprisingly, in 1966, a 10-inch album by the **Carrolls** was released in Romania on the Electrecord label. This eight-track album, included a number of standards such as "Hey, Good Looking", "Mister Postman" and "Sweet Talking Guy". It also featured the Beatles numbers, "This Boy" and "Gonna Loose That Girl".

While this album places the **Carrolls** closest to the Merseybeat scene, the record shows them to be one of the 'softer' groups with quite a 'low key' beat. However, one should also give consideration to the fact that aggressive rock music was not tolerated in Romania at that time, as the government considered it to be inappropriate for the youth of that country to be exposed to that type of music.

The backing group on that album were the **Guys** who were possibly the first British group to play behind the 'Iron Curtain' when they backed **John Burness** on his tour of Bulgaria in 1964. The line-up of the **Guys** was as follows: **Ray Wastle** (lg) **Ian Horn** (org/p) **Brian Hawkins** (bg) and **Dick Mayall** (dr).

The songs, "Hey, Good Looking", "Mr. Postman" and the two **Beatles** numbers featured the lead vocals of **Michael Carroll** and, from his singing, it can be concluded that his musical roots were in the Merseybeat. All

the other tracks were sung by **Irene Carroll**, who proved that she was a good singer but did not have too much in common with Rock 'n' Roll.

On 23rd July 1966, the **Carrolls** played the re-opening concert of the 'Cavern', which also shows that it could not have been a pure cabaret band.

CBS signed the group in 1968 and, in the same year, the singles, "So Gently Falls The Rain", "Ever Since" and "A Lemon Balloon And A Blue Sky" were released.

"Ever Since", coupled with "Come On" seems to be the most interesting but, in the end, it had no greater success than its predecessors or "We're In This Together" from 1969, which was the final release of the **Carrolls** that probably disbanded at that time.

Only **Irene Carroll** continued in professional showbiz when she became **Faith Brown** – a first-class impressionist, entertainer and actress. She is also one of the biggest comedy stars in England and has appeared in a number of successful TV shows.

In spite of this, she continued to sing and later appeared again with a group under the name of **Faith Brown & the Shades** in a line-up with:

Faith Brown	(voc)
Barry 'Baz' Davis	(lg)
Len Wady	(bg)
Pete Saunders	(dr)

Barry Davis, an excellent guitarist, came from the Beat scene as a former member of the **Wild Harks**, the **Connoisseurs**, **King Size Taylor's** new band and the German group, **Mike Warner & His New Stars** from Bielefeld.

The above mentioned line-up was often joined by the resident keyboarders of the clubs in which **Faith Brown & the Shades** performed.

It is not known if **Faith Brown's** final CBS release, "The Game Of Love" or "Anyway That You Want Me" on the Pen label (both from 1970) were recorded with the group or with a studio backing.

In 1972, she switched to PYE where she released four more singles up through 1975, none of which were very successful.

It was during this time that **Faith Brown** married **Len Wady**, who became her husband, bass player and manager all at the same time!

In the end, it can be said that none of the **Carrolls'** or **Faith Brown & the Shades'** recordings got any closer to Merseybeat than the Romanian album, which is certainly a very interesting collector's item today.

Discography :

as the **Carolls** :

Give me time / Darling I want you so much	**UK – Polydor BM 56046 / 1965**
Surrender Your Love / The Folk I Love	**UK – Polydor BM 56081 / 1967**
So Gently Falls The Rain / Nice To See You Darling	**UK – CBS 3414 / 1968**
Ever Since / Come On	**UK – CBS 3750 / 1968**
A Lemon Balloon And A Blue Sky / Make Me Belong To You	**UK – CBS 3875 / 1968**
We're In This Together / We Know Better	**UK – CBS 4401 / 1969**

LP

THE CARROLLS	**ROM – Electrecord EDD 1150 / 1966**

- Surrender Your Love / Hey, Good Looking / No Regrets / Mr. Postman / Sweet Talking Guy / This Boy / Gonna Loose That Girl / The Folk I Love

Faith Brown – solo :

Lock Me In / The Game Of Love	**UK- CBS 4724 / 1970**
Any Way That You Want Me / City Wine	**UK- Pen 766 / 1970**

HOWIE CASEY & THE SENIORS

At first, they were the **Hy-Tones**, sometimes documented as the **Huy-Tones** as they came from Huyton, where they were formed in 1958. The original line-up most probably consisted of **Billy Hughes** (bg/voc), **Jim O'Connor** (rg/voc), **Stan Johnson** (lg), **Stan Foster** (p) and **Derek Gill** (dr).

The Hy-Tones

Derek Gill left and was replaced by **Jeff Wallington** on drums and, shortly after, **Jim O'Connor** was replaced by **Phil Whitehead** (bg/voc), while **Billy Hughes** switched to rhythm guitar. The **Hy-Tones** were also joined by vocalist **Jimmy 'Ginger' Geary** and, a little later by sax-player, **Howie Casey**.

Jim O'Connor, who was the step-brother of **Stan Foster**, quit showbiz for many years and only returned to the scene in 2001, when he occasionally sang with various groups at 'MerseyCats' events.

Stan Johnson left the group, which was then joined by **Brian Griffiths** on lead guitar. Then **Jimmy 'Ginger' Geary** also left to become **Rip Van Winkle** of **Rip Van Winkle & The Rip-It-Ups**, he was replaced by coloured singer **Derry Wilkie** and the group's name was changed to **Derry & The Seniors** at the end of 1959. The group soon became very popular on the Northern scene with their **Little Richard** and **Ray Charles** inspired Rock 'n' Roll. They also made repeated appearances at the famous '2 i's' coffee bar in London where they met German promoter, **Bruno Koschmieder**, who booked them right away.

So **Derry & The Seniors** became the first group from Liverpool to play in Hamburg at the legendary 'Kaiserkeller' in summer 1960.

Tanzpalast der Jugend

Kaiserkeller

Bruno Koschmider-Betriebe · Hamburg, Gr. Freiheit 36

Treffpunkt des modernen jungen Menschen

Gastspiel der populärsten Rock'n Roll Band aus Liverpool

Seniors, mit dem Neger Sänger Derry

und den Nachwuchssängern

After their return to Liverpool, their equipment was destroyed when the 'Top Ten' club in Liverpool burned down. This fact probably led to **Billy Hughes**, **Jeff Wallington** and **Stan Foster** leaving.

Seen in retrospect, this fire disaster led to the birth of a local super group of Liverpool's Sixties' scene, under the name **Howie Casey & the Seniors** in a line-up with:

Derry Wilkie	**(voc)**
Freddie Fowell	**(voc)**
Brian Griffiths	**(lg/voc)**
Howie Casey	**(sax)**
Phil Whitehead	**(bg)**
Frank Wibberley	**(dr)**

The group's name had been changed because **Freddie Fowell** was added to the line-up as a second lead singer. As **'Freddie the Teddy'**, he had formerly been backed by various groups, including the **Five Stars**.

Derry Wilkie & Freddie (Fowell) Starr

Frank Wibberley, a fantastic drummer, had formerly played with the **Four Aces** and the **Rhythm Rockers**.

Howie Casey & the Seniors became the first recording group of the Merseybeat scene when the album, 'Twist at the Top' was released on Fontana in 1962. From that album, the single, "True Fine Mama/Double Twist" was coupled out.

Further singles were "I Ain't Mad At You" (1962) and **Brook Benton**'s "Boll Weevil Song" (1963).

In 1965, their album was reissued under the title, 'Let's Twist' on the Wing label and, for this release, the name was changed slightly to **Wailin' Howie Casey & the Seniors**.

However, the group did not actually exist by that time. Shortly after recording the original album, **Phil Whitehead** had left to join the **Vigilantes** and then later the **Aristocrats**.

For a short time, he was replaced by **Lu Walters**, who came from **Rory Storm & the Hurricanes,** but then he returned to his old group. During his time with **Howie Casey & the Seniors**, **Lu Walters** had recorded the songs, "Gone Gone Gone" and "Nashville Blues". Unfortunately, these songs where he was featured as lead vocalist were never released.

His replacement in **Howie Casey & the Seniors** was **Frank Bowen**, formerly of the **Teenbeats**, **Cliff Roberts' Rockers**, the **Blue Stars** from Glasgow and the **Lonely Ones**.

Howie Casey & the Seniors

But **Howie Casey & the Seniors** only remained together until the middle of 1962 and then they disbanded totally.

The coloured singer, **Derry Wilkie**, whose real name was **Derek Davis**, initially appeared together with **Geoff Stacey & the Wanderers** but then he amalgamated with the **Pressmen** under the name of **Derry Wilkie & the Pressmen**. But that is another story in this book.

Later, the tall show star archetype joined the **Others**, of course under the name of **Derry Wilkie & the Others** and after that, nothing was heard of him on the scene for years. In 1980, he appeared again at the re-opening of the 'Star-Club' in Hamburg and can also be found on the corresponding live sampler. He also toured for a short time with **Screaming Lord Sutch** in Germany, but then returned to Liverpool and, it is said, looked for the right backing group until he sadly died on 22nd December 2001.

Derry Wilkie & the Seniors

Freddie Fowell teamed up with the **Kansas City Five** but then changed his name to **Freddie Starr** and appeared with groups that included **Freddie Starr & the Ventures**, **Freddie Starr & the Midnighters**, **Freddie Starr & the Starr Boys** (the former **Pressmen**) and **Freddie Starr & the Delmonts**, before he started a very successful solo career as an actor and entertainer. He is still a popular TV star these days and sporadically releases records.

Howie Casey first went to Hamburg as a session musician and, amongst others, played with **Tony Sheridan & the Beat Brothers** before he became a member of **King Size Taylor & the Dominoes**. After that he joined the **Pawns** for a short time and then played with the **Krewkats**.

Back in Liverpool, he had short spells with the **Big Three** and the **Griff Parry Five**, but then he re-formed the **Krew**. Later, he was a member of the **Roy Young Band** and **Rigor Mortis**.

These days, he is still a successful session and studio musician and has appeared on many records by well-known artists, including **Paul McCartney** and the **Hollies**. He also still leads his own group – the **Howie Casey Band**.

Brian Griffiths, undoubtedly one of the most talented guitarists from Merseyside, became a member of the **Big Three** and, after that, he formed a trio under the name of the **Seniors** together with **Johnny Gustafson**, a former member of **Cass & the Cassanovas** and the **Big Three**. The third member was **Ian Broad**, the former drummer of the **Five Stars, Gus Travis & the Midnighters** and **Freddie Starr & the Midnighters**. But this band was short-lived and broke up after a tour of Germany.

After the break-up, **Brian Griffiths** was one of the founding members of the **Griff Parry Five** before he joined the **Johnny Gus Set**. After that, he disappeared from the scene and later emigrated to Canada. In 1973, he was a member of the newly-formed **Big Three** that recorded the album 'Resurrection', but then he returned to Canada, where he is still living.

Frank Bowen became the lead guitarist of **Lee Curtis & the All Stars**, then played with the **Pathfinders** and for a short time with **Rory Storm & the Hurricanes**. He then joined **Mike & the Merseymen**, who changed their name to the **Trends** and went down to London. While he was in London he also played with the **Bootleggers**, then he returned to Liverpool in 1965 and became a member of **Earl Royce & the Olympics**. He sadly died at a very young age in 1966.

Frank Wibberley joined the **Lee Eddie Five** and, after that, played with **Emile Ford & the Checkmates**.

Discography :

Double Twist / True Fine Mama	UK- Fontana H 364 / 1962
I Ain't Mad At You / Twist At The Top	UK- Fontana H 381 / 1962
Boll Weevil Song / Bony Moronie	UK- Fontana TF 403 / 1963

LP

TWIST AT THE TOP   UK-Fontana TFL 5180 / 1962

- **Double Twist / The Fly / Yes Indeed / Bony Moronie / Taki Blues / Hey, Hey, Hey, Hey /**

The Boll Weevil Song / Big Daddy / True Fine Mama / Bone Shakin' Annie / Say / Let's Twist Again

(this album was re-released in 1965 on the Wing label - WL 1022 - in England)

Unreleased tracks :

Howie Casey & the Seniors recorded the songs, **"Gone Gone Gone"** and **"Nashville Blues"** with **Lu Walters** as lead vocalist in 1962. Unfortunately, they were never released.

CASS & THE CASSANOVAS

They were one of the very first Rock 'n' Roll groups in Liverpool, if not the first one. Like lots of other very good groups in the first wave, they had their big time prior to the boom and that is why there were no records released by **Cass & the Cassanovas**.

In their early days, they played the clubs and venues in Liverpool and the surrounding areas, where their musical ability ensured they had a large following. During a tour of Scotland they recorded the demo, "After My Laughter Came Tears", with singer **Johnny Gentle**. In their original line-up **Cass & the Cassanovas** consisted of:

Brian 'Cass' Cassar	**(voc)**
Adrian Barber	**(lg)**
Johnny Gustafson	**(bg/voc)**
Johnny Hutchinson	**(dr)**

Brian 'Cass' Cassar left the group as early as 1962. From that moment on they were called the **Big Three** and became one of Liverpool's great Merseybeat legends, but that story can be followed under the **Big Three** in this book.

Brian Cassar initially went down to London in search of international stardom as **Casey Jones**. There he formed a new group under the name **Casey Jones & his Engineers**, which consisted of **Casey Jones** (voc), **Eric Clapton** (lg), **Tom McGuinness** (bg) and **Ray Stock** (dr).

Eric Clapton and **Tom McGuinness** were former members of the **Roosters**. **Ray Stock** then was replaced by **Cozy Powell**, who previously had played with **Pat Wayne & the Beachcombers** from Birmingham (amongst others). Seen in retrospect, this was something like an early super group, but they soon disbanded for unknown reasons.

Eric Clapton became a member of the **Yardbirds** and later played with the **Greek Loone Band**, **John Mayall's Bluesbreakers**, **Cream**, **Blind Faith**, **Delany, Bonnie & Friends** and **Derek & the Dominoes** before he formed his own successful group and became an international superstar.

Tom McGuinness joined **Manfred Mann** and, after that, he formed **McGuinness Flint** and then was a member of the **Blues Band**. Today he is back with the original **Manfred Mann** group who, for legal reasons, appear under the name of the **Manfreds**.

Cozy Powell later became a member of **Ace Kefford Stand** and, after that, played with **Big Bertha**, the **Jeff Beck Group**, **Cozy Powell's Hammer**, **Strange Brew**, **Ritchie Blackmore's Rainbow** and the **Michael Schenker Group**.

Casey Jones amalgamated with the **Midnights** from Bristol, who also adopted the name **Casey Jones & his Engineers** - in a line-up with:

Casey Jones	**(voc)**
Dave Coleman	**(lg/voc)**
Roger Hook	**(rg)**
Jim Redford	**(bg)**
Peter Richards	**(dr)**

In 1963, this group recorded the single, "One Way Ticket", for the Columbia label which, unfortunately, didn't have much success although it was a really good driving Beat number.

Casey Jones & his Engineers then emigrated to Germany where they settled in Hamburg for years and became an integral and somewhat famous part of the 'Star-Club' scene.

They were signed by Bellaphon and released the singles, "Tall Girl" and "Don't Ha Ha", which sold quite well. After these recordings, the band changed their name to **Casey Jones & the Governors** and were signed to the 'Golden 12' label.

With a number of hits including "Jack The Ripper", their new release of "Don't Ha Ha", an adaptation of **Screaming Lord Sutch's** "Don't you just know it", "Yockomo", "Little Girl" and "Come On And Dance", the band continually stepped back into the limelight.

Casey Jones & the Governors

The re-recorded "Don't Ha Ha" was their biggest success and became something of an evergreen of the Beat age in Germany.

In 1967, **Phil Cantley,** a saxophone-player, was added to the line and **Casey Jones** left at that time.

The group continued under the name of the **Gaslight Union** and released some more singles on the German Columbia and Cornet labels, including "Silly Miss Lilly Pfefferkorn", "Stupid Party" or "Do The Kasaboo" (the last one under the name of **Phil Cantley & the Gaslight Union**), none of which were too successful.

But the solo career of **Casey Jones** was also not as successful as he might have thought, and singles such as his really good version of **Solomon Burke**'s "Down In The Valley" or "Mervyn Guy" and "Zebedy Zak" failed to make it.

He also recorded a wild version of "Keep A Knockin'" with a group by the name of the **Casey Jones Government**, but it seems this was only a studio session as this name did not appear again.

Casey Jones is still gigging around in Germany and sometimes releases a record but, so far, none have had much success.

Dave Coleman became a well-known disc jockey with the WDR radio station after the **Gaslight Union** had disbanded at the end of the Sixties.

In the late Seventies, **Jim Redford** appeared on the scene again as a member of **Rangers VSOP**, a follow-up group to the German Sixties recording band, **Frederic & the Rangers**.

Of the other members of the **Governors** nothing was heard of them after that.

Discography :

as **Cass & the Cassanovas** they backed **Johnny Gentle** on

After The Laughter Came Tears	UK-demo unreleased / 1960

as **Casey Jones & his Engineers** :

One Way Ticket / I'm Gonna Love	UK- Columbia DB 7083 / 1963
Tall Girl / Blue Tears	G- Bellaphon BL 1006 / 1964
Don't Ha Ha / Long Gone Train	G- Bellaphon BL 1013 / 1964

EP

DON'T HA HA	G- Bellaphon BL 151 / 1965
- Don't Ha Ha / Blue Tears / Tall Girl / Long Gone Train	

as **Casey Jones & the Governors**:

Slow Down / Mickey's Monkey	G- Golden 12 G 12/01 / 1964
Don't Ha Ha / Nashville Special	G- Golden 12 G 12/27 / 1965
Candy Man / Tallahassee Lassie	G- Golden 12 G 12/32 / 1965

Jack The Ripper / So Long Baby	G- Golden 12 G 12/35 / 1965
Bumble Bee (in German) / Rootin' Tootin' Baby	G- Golden 12 G 12/37 / 1965
Yockomo / Baby Why Did You Say Goodbye	G- Golden 12 G 12/40 / 1966
Little Girl / A Legal Matter	G- Golden 12 G 12/44 / 1966
Come On And Dance / It's Alright	G- Golden 12 G 12/49 / 1966
Dream A Girl / Pretty, Pretty Girl	G- Golden 12 G 12/59 / 1966
Dizzy Miss Lizzy / Casey's New Hand Jive	G- Golden 12 G 12/171 / 1973

(***please note, **Don't Ha Ha** on the 'Golden 12' label was only credited to **The Governors** but featured the lead vocals of **Casey Jones**. The single, **Dizzy Miss Lizzy,** was released at a time when the group was no longer in existence. **Dizzy Miss Lizzy** was from the album, 'Don't Ha Ha', and **Casey's New Hand Jive** from the album, 'Casey Jones & the Governors')

Casey Jones – solo :

Down In The Valley / It Seems I've Waited Too Long	G- Golden 12 G 12/56 / 1966
Mervyn Guy / Sands	G- Dt. Vogue DV 14661 / 1967
Zebedy Zak / Casey's Blue Train	G- Dt. Vogue DV 14872 / 1968

as **The Casey Jones Government** :

Keep On Knocking / Beechwood Park	G- Dt. Vogue DV 14778 / 1968

The Gaslight Union :

Silly Miss Lilly Pfefferkorn / Groovin'	G- Columbia C 23474 / 1967
Destiny Cryin' / Every Now And Then	G- Columbia C 23551 / 1967
Stupid Party / You've Got To Find A New Love	G- Columbia C 23705 / 1967

as **Phil Cantley & the Gaslight Union** :

Do The Kasaboo / I Wouldn't Want To Be An Officer	G- Cornet 5013 / 1968

Dave Coleman – solo :

Mister Gallilei / Alaska Quinn	G- Columbia C 23755 / 1967
Mama Nicolina / Füllt man sich so'n Schatz wie dich in Flaschen	G- Columbia C 23964 / 1968

LPs by **Casey Jones & the Governors** :

DON'T HA HA   G-Golden 12 G12/LP 106/1965

- Don't Ha Ha / Love Potion No.9 / Mickey's Monkey / Parchment Farm /

Slow Down / Too Much Monkey-Business / Sounds Like Locomotion /

Dizzy Miss Lizzy / Talking 'bout You / Do The Dog / Can't Judge A Book /

So Long Baby / Jack The Ripper / Nashville Special

CASEY JONES & THE GOVERNORS   G-Golden 12 G12/LP 108/1966

- Yockomo / Casey's New Hand Jive / Smoking The Blues / My Babe /

Lucille / All You Wanna Do / Hall Of The Mountain King / Come On Everybody /

Baby Why Did You Say Goodbye / Doctor Feelgood / All My Sorrows /

You Got What It Takes / Beautiful Delilah / Guitar Boogie

Songs on compilation albums :

Love Potion No.9	on 'Best Of Beat'	G- Metronome HLP 10.050 / 1965
Mickey's Monkey	on 'Best Of Beat'	G- Metronome HLP 10.050 / 1965
Don't Ha Ha	on 'Beat Hits Vol.2'	G- Bellaphon BWS 305 / 1967
Long Gone Train	on 'Beat Hits Vol.2'	G- Bellaphon BWS 305 / 1967
Tall Girl	on 'Beat Hits Vol.2'	G- Bellaphon BWS 305 / 1967
Blue Tears	on 'Beat Hits Vol.2'	G- Bellaphon BWS 305 / 1967

LEE CASTLE & THE BARONS

This band was formed by **Frank Knight** in Liverpool in early 1962 under the name of **Frank Knight & the Barons**. Right from the start, it was a typical Merseybeat group and they soon became quite popular on Merseyside.

In the original line-up, the band consisted of **Frank Knight** (voc/rg), **Les Stuart** (lg), **Jimmy Bannon** (bg) and **Johnny Rocco** (dr).

Les Stuart was the former leader of the **Les Stuart Quartet** and **Johnny Rocco** the former leader of **Johnny Rocco & the Jets**, while **Jimmy Bannon** came from **Deke Wade & the Ambassadors** and, before that, he had played with the **Phoenix Five**.

When **Johnny Rocco** left, he was replaced by **Bob O'Hanlon**, who had formerly played with **Ken Dallas & the Silhouettes**.

Johnny Rocco, whose real name is **Graham Hodgson**, later emigrated to Spain, where he is still playing guitar in the local clubs.

A little later, **Les Stuart** left to join the **Ventures**, the new backing group for singer, **Freddie Starr**. They later evolved into **Danny Havoc & the Ventures**. After that, he played with the **Kansas City Five**, before he changed his name to **Les Saints** and joined **The Long & The Short**.

His place in the **Barons** was taken by **Jimmy Moran,** aka **Jimmy Martin**, the former leader of **Jimmy Martin & the Martinis**.

Around the same time, the singer, **Ronnie Castle**, who had adopted the stage name **Lee Castle**, was added to the line-up.

When **Frank Knight** left to form **Groups Inc.** , the group changed their name to **Lee Castle & the Barons**.

LEE CASTLE AND THE BARONS

Jimmy Bannon left to join the **Mersey Bluebeats** and was replaced by **Tommy Bennett**, who had no connections to the drummer of the same name, who among others had played with the **Pressmen**.

Bob O'Hanlon joined the **Classics** from St. Helens and, after that, he returned to his original group that, during his absence, had become **Mark Peters & the Silhouettes**.

His place in **Lee Castle & the Barons** was taken over by **Mel Gallagher**, aka **Mel Preston**, the former drummer of the **Classics** and, before that, he had played with the **Zephyrs**.

Jimmy Martin left to join the Liverpool Country-scene and formed the **Idle Hours**, a successful and long-lived group that also released some records.

Accordingly, after all these changes, **Lee Castle & the Barons,** in October 1963, consisted of the following musicians:

Lee Castle	**(voc/rg)**
Mike Liston	**(lg)**
Tommy Bennett	**(bg)**
Mel Preston	**(dr)**

The new lead-guitarist, **Mike Liston,** was a former member of **Bobby Angelo & the Tuxedos,** but he soon left and joined the **Kansas City Five**.

Mike Liston later adopted the stage name of **Mike Snow** and, as such, he joined the **West Five** from London with whom he recorded a great version of the **Rolling Stones** number, "Congratulation".

After that, he played in the backing-group of **She Trinity** and with **Ferris Wheel** before he became a session and studio-musician. As such, he was also featured on the great **Rockin' Horse** album, 'Yes It Is' (see **Kirkbys** story) and, in 1971, he wrote the hit, "Rosetta", for **Georgie Fame**. He later emigrated to Nashville, USA and became a very successful singer and songwriter.

But back to **Lee Castle & the Barons** where **Mike Liston** was replaced by **Johnny Fallon** who came from the **Del Renas.**

With this line-up, **Lee Castle & the Barons** were signed to Parlophone in 1964 and, in the same year, they released the single, "A Love She Can Count On", which was coupled with "Fooling", a song written by another group on the Merseybeat scene - the **Wheels**, that originally hailed from Middleton but had a long residency in Liverpool and formerly were known as **Lee Paul & the Boys**. They also wrote quite successfully for other artists but never released a record in their own right.

Unfortunately, "A Love She Can Count On", only became a local success and so did not help **Lee Castle & the Barons** to achieve any sort of a breakthrough.

After that recording, **Mel Preston** returned to St. Helens where he joined **Cadillac & the Playboys** that later became the **Manchester Playboys**.

He was replaced in **Lee Castle & the Barons** by **Ian Broad**, who formerly had played with **Gus Travis & the Midnighters**, **Freddie Starr & the Midnighters** and **Heinz & the Wild Boys**.

Lee Castle & the Barons did not exist for too long after this - they disbanded sometime in early 1965.

Ian Broad joined **Rory Storm & the Hurricanes** and, after that, went to Italy with **Dave Allen & the Exotics**. He later emigrated to the USA, where he is still living.

Tommy Bennett might have been the musician of the same name who later played with the **Georgians**.

Discography :

A Love She Can Count On / Fooling **UK- Parlophone R 5151 / 1964**

EDDIE CAVE & THE FYX

This is the continuation of the story of the **Terry Hines Sextet** who, after the singer **Terry Hines** was replaced by **Geoff Workman** (org/voc), had continued on the scene as **The Sextet**, the name being only a temporary solution.

Towards the end of 1965, the **Sextet** recruited a new singer named **Eddie Cave**, who had formerly sung with the **Richmond Group**. The band then signed a management deal with **Bob Wooler** and, at his suggestion, they were renamed the **Fix**.

Their music was classic Afro-American Rhythm & Blues and, within a short time, the **Fix** had built a great name for themselves on the local scene. By early 1966 they were booked to play the 'Star-Club' in Hamburg.

Eddie Cave & the Fix at the 'Star Club' Hamburg

In spite of this immediate success, the sax player, **Alby Donnelly**, a former member of the **Plainsmen** and the **Terry Hines Sextet**, left to join the **Clayton Squares**. After that, he was also with the short-lived **T-Squares**, who consisted of ex-members of the **Clayton Squares** and **Karl Terry & the T.T.'s**.

His replacement in the **Fix** was **Ray Renns**, a former member of the **Mysteries** and the **Inmates**, who for a short time had also been a member of the **Terry Hines Sextet**.

The next to leave was band leader, **Bob Hardy** (g/sax), who originally came from **T.L.'s Bluesicians** and had played in the **Terry Hines Sextet**. At that time, he quit showbiz but, by late 1969, he was back on the Liverpool scene, managing the very successful 'Wooky Hollow' theatre club.

The **Fix** signed a contract with PYE and, at the request of the record company, the spelling of the name was changed to the **Fyx**. They went down to London in the following line-up:

Eddie Cave	**(voc)**
Terry Kenna	**(g)**
Pete Newton	**(bg/voc)**
Geoff Workman	**(org/voc)**
Ray Renns	**(sax)**
Dave Irving	**(dr)**

Pete Newton, Geoff Workman, Dave Irving and **Terry Kenna** were the other remaining members of the **Terry Hines Sextet** or the **Sextet**, as they were last named.

In 1966, the single, "It's Almost Good", was released under the name of **Eddie Cave & the Fyx**. It was a straight pop record, produced by **Searchers** drummer, **Chris Curtis,** and featured the backing vocals of **Madelaine Bell** and **Dusty Springfield**. This record did not sell well, although it was presented on the British 'pop' TV programme, 'Ready, Steady, Go'. Accordingly, it was not followed by a second release from the group who continued to play at venues throughout England.

When guitarist, **Terry Kenna** (ex **St. Louis Checks** and **Terry Hines Sextet**), quit to become the manager of Crane's (Liverpool) music shop, the group was joined by **Dennis Swale**, the group's former 'roadie' who had also played with the **Groupiers** and the **Dimensions** earlier in the 60's.

Eddie Cave was replaced by **Steve Aldo**, formerly with **Steve Aldo & the Challengers, King Size Taylor & the Dominoes**, the **Nocturns** and the **Griff Parry Five**.

Dennis Swale soon parted from the group which had now gone back to being called **The Fyx** again.

Paul Pilnick was the new guitarist in the line-up which now also included **Dick Hanson** on trumpet and **Alby Donnelly** on tenor-saxophone.

The **Fyx** were now a Soul band and became one of the busiest and most popular live groups on Merseyside in the late Sixties. In spite of this success, the personnel changes continued and **Ray Renns** and **Dick Hanson** left to be replaced by **Les Smith** (sax) from the **Clayton Squares** and **Steve Collins** (tr).

Fred Smith from the **Bobby Patrick Big Six** took over the drums when **Dave Irving** left and when **Steve Aldo** left to join the **In Crowd**, the new singer was **Colin Areety** who, among others, had formerly sung with the **Almost Blues** and the **Escorts**.

The **Fyx** did not survive for too much longer and finally disbanded in 1968 when **Pete Newton** and **Alby Donnelly** teamed up with **Dave Irving** and **Geoff Workman** again and, together with **Paddy Chambers** and the great Liverpool songstress, **Beryl Marsden,** formed the group **Sinbad**.

This quite short-lived group recorded a great demo with the ballad, "Here We Go Again" which, unfortunately, was never released.

It was in 1969 that **Bob Hardy** needed a resident group for the 'Wooky Hollow' and he recruited his old mates, **Eddie Cave** (voc), **Dave Irving** (dr), **Alby Donnelly** (sax) and **Pete Newton** (bg).

Together with the great guitarist, **Lance Railton**, formerly with **Earl Preston & the T.T.'s** and **Bob Hardy** himself on organ, they became the **Buzz Band**. At some point, **Lance Railton** was replaced by **Paddy Chambers** and, when **Eddie Cave** left, **Bernie Wenton** became the new singer.

Of course, they then became **Bernie & the Buzz Band**, although with the exception of the vocalist, this new group did not have any connection to **Bernie Wenton**'s former recording group of the same name.

When this group disbanded, **Dave Irving** went to London and joined **Sad Cafe**.

Alby Donnelly disappeared from the scene for a while before forming the group, **Supercharge**, which was to become phenomenally successful and achieve international fame.

Bob Hardy quit playing until 1978, when **Terry Connor** persuaded him to join the recording line-up of **Karl Terry & the Cruisers**. This group separated from **Karl Terry** after a year and became **Gaz & the Groovers**. They had also started to work in Germany under the name **Juke**.

In 1984, **Bob Hardy** did a deal with **Alby Donnelly** and **Juke** teamed up with Alby in Germany and became **Supercharge '84**, recording the 'Live At Tina Onassis Wedding' album in early 1985.

In the middle of that year, **Juke** split with Alby and, during the next ten years, **Juke** enjoyed a great deal of success – including a 'number-one' tour as **Ben E. King's** band.

Pete Newton also played with **Karl Terry & the Cruisers** for a while but later became a member of the great Country Rock group, **Kenny Johnson & Northwind**. After that, he appeared with the **Dions**, who had no connection to the Liverpool Sixties group **Roy & the Dions**.

Today he is a member of **Nighttrain**.

Discography :

It's Almost Good / Fresh Out Tears   **UK- PYE 7N 17161 / 1966**

Sinbad :

Here we go again   **UK – demo / 1968**

Advance payment to the Fix from the Star Club (1966)

THE CHANTS

The **Chants** didn't really fit into the Merseybeat scene optically or musically but, they were a very good group and an important part of Liverpool's music scene.

Formed under the name of the **Shades** in the early Sixties, this group consisted entirely of coloured vocalists who did not play any instruments. They were the first group of their kind but, soon there were quite a few similar groups in Liverpool, such as the **Sobells**, the **Conquests** and the **Poppies**, all consisting of coloured singers only.

But the **Chants** were not only the first, they were also the most successful. They found their own style, which always reminded one of the sound of the American vocal groups of the Fifties.

After their name changed to The **Chants**, the group consisted of:

Eddie Amoo	**(lead voc)**
Joey Ankrah	**(voc)**
Edmond Ankrah	**(voc)**
Nat Smeeda	**(voc)**
Alan Harding	**(voc)**

Because the **Chants** depended on live appearances like all the other groups, the vocalists teamed up with the remaining members of **Vince & the Volcanoes**, who changed their name into the **Harlems**, consisting of:

Vincent Ismail	**(lg)**
Robert Eccles	**(bg)**
Dave Preston	**(dr)**

Vinnie Ismail was also known on the scene as **Vinnie Tow** and was the former leader of **Vince & the Volcanos**, who had disbanded a little earlier.

Prior to joining the **Harlems, Dave Preston** had played with **Vince & the Volcanos** and then **Sonny Webb & the Cascades**. He did not stay with the **Harlems** for too long, he then joined the **Secrets**. After that, he played with the **Kinsleys** before becoming a member of the hit group, the **Creation**.

His replacement in the **Harlems** was **John Bedson**, who formerly had played with the **Four Clefs**, the short-lived **Roadrunners (II)** and with the **Challengers**.

Bob Gilmore came in as an additional guitarist, he had also previously played with the **Challengers**.

Vinnie Ismail left and the **Harlems** were joined by **Brendon McCormack**, a superb guitarist who had formerly played with **Rikki & the Red Streaks** and the **Memphis Three**.

The **Chants** recorded their first single, "I Don't Care", in 1963 for PYE, which was not too successful, just like the follow-up, "I Could Write A Book" in 1964.

Their next single, "She's Mine", sounded very much like a **Phil Spector** production but, in spite of good drive and a nice melody, it did not become a chart success for the **Chants**, although it did sell quite well.

"Sweet Was The Wine" (1965) had the same quality and it also sold well. However, it had no chart success and was their last single on the PYE label. Contrary to all the other releases, it is known for sure that, on this single, the **Harlems** were also featured.

The **Chants** switched to Fontana where they recorded a superb single with "Come Back And Get This Loving Baby" in 1966, and it is really hard to understand why this production was not a hit.

It certainly was not the fault of the **Chants**, who did a great job on it.

In the same year, the group also signed a contract with the American MGM label but, the only known release was the single, "Respectable", which apparently sold well in the United States but, as far as it is known, was not released anywhere else.

The Chants

The follow-up in England on the Decca label, was "Lover's Story". It was also released in Germany - their only single over there.

In 1967, the Chants switched to Page One but it was clear from the beginning that their debut for the new label, "Ain't Nobody Home", would not become a major success as it was not commercial enough for that time.

In 1968, RCA signed the **Chants** and, in the same year, released the singles, "A Man Without A Face" and "I Got The Sweetest Feeling". Neither helped the **Chants** achieve any sort of a breakthrough.

Despite the lack of success with their records, the **Chants** have to be counted as one of the leading Liverpool groups of the Sixties and, because they knew how to adapt their musical style to the changing fashion of the times, they existed until the mid 70's.

The Harlems at the Cavern

In 1974, they released "Love Is A Playground" on the little known Fresh Air label and, in 1976, the last single as the **Chants** was "Lucky Old Me" on Chipping Norton but both records already had more of a Disco sound.

At that time, **Chris Amoo** had joined the band, which soon became a top European Disco act as the **Real Thing** and had really big hits including "You To Me Are Everything" or "Can't Get By Without You".

The **Real Thing** was always one of the better Disco groups and are still going strong, even if the line-up has changed a few times! It is only known for sure that **Chris Amoo** is still with them, while **Joey Ankrah** became a solo singer and is still playing the Liverpool clubs these days.

Regarding the **Harlems**, it should be pointed out that, in December 1964, **Vinnie Ismail** and **Rob Eccles**, together with drummer **Johnny Sze** of the **St. Louis Checks,** became the backing group for the great Liverpool songstress, **Beryl Marsden** for a Germany tour with appearances at the 'Star-Club'.

After that tour, the connection broke up and **Rob Eccles** returned to Liverpool and joined **Henry's Handful**. **Johnny Sze** went to Sweden where he joined the **Cherry Stones**, who later evolved into the **Kinetic**.

Vinnie Ismail remained in Germany and became a member of the **Top-Ten All Stars**, the resident group at the famous 'Top-Ten' club in Hamburg. After that, he returned to Liverpool and initially was also a member of **Henry's Handful,** but then he joined the **Valentinos**, who were similar to the **Chants** with the five singers. This group later changed their name into the **Harlems** and recorded the single, "It takes A Fool Like Me" on the DJM label.

Discography :

I Don't Care / Come Go With Me	UK- PYE 7N 15557 / 1963
I Could Write A Book / A Thousand Stars	UK- PYE 7N 15591 / 1964
She's Mine / Then I'll Be Home	UK- PYE 7N 15643 / 1964
Sweet Was The Wine / One Star	UK- PYE 7N 15691 / 1965
Come Back And Get This Loving Baby / Lovelight	UK- Fontana TF 716 / 1966
Lover's Story / Wearing A Smile	UK- Decca F.12650 / 1967
Ain't Nobody Home / For You	UK-Page One POF 016/ 1967
A Man Without A Face / I Don't Need Your Love	UK- RCA 1754 / 1968
I Got The Sweetest Feeling / Candy	UK- RCA 1823 / 1968
Love Is A Playground / Sophisticated Junkyard	UK- Fresh Air 6121.109/1974
Lucky Old Me / I've Been Trying	UK- Chipping Norton CHIP 2 / 1976

Different US-releases :

Respectable / Kiss Me Goodbye	US- MGM K 13008 / 1966

Tracks on compilation-albums :

You Don't Know Like I Know	on **'Silver Soul' Vol. 1**	UK- DJM Silverline DJML 010 / 1970
Progress	on **'Silver Soul' Vol. 1**	UK- DJM Silverline DJML 010 / 1970

(Both of these songs were recorded in 1969)

THE CLAYTON SQUARES

Without any doubt, this was one of Liverpool's leading Rhythm & Blues groups of the Sixties and, beside the **Roadrunners,** one of the most popular ones. The **Clayton Squares** were formed in February 1964 and their management was taken over by none other than **Bob Wooler**, whose far-reaching relationships in the business made it possible for the musicians to become professionals after a very short time.

In their original line-up, the **Clayton Squares** consisted of the following musicians:

Terry Hines	(voc)
Pete Dunn	(lg/org)
Arthur Megginson	(bg)
Mike Evans	(sax/voc)
Eddie Williams	(sax/voc)
Bob Scott	(dr)

Bob Scott was a former member of **Clay & the Classics** and **Pete Dunn** formerly had played with the **Pegasus Four**, the **Flintstones** or **Ogi & the Flintstones**, which were one and the same group, but with different names.

Arthur Megginson left the group and, after a short spell with the **Kruzads,** he apparently quit show business. He was replaced by **Geoff Jones**, who came from the **Georgians** and he probably was the guitarist of the same name who, before that, had played with **Joan & the Demons**.

In March 1964, **Eddie Williams** left the group to join the **Almost Blues**, where he became the lead singer under the name of **Jerkin' George Paul**. He was replaced in the **Clayton Squares** by sax player, **Les Smith**.

In early 1965, **Terry Hines** left to form the **Terry Hines Sextet**, who were also quite successful on Liverpool's Rhythm & Blues scene, but that is another story in this book.

His replacement in the **Clayton Squares** was **Denny Alexander**, who had formerly played with the **Aarons**, the **Secrets** and the **Kinsleys**.

In this line-up, **Bob Wooler** introduced the band to **Andrew 'Loog' Oldham**, who a little later produced their first single, "Come And Get It", for the Decca label, which was also released in Germany. It was a great record with an interesting and commercial Rhythm & Blues sound.

The group, at that time, also recorded a complete album for Oldham which, among others, included a great version of "I've Been Loving You Too Long" and it is very hard to understand why this album was never released.

Instead, in 1966, the **Clayton Squares** released their second single, "There She Is", but this one also failed to make the charts.

The book, 'Beat in Liverpool', which was written by the German, **Jürgen Seuss** in 1966, deals mainly with the **Clayton Squares** as well as with the **Hideaways**, another great Liverpool Rhythm & Blues band. It included an EP insertion which featured one group on either side taken from live performances at the 'Cavern' and the 'Sink', respectively. Unfortunately, it is of such poor recording quality that the record is only interesting for collectors or people who have a deep interest in the Liverpool scene and its groups. The **Clayton Squares** were featured with the songs, "Watch Your Step", "Hey Good Looking" and "Tell Me How Do You Feel", recorded at the 'Cavern'.

Nothing is known of further recordings by the **Clayton Squares,** but it can be taken for granted that there were more songs recorded, especially because of the group's close connection to the Cavern who, at that time, had their own 'Cavern Sound' studios.

However, the **Clayton Squares** existed in this line-up until the end of 1966.

When **Les Smith** left, he was replaced by **Alby Donnelly**, who had formerly played with the **Plainsmen**, the **Terry Hines Sextet** and the **Fyx**.

Les Smith who, at the end of the Sixties, was a member of the **Fyx**, sadly died at a very young age in 1970 in a motorbike accident.

The T-Squares

Pete Dunn also left and was replaced by **Lance Railton**, another great lead guitarist, who was a former member of **Johnny Tempest & the Tornadoes**, which became the **TTs** and backed a number of singers including **'Faron'**, **Earl Preston**, **Cy Tucker**, **Vic Wright**, **Amos Bonny** and **Karl Terry**.

Denny Alexander left and became a member of the **Thoughts**.

Barry Womersley was also a member of the **Clayton Squares** for a short time. He had formerly played with the **Diplomats** and **Rhythm & Blues Inc.** from Southport, as well as with the **Big Three**. He later became a member of **Jasmin T** and **Inner Sleeve**.

The **Clayton Squares** gradually disbanded and **Lance Railton** and the remaining members amalgamated with **Karl Terry** (ex **Karl Terry & the Cruisers**, the **Delemeres** and **Karl Terry & the TTs**) and the remaining members of the **TTs** under the name of the **T-Squares**, who changed their name back to the **Clayton Squares** for a tour of Germany. After this tour, the group disbanded again but was re-formed under the name of the **Clayton Squares** for a second tour of Germany with **Karl Terry** (voc/bg), **Lance Railton** (lg), **Alby Donnelly** (sax), **Pete Hallican** (sax), **Chris Hatfield** (org) and **Paul Hitchmough** (dr).

It is known that **Paul Hitchmough** had previously played with the **Victims**, **Sounds Plus One** and the **Kruzads**, while **Chris Hatfield** came from **Them Grimbles**.

After this tour, the **Clayton Squares** split up completely.

Alby Donnelly later formed **Supercharge**, a band that for years did extremely well in Germany and other European countries.

Mike Evans became a member of the poetry and comedy group, **Liverpool Scene,** before he went down to London where he is still living and looking after the interests of other musicians in a type of musicians' union. In 1977, he was the co-producer of the radio series, 'Merseybeat in Liverpool'.

Karl Terry became a member of **Rory Storm & the Hurricanes** but then formed a new group using the **Karl Terry & the Cruisers** name again. **Lance Railton** and **Chris Hatfield** also played in this group for a time. **Lance Railton** sadly died much too young in 1989.

Paul Hitchmough joined **Curiosity Shoppe** and, in 1990, toured Germany as a member of **Beryl Marsden**'s backing group. He later returned to Germany as a member of **Karl Terry & the Cruisers**.

Discography :

Come And Get It / And Tears Fell	**UK- Decca F.12250 / 1965**
There She Is / Imagination	**UK- Decca F.12456 / 1966**

Besides this, the **Clayton Squares** were featured on an EP which was enclosed in the book, 'Beat in Liverpool', written by **Jürgen Seuss**. On this EP, the **Clayton Squares** can be found with the following live-recordings from the 'Cavern' :

"Watch Your Step", **"Hey Good Looking"** and **"Tell Me How Do You Feel"**   **G- Sonopress EVA 101 / 1966**

Unreleased tracks :

In 1965, **Andrew Loog Oldham** produced a complete album with the **Clayton Squares** of which it is only known that a great version of Otis Redding's, **"I've Been Loving You Too Long"** was featured.

THE CONCORDS

This band was formed in the Anfield/Kensington area of Liverpool in 1962 as an instrumental group under the name of the **Four X's**.

In 1963, they changed their name to the **Concords**, following a suggestion by their manager's wife - long before that similar name was used for the supersonic jetliner. A little later they also changed their musical style, sharing the vocals and playing mainly US Soul influenced material, which was not too well-known in England at that time. From the beginning, the **Concords** consisted of the following musicians:

Ritchie Bennett	**(voc/rg)**
Jim Whitfield	**(lg/voc)**
Ray Adams	**(bg/voc)**
Kenny Meachin	**(dr)**

In 1963, the **Concords** cut a demo of the **Bob Hilliard/Burt Bacharach** song "Any Day Now", which became a favourite on Radio Caroline but was never released on record. Of course, this helped the group's popularity, but it took another year before they were signed by a recording company.

After a very successful tour of Belgium, where they played in front of more than 2,000 people at the 'White House' in Ostend, and then onto Germany, where they stayed for four weeks at a club in Remagen, EMI gave them a contract and, in September 1964, they recorded "Ecstasy" and **Sam Cooke's** "Bring It On Home To Me" for a single. But, for mysterious reasons, this record was never released. This sad fact might have been the reason for two changes in the line-up in 1965.

Ray Adams left the **Concords** to join the re-formed **Pilgrims**, while **Kenny Meachin** also left and disappeared from the scene.

Two new members, **Gordon L. Young** (bg) and **Billy Hewitt** (dr) were recruited.

With this line-up, the **Concords** continued quite successfully on the scene until 1968. Although they never achieved national success or had any record releases, the **Concords** were very popular throughout Lancashire and Cheshire and today are still remembered fondly.

After the split all the members quit show business.

Discography:

Ecstasy / Bring It On Home To Me	UK- EMI (unreleased) / 1964

Additionally, the **Concords** cut a demo with the song, **"Any Day Now"**, in 1963 which became a favourite on Radio Caroline, but was never released on record.

THE CONNOISSEURS

The roots of this Liverpool band go back to 1957, when **Mike Harkess** and **Barry 'Baz' Davis** formed the Skiffle group, The **Wild Harks**, together with **Dave Owin** on guitar and a drummer named **'Tony'**. In 1959, the **Wild Harks** changed their music style and became a Rock 'n' Roll band. This lasted until 1962 when **Mike Harkess** had to join the Army. At that time the **Wild Harks** disbanded.

The original line-up of the Connoisseurs

Back in Liverpool in 1963, **Mike Harkess** met up again with **Barry Davis** and they formed a new group under the name, the **Connoisseurs**. This group also included **Joey Bowers** (bg) and **Geoff Bamford** on drums.

Joey Bowers was a former member of the **Four Jays** and the **Four Mosts**, while **Geoff Bamford** came from the **Memphis Three**. But **Geoff Bamford** did not stay for too long and left to join **Ian & the Zodiacs**, who had a long residency in Hamburg. His replacement in the **Connoisseurs** was **Kenny London**.

In 1964, the group almost disbanded when first **Barry Davis** left to join the new backing group of **King Size Taylor**, followed a little later by **Kenny London**, who disappeared from the scene.

Mike Harkess and **Joey Bowers** then joined forces with a Liverpool trio called the **Mersey Gamblers**, and this new band continued under the name of the **Connoisseurs** in the following line-up:

The Mersey Gamblers

Mike Harkess (voc)

Colin Fabb (rg/voc)

Dave Kent (lg/voc)

Joey Bowers (bg/voc)

Les Mason (dr)

Prior to **Dave Kent** joining the **Mersey Gamblers**, he had played with the **Kingpins**, the **Galaxies** and the **Corvettes**.

Joey Bowers and **Colin Fabb** swapped places on instruments and, in this line-up, the **Connoisseurs** won the 'Northern Beat Contest' in 1965 and came second in the 'All Britain Finals' in London in the same year.

George Martin took the group to the 'Abbey Road' studios where they recorded the **Dave Kent** original, "Make Up Your Mind", as a demo disc, which was not released on record.

The recording line-up of the Connoisseurs

At the end of 1965, the **Connoisseurs** were joined by **Vince Earl** as an additional vocalist. He had formerly played with the **Teenage Rebels** and, after that, led **Vince Earl & the Zeros** and **Vince Earl & the Talismen**. He had also been a member of **Rory Storm & the Hurricanes** for a short time.

Then **Les Mason** left and disappeared from the scene. His replacement was **Jimmy Tushingham**, a former member of the **Four Clefs** and **Rory Storm & the Hurricanes**.

This line-up toured Germany in 1966 and appeared quite often at the well-known 'Star-Palast' in Kiel. Back in England, the **Connoisseurs** recorded another **Dave Kent** song with the title, "Do I Love You" and the standard, "Once In A While" on acetate. Unfortunately, this recording did nothing to help their popularity, especially as they were already a top act in Lancashire anyway.

During 1967, they recorded some more songs on acetate, of which only the following ones are known: "In My Life", "I Look Through You", "I Do" and "Sailor Boy", which were probably all originals, with the exception of the latter.

Joey Bowers left and became a member of the **Cheaters** before he returned to the **Fourmost**, as his former group was now named. In the early Nineties, he was a member of the **Clouds**, who in some way had evolved from the **Fourmost**.

His replacement in the **Connoisseurs** was **Peter Wallace**, who came from the **Mike Cotton Sound** but originally had been a member of **Ian & the Zodiacs**.

Colin Fabb left in 1967 to play Jazz and **Charlie Flynn**, who also came from **Ian & the Zodiacs**, replaced him.

A year later, **Dave Kent** left and his replacement was none other than **Ian Edwards** who, after **Ian & the Zodiacs** split, also had a short stint with the **Fourmost**.

But this line-up also didn't exist for too long and the **Connoisseurs** eventually disbanded sometime in 1969.

Ian Edwards became a member of the **Chesterfields** for a short time, but then retired until he re-formed **Ian & the Zodiacs** in 1999. Sadly, he died unexpectedly on 22 October 2007.

Vince Earl formed the **Vince Earl Attraction** who released two albums in the Seventies. In the later years, he became quite a successful TV actor, but he has managed to keep the **Vince Earl Attraction** going and, at some point, **Charlie Flynn** was also a member.

Dave Kent was still active in a group called **Sounds Sixties** in the Nineties but then he retired.

The **Connoisseurs** occasionally played together again for the 'MerseyCats' in the Nineties, but it is not known who from the Sixties' line-ups beside **Dave Kent** and **Vince Earl** was with them.

In 2000, **Colin Fabb** was a member of the re-formed **Ian & the Zodiacs** and, after the group had parted again from **Ian Edwards**, the remaining **Zodiacs** were also joined by original **Connoisseurs** member, **Barry Davies** who, in 1965, had left **King Size Taylor** to join **Mike Warner & his New Stars** from Bielefeld in Germany. After that, he had played with the **Vince Earl Attraction** and internationally famous groups such as **Jimmy James & the Vagabonds** and the **New Vaudeville Band** before he started a career as solo performer and also recorded in his own right.

Today he is a member of the **Undertakers** and, like **Colin Fabb**, he still appears with the **Zodiacs** from time to time.

Discography :

Make Up Your Mind / —	UK- Abbey Road demo-disc / 1965
Do I Love You / **Once In A While**	UK- Deroy acetate / 1965
In My Life, I Look Through You, Sailor Boy and **I Do**	UK- various acetates / 1966/67

THE CORDES

At the beginning of the Sixties there was a group, formed somewhere in the Childwall area of Liverpool, named **Peter Lewis & the Raiders**.

In 1962, they were joined by bass player, **Dave Dover**, who came from **Deke Wade & the Ambassadors**. The group then consisted of **Peter Lewis** (voc), **Steve Lister** (lg), **Derek Fulwood** (rg), **Dave Dover** (bg/harp) and **Johnny Brown** (dr).

By 1963, the musicians were tired of playing **Cliff Richard & the Shadows** numbers and similar music and they decided to break away from **Peter Lewis**, who went on to form the **Liverpool Raiders**, a sort of religious Beat-group with whom he also recorded on the English Tower-label.

His former group members now shared the vocals and probably continued as the **Raiders** and played more 'rough' Rhythm & Blues music. They then changed the group's name to the **Cordes**. When **Johnny Brown** left and apparently quit show business, the **Cordes** continued in the following line-up:

Steve Lister	**(voc/lg)**
Derek Fullwood	**(rg/voc)**
Dave Dover	**(bg/harp/voc)**
Clive Smith	**(dr/voc)**

Clive Smith, was a former member of the recently disbanded **Mike & the Thunderbirds**.

In the same year, 1963, the **Cordes** recorded two acetates in the Lambda studios in Crosby with the songs, "Clarabella" and "The Evening", which were just demos and never released on record.

They quickly achieved local popularity and played regularly at the many clubs in the city, including the 'Cavern', the 'Mardi Gras', the 'Iron Door', the 'Peppermint Lounge' the 'Victoriana', etc.

At 'Hope Hall' they met up with the **Roadrunners** for the first time, became good friends and after that often appeared together at the same venues.

In September 1964, the **Cordes** recorded an acetate EP in the studios of the Alan Cheetham agency in Manchester, which also included the **Jodimars** song, "Clarabella", again, which apparently was a favourite of theirs at that time as well as the rocking "Betty, Betty, Betty", the standard, "You Are My Sunshine", (the **Ray Charles** version), as well as **Leroy Carr**'s "When The Sun Goes Down".

Around that time, they recorded many of their rehearsals in the front room of **Steve Lister's** house. These tapes are of surprisingly good quality and include standards such as "Roll Over Beethoven", "I Got My Mojo Working", "Watch Your Step", "It Hurts Me So" and "You've Really Got A Hold On Me". Very interesting recordings which show the outstanding quality of the group and especially of guitarist **Steve Lister**.

After the **Cordes** had played regularly at the 'Cavern' for a while, they were chosen to be the first recording group on the new 'Cavern Sound' label. In March 1965, they went into the studio in a cellar in Matthew Street and recorded the songs, "Give Her Time" and "She's Leaving", most probably originals by the group. Although this record has a real order number, it seems it was never released or, if so, only in a very limited

Dave Dover at the Kraal

edition as a demo disc. In 1965, **Dave Dover** was sent down to London by his employers and was replaced in the group by **Mike Byrne** (voc/bg), the former leader of **Mike & the Thunderbirds.** Prior to joining the **Cordes**, **Mike Byrne** had played with **Them Grimbles** and the **Roadrunners**.

From that moment on, the **Cordes** became more of a harmony group. This line-up was re-joined by the returning **Dave Dover**, while **Mike Byrne** put the bass guitar aside and stepped up front as their singer.

It was probably in late 1966 when **Steve Lister** left the group and quit the music business for many years. He was replaced by organist, **Stan Broster** from the **Marescas**.

Clive Smith also left and the drums were taken over by **Terry McCusker**, who had formerly played with **Pete Demos & the Demons**, the **Four Dymonds**, **Rip Van Winkle & the Rip-It-Ups**, the **Valkyries** and the **Roadrunners**. This new line-up changed their name to **Fringe Benefit** and mainly played Tamla Soul material. **Stan Broster** left and was replaced by **Rod Stanson**. In addition, the group was joined by **Brian Farrell** from the **Georgians** as lead singer. He, by the way, was the brother-in-law of **Mike Byrne**, who at that time, switched to keyboards.

In early 1968, **Fringe Benefit** became **Colonel Bagshot's Incredible Bucket Band** (...what a name!) when **Derek Fulwood** was replaced by **Mike Kontzle**, who also came from the **Roadrunners** and, before that, he had played with the **Beatwoods** and **Chick Graham & the Coasters**.

This group cut a version of **Edwin Hawkins'** "Oh Happy Day" on a single for the French Vogue label, coupled with the **Mike Kontzle** original, "Gina", that became a chart success in France and Belgium.

When **Mike Byrne**, **Rod Stanson** and **Mike Kontzle** left, the group became a quartet again when a new member, **Kenny Parry** (key/g/voc), joined the remaining **Brian Farrell**, **Dave Dover** and **Terry McCusker**.

Colonel Bagshots Incredible Bucket Band

The group existed until the early Seventies and, during that time, released the album, 'Oh! What A Lovely War', on the Cadet label, which was originally recorded for the Japanese market where it was obviously also released. With the exception of the **Kenny Parry** number, "I've Seen The Light", all album tracks were written by **Brian Farrell**.

From that album the single, "Smile" was released on Parlophone, a very nice folksy song which, in 1971, was followed by "Georgia Fireball" - once again on Parlophone and, again, a great single.

After that, little was heard of the group, but two years later "She's My Sun" was released on the German Polydor label. This single was not very good and failed to achieve any success.

It was the final release by **Colonel Bagshot's Incredible Bucket Band** who disbanded a little later. **Dave Dover**, **Kenny Parry** and **Terry McCusker** initially continued as a trio under the name, **Nickelodeon**, and later became the group **Bunny** together with girl singer **Linda Millington**.

After the split, **Kenny Parry** became a member of the new **Merseybeats** and then joined **Liverpool Express** and today, together with **Brian Farrell,** still plays in a Country band called **Hambone**. Sometimes they are joined by **Terry McCusker** on drums.

Mike Byrne later appeared again as a solo performer in the Liverpool pubs and he was also the manager of the 'Beatles Museum' in the Albert Dock in Liverpool for a while. After that, he played with various groups such as **Persuader, Rocket 88** and the **Juke Box Eddies** which, without exception, consisted of well-known Merseybeat veterans. Finally, he formed **Mike Byrne & the Sun Rockers**, a very good Rock 'n' Roll group that is still going strong on the scene.

Dave Dover continued in the music business, initially as a session musician and, in the early Eighties, as a member of **Supercharge**. From 1987 until 1994, he played in **Cy Tucker's** band, which sometimes still appeared as **Cy Tucker & the Friars**. After that, he joined the tribute band, **Cocker Power** and, finally, he was with the rock band, **Space Cadets,** who are still in existence.

Of the other original **Cordes** members, **Steve Lister** only lately stepped back onto the music scene as a member of the **Lune Valley Vintage Jazz Band**, which is popular throughout Lancashire and Cumbria. **Derek Fulwood** emigrated to Germany in the Seventies, where he sadly died in 2005 of a heart attack, while **Clive Smith** apparently stopped drumming in the 60's and became a successful salesman.

Discography :

The **Cordes** :

Give Her Time / She's Leaving	UK- Cavern Sound IMSTL 1 / 1965

Unreleased tracks :

Clarabella (one-sided demo)	UK- Lambda acetate / 1963
The Evening (one-sided demo)	UK- Lambda acetate / 1963

Colonel Bagshot's Incredible Bucket Band :

Oh Happy Day / Gina	F - Vogue INT. 80186 / 1969
Smile / Heading Home	UK - Parlophone R 5910 / 1971
Georgia Fireball / One Look In Her Eyes	UK - Parlophone R 5893 / 1971
She's My Sun / Meet Down The Middle	G - Polydor 2058.381 / 1973

LP

'OH! WHAT A LOVELY WAR'	US - Cadet 9037-50010 / 1970

- Six Day War / Lay It Down / Lord High Human Being / Headhunters / I've Seen The Light / Dirty Delilah Blues / Sometimes / That's What I Like To Know / Smile / Tightrope Tamer / Oh! What A Lovely War

THE CROSSBEATS

This Gospel Beat group was formed in the youth-section of the Anglican St. Leonard's church in Bootle under the name of the **Seekers** in early 1963.

When the Australian **Seekers** hit England, it was time for a name change and so for a short time the Liverpool group appeared as the **Sceptres**, but finally decided on the **Crossbeats** as their new name.

They were not really a part of the Merseybeat scene because they did not play the usual songs and the usual clubs, but mainly appeared at various church events. Their exceptional self-composed songs all had religious themes, but their music was pure Merseybeat, even if not in the 'hard' manner.

From the beginning, the **Crossbeats** consisted of the following musicians:

Tony Mathias	**(voc)**
John Boyes	**(lg/voc)**
Eddie Boyes	**(rg/voc)**
John Millington	**(bg/voc)**
Eric Knowles	**(dr)**

It was quite surprising when, in early 1965, the first single by the **Crossbeats** was released.

The songs, "If Only" and "He Wants To Know" were not released on one of the usual record labels, but on the 'Pilgrim' label, which was probably owned by the Anglican Church of England.

This can be deduced from the fact that the label and cover layout seemed quite religious. This release was followed by the **Tony Mathias** composition, "I Know", coupled with "He Waits", a song by **Tony Mathias** and **John Boyes**. Again the same signs: good Merseybeat with religious themes and a religious cover on the Pilgrim label from London. As a result of this release, the **Crossbeats** made some TV appearances and also played a lot of universities, hospitals and prisons all over the country. But, of course, this single did not become a hit success, neither did their follow up, "Step Aside".

At the beginning of 1966, **John Millington** left the group to get married and **Eddie Boyes** switched to bass guitar, while **Sam Pennington,** who had formerly played with the **Questers**, joined the **Crossbeats** as their new rhythm guitarist. **Sam Pennington** also wrote the song, "Busy Man", which was released as their next single in 1966.

In 1967, there was an album by the **Crossbeats** released called 'Crazy Mixed Up Generation', which, besides the songs from the last single, comprised of eight originals by the group.

On 24 March 1967, the group even played the 'Cavern', but as far as it is known, it was their only appearance in this famous Beat cellar.

When **Tony Mathias** got married and left the group, he was not replaced and the members shared the vocals. 1968 brought the last change in the line-up when **Eric Knowles** decided to quit the music business, their new drummer was **John Roberts**, who had previously played with the **Beacons**.

This line-up of the **Crossbeats** continued to perform on the scene until 1975.

Discography :

If Only / He Wants To Know	UK- Pilgrim PSR 7001 / 1965
I Know / He Waits	UK- Pilgrim PSR 7002 / 1965
Step Aside / Forgive Me	UK- Pilgrim PSR 7003 / 1965
Busy Man / Change	UK- Pilgrim PSR 7004 / 1966

LP

| CRAZY, MIXED UP GENERATION | UK- Pilgrim KLP 12 / 1967 |

- Busy Man / Do Not Disturb / Are You Afraid ? / Back Where You Belong /

Snow Covered Mountains / Change / Tears / Time / Crazy Mixed Up Generation /

Do You Remember?

THE CRYIN' SHAMES

The origin of this group began with the formation of the **Bumblies** in 1962 in Liverpool's Norris Green area. Initially, they were just one of a few hundred groups in the Beat metropolis, in spite of their outstanding musical quality. As far as it is known, the group in its original line-up consisted of **Joe Kneen** (voc), **John Bennett** (lg), **Barry Davison** (rg/org), **George Robinson** (bg) and **Charlie Gallagher** (dr).

Founder **George Robinson** was a former member of **Buddy Dean & the Teachers**.

In January 1965, it almost came to a total split-up when **Joe Kneen** and **Charlie Gallagher** left to join the **Calderstones**.

But then **Charlie Crane,** who came from the **Blue Angels,** joined as the new singer and **Dave Ferguson** from the **Countdowns** replaced the leaving **John Bennett**. It is not known who became the new drummer, or even if there was a steady drummer with the **Bumblies** at that time.

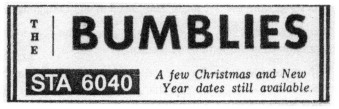

THE BUMBLIES

STA 6040 *A few Christmas and New Year dates still available.*

Dave Ferguson was soon replaced by **Ritchie Rutledge**, another great singer and guitarist, who came from the **Aztecs**.

But this was still not the end of the changes in the line-up and, when **Barry Davison** also left, the **Bumblies,** in the middle of 1965, consisted of:

Charlie Crane	(voc)
Ritchie Rutledge	(lg/voc)
Phil Robert	(org/p)
George Robinson	(bg)
Charlie Gallagher	(dr)

Phil Robert had played together with the returning **Charlie Gallagher** in the **Calderstones** that had recently disbanded.

There was a record released in 1965 by a group with the name of the **Bumblies**, but this, for sure, was not the Liverpool band because the lead guitarist on the single, "I Gotta Tell" was **Terry Ward**, who never appeared in a line-up of the **Bumblies** from Norris Green.

But this release apparently was the reason for the Merseybeat group changing its name to prevent confusion with the recording band. The new name of the group was the **Cryin' Shames**, and so was open to confusion with the US group with the name of the **Cryan' Shames**, but this group obviously was still not known in Europe or the UK at that time.

A little later, **Ritchie Rutledge** put the guitar aside and stepped in front as the second lead vocalist. **Mike Espie** from the **Vaaveros** joined as the new lead guitarist, and so the band became a sextet.

The popularity of the **Cryin' Shames** started to grow and the producer, Joe Meek, became interested and signed them to Decca in late 1965.

With their first single, a moody version of the **Drifters** number, "Please Stay", the **Cryin' Shames** had their first chart success when the record climbed up to No. 26 in March 1966.

Conspicuous on this release are the lisping vocals of **Charlie Crane** but also noticeable is the very good arrangement with a full organ.

It was probably after this release **Charlie Gallagher** left the group and was replaced by **Paul Comerford**, the former drummer with the **Pulsators** and **Tiffany & the Thoughts**.

The Cryin' Shames

It is also said, that the only remaining original member, **George Robinson**, may have been replaced by **Derek Cleary**, but this is not absolutely sure.

Their follow-up single, "Nobody Waved Goodbye", was also a brilliant song with a good arrangement and, it is quite hard to understand why this record did not make the charts, especially because it was in the same style as "Please Stay" – or was it just too similar?

However, it still sold quite well and was not a total flop. In 1966, the group's last single was released with "September In The Rain" - as **Paul + Ritchie & the Cryin' Shames**. However, at that time, **Brian Norris**, a former member of **Earl Preston's Realms,** had taken over on bass guitar.

The name of **Paul + Ritchie & the Cryin' Shames** is a little bit confusing, as from that could be concluded that **Charlie Crane** was no longer with the group. But he definitely was, it's only that he had changed his name from **Charlie Crane** to **Paul Crane**.

Phil Robert had left the group and the new keyboard player, already on that record, was **Pete Byrne**. After **Paul Comerford** left to join the **Escorts** he was replaced by **Tommy Maguire** and the final line-up of the **Cryin' Shames** was complete.

Tommy Maguire was a former member of **Mark Anthony & the Alpha-Beats,** the **Mystery Four** and he was also the successor to **Charlie Gallagher** in the **Calderstones** and, after that, he had played with the **Inmates** and the **T-Squares**.

The **Cryin' Shames,** at that time, were mainly appearing down in London, where at least some of them also played in the **Fruit Eating Bears**, backing the **Merseys**. The line-ups of the **Fruit Eating Bears** and the **Cryin' Shames** were constantly interchanging and, in the end, they both disbanded. However, the **Cryin' Shames** existed for a little longer before they totally disbanded some time in Autumn 1967.

They left a really deep impression behind - because of their only hit, "Please Stay", which on the single was coupled with "What's New Pussycat" - probably the best recording by the **Cryin' Shames**, which was very different from the **Tom Jones'** hit song of the same title.

In 1968, **Pete Byrne** was a member of the Liverpool group, **Mumble** and, in the same year, **Ritchie Rutledge**, who today is still quite popular in Liverpool, became a member of the **Hideaways**.

The **Hideaways** changed their name to **Confucius** a little later and **Ritchie Rutledge** was featured on their only single. In 1972, he played for a short time with the **Swinging Blue Jeans** and, after that, he was a member of **Blackwater Park** and **Grimms**.

Brian Norris joined the **Dimensions** that soon evolved into the cabaret-trio **Pendulum** and **Tommy Maguire** later played with the **New Merseybeats** and **Karl Terry & the Cruisers**.

Gary Walker and Rain

Paul Crane (voc/g) together with **Joey Molland** (lg) from the **Fruit Eating Bears** teamed up with **Gary Leeds** of the **Walker Brothers** on drums and the London bass guitarist, **John Lawson** in the group, **Gary Walker & Rain**. They became very popular, especially in Japan, where they released the majority of their very collectable records, some of those numbers were written by **Paul Crane**.

When **Gary Walker & Rain** disbanded in early 1969, **Paul Crane** became a record-producer and, in 1970, under the name of **Charlie Crane** again, released a solo single with "Come Day, Go Day Man", which was written by Liverpudlian, **Alan Crowley**, but it was not too successful.

Suddenly in 1973, the name **Cryin' Shames** appeared again on the scene when the single, "I'm Gonna Tell The World" with its flip-side, "I Don't Believe It" was released on the York label.

Both songs were co-written by **Charlie Crane**, together with a certain 'Marshal' on the A-side, and a certain 'Mitchell' on the B-side, who might have been members of the **Cryin' Shames** at that time.

The record was in the commercial and modern sound of that time and "I'm Gonna Tell The World" reminded one a little bit of the **Cryin' Shames** sound of the Sixties, but mainly because of the vocals of **Charlie Crane**.

After that release, nothing was heard again of the 'new' **Cryin' Shames**, who most probably disbanded after the record, as they had likely only used that name for the recording session with **Charlie Crane**.

Charlie Crane sadly died much too young sometime in the Seventies (?).

The original **Cryin' Shames** bass-guitarist, **George Robinson**, along with a female partner is still performing under the name of the **Cryin' Shames Duo**. The original drummer, **Charlie Gallagher**, and one-time **Bumblies** group-member, **Dave Ferguson**, are both members of a group that also performs under the **Bumblies** name again.

None of the other members of the **Bumblies** or the **Cryin' Shames** appeared on the scene again.

Discography :

Please Stay / What's New Pussycat	**UK- Decca F.12340 / 1966**
Nobody Waved Goodbye / You	**UK- Decca F.12425 / 1966**
September In The Rain / Come On Back	**UK- Decca F.12483 / 1966**
I'm Gonna Tell The World / I Don't Believe It	**UK- York YR 202 / 1973**

(please note that "**September In The Rain**" was released as **Paul + Ritchie & the Cryin' Shames**)

Charlie Crane – solo :

Come Day, Go Day Man / Face On The Wind	**UK- Decca F.13089 / 1970**

THE CURIOSITY SHOPPE

As can be seen from the group's name, they were part of something that was really the third generation of the Merseybeat wave. The story started when **Billy Hargreaves** left the **Aztecs** in 1966 and joined another Liverpool group with the name of the **Mistake**, where he met **Harry Shaw** and **Sam Rothwell**.

When the line-up of this group started to crumble away in 1967, the above named three members recruited other musicians and continued under the name **Curiosity Shoppe**, in a line-up with:

Harry Shaw	**(voc)**
Mick Rowley	**(lg/voc)**
Sam Rothwell	**(key/voc)**
Billy Hargreaves	**(bg)**
Bill Geeleher	**(dr)**

Bill Geeleher was a former member of the **Modes** and the **Calderstones**. Unfortunately, **Mick Rowley**'s former group is not known.

Of course, the music of **Curiosity Shoppe** was no longer pure Merseybeat but, in line with the fashion of that time, it had a certain psychedelic touch.

The group went down to London to play the club scene where they became quite popular. They were signed to the Decca sub label, Deram and, in 1968, had their first single released with "Baby I Need You". A very interesting record that was also released in Europe but, in the end, it was not commercial enough to become a chart success.

They returned to Liverpool and, when they had to go down to London again, **Bill Geeleher** left the group and disappeared from the scene.

Paul Hitchmough came in as his replacement. He was a well-known Merseybeat drummer who had already played in many groups including the **Hangmen**, the **Victims**, the **Corals**, **Sounds plus One**, the **Kruzads** and **Clayton Squares**.

The **Curiosity Shoppe** continued playing all over England for another two years and then disbanded in 1971.

Mick Rowley probably quit show business as did **Billy Hargreaves**.

Paul Hitchmough also disappeared from the scene but, in the Nineties, he was back with the **Beryl Marsden Group**. He then joined **Karl Terry & the Cruisers** before withdrawing again from the music scene. However, he continued to play sporadically with different groups, not becoming a steady member of any of them.

Of **Sam Rothwell**, it is known that he joined **Confucius** and later he played with the re-formed **Merseybeats**.

Harry Shaw also continued in showbiz and later played with groups such as **Export** and **Garth Rockett & the Moonshiners**.

In 2003, there was a reunion concert which, besides all the other original members, included **Paul Hitchmough** on drums again. But this was a one-off thing and not repeated - yet!

Discography :

Baby I Need You / So Sad   **UK- Deram DM 220 / 1968**

LEE CURTIS & THE ALL STARS

Lee Curtis, whose real name is **Peter Flannery**, was an ideal Rock 'n' Roll star. If one takes his good looks, his tall slim figure, his toothpaste smile, his pleasant aura and his great voice, it's not surprising that his success was almost pre-programmed. He started his career as a singer at the beginning of the Sixties with the Liverpool group, the **Detours**.

Lee Curtis & the Detours appeared regularly at Liverpool clubs until the end of 1962. Then he parted from the group, who continued as the **Detours**, but that is another story in this book. **Lee Curtis** then formed a new group under the name of **Lee Curtis & the All Stars**, which in the original line-up consisted of:

Lee Curtis	**(voc)**
Frank Bowen	**(lg)**
Tony Waddington	**(rg/voc)**
Wayne Bickerton	**(bg/voc)**
Bernie Rogers	**(dr)**

Bernie Rogers was a former member of the **Travellers**, and **Johnny Saint & the Travellers**, while **Wayne Bickerton** had formerly played with the **Bobby Bell Rockers** and **Steve Bennett & the Syndicate**.

Tony Waddington was a former member of **Gene Day & the Django-Beats**, the **Comets** and **Steve Bennett & the Syndicate**, and **Frank Bowen** had previously played with the **Teenbeats**, **Cliff Roberts' Rockers**, the **Blue Stars** and the **Lonely Ones**, as well as with **Howie Casey & the Seniors**.

Bernie Rogers left in 1963 to join **Denny Seyton & the Sabres**, and his replacement in the **All Stars** was none other than **Pete Best**, the former drummer with the **Blackjacks** and the **Beatles**.

In this line-up, **Lee Curtis & the All Stars** were featured on the Decca compilation, 'Live At The Cavern', with the songs, "Jezebel" and "Skinny Minnie". It was also this group that cut the singles, "Let's Stomp" and "What About Me", on the Decca label, which were released after the **Lee Curtis** solo single, "Little Girl".

They all failed to make the charts, although "What About Me" was an especially good record.

The **All Stars** also recorded the very interesting acetate, "Hide And Seek", without **Lee Curtis**. That was coupled with the great instrumental, "Czardas", which made it clear what an excellent guitarist **Frank Bowen** was.

Lee Curtis - Chuck Berry Club - Bielefeld (Germany)

In 1964, for some unknown reason, **Lee Curtis** parted from the group. Initially, they continued to perform under the name of the **Original All Stars** and then later, as **Pete Best & the Original All Stars**.

Frank Bowen left and became a member of the **Pathfinders** and, after that, he had a short stint with **Rory Storm & the Hurricanes**. Later he played with **Mike & the Merseymen**, who a little later changed their name to the **Trends** and went down to London.

After a short spell with the **Bootleggers** in London, **Frank Bowen** returned to Liverpool and joined **Earl Royce & the Olympics**. He sadly died much too young in the Sixties.

His replacement in the **Original All Stars** was **Tommy McGuirk**, a former member of the **Comets** and the **Aarons**.

A little later the band's name was changed into The **Pete Best Four**, which then evolved into the **Pete Best Combo**, but that again is another story in this book.

Lee Curtis formed a new group under the name of **Lee Curtis & the All Stars** and, for the first time, toured Germany, where he became a top act at the 'Star-Club' in Hamburg.

LEE CURTIS & THE ALL STARS

Besides **Lee Curtis**, this band consisted of **Paul Pilnick** (lg), **George Peckham** (rg), **Dave 'Mushy' Cooper** (bg) and **Don Alcyd** (dr).

Don Alcyd was a former member of **Tommy & the Metronomes** and **Faron & the Tempest Tornadoes**, as well as the Liverpool **Renegades**, from which **George Peckham** also came.

Dave Cooper had previously played with the **Topspots**, **Bob Evans & the Five Shillings** and the **Vegas Five** which, in some way, all were predecessor groups of the **Undertakers**. He also had a short spell with **Faron's Flamingos**. **Paul Pilnick** came from **Vince & the Volcanoes**.

Despite their very successful German tour, **Lee Curtis & the All Stars** disbanded soon after. **George Peckham** and **Paul Pilnick** (under the name **Paul St. John**) initially joined **Groups Inc.**, after that **George Peckham** met up with **Dave Cooper** again in the **Pawns**, while **Paul Pilnick** became a member of the **Big Three**.

Dave Cooper later played with the **Vauxhalls** and the **Fruit Eating Bears** and **Don Alcyd** went down to London as a session musician but then returned to Liverpool and joined the **Delmonts**.

Back: George Peckham, Don Alcyd & 'Mushy' Cooper. Front: Paul Pilnick & Lee Curtis

Lee Curtis amalgamated with some members of the **Casuals** from Southport, who were **Simon Hind** (rg), **Mike Bankes** (bg) and **Joe Walsh** (dr), who was a former member of the **Teenbeats** and the **T.J's.**

Simon Hind and **Mike Bankes** were both former members of the **Commancheros** from Lincoln.

As **Dudley Knowles**, the **Casuals** lead guitarist, did not want to go to Germany, they recruited **Mike Cummins**, who came from Formby and whose former group is not known.

Under the name of **Lee Curtis & the All Stars,** they went over to the 'Star Club' again and they were just as successful as the previous line-up but, for unknown reasons in 1965, they disbanded again.

Lee Curtis and **Joe Walsh**, together with the returning **Paul Pilnick,** formed a new group - once again under the name of **Lee Curtis & the All Stars** and this line-up became the most successful and longest lasting of them all.

The band then consisted of:

Lee Curtis	**(voc)**
Paul Pilnick	**(lg)**
Christopher P. Dannis	**(rg)**
Robert F. Garner	**(bg)**
David McShane	**(sax)**
Joe Walsh	**(dr)**

Robert Garner and **Dave McShane** both came from the recently disbanded **Ice Blues**. Before that, **Robert Garner** had played with the **Brokers** from Warrington and **Tony Sheridan & the Beat Brothers**, he also had a short spell with the **Merseybeats**.

Lee Curtis & the All Stars recorded for the 'Star-Club' label and their legendary single, "Extacy" was voted 'record of the week' on Radio Caroline but, it was a German release and Philips missed a great chance by delaying the British release. This misfortune was probably the reason that "Extacy" did not chart and so there was no major breakthrough for the group.

Their next single, a cover-version of "Shame and Scandal In The Family", compared to "Extacy", was terrible and deserved to be a flop. If they only had swapped the sides on the record as "Nobody But You" was the far better song . . .

This line-up also recorded two albums with the titles, 'Star-Club Show 3' and 'It's Lee'. The first one was a very good album, on which everything a real fan wanted, from Rock 'n' Roll - to Beat - to great Blues ballads can be found.

All these records were released on the German 'Star-Club' label and **Lee Curtis & the All Stars** were considered to be one of the stars of the so-called 'Star-Club' scene but, because they had such a long residency in Germany, they 'missed the boat' in England.

In 1966, **Lee Curtis & the All Stars** disbanded again. **Robert Garner** became a member of the **Mark Four**, which, a little later, evolved into the hit group, **Creation,** that had international chart success with records such as "Painter Man" and "Tom Tom".

Joe Walsh joined **Ian & the Zodiacs** and, after that, disappeared from the scene. However, in the Eighties, he was back with the newly formed **Undertakers** before he quit show business.

Paul Pilnick, a really fantastic guitarist, appeared again as a member of the groups, **Stealer's Wheel**, **Badger**, **Sinbad**, **Deaf School** and **Jake**.

Lee Curtis remained in Germany and formed a new backing group which, besides the Scot, **Dave Watt** (lg) and the Germans, **Edgar Köhler** (dr) and **Frank 'Piggy' Jarnach** (org/p) also included **Simon Hind** (bg) again.

Frank Jarnach was the former leader of the Hamburg group, **Piggy & the Jokers**, while **'Eddie' Köhler** had previously played with the **Jaguars** from Herford and the **Green Onions** from Bielefeld, but he was soon replaced in the **All Stars** by **Wolfgang Krüger**.

This band did not last for too long and then **Lee Curtis** went solo. For a short time, the group continued under the name of the **All** and recorded the single, "You Don't Have To Say", for the German Fontana label, which did not sell too well.

Lee Curtis recorded two more singles with a great version of **Del Shannon**'s "Kelly" and the **Every Mother's Son** success, "Come On Down To My Boat". Neither became hits, although "Kelly" most probably was his best record ever.

He then had a bad car accident, which was followed by complicated operations. He returned to Liverpool and quit show business for years but. when the 'Star-Club' was re-opened in 1980, he was back on the scene and, since then, he has toured Germany at regular intervals, most of the time backed by the **Bonds '81** and his former pianist, **'Piggy' Jarnach,** is always with him.

Lee Curtis still loves to sing in Germany, where he was a big star in the Sixties and where he is not forgotten today.

Discography :

as **Lee Curtis & the All Stars** :

Let's Stomp / Poor Unlucky Me	UK- Decca F.11690 / 1963
What About Me / I've Got My Eyes On You	UK- Decca F.11830 / 1964
Extacy / A Shot Of Rhythm & Blues	UK- Philips BF 1385 / 1965

(*** please note that **Extacy / A shot of Rhythm & Blues** was originally recorded in Germany on **'Star-Club'** **148.504** in 1965)

Different German releases :

Shame And Scandal In The Family / Nobody But You	G- Star-Club 148.542 / 1965
Kelly / Mohair Sam	G- Star-Club 148.553 / 1965

Lee Curtis – solo :

Little Girl / Just One More Dance	UK- Decca F.11622 / 1963

Different German release :

Come On Down To My Boat / Concerto For Her	G- Star-Club 148.590 / 1966

The All Stars (without Lee Curtis) :

Hide And Seek / Czardas	UK- acetate demo / 1963

The All (final line-up of the **"All-Stars"** without Lee Curtis) :

You Don't Have To Say / I Don't Go Back	G- Fontana 269.374 / 1967

LPs as **Lee Curtis & the All Stars** :

'STAR-CLUB SHOW 3'   G- Star Club 158.002 / 1965

- Memphis Tennessee / Mess Of Blues / When I Get Paid / It's Only Make Believe /

I've Got My Eyes On You / Boys / Boppin' The Blues / My Babe / Where Have All The Flowers Gone /

Blue Suede Shoes / Let's Stomp / Hello Josephine / Can't Help Falling In Love

IT'S LEE'   G- Star Club 158.017 / 1965

- Shame And Scandal In The Family / Um Um Um Um Um / Stand By Me /

Little Egypt / Stupidity / Slow down / Jezebel / Wooly Bully / Irresistible You /

It's No Good For Me / Mickey's Monkey / Sticks And Stones / One Night / Nobody But You

Tracks on compilation albums :

"Skinny Minnie"	on 'At The Cavern'	UK- Decca BLK 16294 / 1964
"Jezebel"	on 'At The Cavern'	UK- Decca BLK 16294 / 1964
"Extacy"	on 'Star-Club Informationsplatte'	G- Star-Club 111.371 / 1965
"Um Um Um Um Um"	on 'Star-Club Scene '65'	G- Star-Club 158.018 / 1965
"Extacy"	on 'Sweet Beat'	G- Star-Club 158.022 / 1965
"Extacy"	on 'Beater's Hitparade'	G- Philips 75283 P 13 / 1967

Unissued tracks :

As unissued tracks of **Lee Curtis,** the songs, **"No Other Love"** and **"Lovesick Blues",** are known, which were probably both recorded on acetate in 1963.

THE CYCLONES

After **Peter Fleming**, better known as **Mark Peters**, had disbanded his old group, **Dean Fleming & the Flamingos**, he and his brother, **Steve 'Tiger' Fleming,** formed **Mark Peters & the Cyclones** in Liverpool in 1960. The band, at that time, consisted of **Mark Peters** (voc), **Vic Grace** (lg/voc), **Steve Fleming** (p/org), **Frank Dudley** (bg) and **Les Watkins** (dr).

Within a year, **Mark Peters & the Cyclones** were established among the leading Liverpool groups and, in October 1961, they were voted No. 8 in the popularity poll of the 'Mersey Beat' newspaper.

But this line-up did not last too long and the first to leave was **Frank Dudley**, who was replaced by **Tony Webster** who, according to the 'Mersey Beat', was the former guitarist of **Tommy & the Metronomes** or **Tommy Lowe & the Metronomes**, as they were sometimes billed.

About the same time, **Les Watkins** left to join **Lee Shondell & the Boys** and he was replaced on drums by **Roy Cresswell**, a former member of the **Travellers**, who also appeared as **Johnny Saint & the Travellers**.

A little later the group almost disbanded totally when **Vic Grace** left to form the **Hi-Cats**. After that, he was a member of both **Danny Havoc & the Ventures,** who then evolved into the **Secrets**, which is another story in this book.

Mark Peters and his brother **Steve Fleming** teamed up with the **Silhouettes**, who had just separated from singer, **Ken Dallas**, and this group then continued under the name of **Mark Peters & the Silhouettes**, also another story.

Roy Cresswell and Tony Webster formed a new group and continued under the name of the **Cyclones** in the following line-up:

Freddie Ennis	(voc/bg)
Tony Webster	(lg/voc)
Bill Wesley	(sax)
Roy Cresswell	(dr)

Freddie Ennis was also a former member of **Johnny Saint & the Travellers** and, prior to joining the **Cyclones,** he had played with **Karl Terry & the Cruisers.**

This new line-up of the **Cyclones** was signed by Oriole in 1963 and in that same year the single, "Nobody", was released. But this record wasn't successful and no further releases followed.

After that, **Bill Wesley**, whose real name is **Billy Burton**, left to join the **Pete Best Combo**, with whom he also went to the USA. He later played with the **Denims** and with **Karl Terry & the Cruisers.**

The remaining members continued as a trio and a little later changed their name into the **Few**. Initially, it had been planned to change it to the **Blues**.

They were quite successful and popular on the Merseybeat scene and played all the major venues in Merseyside. Unfortunately, they did not have any national success.

It is a little confusing that the **Few** were often introduced as 'Oriole recording artists' although there was never a release under that name. The reason was probably the fact that the group recorded with Oriole as the **Cyclones**, but it might also be possible that the **Few** made some further recordings for Oriole which were not released.

The group continued to be busy on the scene but, in early 1964, disbanded totally.

THE FEW   Oriole

Sole Representation
THE ARCADE VARIETY AGENCY   49a Bold Street, Liverpool, 1.
ROYal 1409   ROYal 8897

Tony Webster, once again according to the 'Mersey Beat' newspaper, became a member of the **Runaways**, which was the group that backed singer, **Bill Kenwright,** on his single, "I Want To Go Back There Again", in 1967 but, again, that is another story which can be followed in this book.

Of **Billy Burton**, it is known that he later emigrated to South Africa where he lived for many years. In the early Nineties, he returned to Liverpool, played with **Karl Terry & the Cruisers** and, after that, gigged around with various groups.

Freddie Ennis, who kept playing on the scene, later emigrated to Australia, where he is still living. Unfortunately, what happened to **Roy Cresswell** after the **Few** disbanded, is not known.

Discography :

Nobody / Little Egypt   UK- Oriole CB 1898 / 1964

RICK E. DARNE & THE TOPLINS

Very little information was available about this group. It was formed under the name of the **Overlanders** in Chester in the early Sixties but later changed its name to **Rick E. Darne & the Dee-Fenders**.

In 1965, the group entered the so-called 'Toplin Beat Contest', which was sponsored by the Rael Brook Company in Liverpool, 'Toplin' being their speciality fabric. The first prize was a recording contract, on condition that the winning group changed their name into the **Toplins**.

CALLING ALL BEAT GROUPS

WHO WILL BE THE TOPLINS?

RAEL-BROOK BEAT CONTEST

£250 IN PRIZES

HEATS START 17th FEBRUARY

DO YOU WANT TO WIN FAME AND FORTUNE IN 1964?

Then HURRY! HURRY!

Only a limited number of entries can be accepted for this BIG OPPORTUNITY CONTEST.
Get your entry forms from your Rael-Brook stockist. The Cavern Club, or record and music stores throughout the North West. Entry forms can be obtained by post from the Cavern Club, Mathew Street, Liverpool.

HEATS AND SEMI-FINALS TO BE HELD AT LIVERPOOL'S FAMOUS

CAVERN CLUB

DON'T DELAY — ENTER TODAY

Rick E. Darne & the Dee-Fenders were the winners and so became **Rick E. Darne & the Toplins** - including the following musicians:

Rick E. Darne   (voc)

Vic Stamper

Dennis Collins

Dave Beatty

Tony Koziol

It seems that the recording contract was something of a false promise as nothing is known of a single released by **Rick E. Darne & the Toplins**.

Nevertheless, the group became a local attraction in Liverpool and, in July 1965, they were the bill topper at the Beat events on the 'Royal Iris', the legendary Beat ship on the River Mersey.

But after that, little was heard of the band until December 1965.

At that time, a private single (or was it the promised record?) with the Christmas-Beat songs, "Sleigh Bells" and "Christmas Message", was released on the Unicord label.

Both songs were composed by Liverpool songwriter, **Ron Anderson**. However, the record did not attract much attention in the marketplace and it is doubtful that it was ever distributed in the stores. **Rick E. Darne** probably left the group after that as the **Toplins** were then taken over as a quartet by 'Cavern Artists' management.

So what is left of **Rick E. Darne & the Toplins** is just that private Christmas single, which is a most admired collector's item today. Unfortunately, it did not really help the group at that time, as it never had much of a chance at creating any sort of impact after the Christmas season.

As the music press did not take too much notice of the group after this, it is not known when they disbanded or what happened to the musicians, as none of them ever appeared on the scene again.

Discography :

Sleigh Bells / Christmas Message   **UK- Unicord UP 663 / 1965**

STEVE DAY & THE KINSMEN

This story starts with the formation of the Beat-group, the **Masqueraders** in the early Sixties. Most probably in Wallasey on the Wirral, the west side of the River Mersey.

The group originally consisted of **Ricky Dickinson** (voc/rg), **Adrian Flowerday** (lg/voc), **Alan Peers** (bg) and **Tony Aldridge** (dr).

Adrian Flowerday was a former member of **Dave & the Rave-Ons**.

When **Ricky Dickinson** left the group and disappeared from the scene, he was replaced by **Tom Earley**, who came from Birkenhead's **Pathfinders**. A little later, the group's name was changed to the **Kinsmen**.

The Masqueraders (1963)

Ricky Dickinson, Tony Aldridge, Alan Peers, Adrian Flowerday

The Kinsmen (1963)

Tom Earley returned to the **Pathfinders** and then **Tony Aldridge** followed him. The two remaining **Kinsmen** recruited new members and, in May 1963, amalgamated with **Rod Pont**, who, under the stage name of **Steve Day**, had formerly led the groups, **Wump & His Werbles**, **Steve Day & the Jets** (formerly the backing group for **Johnny Rocco** under the name of **Johnny Rocco & the Jets**), and its follow-on band, the very popular **Steve Day & the Drifters**.

The **Drifters**, after **Steve Day** had left, first continued as the backing group for **Gus Travis**, and later went solo under the name of the **Rainchecks**, but that is another story.

Steve Day & the Kinsmen, as the group was called from that time on, appeared in the following line-up:

Steve Day	**(voc)**
Adrian Flowerday	**(lg/voc)**
Kingsley Foster	**(rg)**
Alan Peers	**(bg)**
Steve Skelly	**(dr)**

Kingsley Foster and **Steve Skelly** both came from the **Kingfishers** and **Steve Day** had also sung with the **Kingfishers** previously. For a short time before **Steve Skelly** joined, **Tommy Bennett** had played drums with the **Kinsmen**. He came from the **Pathfinders** and had swapped places with **Tony Aldridge**. When **Steve Skelly** took over from him, **Tommy Bennett** joined the **Pressmen**.

Steve Day & the Kinsmen, in the end, were more successful than **Steve Day & the Drifters**, but for mysterious reasons their name did not have the same impact on the scene as **Steve Day's** former group.

Steve Day & the Kinsmen

In 1964, EMI became interested in **Steve Day & the Kinsmen** and recorded the songs, "Last Bus Home" and "You Ask Me Why", but only as a demo on acetate which, unfortunately, was not followed by an official record release. Both songs were written by the group and both were really nice Beat numbers.

After this, no more songs were recorded by the group, which is hard to understand because it was certainly one of the really good groups from Merseyside who existed quite successfully on the live scene for a long time and probably did not disband before the end of the Sixties, although there must have been some more changes in the line-up during that time.

Adrian Flowerday had already left the group in 1965 to join the **New Pressmen** and, in June of that year, **Kingsley Foster** became a member of the **Pathfinders**, where he switched to organ.

It is not known who were the replacements in **Steve Day & the Kinsmen**.

Steve Day himself was active in the Liverpool pub and cabaret scene until the mid-Seventies and, after a break, he formed a new group under the name **Steve Day & the Kinsmen** at the beginning of the Eighties. However, this group only lasted for a short time and it is not known if any of the old members were featured in it.

After that, **Steve Day** quit show business but stepped back onto the scene with the birth of 'MerseyCats', but more as a compere and disc jockey, than as a singer.

There were no plans for forming a new group and plans to release a solo single under the direction of **Billy Kinsley** (a member of the **Merseybeats** and **Liverpool Express**) were also discarded.

In 1995, **Steve Day** emigrated to Portugal where he worked as disc jockey, but sadly died of throat cancer very soon after.

Unfortunately, what happened to **Alan Peers** and **Steve Skelly** after the **Kinsmen** had disbanded is not known. None of them appeared on the scene again.

So what is left from **Steve Day & the Kinsmen** is a nice demo, which provides good material for a late release.

Discography :

Last Bus Home / You Ask Me Why   UK- EMI - acetate / 1964

THE DEFENDERS

Initially, there were the four friends, **John Conrads** (dr), **Keith Alcock** (bg), **Kenny Baker** (lg) and a rhythm guitarist, whose name has been lost with the passing of time, who formed a group in the Anfield area of Liverpool in the very early Sixties. They were joined by the singer, **Dave Bell,** and the group became **Dave Bell & the Bell Boys**.

The Bell Boys - L to R: Unknown (rg), John Conrads, Kenny Baker & Keith Alcock

This group did not last too long as **John 'Bob' Conrads** and **Keith Alcock** (aka **Keith Karlsson**) went on to play with **Jet & the Valiants** and **Jet & the Centerbeats.**

After that they formed the **Nomads**, who were featured on the Oriole compilation, "This Is Merseybeat" Vol. 2 and who very soon evolved into the **Mojos**.

Dave Bell disappeared from the scene.

The 'early' Defenders

Kenny Baker teamed up with **John Williamson** (voc), **Graeme Pugh** (rg/voc), **Phil Howard** (bg/voc) and **Albie Skelton** (dr), who were playing local youth and social clubs during 1962 under the name, **Johnny Wilde & the Bopcats.**

Albie Skelton was then replaced by **Les Reynolds** and the group's name was changed to the **Defenders**.

The Defenders with Wally Dene (front)

Dave Forshaw took over their management and they started performing at the major dance halls and ballrooms throughout Merseyside, including the 'Grafton', St. John's Hall in Bootle, Litherland Town Hall, the 'Jive Hive' in Crosby and the Orrell Park Ballroom.

In 1963, John Williamson temporarily left the group. During his absence, he was replaced by two different singers: Paul La Celle, who was better known as Paul Valance of Paul Valance & the Tremors fame. Paul Valance did not stay for too long, his replacement was Wally Dene, who left when John Williamson returned.

After Graeme Pugh left the group (he later emigrated to Australia), the Defenders were:

John Williamson	(voc/rg)
Kenny Baker	(lg/voc)
Phil Howard	(bg/voc)
Les Reynolds	(dr/voc)

In this line-up they took part in a Beat group competition organised by the 'Liverpool Echo', in which approximately 250 groups from the northwest participated.

The Defenders placed fourth after playing an instrumental version of "Swan Lake" in typical Shadows style.

This was doubtless a considerable success and opened the door for the Defenders to play all the 'top' venues in Liverpool, including the 'Cavern', the 'Locarno', the 'Iron Door', the 'Mardi Gras' and the 'Peppermint Lounge'. They also had engagements throughout England.

It was in 1964 that Phil Howard decided to join the Four Originals and his leaving led to the Defenders disbanding. Kenny Baker became a member of the Lee Eddie Five, but when this group also disbanded a few months later, he and the bass-guitarist of that group, Jeff Nixon, teamed up again with John Williamson and Les Reynolds and re-formed the Defenders.

Jeff Nixon did not stay for too long and went on to join Emile Ford & the Checkmates. His replacement was Ray Clegg, a former member of Wallasey's Vampires. When Les Reynolds left around the same time, Jimmy Taylor took over on drums but he was replaced a little later by Robbie Webster.

This line-up of the Defenders was chosen by Radio Caroline DJ, Mike Aherne to back him on his recording of "I love you Betty", which he had written himself - later on, it got some plays on Radio Caroline.

As there was still some paid time left in the Kensington studios of Percy Phillips after recording that acetate, the Defenders used that opportunity to record the Spotnicks style instrumental, "Spanish Armada", coupled with the very interesting vocal number, "Mr. Soul", which included a sax player, unfortunately, his name is not known.

On this acetate, Kenny Baker played lead guitar on "Spanish Armada" and the organ on "Mr. Soul". In addition, another acetate was recorded around the same time, which, besides "Spanish Armada" again, included the songs, "What Am I To Do", "Why, Why, Why" and "What Am I Gonna Do", probably all originals by the group.

The 'new' Defenders

Amos Bonny

The Defenders later added an organ player to their line-up with **Tommy Hammond**, who was also a good singer.

When **Tommy Hammond** left, **Amos Bonny**, who had previously sung with **Amos Bonny & the TTs,** joined as lead vocalist. After six months, he left to join the **Easybeats** and was later a member of a band called **Mumble**.

In 1966, back to a four-piece again, the **Defenders** became the backing group for the great Liverpool songstress, **Irene Green**, who was known on the scene as **Tiffany** and who had formerly sung with **Tiffany's Dimensions** and recorded with **Tiffany & the Thoughts**.

This co-operation did not last too long and the **Defenders** continued performing in their own right once again.

A little later, while playing at the 'Cavern', they were spotted by a Greek talent scout who called himself 'Orango' and he booked the **Defenders** to play the casinos and night clubs along the French Riviera. As **Robbie Webster** was not able to go, **Tommy Limb** (ex **Ricky Gleason & the Topspots** and **Mersey Monsters**) took his place on drums for that tour.

As some members became homesick or had other obligations in Liverpool, the **Defenders** disbanded after a summer season playing the Casinos in Biarritz. However, it is interesting to note that while they were in Biarritz, they were spotted by a talent scout and offered the chance to record in Paris. This did not happen, as at that time the recording engineers went on a strike which could have lasted for weeks and the group did not have the time to stay in France that long.

Instead of being a chance for a greater career, this was the end for the **Defenders** in late 1966.

The Defenders in Biarritz

John Williamson later went on to play and sing solo and of **Ray Clegg,** it is said that he later went to America with **Mungo Jerry,** while **Robbie Webster** quit the music business to become a pilot with British Airways.

The Myths - L to R: 'Mars', John Bedson, Doug Hughes, Bob Gilmore & Kenny Baker

All the other members apparently quit showbiz at that time too – with the exception of **Kenny Baker.** He was approached by a group called the **Myths,** who had an offer to play the American military bases in Germany for seven (!) months.

Kenny Baker accepted and so the **Myths** went to Germany in a line-up with **Doug Hughes** (voc/rg), **Bob Gilmore** (lg), **Kenny Baker** (org/g), a certain **'Mars'** (bg/voc) and **John Bedson** (dr/voc).

John Bedson was a former member of the **Four Clefs,** the **Challengers** and the **Harlems,** while **Bob Gilmore** had also played with the **Challengers** and the **Harlems** previously.

Unfortunately, this highly interesting group broke up again after their return to Liverpool.

Kenny Baker quit the music business for some years but in the Seventies, came back as a member of the **Signs,** who in the interim had evolved into a cabaret group.

Nearly 40 years after their split, the **Defenders** came together again to play as a surprise at the 60th birthday party of their former manager **Dave Forshaw** in a line-up with **John Williamson** (voc/g), **Kenny Baker** (lg/key), **Graeme Pugh** (rg/voc), **Phil Howard** (bg/voc) and **Robbie Webster** (dr).

This one-off show was recorded and showed them to be in really good musical condition. Unfortunately, it did not lead to the group reforming.

Phil Howard sadly died in 2004, while still a member of the **Four Originals.**

Discography :

Spanish Armada / Mr. Soul	**UK- Kensington-acetate / 1964**
Why, Why, Why / What Am I To Do / Spanish Armada / What Am I Gonna Do	**UK- Kensington-acetate EP / 1964**

as backing-group for **Mike Aherne:**

I Love You Betty /	**UK- Kensington acetate / 1964**

THE DELMONT FOUR

This group was formed by two brothers, **Terry** and **Kevin Lappin** in Liverpool as a four-piece in 1963, and there was no connection to another Liverpool group with the name, **Rick & the Delmonts**, which featured **Ricky Yates** as lead vocalist.

The **Delmont Four** had a very high musical standard and established themselves very quickly on the Merseybeat scene. At that time, the group consisted of the following musicians:

Terry Lappin	(voc/rg)
Allan Davies	(lg)
Kevin Lappin	(voc/bg)
George Roberts	(dr)

George Roberts most probably was not a founding member of the group, as he had already played with the **Pacemakers**, **Jeannie & the Big Guys** and the **Excheckers** from Chester, as well as with **Freddie Starr & the Starr-Boys** in Germany.

As it seems, he did not stay for too long with the **Delmont Four**. Initially, he became the roadie for the **Takers**, then after a very short spell with **Amen Corner,** he joined the **Mindbenders** from Manchester.

He then continued on the scene as a freelance drummer, but in the early Eighties became a member of **Rogues Gallery**.

His replacement in the **Delmont Four** was **Don Alcyd**, who had formerly played with **Tommy & the Metronomes**, **Faron & the Tempest Tornadoes**, the **Renegades** from Liverpool and **Lee Curtis & the All Stars**.

This line-up of the **Delmont Four** recorded a private EP on the Unicord label a little later, with the songs "Reet Petite", "Blue Moon", "First Taste Of Love" and "Before You Accuse Me".

In 1964, the **Delmont Four** toured Germany as the backing group for Chester's songstress, '**Jeannie**', of **Jeannie & the Big Guys**, but this connection did not last for too long.

In early 1965, **Don Alcyd** left and was replaced by **Johnny Gee**, a former member of Liverpool's **Tokens** and the **Secrets**.

Still in the same year, the **Delmont Four** were called into the studio to record some songs for the compilation 'Liverpool Goes Country', on which the group was only featured with the song, "Beyond The Shadow" - a nicely done number, but it seems this was their only step into Country music.

With this song, plus their nice version of "Sea Of Heartbreak", they were featured on a split EP together with **Tom O'Connor** on the Rex label.

For these recordings their name was shortened into the **Delmonts**, and they continued with that name from then on.

When popular singer, **Freddie Starr** was looking for a new backing group, he became aware of them and they amalgamated as **Freddie Starr & the Delmonts**.

The singer's real name is **Freddie Fowell**, and he had previously sung with **Howie Casey & the Seniors**, the **Kansas City Five**, **Groups Inc.**, **Freddie Starr & the Ventures**, **Freddie Starr & the Midnighters** and **Freddie Starr & the Flamingoes**. With the latter, he had recorded as **Freddie Starr & the Starr Boys**. **Freddie Starr & the Delmonts** toured Germany quite successfully in 1965 and, after their return, they continued for a long time together.

Freddie Starr & the Delmonts

But the group did not make any more records, and it is also not known if they cut acetates or made test recordings. This is quite hard to understand, as it was a great group and very popular in the north of England.

It was at the end of the Sixties when **Freddie Starr** left the **Delmonts**. He started a very successful career as an entertainer and today is one of the better known TV stars in the UK.

The **Delmonts** continued together as a group, although it is not known if there were any personnel changes in the line-up.

In 1971 the single, "A Ra Chicera" was released on the Spiral label but, unfortunately, it had no great success. That was the last anyone heard of the **Delmonts**, who had become part of the cabaret-scene and probably split up sometime in the Seventies.

Of the individual members, only **Johnny Gee** re-appeared on the scene later on as a member of **Pikkins**.

In the end it can be said that the **Delmont Four** or the **Delmonts** never made the headlines, but they were one of the really good and interesting Liverpool bands, still remembered today.

Discography :

Reet Petite / Blue Moon / First Taste Of Love / Before You Accuse Me	UK- Unicord acetate-ep / 1963
A Ra Chicera / Sorry For My Jealousy	UK- Spiral / 1971

Split EP with Tom O'Connor :

'TOM O' CONNOR MEETS THE DELMONTS'   UK- Rex EPR 5003 / 1966

The Delmonts : **Sea Of Heartbreak** and **Beyond The Shadow**

Tom O'Connor (backed by the **Delmonts**) : **Pretty Pictures** and **I Can't Imagine What Went Wrong**

Songs on compilation albums :

Beyond The Shadow   on **'Liverpool Goes Country'**   UK- Decca-Rex LPR 1002 / 1965

THE DEL RENAS

This group originated from the **Deltics**, a Skiffle trio which was formed in Wavertree/Garston area of Liverpool in 1958 by **Brian Young** (g), **Brian James** (p) and **Brian Dean** (dr).

A little later, the singer **Ray Walker** joined and the band then called themselves **Ray & the Del Renas**. The name 'Del Rena' was adopted from a Liverpool shipping line.

Ray Walker & the Del Renas

In 1959, the group was joined by the two guitarists, **Terry Fisher** (lg) and **Derek Green** (rg) and their music changed to Rock 'n' Roll. They became very popular with **Ray Walker** singing in the style of **Roy Orbison** and **Del Shannon**.

Ray & the Del Renas were probably the first Merseyside group to feature an electric organ, playing instrumentals such as "Telstar" and "Red River Rock".

In 1960, the female singer **Joan Molloy** joined them as an additional member. She left in 1961 and it's believed, that under her real name of **Joan Woolton**, she became the lead singer for **Joan & the Demons**.

Brian Young also left in the same year and disappeared from the scene, he was replaced by **John Withy**. The band, at that time, often appeared at the major venues, such as the 'Cavern', the 'Iron Door', the 'Downbeat', the 'Orrell Park Ballroom' and the 'Tower Ballroom' in New Brighton.

In 1962, **Ray Walker** left to join the **Escorts**, but after a short time he disappeared from the scene.

He, by the way, is not the musician of the same name who played with **Ogi & the Flintstones**.

Brian Dean also left and the new drummer was **Eddie Edwards**, who came from the **Flames** but he did not stay for too long and joined the **Nashpool Four**, who for some time also appeared as the **Nashpool**. After that, he had a short spell (like all their drummers) with **Rory Storm & the Hurricanes** and then played with the **Beechwoods** before he also disappeared from the scene.

Ian Howe became the new drummer with the **Del Renas**, as they were called now.

John Withy and **Brian James** teamed up to sing harmony in the style of the **Everly Brothers**, but a little later the group changed their musical style to Rhythm & Blues and Beat with all the members sharing the vocals. All these changes are quite hard to understand because the band was really successful. They were voted No. 9 in the popularity poll of the 'Mersey Beat' newspaper in October 1961, which was quite an achievement if one considers how many groups were already around in Liverpool at that time.

However, in March 1963 the band was offered an engagement at the 'Star-Club' in Hamburg, but not all members were able to go. Therefore, **Brian Dean** returned and took over his old place on drums, while **Terry Fisher** and **Derek Green** were replaced by **Johnny Fallon**.

They then went to Hamburg for a few months and when they returned to Liverpool, they recorded for both volumes of 'This Is Merseybeat'- in the same line-up with:

Brian James	**(p/voc)**
Johnny Fallon	**(g/voc)**
John Withy	**(bg/voc)**
Brian Dean	**(dr)**

The **Del Renas** were featured on the above mentioned Oriole compilations with very nice versions of "Sigh, Cry, Almost Die", "Nashville Blues" and "When Will I Be Loved".

At that time, they again sounded like the **Everly Brothers**, but these were the only recordings by the group that continued under the name of the **Del Renas** and they were quite successful on the scene until they disbanded totally for unknown reasons in 1964.

Of the individual members, only **Brian Dean** and **Johnny Fallon** appeared again on the scene, **Johnny Fallon** as a member of **Lee Castle & the Barons**, while **Brian Dean** joined the **Coins**, which was not the group of the same name that evolved from the **Young Ones**.

It's hard to understand why there were not more records released by the **Del Renas** as their three songs on the compilation sounded great and proved that they were one of the better Liverpool groups.

When the earlier **Del Renas** members, **Terry Fisher**, **Derek Green**, whose real name is **Derek Gretty**, and **Ian Howe** turned down the offer to go to Hamburg and were left behind in Liverpool, they formed a trio under the name of the **Motifs**. They were also quite successful on the local scene and appeared regularly at all the major venues and in 1963, they recorded an acetate at the Deroy studios in Hest Bank, Lancashire with "Nobody But You" plus three **Chuck Berry** numbers.

The **Motifs** existed until late 1966, and then disbanded totally and the individual members disappeared from the scene for years - until 1987, when **Terry Fisher** and **Derek Green,** for a short time, teamed up again as a cabaret duo under the name of **Contraband**.

These days, **Derek Green** and **Terry Fisher** are members of the **Four Originals**, a successor-group of **Dale Roberts & the Jaywalkers**. They sometimes also appear as the **Jaywalkers**.

When, in 1990, **Terry Fisher** became a member of the 'MerseyCats' organisation, he tried for years and years to get the **Del Renas** back together again and finally succeeded, even if the group only appears occasionally for the 'MerseyCats' events – in a line-up with **Terry Fisher** (lg/voc), **John Withy** (rg/voc), **Brian James** (p/org/voc), **Derek Green** (bg/voc) and **Ian Howe** (dr).

With that the full 1963 line-up has come together again and the **Del Renas** are thus the only original Merseybeat group in Liverpool. What a fantastic thing!

Discography :

Songs on compilation-albums :

Sigh, Cry, Almost Die	on 'This Is Merseybeat' Vol. I	**UK- Oriole 40047 / 1963**
Nashville Blues	on 'This Is Merseybeat' Vol. II	**UK- Oriole 40048 / 1963**
When Will I Be Loved	on 'This Is Merseybeat' Vol. II	**UK- Oriole 40048 / 1963**

as **The Motifs :**

Nobody But You / School Days / Let It Rock / All Aboard   **UK– Deroy acetate-EP / 1963**

THE DENNISONS

This Liverpool group was formed in 1961 in the area of Aintree and, from the beginning, was a very typical Merseybeat group.

While the **Dennisons** remained more or less unknown on the European continent, they became one of the leading groups in Northern England and many people were convinced that they would make it to the top. They started their career with a residency at the BICC-club in Melling, but very soon were booked to play the 'Cavern', where they caused such a sensation, that compere and DJ **Bob Wooler** described them with the words "they created the biggest impression in Liverpool since the Beatles".

No doubt, it was a fantastic group and already within their first year of existence, they went into a studio and recorded the song, "Tutti Frutti" on acetate, which was never released as an official record.

In their original line-up the, Dennisons consisted of:

Eddie Parry	**(voc/g)**
Steve McLaren	**(lg/voc)**
Ray Scragge	**(rg/voc)**
Alan Willis	**(bg/voc)**
Clive Hornby	**(dr)**

In 1963, the **Dennisons** signed with Kennedy Street Enterprises and turned professional. That was the reason **Alan Willis** decided to leave, as he did not want to give up his job.

His replacement was **Terry 'Tex' Carson**, but this was the only change in the line-up for years.

The Dennisons
— Decca Records

Kennedy Street Enterprises Ltd.
Kennedy House,
14 Piccadilly, Manchester 1.
CENtral 5423

Their outstanding success soon attracted the interest of various record-companies and still, in 1963, the **Dennisons** were signed to Decca.

Their national breakthrough came when they were featured on the legendary Decca sampler, 'Live At The Cavern' with the songs, "Devoted To You" and "You Better Move On", which really created a great impression.

This was very quickly followed by their first single, "(Come On) Be My Girl", a great Beat record that was written by **Eddie Parry** and **Steve McLaren** and climbed the charts to No. 46.

This, without a doubt, was a good start and a great success for their debut on the record market, which was enhanced by their follow-up, an interesting version of **Rufus Thomas**' "Walking The Dog", which reached No. 36.

But this was also the last chart success for the **Dennisons**, although their next single, "Nobody Like My Baby" was a very good record that had all the hallmarks of a successful hit.

In 1964, the **Dennisons** also recorded the **Coasters** hit, "Yakety Yak", as well as an interesting version of **Joe Brown**'s "A picture of you", but neither of these numbers were released. They continued as a very busy live act in Northern England and appeared regularly at the 'Cavern' and all the other major venues.

In 1966, **Eddie Parry** left the group and quit show business.

The Dennisons

Ray Scragge then took over as their lead vocalist and, after the **Dennisons** had continued as a quartet for some time, they were joined by the great coloured singer, **Colin Areety**, a former member of the **Conquests** and the **Almost Blues**.

Their music, not at least through the addition of their new singer, became more Soul influenced and it was probably at that time, when **Stevie Wonder**'s "Makin' Whoopee" was recorded by them, but not released.

About one year later, the **Dennisons** disappeared from the scene and only **Colin Areety** continued in the music-business. Initially, he joined the **In Crowd** and after that sang with the **Michael Henri Group**. He then started an impressive solo-career in the Northern club scene and also recorded in his own right in the Seventies. He was very popular in Liverpool and the surrounding areas of Blackpool and Manchester until he sadly died in 2007.

In 1991, **Terry Carson** died from multiple sclerosis and this sad occasion brought the remaining **Dennisons** together again for one concert, but for unknown reasons, the group did not continue on after that.

Eddie Parry sadly also died in 1995 aged 49 and the cause of his death was most probably a heart attack.

When in 1997 **Ray Scragge** was diagnosed with lung cancer, he decided to make the best out of the time that was left for him and formed the **New Dennisons** that, besides him, consisted of **Dave Keighley** (ex **Pilgrims**) on lead guitar, **Mike Rudzinsky** (ex **Avengers**) on bass-guitar and ex **Four Sounds** drummer, **Alan Denton**. They recorded a CD and played the scene until **Ray Scragge** died in February 2001.

Steve McLaren, who later played the classical guitar, died in 2007 and was followed in July 2008 by **Clive Hornby**, who had become very popular as an actor when he played the role of Jack Sugden in the daily British TV soap 'Emmerdale'. He died of hypoxia.

What a tragic end to the story of this great Merseybeat group . . . .

Discography :

Tutti Frutti / ?		UK- ??? acetate / 1962
Come On Be My Girl / Little Latin Lupe-Lu		UK- Decca F.11691 / 1963
Walking The Dog / You Don't Know What Love Is		UK- Decca F.11880 / 1964
Nobody Like My Baby / Lucy (You Sure Did It This Time)		UK- Decca F.11990 / 1964

Songs on compilation-albums :

Devoted To You	on **'Live At The Cavern'**	UK-Decca BLK 16294 / 1964
You Better Move On	on **'Live At The Cavern'**	UK-Decca BLK 16294 / 1964

Unissued tracks :

In 1964, The **Dennisons** recorded the **Coasters** number, **"Yakety Yak"** and **Joe Brown**'s **"A Picture Of You"** for Decca, which for unknown reasons, were not released.

With **Colin Areetey** as lead-singer, they recorded **"Makin' Whoopee"**, which also was not released.

THE DETOURS

This group originated from the **Farenheits**, which were formed in Liverpool in the very early Sixties. After singer **Alan Peters** (<u>not</u> identical to the member of the **Almost Blues**) had left and quit show business along with some other changes in the line-up, this band became the **Detours** and probably continued as an instrumental group.

This changed when, in 1962, the **Detours** became the backing group for singer **Lee Curtis** and, from that time on, appeared as **Lee Curtis & the Detours** on the scene.

In the interim, drummer, **Jimmy Wade** had left and joined **Eddie Dean & the Onlookers**.

Lee Curtis & the Detours became a busy and successful live act in Liverpool's Merseybeat scene and appeared at all the major venues. But in 1962, the singer parted from the group and formed a new band under the name of **Lee Curtis & the All Stars**, but that is a story of its own.

The **Detours** then continued as a vocal/instrumental group in a line-up with:

Richard Quilliam	(voc/lg)
Pete Brown	(rg)
Charlie Robinson	(bg)
John Puddifer	(dr)

For a short time, they also backed girl singer, **Barbara Dee**, who actually was a disc jockey and had made her first appearances as a singer with the **Mersey Monsters** as her backing group.

Barbara Dee & the Detours became a successful live act in Liverpool, but then their ways separated.

In 1964, the **Detours** were engaged to appear at the 'Star-Club' in Hamburg, where they went down very well, which proves that they must have been very good musically.

This makes it all the more difficult to understand why the group split very soon after replacing **Pete Brown** with **Billy Churchill**.

Richard Quilliam and **Charlie Robinson** (aka **Charly King**) joined the **Tokens** from Liverpool, while all the others disappeared from the scene.

In October 1965, the **Detours** were re-formed by founding member, **Richard Quilliam** together with **Billy Churchill** - in a line-up with:

Ricky Yates	(voc)
Richard Quilliam	(lg/voc)
Billy Churchill	(rg)
James Carnaby	(bg)
Kenny Guy	(dr)

Ricky Yates was the former leader of **Rick & the Delmonts**, who had no connection to the backing group of **Freddie Starr** named the **Delmonts** or the **Delmont Four**, respectively.

Kenny Guy had formerly played with the **Bonnevilles** and the **Kingbees**. Furthermore, it is of interest to note that **James Carnaby's** real name is **Jimmy Connell**.

The **Detours** in this line-up moved to the south of England, probably to London, where they placed second in a big Beat contest, which of course helped their popularity in their new location. In spite of that success, there were some changes in the line-up when **Richard Quilliam**, **Billy Churchill** and **James Carnaby** left and returned to Liverpool.

The new members were **Vinnie Ismail** (g) and **Tommy Husky** (sax) from Liverpool, as well as **Sid Gardner** (bg). **Vinnie Ismail** was a former member of **Vince & the Volcanoes**, the **Harlems**, the **Top-Ten All Stars** (Germany) and **Henry's Handful**, while **Tommy Husky** had played with the **Deejays**, the **Nashpool** and **Earl Preston's Realms**.

In this line-up, the **Detours** were signed by CBS in 1967 and a little later had their first single released with "Run To Me Baby". One year later the follow-up, "Whole Lot Of Lovin' " was released, but it also did not make a great impression on the scene, which might have been the reason for CBS dropping the band.

The **Detours** then teamed up with singer, **Gene Latter** from Cardiff's **Shake Spears** and released a third single, this time on the Spark label under the name of **Gene Latter & the Detours**. But when "My Life Ain't Easy" was released, there had already been some personnel changes and, a little later, the **Detours** disbanded totally.

Vinnie Ismail became a member of the **Valentinos**, who later changed their name into the **Harlems** and recorded one single as **Harlem** on the DJM label. It is said that **Ricky Yates** and **Kenny Guy** backed the

Valentinos for a time, but then went back to Liverpool and probably re-formed the **Detours**. Of that line-up it is known that **Jimmy Ikonomides**, a former member of the **Mafia Group**, the **Calderstones** and the **Kruzads** played the bass-guitar.

This line-up did not exist for too long and **Kenny Guy** joined **Karl Terry & the Cruisers**, where he played for quite some time prior to becoming a member of **Kenny Johnson & Northwind**.

Sometime later, **Vinnie Ismail** was also a member of **Karl Terry & the Cruisers** but, after that, quit show business. He died sometime in the late Eighties.

In the Seventies, **Ricky Yates** was a member of **Capricorn** and then he also turned away form showbiz. He sadly died in 2005.

Gene Latter carried on as solo singer and released some quite successful singles, while **Tommy Husky** became a successful session musician as a sax player and, in the Nineties, he also released some solo albums. Nothing more was heard of the other members of the **Detours** after that.

Discography :

as **The Detours** :

Run To Me Baby / Hanging On	**UK- CBS 3401 / 1967**
Whole Lot Of Lovin' / Pieces Of You	**UK- CBS 3712 / 1968**

as **Gene Latter & the Detours** :

My Life Ain't Easy / Angie	**UK- Spark SRL. 1015 / 1968**

GERRY DE VILLE & THE CITY KINGS

During his school days, the Liverpool guitarist, **Dave Passey** started to play Skiffle and formed his first group in the late Fifties.

In the beginning, there were quite a few personnel changes as well as various group-names involved until a steady line-up was established in 1960 with **Alan Kennett** (voc), **Dave Passey** (lg), **Joey Harrison** (rg) and **Dave Fidler** (dr). There was no bass-guitarist at that time, but this line-up eventually became the first **City Kings**.

By 1962, the line-up, with the exception of **Dave Passey,** had completely changed again and the **City Kings** had become a Rock 'n' Roll group. In the same year, they were joined by the singer, **Gerry Hale,** who formerly, under the name of **Gerry Temple,** had sung with the **Mysteries** and then later adopted the stage name of **Gerry Bach,** when he fronted **Gerry Bach & the Beathovens**.

He changed his name again and the group now became **Gerry De Ville & the City Kings** in a line-up with:

Gerry De Ville	(voc)
Dave Passey	(lg/voc)
Jimmy Carter	(rg/voc)
Ritchie Mitchell	(bg/voc)
Pete Rogers	(dr)

Ritchie Mitchell and **Jimmy Carter** were both former members of the **Aarons**, while the former group of **Pete Rogers** is not known.

Gerry De Ville & the City Kings, within a short time, became very popular on the Merseybeat scene and so it was not really surprising, when in 1964, Parlophone invited them to London for test recordings. Unfortunately, it is not known which songs they recorded at that session, as in the end, they did not get a contract and so nothing was released.

This fact did not prevent the group from building up a good name on the music scene, although tours through Scotland and northern England did not bring the success that was hoped for and which was obviously deserved.

Gerry De Ville & the City Kings were one of the interesting Liverpool bands, but information about them is very hard to find because the press did not pay too much attention to the group.

The Beat-paper, 'Combo' had a column written by **Gerry De Ville,** in which he wrote about the Merseybeat scene and it's groups, but for mysterious reasons he never wrote about his own group.

When **Jimmy Carter** left in early 1964 and disappeared from the scene, the group continued as a quartet.

At the end of the same year, **Ritchie Mitchell** also left and became a member of **Phil Brady & the Ranchers**.

His replacement in **Gerry De Ville & the City Kings** was **Malcolm Shelbourne,** who was a former member of **Clay Ellis & the Raiders** and **Savva & the Democrats**.

A little later, **Peter Rogers** left and was replaced by **Bill Robinson,** who also came from the just disbanded **Savva & the Democrats**.

This again was a great line-up, that stayed together until 1968, they were really popular and had a large following on Merseyside.

Then **Billy Robinson** left and his place on drums was taken over by **Maurice Daniels**, who formerly had played with **Alby & the Sorrals** and the **Coins**.

Malcolm Shelbourne also left and was replaced by **Chris Turner.**

Then in 1969, **Ritchie Galvin** took over on drums from **Maurice Daniels**. The new drummer was a former member of the **Galvanisers**, **Earl Preston & the TT's**, as well as **Earl Preston's Realms**.

This must have been the line-up that released "Alone In The Night" , their only single on the little known Virginia label. This record, which was only credited to **Gerry De Ville**, may have been a private release, that unfortunately, had no great success. The A-side as well as the B-side, "You Never Tell Me", were both **Gerry Hale** originals, but not really Merseybeat anymore.

In 1970, **Mal Shelbourne** and **Billy Robinson** returned to the group, while **Chris Turner** disappeared from the scene and **Ritchie Galvin** joined a Country band called **Western Union**. He continued to play Country music until he died in July 2001.

In 1972, founder, **Dave Passey** left and after that played with the cabaret groups, **Adidas**, **Bulldog** and **Peyton Place**, he was replaced in **Gerry De Ville & the City Kings** by **Dave Blackstone** who, in the Sixties, had played with the **Tabs**. **Dave Blackstone** did not stay with them for too long and later appeared again as a member of **Johnny Guitar & his Hurricanes**, **Karl Terry & the Cruisers** and **Mayday**. He sadly died a few years ago. **Billy Sharrock** then took over on lead-guitar.

Gerry De Ville & the City Kings existed for at least another ten years and, it is known that, in the early Eighties, **Alex Paton** was their drummer, who in the Sixties had played with the **Toledos**, the **Mersey Four** and **Tony Carlton & the Merseyboys**, among others. It can be taken for sure that there were more personnel changes in the line-up over the years, particularly as the group became a popular part of the cabaret-scene.

Gerry Hale became a university lecturer and ran his own hairdressing-salon and, besides this, he continued as a solo-performer in the local clubs. Sadly, he died of a heart attack in December 2012.

Of **Malcolm Shelbourne,** it is known that, in the Seventies, he became a member of **Purple Grass**, that later was renamed **Rainbow**, where he played until 1982 and then quit the music-business.

Dave Passey, in 1979, moved to Wakefield where he joined the show band, **Frank Hepworth & the Kalahari Bushmen**, he then became a long time member of **Heartbeat** from Holywell in North Wales. After that, he teamed up again with former **City Kings** member, **Chris Turner** in the cabaret-duo, **Gaz & Dave**, that played together until 2006.

Discography :

Alone In The Night / You Never Tell Me   **UK- Virginia V 101 / 1969**

Besides this recording, **Gerry De Ville & the City Kings** made some test recordings for Parlophone in 1964, of which nothing was ever released so, unfortunately, it is not known which songs were recorded in these sessions.

THE DIMENSIONS

This group was formed under the name, **J.C. & the Strollers** in Liverpool in 1960, **J.C.** being the initials of **Jimmy Clarke**, the bandleader.

In 1963, after the original drummer had left, their name was changed to the **Four Dimensions**. The line-up then consisted of **Jimmy Clarke** (voc/bg), **Ray Jones** (lg), **Kenny McGunahan** (rg) and **Mike Easthope** (dr).

The **Four Dimensions** were very busy on the local scene and established a good name for themselves, but they nearly disbanded when, in quick succession, both guitarists left and disappeared from the scene.

Manager
GEOFF LEACK
48 Brownmoor Lane
LIVERPOOL 23
(WATerloo 4260)

Representation
PEPPERMINT PROMOTIONS
37/43 LONDON RD
LIVERPOOL 3
(NORTH 0753)

Jimmy Clarke and **Mike Easthope** then formed a new group under the old name and were joined by **Jimmy Lynch** (lg), who came from the **Black Cats** and **Graeme Pugh** (rg). A little later this group was joined by the girl singer, **Irene Green**, better known as **'Tiffany'**, who was formerly in the original line-up of the **Liverbirds**, who became a very popular all girl vocal/instrumental group, especially in Germany.

Under the name **Tiffany's Dimensions**, the band was booked for a tour of Scotland. For that tour, the musicians had to become professionals but **Jimmy Lynch** didn't agree and did not want to leave Liverpool. He was replaced by **Tony Raynor**, who normally was a member of **Blues Unlimited** and only stood in for him on this tour. While in Scotland, their entire equipment was stolen, leading to the band splitting up.

Tony Raynor probably returned to **Blues Unlimited** while **Graeme Pugh** disappeared from the scene. **Jimmy Clarke** and **'Tiffany'** re-formed the group with **Karl Terry** (rg) and **Les Williams** (lg), as well as with another drummer, who was very soon replaced by the returning **Mike Easthope**.

Karl Terry (the 'Sheik Of Shake') and **Les Williams** both came from **Group One** and before that, **Karl Terry** was the leader of **Karl Terry & the Cruisers**,

while **Les Williams** originally was a member of **Terry & the Tuxedos** and **Billy Butler & the Tuxedos**.

Karl Terry then left to join the **Delemeres** from Newcastle and later played in various Merseybeat groups, including **Rory Storm & the Hurricanes**, **Karl Terry & the TT's** and the **Clayton Squares**, before he re-formed **Karl Terry & the Cruisers**.

In 1965, **Tiffany & the Dimensions** were signed by Parlophone and it is said that **George Martin** was so enthusiastic about them that he wanted to build two separate acts.

So **'Tiffany'** split from the group and started a solo career. Sometime later she was backed by the **Thoughts** under the name of **Tiffany & the Thoughts**, but her time with them can be followed in a separate story.

The former **Four Dimensions** or **Tiffany's Dimensions** now continued under the name the **Dimensions** with the following line-up:

Jimmy Clarke	(voc/rg)
Les Williams	(lg/voc)
Dennis Swale	(bg)
Mike Easthope	(dr/voc)

Dennis Swale, the cousin of **Les Williams**, had previously played with **Terry & the Tuxedos** and the **Croupiers**.

In 1965, the **Dimensions** recorded their great version of "Tears On My Pillow", which is a Merseybeat classic and probably one of the most beautiful ballads that ever came out of Liverpool. It is a real masterpiece with excellent vocals. Unfortunately, it failed to become a chart success, although it must have sold very well.

Around that same time, the group cut an acetate with the two ballads, "I'll Take You Home Again Kathleen" and "I Wonder If I Care As Much", as well as one standard rocker, "Hello Josephine".

"I'll Take You Home Again Kathleen" was a great song and the heights **Jimmy Clarke** reached with his voice are unbelievable. It is a shame that this song was never released!

In 1966, **Dennis Swale** left the group. He initially became a roadie with **Earl Preston's Realms**. After that, he played with **Eddie Cave & the Fyx**, the **Buzz Band** (not identical to **Bernie & the Buzz Band**) and the **St. Ive's Trio**, before he disappeared from the scene for years.

In 1978, he was back as a member of **Karl Terry & the Cruisers**, he then played with a group called **Honey** and after that became a member of **Faron's Flamingos**.

After he had left in 1966, the **Dimensions** continued as a trio and then in 1967, when **Mike Easthope** left to join **Shane Fenton & the Fentones**, the remaining **Jimmy Clarke** and **Les Williams** continued as a duo under the name of the **Two Dimensions** (what else?) on the cabaret scene, before they also separated.

Jimmy Clarke is known to have moved to the north east of England and continued as a solo performer.

It was probably right at the end of the Sixties, that **Les Williams** together with **Brian Norris** (bg) and **Alan Noone** (dr) teamed up with **Irene Green** again in a new version of **Tiffany's Dimensions**.

Brian Norris was a former member of **Earl Preston's Realms** and the **Cryin' Shames**, while **Alan Noone** formerly had played with the **Vampires** from St. Helens, the **Riot Squad**, **Mark Peters & the Method** and the **Dave Alan Set**.

This relationship apparently did not last too long and, in 1970, **Les Williams** and **Brian Norris** together with the returning drummer **Mike Easthope** formed a trio, under the name of the **Dimensions** again.

This group soon changed their name to **Jet**, and then into **Pendulum**.

In 1978, this line-up as the **Dimensions** was featured on the revival sampler, 'Mersey Survivors' with the songs ,"Little Queenie", "Something Else", "Drift Away" and "Another Saturday Night".

After this record, the group continued as **Pendulum** on the club and cabaret scene for many years.

Brian Norris later was replaced by **Ted Thompson**, who in the Sixties was a member of **Savva & the Democrats**.

When this trio split, **Mike Easthope** and **Les Williams** quit show business.

In 1989, there was a group with the name, the **Dimensions** on the scene again, formed by **Dennis Swale**, but, besides him, there was no connection to the **Dimensions** of the Sixties.

Les Williams returned to the scene through the 'MerseyCats' organisation and became a member of the newly-formed **Mojos** under the leadership of **Nicky Crouch**. Later, he joined the re-formed **Black Knights**, where he is still playing today.

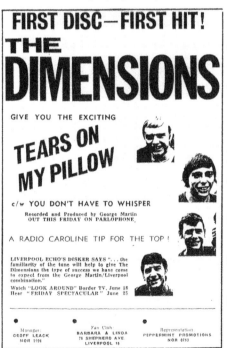

Discography :

Tears On My Pillow / You Don't Have To Whisper
                                        UK- Parlophone R 5294 / 1965

Tracks on compilation albums :

Another Saturday Night	on 'Mersey Survivors' **UK- Raw RWLP 104 / 1978**
Little Queenie	on 'Mersey Survivors' **UK- Raw RWLP 104 / 1978**
Something Else	on 'Mersey Survivors' **UK- Raw RWLP 104 / 1978**
Drift Away	on 'Mersey Survivors' **UK- Raw RWLP 104 / 1978**

Unreleased tracks:

I'll Take You Home Again Kathleen / I Wonder If I Care As Much / Hello Josephine
UK- EMI (?) acetate / 1966

THE DIONS

This is the story of an unlucky Merseybeat group and their manager, who ended up becoming more successful than the band.

It all started in Liverpool in the early Sixties when the band, **Roy & the Dions** was formed with **Roy Brooks** (voc/rg), **Mike Johnson** (lg), **Gerry Osborne** (bg) and a drummer, whose name is not known.

Roy & the Dions appeared regularly at all the major venues on Merseyside, including the 'Cavern', and so became quite popular on the scene. At the end of 1963, the group almost disbanded when **Roy Brooks** and the unknown drummer left.

Roy Brooks, by the way, never appeared again on the scene.

Mike Johnson and **Gerry Osborne** recruited other musicians and then continued under the name of the **Dions** in the following line-up:

Arthur Patterson	**(voc)**
Mike Johnson	**(lg/voc)**
Stan Alexander	**(rg/voc)**
Gerry Osborne	**(bg/voc)**
John Sticks	**(dr)**

John Sticks' real name is **John Foster**. He is the cousin of **Ringo Starr** and had, for a very short time, previously played with the **Escorts**.

Stan Alexander was a former member of the **Black Velvets**, a good group that was managed by a young Liverpudlian, **Daryl Philip Core**, a trained opera singer, who then also took over the management of the **Dions**.

1964 should have been a big year for this really young group. To begin with, the **Dions** were chosen from hundreds of other groups to be featured in the film, 'Ferry Cross The Mersey', alongside **Gerry & the Pacemakers** and other well-known Liverpool groups.

But it soon turned out that some of this film had to be 'trimmed back' and, unfortunately, the **Dions** were one of the groups that had to be 'cut'.

The **Dions** had needed the publicity of the film so badly and, of course it had been a great chance for them. This negative development apparently was the reason for them disbanding shortly after that decision. But in the meantime, German promoters had showed interest in booking them for a tour, and so they re-formed in the former line-up with the exception of **Mike Johnson**, whose replacement was **Robin Bruce** on lead guitar, and besides this, **Andy O'Hagan** (harp) came in as an additional member.

The German tour was quite successful and, amongst other places, the **Dions** appeared at the 'Star-Club' in Hamburg. In spite of all this, a major breakthrough did not happen for the band, who continued playing in Liverpool and the surrounding area.

Towards the end of 1965, as it seems, the **Dions** disbanded totally, but then **Stan Alexander** and **Andy O'Hagan**, together with **Alan Currie** (org), **Ian Collier** (bg), **Derek Marl** (sax) and **Billy Geeleher** (dr) continued under the name of **Dions Sole Band**.

Billy Geeleher was a former member of the **Mode** and the **Calderstones**, while **Derek Marl** had previously played with the **Michael Allen Group** and the **Secrets**.

It was most probably in early 1966, that the **Dions Sole Band** changed their name to the **Times** and besides playing in their own right, also became the backing group for the Liverpool vocal trio, the **Signs**, another story in this book which also includes the continuation of the **Times** story.

In the meantime, **Darryl Philip Core** had given up management and concentrated on his singing career. He initially used the stage name **Paul Dean** and appeared together with the **Clansmen** from Burscough/Southport, but this association did not last for too long and ended after a series of gigs and the recording of two or three acetates.

He then changed his stage name to **David Garrick** and was signed by PYE in 1965.

A little later, he had his first single out with "Go" on the Piccadilly label, which had no success, just like the follow-up, "One Little Smile".

On his next single, **David Garrick** recorded a version of "Lady Jane" which earned a national breakthrough for him when it climbed up to No. 28 in the charts in 1966. The **Iveys**, who included Liverpool musicians and later became very famous as **Badfinger**, may have backed him on that single.

The follow-up, "Dear Mrs. Applebee" stopped at No. 22 but became a monstrous hit in Germany and throughout Europe.

The Times

David Garrick then went to Germany for quite a long time with his own backing group named **Dandy**, which, for sure, was identical with the **Iveys**.

In Germany, he had another big hit with "Please Mr. Movingman", a catchy pop tune in the same style as "Dear Mrs. Applebee". While he was in Germany he had a long string of hits, including

DAVID GARRICK

the previously mentioned, "Please Mr. Movingman", "Rainbow", "A Little Bit Of This" and "Don't Go Out Into The Rain", all catchy pop tunes, none of which had any connection to Beat music anymore.

After some flops, he concentrated on opera singing and he should have been very successful with this. The wave of the Sixties revivals brought him back into the limelight in the early Nineties, although there was no comparison with his success of the late Sixties.

Discography :

The Dions :

This group never released a record but definitely recorded some songs for the film, 'Ferry Cross The Mersey', in 1964. Unfortunately, the film had to be 'trimmed back' and the **Dions** were one of the groups that were 'cut'. That is why it is not known which songs were recorded.

David Garrick :

Go / When The World Was Our Own	UK- Piccadilly 7N 35231 / 1965
One Little Smile / We Must Be In Love	UK- Piccadilly 7N 35263 / 1965
Lady Jane / Let's Go Somewhere	UK- Piccadilly 7N 35317 / 1966
Dear Mrs. Applebee / You're What I'm Living For	UK- Piccadilly 7N 35335 / 1966
I Found A Love / A Broken Heart	UK- Piccadilly 7N 35371 / 1968
Ave Maria / Please Stay	UK- Piccadilly 7N 35398 / 1967
Rainbow / I'll Be Home	UK- PYE 7N 17509 / 1968
A Little Bit Of This / Flutterby Butterfly	UK- PYE 7N 17610 / 1968

Different German releases :

Please Mr. Movingman / A Broken Heart	G- Hit-Ton HT 300 082 / 1967
A Certain Misunderstanding / I'm Looking Straight At You	G- Hit-Ton HT 300 090 / 1967
Hey Mr. Möbelmann / Zeig Den Anderen Nicht Dein Herz	G- Hit-Ton HT 300 098 / 1967
Don't Go Out Into The Rain / Theme For A Wishing Heart	G- Hit-Ton HT 300 124 / 1968
Maypole Mews / I'd Like To Get To Know You Better	G- Dt. Vogue DV 14.840 / 1968
Poor Little Me / Molly With The Hair Like Silver	G- Dt. Vogue DV 14.935 / 1969
Ave Maria / Only A Rose	G- Dt. Vogue DV 14.967 / 1969

Rüdesheim Liegt Nicht An Der Themse / Lady Marmalade	G- Columbia 006-28777 / 1969
Lieber Dr. Eisenbart / Mein Herz Ist Doch Kein Bienenhaus	G- Columbia 006-29810 / 1969
Heya Mississippi Girl / Piccadilly Lady	G- Columbia 006-29862 / 1970
Bake Me A Woman / House In The Heart	G- Columbia 006-91313 / 1970

EP's (French releases) :

'DEAR MRS. APPLEBEE'   F- Vogue PNV 24182 / 1967

- Dear Mrs. Applebee / Lady Jane / You're What I'm Living For / Let's Go Somewhere

'I'VE FOUND A LOVE'   F- Vogue PNV 24187 / 1967

- I've Found A Love / A Broken Heart / It's Not That Easy / I'm Looking Straight At You

LP's (English and German releases) :

'A BOY CALLED DAVID'   K-Marble Arch MAL 822/1967

- So Much Love / I'm Looking Straight At You / A Groovy Kind Of Love / Dear Mrs. Applebee /

Liza Brown / You Don't Know / Dandy / I've Been Loving You Too Long / Lady Jane /

Ain't Gonna Lie / When The World Was Our Own / Master John / It's Not That Easy /

The Man Who Took The Valise Off The Floor Of Grand Central Station At Noon

'DON'T GO OUT INTO THE RAIN'   G-Hit-ton HTSLP 340042/ 1968

- I Go The Feelin' / Somewhere / Don't Go Out Into The Rain (You're Gonna Melt, Sugar) /

What Becomes Of The Broken Hearted / Theme For A Wishing Heart / Dancing In The Street /

The Gentle People / Unchained Melody / Then You Can Tell Me Goodbye / That's How Love Goes /

Please Stay / I've Found A Love

As: **David Garrick & Dandy** :

'BLOW-UP LIVE !' (live from the 'Blow-Up', Munich)   G-Hit-ton HTSLP 340058/ 1968

- See See Rider / Mr. Pleasant / Words / Simon Says / If I Were A Carpenter /

Medley : Rainbow, Please Mr. Movingman, Lady Jane, Dear Mrs. Applebee /

River Deep Mountain High / Dandy / Gimme Little Sign / Dedicated Follower Of Fashion /

World / Bend Me, Shape Me

VINCE EARL & THE TALISMEN

The **Talismen** were formed on the Wirral, probably in Wallasey, in 1962 and very soon became one of the local top acts on the west side of the River Mersey.

It was in 1963 that they were joined by singer, **Vince Earl**, who had started his career with the **Teenage Rebels** and after that he had become quite popular on the scene with his group, **Vince Earl & the Zeros**.

The **Talismen** then changed their name to **Vince Earl & the Talismen** and appeared in the following line-up:

Vince Earl	(voc)
Geoff Pollit	(lg/voc)
John Bethel	(org/voc)
Tony McDonough	(bg/voc)
Alan Jaecock	(dr)

All members of the **Talismen** were experienced musicians that had played in other groups previously.

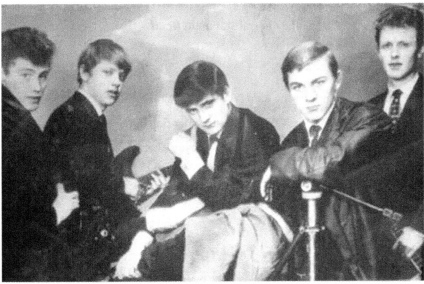

Vince Earl & the Talismen

Tony McDonough was a former member of the **Travellers** from Wallasey, while both **Geoff Pollit** and **Alan Jaecock** (whose name is sometimes documented as **Jake Alcock**), may have previously played in the **Thunderbeats**. If so, it was not the **Thunderbeats** from Preston that had **Keef Hartley** on drums. Unfortunately, the group **John Bethel** had previously played in, is not known.

As **Vince Earl & the Talismen** became more and more successful, they turned professional and, within a short time, signed a recording contract with Oriole. But then they were put on ice and, as far as it is known, there was never a record released. Maybe this was because of the takeover of Oriole by CBS and unfortunately, the connection to Liverpool was not as close with CBS as it was with Oriole.

Consequently, **Vince Earl & the Talismen** had to survive on their live appearances and it seems they did not have a problem with that because they were really busy in Liverpool and the surrounding areas.

But, because of the recording contract flop, the group did not achieve national stardom, and nothing is known about the group ever touring the European continent.

At the end of 1964, **Vince Earl** left to join the **Connoisseurs**, and later became a member of **Rory Storm & the Hurricanes**.

In 1965, the **Talismen** were joined by **Karl Terry** (voc/g) and **Gordon Evans** (aka **Gordon Loughlin**) (bg), who came from the recently disbanded **T.T.s** but, they only had a short spell with the **Talismen** and then went back to re-form the **T.T.s**. Soon after that, they both joined up with the rest of the just disbanding **Clayton Squares** under the name of the **T-Squares**.

The **Talismen** continued as a four-piece and, in 1966, recorded an acetate with the songs, "Break My Heart" and "Wall".

Around that time, **Dave Keegan** joined the group but, it is not known if he was an additional guitarist or a replacement for **Geoff Pollit**.

However, the **Talismen** broke up soon after and all the members disappeared from the scene - with the exception of **Dave Keegan**, who joined the **Locations**, that a little later continued under the name of the **Talismen**. (For more details about that, see the story of the **Victims**).

Tilly and the Talismen

As it seems, the new **Talismen** did not exist for too long either – at least not under that name, as still, in 1966, **Geoff Pollit**, **Tony McDonough** and **Alan Jaecock** together with the girl-singer, **Joyce Bennett**, appeared again under the name of **Tilly & the Talismen**. This was more of a cabaret-group that continued to play on the scene for quite some time.

It is not known when **Tilly & the Talismen** broke up or what happened to the members after that.

In or around 2008, there was a group under the name of the **Talismen** that appeared sporadically in the clubs and pubs on the Wirral and it is known that **Tony McDonough** and **Alan Jaecock** were two of the members.

In the late sixties, **Vince Earl** formed the **Vince Earl Attraction** with **Graham Jones** (lg), **Barry Triggs** (org/p), **Ray Whitehead** (bg) and **Jimmy Jordan**, the former drummer of **Earl Royce the Olympics**. This also was more of a cabaret group and, after **Jimmy Jordan** was replaced by **Billy Dunlop** in late 1973, they released an album with the title, 'First' on the 'Liverpool Sound'-label (LS 1778).

After **Ray Whitehead** left, **Vince Earl** took over on bass guitar and, in 1974, the **Vince Earl Attraction** released their second album, 'Can't Get Enough' on Amazon records (unnumbered).

In 1992, **Vince Earl** appeared again with the **Connoisseurs** at a concert for the 'MerseyCats' organisation. He is now quite a popular TV actor but, he has kept the **Vince Earl Attraction** going to this day and for a time, guitarist **'Baz' Davis** (ex **Connoiseurs**, **King Size Taylor**, etc.) was a member. In addition, **Charlie Flynn** (ex **Ian & the Zodiacs** and **Connoisseurs**), **Steve Fleming** (ex **Mark Peters & the Silhouettes**), and **Dave Lovelady** (ex **Fourmost**) played with that group.

Discography :

Vince Earl & the Talismen had signed a recording contract with Oriole, but there was never anything released.

The Talismen :

Break My Heart / Wall   **UK- ??? Acetate / 1966**

THE EASYBEATS

It is important to point out that there was absolutely nothing in common between the Australian hit group the **Easybeats** and this Liverpool band, which was formed in 1961. But there is a connection between them and this connection is the Liverpool drummer, **Gordon 'Snowy' Fleet**, who was with the **Four Musketeers** and, for a short time, with the **Mojos** in the early Sixties. He was an admirer of the Liverpool **Easybeats** and followed them around before he emigrated to Australia.

Over there, he continued in the music business as a drummer and, when his group was looking for the right name, he remembered his time in Liverpool and suggested **The Easybeats**, which was accepted by the other musicians - the rest is history.

The Liverpool **Easybeats** were formed by **Frank Townsend** under the name, the **Texans**, and, from the beginning, their manager was **Gerry Jackson**, the brother of **Searchers** vocalist **Tony Jackson**.

It must have been some time in 1962 that lead guitarist, **Frank McTigue,** left to form the **Crusaders**, that later became the **Kruzads**, another story in this book.

However, he did not stay away for too long and returned to the **Easybeats** while their original bass guitarist, **Eddie Hill** joined the **Kruzads** as their new lead guitarist.

Accordingly, in 1963, the line-up of the **Easybeats** consisted of:

Frank Townsend	(voc/rg)
Jim Doran	(lg/voc)
Frank McTigue	(bg/voc)
Robert Ninnim	(dr)

Jim Doran was the new member who had taken over on lead guitar when **Frank McTigue** had left for the **Kruzads**, so on his return **Frank McTigue** continued with the band as their bass guitarist.

The **Easybeats** at that time were the only known Liverpool group whose sound was influenced by American Surf music and the group very soon became one of the top club attractions in Liverpool and the surrounding areas. They then signed a contract with the London-based Ponte & Oates agency and went down to London for a long residency.

For a short time, the group changed their name to the **Dealers** and during this time they cut the song, "Girl From New York City", from a live performance at the famous 'Marquee' club. On the actual acetate, the song was coupled with an interesting version of "Stagger Lee" and it was intended to be released as a single. Unfortunately, the group fell out with their London management agency. They returned to Liverpool, went back to their former management and their old name and, of course, the planned single release was cancelled!

Robert Ninnim left the group, he was later a member of a group called **Tyme & Motion**.

His replacement was **Pete Orr**, a former member of the **Hi-Cats, Groups Inc.**, as well as **Freddie Starr & the Ventures, Danny Havoc & the Ventures** and **Danny Havoc & the Secrets**, which were basically one and the same group under different names and with slightly varied line-ups.

Soon after this, the **Easybeats** were booked for a big festival in South Wales and there a certain **Kit Lambert** approached them with a song written by **Pete Townsend** of the (as yet) unknown group called **The Who**. He wanted the **Easybeats** to record it and so the group left the festival, went straight into a studio and cut an acetate of "The Kids Are Alright". When **Kit Lambert** heard it, he was enthusiastic about the arrangement and recording and wanted to release it on single and to sign the **Easybeats** to his stable. But because of their experience with their former London agency, the **Easybeats** turned the offer down. So the song with the **Easybeats** arrangement idea was recorded a little later by **The Who**, and became a million seller. Meanwhile, **Pete Orr** had left the group who then recruited **Frank Cork** from the London scene as their new drummer .

In 1966, **Frank Townsend** left the **Easybeats** and went back to London to join **Tony Rivers & the Castaways**, another great harmony group who later changed their name to **Harmony Grass**.

While in London, **Frank Townsend** lived together in a flat with the **Fruit Eating Bears** from Liverpool who were down there as the backing group for the **Merseys**. Probably for that reason, it is sometimes stated that **Frank Townsend** had joined them but, that is definitely not true. When he returned to Liverpool, he became a member of the **Escorts**.

His replacement in the **Easybeats** in 1966 was **Pete Carter**, but he did not stay for long and was replaced by **Adrain Lord**, whose real name is **Adrian Wilkinson**, and who was a former member of the **Missouri Drifters**, the **Nomads** (who became the **Mojos**), the **Mastersounds** and the **Bluesville Bats**, as well as Liverpool's **Faces**. He also played with the **Mersey Five** in Germany and, on his return to Liverpool, had been a member of **Them Grimbles**. He did not stay with the **Easybeats** for long and then he disappeared from the scene.

The new singer was **Ronnie Cotton**, better known as **Amos Bonny**, who had formerly sung with **Amos Bonny & the T.T.s** and the **Defenders**.

The **Easybeats** continued in this line-up on the local scene until they finally broke up in 1968.

The Beechwoods

Amos Bonny joined a group called **Mumble**, while **Frank McTigue** together with **Jim Doran** became members of the **George King Group** which, besides them consisted of former **Excerts** and **Georgie's Germs** members, **John Hodgson** and drummer, **Barry Robinson**.

John Hodgson was replaced in the **George King Group** by **Frank Townshend** and when the **George King Group** broke up, **Frank McTigue** had a short spell with the **Big Three** and the **Alan Price Set** before he quit showbiz for years. In the Seventies he was a member of a group called **Faith**.

Jim Doran teamed up again with **Frank Townsend** and, together with **George Cassidy** (ex **Dingle Dices, Clay & the Classics**, the **Masterminds** and **Fruit Eating Bears**) formed the group **The Beechwoods**, again a great harmony group in the style of the **Easybeats**.

In addition to those three, the group consisted of **John Larkin** (lead-voc), **Billy Pimlet** (lg/voc) from the **Inmates** and **Eddie Edwards** (dr), a former member of the **Flames**, **Del Renas**, **Nashpool Four** and **Rory Storm & the Hurricanes**. At a later date, **Kevin Short**, the former bass guitarist of the **Notions**, may have played with the group.

The **Beechwoods** continued quite successfully on the scene and are said to have recorded again, but no further information could be found.

Taste of Honey

In 1969, the band name was changed to **Taste Of Honey** and sometime later an album was released on the little known Rediffusion label which, without exception, featured **Beach Boys** songs and was accordingly entitled, 'Pay A Tribute To The Beach Boys'.

In addition, there was said to have been a single released called "Goody Goody Gumdrops", but again, no further details could be found. Sometime in the early Seventies, **Taste Of Honey** split up and, with the exception of **Frank Townsend**, probably all the members quit show business.

A few years back, **Frank Townsend** teamed up again with **Jim Doran** and **Dave Morgan** from the **Clouds** in a harmony vocal/guitar trio, using the name of **The Easybeats** again. This group is still going on the scene, even if they are not playing regularly. Sometimes they are joined by **Frank McTigue** again.

Discography :

as **The Dealers** :

Girl From New York City (live-version) / Stagger Lee   UK- acetate / 1964

as **The Easybeats** :

The Kids Are Alright   **UK- one sided acetate / 1965**

Taste Of Honey :

LP '**PAY A TRIBUTE TO THE BEACH BOYS**'   **UK-Rediffusion R.I.M. ZS 01-22 / 1969**

- **California Girls / Then I Kissed Her / God Only Knows / Why Do Fools Fall In Love /**

I Can Hear Music / You're So Good To Me / Fun, Fun, Fun / Darlin' / Help Me Rhonda /

Sloop John B / Do It Again / Barbara Ann

JASON EDDIE & THE CENTERMEN

This group was formed as **Vance Williams & the Rhythm Four** in Liverpool in 1962. In January 1963, the vocalist, **Vance Williams** left and was replaced by the songstress, **Beryl Ward**, and correspondingly ,the name was changed into **Beryl Ward & the Centermen**. But the vocalist problem was not resolved, as **Beryl Ward** left them in the same year. Her place then was taken by **Albert Wycherley**, the brother of Liverpool's Rock 'n' Roll hero, **Billy Fury**, whose real name was **Ronald Wycherley**.

Like his brother, **Albert Wycherley** also changed his name - to **Al Trent**. From that moment on, the band's name was changed to **The Centermen with Al Trent** and the line-up included the following musicians:

Al Trent	(voc)
Terry Barrett	(lg)
John Kirkpatrick	(p/voc)
Cy Richmond	(bg)
Bill Conroy	(dr)

Peak Promotions RING SEFTON 3398

THE CENTERMEN with AL TRENT

John Kirkpatrick was a former member of the **Travellers**, **Karl Terry & the Cruisers** and **Lee Shondell & the Boys**, while **Charles 'Cy' Richmond** was a former member of the **Delacardos**.

Terry Barrett left quite soon and later was a member of the **Silver Set** and **Cy Tucker & the Friars**.

He was replaced by **John Peters**, who had formerly played with the **Arrows**.

In 1964, the **Centermen** were signed by Parlophone, but this was not followed by a record release at that time, although it can be taken for granted that some test recordings were made. Despite the fact that the group failed to achieve national success, the musicians became professionals, as they apparently had numerous engagements throughout the north of England.

In 1965, the name of the band was changed into **Jason Eddie & the Centermen**, which was not caused by any changes in the line-up, only because **Al Trent** had changed his name to **Jason Eddie**.

In November 1965, the band had their first single released with "What'cha Gonna Do Baby", which was not too successful, although seen in retrospect it was their best record.

The follow-up came in 1966 with a very strange version of **Guy Mitchell's** classic, "Singin' The Blues", both records were produced by **Joe Meek**.

Joe Meek is known to have produced some very bad records with various Beat groups of that time, but this was absolutely the worst of all and the record is not even worth listening to, although this certainly wasn't the fault of **Jason Eddie & the Centermen**. Not too much imagination is necessary to create various good arrangements for this song, but this version was really perverted with its nerve-wracking guitar which never ceased and allegedly was played by **Ritchie Blackmore**.

However, this was the last record by **Jason Eddie & the Centermen**, and the group disbanded at the end of the Sixties after they had recorded the song, "Mr. Busdriver" in 1968, that was later released on a Merseybeat compilation CD.

John Kirkpatrick later became a member of the **Albion Dance Band** and **Billy Conroy** appeared again on the scene in 1992 as a member of **Karl Terry & the Cruisers** before he quit show business.

All the other former members of **Jason Eddie & the Centermen** never appeared on the scene again. **Albert Wycherley**, much later, came back as a singer, impersonating his brother. **Billy Fury**. He sadly died in September 2011

Discography :

| What'cha Gonna Do Baby / Come On Baby | UK- Parlophone R 5388 / 1965 |
| Singin' The Blues / True To You | UK- Parlophone R 5473 / 1966 |

Unreleased tracks :

Mr. Busdriver

UK- acetate / 1968

LEE EDDIE & THE CHEVRONS

The **Chevrons** were formed in Liverpool in 1962 and were one of the more popular groups in the British capital of Beat, but they never had any real outstanding success.

At the end of 1963, the group was joined by singer, **Brian Lee**, better known on the scene as **Lee Eddie**, who had previously led the **Lee Eddie Five**, who had also been quite successful and have their own story in this book.

Due to the popularity of the new singer, the band changed its name to **Lee Eddie & the Chevrons** and the line-up at that time consisted of:

Lee Eddie	**(voc)**
Alan Ryan	**(lg)**
Arthur Boughey	**(bg)**
Mike Logan	**(org)**
Andre Eustance	**(dr)**

In 1964, an acetate was recorded by **Lee Eddie & the Chevrons** with the **Roy Orbison** success, "Running Scared" and the folk song, "Born On The Wind".

Both were very nice, melodic numbers but with weak sound quality. This demo was made for EMI and unfortunately, it was not followed by a real record release.

At the end of 1964, **Mike Logan** left to join the **Denny Seyton Group**, which, for a short time, may have continued as the **Lovin' Kind**, but then, under the name of the **Motowns,** they went to Italy for a long residency where they recorded and became very popular.

His replacement in the **Chevrons** was a guitarist called **'Anton'**, whose surname or real name is not known.

Because of the fact that (with the exception of Lee Eddie) all the members had an 'A' as the first letter of their Christian names, the group sometimes jokingly was announced as **'Four A's & one Lee'** in the music newspapers.

The group probably disbanded in 1964 as singer, **Lee Eddie** appeared on the scene with a new group under the name of the **Lee Eddie Show Group** around that time.

But of course there is also the possibility that this was only a change of the group's name, as none of the other members of the **Chevrons** appeared in any other bands after that.

Discography :

Running Scared / Born On The Wind   UK - EMI acetate-demo / 1964

THE LEE EDDIE FIVE

This was one of the pioneering groups of Liverpool's Fifties' music scene, formed as a Skiffle band under the name of the **Lee Eddie Five** in 1957. They switched to Rock 'n' Roll and became a significant band on Merseyside - with the following line-up:

Lee Eddie	**(voc)**
Norman Scroggei	**(g/voc)**
Pete McFayden	**(g/voc)**
Jeff Nixon	**(bg/voc)**
John Nugent	**(dr)**

The real name of **Lee Eddie** was **Brian Lee** and he was probably the founder of the group which, unfortunately, was never signed by a recording company, although the **Lee Eddie Five** did some recording sessions, but most probably on a private basis.

Despite the fact that the group had a really good name and a large following in the north of England, it never achieved national importance or popularity and, as far as it is known, never played outside England.

In 1963, **John Nugent** left the group and for a while disappeared from the scene, but then he became the drummer for the **Four Originals**, which was a sort of follow-up group of the popular **Dale Roberts & the Jaywalkers**. He stayed with that group until 1973 and then apparently quit playing.

He was replaced in the **Lee Eddie Five** by **Frank Wibberley**, who had formerly played with the **Rhythm Rockers** and the **Four Aces**, as well as with **Derry & the Seniors** and **Howie Casey & the Seniors** respectively.

It was in early 1964 that **Norman Scroggei** left to join **Mark Peters & the Silhouettes**. He continued to play with the **Silhouettes** after **Mark Peters** left them and, after that, he played with the **Three Cheers**, who later changed their name to **Phase Three**.

He was replaced by **Kenny Baker**, the former lead guitarist of the just disbanded **Defenders**. This line-up of the **Lee Eddie Five** only continued for a short time and then disbanded without having achieved any major success.

Lee Eddie then amalgamated with the Liverpool group **The Chevrons** under the name of **Lee Eddie & the Chevrons**, with whom he later cut a nice acetate.

After that, he was the leader of the **Lee Eddie Show Group**, before he disappeared from the scene.

Frank Wibberley joined **Emile Ford & the Checkmates**.

Jeff Nixon and **Kenny Baker** re-formed the **Defenders**, but **Jeff Nixon** very soon followed **Frank Wibberley** to **Emile Ford & the Checkmates** and later, both were probably members of the **Original Checkmates** after **Emile Ford** had started his solo-career.

Nothing was heard of **Pete McFayden** who disappeared from the scene.

Discography :

The **Lee Eddie Five** never released an official record but they had some private recording sessions. Unfortunately, it is not known which songs were recorded and if there were any acetates made of them.

The Lee Eddie Five.

WE GUARANTEE A GREAT SHOW
Every FRIDAY and SATURDAY at . . . . **AINTREE INSTITUTE**

Buses 20, 21, 30, 61, 91, 92, 93, 95, 96, 500 to the Black Bull—we're next door

LOOK! This Friday— DOMINOES With their new Kingsize sound
          LEE EDDIE 5 Liverpool's Livesome Fivesome

LOOK! LOOK! This Saturday— GREAT BOPPIN' BEATLES ! ! This Saturday
          plus Johnny Sandon and the Searchers

IT'S ALWAYS AI AT THE AI——YOUR WEEKEND DANCES

CLAY ELLIS & THE RAIDERS

This group was formed in Wallasey, on the west side of the River Mersey in 1961 and was certainly one of the area's first and very important Beat bands who, within a short time, also became very popular in the Beat metropolis of Liverpool.

In the original line-up, **Clay Ellis & the Raiders** consisted of the following musicians:

Clay Ellis	**(voc)**
John Edmunds	**(lg)**
Les Belamere	**(rg)**
Malcolm Shelbourne	**(bg)**
Kenny Cochran	**(dr)**

But this line-up did not last too long and when **John Edmunds** returned to London (where he hailed from) and **Les Belamere** also left, only one new guitarist, **Bobby Turner**, was added to the group.

In 1963, **Clay Ellis & the Raiders** went into the studio and recorded an EP with the songs, "Put The Blame On Me", "I'm A Fool For You", "Here's Hopin' ", "Smile A Little Smile For Me" and "I'm A Hog For You" which unfortunately, was only released as a demo on acetate.

It seems, this very good group was never signed by a major recording company and so did not make any sort of a national breakthrough. However, they were well accepted on the scene and had plenty of engagements on the Wirral and also in Liverpool and the surrounding areas.

In late 1963, **Clay Ellis & the Raiders** disbanded for unknown reasons.

Clay Ellis teamed up with the **Corsairs** from Liverpool under the name of **Clay Ellis & the Corsairs**, but this connection only lasted for a short time and then **Clay Ellis** formed a new group under the name of **Mr. Lee & Co.**, which is a another story in this book.

Malcolm Shelbourne joined **Savva & the Democrats**, who also hailed from Wallasey, where he played until that group broke up in 1965. He then became a member of **Gerry De Ville & the City Kings**, where he played until 1972. He then joined **Purple Grass**, who a little later changed their name to **Rainbow**. When this group disbanded in 1982, **Malcolm Shelbourne** quit showbiz and went back to a normal job.

After **Clay Ellis & the Raiders** disbanded, **Kenny Cochran** joined the **Koobas,** who also hailed from the west side of the River Mersey and later became quite popular throughout England and on the European continent. But **Kenny Cochran** did not stay with them for too long and became a member of the backing group for the **Excelles**. When the **Excelles** went down to London, **Kenny Cochran** left and, it seems, quit show business.

Bobby Turner later appeared again as a member of the **Black Abbots**, who hailed from Chester.

It is really sad that **Clay Ellis & the Raiders** never had a real record released which could have helped the group to make the breakthrough it doubtlessly deserved, as it was one of the very good bands on the Merseybeat scene.

Clay Ellis sadly died much too young in 1996.

Discography :

EP (without title)   **UK- Eroica-acetate / 1963**

- Put The Blame On Me / I'm A Fool For You / Here's Hopin' /

Smile A Little Smile For Me / I'm A Hog For You

THE ESCORTS

This was a typical Merseybeat group and certainly one of the very best, even if they didn't have much international chart success.

Formed in Liverpool in 1962, the **Escorts** mainly consisted of very young musicians, and these teenagers, of course, had to obtain some musical experience. But the day was not too far away when the **Escorts** would prove the outstanding musical quality they possessed.

Originally the group was a five-piece with **Ray Walker** as their lead singer, who was probably the most experienced as he was the former leader of **Ray & the Del Renas**.

But **Ray Walker** left shortly after the group was first formed and disappeared from the scene. He should not be confused with the guitarist of the same name, who played with **Ogi & the Flintstones**.

Around the same time, their drummer **John Foster**, who had changed his name to **John Sticks** and who was a cousin of **Ringo Starr**, also left to join the **Dions,** formerly known as **Roy & the Dions**.

The **Escorts** added a new drummer and continued as a four-piece in the line-up with:

Terry Sylvester	(lg/voc)
John Kinrade	(rg/voc)
Mike Gregory	(bg/voc)
Pete Clarke	(dr)

Pete Clarke was a great drummer, he had previously played with **Vince & the Volcanoes** and **Groups Inc.** All the other members were newcomers to the scene.

In this line-up, the **Escorts** took part in a Beat contest sponsored by the 'Record Mirror' newspaper and won. The **Merseybeats** took second place and **Freddie Starr & the Midnighters** came in third.

The prize was a recording contract with Fontana and, in 1963, the first single by the **Escorts** was released. "Dizzy Miss Lizzy" was a No. 1 hit in Texas, but had no great chart success in England or elsewhere, although it was a great driving version of the **Larry Williams** Rock 'n' Roll classic.

With their follow-up, "The One To Cry", the **Escorts** placed at No. 49 in the British charts, while their third single, "I Don't Want To Go On Without You" failed to enter the top 100.

This song later became a really big hit for the **Moody Blues** from Birmingham.

In the meantime, the **Escorts** had become firm favourites in Liverpool and they were also the resident group at the famous 'Blue Angel' club.

THE ESCORTS

166

Pete Clarke left to join the **Krew** (also known as **The Crew**) and, after that, he became a member of **Them Grimbles**. Then he had a short stint with **5 A.M. Event**, that recorded the single, "Hungry", which was produced by **Searchers** drummer, **Chris Curtis** for PYE in 1966. **5 A.M. Event** was a Canadian group that made Liverpool their home for two years, they were formerly known as the **Crescendos**.

His replacement in the **Escorts** was **Kenny Goodlass**, again a great drummer, who formerly had played with the **Panthers** and the **Kirkbys**.

In 1965, another great record, "C'mon Home Baby", was released (their only release that year). This song was also released on the German 'Star-Club' label as the reverse side of "Dizzy Miss Lizzy". It also had no chart success but, at least it helped the **Escorts** to achieve some popularity in Germany.

In 1966, the group had its last single out on the Fontana label with "Let It Be Me", but this wonderful melodic **Gilbert Becaud** song again failed to get into the charts.

The **Escorts** switched to Columbia and, in 1966, released their final single with the great songs, "From Head To Toe" and "Night Time", which some people say was their best record. It is curious that this single was released in Germany on the Dt. Vogue label, which normally was the German connection for PYE records. However, even this interesting record did not enter the charts.

Prior to this record, **Terry Sylvester** had left the **Escorts** to become a member of the **Swinging Blue Jeans** and from there he joined the **Hollies**. Initially, he was replaced by **Frank Townshend**, who originated from Liverpool's **Easybeats** and, prior to joining the **Escorts,** he had played with **Tony Rivers & the Castaways** from London. **Frank Townshend** did not stay for too long and became a member of the **Beechwoods**, a successor group of the **Easybeats**, that later recorded under the name of **Taste Of Honey**.

His replacement in the **Escorts** was **Paddy Chambers** who had been in the line-up that had recorded their final single. He was a former member of well known groups including **Faron's Flamingos**, the **Big Three**, the **Eyes** and **Paddy, Klaus & Gibson**.

Pete Clarke came back to replace **Kenny Goodlass**, who had left to join the **Swinging Blue Jeans** for a short time, he then played with the **Fruit Eating Bears**, the backing group for the **Merseys**.

Pete Clarke left to join the **Liverpool Scene** and was replaced by **Paul Comerford**, a former member of the **Pulsators**, the **Thoughts** and the **Cryin' Shames**. Later, there was another change on drums when **Paul**

Comerford left to join the **Times** and was replaced by **Tommy Kelly**, who had formerly played with **Danny Royl & the Strollers**, the **Sensations**, the **Young Ones**, **Rikki Janson & the Q-Kats** (all one group with different names) and **Earl Preston's Realms**. For a short time, **Bruce McCaskell** was also with the **Escorts** (on their last German tour), having formerly played with the **Bluegenes**, the **Kansas City Five** and with **Groups. Inc.**, but it is not known for sure if he was a member of the group or of the crew.

The Escorts with Paddy Chambers

In 1968, the **Escorts**, one of the most underrated Liverpool groups, disbanded totally.

Mike Gregory had a short spell with the **Hollies** and then became a member of the **Swinging Blue Jeans**, where he played until 1972. After that, he and **Paddy Chambers** were members of **Big John's Rock 'n' Roll Circus**. He later appeared again on the **Bay City Rollers album,** 'Once Upon A Star'.

Bruce McCaskell later became the manager of the **Average White Band**, he sadly died at Christmas 1993 from a heart attack.

Kenny Goodlass was a member of the newly formed **Merseybeats** until 1980 and from 1993 until 1996 he was the drummer with **Karl Terry & the Cruisers** but later returned to his re-formed original group, the **Kirkbys**.

Paddy Chambers, after his membership in **Big John's Rock' n 'Roll Circus** together with **Beryl Marsden**, was a member of the great Liverpool Soul band, **Sinbad,** and later was the leader of **Paddy Chambers & the Java Jive**. He sadly died in the Nineties.

Terry Sylvester left the **Hollies** in the mid 80's and, it was reported that he would form the **New Escorts**, but there was never anything heard about such a group. **Terry Sylvester** continued to make solo records, he later emigrated to the USA where he is still a popular musician.

John Kinrade and **Tommy Kelly** apparently quit show business and went back to normal day jobs.

Discography

Dizzy Miss Lizzy / All I Want Is You	**UK- Fontana TF 453 / 1964**
The One To Cry / Tell Me Baby	**UK- Fontana TF 474 / 1964**
I Don't Want To Go On Without You / Don't Forget To Write	**UK- Fontana TF 516 / 1964**
C'mon Home Baby / You'll Get No Lovin' That Way	**UK- Fontana TF 570 / 1965**
Let It Be Me / Mad Mad World	**UK- Fontana TF 651 / 1966**
From Head To Toe / Night Time	**UK- Columbia DB 8061 / 1966**

Different German release :

Dizzy Miss Lizzy / C'mon Home Baby	**G- Star-Club 148.540 / 1966**

(All above recordings were re-released on the album 'From The Blue Angel' on the Edsel label (FORD 1) in 1982)

THE EXCELLES

This five-piece vocal group was formed in 1963 by twin brother and sister **Frank** and **Maureen Collins** in Speke, South Liverpool.

Their music focused on the Motown sound, and so the **Excelles** were one of the outstanding vocal groups on the Liverpool music scene. But this does not mean that they were a real Soul band, they just took the songs and the rhythm of the Motown scene and mixed it up with a real Beat.

In the beginning, the **Excelles** consisted of the following members:

Frank Collins	(voc/g)
Maureen Collins	(voc)
Carrol Carter	(voc)
Vicky Bird	(voc)
Patrick McHugh	(voc)

For their first live appearances, the **Excelles** teamed up with various local groups before they formed their own backing group in 1964.

This band had no name and, besides an organist, it also included **Pete Williams** (bg) and **Kenny Cochran** (dr), who both came from the **Kubas**.

Kenny Cochran had previously played with **Clay Ellis & the Raiders** and **Pete Williams** with **Roy Montrose & the Midnights**.

The **Excelles** then appeared at all the major venues on Merseyside, including the 'Cavern', where they were recorded together with the **Hollies** for the radio programme, 'Sunday Night At The Cavern', in 1964. They became very popular in the north of England, but for mysterious reasons did not sign a recording contract.

Vicky Bird was the first to leave and probably quit show business, she was not replaced in the **Excelles**. When

The Excelles at the Cavern

Maureen Collins also left the group to get married, she was replaced by **Dyan Birch**, the sister of **Pamela Birch**, who played in the **Liverbirds**.

This change probably happened in 1966 and, for a short period around that same time, they were also backed by the popular Liverpool group, the **Notions**. One year later the group decided to turn professional and moved down to London.

Their backing group split because **Kenny Cochran** and **Pete Williams** wanted to stay in Liverpool. Neither of them appeared on the scene again.

The **Excelles** formed a new backing group and amalgamated with them under the name of **Arrival**, and the line-up was as follows:

Frank Collins	(voc/g)
Carrol Carter	(voc)
Dyan Birch	(voc)
Paddy Hough	(voc)
Don Hume	(org/p)
Tony O'Malley	(bg)
Lloyd Courtney	(dr)

Arrival

Paddy Hough of course was identical to **Patrick McHugh** and **Don Hume** might have been the organist, that had previously played with the **Excelles** in Liverpool, but this is not certain.

With their new name, the group became very popular in the capital of England and they were soon signed by Decca.

In 1969, their first single, "Friends", was released and this great Soul influenced record climbed up to No. 8 in the British charts. **Arrival** were also quite successful on the European continent with this debut single.

This release was followed by the album, 'Arrival', which was a little bit disappointing after that superb single, which was also included on that LP. Other nice tracks were the Gospel influenced songs, "Prove It", "See The Lord" and "Take Me", as well as the melodic "Not Right Now", while their version of the **Doors** hit "Light My Fire" was not bad, but a little bit too jazzy.

In May 1970, "I Will Survive", another strong single was released, which stopped at No. 16 in the charts. This new success was followed by some more television appearances and radio shows, both in the UK and also in Europe, but surprisingly not by a follow-up single, which after that success is very hard to understand.

Because of various personnel changes, it took **Arrival** two years until they signed a new recording contract, this time with CBS, where, in 1972, their second album, also titled 'Arrival' was released.

At that time, **Carrol Carter** and **Don Hume** had left the group and **Arrival** was joined by **Raphael Pereira** as an additional guitarist and the place on piano was taken over by **Tony O'Malley**, while the new bass guitarist was **Philip Chen**, who was replaced, on the album, by **Lee Sutherland**.

Glen Lefleur replaced **Lloyd Courtney** who left and became a member of the hit group the **Casuals** who, in 1967, had a huge international hit with "Jesamine". It should be noted that there was also a Liverpool group called the **Casuals**, but there is no connection between these two groups.

1973 saw another album release by the group, this time with the title, 'Heartbreak Kid', from which the single, '(The Theme From) The Heartbreak Kid', was coupled out and became a real flop, although the B-side "Sweet Summer", a **Dyan Birch/Frank Collins** original, was quite nice.

In Germany, this record was followed by another single with the titles, "Love Song" and "Out Of Desperation", which was released on the German CBS label in 1973. Nothing is known of a corresponding release for the British market.

This apparently was the final record by **Arrival**, who broke up quite soon after its release.

Frank Collins, **Paddy McHugh** and **Dyan Birch** became members of the progressive group **Kokomo**.

In 1977, all three were featured on the **Brian Ferry** album, 'In Your Mind' and, in 1978, **Dyan Birch** and **Frank Collins** also appeared on an album by **Andy Desmond**.

Both Decca singles of **Arrival** were re-released. "I Will Survive" in 1975 and "Friends" in 1978, but there was no chart entry for them at that time.

Discography :

The **Excelles** never released an official record under that name but, in 1964, a live performance by them was recorded for the Radio programme, 'Sunday Night At The Cavern'. Unfortunately, the songs that were recorded from that performance are not known.

as **Arrival** :

Friends / Don't Turn His Love Away	**UK- Decca F.12986 / 1969**
I Will Survive / See The Lord	**UK- Decca F.23026 / 1970**
The Theme From 'The Heartbreak Kid' / Sweet Summer	**UK- CBS 1350 / 1973**

Different German release :

Love Song / Out Of Desperation	**G - CBS 7035 / 1973**

LPs :

'ARRIVAL'   UK-Decca SKL 5055 / 1970

- Live / Light My Fire / No Good Advice / Prove It / See The Lord / Sit Down And Float /

Don't Turn His Love Away / Take Me / La Virra / Not Right Now / Hard Road

'ARRIVAL'   UK – CBS 64733 / 1972

- Glory Be / So It Is Written / Not Gonna Worry / You, Love And Me / Family Tree /

Part Of My Dream / Not Preconceived / Have A Drink On Your Father / Understanding /

Weary Sad, Weary Down

'HEARTBREAK KID'   UK – CBS 70125 / 1973

A CHRISTMAS MESSAGE FROM CAVERN ARTISTES . . .

"We hope all our fans have a very happy time this coming Christmas. Thanks for your support during the past year and we look forward to seeing you in the New Year."

MICHAEL ALLEN GROUP
CLAYTON SQUARES
EXCELLES
HIDEAWAYS
KUBAS
NOTIONS
EARL PRESTON'S REALMS
ST. LOUIS CHECKS

SOLE REPRESENTATION:
CAVERN ARTISTES LTD.
8—12 MATHEW STREET,
(off North John Street) Liverpool 2. CEN. 2874

THE EXCERTS

Here everything started in Speke, on the outskirts of Liverpool in the very early Sixties, when the group, **The Abstracts** was formed by friends **John Hodgson** (lg/voc), **Barry Robinson** (rg/voc), **Bill Cole** (bg/voc) and **Ray Timmins** (dr).

They played the youth and church clubs in the immediate vicinity but they broke up when **Barry Robinson** left to join the already established **Billy & the Heartbeats** as their drummer, whose line-up then consisted of **Billy Formby** (voc), **Arthur Roberts** (lg), **Glenn Smith** (rg/voc), **Harry Millington** (bg), **Barry Robinson** (dr).

Billy & the Heartbeats initially played a lot of **Cliff Richard** and similar 'pop' music but this changed, when still in 1963, singer **Billy Formby** left because the other members no longer wanted to play that 'soft music'.

The Abstracts
L to R: Barry Robinson, Ray Timmins, John Hodgson & Bill Cole

Glenn Smith took over the lead vocals and the group continued on as the **Heartbeats**.

Arthur Roberts was replaced by **John Hodgson** and, shortly after that, **Glenn Smith** also parted from the group. His replacement was **Alan Bradshaw** as the new rhythm guitarist.

Now that the changes had started, it was time for a new beginning and a new name – **The Excerts**. **Harry Millington,** for some reason, did not agree with this and left the group. **Alan Bradshaw** was also unhappy with the new direction and vacated his place for the returning **Arthur Roberts**.

Accordingly, in early 1964, the **Excerts** consisted of:

Brian McTigue	(voc/perc)
John Hodgson	(lg/voc)
Arthur Roberts	(rg)
Thomas Shire	(bg/voc)
Barry Robinson	(dr)

THE STARLIGHT ★ ☆ ★

MERSEYSIDE'S MOST EXCITING BEAT CLUB

THIS WEEK'S ATTRACTIONS
THURSDAY: SOUTHBANK 4 & THE STRETTONS
FRIDAY: THE EXCERTS — SATURDAY: THE PRESSMEN
SUNDAY: THE CITY BEATS   LIMITED FREE MEMBERSHIP
                          MINIMUM AGE 17
96b WAVERTREE ROAD, LIVERPOOL 7 (Entrance in June Street)

Unfortunately, it is not known which group **Thomas Shire** came from and **Brian McTigue** was apparently a newcomer to the scene. He, by the way, was the brother of **Frank McTigue** of the **Easybeats**.

The **Excerts** became very popular locally and also started to play the clubs in downtown Liverpool.

In the middle of 1964, the group took part in a Beat contest at the 'Cavern' and won which, besides the prize and a sensational parade through the city centre, of course meant further bookings at the most popular music club of that time. Their first full time appearance at the 'Cavern' was in October 1964 and, from then on they played the famous cellar quite regularly throughout 1965.

In late 1964 or early 1965, the **Excerts** went into **Alan Cheetham's** A.G.C. studio in Stockport and cut an interesting demo with the title, "24 Manhattan Place", which was written by **John Hodgson**. The flipside featured a **John Lee Hooker** number, "Crawling Kingsnake".

This demo was not followed by an official record and so it did not help the group's popularity.

Ray Timmins replaced **Barry 'Basher' Robinson**, who left for a short stint with **Gerry De Ville & the City**

TOMMY SHIRE   BRIAN McTIGUE   BARRY ROBINSON   JOHN HODGSON   ALBY BRADSHAW
BASS GUITAR   LEAD SINGER   DRUMS   LEAD GUITAR   RHYTHM GUITAR

The Excerts

Kings. After that, he formed his own group under the name of **The Sect** but, after their first appearance at the 'Cavern', the name, following a **Bob Wooler** suggestion, was changed to **The Kop**.

For unknown reasons, **Brian McTigue** left the **Excerts** in early 1966 and apparently quit show business. The group continued on as a four-piece with all of the members sharing the vocals.

They changed their name to **Georgie's Germs** and appeared under that name for the first time at re-opening night of the 'Cavern' on the 23rd July 1966.

Towards the end of that year, **Barry Robinson** returned and took over his old place again, replacing **Ray Timmins**. Nothing was ever heard of **Ray Timmins** again.

Georgie's Germs continued to play regularly at the 'Cavern' until they split up sometime in 1967. **John Hodgson** and **Barry Robinson** stayed together and formed the **George King Group** with the ex-**Easybeats** members, **Frank McTigue** (voc/bg) and **Jimmy Doran** (voc/rg).

This line-up did not last for too long. **John Hodgson** went on to play with the **Almost Blues** and was replaced by **Frank Townsend**, also formerly with the **Easybeats**, and prior to joining the **Excerts,** he had played in other groups.

The **George King Group** did not last for too long after this and broke up when **Barry Robinson** also left and joined the **Almost Blues**.

Later, **John Hodgson** played with the great Country Rock group, **Kenny Johnson & Northwind**, where he met up with his old mate, **Arthur Roberts** again.

Barry 'Basher' Robinson later became a member of the group, **Faith**, where he played for a very long time.

Thomas Shire apparently quit show business after **Georgie's Germs** had disbanded and he sadly died of cancer, aged 32.

Discography :

24 Manhattan Place / Crawling Kingsnake   **UK- AGC - acetate / 1964**

THE EXCHECKERS

This band was formed in Chester in the early Sixties and, after a short time, turned professional as they were apparently doing very well with plenty of appearances in their hometown, the Beat-metropolis, Liverpool and also in the Manchester area.

In the original line-up the **Excheckers** consisted of the following musicians:

Peter Johnsson	(voc/lg)
Phillip Blackwell	(p/voc)
John Pickett	(bg)
George Roberts	(dr)

George Roberts was a former member of **Jeannie & the Big Guys**, who were originally known as the **Pacemakers** (not to be confused with **Gerry & the Pacemakers**) and, for a short time, as **Four Hits & A Miss**.

In 1964, the **Excheckers** were signed to Decca and a little later their first single, "All The World Is Mine",

The Excheckers - original line up

was released. A nice Beat record which, unfortunately, did not achieve the success that it deserved and so did not help the group's popularity.

The **Excheckers** then went to Germany for an extended period and, during this time, they were signed to Dt. Vogue. During their stay over there, they recorded the German versions of "Memphis Tennessee" and "Big Bad John" on a single in 1965, of which the latter song is more than similar to "Unhappy Girls" of the **Searchers** on their 'Sugar & Spice' album.

For that single, as well as for the follow-up "Boys", which was also sung in German and coupled with a song of **Shorty Miller & the Raylads**, the **Excheckers,** by request of the record company, had changed their name into the **Liverpool Beats**.

It is an interesting fact that Dt. Vogue also released an album by the **Excheckers** using the pseudonym of the **Liverpool Beats** titled, 'This Is Liverpool', which allegedly was a live-recording from Liverpool's 'Iron Door'.

In this connection, it is important to point out that these **Liverpool Beats** were not identical to the group of the same name that released the album, 'The New Merseyside-Sound', on the American 'Rondo' label, because that group probably consisted of studio musicians who used the name **Billy Pepper & the Pepperpots** which, most probably was a session-group.

The German album, 'This Is Liverpool', featuring the Chester group, the **Excheckers** as the **Liverpool Beats,** is a very rare and extremely desirable collectors' item today, just like their singles in the German language.

The **Excheckers** as the **Liverpool Beats** were also featured on the two Swiss compilations, 'Beat' and 'Yeah Yeah', in 1964 on the Elite Special label with the songs, "Let's Get Together" and "Walking The Dog".

Also, under the name of the **Liverpool Beats,** they can be found on the German compilation, 'Original Beat aus England' from 1964 with the songs, "Poison Ivy" and "Hello Josephine", which were both taken from their live album.

On this obscure compilation on the Pop label, a total of eight numbers were featured under the name of the **Liverpool Beats**, but only the song, "Don't Let Me Be Misunderstood", might have been played by the

Excheckers. Even that does not seem too probable because the sound is totally different from their other recordings. The other songs under the **Liverpool Beats** name, "Lucille", "Tutti Frutti", "Rip It Up" and "Mean Woman Blues" were taken from the live-album of **Freddie Starr & the Starr Boys**, and the song, "I'll Never Find Another You", was done by an unknown group with female lead-vocals and has absolutely no connection to the **Liverpool Beats** or **Excheckers**, respectively.

However, on one of their last appearances at the 'Star Palast', the **Excheckers** were on the same bill as **Freddie Starr & the Starr Boys**, who still had a few weeks left to play in Germany.

The drummer for **Freddie Starr & the Starr Boys - Aynsley Dunbar** for some reason desperately wanted to return to Liverpool and, so it happened in the end, the two drummers swapped groups.

George Roberts continued to play with **Freddie Starr & the Starr-Boys** in Germany, while **Aynsley Dunbar** returned with the **Excheckers** to Merseyside.

On his return to Liverpool, **George Roberts** initially became the roadie for the **Takers** but then he joined the **Delmont Four**.

Aynsley Dunbar was the former drummer with the **Merseysippi Jazz Band** and **Derry Wilkie & the Pressmen**, after that he joined **Freddie Starr & the Starr Boys** (also known as the **Flamingoes**).

Probably with him on drums, the **Excheckers** soon went back to Germany where they were signed to Ariola and their first single on that German label was "Buzz, Buzz, Buzz", which, in spite of the not too intelligent title, was a great Beat record with an incredible drive.

It sold quite well but did not get any chart honours, just like their follow-up, "Mama Didn't Know" of 1965, which was a little bit too commercial and not as strong as their preceding release. These Ariola recordings were released under the name of the **Excheckers**.

There is nothing known about further releases on the European market and, after their return to England, the **Excheckers** continued to perform for some time. However, probably before their final Ariola single, **John Bell** had replaced **Aynsley Dunbar**, who in March 1965 had become a member of the **Mojos** and, after that, he played with **John Mayall's Bluesbreakers**, the **Aynsley Dunbar Retaliation**, **Journey**, **Jefferson Starship** and other famous groups.

Not long after this the **Excheckers** disbanded, none of the individual members appeared on the scene again.

Discography :

as **The Excheckers** :

All The World Is Mine / It's All Over	UK- Decca F.11871 / 1964

different German releases :

Buzz, Buzz, Buzz / You Are My New Love	G- Ariola 18.596 AT / 1964
Mama Didn't Know / Do The Bird	G- Ariola 18.598 AT / 1965

as **The Liverpool Beats** :

Memphis Tennessee / Big Bad John	G-Dt.Vogue DV 14173 / 1964
Boys / <u>Shorty Miller & the Raylads</u> : Hey, Hey Shorty	G-Dt.Vogue DV 14201 / 1964

LP as **'The Liverpool Beats'** :

THIS IS LIVERPOOL	G-Dt. Vogue LDV 17005 / 1964

- I Wanna Be Your Man / Roll Over Beethoven / 24 Hours From Tulsa / My Prayer /

My Baby Left Me / I'm Talking About You / Here's Hoping / Little Queenie /

Poison Ivy / Memphis Tennessee / Thou Shalt Not Steal / Hello Josephine

(recorded live at the 'Iron Door', Liverpool)

Tracks on compilation albums :

as **'The Liverpool Beats'** :

"Walking The Dog"	on 'Beat'	CH- Elite Special SOLP-S-33-250 / 1964
"Let's Get Together"	on 'Yeah Yeah'	CH- Elite Special SOLP-S-33-251 / 1964
"Poison Ivy"	on 'Original Beat aus England'	G- Pop Z 10006 / 1964
"Hello Josephine"	on 'Original Beat aus England'	G- Pop Z 10006 / 1964
"Don't Let Me Be Misunderstood"	on 'Original Beat aus England'	G- Pop Z 10006 / 1964

(***please note that it is not certain if the song, "Don't Let Me Be Misunderstood", was really played by the **Liverpool Beats** as it was too different in sound. All the other songs which were included on the German compilation under the name of **The Liverpool Beats** were certainly not played by them. - see story for detailed information)

THE EXECUTIONERS

This group was formed in the early Sixties somewhere on the Wirral, probably in Birkenhead.

Alan Webster (lg), **Rodney Lewis** (bg) and drummer **Alexander Carroll** went under the name of the **Threebeats** in 1961. A few months later, they added a rhythm guitar to the line-up and changed their name to the **Executioners**.

They became very popular locally and soon began performing at the major Birkenhead venues such as the 'Majestic' and the 'Cubik', as well as the Tower Ballroom in New Brighton.

Obviously, it was time to conquer the Liverpool scene and on the 22nd March 1963, the **Executioners** had their first appearance at the 'Cavern'. Even though they had established themselves, the lead guitarist and singer **Alan Webster** left the group in 1963 and became a member of the **Young Ones** from Birkenhead before he disappeared from the scene. He apparently emigrated to Australia later on and it is believed that he continued in the music business down there.

The **Executioners**, as they were named from the beginning, continued in the following line-up:

Rod Lewis	**(voc/bg)**
Ray Milne	**(rg/voc)**
Graham Dixon	**(lg/voc)**
Alexander Carroll	**(dr)**

Alexander Carroll did not stay for too long and was replaced by **Frank McLaughlin** on drums, who came from the **Atomics**.

This line-up of the **Executioners** became very popular in downtown Liverpool and started to play regularly at the 'Cavern', as well as at many of the other Merseyside venues but without making much headway.

However, in 1964, they were chosen, along with other groups including the **Four Clefs** and **Reds Inc.**, to be part of the new Merseybeat compilation, 'Cavern Alive', and were recorded by **John Schroeder** for Oriole. Unfortunately,

this record, for mysterious reasons, was not released and therefore, it is only known that **Chan Romero**'s, "Hippy Hippy Shake" was amongst the songs that were recorded by the **Executioners**. This non-release could have been the reason for **Graham Dixon** leaving the group and he continued to play in various dance bands. His replacement was a certain **Richard Mumford**, a former member of the **Tributes**.

It was probably this line-up that recorded a demo-disc with the **Alan Webster** original, "Time Will Tell", for **Brian Epstein** in the Kensington studios of **Percy Phillips**. A nice song that later was covered by other Merseybeat groups but it did not help the **Executioners** at that time.

They continued to play on the Merseyside scene and had a large following but nothing is known about further recordings or any outstanding success.

Towards the end of 1965 they disbanded. **Rod Lewis** continued to play in a cabaret-duo and it's believed that sometime later **Richard Mumford** was a member of the **Pathfinders**, before he quit showbiz.

Ray Milne became a fireman and sadly died a few years ago of cancer.

Frank McLaughlin, after the split with the **Executioners**, disappeared from the scene for a while, but then he was back with a group called the **New Executioners**, which besides him consisted of **Terry Amos** (lg/voc), **Dave Ward** (rg/voc) and **Chris Kelly** (bg/voc).

This band was not that successful and did not survive for too long. **Terry Amos** became a member of the **Intruders**, while **Frank McLaughlin** joined a Country group by the name of **The Texas Reds**, with whom he also toured the American military bases in Germany.

Discography :

Time Will Tell / I've Been There   **UK- Kensington acetate / 1964**

In 1964, before this acetate was cut, the **Executioners** were recorded by **John Schroeder** with three or four songs for the new Oriole Merseybeat compilation, 'Cavern Alive', which in the end was never released. It is only known that **Hippy Hippy Shake** was amongst the songs that were recorded.

THE EYES

This group was formed in Liverpool in 1964 and, like the **Liverbirds** and **Ian & the Zodiacs**, they had a long residency in Germany, where they became popular and successful on the so-called 'Star-Club' scene.

In spite of this, they were a real Merseybeat group consisting of the following musicians:

Paddy Chambers	(lg/voc)
John Frankland	(rg/voc)
Lewis Collins	(bg/voc)
Gibson Kemp	(dr/voc)

All members were experienced musicians who had previously played in other well known groups.

The Eyes - original line-up with Lewis Collins

Paddy Chambers was a former member of **Faron's Flamingos** and the **Big Three**, while **John Frankland** came from **King Size Taylor & the Dominoes**.

Lewis Collins had played with the **Renegades** from Liverpool, the **Kansas City Five** and the **Georgians** - in the first two groups as the drummer, before he switched to the bass guitar.

Gibson Kemp had started his career with the **Night People**, before he became a member of **Tommy & the Satellites**, the **Memphis Three** and after that he played with **Rory Storm & the Hurricanes** and **King Size Taylor & the Dominoes**.

Lewis Collins left to return to Liverpool where he joined the **Mojos** and he was replaced in the **Eyes** by the German **Klaus Voormann**.

In this line-up the single, "She", was recorded, with the 'Star-Club' standard, "Peanut Butter", on the reverse side. This record, in contrast to the musical quality of the group, was not very good and did not become a great success in Germany, where it was released exclusively.

But prior to this single, the **Eyes** had already been in the studio where the songs, "Another Saturday Night", "Love Is A Swinging Thing", "Twenty Flight Rock" and "Baby Baby" were recorded. "Baby Baby", by the way, was the **Supremes** hit success, "Where Did Our Love Go".

These songs were released on the two Swiss compilations, 'Beat' and 'Yeah Yeah', on the Elite Special label.

John Frankland was replaced for a short time by **Johnny Phillips** (sax), who came from the **Roadrunners**. When **John Frankland** returned to the **Eyes**, **Johnny Phillips** went on to play with the **Krew** (aka **The Crew**). When **John Frankland** quit show business in 1965 to get married to a girl from Hamburg, the others continued as a trio under the name of **Paddy, Klaus & Gibson**.

They were signed by PYE and, in 1965, their first single was released with "I Wanna Know", which was the English version of the winning song of the French Eurovision Song Contest "N'avoue Jamais", by **Guy Mardel**. Correspondingly, it was quite an unusual record for a group like **Paddy, Klaus & Gibson** and there was no connection to the roots of Merseybeat in this release.

Their following single, "No Good Without You Baby", was better, but also not really successful, just like the third and final release by the band, "Teresa", although this was a very nice and melodic song, even if it was not 'hard' Beat anymore.

It seems that **Brian Epstein**, who had taken over the group's management, tried to make something like the new **Walker Brothers** out of **Paddy, Klaus & Gibson**, but this failed in the end.

The trio disbanded in 1966 and **Klaus Voormann**, who had also designed the cover of the **Beatles** album 'Revolver', became a member of **Manfred Mann**. After that he was sometimes regarded as a fifth member of the **Beatles** because he had played on some sessions with them but, of course, without becoming a steady member.

Gibson Kemp joined **Lee Curtis & the All Stars** for a short time in one of their last line-ups, but then became a member of the 'Star-Club' band, the **Giants,** from Hamburg. Around this time, he also had a solo single released on the German Polydor label.

Later, he played in the backing group of the **Les Humphries Singers** before he became a studio musician and then a producer for Phonogram, first in Hamburg and then in London, before he went to Australia. He later returned to Hamburg where he is still living today.

Paddy Chambers joined the **Escorts**, where he played until the group split up in 1967. He then became a member of **Big John's Rock 'n' Roll Circus** and, after that, played with **Sinbad** and then led **Paddy Chambers & the Java Jive** until he sadly died much too young in 2000.

Lewis Collins later had a successful career as an actor (one of his roles was 'Bodie' in the British TV show 'The Professionals') but, in 1983, he started to record some solo singles again from time to time.

Discography :

as **The Eyes** :

She / Peanut Butter   **G - Star-Club 148.519 / 1965**

Tracks on compilation albums :

Baby Baby (Where did our love go)	on 'Beat'	CH- Elite Special SOLP-S-33-250 / 1964
Another Saturday Night	on 'Beat'	CH- Elite Special SOLP-S-33-250 / 1964
Love Is A Swinging Thing	on 'Yeah Yeah'	CH- Elite Special SOLP-S-33-251 / 1964
Twenty flight Rock	on 'Yeah Yeah'	CH- Elite Special SOLP-S-33-251 / 1964

as **Paddy, Klaus & Gibson** :

I Wanna Know / I Tried	UK - PYE 7N 15906 / 1965
No Good Without You Baby / Rejected	UK - PYE 7N 17060 / 1966
Teresa / Quick Before They Catch Us	UK - PYE 7N 17112 / 1966

Gibson Kemp – solo :

Make Love Not War / My Magic Room   **G - Polydor 52975 / 1967**

(***please note that the A-side of **Gibson Kemp's** solo single was an instrumental soundtrack number for the film of the same name, which was written by **Gibson Kemp**. The B-side is sung by **Gibson Kemp**, but was recorded together with the **Giants** from Hamburg and had been released previously, also in 1967, by the **Giants** - on the reverse side of their single, "Even The Bad Times Are Good" - Polydor 52963)

FARON'S FLAMINGOS

This group originated from the **Hi-Hats**, a Skiffle group formed in a Liverpool bicycle club at the end of the Fifties. The **Hi-Hats** then evolved into the **Ravens**, a Beat group that initially appeared with **Mike McPhillips** as their vocalist under the name **Robin & the Ravens**.

Mike McPhillips was replaced by **Billy 'Faron' Ruffley**, who had previously sung with the **Tempest Tornadoes** under the name of **Faron & the TTs**. There were probably also some more changes in the line-up and, following a suggestion by **Bob Wooler**, the name of the group was changed from the **Ravens** into **Faron & the Flamingos**. A little later they became **Faron's Flamingos**.

Within a very short time, the group became one of the local attractions - in the following line-up:

Billy 'Faron' Ruffley	(voc)
Nicky Crouch	(lg/voc)
Billy Jones	(rg/voc)
Eric London	(bg/voc)
Trevor Morais	(dr)

Trevor Morais, a really great drummer, was a former member of the **Cadillacs**, while it seems likely that **Nicky Crouch**, **Eric London** and **Billy Jones** were the remaining members of the original group.

In January 1962, **Eric London** left to join **Group One** and his replacement in **Faron's Flamingos** was **Dave 'Mushy' Cooper**, a former member of the **Topspots** (which was not the group of the same name that backed **Ricky Gleason**). After the **Topspots**, **Dave Cooper** had played with **Bob Evans & the Five Shillings** and **The Vegas Five**. All three groups were, in some way, predecessor bands of the **Undertakers**.

Pam Conelly then joined **Faron's Flamingos** as an additional singer, but left a little later, as did **Billy Jones**. Both disappeared from the scene.

The new members were **Paddy Chambers** (rg/voc), who had formerly played with the **Creoles** and **Steve Bennett & the Syndicate**, and **Barbara Harrison** (voc), who had previously sung with the **Hi-Cats** and **Johnny Templer & the Hi-Cats**.

When, in January 1963, **Dave Cooper** left and joined the **Pawns**, 'Faron' himself took over on bass guitar, and the band continued as a quartet, **Barbara Harrison** also left to join **Danny Havoc & the Ventures**, who later became the **Secrets**. After that she sang with the **Kansas City Five**.

Shortly after that change, **Faron's Flamingos** were signed by Oriole and featured on the legendary compilation albums, 'This Is Merseybeat' Vol. 1 and Vol. 2 with the songs, "Let's Stomp", "Shake Sherry",

"Talkin' 'bout You" and "So Fine". The first two of these songs were later released on a single but, unfortunately, had no chart success, although it had a great 'rough' Beat, just like the follow-up, "See If She Cares" with its superb B-side, "Do You Love Me", which a little later became a tremendous hit for **Brian Poole & the Tremeloes**.

FARONS FLAMINGOS

Faron's Flamingos disbanded in early 1964, when **'Faron'**, also called 'The Panda Footed Prince Of Prance' and **Paddy Chambers** joined the **Big Three**.

After that, **'Faron'** emigrated to France where he was a member of a group called **Blue Suede**.

Paddy Chambers later played with the **Eyes** (that evolved into **Paddy, Klaus & Gibson**), the **Escorts**, **Big John's Rock 'n 'Roll Circus**, **Sinbad** and finally he appeared with his own group under the name, **Paddy Chambers & the Java Jive** – until he sadly died in 2000.

Nicky Crouch became a member of the **Mojos** or **Stu James & the Mojos** respectively, before he disappeared from the scene for years. Then he came back with a group called **Ace Of Clubs** and, in the early Nineties, played with the re-formed **Cliff Roberts' Rockers** before he disappeared again for a while and then re-formed the **Mojos**, which includes **Eric London** and other well-known Merseybeat musicians and is still playing today.

Trevor Morais initially formed his own band under the name of the **Trevor Morais Combo** who also backed Manchester songstress, **Lorraine Gray** for a short time. After that he joined **Ian Crawford & the Boomerangs** from Manchester, but returned to Liverpool and had a short spell with **Rory Storm & the Hurricanes**. He then went back to Manchester and became a member of the **Peddlers** where he played until they split up in the Seventies. He appeared again in the **Elkie Brooks** backing group, and after that as a member of **Stealer's Wheel**.

Billy 'Faron' Ruffley returned to Liverpool in the mid-Seventies and formed the new **Faron's Flamingos**, who were also featured on the revival sampler, 'Mersey Survivors' in 1978 (UK- Raw RWLP 104) with the songs, "Some Other Guy" and "Let's Twist Again". But this group had more of a session character and, besides 'Faron', only **Chris Evens** was known.

From that session a single was also released with a strong version of "Bring It On Home To Me" coupled with a totally disappointing version of **Eddie Cochran**'s "Come On Everybody" (UK-Raw 27).

After that, 'Faron' had a steady line-up again for his **Flamingos** which, at one time, also included **Brian Jones** (sax) who in the Sixties was a member of the **Undertakers** and later played with the **Glitter Band**. However, **Brian Jones** left the **Flamingos** and returned to **Gary Glitter** before joining the great Liverpool Soul band **Y-Kickamoocow**. Later, he was a member of **Nighttrain** and he also appeared with the re-formed **Kirkbys** and his old group, the **Undertakers**.

In 1987, **Faron's Flamingos** toured Germany under the wing of **Horst Fascher**, the former manager of the legendary 'Star-Club' in Hamburg.

'Faron', whose singing was still as good as in the Sixties, presented himself to the audience in a very professional manner and did full credit to his nickname as the 'Panda Footed Prince Of Prance'.

There was no doubt he was still a Rock 'n' Roller from tip to toe, supported by a good group with the line-up of **Phil Melia** (lg/voc), **Graham Price** (bg), **Steven Robertson** (sax) and **Derek Smallridge** (dr).

Phil Melia was a former member of **Mojo Filter**, while **Graham Price** came from **Supercharge** and, **Derek Smallridge** was also a pioneer of Liverpool's music scene.

But the line-up of the band kept steadily changing and **Phil Melia**, who later played with the **Pete Best Band**, was replaced by **Steve Roberts**, the younger brother of **Cliff Roberts**, the leader of the pioneering Liverpool group **Cliff Roberts' Rockers**.

Graham Price was replaced by **Dennis Swale** who, in the Sixties, had been with groups such as **Terry & the Tuxedos**, the **Croupiers**, the **Four Dimensions** and the **Fyx**.

The preceding line-up had been great but this new one was excellent and exactly what is expected of a Rock 'n' Roll band. Unfortunately, it only lasted until 1989 and then **Steven Robertson** joined **Geoff Nugent's Undertakers**. **Steve Roberts** changed to the **Fourmost**, then later joined his brother's band the **Cliff Roberts' Rockers**. **Dennis Swale** started an agency before forming a new band under the name of the **Dimensions** and **Derek Smallridge** joined a circus orchestra.

But 'Faron' got a good band together again under the name of **Faron's Flamingos**, which also included **Chris Evens** on guitar again, as well as **Bernie Rogers** on drums who, in the Sixties, had played with **Lee Curtis & the All Stars** and **Denny Seyton & the Sabres**.

In 1992, 'Faron' had a heart attack and was seriously ill for some time but, after that, he was back with his band again, playing the bass guitar and jumping around as before - until he had a second heart attack in 1996.

After that, he never got a steady group together again and he only appears from time to time at the 'MerseyCats' events, where he sings with various groups.

Discography :

See If She Cares / Do You Love Me	UK- Oriole CB 1834 / 1963
Shake Sherry / Give Me Time	UK- Oriole CB 1867 / 1963
Let's Stomp / <u>Rory Storm & the Hurricanes</u>: I Can Tell	UK- Columbia 43018 / 1964

Tracks on compilation albums :

Let's Stomp	on 'This Is Merseybeat' Vol.1	UK- Oriole PS 40047 / 1963
Talkin' 'bout You	on 'This Is Merseybeat' Vol.1	UK- Oriole PS 40047 / 1963
Shake Sherry	on 'This Is Merseybeat' Vol.2	UK- Oriole PS 40048 / 1963
So Fine	on 'This Is Merseybeat' Vol.2	UK- Oriole PS 40048 / 1963
Do You Love Me	on 'Group-Beat '63'	UK- Realm RM 149 / 1963
See If She Cares	on 'Group-Beat '63'	UK- Realm RM 149 / 1963
Let's Stomp	on EP "Take Six"	UK- Oriole EP 7080 / 1963

THE FOUR CLEFS

This was certainly one of the most important and popular groups on Liverpool's early Merseybeat scene. Although they never had a breakthrough or any major success, the **Four Clefs** were always there where it happened and they always placed well in the monthly popularity poll run by the 'Mersey Beat' newspaper.

Formed in 1961 in the area of **Crosby**, this group, besides the normal standards, concentrated mainly on **Buddy Holly** material and were often named as 'Liverpool's own Crickets'.

In their original line-up the **Four Clefs** consisted of:

Arthur Raynor	(voc/g)
Norman Trump	(g)
Frank Morris	(bg)
John Bedson	(dr)

John Bedson was the first to leave, he became a member of the short lived **Roadrunners (II)**, that had nothing in common with the popular Liverpool R&B group of the same name.

When the **Roadrunners (II)** broke up, he joined the **Challengers** who, at that time, backed **Tommy Quickly** and who later amalgamated with coloured singer, **Steve Aldo** as **Steve Aldo & the Challengers**, but that is another story in this book. **John Bedson** then joined the **Harlems** and later played with the **Myths**.

His place on drums with the **Four Clefs** was taken by **Jimmy Tushingham**, who was apparently a newcomer on the scene.

In 1962, **Norman Trump** left the group on a temporary basis and for approximately three months was replaced by **Derek Watling**. But then he returned to the **Four Clefs** and took his old place again while **Derek Watling** disappeared from the scene.

Les Ackerley, owner of the famous 'Iron Door', took over the management of the group and the **Four Clefs**, of course, became regulars at his club where they were recorded in late 1962 or early 1963. This was around the same time as the **Searchers** also recorded there and, as a result of that session, the **Searchers** obtained a recording contract with PYE, while the **Four Clefs**, for some reason, were not signed to a recording company.

The **Four Clefs** 'Iron Door' recording was most probably cut on acetate but nobody knows what happened to it and it is therefore not known which songs were recorded at that session.

In 1964 the **Four Clefs** were recorded again, this time by **John Schroeder** for the planned Oriole sampler, 'Cavern Alive', but this was never released and so it is only known that "Memphis Tennessee" was amongst the four or five songs that were recorded by the **Four Clefs**.

A little later, the group was offered a European tour but **Arthur Raynor** decided to leave the group and join **Chick Graham & the Coasters**, where he took over the lead vocals when **Chick Graham** left the group. When the **Coasters** split in 1965, **Arthur Raynor** became a solo entertainer on the cabaret circuit where he is highly regarded and still continues to perform today under the stage name **Tony Marsh**.

After he left, the **Four Clefs** disbanded totally and **Frank Morris** and **Norman Trump** apparently quit the music business. **Jimmy Tushingham** went on to join **Rory Storm & the Hurricanes**. After that he was a member of the **Connoisseurs** until they finally disbanded in 1969.

Discography :

Nothing was ever released by the **Four Clefs** but, in 1963, they were recorded at the 'Iron Door' and from that session most probably an acetate was cut that went missing and so it is not known which songs were recorded. In 1964, the **Four Clefs** were chosen to be featured on the Oriole sampler, 'Cavern Alive' and recorded four or five numbers under the wing of **John Schroeder**. But this record was not released in the end and so it is only known that **Memphis Tennessee** was amongst the recorded songs.

THE FOUR JUST MEN

Although counted as part of the Manchester scene, this group actually was a true Liverpool outfit.

In 1961, a certain **Demetrius Christopholus** took part in a vocalist contest at the Grafton Ballroom in Liverpool and won. Encouraged by this success, he asked some friends to form a group with him and a few months later **Dee Fenton & the Silhouettes** had their first appearance – in a line-up with vocalist **Dee Fenton** (aka **Demetrius Christopholus**), **Peter Turner** (g), **Harry Bear** (bg) and **Larry Arendes** (aka **Larry King**) on drums.

Dee Fenton & the Silhouettes

At the end of 1962 guitarist, **John Kelman** joined the group, having formerly played with the **Dons** and the **Five Stars**. **Harry Bear** left and **Peter Turner** took over on bass guitar.

At that time, **Dee Fenton & the Silhouettes** were really popular in Liverpool and always placed within the first 20 groups in the popularity polls of the 'Mersey Beat' newspaper. They became much more successful when 'Kennedy Street Enterprises' took over their management and made them change their name into **Four Just Men** and to settle down in Manchester in the following line-up:

Demetrius Christopholus	**(voc/rg)**
John Kelman	**(lg/voc)**
Peter Turner	**(bg)**
Larry King	**(dr)**

The singer's name leaves no doubt that he was of Greek origin, just like **Savva Hercules**, the singer of the Liverpool beat group **Savva & the Democrats**.

In 1963, **John Kelman** left to go back to Liverpool and joined **Freddie Starr & the Midnighters** that, almost without exception, consisted of former members of the **Five Stars**.

He was replaced by **Harold 'Lally' Stott** from Prescot who had formerly played with the **Phantoms** and the **Vaqueros**.

But still in 1964, **John Kelman** returned to the **Four Just Men** and took over his old place again, while **Lally Stott** went to Liverpool to join the **Denny Seyton Group**. **Lally Stott** later went to Italy with the **Motowns** and became a very successful songwriter, but that is a different story that can be followed under **Denny Seyton & the Sabres** in this book.

The **Four Just Men** recorded the original, "Half Past Five" for Decca in 1964, but this was not released. They also wrote and played the theme music for TV's 'Friday Night' and maybe because of this they caught the attention of EMI where they were signed to the Parlophone label.

Their first single, "That's My Baby", was a real classic Merseybeat record, coupled with the very nice "Things Will Never Be The Same". In spite of it's quality, it failed to make the charts and the deserved breakthrough.

"That's My Baby" somehow became quite popular in Germany, where it was covered by various German beat groups, although the record was never released over there.

When the single was just freshly released, another group claimed the name of the **Four Just Men** as their own. Accordingly, the Liverpool outfit changed its name to **Just Four Men** and under that name "That's My Baby" was re-released in 1964.

Peter Turner left and apparently quit show business. His replacement in **Just Four Men** was **Keith Shepherd**, who came from Manchester's **Johnny Martin & the Tremors**.

Probably with this line-up, their next single, "There's Not One Thing", was released – again, a great song coupled with a great B-side, "Don't Come Any Closer", but also again, without any further success.

Keith Shepherd left and was replaced by **Stuart Sirett**, something of a musical globetrotter, who formerly had played with the Manchester groups, **Bing Stanley & the Dominator Four**, the **Javalins**, **Deke Rivers & the Big Sound**, **Wayne Fontana & the Jets**, **Johnny Peters & the Crestas** and **Johnny Peters & the J.P.s**.

It was not really surprising that he did not stay for too long and then he joined the **Black Cat Bones**. After that he played with **Wayne Fontana & the Opposition** and then in a cabaret duo called **Musicbox**.

The **Just Four Men** were joined by **Barry Ashall** and, probably with this line-up, the band was offered the **Burt Bacharach** song, "Trains And Boats And Planes" for their next release.

The group recorded it but, in the end, did not want it to be released. It was given to **Billy J. Kramer** and became a huge hit. The originals, "Tomorrow", "Norman Needs A Man", "I Just Can't Make Up My Mind", "Thinkin' About Your Love" and "Shelter Of Your Arms" were probably also recorded at these recording sessions, but never released.

Just Four Men went on a 30-day tour through the UK with **Del Shannon** and the **Shangri-Las** and, after that, on a short tour with the **Rolling Stones**. This was followed by a six-week engagement together with **David Garrick** in Paris, but none of this brought the sought after breakthrough.

When they came back from France, they joined singer **Pete MacLaine** for a time under the name **Pete MacLaine & the Four Just Men**.

Pete MacLaine, of course, was very popular on the Manchester scene, being the former singer with **Pete MacLaine & the Dakotas** and **Pete MacLaine & the Clan**. This new connection did not record and when the **Four Just Men** separated from **Pete MacLaine**, the group decided on a fresh approach with a new sound and a new name. So, in 1966, the legendary freak-beat outfit, **Wimple Winch** was born. The group was signed to Fontana and the first release under their new name was "What's Been Done", coupled with "I Really Love You". Both songs were still Merseybeat at its best, but on the follow-up, "Save My Soul", the psychedelic touch was already there. That single hit the top of the local charts and

remained there for ten weeks but was not matched by sales in the rest of the country, for whatever reason.

The unusual "Rumble On Mersey Square South" was their third release and is very often named as their best single, but the public at large apparently did not like it, as it took them nowhere.

It was probably in early 1968 that **Wimple Winch** disbanded and the musicians went their separate ways.

John Kelman joined **Terry Rowland & the Explosions** for a short time, but then it seems he went back to Liverpool and quit show business, as did **Barry Ashall**.

Dee Christopholus was later featured in the musical 'Hair' but then concentrated on writing songs and later also became a record producer for the GTO label.

Larry King joined a band called **Sponge**, who were also the backing group for **Dave Berry** for a while. This group, still with **Larry King**, later changed its name to **Pacific Drift** and recorded one single and an interesting progressive album, 'Feelin' Free' for Deram in 1970.

When this group split, **Lawrence Arendes,** aka **Larry King**, concentrated on photography but also kept playing – later with **Mr. Suit**, the residential group at 'The Hangout' in Liverpool.

Discography :

as **The Four Just Men** :

That's My Baby / Things Will Never Be The Same	**UK- Parlophone R 5186 / 1964**

as **Just Four Men** :

That's My Baby / Things Will Never Be The Same	**UK- Parlophone R 5208 / 1964**
There's Not One Thing / Don't Come Any Closer	**UK- Parlophone R 5241 / 1965**

Different US-release (as **The Four Just Men**) :

There's Not One Thing / <u>Freddie & the Dreamers</u> : Send A Letter To Me	**US- Tower 163 / 1965**

Tracks on compilation albums :

That's My Baby	on 'I'm Telling You Now'	**US- Tower DT 5003 / 1965**
Things Will Never Be The Same	on 'I'm Telling You Now'	**US- Tower DT 5003 / 1965**

as **Wimple Winch** :

What's Been Done / I Really Love You	**UK- Fontana TF 703 / 1966**
Save My Soul / Everybody's Worried About Tomorrow	**UK- Fontana TF 718 / 1966**
Rumble on Mersey Square South / Typical British Workmanship	**UK- Fontana TF 781 / 1966**

(*** please note that some copies of the last single were miss-pressings and had **"Atmospheres"** as B-side)

Unreleased tracks:

as **Four Just Men** or **Just Four Men** :

'Friday Night'	TV-music theme recording / 1964
'Half Past Five'	UK- Decca demo / 1964
Nightmare / Working Day Blues	UK- ??? acetate / 1964

Further unreleased tracks from Parlophone recording sessions are

"Trains And Boats And Planes", "Tomorrow", "Norman Needs A Man",

"I Just Can't Make Up My Mind","Thinkin' About Your Love", "Shelter Of Your Arms" - probably all from 1965

as **Wimple Winch** :

"Atmospheres", "Three Little Teddy-Bears", "You're A Big Girl Now", "Coloured Glass", "Those Who Wait", "Sagitarius" and "The Last Hooray" - probably all from the Fontana recording sessions in 1966/67

"Marmalade Hair", "Bluebell Wood", "Lollipop Minds", "Pumpkin pie" - all independent recordings from 1967

THE FOURMOST

It all started with the duo, **The Two Jays**, which was formed by **Brian O'Hara** and **Joey Bowers** in Liverpool in the late Fifties in the style of the **Everly Brothers**.

After that, both musicians had a short spell with one of **Gerry Marsden's** Skiffle groups before they formed a band under the name of **The Four Jays**. This name was changed to **The Four Mosts** a little later, following a suggestion by **Bob Wooler**.

When **Brian Epstein** took over their management in 1963, he shortened that name to the **Fourmost**. Shortly before the final name change, **Joey Bowers** (g/voc) left the group to join the **Connoiseurs** and, after that, he became a member of the **Cheaters**.

The Four Jays
L to R: Billy Hatton, Brian Redman, Mike Millward & Brian O'Hara

Accordingly in 1963, the **Fourmost** consisted of the following musicians:

Brian O'Hara	(voc/rg)
Mike Millward	(lg/voc)
Billy Hatton	(bg/voc)
Brian Redman	(dr)

Mike Millward was the new member of the **Fourmost**, having previously played with **Bob Evans' Five Shillings**.

Billy Hatton was a former member of the **Beat Cats**.

Brian Redman left to join **King Size Taylor & the Dominoes** and later played with **Sonny Webb & the Cascades** from which the internationally successful Country band, the **Hillsiders** evolved.

The new drummer with the **Fourmost** was **Dave Lovelady**, a former member of **Ian & the Zodiacs** and **King Size Taylor & the Dominoes**.

With this line-up, the group was signed by Parlophone and their first single, "Hello Little Girl", became a top 10 hit in 1963 when it climbed up to No. 9 in the charts.

This great debut success was followed by "I'm In Love" (No. 17 in 1963), "A Little Lovin' " (No. 6 in 1964), "How Can I Tell Her" (No. 33 in 1964), their good version of the Four Tops success, "Baby I Need Your Loving" (No. 24 in 1964), and the Leiber/Stoller composition, "Girls, Girls, Girls" (No. 33 in 1965), which was more comedy than Merseybeat.

However, the **Fourmost** had six big chart hits from their first seven singles, which was an outstanding success. Only "Everything In The Garden" (1965) did not enter the charts, although it was one of their better recordings.

In the meantime, the **Fourmost** were featured in the film, 'Ferry Cross The Mersey', with the song, "I Love You Too", which was included in both the British and German release of the corresponding soundtrack album.

In November 1965, the **Fourmost** had their first album out with the title, 'First and Fourmost', that showed them to be very varied in their music, which was not altogether positive. There were real rockers such as "The Girl Can't Help It" or "Heebie Jeebies", Soul influenced material like "The In-crowd", "Some Kind Of Wonderful" or "Something's Got A Hold On Me", Country songs including "Sure To Fall", really good Merseybeat such as "Till You Say You'll Be Mine" and the great "My Block", the swing number "Bound To Lose My Heart", and songs like "Girls, Girls, Girls" and "Baby Sittin' Boogie", which showed that the group's trend was more towards being a comedy band than a Beat group.

It can be said that the **Fourmost** were the first cabaret group on the Merseybeat scene although, in 1966, they released a nice Beat ballad with the Lennon/McCartney composition, "Here, There And Everywhere". But their follow-up to this, "Auntie Maggie's Remedy", was a real comedy song again, and only from the B-side, "Turn The Lights Down", could it be figured that this group originated from the Merseybeat scene.

In the meantime, **Mike Millward** had become ill with leukaemia and for a short time was replaced by **Bill Parkinson**. But he returned to the **Fourmost** and **Bill Parkinson** went on to become a member of **Chris Lamb & the Universals** and, after that, played with the **Circles**, who also sometimes backed **Screaming Lord Sutch** under the name of the **Savages**. He then joined the backing group of **Tom Jones** (what a contrast!) and became a successful songwriter. As such, he wrote "Mother Of Mine", which was a big international hit for **Neil Reid**.

In December 1965, **Mike Millward** left the **Fourmost** again because of his illness and sadly died a little later, which was a big shock for the entire Liverpool music scene, as he was a really likeable guy. He was replaced by **George Peckham**, a former member of Liverpool's **Renegades**, **Lee Curtis & the All Stars**, the **Pawns**, **Groups Inc.**, the **Kinsleys** and **Earl Royce & the Olympics**.

The Four Mosts

FORMERLY THE FOUR JAYS

BRO 3454
WAT 4338

When **George Peckham** left, **Ian Edwards**, who had just disbanded **Ian & the Zodiacs**, took over but a little later he joined the **Connoisseurs** and the original member, **Joey Bowers,** returned to the **Fourmost**.

In 1969, **Paul McCartney** produced the single, "Rosetta", with the **Fourmost** on the CBS label, quite a poor production and the better side on that record was the B-side, "Just Like Before". This record did not sell too well and had no chart success, nor did the far better "Apples, Peaches, Pumkin' Pie" from the previous year.

For the release of their next single, "Maxwell's Silver Hammer", the **Fourmost** used the name of **Format**. This, by the way, was the only single that was ever released by them in Germany but it never became a big seller. The follow-up, "Easy Squeeze", again did not make any progress on the record market and it was their final recording for CBS.

1972 saw the final single release by the **Fourmost** with the songs, "Goodnight Sweet Dreams" and "Memphis", on the obscure Phoenix label.

In 1975, the **Fourmost** released a second album entitled 'The Fourmost', which included studio versions of their live act, such as "Down At The Club", "I've Got You Under My Skin", "Save The Last Dance For Me", "Without You", "Rag Doll" and "Will You Still Love Me Tomorrow". This was not too bad, but also no 'knockout'.

The end for the **Fourmost** came in 1979, when **Joey Bowers**, **Bill Hatton** and **Dave Lovelady** decided to form the cabaret band, **Clouds**, which also included **Steve 'Tiger' Fleming** (org), who had formerly played with various Merseybeat groups including, **Mark Peters & the Cyclones**, **Mark Peters & the Silhouettes**, and later with the newly formed **Merseybeats**.

When **Clouds** split, **Steve Fleming** and **Dave Lovelady** joined the **Vince Earl Attraction**, where they played together with other well-known Merseybeat musicians for quite a long time.

Brian O'Hara amalgamated with another Liverpool group under the name of the **Fourmost** but, in 1982, he left that band and became a compere and solo entertainer in the cabaret scene until he sadly committed suicide in 1999. The group continued under the name of **The Fourmost** with a line-up of **Billy Haisman** (voc/bg), **Ronnie Hughes** (lg/voc), **Bernie Crossley** (rg/voc) and **John Campbell** (dr/voc).

But they were no longer a cabaret band and their live programme included the old hit songs of the **Fourmost**, as well as stuff of the **Beach Boys, Four Seasons**, and so on.

Prior to **Brian O'Hara's** death, the original **Fourmost** came together again a few times for the 'MerseyCats' organisation, but these were only occasional performances and they never gave the impression that they seriously tried a comeback. Maybe one day . . .

Discography :

Hello Little Girl / Just In Case	UK- Parlophone R 5056 / 1963
I'm In Love / Respectable	UK- Parlophone R 5078 / 1963
A Little Lovin' / Waiting For You	UK- Parlophone R 5128 / 1964
How Can I Tell Her / You Got That Way	UK- Parlophone R 5157 / 1964
Baby I Need Your Loving / That's Only What They Say	UK- Parlophone R 5194 / 1964
Everything In The Garden / He Could Never	UK- Parlophone R 5304 / 1965
Girls, Girls, Girls / Why Do Fools Fall In Love	UK- Parlophone R 5379 / 1965
Here, There And Everywhere / You've Changed	UK- Parlophone R 5491 / 1966
Auntie Maggie's Remedy / Turn The Lights Down	UK- Parlophone R 5528 / 1966

Apples, Peaches, Pumkin Pie / I Couldn't Spell		UK- CBS 3814 / 1968
Rosetta / Just Like Before		UK- CBS 4041 / 1969
Easy Squeeze / Do I Love You		UK- CBS 4461 / 1970
Goodnight Sweet Dreams / Memphis		UK- Phoenix S NIX 126 / 1972

Different US-release

If You Cry / A Little Bit Of Loving	US-Atco 45-6307 / 1964

Eps :

FOURMOST SOUNDS	UK-Parlophone GEP 8892/ 1963

- I'm In Love / Respectable / Hello Little Girl / Just In Case

HOW CAN I TELL HER	UK-Parlophone GEP 8917/ 1964

- How Can I Tell Her / You Got That Way / A Little Lovin' / Waiting For You

LP FIRST AND FOURMOST	UK-Parlophone PMC 1259/ 1965

- Till You Say You'll Be Mine / Yakety Yak / Girls, Girls, Girls / My Block / So Fine / Some Kind Of Wonderful / The Girl Can't Help It / Today I'm In Love / The In-crowd / Baby Sittin' Boogie / Heebie Jeebies / Sure To Fall (in love with you) / Bound To Lose My Heart / Something's Got A Hold On Me

LP THE FOURMOST	UK- private release SOF 001 / 1975

- Down At The Club / My Eyes Adored You / Zing Went The Strings Of My Heart / I've Got You Under My Skin / Save The Last Dance For Me / The Girl Can't Help It / Without You / Take Your Finger Out Of Your Mouth / Rag doll / Will You Still Love Me Tomorrow

(*** please note that this album was a private release by the band for sale at gigs only)

Tracks on compilation-albums :

I Love You Too	on 'Ferry Cross The Mersey'	UK-Columbia 33 SX 1676 / 1964

as **Format** :

Maxwell's Silver Hammer / Music Man	UK- CBS 4600 / 1969

Unissued tracks :

Among the unissued tracks of the **Fourmost** are the songs, "**Little By Little**" (1964), "**Running Bear**" (??) and "**Love Of The Common People**" (probably 1969).

GERRY & THE PACEMAKERS

This legendary Merseybeat group originated with the **Mars Bars**, a Skiffle group formed in Liverpool in the late Fifties that consisted of **Gerry Marsden** (voc/g), **Dixie Dean** (g), **Jimmy Tobin** (bg), **Tommy Ryan** (wb) and **Freddie Marsden** (dr).

When, a little later, **Arthur McMahon** (p) joined, the name of the group was changed to **The Gerry Marsden Skiffle Group**.

The Star Club Hamburg - Faron with the Pacemakers

Arthur McMahon, by the way, was the same person as **Arthur Roy**, the former leader of **Arthur Roy & the Rockers**. This line-up was probably joined by the **Two Jays** for a short time, which were **Joey Bowers** and **Brian O'Hara**, who then formed the **Four Jays**, which later became the **Fourmost**.

Jimmy Tobin and **Tommy Ryan** left and disappeared from the scene. Then **Dixie Dean** left to join the **Kruzads** and from 1972 until 1974 he was a member of **McGuinness Flint**.

The brothers **Gerry** and **Freddie Marsden** together with **Arthur McMahon** continued as a trio under the name of the **Gerry Marsden Trio**.

When the members of the **Gerry Marsden Trio** decided to continue as a Beat group, they looked for a bass guitarist and they wanted **Keith Draper**, but he decided to join **Alby & the Sorrals** instead. So **Les Chadwick** was recruited and the group changed its name to **Gerry & the Pacemakers**.

The next to leave was **Arthur McMahon** who joined the **Nocturns** and accordingly, the group now consisted of:

Gerry Marsden	(voc/lg)
Les Maguire	(p/voc)
Les Chadwick	(bg/voc)
Freddie Marsden	(dr)

The new member, **Les Maguire,** had formerly played saxophone with the very early **Undertakers**.

In this line-up, **Gerry & the Pacemakers** recorded all their Sixties material, which was released on the Columbia label.

Some people like to say that this band grew up in the slipstream of the **Beatles** and was no more than a 'fare dodger', but this is nonsense because, for some time, **Gerry & the Pacemakers** were as successful and as popular in Liverpool as the **Beatles**. They had a different sound and their own hits, which had no connection to the Fab Four's. Amongst them was the first No. 1 hit ever to come out of Liverpool.

Their most successful records were "How Do You Do It" (No. 1), "I Like It" (No. 1), "I'm The One" (No. 2), "You'll Never Walk Alone" (No. 1), "Don't Let The Sun Catch You Cryin' " (No. 6), "Ferry Cross The Mersey" (No. 8), "I'll Be There" (No. 15), "Walk Hand In Hand" (No. 29) and "Girl On A Swing".

"You'll Never Walk Alone" became the anthem for Liverpool Football Club and is played at all their matches. From there it spread around to all the football stadiums in the world.

"Ferry Cross The Mersey", of course, was the title song of the motion picture which, besides **Gerry & the Pacemakers** in the main role, featured the Liverpool artists **Earl Royce & the Olympics**, the **Black Knights**, the **Blackwells**, the **Koobas**, the **Fourmost** and **Cilla Black**.

Even if this musical film was not a bestseller, it is an interesting and important, visual and historical document of the unique Liverpool Beat era. The title song was later re-released by lots of other artists and brought in quite a lot of money for the composer **Gerry Marsden**.

When, at the end of the Sixties, the Beat began to loose more and more ground, **Gerry Marsden** disbanded the **Pacemakers** and accepted a part in the musical, 'Charlie Girl', from which a record of him together with **Derek Nimmo** was released, but "Liverpool/Charlie Girl" was quite a poor single and had no great success.

Freddie Marsden was so annoyed about his brother disbanding the group, that he never spoke to him again. He went back to a normal day job and never returned to show business. He sadly died in December 2006.

Les Chadwick emigrated to Australia where he owned a music shop in Sidney and **Les Maguire** became a sailor but, in 1999, he stepped back into the music business as a member of the re-formed **Ian & the Zodiacs**, who, after **Ian Edwards** had left, continued under the name of the **Zodiacs** and, as such, they still occasionally appear today.

Gerry Marsden continued in the music business and recorded some nice solo singles including "Please Let Them Be" and the fantastic "My Home Town", until he formed a new group under the name of **Gerry & the Pacemakers** in the mid-Seventies.

In 1977, this group toured Germany again, with the line-up of **Gerry Marsden** (voc/lg), **Mark Kirkpatrick** (bg), **Bob Haddrell** (org) and **Keith Hall** (dr).

Mark Kirkpatrick was a former member of **Venom**, while **Keith Hall** had been a professional musician since the age of 12 and, amongst others, had played with **Picketywitch**.

Bob Haddrell came from a Jazz background and a little later was replaced by **Alan Greenwood** (p/org) who, for Rock 'n' Roll music, was much better and, as a session musician, had formerly played with various groups.

In 1978, a TV film about **Gerry & the Pacemakers** was shown in England and Germany which made it very clear how popular the pleasant singer with the inimitable grin and his group still were at that time, even if very good singles such as the second take of "You'll Never Walk Alone", "Unchained Melody" and "Oh My Love" did not become chart hits.

In the mid-Eighties, **Gerry Marsden** had a hit comeback when he was the leader of the session group **Crowd**, which also included **Frank Allen** of the **Searchers**, **Joe Fagin** (formerly **The Strangers**), **Paul McCartney**, as well as a lot of other popular musicians. They recorded the benefit record, "You'll Never Walk Alone", for the victims of the fire disaster in Bradford's football stadium. This record became a chart topper.

In 1989, Gerry Marsden was a member of another session group which also included **Paul McCartney**, **Holly Johnson** (of **Frankie Goes To Hollywood**) and the **Christians**. This session, which had no special name, recorded another benefit record for the victims of the terrible and unforgettable disaster in the Hillsborough football stadium in Sheffield, which happened during the match between 'Liverpool FC' and 'Nottingham Forest'.

This record, a re-arranged version of **Gerry Marsden**'s "Ferry Cross The Mersey", became another top 5 hit. Some people may say **Gerry Marsden** only had his later successes because of these benefit records but, this would be unfair, as he is as good a musician today as he ever was, which is especially clear from the later records by **Gerry & the Pacemakers**. The only exception here is the 'Lennon/McCartney Songbook' LP by **Gerry Marsden** alone, which was released by K-tel in 1985. From the point of view of a real Beat fan, it can only be described as extremely gruesome and boring with all that synthesizer and drum-machine noise. It is hard to understand how a pioneer of the Beat movement like **Gerry Marsden** could condescend to do something like this.

But even this unfortunate slip-up does not change the fact that the group, **Gerry & the Pacemakers,** truly deserves to be called a legend of the unique Merseybeat era.

Discography :

How Do You Do It / Away From You	UK- Columbia DB 4987 / 1963
I Like It / It Happened To Me	UK- Columbia DB 7041 / 1963
You'll Never Walk Alone / It's Alright	UK- Columbia DB 7126 / 1963
I'm The One / You've Got What I Like	UK- Columbia DB 7189 / 1964
Don't Let The Sun Catch You Cryin' / Show Me That You Care	UK- Columbia DB 7268 / 1964
It's Gonna Be Alright / It's Just Because	UK- Columbia DB 7353 / 1964
Ferry Cross The Mersey / You, You, You	UK- Columbia DB 7437 / 1964
I'll Be There / Baby, You're So Good To Me	UK- Columbia DB 7504 / 1965
Walk Hand In Hand / Dreams	UK- Columbia DB 7738 / 1965
La la la / Without You	UK- Columbia DB 7835 / 1966
Girl On A Swing / Fool To Myself	UK- Columbia DB 8044 / 1966

Different French release :

You'll Never Walk Alone / Jambalaya	F- Columbia 7 XCA 10.054 / 1964

Different German releases :

Pretend / Why Oh Why	G- Columbia C 22929 / 1965
Girl On A Swing / The Way You Look Tonight	G- Columbia C 23325 / 1966

Different US-releases :

It's Gonna Be Alright / Skinny Minnie	US- Laurie 3293 / 1965
I Like It / Jambalaya	US- Laurie 3271 / 1964
Give All Your Love To Me / You're The Reason	US- Laurie 3313 / 1965
Looking For My Life / Bright Green Pleasure Machine	US- Laurie 3370 / 1966

Different Danish release :

A Shot Of Rhythm And Blues / Jambalaya	DK – Columbia DS 2232 / 1964

Different Canadian releases :

Jambalaya / Summertime	CAN – Capitol 72168 / 1964
Ferry Cross The Mersey / Reelin' And Rockin'	CAN – Capitol 72216 / 1964

Different Australian release :

Give All Your Love To Me / The Wrong Yo Yo   AUS – Columbia DO 4604 / 1965

Gerry Marsden – solo :

Please Let Them Be / I'm Not Blue   UK- CBS 2784 / 1967

Gilbert Green / What Makes Me Love You   UK- CBS 2946 / 1967

In The Year Of April / Everyday   UK- Nems 3831 / 1968

Every Little Minute / In Days Of Old   UK- Nems 4229 / 1969

I've Got My Ukelele / What A Day   UK- Decca F. 13172 / 1971

Amo Credo / Come Break Bread   UK- Phoenix 129 / 1972

Gerry Marsden & Derek Nimmo :

Liverpool / Charlie Girl   UK- CBS 3575 / 1968

EPs :

HOW DO YOU DO IT   UK-Columbia SEG 8257/ 1963

- How Do You Do It / Away From You / I Like It / It Happened To Me

YOU'LL NEVER WALK ALONE   UK-Columbia SEG 8295/ 1963

- You'll Never Walk Alone / Jambalaya / Chills / A Shot Of Rhythm & Blues

I'M THE ONE   UK-Columbia SEG 8311/ 1964

- I'm The One / You've Got What I Like / You Can't Fool Me / Don't You Ever

DON'T LET THE SUN CATCH YOU CRYIN'   UK-Columbia SEG 8346/ 1964

- Don't Let The Sun Catch You Cryin' / Show Me That You Care / Summertime / Where Have You Been

IT'S GONNA BE ALRIGHT   UK-Columbia SEG 8367/ 1964

- It's Gonna Be Alright / It's Just Because / Maybelline / You're The Reason

GERRY IN CALIFORNIA   UK-Columbia SEG 8388/ 1965

- Skinny Lizzie / My Babe / Away From You / What'd I Say

HITS FROM 'FERRY CROSS THE MERSEY'   UK-Columbia SEG 8397/ 1965

- It's Gonna Be Alright / I'll Wait For You / Ferry Cross The Mersey / Why Oh Why

RIP IT UP   UK-Columbia SEG 8426/ 1965

- Rip It Up / Reelin' And Rockin' / Whole Lotta Shakin' Goin' On / You Win Again

Different French releases :

YOU'LL NEVER WALK ALONE   F-Columbia ESRF 1446 / 1963

- You'll Never Walk Alone / Jambalaya / A Shot Of Rhythm & Blues / Where Have You Been

DON'T LET THE SUN CATCH YOU CRYIN' / I'M THE ONE   F-Columbia ESRF 1549 / 1964

- Don't Let The Sun Catch You Cryin' / Show Me That You Care / You've Got What I Like / I'm The One

FERRY CROSS THE MERSEY   F-Columbia ESRF 1637 / 1965

- Ferry Cross The Mersey / You, You, You / It's Gonna Be Alright / It's Just Because

LPs :

HOW DO YOU LIKE IT   UK-Columbia SX 1546 / 1963

- Shot of Rhythm & Blues / Jambalaya / Where Have You Been / Here's Hoping / Pretend / Maybelline / You'll Never Walk Alone / Wrong Yo-yo / You're The Reason / Chills / You Can't Fool Me / Don't You Ever / Summertime / Slow Down

FERRY CROSS THE MERSEY   UK-Columbia SX 1693 / 1965

- It's Gonna Be Alright / Why oh Why / Fall In Love / Think About Love / This Thing Called Love / Baby You're So Good To Me / I'll Wait For You / She's The Only Girl For Me / Ferry Cross The Mersey / + The Fourmost : I Love You Too + George Martin Orchestra : All Quiet On The Mersey-Front + Cilla Black : Is It Love

YOU'LL NEVER WALK ALONE   UK-Regal SREG 1070 / 1967

- same songs as on 'How Do You Like It' - album

Different US-releases :

DON'T LET THE SUN CATCH YOU CRYIN'   US-Laurie SLP 2024 / 1964

- Don't Let The Sun Catch You Cryin' / I'm The One / Away From You / Jambalaya / Mabellene / You'll Never Walk Alone / How Do You Do It / You're The Reason / Don't You Ever / Summertime / Slow Down / Show Me That You Care

SECOND ALBUM US-Laurie SLP 2027 / 1964

- I Like It / A Shot Of Rhythm & Blues / Where Have You Been / Here's Hoping / Pretend / The Wrong Yo-Yo / Chills / You Can't Fool Me / It's Happened To Me / It's All Right / Slow Down / Jambalaya

FERRY CROSS THE MERSEY US-United Artists UAS 6387/ 1965

- songs of **Gerry & the Pacemakers** are the same as on UK-release + <u>The Black Knights</u> : "I Gotta Woman", <u>Earl Royce & the Olympics</u> : "Shake A Tail Feather", <u>The Blackwells</u> : "Why Don't You Love Me"

I'LL BE THERE US-Laurie SLP 2030 / 1965

- I'll Be There / What'd I Say / Rip It Up / You Win Again / You You You / Now I'm Alone / My Babe / Reelin' And Rockin' / I Count The Tears / Whole Lotta Shakin' Goin' On / It'll Be Me / Skinny Minnie

GREATEST HITS US-Laurie SLP 2031 / 1965

- Ferry Cross The Mersey / How Do You Do It / I'm The One / My Babe / Away From You / I'll Be There / It's Gonna Be Alright / Pretend / I Like It / Chills / It'll Be Me / Don't Let The Sun Catch You Crying

GIRL ON A SWING US-Laurie SLP 2037 / 1966

- Girl On A Swing / The Way You Look Tonight / Guantanamera / Pretty Flamingo / At The End Of The Rainbow / Looking For My Life / The Big Bright Green Pleasure Machine / See You In September / Who Can I Turn To / Without You / Strangers In The Night / La La La

<u>Tracks on compilation-albums :</u>

It's Gonna Be Alright	on 'Liverpool'	G- Columbia C 83777 / 1964
It's Just Because	on 'Liverpool'	G- Columbia C 83777 / 1964
Whole Lotta Shakin' Goin' On	on 'Liverpool '65'	G-Columbia SMC 83990 / 1965
Rip It Up	on 'Liverpool '65'	G-Columbia SMC 83990 / 1965
You Win Again	on 'Liverpool '65'	G-Columbia SMC 83990 / 1965
Pretend	on 'Liverpool Hop'	G-Columbia SMC 83983 / 1965
How Do You Do It	on 'The Best Of The Liverpool Sound'	F- Columbia FPX 272 / 1964

<u>Unreleased tracks :</u>

The only known unreleased tracks by **Gerry & the Pacemakers** are "**Come Back To Me**", "**When Oh When**" and "**Hallelujah I Love Her So**", probably all from 1963/1964.

For collectors it might be of interest to know that all three songs were included in the 1984 album, '**The Very Best Of Gerry & the Pacemakers**' (UK- MFP 41 5654 1).

In addition, **Gerry Marsden** cut the one-sided EMIDISC acetate, "**I Ain't Got Time**", probably in the late Sixties/early Seventies.

RICKY GLEASON & THE TOPSPOTS

To clear up one thing in advance, this group did not have any connection with the **Topspots** from the Wirral, the predecessor group of the **Undertakers**.

This band was formed in the area of Litherland by **Derek Banks** (aka **Ricky Gleason**) under the name of **Denny & the Escorts** in 1962. They became quite popular on the local scene but they were never an outstanding success.

In 1963, when **Dave Forshaw** took the group under his wing, the name was changed to **Ricky Gleason & the Topspots** and the line-up at this time consisted of the following musicians:

Ricky Gleason	(voc)
Len Burman	(g/voc)
Graham Little	(g)
Kelvin Harrison	(bg/voc)
Tommy Limb	(dr)

Kelvin Harrison, for sure, was not an original member, as he formerly had played with **Tommy & the Satellites**.

In 1963, the group was signed to Oriole and, according to **Ricky Gleason,** was featured on the third volume of the legendary samplers, 'This Is Merseybeat', with the songs, "I'm A Hog For You" and "Johnny B. Goode". This third volume was allegedly released in the United States only and in a very small edition. In general there is nothing known about such a release, but who can claim that it is not true, especially if it is considered that Oriole as record label had a strong connection to the USA?

However, it is a fact that in 1963, **Ricky Gleason & the Topspots** recorded two Kensington acetates and the first one, amongst other songs, also included "I'm A Hog For You".

While the first acetate was an EP, the second one was a single with the songs, "Talk About You" and "You're No Longer Mine", probably both originals by the group.

In 1963, **Ricky Gleason & the Topspots** were booked to play the 'Star-Club' in Hamburg where they went down well. During their stay in Hamburg, the group is said to have been recorded by the German Polydor label but, again, there is nothing known about a release. This does not necessarily mean that nothing was released because the German Polydor label was well known for sometimes releasing records under incorrect or different band names.

In 1964, **Len Burman** left the group and disappeared from the scene while **Kelvin Harrison** joined **J.J. & the Hi-Lites**, which a little later became the **Mersey Monsters**. He later played with the **Rebels**.

The new members in **Ricky Gleason & the Topspots** were **Keith Dodd** (g) and **Kenny Rees** (bg/voc).

Keith Dodd was a former member of the **Gerry Bach & the Beathovens** while **Kenny Rees** had previously played with the **Black Velvets**.

A little later, **Ricky Gleason** also left the group who continued under the name of the **Topspots** - probably with **Kenny Rees** on lead vocals.

The Topspots at the Star Club Hamburg

RICKY GLEASON & THE TOPSPOTS
Would like to wish all friends, fans, promoters etc especially Dave Forshaw, Don Read and Bill and Virginia of 'Mersey Beat'----ALL THE BEST FOR THE COMING SEASON

MERSEYSIDE'S NEW No.1 GROUP----

RICKY GLEASON
AND THE
TOPSPOTS
(B.B.C. RECORDING ARTISTES)
Just back from the Star Club

Manager:
DAVID FORSHAW Enterprises
6 DALEY PLACE
BOOTLE 20
AINtree 9654

London Representative:
DON READ LTD.,
4 WEIGHHOUSE STREET
LONDON W.1.
HYDE PARK 5164

Ricky Gleason at first formed the group, **Ricky Gleason & the Nighthawks**, but then joined the **Rebels**, formerly known as **Ian & the Rebels** and, with **Ricky Gleason,** they sometimes appeared under the name of **Ricky Gleason & the Rebels**.

This new connection also did not last for too long and **Ricky Gleason** then teamed up with the **Renicks**, another group out of **Dave Forshaw's** stable. This group, that initially appeared as **Ricky Gleason & the Renicks**, was somehow in the process of disbanding and the remaining **Renicks'** members, together with **Ricky Gleason,** then continued on as **Ricky Gleason & the New Topspots**.

When this group disbanded in the late Sixties, **Ricky Gleason** became a member of the **St. Ive's Trio** and, until 1975, he sang in a cabaret duo together with **David May**, a former member of **Mark Peters & the Silhouettes** and **Rory Storm & the Hurricanes**. Then **Ricky Gleason** quit show business for many years.

But, back to the **Topspots** who continued together until 1965 and, during that time, cut two more acetates on Deroy.

The first one, recorded immediately after the departure of **Ricky Gleason**, included the songs, "Jam", "Nothin's Shakin' ", "Chills" and "Little Latin Lupe-Lu".

The second one (recorded in 1965) included "True Love", "Milkcow Blues", "What Is This Feeling" and "Welcome To My World".

When the **Topspots** split up, drummer **Tommy Limb** became a member of the **Mersey Monsters** and **Kenny Rees** joined the new **King Size Taylor** group before he disappeared from the scene.

Of **Keith Dodd** it is known that he joined the **Principals**, that later evolved into a cabaret-group. All the other members probably quit showbiz at that time.

In 1998, there was a revival concert by **Ricky Gleason & the Topspots** for the 'MerseyCats' at the 'Aintree Institute' with **Ricky Gleason**, **Kelvin Harrison**, **Graham Little** and **Tommy Limb**.

For unknown reasons, **Keith Dodd** did not show up for that event, so **Geoff Nugent** of the **Undertakers** stood in for him.

Around ten years later, **Ricky Gleason & the Topspots** re-formed in the same line-up from 1964 with one exception. **Graham Little** was no longer with them and his place was taken by **Keith Hubbard**, the original guitarist for the **Rebels**.

The group had quite a few appearances on the scene again but, unfortunately in 2010, **Keith Dodd** had to give up playing because of problems with his hearing.

At that time **Keith Hubbard** took over on lead-guitar and the group continued as a quartet that, besides **Keith Hubbard** and **Ricky Gleason,** still includes **Tommy Limb** and **Kelvin Harrison**.

Discography :

Derek Banks once stated that **Ricky Gleason & the Topspots** were featured on the third volume of the Oriole samplers, 'This Is Merseybeat' with the songs, "**I'm A Hog For You**" and "**Johnny B. Goode**".

This album allegedly may have been released only in the USA and in a very small edition, which seems improbable, but not impossible.

In addition, **Ricky Gleason & the Topspots** recorded in Germany in 1963 for the Polydor label, but there is nothing known about a release under the name of **Ricky Gleason & the Topspots**.

as **Ricky Gleason & the Topspots** :

Remember Me / I'm A Hog For You /	
Pistol Pickin' Mama / Now I Know	UK- Kensington acetate-EP / 1963
Talk About You / You're No Longer Mine	UK- Kensington acetate / 1963

as **The Topspots** :

Jam / Nothin's Shakin' / Chills / Little Latin Lupe-Lu	UK- Deroy acetate-EP / 1964
True Love / Milkcow Blues /	
What Is This Feeling / Welcome To My World	UK- Deroy acetate-EP / 1964

CHICK GRAHAM & THE COASTERS

In the beginning, this group was called **The Sandstormers** and, in 1962, under the name of the **Phantoms**, they became the backing group for a singer named **Billy Forde**, whose real name was **William Howard Ashton** and who later, as **Billy J. Kramer**, achieved international stardom.

Billy Forde & the Phantoms were one of hundreds of Liverpool amateur beat groups specialising in the imported U.S. Rock 'n' Roll sound.

Ted Knibbs took over their management and following his advice they changed their name to **Billy Kramer & the Coasters**.

Ted Knibbs' influence apparently worked well on the group, as they came third in the 'Mersey Beat' newspaper popularity-poll in 1963. Shortly thereafter, following an appearance at the 'Cavern', **Brian Epstein** became interested in taking over the management of **Billy Kramer & the Coasters** and recorded the demo, "She's My Girl", with them – most probably in **Percy Phillips'** Kensington studios.

However, with the exception of **Billy Kramer**, none of the group members wanted to take

BILLY KRAMER
WITH
THE COASTERS

the step forward into the professional music business. So **Brian Epstein** only signed the singer and, for his backing group, **Brian Epstein** selected the **Dakotas** from Manchester, the former backing group of **Pete MacLaine**.

The name of this new group was **Billy J. Kramer** <u>with</u> the **Dakotas** - the band in some way had to stay individual as they also recorded without Billy J. in their own right. But that is a completely different story.

The **Coasters** continued under the management of **Ted Knibbs** and he brought them together with the boyish looking singer **Graham Jennings**.

Chick Graham

206

Under the name **Chick Graham & the Coasters**, the group had a real impact on the scene and turned professional in 1963 - in the following line-up:

Chick Graham	(voc)
Arthur Ashton	(lg/voc)
Ray Dougherty	(rg)
George Braithwaite	(bg)
Tony Sounders	(dr)

Tony Sounders is sometimes documented as **Tony Saunders** or under his real name, which is **Tony Sanders**.

Arthur Ashton, by the way, is a cousin of **Billy J. Kramer**, he had formerly played with the **Confederates** together with **Mike Pender** of the **Searchers**.

George Braithwaite left and probably quit the music business. His replacement was **Arthur Raynor**, a former member of the **Four Clefs**. He took over the rhythm-guitar, while **Ray Dougherty** switched to bass.

In 1964, **Chick Graham & the Coasters** were signed to Decca and, in the same year, released two nice Beat singles with "Education" and "A Little You". The latter had some minor success but did not enter the charts. "A Little You", in 1965, became a big chart success for **Freddie & the Dreamers** from Manchester, although their version, for sure, was no better than the one by **Chick Graham & the Coasters**.

Also recorded were versions of "Ciao Ciao Bambino" and the **Shirelles** number, "Will You Still Love Me Tomorrow", which were meant to be included on a Decca EP by the group which, for mysterious reasons, was not released.

In spite of their bad luck with the records, **Chick Graham & the Coasters** had a large following in the north of England and their popularity also reached down as far as London.

So they existed very well on the scene for quite some years until for unknown reasons a series of changes started in the line-up.

The first to leave was **Arthur Ashton**, who joined **Mark Peters & the Silhouettes** and later played with **Ian & the Zodiacs**. He was replaced by **Mike Kontzle**, who came from the **Beatwoods**.

Arthur Raynor, at that time, took over the lead-guitar and **Mike Kontzle** played rhythm.

Tony Sounders followed **Arthur Ashton** to **Mark Peters & the Silhouettes** and later became a member of the **Squad**, formerly known as the **Riot Squad**, that ultimately evolved into **Mark Peters & the Method**.

The new drummer with the **Coasters** was **Jimmy Lacey**, a former member of the **Profiles** and **Johnny Templer & the Hi-Cats**.

For mysterious reasons, **Chick Graham** decided to leave the group and to quit show business. He never appeared on the scene again.

Arthur Raynor became the new frontman and the group, for a short while, continued as the **Coasters** but then broke up totally.

Arthur Raynor changed his name to **Tony Marsh** and became a very successful solo artist on the cabaret scene, where he is still going strong today.

Jimmy Lacey joined the **Three Cheers** who later may have evolved into the Polydor recording group, **Phase Three**.

Mike Kontzle became a member of the **Roadrunners** and later appeared with **Colonel Bagshot & his Incredible Bucket Band**.

The other members of **Chick Graham & the Coasters** did not appear on the scene again. Only the group's name remains as a legend of Merseybeat.

Discography :

as **Billy Kramer & the Coasters** :

She's My Girl	UK – one sided acetate demo / 1963

as **Chick Graham & the Coasters** :

Education / I Know	UK-Decca F.11859 / 1964
A Little You / Dance, Baby, Dance	UK-Decca F.11932 / 1964

Unissued tracks :

In 1964, **Chick Graham & the Coasters** recorded the songs, "**Will You Still Love Me Tomorrow**" and "**Ciao Ciao Bambina**", at Decca for an EP which, for unknown reasons, was never released.

THE GRIFF PARRY FIVE

This group was formed in Liverpool in February 1964 by **Ron Parry**, the former drummer with **Joe Brown & the Bruvvers** and **Brian 'Griff' Griffiths**, who had formerly played with **Derry & the Seniors**, **Howie Casey & the Seniors** and **the Big Three**.

Right from the start, the **Griff Parry Five** consisted of the following musicians:

Steve Aldo	**(voc)**
Brian Griffiths	**(lg/voc)**
Vinnie Parker	**(p/org)**
Fran Galloway	**(bg/sax)**
Ron Parry	**(dr/voc)**

Steve Aldo, whose real name is **Eddie Bedford**, had previously sung with **Steve Aldo & the Challengers**, the **Nocturns** and with **King Size Taylor & the Dominoes**.

Francis Galloway was also a former member of **King Size Taylor & the Dominoes**, who had just disbanded.

In this line-up, the **Griff Parry Five** also appeared as the backing group for **King Size Taylor** at some gigs in England.

In 1964, the band was signed to Decca and recorded the songs, "Don't Make My Baby Blue", "Irresistible You" and the **Crests** success, "Sixteen Candles" (according to an announcement in the 'Mersey Beat' newspaper). For some mysterious reason, none of them were ever released.

Finally, their first single was released with a very strong version of **Marvin Gaye**'s "Can I Get A Witness", under the name of **Steve Aldo**.

Unfortunately, this single, which was coupled with **Jimmy Reed's** Blues classic, "Baby What You Want Me To Do", had no chart success, and so remained the only release by the group.

The **Griff Parry Five** for a short time were also joined by **Howie Casey**, after he had been with the **Big Three** for a short spell. However, he then went on to reform the **Krew**, where he had also played previously, when this group was active in France under the name of the **Krewkats**.

King Size Taylor & the Griff Parry Five

It was probably in late 1964 that **Ron Parry**, **Brian Griffiths** and **Vinnie Parker** left to team up with **Johnny Gustafson** in the **Johnny Gus Set**, which is another story in this book.

Because the 'name giving' musicians had left, the group could not continue under the **Griff Parry** name so the remaining **Steve Aldo** and **Fran Galloway** recruited **Spike Jones** (org) and **Brian Low** (dr) plus a guitarist, whose name is not known, and they continued on as the **Steve Aldo Quintet**.

It is not absolutely sure, but possible and with a certain plausibility, that this line-up recorded the single, "Everybody Has To Cry", that once again was only released under the name of **Steve Aldo** on Parlophone in 1964.

The **Steve Aldo Quintet** disbanded when **Steve Aldo** left to follow former member, **Howie Casey** to the **Krew**. When this band also split up, **Steve Aldo** joined the **Fyx** and then became a member of the **In-Crowd**, before he was backed by the **Fairies** for a short time.

Later, **Steve Aldo** was a Jazz singer but then disappeared from the scene.

Fran Galloway wanted to form a new group together with **Daryl Dougdale** (org) of the **Johnny Gus Set**, drummer **Pete Clarke** of the **Escorts** and a certain **Nick La Grec** aka **Nick Carver** (voc/sax) out of the

Roadrunners. Unfortunately, the name of the band is not known, or even if this band ever became a reality.

For sure it is known that **Fran Galloway** became a member of the **Freddie Kelly Combo**, who played more of a night-club style of music. In early 1968, he played with the group, **Lallypop** in Italy, which was formed by **Lally Stott** after he had left the **Motowns**.

Fran Galloway remained in Italy and became a member of **I Baronetti** and then he played in the backing group of the Italian pop-singer, **Nada**, who became very popular after her success at the San Remo Festival and sold 700,000 (!) copies of her record, "Que fredda fa" in one day.

From there, **Fran Galloway** joined the **Four Kents**, a group made up of former American G.I.s, in the style of the **Four Tops**, who also had a hit-record in Italy with "Sei lontano".

He then returned to Liverpool and became a member of the **In Crowd**, but then, as a professional session-musician, backed various Blues performers on their UK tours.

Discography :

In 1964, the **Griff Parry Five** recorded for Decca the songs, "Sixteen Candles", "Irresistible You", "Don'tMake My Baby Blue", and probably two others, but there was never anything released.

The following records were released under the name of **Steve Aldo** although, on the first one, the whole line-up of the **Griff Parry Five** was featured and, on the second one, most probably the complete **Steve Aldo Quintet** :

as **Steve Aldo** :

Can I Get A Witness / Baby What You Want Me To Do	UK- Decca F.12041 / 1964
Everybody Has To Cry / You're Absolutely Right	UK- Parlophone R 5432 / 1964

GROUP ONE

This true Liverpool group was formed in the beginning of 1962 by experienced musicians, who had all previously played in other established groups on the Merseybeat scene – a fact that made some people talk about them as a local super-group.

Anyway, they had left their former bands because they did not want, for whatever reasons, to become professionals in the music business.

Group One, in their first line-up, consisted of:

Dave Williams	**(voc/lg)**
Eric London	**(rg/voc)**
Keith Stokes	**(bg/voc)**
Harry Prytherch	**(dr)**

Dave Williams was a former member of the **Firecrests** and the recently disbanded **Dale Roberts & the Jaywalkers**, while **Eric London** had previously played with the **Ravens** (or **Robin & the Ravens**) who later became **Faron's Flamingos**.

Keith Stokes and Harry Prytherch were former members of the Remo Four, or the Remo Quartet, as this group was originally named.

In November 1962, Eric London left and quit show business and only lately appeared again as a member of the re-formed Mojos, where he is still playing.

He was replaced in Group One by Brian Hilton, a former member of Vince Earl & the Zeros.

One month later, Group One was placed at number 13 in the popularity poll of 'Mersey Beat' newspaper - a really a big success if one considers that, at this time, there were hundreds of Beat groups around in Liverpool. This excellent placing in the 'Mersey Beat' poll is a real indicator of the popularity of Group One, who a little later were featured on various TV and radio programmes.

Oriole became interested in signing them and probably did, although there never was a record released. Dave Williams left the group and became a founder-member of the Four Originals which was something of a successor group to his old band, Dale Roberts & the Jaywalkers, that still performs on the scene with him on lead-guitar.

Group One

His replacement in **Group One** was **Karl Terry** (voc/g), the legendary 'Sheik of Shake', who had formerly led his own group **Karl Terry & the Cruisers**.

A little later, **Brian Hilton** also left to join **Sonny Webb & the Cascades**, who then became the **Hillsiders**. He was replaced by **Les Williams** who was a former member of **Terry & the Tuxedos** and **Billy Butler & the Tuxedos**.

Group One, in addition to the **Searchers**, the **Undertakers** and **Ogi & the Flintstones** were one of the groups who regularly performed at the 'Iron Door'.

In 1964, the group disbanded totally without having had any national success, but they were very popular throughout the north of England and, let's face it, that says a lot for an amateur band, doesn't it?

Karl Terry joined Newcastle's **Delemeres**, who were the resident group at Liverpool's 'Locarno' dance hall and then he became a member of **Amos Bonny & the TT's**, who a little later were re-named **Karl Terry & the TT's**. After that, he had a very short spell with the **Talismen** but then re-formed the **TT's**, before the remaining members of this group and the remaining members of the **Clayton Squares** amalgamated as the **T-Squares**. He later re-formed **Karl Terry & the Cruisers** again and is still playing the Liverpool pub circuit.

Les Williams became a member of **Tiffany's Dimensions**, he also had a short spell with the **Talismen,** before he re-joined the **Four Dimensions**, that later shortened their name to the **Dimensions**, before they changed it to **Jet** and after that to **Pendulum**.

He later joined the re-formed **Mojos**, but left them to join the re-formed **Black Knights**, where he is still playing today.

Harry Prytherch quit show business in the Sixties, as did **Keith Stokes**.

In 1993, **Group One** was re-formed for the 'MerseyCats' organisation in the original line-up of 1962 with **Dave Williams, Keith Stokes, Eric London** and **Harry Prytherch**, but the group only played sporadically at 'MerseyCats' benefit concerts. **Keith Stokes** sadly died in 2010.

Discography :

Group One never released a record but probably recorded some songs for Oriole in 1963. Certainly there were also some sessions for various TV and radio shows recorded but, unfortunately, the songs are not known - with the exception of "**Pretend**", which was recorded live for the BBC in October 1963.

GROUPS INC.

At the end of 1962 when **Freddie Starr** was still appearing with the **Kansas City Five,** he was offered a French tour and, obviously, he wanted the group to go with him. But as most of the musicians did not want to turn professional, only **Bruce McCaskill** and **Peter Cooke** of the **Kansas City Five** accepted the offer. They found further members in **Sid Edwards** (bg), formerly with the **Flames, Nutrockers** and **Lee Shondell & the Capitols** and a drummer, **Pete Orr** from the **Hi-Cats.** This line-up was also joined by the female singer, **Wendy Harris,** as it was a presupposition for the tour to have a female in the line-up. **Wendy Harris** had just returned from a tour of France with the **TT's.**

This new line-up was named **Groups Inc.,** but broke up after their return from France.

Sid Edwards and **Pete Orr** were founder members of the **Ventures,** who, a little later, became the backing group for **Freddie Starr** for a time, while **Wendy Harris** disappeared from the scene.

Bruce McCaskill and **Peter Cooke** formed a new group under the name of **Groups Inc.,** that were occasionally called the **G.I's.** This new line-up then consisted of:

Frank Knight	(voc/g)
Peter Cooke	(lg/voc)
Bruce Monroe	(rg/voc)
Pete Jones	(bg)
Pete Clarke	(dr)

Bruce Monroe, of course, was **Bruce McCaskill,** who originally was the founder of the **Bluegenes,** the predecessor group of the **Swinging Blue Jeans** and after that he was the founder and bandleader of the **Kansas City Five.**

WHAT HAS FRANK KNIGHT GOT UP HIS SLEEVE? . . .

WATCH THIS SPACE FOR NEWS OF

GROUPS INC.

with

FRANK KNIGHT

Peter Cooke had started with the **Topspots,** (not **Ricky Gleason**'s group) and then played with **Dee & the Dynamites,** the short-lived **Roadrunners (II)** and the **Kansas City Five.**

Frank Knight was the former leader of **Frank Knight & the Barons,** who after his departure became **Lee Castle & the Barons.**

Pete Jones came from Liverpool's recently disbanded **Renegades** and, before that, he had played with the **Crosbys,** while **Pete Clarke** came from **Vince & the Volcanoes.**

This line-up of **Groups Inc.** did not last for too long because **Frank Knight** left and was replaced by **George Peckham,** a former member of the **Skylarks,** the **Renegades** and **Lee Curtis & the All Stars.**

Peter Cooke left to join **Earl Royce & the Olympics** and, after that, he played with the **Trend** (without an 's') and, in the Seventies, he was a member of the newly formed **Faron's Flamingos.**

Frank Knight

He was replaced in **Groups Inc.**, by Paul St. John, whose real name was **Paul Pilnick** and who had previously played with **Vince & the Volcanoes** and **Lee Curtis & the All Stars**.

Pete Jones also left to join the **New Avengers** and was replaced by **Robert Allen**.

With the exception of **Bruce McCaskill** (aka **Bruce Monroe**) and **Pete Clarke**, the whole line-up had changed within a very short time and so **Groups Inc.**, now appeared in the following line-up:

George Peckham	(voc/g)
Paul St. John	(lg)
Bruce Monroe	(rg/voc)
Robert Allen	(bg)
Pete Clarke	(dr)

In spite of all the changes, the band managed to maintain a really good musical quality and they were very popular throughout Merseyside. They may also have gone to France again with **Freddie Starr** and a different girl-singer. **Groups Inc.** then became something like the resident group at the famous 'Iron Door' but also appeared quite often at the 'Cavern' and all the other Liverpool venues.

Because of the steadily changing line-up, the band never signed a recording contract and also never had the chance of a national breakthrough.

It was in 1964 when **Groups Inc.** disbanded totally and the individual members joined other groups.

Pete Clarke became a member of the **Escorts** and later played with the **Krew** (better known as **The Crew**), **Them Grimbles** and the **5 A.M. Event**, before he re-joined the **Escorts**. In 1966, he was a member of the **Fruit Eating Bears** and later became a founding member of **Liverpool Scene**, who musically did not really belong to the Merseybeat scene anymore.

Bruce McCaskill (Monroe) also became a member of the **Escorts** but probably one of the road crew and not of the band. After that, he was the road manager for **Eric Clapton** and then became the very successful manager of the **Average White Band**. He sadly died, much too young, in 1994.

George Peckham joined the Pawns, then he moved on to the **Kinsleys** but they very soon disbanded. After that he appeared with **Earl Royce & the Olympics** and later became a member of the **Fourmost**. Paul Pilnick (St. John) initially played with the **Big Three** but then re-joined **Lee Curtis & the All Stars**. After that he played with various successful groups including **Stealer's Wheel** and **Deaf School**.

In 1978, the band name, **Groups Inc.**, appeared again on the revival sampler, 'Mersey Survivors', but only for this recording session and, with the exception of **George Peckham** and **Pete Jones**, probably none of the former members were included.

On that interesting compilation, **Groups Inc.** made a good impression in performing **Arthur Alexander**'s classics, "Where Have You Been" and "Soldier Of Love".

Unfortunately, these were the only releases of **Groups Inc.**, for certain one of the good and very interesting groups of the unique Merseybeat era.

Discography :

There never was a record released by **Groups Inc.** in the Sixties and, as far as it is known, no acetates or demos were recorded.

But, in 1978, the band name appeared again with **George Peckham** and **Pete Jones** of the Sixties line-up, when **Groups Inc.** was featured on the following compilation:

"**Where Have You Been**"	on '**Mersey Survivors**'	**UK-Raw RWLP 104 / 1978**
"**Soldier Of Love**"	on '**Mersey Survivors**'	**UK-Raw RWLP 104 / 1978**

THE JOHNNY GUS SET

This group was formed by **Johnny 'Gus' Gustafson** in Liverpool in 1965 after he had formerly played with the groups, **Cass & the Cassanovas**, the **Big Three**, the **Seniors** and the **Merseybeats**.

The original line-up of the **Johnny Gus Set** consisted of the following musicians:

Johnny Gustafson	**(voc/bg)**
Brian 'Griff' Griffiths	**(g/voc)**
Vinnie Parker	**(org)**
Ron Parry	**(dr)**

Brian 'Griff' Griffiths was a former member of **Derry & the Seniors** (who became **Howie Casey & the Seniors**), the **Big Three**, the **Seniors** and the **Griff Parry Five**, while **Ron Parry** had formerly played with **Joe Brown & the Bruvvers** and the **Griff Parry Five**.

Vinnie Parker, who had also been in the **Griff Parry Five**, did not stay for too long and the **Johnny Gus Set** continued on as a trio.

They were signed by Polydor and, in 1965, recorded the single, "Just To Be With You", that had little success, although it was also released in Germany on the black International label of Polydor.

In May 1965, **Daryl Dougdale** (org), the former leader of the **Daryl Dougdale Trio,** joined the group but left them in July of the same year to form a new group with **Francis Galloway** (bg/sax), **Pete Clarke** (dr) and **Nic La Grec** aka **Nick Carver** (voc/sax). As there was nothing further heard about this group, it is doubtful that it ever became a reality. The **Johnny Gus Set** once again became a trio and recorded a new single in December 1965. Their version of "Take Me For A Little While" was also released on Polydor but only in England and, this time, it was only credited to **Johnny Gustafson**.

Unfortunately, as this single achieved little success, the group disbanded in early 1966.

Johnny Gustafson, together with **John Banks** of the just disbanded **Merseybeats**, formed the duo **Johnny & John** and, for a time, they were backed by the **Thoughts** from Liverpool, who also backed them on their only single, "Bumper To Bumper", which did not have any better success.

After that, both **Johnny Gustafson** and **John Banks** joined the **Quotations**, a London-based group who released a great single with "Cool It/Mark Of Her Head" where the B-side was written by **Johnny Gustafson**.

For a short time **John Banks** played with **Rupert's People,** who also recorded as **Johnny B. Great**.

Johnny Gustafson briefly appeared with **Episode Six** and later became a member of **Quartermass** and **Hard Stuff**. He also played on the **Roxy Music** album, 'Stranded', and, after that, he sang the part of 'Simon Zealotes' in the musical, 'Jesus Christ Superstar', where he was featured on the original album. In 1973, he re-formed the **Big Three** together with former member, **Brian Griffiths**, as well as with the drummer, **Nigel Olson**, who had previously played with **Plastic Penny**, the **Spencer Davis Group** and in **Elton John**'s backing group **Dodo**.

This new line-up of the **Big Three** recorded the album, 'Resurrection', and then disbanded.

Brian Griffiths emigrated to Canada but **Johnny Gustafson** appeared again at the end of the Seventies with the **Ian Gillan Band** and, in the Eighties, he was a member of a London band which appeared under two different names, **Rowdy** and also as the **Rock Band**. Finally, **Johnny Gustafson** was a member of the **Pirates**, who had evolved from **Johnny Kidd's** former backing group of the same name. Nothing more was heard of the other members of the quite short-lived **Johnny Gus Set**.

Single discography:

Just To Be With You / Sweet Day   UK- Polydor 56 022 / 1965

as **Johnny Gustafson** :

Take Me For A Little While / Make Me Your Number One   UK- Polydor 56 043 / 1965

Johnny (Gustafson) **& John** (Banks) :

Bumper To Bumper / Scrape My Boot   UK- Polydor 56 087 / 1966

(*** please note that the second single was only released under the name of **Johnny Gustafson** but he was backed by the **Johnny Gus Set**. The duo **Johnny & John** was backed by the **Thoughts** from Liverpool on their only single.)

THE HIDEAWAYS

This pure Rhythm & Blues band was formed by three Liverpudlians, one American and a musician of Cantonese descent, in Liverpool at the end of 1963.

In this multinational line-up, the **Hideaways,** with their exceptional musical quality, became a really important part of the Liverpool scene within a very short time. Unfortunately, Rhythm & Blues was not as popular at that time as the more commercial Merseybeat and, for that reason, the group was not paid the attention that it deserved. However, in less than a year, the **Hideaways** had become one of the leading Rhythm & Blues bands in the north of England - in a line-up with:

Ozzi Yue	(lg/voc)
Frank O'Connor	(voc/rg)
Judd Lander	(harp /voc)
John Shell	(bg/voc)
John Donaldson	(dr)

At the end of 1964, **John Shell** was called up by the US army to serve in the Vietnam war, which was possible because, in spite of his long-time residency in England, he was still an American citizen.

In 1967 he lost his life in this controversial war - a real loss!

His replacement in the **Hideaways** in 1964 was **Dave Collins**, another Liverpudlian, who had formerly played with the **Hi-Cats** and their continuation groups, **Freddie Starr & the Ventures**, **Danny Havoc & the Ventures** and the **Secrets**.

The **Hideaways** appeared regularly at all the major clubs in Liverpool and the surrounding area, but it took until 1966 for the **Hideaways** to be recorded for the first time.

This was not an official record but contained live recordings from the 'Sink' club in Liverpool, which, together with two numbers by the **Clayton Squares,** were

The Hideaways with Judd Lander - Christmas 1964

featured on an EP included with the German book, 'Beat in Liverpool', written by Jürgen Seuss.

On this record, the **Hideaways** were featured with "Momma Keep Your Big Mouth Shut" and their version of **Arthur Alexander**'s "Black Night". Unfortunately, the sound quality of this record is pretty poor and so the EP is only of interest to collectors or other individuals who are interested in the Liverpool music scene of the Sixties.

In addition to the **Clayton Squares**, the **Hideaways** were heavily featured in the above mentioned book. The **Hideaways** were a very good group so it is a mystery why, at that time, no official record was released. Another important and interesting fact is that the **Hideaways** played the 'Cavern' more times than any other band - a total of 412 gigs! These appearances also included the final gig before the 'Cavern' was closed in February 1966, as well as the first night when it was re-opened in July 1966.

In late 1966 or early 1967, **Judd Lander** left the group and a little later joined **Selofane** from Liverpool who, in 1967, cut two excellent singles for CBS, but that is another story.

Judd Lander went down to London with **Selofane** where he later became a very successful session and studio musician, working with many of the big name stars. Among others, he can be heard playing that great harmonica on the hit record, "Karma Chameleon", by **Boy George's Culture Club**.

Ritchie Rutledge, who had previously played with the **Aztecs** and the **Cryin' Shames,** joined the **Hideaways** as an additional singer, sharing the lead vocals with **Frank O'Connor** and **Ozzi Yue**.

Dave Collins left and was replaced by **Chris Finley**, a former member of the **Runaways**, the **Kruzads**, the **Masterminds** and the **Fruit Eating Bears**.

It was most probably this line-up that recorded the **Yardbirds** song, "I Wish You Would", the **Sammy Davis'** "But Not For Me", as well as the group's originals, "Life's A Drag", "The Times I Wish", "I Know What You're Thinking" and "Sally Go Round The Moon" for RCA. The last two of these songs were supposedly planned for a single, that was publicized but, unfortunately, never released.

The Hideaways as Confucius

By then. the **Hideaways**, following the fashion of that time, had dropped the 's' from their name and so articles and leaflets for that record featured the name **Hideaway**. This obviously was not the right solution as the group very soon changed their name completely into **Confucius**.

When **John Donaldson** left and quit showbiz, **Phil Chittick** joined the group as their drummer.

In late 1968, **Confucius** recorded their only single with "The Brandenburg Concerto" for RCA, which was a nice and very commercial record, but no longer comparable with their original sound anymore.

This record, which was coupled with the **Frank O'Connor** and **Chris Finley** original, "The Message", in spite of it's catchy melody and good drive, did not have any chart success and so the band did not achieve the undoubtedly deserved breakthrough.

Confucius most probably disbanded in the very early Seventies. **Phil Chittick** appeared again with the new **Merseybeats** and then played with **Cy Tucker & the Friars**. **Chris Finley** also joined the new **Merseybeats**, then he became a member of **Herman's Hermits** and after that played with a number of different bands.

In 1972, **Ritchie Rutledge** became a member of the **Swinging Blue Jeans** and **Frank O'Connor** teamed up with **Alan Crowley** (ex **Billy Butler & the Tuxedos**) in the cabaret duo, **Two's Company**, before he started a solo career and released some nice solo singles, in particular, "Liverpool - It All Came Tumbling Down", is a very good one. He wrote this song at the same time as his brother **Freddie O'Connor** wrote a book of the same title.

In 1989, **Frank O'Connor** and **Ozzi Yue,** along with some other famous Liverpool musicians including **Mike Pender** of the **Searchers, Tony Crane** and **Billy Kinsley** of the **Merseybeats, Kenny Parry** of **Liverpool Express** and **Alan Crowley, John O'Brian** and **Billy Butler** (all formerly of **Billy Butler & the Tuxedos**), were part of the session group, the **Class Of '64,** which recorded an album of original songs written by **Frank O'Connor** and **Alan Crowley.** Even if it was more Country influenced, it was a really good album which also clearly showed the song writing talent of Frank and Alan.

In 1991, the **Class Of '64** also recorded a memorial cassette with "Cavern Days" which, unfortunately, was not released on record. Of course it was a different line-up but also included **Frank O'Connor** again.

Ozzi Yue later became a really successful actor but he also kept in touch with his musical roots and he still leads his own group, **Yue Who,** which is quite a successful act on the Liverpool club scene.

After a short appearance at the Matthew-Street Festival in Liverpool in 2009, the **Hideaways** accepted an invitation from the German 'Beat-Club '66' and, amongst others, took part in their 'Merseybeat Open Air' concert in July 2010 in Bielefeld where they were a big 'hit' with the audience.

A great performance on which **Billy Kinsley** replaced **Frank O'Connor**, while the rest of the line-up consisted of **Ozzie Yue, Judd Lander, Chris Finley** and **John Donaldson** with **Dave Goldberg** on keyboards added to the line-up as a guest musician. They presented themselves as a great group of entertainers, in particular the audience was especially enthusiastic about **Ozzi Yue** and his singing abilities.

Discography :

The group never released an official record under the name of **The Hideaways** but live-recordings from the 'Sink', together with the **Clayton Squares,** can be found on an EP that was included with the German book, 'Beat in Liverpool', by **Jürgen Seuss** – see text.

EP **'Beat in Liverpool'**   G – Sonopress EVA 101 / 1966

The Hideaways : **Black Night / Momma Keep Your Big Mouth Shut**

The Clayton Squares : **Watch your step / Hey good looking / Tell me how do you feel**

as **Confucius** :

The Brandenburg Concerto (That's what I was) / The Message   UK- RCA 1923 / 1968

Unreleased tracks :

In 1967/1968 the following numbers were recorded as **'Hideaway'** for RCA but, unfortunately, never released:

"I Wish You Would", "But Not For Me", "Life's A Drag", "I Know What You're Thinking", "The Times I Wish" and **"Sally Go Round The Moon".**

THE TERRY HINES SEXTET

Bob Hardy

This real Rhythm & Blues group was formed in Liverpool by former members of the recently disbanded **T.L.'s Bluesicians** in early 1965 – namely **Bob Hardy** (g/sax), **Phil Perry** (p) and **Pete Newton** (bg). For more information, see the **T.L.'s Bluesicians** story in this book.

They teamed up with the vocalist, **Terry Hines**, who had just parted from the **Clayton Squares**, the sax-player **Ray Renns** from the **Inmates** and **Dave Irving** on drums.

Phil Perry and **Ray Renns** did not stay for too long and, while **Phil Perry** stopped playing, **Ray Renns** later appeared again as a member of the **Fyx**.

With the new members, the **Terry Hines Sextet** now consisted of the following musicians:

Terry Hines	(voc)
Bob Hardy	(g/tr/sax)
Terry Kenna	(lg)
Pete Newton	(bg)
Alby Donnelly	(sax)
Dave Irving	(dr)

Terry Kenna was a former member of the **St. Louis Checks**, while **Dave Irving** had previously played in a Modern-Jazz trio.

Alby Donnelly, for a very short time, had also played with the **St. Louis Checks** and, before that, he had been a member of the **Plainsmen**.

The **Terry Hines Sextet,** within a short time, became very popular on the scene and, still in 1965, went into the CAM studio and recorded the songs, "Caldonia" and "Back Door Blues". Of these two, "Caldonia" especially is a real knockout.

In July 1965, the group also recorded at the famous 'Marquee' in London for a commercial radio station, but it is not known which songs were played at that gig. A little later, the **Terry Hines Sextet** provided the music for the 'Jack Of Spades', a play featured in Liverpool's 'Commonwealth Arts Festival' at the 'Everyman' Theatre.

It was here that **Terry Hines** discovered his love of the theatre and left the group in October 1965 to concentrate on his new career.

Geoff Workman (voc/org/p), formerly of the **Feelgoods,** then joined the band which changed its name, for a short period, to **The Sextet** before recruiting a new vocalist/frontman with **Eddie Cave**, who formerly had sung with the **Poets** which then evolved into the **Richmond Group**.

This line-up, following a suggestion of **Bob Wooler** who became the band's manager and agent, changed its name to the **Fix**. But that is another story in this book.

Discography :

In 1965, the **Terry Hines Sextet** recorded the songs, "**Caldonia**" and "**Back Door Blues**", at the CAM studio in Moorfields on a reel-to-reel tape. Unfortunately, these numbers were never released on record but were featured on the Mayfield-CD, 'This Is Merseybeat Vol. 3' in 2002.

IAN & THE ZODIACS

Two groups were formed in the Crosby area of Liverpool in 1958 which were both predecessor groups to **Ian & the Zodiacs**. These groups were **The Deltones** and **The Zodiacs**.

The **Deltones** originally consisted of **Paul Dougherty** (voc), **Ian Edwards** (voc/g), **Geoff Bethel** (p/org), **George Hodges** (bg) and **Peter 'Mesh' Stephenson** (dr).

In 1960, **Geoff Bethel** joined **King Size Taylor & the Dominoes** and **Ian Edwards** became a member of the **Zodiacs** while the remaining three musicians, together with **Dave Edwards** (lg), continued as a band under the name **St. Paul & the Angels** but later changed their name back to the **Deltones**.

They disbanded in 1963 and only **'Mesh' Stephenson** appeared again in the late Nineties - as a member of the re-formed **Dominoes**, that were sometimes joined by **King Size Taylor**.

The **Zodiacs** originally consisted of **John Kennedy** (voc/g), **Pete Griffiths** (bg), **Pete Pimlett** (g), **Jerry Garagan** (p), a sax-player by the name of **Dave**, and **Dave Lovelady** on drums.

Johnny Kennedy left in 1960 to become a member of **King Size Taylor & the Dominoes** and, after that, he appeared with **Carl Vincent & the Counts**. The **Zodiacs** were joined by **Ian Edwards** of the **Deltones**, but the group nearly disbanded when **Pete Griffiths** was killed in a motorbike accident. At the same time, **Jerry Garagan** and the sax-player, **Dave** left.

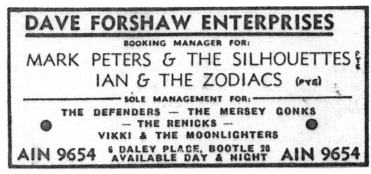

DAVE FORSHAW ENTERPRISES

BOOKING MANAGER FOR:

MARK PETERS & THE SILHOUETTES &
IAN & THE ZODIACS (PYE)

SOLE MANAGEMENT FOR:

THE DEFENDERS — THE MERSEY GONKS — THE RENICKS — VIKKI & THE MOONLIGHTERS

AIN 9654 6 DALEY PLACE, BOOTLE 20 **AIN 9654**
AVAILABLE DAY & NIGHT

The remaining, **Ian Edwards**, **Pete Pimlett** and **Dave Lovelady**, were then joined by **Peter Wallace** (bg) and changed their name to **Ian & the Zodiacs**.

But this line-up only lasted for one year and then **Pete Pimlett** left and apparently quit show business, while **Dave Lovelady** became a member of **King Size Taylor & the Dominoes**.

Ian Edwards and **Peter Wallace** were then joined by **Charlie Flynn** (g/voc), **Geoff Bethel** (p/org) and **Cliff Roberts** (dr), who all came from **King Size Taylor & the Dominoes**.

Charlie Flynn had previously played with the **Bobby Bell Rockers** and **Geoff Bethel** (of course) had played with the **Deltones**.

With all these changes, **Ian & the Zodiacs** in 1961 consisted of:

Ian Edwards	(voc/g)
Charlie Flynn	(g/voc)
Peter Wallace	(bg)
Geoff Bethel	(p/org)
Cliff Roberts	(dr)

This line-up lasted for some time and, in 1963, was chosen to be featured on the Oriole compilations, 'This Is Merseybeat' Vol. 1 and Vol. 2, with the songs, "It Ain't Necessarily So", "Let's Turkey Trot" and "Secret Love".

A little later, **Ian & the Zodiacs** had their first single released on the same label with a great version of the **Marvelettes** number, "Beechwood 4-5789", but, unfortunately, it was unsuccessful. A few weeks later, the album tracks, "Let's Turkey Trot" and "It Ain't Necessarily So", were also released on a single but under the name of **Wellington Wade**.

Charlie Flynn had used this name when he wrote the B-side of the first single and it is hard to explain why this name was chosen by Oriole for the second single, because it was clearly the recordings that were done by **Ian & the Zodiacs** for the compilation. However, this record also did not make it, although the magazine, 'Reveille', saw a bright future for the 'new talented singer', **Wellington Wade** . . . .?

Despite the two unsuccessful singles, 1963 turned out to be a good year for **Ian & the Zodiacs** as they were booked to play the 'Star-Club' in Hamburg, where they went down very well.

Geoff Bethel had left the group before the trip to Hamburg and, just for that tour of Germany, he was replaced by **Mike Partridge**, who came from Birmingham's 'Brumbeat' scene. After the tour, he left again and **Ian & the Zodiacs** continued as a four-piece.

When **Cliff Roberts** left to join the new **King Size Taylor** band in 1964, he was replaced by **Geoff Bamford**, the former drummer with **Rikki & the Red Streaks**, the **Memphis Three** and the **Connoisseurs**.

In 1965, the group released the single, "Just The Little Things I Like", under the name, **Ian Edwards & the Zodiacs,** on Fontana, as well as the album, 'Gear Again', on the Wing label, which featured cover versions of the big hits of that time.

In the meantime, **Ian & the Zodiacs** had been back to Germany where they were already major stars on the so-called 'Star-Club' scene. The group also became quite popular in the United States after the album, 'Ian & the Zodiacs', was released over there. This was a great long player, which was also released in Germany as 'Star-Club Show 7' on the 'Star-Club' label, but for mysterious reasons was never issued in Great Britain.

For the German market, "Message To Martha" was coupled out as a single, followed by further great singles, such as "So Much In Love", "Bitte Komm Wieder", the superb "Leave It To Me", "No Money No Honey" and "Na-na-na-na-na" - all recorded in 1966. The German version of "Message To Martha", which was not released at that time, was eventually released in 1999!

Besides this, **Ian & the Zodiacs** had two more great albums released in Germany with the titles, 'Just listen to ...' and 'Locomotive', while in England and USA, only a few more singles were issued.

It is very hard to understand why the English market failed to pay more attention to this excellent group. It was one of the Liverpool groups that had a great influence on the German music and band scene and was regarded as one of the best beat groups that ever came out of England.

In 1966, one more double album was released on the English Fontana label, but this one, under the pseudonym of **The Koppykats,** featured exceptional cover versions of the **Beatles** hits. It became the

biggest selling success for **Ian & the Zodiacs** in England and was also released in Europe. In Germany it was issued as two single albums with the titles, 'The Beatles Best Done By The Koppykats' and 'More Beatles Best Done By The Koppykats', of which the songs, "Help" and "Nowhere Man", were coupled out as a single on the obscure 'Pop Ten' label. Without doubt, these records were played, sung and produced very well but were not half as interesting as the other albums by **Ian & the Zodiacs.**

Meanwhile, there had been some more changes in the line-up. **Peter Wallace** had left in August 1966, he initially joined the London-based group, the **Mike Cotton Sound,** but then he returned to Liverpool where he joined the **Connoisseurs**.

He was replaced in **Ian & the Zodiacs** by **Tony Coates** from Liverpool, who formerly had played with the **Hungry I's**, the **Corsairs** and **Mark Peters & the Method**.

Geoff Bamford had also returned to Liverpool, where he disappeared from the scene and his replacement was **Fred Smith**, a former member of the **Bobby Patrick Big Six** and **Tony Sheridan & the Big Six**, but he did not stay for too long and later became a member of the **Kevin Ayers Band**.

The new drummer with **Ian & the Zodiacs** in 1967 was **Joe Walsh**, who had previously played with the **Teenbeats**, the **TJs** and finally with **Lee Curtis & the All Stars**.

In March 1967, **Charlie Flynn** followed **Peter Wallace** to the **Connoisseurs** and he was replaced by **Arthur Ashton**, a former member of the **Confederates, Billy Forde & the Phantoms** and the follow-on groups, **Billy Kramer & the Coasters** and **Chick Graham & the Coasters**, he had also played with **Mark Peters & the Silhouettes**.

The German, **Klaus Doldinger,** occasionally joined **Ian & the Zodiacs** on their records as their organist. He had previously, under the name of **Paul Nero**, led his own group, the **Blue Sounds Inc.**.

In July 1967, **Ian & the Zodiacs** disbanded totally when **Ian Edwards** returned to Liverpool, where he became a member of the **Fourmost** - but only for a short time, and then he also joined the **Connoisseurs**.

After that, he played with the **Chesterfields** before he quit show business for many years.

Tony Coates remained in Hamburg and joined the **Hi-Fis**, but then returned to Liverpool and joined the **Steve Allan Set**, that, in 1969, became **Paper Chase**. After that, he was a member of the new **Merseybeats** that recorded as **Crane**, and then he joined **Liverpool Express**. Later on, he played with the **Vince Earl Attraction**.

Arthur Ashton emigrated to the USA and **Joe Walsh** became a member of the newly formed **Undertakers** before he also quit the music business.

It is very hard to understand why this fabulous group never had greater international chart success. Even though they were one of the legendary Liverpool groups, this simply does not do enough justice to their excellent musical ability and their outstanding reputation on the European music scene of the Sixties.

In the end, it can be said that England missed out on one of their very best groups of that time.

In 1999, **Ian Edwards** stepped back onto the music scene and re-formed **Ian & the Zodiacs** together with former **Gerry & the Pacemakers** member, **Les Maguire** (p/org/voc), **Colin Fabb** (bg/voc), who, in the Sixties, was a member of the **Connoisseurs**, and **Malcolm Little** (lg). The drummer for that new group, **Carl Hardin**, was a member of **Paul Dean & the Tuxedos** in the Sixties, a band made up of British servicemen based in Bielefeld in Germany and, after that, he had played with various beat groups in England.

In this line-up, **Ian & the Zodiacs** toured Germany in 2000 and, for sure, their gig in Bielefeld went down a bomb.

In 2003, the group parted from **Ian Edwards** for unknown reasons and, with the singer, **Neil Lancaster**, and **Barry 'Baz' Davis** as new lead guitarist, continued on as the **Zodiacs**.

Barry Davis was an original member of the **Connoisseurs** and, after that, he had played with **King Size Taylor**, **Mike Warner & the New Stars** (from Bielefeld), the **New Vaudeville Band** and **Jimmy James & the Vagabonds**. Today, besides playing with the **Zodiacs,** he is also a member of the **Undertakers**.

Ian Edwards quit show business again but then tried a new comeback with different backing groups. He sadly died unexpectedly on 22nd October 2007, which was not only a shock for the Merseybeat scene, but also a tragic loss.

Single discography :

Beechwood 4-5789 / Can You Think Again	UK- Oriole CB 1849 / 1963
No Money, No Honey / Where Were You	UK- Fontana TF 708 / 1966
Wade In The Water / Come Along Girl	UK- Fontana TF 753 / 1966

as **Wellington Wade** :

Let's Turkey Trot / It Ain't Necessarily So	UK- Oriole CB 1857 / 1963

as **Ian Edwards & the Zodiacs** :

Just The Little Things I Like / This Won't Happen To Me	UK- Fontana TF 548 / 1965

Different German releases as **Ian & the Zodiacs** :

Message to Martha / Spartacus	G- Star-Club 148.514 / 1965
So Much In Love With You / All Of Me	G- Star-Club 148.535 / 1965
Bitte Komm Wieder / All Of Me	G- Fontana 269.325 / 1965
Leave It To Me / Why Can't It Be Me	G- Star-Club 148.543 / 1966

| No Money, No Honey / Ride Your Pony | G- Star-Club 148.548 / 1966 |
| Na-Na-Na-Na-Na / Any Day Now | G- Star-Club 148.572 / 1966 |

Different US releases as **Ian & the Zodiacs** :

Livin' Lovin' Wreck / Crying Game	US-Philips 40244 / 1965
Good Morning Little Schoolgirl / Message To Martha	US-Philips 40277 / 1965
So Much In Love / This Empty Place	US-Philips 40291 / 1965
Leave It To Me / Why Can't It Be Me	US-Philips 40343 / 1966

as **The Koppykats** :

| Help / Nowhere Man | G- Pop Ten 6805.015 / 1966 |

EP – discography :

IAN & THE ZODIACS (6 tracks 33rpm Jukebox- EP)

Good Morning Little Schoolgirl / The Crying Game / Jump Back / So Much In Love / Clarabella /

Baby, I Need Your Loving   US – Phillips PHS-807-C / 1965

LP discography :

GEAR AGAIN   UK- Wing WL 1074 / 1965

- Eight Days A Week / It's All Over Now / The Rise And Fall Of Flingel Bunt / We're Through /

Tired Of Waiting For You / I Feel Fine / All Day And All Of The Night / Game Of Love /

When You Walk In The Room / Um-Um-Um-Um-Um / A Hard Day's Night / Silhouettes

Different German releases :

STAR-CLUB SHOW 7   G- Star-Club 158.007 / 1965

- Good Morning Little Schoolgirl / Rockin' Robin / The Crying Game / Message To Martha /

Jump Back / This Empty Place / So Much In Love With You / Livin' Lovin' Wreck / Clarabella /

Spartacus / Baby I Need Your Lovin' / It's Alright / A Hard Day's Night

JUST LISTEN TO IAN & THE ZODIACS   G- Star-Club 158.020 / 1966

- The 'In' Crowd / Make It Easy On Yourself / I Need You / Face In The Crowd /

It's A Crying Shame/ Nature Boy / Can't Stop Running Away / Headin' Back To You / Donna Donna /

Believe Me / Strong Love / As You Used To Do / What Kind Of Fool / No, Not Another Night

LOCOMOTIVE   G- Star-Club 158.029 / 1966

- Ride Your Pony / Respect / See-Saw / Where Were You / Cool Jerk / This Won't Happen To Me /

Come On Along Girl / Going To A Go-Go / Wade In The Water / Get Out Of My Life Woman /

No Money, No Honey / Thinkin' About You Girl / Working In The Coal-Mine / Soulful Dress

as **The Koppykats** :

THE BEATLES BEST DONE BY THE KOPPYKATS   G-Fontana 700.153 WGY/1966

- You Can't Do That / Little Child / All My Lovin' / Eight Days A Week / I'll Follow The Sun /

Long Tall Sally / I Feel Fine / A Hard Day's Night / The Things We Said Today / I'm A Loser /

I Saw Her Standing There / Roll Over Beethoven

MORE BEATLES BEST DONE BY THE KOPPYKATS   G-Fontana 701.543 WPY/1966

- Nowhere Man / Norwegian Wood / We Can Work It Out / Yesterday / Day Tripper /

I'm Looking Through You / Help / You've Got To Hide Your Love Away / Ticket To Ride /

I'm Down / Dizzy Miss Lizzy / Please Mr. Postman

(*** please note that these two LPs were released in England as double album on Fontana)

Different US releases :

IAN & THE ZODICAS   US-Philips PHS 600-176 / 1965

- same as the German 'Star-Club Show 7' only without "**Livin' Lovin' Wreck**"

Tracks on compilations :

Let's Turkey Trot on 'This Is Merseybeat' Vol. 1	UK - Oriole PS 40047 / 1963
Secret Love on 'This Is Merseybeat' Vol. 2	UK - Oriole PS 40048 / 1963
It Ain't Necessarily So on 'This Is Merseybeat' Vol. 2	UK - Oriole PS 40048 / 1963
That's Nice (live) on 'Beat und Prosa live im Star-Club'	G-Philips (Twen) 843.933 / 1966
Ride Your Pony (live) on 'Beat und Prosa ....'	G-Philips (Twen) 843.933 / 1966
No Money, No Honey (live) on 'Beat und Prosa ....'	G-Philips (Twen) 843.933 / 1966
Intro Let's Go / No Money No Honey on Beat-Club	G-Philips (Bild und Funk) 111.576 / 1967
Take A Message To Martha on 'Beater's Hitparade'	G-Philips 75283 P.13 / 1967

THE INCAS

This band was formed in 1963 by **Terry Broughton** and **Bob Martin** in St. Helens, which is not very far from Liverpool. Before that, both of them had played in a school band called **The Falcons**.

Initially, the **Incas** played a lot of **Cliff Richard & the Shadows** numbers, as well as related material, but they ultimately evolved into a real Beat group.

It did not take too long until they became popular on the local scene and appeared regularly at such well known venues as the 'Plaza' in St. Helens, the 'Orrell Park Ballroom', as well as at the 'Cavern' and the 'Peppermint Lounge' in Liverpool. At that time, the **Incas** consisted of the following musicians:

Jed White	**(voc)**
Terry Broughton	**(g/voc)**
John Crogan	**(g/voc)**
Bob Martin	**(bg/voc)**
Alf Anslow	**(dr**)

Jed White, **John Crogan** and **Alf Anslow** were all newcomers to the music business. **Jed White** did not stay for too long and most probably quit show business as he did not appear on the scene again. He was not replaced in the **Incas**, who continued as a four piece with all of the members sharing the vocals.

It was in early 1966 that **Terry Broughton** and **John Crogan** also left the group, they continued playing together under the name of the **Morning Duo** until **John Crogan** emigrated to Canada in 1970, where he is still living.

Terry Broughton quit the music business but stepped back into it in 1990 when he joined a group with the name, **Old Kids On The Rocks** - do you see any relationship to **New Kids On The Block**?

But back to the **Incas**: The remaining members, **Bob Martin** and **Alf Anslow,** formed a new group in early 1966 under the old name, which also included **Martin O'Brian** as their lead singer.

Martin O'Brian was a former member of the popular **Federal Five** from St. Helens who, at some point, had changed their name into the **Streamers**.

Unfortunately, the guitarist or guitarists of that new line-up are not known, but it may have been **Phil Ganson** or **'Shirt' Clayton**, if not both, who were also former members of the **Federal Five** and the **Streamers** respectively, who apparently had just disbanded at that time.

Therefore, it is possible that **Bob Martin** and **Alf Anslow** not only teamed up with **Martin O'Brian**, but also with other remaining members of his former group, but that is only a supposition.

Norman Thomas became their manager and somehow he acquired a recording contract with Parlophone for the group, who in the same year released a great Beat record with the songs, "One Night Stand" and "I'll Keep You Holding On".

The single sold well but, in the end, failed to make the charts so it was not followed by another record. Around the same time, a group with the name of the **Incas** was featured with one song on a flexi disc from Keele University (Lyntone LYN 765/5). This might have been the **Incas** from St. Helens, but this is not certain and, unfortunately, the song featured on that EP, together with three other groups, is also not known.

However, after their Parlophone release, little was heard of the **Incas** and they soon disappeared from the scene. Unfortunately, what happened to the individual musicians after the split is not known.

Discography :

One Night Stand / I'll Keep Holding On   **UK- Parlophone R 5551 / 1066**

(In addition, there was a flexi EP from the Keele University released in the Sixties (Keele Rag Record Lyntone LYN 765/6). On this EP, the **Incas** and three other bands were featured. This may have been the **Incas** from St. Helens, but this is not absolutely certain)

TONY JACKSON & THE VIBRATIONS

This group was formed in 1964 by Liverpudlian **Tony Jackson**, who had started his career in the Fifties as a guitarist/vocalist with the **Martinis** Skiffle group prior to going solo under the name, **Clint Reno**. After that, he became the lead vocalist and bass guitarist with the **Searchers**, who initially backed **Johnny Sandon** before they became internationally famous in their own right.

Tony Jackson's lead vocals can be heard on the worldwide hits, "Sweets For My Sweet" and "Sugar And Spice". After he parted from the **Searchers** (for mysterious reasons), he formed his own group under the name of **Tony Jackson & the Vibrations**, which consisted of non Liverpool musicians. The reason why he turned his back on the Liverpool Merseybeat scene in such a way was probably only known to **Tony Jackson**, but it is possible that it was an act of defiance stemming from his break up with the **Searchers**. However, **Tony Jackson & the Vibrations** were a very good group and in their original line-up consisted of:

Tony Jackson	**(voc/bg)**
Ian Bruisel	**(g/voc)**
Martin Raymond	**(org/voc)**
Paul Francis	**(dr)**

Tony Jackson & the Vibrations

Paul Francis hailed from Beckenham and was a former member of the **Rolf Harris Band** and **Bobby Christo & the Rebels** from the London scene.

Martin Raymond was from Croydon and had previously played with the **Westmister Five**. While **Ian Bruisel**, who sometimes also used the name of **Ian Leighton**, hailed from Streatham.

Tony Jackson and his new group were signed by PYE, the same label where he had also recorded with the **Searchers**. The first single by **Tony Jackson & the Vibrations** was a very strong version of **Mary Wells'** "Bye Bye Baby" coupled with the great **Bobby Parker** classic, "Watch your step".

The record climbed up to No. 25 in the British charts and this debut success was followed by another **Mary Wells** original but, "You Beat Me To The Punch" was not as successful as its predecessor.

"Love Potion No. 9" didn't make the charts either but, if it was compared to the **Searchers** version, it is easy to hear that **Tony Jackson & the Vibrations** played a much 'harder' version. It was more Rock than the harmony styled **Searchers** sound.

In 1965, **Tony Jackson & the Vibrations** recorded their final single for PYE with "Stage Door", a really great, melodic song which deserved to be successful but did not make it in the end.

The band changed its name to **The Tony Jackson Group** in early 1966 and, a few months later, **Martin Raymond** left.

His replacement was **Ian Green**, a former session musician who had just worked with the **Everly Brothers** on their album, 'Two Yanks in London'.

The **Tony Jackson Group** was signed to CBS and their first single for the new label was the strong "You're My Number One", but it also failed to become a chart success.

The follow-ups were "Never Leave Your Baby's Side", "Follow Me" and "Anything Else You Want", which were all released in 1966.

At the end of that year, the group was joined by **Dennis Thompson** as bass guitarist, while **Tony Jackson** concentrated on the vocals.

One more EP was released on the CBS label. It consisted exclusively of songs from the former singles – this EP was also released in France.

The **Tony Jackson Group** became a quartet again when **Ian Green** left in early 1967.

Ian Bruisel's brother, Jimmy, had a Portuguese girlfriend and her father ran a recording studio and a radio station in Lisbon. The group went to Portugal on holiday in 1967 but also accepted some gigs in the sunny south. On this holiday tour, the **Tony Jackson Group** was taken into the above mentioned studio where an EP was recorded on the studio-owned label 'Estudio' with the songs, "Just Like Me", "He Was A Friend Of Mine", "Understanding" and "Shake".

EP Cover for the 'Estudio' release with Tony Jackson, Paul Francis, Denis Thompson & Ian Bruisel

This record is a desired collector's item these days but, in 1967, it was unsuccessful, probably because this small, private label had no real commercial distribution system.

Quite soon after, the **Tony Jackson Group** returned to England and disbanded.

Dennis Thompson emigrated to the USA, while **Paul Francis** opened a recording studio, probably in the Liverpool area.

Ian Bruisel quit show business and, in 1987, he died of a brain haemorrhage.

Tony Jackson later became the manager of a golf club near Liverpool.

When **Mike Pender** separated from the **Searchers** in 1986 to form his own group under the name **Mike Pender's Searchers**, it was rumoured that **Tony Jackson** would join this new band, but it did not happen in the end.

In 1990, **Tony Jackson** and **Paul Francis** re-formed **Tony Jackson & the Vibrations** with new members, **Colin Free** (lg), **Steve English** (bg) and **Chris Teeder** (key). Unfortunately, without a major breakthrough and with no record releases, they did not exist for too long.

Tony Jackson sadly died in August 2003.

Single discography :

Bye Bye Baby / Watch Your Step	**UK- PYE 7 N 15685 / 1964**
You Beat Me To The Punch / This Little Girl Of Mine	**UK- PYE 7 N 15745 / 1964**
Love Potion No. 9 / Fortune Teller	**UK- PYE 7 N 15766 / 1964**
Stage Door / That's What I Want	**UK- PYE 7 N 15876 / 1965**

as **The Tony Jackson Group** :

You're My Number One / Let Me Know	**UK- CBS 202.039 / 1966**
Never Leave Your Baby's Side / I'm The One She Really Thinks A Lot Of	**UK- CBS 202.069 / 1966**
Follow Me / Walk That Walk	**UK- CBS 202.297 / 1966**
Anything Else You Want / Come And Stop	**UK- CBS 202.408 / 1966**

EP discography

THE TONY JACKSON GROUP   **UK- CBS 5726 / 1966**

- You're My Number One / Let Me Know / I'm The One She Really Thinks A Lot Of /

Never Leave Your Baby's Side

(*** please note that this EP was also released on French CBS under the same order number with the title, 'You're My Number One')

Different Portuguese release:

TONY JACKSON GROUP   **P - Estudio** (without number) **/ 1967**

- Just Like Me / Understanding / Shake / He Was A Friend Of Mine

JEANNIE & THE BIG GUYS

In the beginning, they were the **Pacemakers**, a four-piece group formed in Chester in 1960.

The Pacemakers

While playing the local scene, they rehearsed in the 'George' pub and the owner, Mr. Hughes, had a daughter that sometimes joined the **Pacemakers** at their rehearsals for a few songs.

Rita Hughes was a really good singer and, at some point during 1962, she was added to the line-up, who from then on appeared as **Four Hits & A Miss**. They very likely would have had to change their name at that time anyway in order to prevent confusion with the up-coming **Gerry & the Pacemakers** from Liverpool.

The Chester group with it's new girl-singer became very popular on the scene and in 1963 they were signed to the PYE label. The record company did not like the group's name as it was too ambiguous, the group finally became **Jeannie & the Big Guys** in the following line-up:

Jeannie	(voc)
David Jones	(g/voc)
Geoff Dawson	(g/voc)
Owen Rickets	(bg/voc)
George Roberts	(dr)

Still in 1963, **Jeannie & the Big Guys** recorded the single, "Don't Lie To Me", which was coupled with the **Shirelles** classic, "Boys", a song often covered by other Liverpool groups including the **Beatles** and **Lee Curtis & the All Stars**.

Jeannie & the Big Guys

In January 1964, **George Roberts** left the group to join the **Excheckers** and, after that, he played with the **Delmonts**, had a short spell with **Amen Corner** and, in late 1965, joined the **Mindbenders**. He then became a freelance drummer but, in the early 80's, he was a member of **Rogues Gallery**.

In 1964, he was replaced in **Jeannie & the Big Guys** by **Terry Lynch**, who most probably came from **Ricky Darne & the Dee-Fenders** that, a little later, became **Rick E. Darne & the Toplins**, another story.

With this line-up, the second single by **Jeannie & the Big Guys** was released, but their cover version of "Sticks And Stones" did not achieve any chart success.

Shortly after this, **Jeannie** left to go solo and the group continued for a while under the name of the **Big Guys** but then disappeared from the scene.

Cor!

Gorgeous girl with the dark brown hair is Jeannie. Guys down in the South of England will have the benefit of Jeannie's looks from June onwards when she goes on a Southern tour.
Backing her on her public engagements is Earl Royce and the Olympics.

Of the members, it is only known that **Owen Rickets** later played in one of the early line-ups of the re-formed **Faron's Flamingos**.

Jeannie for a short time was backed by **Earl Royce & the Olympics** from Liverpool but, still in 1964, toured Germany with the **Delmont Four**.

In the same year, she was signed to Parlophone and her first solo single ,"I Love Him", was released under the name **'Jeannie'**.

After that, she changed her name to **Cindy Cole**, got a recording contract with Columbia and, from November 1964 onwards, she was backed by the **Fugitives** from Chester, who could have been an offshoot of the former **Big Guys**.

In April 1965, the single, "A Love Like Yours", was released under the name **Cindy Cole** but, like its predecessors, it did not become a hit. Neither did the follow-up, "Just Being Your Baby (turns me on)". Despite this lack of success, she was one of the really good female singers on the British Beat scene.

She, and her new backing group, never made a major breakthrough and, at the end of the Sixties, **Cindy Cole** and the **Fugitives** disappeared from the scene without much attention being paid to the fact.

It is known that, in later years, **Rita Hughes**, who, besides being a very beautiful and talented singer, had some prestige cabaret bookings.

She died unexpected and far too young in April 1989 - at the age of 42.

The Fugitives

Rita (Jeannie) Hughes

Jeannie and the Big Guys

L to R: Owen Rickets, George Roberts , Rita (Jeannie) Hughes , Dave Jones & Geoff Dawson

Single discography

as **Jeannie & the Big Guys** :

Don't Lie To Me / Boys	UK- PYE 7 N 35147 / 1963
Sticks And Stones / I Want You	UK- PYE 7 N 35164 / 1964

'Jeannie' – solo :

I Love Him / With Any Other Girl	UK- Parlophone R 5343 / 1964

as **Cindy Cole** :

A Love Like Yours / He's Sure The Boy I Love	UK- Columbia DB 7519 / 1965
Just Being Your Baby / Lonely City Blue Boy	UK- Columbia DB 7973 / 1966

(*** please note that on the last two singles, **Cindy Cole** (aka Jeannie) was most probably backed by the **Fugitives** who, at that time, were her regular backing group)

DAVID JOHN & THE MOOD

Original Line up with
Robb Deka & Rick Greenwood

This band hailed from Preston, Lancashire and, without a doubt, was the number one group of its hometown.

It is possible that the group originated in 1962 under the name of the **Mood Rhythms** by singer **David John Smith**, but this information seems a little doubtful.

David John was a member of the **Bobcats** and the **Thunderbeats**. After that, he had joined the very short-lived **Questions** that also included **Reg Welch** (lg), who came from the **Rebels** and **Peter Atkinson** (rg) and **John Brierley** (bg) from the **Thunderbeats**, as well as **Gene Carberry** (dr), a former member of the **Crusaders**. The **Questions** only played four gigs - the last one was at the 'Daily Herald Beat Festival' in Liverpool in 1963 where they backed **Ricky Valence**. This obviously creates some doubt regarding the 1962 formation.

Reg Welch and **John Brierley** went on to play with **Freddie Starr & the Midnighters** and **Gene Carberry** (after a tour of Poland with the **Atoms**) became a member of the **Prestons**, which is another story in this book.

David John joined the **Falcons** which, besides him, consisted of **Robb Deka** (p/voc), **Peter Illingworth** (g/voc), **Rick Greenwood** (bg) and **Freddie Isherwood** (dr).

Peter Illingworth was a former member of the **Bruff Boys** and the **Travellers**, formerly known as **Wendy & the Travellers**.

Drummer **Freddie Isherwood** (sometimes named **Mal Isherwood**) came from the **Corries**, while **Robb Deka** and **Rick Greenwood** had previously played with the **Crusaders**.

This line-up of the **Falcons** changed their name into **David John & the Mood** in 1963.

Robb Deka, whose real name is **Robert Eccles** and who may have also played in the backing group of **Julie Grant**, left in 1963 and went down to London for test recordings on which he was backed by a trio, that a little later became the **Puppets**, which are also featured in this book. After that, he returned to Lancashire and joined the **Prestons**.

Rick Greenwood also left and, accordingly, **David John & the Mood** in early 1964 consisted of:

David John	(voc)
Peter Illingworth	(lg/voc)
Peter Atkinson	(rg/voc)
John Brierley	(bg/voc)
Freddie (Mal) Isherwood	(dr)

David John & the Mood were signed by Decca for their new sub-label, Vocalion, which was quite a surprise as the group had not yet had any outstanding success.

In May of the same year, their first single, "A Pretty Thing", was released coupled with "To Catch That Man". Both numbers were not really commercial but a very interesting mixture of Rhythm & Blues and Mod sound. This record was not very successful, mainly because both the group and the label were still unknown at that time. In addition, in 1964, the commercial Merseybeat still played a leading role in the music business. But it seems "A Pretty Thing" did not sell too badly, as the group's next single was planned for release on the Decca label.

Still in 1964, the song, "It's So Exciting", was recorded and announced in the 'Mersey Beat' newspaper, but it is uncertain whether it was really released as it was never mentioned in any discography and is also not found in the Decca catalogue.

However, the popularity of the group started to grow and the music press showed more and more interest in them. Suddenly **David John & the Mood** became quite a well known name, and not only in the north of England.

The group was then signed to Parlophone and two more singles, produced by **Joe Meek**, were released in 1965.

"Bring It To Jerome" was a great number, again the typical mixture of Rhythm & Blues and Mod sound, as was the B-side, "I Love To See You Strut". Unfortunately, this record also failed to make the charts.

Their other single, "Diggin' For Gold", was much 'weaker' and it also failed to get **David John & the Mood** into the headlines, let alone any chart success.

In the middle of 1966, **David John** disbanded the group and, for a short time, joined **Sound Five**, who later changed their name to **Barbed Wire Soup**. He also guested with an outfit called **Three-D**, which consisted of former **Puppets** members and, with **David John** as their lead vocalist, evolved into the recording group **Thundermother**.

Peter Illingworth joined **Purple Haze**, who later recorded as **Little Free Rock**.

Single discography :

A Pretty Thing / To Catch That Man	UK- Vocalion V 9220 / 1964
It's So Exciting /	UK- Decca ??? / 1964
Bring It To Jerome / I Love To See You Strut	UK- Parlophone R 5255 / 1965
Diggin' For Gold / She's Fine	UK- Parlophone R 5301 / 1965

(*** please note that it is not known for sure if "**It's So Exciting**" was really released after it was recorded for Decca. It was announced in the music press but is not found in the official Decca catalogue)

THE JYNX

Whether or not this band should be featured in this book may be open to debate, as it is not known exactly where they came from.

They appeared on the scene suddenly in 1962 and insiders regard them as part of the Liverpool/Merseybeat scene. This is somewhat questionable as there was never anything written about them in the Liverpool music papers such as the 'Mersey Beat' or the 'Combo' – their name did not even show up in any of the Liverpool club's advertisements, although there is a photo existing of them, taken at the 'Cavern'.

However, they were 'there' and sounded very much like Merseybeat and were of outstanding musical quality, judging by their only single.

The **Jynx** consisted of the following musicians:

Keith Wells	(voc)
Brian Ashley	(g/voc)
Gordon Lincoln	(g)
George Hunt	(bg/voc)
C. John Curtis	(dr)

The group was signed to Columbia in 1964 and, in June of that same year, their first single was released with the songs "How" and "Do What They Don't Say", which were great songs and excellent examples of Beat music at its best.

The song "How" was written by **Gordon Wingrove** and "Do What They Don't Say" by **Keith Street**, both unknown songwriters, but who were possibly identical with **Gordon Lincoln** and **Keith Wells** of the band. This fantastic single was produced by **Norrie Paramor**.

The **Jynx** were also featured with both of these songs on the French sampler, 'The Best Of The Liverpool Sound', and, in spite of stiff competition from groups such as **Tony Rivers & the Castaways**, the **Dave Clark Five**, **Freddie & the Dreamers, Gerry & the Pacemakers, Mike Sheridan & the Nightriders, Chris Farlowe & the Thunderbirds** and others, they certainly created the best impression on that record.

With regard to the **Jynx**, it seems that recording directors, producers, managers, promoters and the press all made the same mistake in not taking more notice of this group. They should have been pushed a little more and probably would have become big stars in the Beat business, because they had the right musical quality and the right sound.

At the end of the Beat boom, the **Jynx** disappeared from the scene and no one really noticed. It was as though they had just been another 'one record band'.

If it hadn't been for this one excellent record, probably one of the best of that era, it would have been as if they never existed.

Single discography :

How / Do What They Don't Say   UK- Columbia DB 7304 / 1964

Tracks on compilations :

"How"   on **'The Best Of The Liverpool Sound'**   F- Columbia FPX 272 / 1964
"Do what they don't say"   on **'The Best Of The Liverpool Sound'**   F- Columbia FPX 272 / 1964

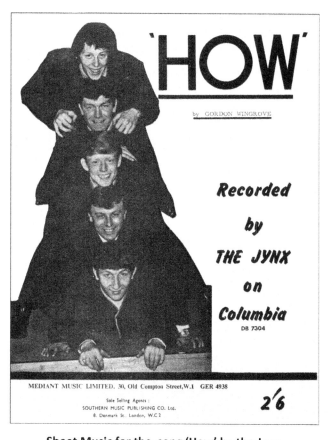

Sheet Music for the song 'How' by the Jynx

THE KANSAS CITY FIVE

As can be concluded from their name, this group's music was initially oriented towards Rock-A-Billy, influenced by **Carl Perkins** and also **Jerry Lee Lewis**, which could be heard in their heavily featured piano, and is likely the reason their musical style became more Rock 'n' Roll with time.

The **Kansas City Five** were formed by ex-**Bluegenes** founder member **Bruce McCaskill** in Liverpool in 1962 and within a short time became very popular and successful on the local scene.

Their original line-up consisted of the following musicians:

Bruce McCaskill	(voc/g)
Peter Cooke	(voc/g)
Tommy Hughes	(p/voc)
Alan Stratton	(bg)
Colin Middlebrough	(dr)

Peter Cooke had previously played with the **Topspots**, **Dee & the Dynamites** and with the short-lived **Roadrunners (II)**, who were not the Rhythm & Blues group that became well known a little later.

Tommy Hughes had started his career with the **Pinetop Skiffle Group,** he then became a member of the **Bluegenes** who, of course, were the predecessors of the **Swinging Blue Jeans**.

Alan Stratton was a former member of the **Black Cats**, one of the very early and important Liverpool groups, while **Colin Middlebrough** came from the **All Blacks Skiffle Group**.

From August until November 1962, the **Kansas City Five** were the regular backing group for singer **Freddie**

Fowell, a former member of **Howie Casey & the Seniors**, who a little later changed his name to **Freddie Starr** and was the lead singer for **Freddie Starr & the Ventures**, **Freddie Starr & the Midnighters**, **Freddie Starr & the Starr Boys** (also known as **Freddie Starr & the Flamingoes**) and **Freddie Starr & the Delmonts**.

After **Freddie Starr**, who later became a well-known British TV star, had separated from the **Kansas City Five**, the group was joined by **Robbie Hickson**, who had previously sung with **Alfie Diamond & the Skiffle Kings**, the **Casuals** (not the hit group of the same name), and the **Topspots**. He was also 'Dee' of **Dee & the Dynamites**. The last two groups were forerunner bands of the **Undertakers**.

Although the band was a six piece now, it continued under the name of the **Kansas City Five**.

They became the resident group at the famous 'Iron Door' and sometimes also backed the great Liverpool songstress **Beryl Marsden** at her gigs.

At the end of 1962, **Bruce McCaskill** and **Peter Cooke** left and, together with other musicians, formed a backing-group for **Freddie Starr** for his French tour. This newly-formed band was the foundation for **Groups Inc.**

After **Groups Inc.**, **Peter Cooke** became a member of **Earl Royce & the Olympics**, where he also used the stage name **Pete Melody**. He later formed a new group under the name the **Trend** and, in the Seventies was a member of the newly-formed **Faron's Flamingos**, after that, he continued to perform on the cabaret scene.

Bruce McCaskill, who sometimes also appeared as **Bruce Monroe**, joined the **Escorts**. But it is not certain if he was a member of the group or the crew. After that, he was road manager for **Eric Clapton** for a time, he later became the manager of the **Average White Band**.

But back to the **Kansas City Five**, who were left as a four-piece but became a quintet again when they were joined by **Les Stuart** as their new guitarist in 1963. He was the former leader of the **Les Stuart Quartet** and, after that, had played with **Frank Knight & the Barons** and **Danny Havoc & the Ventures**.

It was probably in 1963 that **Robbie Hickson** left and apparently quit show business, he was not replaced and **Les Stuart** took over the lead vocals. At this time, the **Kansas City Five** became the resident group at the 'Odd Spot', a popular Liverpool live club run by their manager, **Jim Turner**.

Around that time, they were joined by songstress, **Barbara Harrison**, who sometimes also used the stage name '**Deanne**' and who had previously sung with the **Hi-Cats**, **Faron's Flamingos** and **Danny Havoc & the Ventures**.

Les Stuart then left to join the **Long & Short**, where he used the stage name **Les Saints**.

His replacement in the **Kansas City Five** was **Mike Liston**, a former member of **Bobby Angelo & the Tuxedos** and **Lee Castle & the Barons**.

The next to leave was **Colin Middlebrough**, who later joined the **Four Originals**, that had evolved from the very popular **Dale Roberts & the Jaywalkers**.

He was replaced in the **Kansas City Five** by **Lewis Collins**, who came from Liverpool's **Renegades**.

Probably with this line-up the band toured France and Germany, where they are also likely to have appeared at the 'Star-Club' in Hamburg, although no record can be found of it.

Despite the success the **Kansas City Five** had on Merseyside, they split totally in 1964 without having achieved any national recognition.

Mike Liston joined the **Classics** from Liverpool and later became a successful session musician and record producer in Nashville.

Lewis Collins joined the **Georgians**, where he switched to bass guitar. After that, he was the bass guitarist with the **Eyes** and the **Mojos**. He later became a successful British TV actor (do you remember 'Bodie' of the 'Professionals'?) and, in 1983, started to record again, but without any great success.

Barbara Harrison continued as a solo singer. She was signed by Decca but, as far as it is known, there was never anything released. She then simply faded from the scene.

Alan Stratton became a member of **Johnny Marlowe & the Whip-Chords**, where he remained until the group disbanded in 1966. He then joined the **Fables** and, in the early Seventies, was a member of the **Chesterfields**, where he replaced **Ian Edwards**.

The **Chesterfields**, with a line-up that included ex **Stereos** guitarist, **Irvin Banks**, **Alan Stratton** (bg) and **Dave Smith** (voc), recorded an EP on the 'Liverpool Sound' label in 1973 (LS 1740 EP) with the songs, "Things", "Girl From Ipanema", "Matrimony" and "Wham Bang". On this acetate, **Tommy Hughes** (p), **Ray Smith** (sax) and **Les Reynolds** (dr) were also featured as guest musicians. In 1974, **Dave Smith** was replaced by **Malcolm Andrews** (voc/g), a former member of the **Mastersounds** and the **Kruzads**. After the **Chesterfields'** record, **Tommy Hughes** quit show business but later came back as a member of the re-formed **Mojos**, where he is still playing today.

In 1991, the **Kansas City Five** were re-formed for appearances at the 'MerseyCats' events with the original members, **Alan Stratton**, **Robbie Hickson**, **Peter Cooke**, **Tommy Hughes** and **Colin Middlebrough**, who is these days still a steady member of the **Four Originals**.

On one occasion, the **Kansas City Five** were also joined by founder, **Bruce McCaskill**, who sadly died unexpectedly on 24th December 1993.

In 1994, **Alan Stratton** became a temporary member of **Karl Terry & the Cruisers**, where he played the double bass when this band toured Germany. He was also featured in the line-up when **Karl Terry & the Cruisers** cut the great album, 'Rock 'n' Roll - that's all', for the German 'Merseyside' label.

SONNY KAYE & THE REDS

Real Liverpudlians would say this group was from 'over the water', as it was formed in the coffee bar, 'El Cappucino' in Runcorn on the opposite side of the River Mersey by **Frank Keenan**, in 1961. The founder was, of course, the one who then adopted the stage name **Sonny Kaye**.

In their original line-up, **Sonny Kaye & the Reds** consisted of **Sonny Kaye** (voc), **Bill Mullan** (lg/voc), **Tony Moffatt** (rg), **Harry Nelson** (sax), **Ronald Quine** (bg) and **Harry Cosgrove** on drums. **Bill Mullan** had previously played with the **Dominoes** and **Dean Sabre & the Ghosts**, while all the others were probably newcomers to the scene.

In this line-up, the group soon became very popular on the local scene and, in August 1962, they won the 'Widnes/Runcorn Popularity Poll', a contest held by NEMS at the Deacon Road Labour Club. A few weeks later, **Sonny Kaye & the Reds** appeared on the same bill at the Queens Hall in Widnes with the **Beatles** and **Billy J. Kramer & the Dakotas**.

In spite of this success, the line-up started to change and, with the exception of **Sonny Kaye** and **Bill Mullan**, all the other members left one after the other. However, in 1963, **Sonny Kaye & the Reds** consisted of:

Frank Keenan	(voc)
Bill Mullan	(lg/voc)
John Ashton	(bg)
Terry Lewis	(dr)

It is not known in which groups the new members had played previously but it is sure that **John Ashton** came from somewhere in the St. Helens area and was not the bass-guitarist of the same name, who played in the Widnes groups the **Cheetahs** and **Vic Takes Four**.

Sonny Kaye & the Reds wore red suits at their gigs and one highlight in their live programme was a terrific version of "Moon River".

Their manager, **Eric Hayes**, got them signed to 'Darville Entertainments' and, from then onwards, the group appeared regularly at the major Liverpool clubs such as the 'Cavern' and the 'Iron Door'. They soon became very popular on the Merseybeat scene.

In the meantime, the lead guitarist's brother, **Paddy Mullan,** was added to the line-up on bass guitar, while **John Ashton** switched to rhythm.

Still, in 1963, **Sonny Kaye & the Reds** recorded an acetate on 'Northampton Sounds' with the songs, "Long Tall Sally" and "Jacky". The latter one was an original, written by **Sonny Kaye** and **Bill Mullan**.

'Darville Entertainments' arranged a tour of Germany for the band, where it appeared at the 'Star-Palast' clubs in Kiel, Eckernförde, Rendsburg, Lüneburg, as well as at the 'Beat-Club' in Dortmund, which was also part of the 'Star-Palast' chain. At the end of this really successful tour, they also played Mainz. Just for that tour, **Sonny Kaye & the Reds** had been joined by **Gary Lloyd** as an additional guitarist. Back in England they took part in the Fontana record company competition, 'Kings Of The Big Beat', and won. They went down to London and did a recording test for the Fontana label. Unfortunately, nothing was released on record and it is also not known which songs were recorded at that session.

John Ashton was temporarily replaced in the group by **Derek Gilbert**, who came from the **Paladins**, but this was only for a few gigs and then **John Ashton** returned and **Derek Gilbert** probably went back to his old group.

In September 1964, **Sonny Kaye** left show business for health reasons (as it was rumoured) and the group continued as a four-piece.

They changed their name to **We Few** and, when they were joined by the girl singer, **Rita Mather**, they continued as **We Few & Rita**. But this was not for too long and **Rita Mather** left to team up with the **Squad** from Liverpool, formerly known as the **Riot Squad**, that now appeared as the **Squad & Rita**. After that, she sang with the **Vogue** from St. Helens, with whom she recorded as **Rita & the Vogue**. In the late Sixties, she was a member of the **Crusaders** from Widnes but then started a solo-career under the name of **Toni West**. She is still singing in the clubs under that name .

SONNY KAYE & THE REDS
Sole Representation
DARVILLE ENTERTAINMENTS WALLASEY CHESHIRE.

In 1965, **Sonny Kaye** returned to his group, but he did not stay for too long.

When he left again, former tour member, **Gary Lloyd,** returned and the band was also joined by **Bobby Didsbury** as an additional singer, who was a former member of the **Dominoes** and **Dean Sabre & the Jets**.

At that time, the group's name was changed again, this time to **Reds Inc.** and, as such, the group recorded the songs, "Shake, Rattle And Roll" and the **Larry Williams** classic, "Lawdy Miss Clawdy", for the Oriole sampler, 'Cavern Alive', and probably some more, but no further details are known, because this record was never released. Subsequently, another acetate was made of the two named songs, again on Northampton Sounds.

It was probably in 1966 when **Sonny Kaye** returned again and the name of the band was changed back to **Sonny Kaye & the Reds**.

Sometime in the sixties, **Bobby Didsbury** left the UK and emigrated to Australia.

In March 1968, **Sonny Kaye & the Reds** took second place in the very popular British TV-show ,'Opportunity Knocks', but, again, this major success was not followed by a recording contract.

It is said that some time later original drummer, **Harry Cosgrove,** replaced **Terry Lewis** for a time, but then **Terry Lewis** (who in the meantime had been the resident drummer at the 'Linnets' pub in Runcorn) returned to the group.

It was in the early Seventies that **Sonny Kaye & the Reds** finally disbanded. It is known that sometime later **Bill Mullan** was a member of **Salamander** and **Kokomo,** before he played with **Skytrain.**

In 1983, **Sonny Kaye & the Reds** played a reunion concert at the 'Linnets' in Runcorn, and as far as it is known, with the 1964 line-up. **Paddy Mullan** sadly died from diabetes in the second half of the Eighties so, unfortunately, there was no possibility of a later repetition.

After that, **Bill Mullan** and **John Ashton** were the only ones that continued to perform on the local scene.

Sonny Kaye who, in the meantime, had worked as a disc jockey, died unexpectedly and much too young in April 1994. At his funeral a Jazz band played "When The Saints Go Marching In".

After the death of **Sonny Kaye, Bill Mullan, John Ashton** and **Terry Lewis** always had plans to reform the group – until **Terry Lewis** died of a massive heart attack in April 2011. After that, **Bill Mullan** and **John Ashton** continued as a duo under the name of **Tupelo Junction** for a few months but then also gave up performing.

Discography :

As: **Sonny Kaye & the Reds** :

Jacky / Long Tall Sally   UK - 'Northampton-Sounds' acetate / 1963

As: **The Reds Inc.** :

Shake, Rattle & Roll / Lawdy Miss Clawdy   UK - 'Northampton-Sounds' acetate / 1965

In addition, **Sonny Kaye & the Reds** recorded for Fontana after the group had won the 'Kings Of The Big Beat' competition but, unfortunately, there was never anything released.

It is also possible that besides "**Shake, Rattle And Roll**" and "**Lawdy Miss Clawdy**" the **Reds Inc.** recorded some more songs for the Oriole sampler, 'Cavern Alive', which, in the end, was also not released.

THE KINETIC

It all started when **Beryl Marsden** was booked to play at the 'Star-Club' in Hamburg in December 1964. She needed a backing group, so the management hurriedly recruited **Vinnie Ismail** (lg/voc) and **Rob Eccles** (bg) from the **Harlems**, both of whom were also former members of **Vince & the Volcanoes**.

The drummer was **Johnny Sze**, who came from the **St. Louis Checks** but, before that, he had been a member of the **Satanists**. This line-up played a few shows with **Beryl Marsden** in Hamburg as the **Harlems**, but they may also have had some appearances as the **Blue Boys**.

In early 1965, this connection split up and, while **Rob Eccles** returned to Liverpool and joined **Henry's Handful**, **Vinnie Ismail**, who is also known as **Vinnie Tow**, remained in Hamburg and joined the **Top Ten Allstars**, the resident group at the famous 'Top Ten' club. He then also returned to Liverpool and joined **Henry's Handful**. After that, he was a member of the **Valentinos**, who later recorded as **Harlem**. In the Eighties, he played with **Karl Terry & the Cruisers**.

Drummer, **Johnny Sze,** after a time jamming in Hamburg, went to Sweden and became a member of the **Cherry Stones**.

The **Cherry Stones** were a Swedish group who, a few months previously, had released an interesting single with "Muddy Hands /Go Away" (HMV X 8661) but, for mysterious reasons, had disbanded shortly after that.

The **Cherry Stones** now consisted of the Liverpudlians, **Bob Weston** (lg) and **Johnny Sze** (dr/voc), **Andy Mowbray** (voc/harp) and two Swedes, **Lennart Blomkvist** (rg) and **Leif Matses** (bg), who probably were the remaining members of the original Swedish recording line up.

After playing the clubs in and around Stockholm for a time, the **Cherry Stones** were booked to support the **Kinks** on their tour of Finland. The group went down very well but, after a few gigs got sacked – did they go down too well?

Whatever the reason, somehow it happened that the German, **Jo May,** took over their management and brought them to Germany. Very soon a great version of the **Timi Yuro** number, "What's The Matter Baby", was released on their new manager's own label. Unfortunately, it was not distributed too well and so it had limited success.

Jo May got the group a gig, opening an Art Gallery in Munich. The French owner, **Madame Renai,** was enthusiastic about the **Cherry Stones** and asked them if they were also interested in playing in Paris. Of course they were – with the exception of the two Swedes, who returned home.

The remaining three recruited other Liverpool (?) musicians and continued as the **Kinetic** in the line-up with:

Andy Mowbray	(voc/harp)
Bob Weston	(lg)
Mick Humphries	(org/p)
Geoff Capper	(bg)
Johnny Sze	(dr)

The Kinetic

The new member, **Mick Humphries,** was sometimes reported as **Michael Humby** by the music newspapers and therefore, it is not known what his real name was. Regardless, this is the group that went to Paris and their management was then shared between **Jo May** for Germany and **Madame Renai** for France.

After the **Kinetic** had successfully supported some really big name artists of that time, including **Cat Stevens**, **Jimi Hendrix** and the **Spencer Davis Group**, they were signed to Disques Vogue, a major record company in France.

In 1966, their first EP, 'Suddenly Tomorrow', was released. All songs on that EP were originals by the **Kinetic**. It apparently sold quite well as, in 1967, it was followed by another EP, 'Live Your Life', which was also a good seller. A complete album of their own material was then released, also entitled 'Live your life'.

In between, the group toured Germany again and also played the 'Star-Club' in Hamburg but, it can be said that the **Kinetic** had settled down in Paris and mainly toured in France at that time.

They became a very successful part of the French music scene and remained there until the early Seventies. However, when the group was asked to go to Spain, **Bob Weston** did not agree and went back to Sweden for a while but then returned to England and later was a member of **Fleetwood Mac**.

All the others went straight back to England and wanted to reform the group again, which for unknown reasons, did not happen.

During the time of the big Beat boom, the **Kinetic** had always played in Sweden, Germany or France. Consequently, they were not paid too much attention on the Merseybeat scene. Judging by their records, it can be said that England missed out on another great group.

Discography :

EP '**Suddenly Tomorrow**'   **FR- Vogue EPL 8520 / 1966**

- Suddenly Tomorrow / Letter To Rosetta / Time Of Season

EP '**Live Your Life**'   **FR- Vogue EPL 8544 / 1967**

- Live Your Life / Hall Of The Viking / Sunny Cloud / The Train

LP '**Live Your Life**'   **FR- Vogue CLVLX 148 / 1967**

- Live Your life / Hall Of The Viking / Letter To Rosetta / Child's Song / Sunny Cloud /

Suddenly Tomorrow / Willy 'D' Fixer / Time Of Season / The Train / Jam Around

as **The Cherry Stones** :

What's The Matter Baby / The Things She Says   **G- JMP 19 702 / 1966**

THE KINSLEYS

This band was formed by **Billy Kinsley** in Liverpool in April 1964. He had previously played with the **Pacifics**, the **Mavericks** and, of course, the **Merseybeats**.

As it seems, he and the other members of this new group had major problems choosing a name and, initially, names including the **Rivals** and the **Nameless Ones** were discussed. One of their first appearances was made under the latter name, before they decided to call the band **The Kinsleys**.

Of course, the group profited from the popularity of their leader gained through his membership in the **Merseybeats** but this, for sure, was not the only reason for their great success locally.

The **Kinsleys** in fact were a really good group and in the original line-up consisted of:

Billy Kinsley	(voc/bg)
Dave Percival	(g/voc)
Denny Alexander	(g/voc)
Dave Preston	(dr/voc)

All members were experienced musicians - **Denny Alexander** had previously played with the **Aarons** and the **Secrets**, while **Dave Preston** was a former member of the **Harlems** and the **Secrets**.

Dave Percival came from the original trio line-up of the **Pawns** and, before that, he had played with the **Climbers**. He possibly was the musician named **Dave Percy**, who had also played with the **Roadrunners**.

But **Dave Percival** did not stay for too long. He then joined the newly-formed **Epics** who, unfortunately, never got to perform in public.

His place in the **Kinsleys** was taken by **Tommy Murray**, who had formerly played with the **Memphis Rhythm & Blues Combo**.

It was probably this line-up that recorded the songs, "Goodbye" and "Do Me A Favour", both great Merseybeat songs which, unfortunately, were never released.

The reason for that might have been **Billy Kinsley** leaving when, at the end of 1964, he re-joined the **Merseybeats**, where he remained until that group disbanded in 1966. After that, he and **Tony Crane** of the **Merseybeats** formed the duo the **Merseys** and had a big hit with their version of "Sorrow", as well as some other records that sold well. They then changed their name to the **Crackers** but only released one more single. After that, **Billy Kinsley** had a short spell with the **Swinging Blue Jeans** and, in 1970, he and **Jimmy Campbell** (ex **Kirkbys**) were members of **Rockin'**

Horse, who released an absolutely great single with "The Biggest Gossip In Town", which was pure Merseybeat at its best. He then joined **Gerry & the Pacemakers** for a short time and, after that, formed **Liverpool Express** in the early Seventies. This group had a string of hits before it disbanded and **Billy Kinsley** joined the **Cheats**. Later he re-formed **Liverpool Express** and, since 1993, he has been back with the **Merseybeats**.

But back to the **Kinsleys,** who did not disband when **Billy Kinsley** left in 1964.

Denny Alexander also left and initially he wanted to form a new group together with **Tommy McGuirk**, with whom he had played in the **Aarons** and who, in the meantime, had been a member of the **Pete Best Four**.

This did not happen and so, in early 1965, **Denny Alexander** became a member of the **Clayton Squares**.

Dave Preston and **Tommy Murray** then teamed up with **Tim Dougdale** (voc/g) of the **Georgians**. They initially continued on as a trio under the name of the **Kinsleys**.

Then they were joined by **George Peckham** (voc/bg), who had formerly played with the **Renegades** from Liverpool, the original

Pawns, **Lee Curtis & the All Stars**, the re-formed **Pawns** and **Groups Inc**. In 1965, he left the **Kinsleys** to join **Earl Royce & the Olympics** and later became a member of the **Fourmost**.

In July 1965, **George Peckham** was replaced by **Mike Hart**, who came from the **Richmond Group**, after having previously played with the **Roadrunners** and the **Krew**.

At the end of that same year, the **Kinsleys** disbanded totally without ever having recorded again.

Tommy Murray joined the **Krew** and, after that, played with a group called **Mumble**.

Dave Preston became a member of the **Mark Four** from Cheshunt, who, a little later, had international success as **Creation**.

Mike Hart formed **Henry's Handful** and, after that, appeared for a short time with another group called **Mike Hart & the Moondogs** before becoming a founding member of **Liverpool Scene**.

After that, **Mike Hart** went solo, while **Tim Dougdale** disappeared from the scene.

Discography :

There was no official record released by the **Kinsleys** but the group recorded two great songs with "**Goodbye**" and "**Do Me A Favour**" in 1964, probably for Fontana.

THE KIRKBYS

From the band's name, it can already be concluded that they originated from the Liverpool suburb Kirkby, where they were formed in 1961 by **Jimmy Campbell** together with **John Lloyd**, **Kenny Goodlass** and the singer, **Gerry Savage,** under the name, **The Tuxedos**.

When **Gerry Savage** left, the group was joined by **Joey Marooth** and **Alby Power** and very soon changed their name to **The Panthers**.

In 1962, the **Panthers** cut a Kensington acetate with the songs, "For You" and "Searchin' ", but, a little later, changed their name to the **Kirkbys** and recorded an EMI acetate with five tracks, of which only the song, "Feel So Bad", is known to have been included.

A little later, when they decided to become professionals, the **Kirkbys** consisted of the following musicians:

Joey Marooth	(voc)
Jimmy Campbell	(g/voc)
John Lloyd	(g/voc)
Alby Power	(bg/voc)
Kenny Goodlass	(dr)

They very soon became one of the leading groups on Merseyside and occasionally they also backed boxing champion, **John Conteh**, who also hailed from Kirkby and who had started a singing career!

The **Kirkbys** were signed to RCA and, in 1965, their first demo, "Cos' My Baby's Gone", was recorded, which was only released in Finland with "She'll Get No Lovin' That Way" on the B-side. The single was apparently quite successful. The A-side was a great song - an original by the group which was written by **Jimmy Campbell**, a very talented songwriter.

Around the same time, the **Kirkbys** toured Germany quite successfully, playing lots of gigs in the South.

Their follow up single, "It's A Crime", was released in England - again a very strong Beat record. Unfortunately, it had limited success but, today it is a highly desired and expensive collector's item.

After that record was released, **Kenny Goodlass** left to join the **Escorts** and later had a short spell with the **Swinging Blue Jeans** before he became a member of the **Fruit Eating Bears**, who also backed the **Merseys** on their hit single, "Sorrow", in 1966.

He was replaced in the **Kirkbys** by **Mervyn Sharp**, who came from the **Pulsators.** This line-up cut the single, "Don't You Want Me No More", which, again, was only released in Finland and seems to have been a minor hit over there.

"Don't You Want Me No More" and the B-side, "Bless You", both **Jimmy Campbell** originals, were great songs in the very popular **Byrds** style and normally would have been successful in England as well as in Europe. So it's hard to understand why it was never released anywhere else. However, it appears that after the release, the **Kirkbys** spent some time in Scandinavia but nothing is known about any further recordings.

In 1967, **Mervyn Sharp** left the group and disappeared from the scene. He was replaced by the returning **Kenny Goodlass** and, a little later, the group's name was changed to **23rd Turn-Off**, the number of the motorway exit to Kirkby.

The band was signed to Deram and, in 1968, the single, "Michelangelo", was released.

However, this record was not too successful and the group with the unusual name, **23rd Turn-Off**, disbanded, probably in early 1969.

Together with **Dave Harrison** from the **Jacobeats** on drums and Jimmy's brother, **Pete Campbell,** on bass guitar, **Jimmy Campbell**, **John Lloyd** and **Joey Marooth,** at that time, formed the **Clique**. Pete Campbell, who was a former member of **Karl Terry & the Cruisers**, the **Beathovens**, the **Fontanas** and the **Mersey Five**, had just come back from Germany, where he had a long residency with the Scottish group **John O'Hara & the Playboys**.

While the **Clique** were playing the clubs in and around Merseyside, **Jimmy Campbell** also recorded the solo album, "Son Of Anastasia", and the two singles, "On A Monday" and "Lyanna".

In 1970, he got together with former **Merseybeats, Kinsleys** and **Merseys** member, **Billy Kinsley,** and formed the group, **Rockin' Horse**, that cut an album with the title, 'Yes It Is', from which the great single, "Biggest Gossip In Town", was coupled out. This was a great Merseybeat song and, although the album was really interesting, the other tracks didn't compare to it.

These recordings were made with the session musicians, **Bobby Falloon** (g), **Stan Gorman** (dr) and **Mike Snow** (p/org), but when it came to live-appearances, **Rockin' Horse** was identical with the **Clique**, with the addition of **Billy Kinsley** of course.

It was probably still in 1970 that **Rockin' Horse** backed **Chuck Berry** on his British tour but, besides this tour, the group was not too active under that name and a little later it was given to another Liverpool group that released further singles on the 'Randy' and 'Pyramid' labels.

The **Clique** continued on the scene for some time but **Jimmy Campbell** also continued to record solo and, still in 1970, his second album, "Half-Baked", and the great single, "Don't Leave Me Now" were released.

It is not exactly known when the **Clique**, a very successful club-band, finally broke up.

In 1979, **John Lloyd** appeared on the scene again in a duo with **Earl Preston** under the name of the **Raffles**, which existed until the early Eighties. He then disappeared from the scene.

Joey Marooth emigrated to Australia but later returned to Liverpool, where he did not join another group.

Kenny Goodlass later played with the newly-formed **Merseybeats** and, from 1992 until 1995, he was a member of **Karl Terry & the Cruisers**, who recorded the album, 'Rock 'n' Roll – That's All', in Germany.

In the mid-Nineties, the **Kirkbys** were re-formed by the original members, **Joey Marooth**, **John Lloyd**, **Alby Power** and **Kenny Goodlass**. The top-class saxophonist, **Brian Jones**, a member of the **Undertakers** in the Sixties, was added to this line-up, as well as **Dave Goldberg** (who was also still playing with the **Merseybeats**) on keyboards. Unfortunately, **Jimmy Campbell** was too ill and only joined his old group on stage at some of their gigs.

They were a very good and a very interesting group that didn't just play all the old standards over and over again.

Alby Power had to leave for health reasons and his place in the **Kirkbys** was taken by **Alan Crooks**. **Alby Power** sadly died on 22 September 2004, aged 59, and **Jimmy Campbell** also left us on 12th February 2007, at the age of 63.

The **Kirkbys** only appear occasionally these days, but their performance is always worth watching.

Single discography :

as **The Kirkbys** :

It's A Crime / I've Never Been So Much In Love	UK- RCA 1542 / 1965

Different Finnish releases :

Cos' My Baby's Gone / She'll Get No Lovin' That Way	SF- RCA FAS 942 / 1965
Don't You Want Me No More / Bless You	SF- RCA FAS 948 / 1966

as **23rd Turn-Off** :

Michelangelo / Leave Me Here	UK- Deram DM 150 / 1968

Jimmy Campbell – solo :

On A Monday / Dear Marge	UK- Fontana TF 1009 / 1969
Lyanna / Frankie Joe	UK- Fontana TF 1076 / 1970
Don't Leave Me Now / So Lonely Without You	UK- Fontana 6007025 / 1970

LP "SON OF ANASTASIA"	UK- Fontana STL 5508 / 1969

- When I Sit Down To Reason / Mother's Boy / Another Vincent Van Gogh / Penny In My Pocket / Bright Side On The Hill / Dear Marge / Lyanna / They All Come Marching Home / On A Monday / Lovely Elisa Cope Is Dead / You'll Break My Heart In Two / Tremendous Commercial Potential / Adrian Henry's Party-Night / Another Springtime / Michelangelo / Painting A Sign

LP "HALF BAKED"   UK-Vertigo 6360 010 / 1970

- Green Eyed American Actress / Loving You Is All I Do / So Lonely Without You / In My Room That's Right
- That's Me / I Will Not Mind / Dulcie (It's December) / Forever Grateful / Half Baked / Closing Down The
Shop / Don't Leave Me Now

(*** please note that the songs, "Green Eyed American Actress", "So Lonely Without You" and "That's
right - That's Me", were recorded with Rockin' Horse)

Rockin' Horse :

Biggest Gossip In Town / You Say   UK- Philips 6006 156 / 1970

Julian The Hooligan / Stayed Out Late Last Night   UK- Philips 6006 200 / 1970

(*** please note that later releases by Rockin' Horse on the 'Randy' and 'Pyramid' labels were by a different
group)

LP "YES IT IS"   UK- Philips 6308 075 / 1970

- Biggest Gossip In Town / Oh Carol I'm So Sad / You're Spending All My Money / Baby Walk Out With
Your Darlin' Man / Don't You Ever Think I Cry / Yes It Is / Stayed Out Late Last Night / Delicate Situation /
Son, Son / Golden Opportunity / I'm Trying To Forget You / Julian The Hooligan

Unissued tracks (acetates) :

as The Panthers:

For You / Searchin'   UK - Kensington-acetate / 1962

as The Kirkbys :

Feel So Bad + four other tracks   UK - EMI - acetate / 1963

Besides this, the following album without a title was recorded on acetate :

Dreaming / Friends And Relations / Penny In My Pocket / Flowers Are Flowering /

I'll Be With You / Mother's Boy / I'll Be Round / Michael Angelo   UK - Emidisc acetate-album / 1966

as 23rd Turn-Off :

Michelangelo (alternative version) / Dreaming   UK - Deram - acetate / 1967

THE KLUBS

This was a group from the second Merseybeat generation as it was only formed in 1963 at the Birkenhead Institute School by **John Reid**, **Trevor Griffiths** and **Malcolm Bickley**.

They started as a six-piece Rhythm & Blues group with an ever changing line-up. Before they became popular in the Liverpool area, they won a national Beat contest on the Isle of Man in August 1965 and were presented with a large silver cup by the famous DJ, **Jimmy Saville,** and £250, which was an astronomical sum at that time.

When **Mal Bickley** sacked the original drummer called '**Tommy**', for unknown reasons, it caused a dispute in the band with the result that **Mal Bickley** also left. He continued with session work before he became a solo artist and later got involved with the theatre-scene.

A new bass-guitarist joined named **Tony Woods**, who also did not stay for too long. After he had parted from the group, the **Klubs,** in 1965, consisted of the following musicians:

Paddy Breen	(voc)
Alan Walker	(voc/harp)
Trevor Griffiths	(lg/voc)
John Reid	(rg/voc)
Norris Easterbrook	(bg/voc)
Kenny Marshall	(dr)

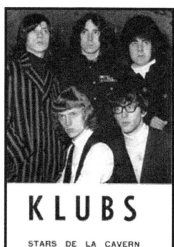

KLUBS

STARS DE LA CAVERN
ET DE LA TÉLÉVISION

Norris Easterbrook was a former member of the **Legends**.

The group now played a sort of Rhythm & Blues in the 'harder' style of the **Rolling Stones** and the **Pretty Things**. Besides venues in Liverpool, they also appeared quite regularly in London, where they mainly played the 'Tiles' in Oxford Street and the famous 'Marquee Club'.

In early 1966, **Alan Walker** left the group which continued as a quintet and perfected such an explosive stage act that they were also nicknamed **The Wild Wild Klubs** - a name that was also used in some advertisements and announcements. In the meantime, they had become really popular in their hometown and appeared at all the major venues in and around Merseyside.

At the end of 1966, 'Cavern Enterprises' took over the management of the **Klubs**. They then became regulars at the 'Cavern', where they often shared the bill with famous artists such as, **Chuck Berry**, **Chris Farlowe & the Thunderbirds**, **John's Children** and the American group, the **Coasters**.

They were probably one of the groups with the most appearances at the 'Cavern' in 1967.

The **Klubs** also went to France for a long tour which apparently wasn't too successful as, in the end, **Alf Geoghegan**, at that time owner of the 'Cavern', had to go over to France to bring them back. **Kenny Marshall** left the group and a little later died in a boating accident on the River Dee.

His replacement was **Peter Sinclair-Tidy**, the former drummer with the **Crazy Chains**.

It was probably with this line-up that the **Klubs** recorded the one-sided demo, "Livin' Today", on Chart Records, which in some way was connected to the 'Cavern'. After that, a Granada TV talent show presented them singing their original song, "Only John Tring", and probably because of that, in 1967, the **Klubs** were invited by EMI to the Abbey Road Studios for some test recordings.

Under the wings of **David Paramor**, they recorded a new version of their song, "Livin' Today", as well as the **Cream** success, "NSU", and the **John's Children** number, "Desdemona", but in the end, their wild sound was declared un-recordable and so nothing was released.

In 1968, the group went down to London again where they were discovered by producer, **Don Arden**, who took them to the Decca studios. Two sessions produced recordings of the **Beatles** number, "Drive My Car", **Arthur Brown**'s smash hit, "Fire", and two originals, "Midnight Love Cycle" and "Ever Needed Someone". For the release, **Don Arden** wanted the band to change their name to **Revolution,** which the musicians absolutely refused to do and so, once again, the recordings were never released.

The **Klubs** were added to the BBC's **Pink Floyd** concerts as a support act in 1968 and, after that, returned to Liverpool.

Jim McCulloch, a local nightclub owner, took over their management and recorded them for his label, 'CAM' records, which he shared with **Charlie Weston**.

The 'CAM' recordings included the original numbers, "Indian Dreams", "Can't Ebenezer See My Friend", "Oh Baby", "I Found The Sun" and a new version of "Ever Needed Someone", the last two were chosen for a release on single. So, in late 1968, the only single by the **Klubs** was released, but 'CAM' did not have a real distribution system and accordingly, the record only sold quite well on Merseyside. It was a very interesting record with a nice ballad on the A-side and a solid beat on the flipside, both with a slightly psychedelic influence. Of course, it was no longer the Merseybeat of the early Sixties but the melodies of both songs were quite commercial and so was the musical arrangement.

In 1969, the **Klubs** started to 'come apart' after another engagement at the 'Marquee Club' in London. The first to leave was **Norris Easterbrook** in May 1969, followed by **Trevor Griffiths** in August of the same year.

Trevor Griffiths became a solo artist on the cabaret scene and then he formed a duo with **Alan Greer**, a former member of **Wayne Calvert & the Cimarrons** and **Me & Them**, that was also the backing group for **Chris Andrews** for a time. After **Norris Easterbrook** and **Trevor Griffiths** had left, the **Klubs** continued as a trio and, in 1969, recorded another demo with "The Stripper" and a new arrangement of "Can't Ebenezer See My Friend" for DJM, which again was not followed by a release.

Norris Easterbrook returned to the group which, under its old name, had developed into a Heavy Metal band. However, the **Klubs** split up totally when **John Reid** formed **Strife** with **Paddy Breen** and **Trevor Griffiths**.

Strife became quite successful in the European Heavy Metal scene and recorded two or three albums, but **Paddy Breen** left after a short time and returned to Liverpool.

There, he teamed up again with **Peter Sinclair-Tidy** and guitarist, **Steve Wright**, under the name of **Wardog**. When this group split, **Peter Sinclair-Tidy** joined **Shane Fenton & the Fentones** but, in 1976, he teamed up again with **Paddy Breen** and guitarist, **Steve Burkhill**, in **Goldilox**, who later changed their name to **Skytrain**.

Trevor Griffiths had also left **Strife** to join **Alan Greer** in the **Lettermen,** which also included **Ronnie Crampton** (bg/voc) and **Tony Mac** (dr/voc). The **Lettermen** cut an interesting album, 'First Class', on the Stag label, this is a very sought after album today.

In 1979, **Trevor Griffiths** teamed up with **Norris Easterbrook** again in a group called **Night Moves**. They played the cabaret circuit until the early Eighties.

At Christmas 1991, there was a **Klubs** reunion at 'MerseyCats', after that they were banned from participating in any further concerts because they played 'too loud and too wild'- the **Wild Wild Klubs** – eh!

In 1999, an album by the **Klubs** with all the surviving material from the Sixties was released on the Tenth Planet label, which was declared as 'album of the year' by the famous music magazine, 'Record Collector'.

This resulted in another reunion of the group in May 2000 at the 'Cavern' where they appeared in the original Sixties line-up, with the exception of **Trevor Griffiths**, who was ill at that time.

The **Klubs** continued as a four-piece on the scene until the end of that year. Their final appearance was in November 2000 at the 'International Guitar Festival'.

Norris Easterbrook and **Steve Burkhill** still play together in a three-piece Rock band, sometimes appearing under the name, the **Klubs,** at local Merseyside venues.

Discography :

I Found The Sun / Ever Needed Someone	UK- CAM Records CAM 681 / 1968

Unissued tracks:

Livin' Today (one-sided demo)	UK- Chart Records acetate / 1967
The Stripper / Can't Ebenezer See My Mind	UK- DJM Demo / 1969

In addition, the **Klubs** recorded the following songs, which apparently got stuck in the archives:

Old John Tring	TV-Granada talent-show / 1967
NSU, Desdemona, Livin' Today	Test-Recordings for EMI / 1967
Drive My Car, Fire, Midnight Love Cycle, Ever Needed Someone	Test-Recordings for Decca / 1968
Indian Dreams (2 versions), Can't Ebenezer See My Mind, Oh Baby	CAM-Recording Session / 1968

THE KOOBAS

Here, everything started in 1961 on the Wirral with the group **Roy Montrose & the Midnights** that, besides the vocalist, **Roy Montrose,** also included the brothers, **Roy Morris** (lg) and **John Morris** (dr), as well as **Pete Williams** (bg) and **Dave Austin** (rg).

STEADILY BUILDING A BIG NAME FOR THEMSELVES

In 1962, **Dave Austin** left and emigrated to Canada. For a short time he was replaced by the singer's brother, **Robert Montrose**, and then **Stu Leithwood** took over on rhythm-guitar. At that time, the group changed it's name into **The Kubas.**

A little later, **Roy Montrose** left and continued with his brother, **Robert Montrose** in a duo called **Take Two** and later he performed on his own as singer/ guitarist under the name of **Roy Malcolm**.

He was not replaced as **Stu Leithwood** took over the lead vocals. When **John Morris** decided to become the roadie for the group, the **Kubas** were joined by **Kenny Cochran**, who came from **Clay Ellis & the Raiders.** Accordingly, they appeared in the following line-up:

Stu Leithwood	**(voc/rg)**
Roy Morris	**(lg/voc)**
Pete Williams	**(bg/voc)**
Kenny Cochran	**(dr)**

In 1963, the group was chosen to take part in the motion picture, 'Ferry Cross The Mersey', with **Gerry & the Pacemakers** in the main role. For this film, the **Kubas** recorded the originals, "Steady Girl" and "Oh Little Fool", which were not too impressive and were not featured on any of the corresponding soundtrack albums.

In spite of this, the group was signed to Columbia and, a little later, their first single was released with an interesting version of "Magic Potion", coupled with "I Love Her", which was the song ,"Steady Girl", from the above-mentioned film.

But this line-up did not last too long as **Kenny Cochran** and **Pete Williams** left to join the backing group of the **Excelles**, a newly-formed Liverpool vocal group who later became the hit group, **Arrival**. The new members of the **Kubas** were **Tony O'Reilly** (dr) and **Keith Ellis** (bg/voc), both were former members of the **Pilgrims**.

Due to legal reasons, the spelling of the group's name was changed to **Koobas** and, under this name, a second single was released in 1965, this time on PYE.

"Take Me For A Little While" sold better than their debut release but, unfortunately, it also failed to make the charts. These two records, of course, helped the band's popularity on Merseyside.

ᵀʜᵉKOOBAS

Despite this positive development, it can be said that the **Koobas** were one of the unlucky Liverpool groups, as their first German tour, with appearances at the famous 'Star-Club' in 1963, did not bring the expected breakthrough. Then, when the big boom in Liverpool started, the band had accepted a long residency in Spain and, accordingly, not too much notice was taken of them by producers, promoters and so on. But in 1965, they had the chance of a great breakthrough when they supported the **Beatles** on their UK tour.

Once again, nothing happened to improve the fortunes of the band, perhaps with the exception of the fact that they were chosen to take part in the film, 'Merry Go Round The Roses', from which an EP was recorded by them. But the bad luck stuck and this very interesting EP was never released.

The next single by the **Koobas** with the songs, "You'd Better Make Up Your Mind" and "A Place I Know", was not as commercial as its predecessors and, once again, failed to become a success which probably led to the end of their contract with PYE.

The **Koobas** switched back to Columbia and, in 1966, their best single ever was released with "Sweet Music". Great, 'rough' and truthful Beat, just like the B-side, "Face", but, once again, it was mysteriously ignored by the public at large. This record was also released in Germany, where it had limited success, although the sales were not that bad.

It was simply too late for the **Koobas** to jump on the big success train, although they certainly were one of the good and very interesting Liverpool bands.

Their follow-ups, "Sally" and "Gipsy Fred", were also not too successful, while their next single, a great version of **Cat Stevens**' "First Cut Is The Deepest", was a real highlight but once again failed to make the charts. This was the final single by the **Koobas** for the British market and the band had almost been forgotten when suddenly and surprisingly an album with the title, 'The Koobas', was released in 1969, from which one more single was coupled out with 'Where Are The Friends', especially for the French market. This long player, of course, was no longer Beat but more the Psychedelic sound, popular at the time. Accordingly, the album must have been a bit disappointing for the Beat freaks perhaps with the exception of their bluesy version of **Erma Franklin**'s "A Little Piece Of My Heart", which was perfect and in every respect - the best number on that album.

An interesting addition to this story is the fact that the three guitarists' silhouettes on the record sleeves of the German Ariola label for their 'Star Club' series were the **Koobas**, although they never had a contract with, or any other connections to Ariola.

Shortly after the release of the **Koobas** album, probably still in 1969, this highly-underrated group disbanded totally and **Tony O'Reilly** was associated with **Yes** and **Bakerloo** but, after that, became the resident drummer in a Liverpool club.

Keith Ellis became a member of **Van der Graaf Generator** and then played with the **Misunderstood** and **Juicy Lucy**. After that he went to America and, from the mid to the late Seventies, was a member of **Boxer**, before he joined **Iron Butterfly**, where he played until 1978 when, during a Germany tour of that group, he died in Darmstadt.

Stu Leithwood became a member of **March Hare** and **Roy Morris** joined the **Alan Reeves Combo**, which was based in France.

Single discography :

Magic Potion / I Love Her	UK- Columbia DB 7451 / 1964
Take Me For A Little While / Somewhere In The Night	UK- PYE 7 N 17012 / 1965
You'd Better Make Up Your Mind / A Place I Know	UK- PYE 7 N 17087 / 1966
Sweet Music / Face	UK- Columbia DB 7988 / 1966
Sally / Champagne And Caviar	UK- Columbia DB 8103 / 1967
Gypsy Fred / City Girl	UK- Columbia DB 8187 / 1967
First Cut Is The Deepest / Walking Out	UK- Columbia DB 8419 / 1967

Different French release :

Where Are The Friends / Royston Rose	F- Columbia CF 165 / 1969

(*** please note that the first UK single was released under their original name - **The Kubas**)

LP discography

THE KOOBAS	UK- Columbia SCX 6271 / 1969

- Royston Rose / Where Are The Friends / Constantly Changing / Here's A Day / Fade Forever /

Barricades / A Little Piece Of My Heart / Gold Leaf Tree / Mr. Claire / Circus

Unreleased tracks :

When the **Koobas** took part in the motion picture, 'Merry Go Round The Roses', an EP was recorded by them which, unfortunately, never saw the light of day in the record market. That is why it is not known which songs were recorded at that time.

BILLY J. KRAMER WITH THE DAKOTAS

In the beginning of the Sixties, the group, **Billy Forde & the Phantoms,** was formed in Liverpool and, when **Ted Knibbs** took over their management, he changed their name to **Billy Kramer & the Coasters**. It was a real amateur outfit but, within a short time, became very popular on the scene. In 1962, they reached the number 3 spot in the 'Mersey Beat' newspaper popularity poll.

Probably because of that success, **Brian Epstein** became interested in managing the up and coming group and **Billy Kramer & the Coasters** recorded the demo, "She's My Girl", a song by Liverpool songwriter, **Ralph Bowdler**.

Brian Epstein took it to EMI and they became interested in signing the band. But, with the exception of **Billy Kramer**, whose real name is **William Howard Ashton**, none of the **Coasters** wanted to become professional musicians. So, the singer separated from the group and signed a contract with **Brian Epstein**.

The **Coasters** continued together under the wing of **Ted Knibbs** and found a new singer in **Chick Graham**. In 1963, they also turned professional under the name of **Chick Graham & the Coasters**.

Brian Epstein changed his singer's name from **Billy Kramer** to **Billy J. Kramer** and arranged a co-operation between him and the Manchester band, **The Dakotas**, who formerly had backed **Pete MacLaine**. It should be pointed out here that the 'J' was added to his name because **Brian Epstein** thought it sounded more interesting and not because **Billy J. Kramer** was a big fan of **'J'ohn Lennon**, as it is often claimed by poorly informed people.

However, the correct name for the new amalgamation was **Billy J. Kramer <u>with</u> the Dakotas**, because the **Dakotas** also recorded solo and had two chart hits with the instrumentals, "Magic Carpet" and "The Cruel Sea", in 1963. However, their 1964 follow-up, "O' Yeh", failed to make the hit parade.

Billy J. Kramer with the Dakotas were voted 'the best new group of the year' by the national music paper, 'Melody Maker', in 1963. That fact alone makes it clear how popular the group was throughout the UK. Their line-up at that time was:

Billy J. Kramer	(voc)
Mike Maxfield	(g)
Robin McDonald	(g)
Ray Jones	(bg)
Tony Mansfield	(dr)

Mike Maxfield was a former member of **Don Curtis & the Coasters**, one of the first Manchester groups that also appeared regularly on the Liverpool scene.

Tony Mansfield's real name is **Tony Bookbinder,** a brother of **Elkie Brooks** who later became a major recording star.

The first single released by the Liverpool/Manchester connection, "Do You Want To Know A Secret", was written by **John Lennon** and **Paul McCartney** and went straight to number 2 in the British charts in 1963. Then with the follow-up, "Bad To Me", **Billy J. Kramer with the Dakotas** had their first chart topper later in the same year. This success was followed by "I'll Keep You Satisfied" (No. 4 in 1963), their biggest hit, "Little Children" (No. 1), and, "From A Window" (No. 10), both in 1964.

Their next single, "It's Gotta Last Forever", did not chart, but the **Burt Bacharach** song, "Trains And Boats And Planes", was another 'Top 20' hit for the group and reached No. 12 in 1965.

Billy J. Kramer with the Dakotas also charted in the USA with some of these records, where they were very popular at that time. In England, the group had a special tour programme under the name, 'The Billy J. Kramer Pop Parade'. However, in the rest of Europe, they were mysteriously unsuccessful with their records, which had limited distribution in other countries. For example, in Germany, where Merseybeat was very popular, only "Do You Want To Know A Secret" was released.

In 1965, **Ray Jones** left and was replaced by **Ken Sherrat**, who came from Stoke's **Marauders**.

Mike Maxfield, who still sporadically played with **Don Curtis & the Coasters,** also left and became the manager of the Manchester group, **Ivan's Meads**.

He was replaced by **Mick Green**, a former member of **Johnny Kidd & the Pirates**.

In 1966, **Tony Mansfield** temporarily replaced **Bobby Elliott** in the **Hollies**. When **Bobby Elliott** returned to the **Hollies, Tony Mansfield** had a short spell with **Dave Berry & the Cruisers**. After that, he apparently quit show business for quite a while but, in 1981, was back on the scene as a member of **New Music**.

For a while, **Roy Dyke** of the **Remo Four** stood in for him with the **Dakotas** but then **Frank Farley** took over that position. **Frank Farley** had also previously played with **Johnny Kidd & the Pirates**.

In the meantime, further singles including "Neon City", "We're Doing Fine" and the nice ballad, "Take My Hand", were released, but all failed to make the charts.

When **Ken Sherrat** left to join the newly-formed **Tennesseans**, **Billy J. Kramer** also separated from the **Dakotas** who found a new singer in **Lou Rich** and released two more singles with "I'm An 'ardworking Barrow-man" and "Can't Break The News".

Then **Mick Green**, **Frank Farley** and the only remaining original member, **Robin McDonald,** became the new **Rebel Rousers** for the great singer **Cliff Bennett**. When the **Rebel Rousers** disbanded, only **Mick Green** appeared again - as a member of the re-formed **Pirates**.

But this is not the end of the **Dakotas** story as they were re-formed by founding members, **Tony Bookbinder** and **Mike Maxfield,** together with **Eddie Mooney** (voc/bg) and **Pete MacDonald** (key). The group kept very busy on the scene but a new co-operation with **Billy J. Kramer** never took place.

After he had left the **Dakotas** in 1967, **Billy J. Kramer** went solo and for a while was backed by the **Remo Four** on live appearances. His records, "Sorry", "Town Of Tuxley" (both in 1967), "1941" and "A World Without Love" (both in 1968) as well as "Colour Of My Love" (1969) did not make the charts, although they were quite interesting.

He continued recording for different labels and, in 1971, he released "And The Grass Won't Pay No Mind" on Polydor as the only record under his real name **William Howard Ashton**.

He later formed a new backing group that, in England, toured as the **B.J.K.-Band** but also used the name of the **Dakotas** sometimes.

In 1977, the line-up of this group consisted of **Max Milligan** (g), **Chris Cole** (org/p), **Mike Clustin** (bg) and **John Dillon** (dr).

Max Milligan, **Mike Clustin** and **John Dillon** were former members of a band called **Breeze**, while **Chris Cole** was a former classical musician. In this line-up, they toured Germany as **Billy J. Kramer & the Dakotas** for the first time since the Sixties. Unfortunately, this tour wasn't too successful and, accordingly, not repeated.

Around this time, **Billy J. Kramer** also released some good singles such as the melodic "Warm Summer Rain" (1977), the very interesting "Ships That Pass In The Night" and, in 1982, the 'Merseybeatish' "Dum Dum" as B-side of the not so good "Rock It".

1983 saw the release of the really nice single, "You Can't Live On Memories", written by himself. The song describes his own career ending with the meaningful words, 'but that was all in the past, you can't live on memories, they won't last'. How right he was!

He later emigrated to the USA and there he released a new album with quite good second takes of his big Sixties hits on one side, as well as some interesting new songs on the other. The title of that long player was 'Kramer vs. Kramer' (US-Attack ATA 007 / 1986).

Single discography

as **Billy Kramer & the Coasters** :

She's My Girl / (probably only one-sided)	UK- Epstein-demo (acetate) / 1963

as **Billy J. Kramer with the Dakotas** :

Do You Want To Know A Secret / I'll Be On My Way	UK-Parlophone R 5023 / 1963
Bad To Me / I Call Your Name	UK-Parlophone R 5049 / 1963
I'll Keep You Satisfied / I Know	UK-Parlophone R 5073 / 1963
Little Children / They Remind Me Of You	UK-Parlophone R 5105 / 1964
From A Window / Second To None	UK-Parlophone R 5156 / 1964
It's Gotta Last Forever / Don't You Do It No More	UK-Parlophone R 5234 / 1965
Trains And Boats And Planes / That's The Way I Feel	UK-Parlophone R 5285 / 1965
Neon City / I'll Be Doggone	UK-Parlophone R 5362 / 1965
We're Doing Fine / Forgive Me	UK-Parlophone R 5408 / 1966
Take My Hand / You Make Me Feel Like Someone	UK-Parlophone R 5482 / 1966

Different US release :

Twilight Time / Irresistible You	US- Imperial 66115 / 1965

Different Spanish release :

Little Children / Pride	ES – Odeon SD 5959 / 1964

Different Canadian release :

The Twelfth Of Never / Twilight Time	CAN – Capitol 72303 / 1965

Billy J. Kramer – solo :

Sorry / Going, Going, Gone	UK-Parlophone R 5552 / 1967
Town Of Tuxley / Chinese Girl	UK-Reaction 591014 / 1967
1941 / His Love Is Just A lie	UK-Nems 56-3396 / 1968
A World Without Love / Going Through It	UK-Nems 56-3635 / 1968
Colour Of My Love / I'm Running Away	UK-MGM 1474 / 1969

as **Wiiliam Howard Ashton** :

And The Grass Won't Pay No Mind /	UK-Polydor ??? / 1971

The Dakotas – solo :

The Cruel Sea / The Millionaire	UK-Parlophone R 5044 / 1963
Magic Carpet / Humdinger	UK-Parlophone R 5064 / 1963
O' Yeh / My Girl Josephine	UK-Parlophone R 5203 / 1964
I'm An 'ardworking Barrow-man / 7 lbs Of Potatoes	UK-Page One 018 / 1967
Can't Break The News / The Spider And The Fly	UK-Philips 1645 / 1968

EP discography

as **Billy J. Kramer with the Dakotas** :

THE KRAMER HITS   UK-Parlophone GEP 8885 / 1963

- Do You Want To Know A Secret / I'll Be On My Way / Bad To Me / I Call Your Name

I'LL KEEP YOU SATISFIED   UK-Parlophone GEP 8895 / 1963

- I'll Keep You Satisfied / I Know / Dance With Me / It's Up To You

I'LL KEEP YOU SATISFIED No.2   UK-Parlophone GEP 8907 / 1964

- Little Children / They Remind Me Of You / Beautiful Dreamer / I Call Your Name

FROM A WINDOW   UK-Parlophone GEP 8921 / 1964

- From A Window / Second To None / Dance With Me / The Twelfth Of Never

BILLY J. PLAYS THE STATES   UK-Parlophone GEP 8928 / 1965

- Sugar Babe / Twilight Time / Irresistible You / Tennessee Waltz (all live-recordings)

Different French release :

BILLY J. KRAMER / THE DAKOTAS   F- Odeon SOE 3743 / 1964

- Bad To Me / Do You Want To Know A Secret / The Cruel Sea / The Millionaire

EP by **The Dakotas** :

THE DAKOTAS   UK-Parlophone GEP 8888 / 1963

- The Cruel Sea / The Millionaire / Magic Carpet / Humdinger as **Billy J. Kramer with the Dakotas :**

LISTEN   UK-Parlophone PMC 1209 / 1964

-Dance With Me / Pride / I Know / Yes / Twelfth Of Never / Sugar Babe /

Da Doo Ron Ron / It's Up To You / Great Balls Of Fire / Tell Me Girl / Anything

That's Part Of You / Beautiful Dreamer / Still Waters Run Deep / I Call Your Name

Different US releases :

LITTLE CHILDREN   US-Imperial LP 12267 / 1964

- Little Children / Da Doo Ron Ron / Dance With Me / Pride / I Know /

They Remind Me Of You / Do You Want To Know A Secret / Bad To Me /

I'll Keep You Satisfied / Great Balls Of Fire / It's Up To You / Tell Me Girl

I'LL KEEP YOU SATISFIED / FROM A WINDOW   US-Imperial LP 12273 / 1964

-I'll Keep You Satisfied / I Call Your Name / Beautiful Dreamer / The Twelfth Of Never /

Sugar Babe / I'll Be On My Way / From A Window / Second To None / Anything

That's Part Of You / Still Waters / Yes / The Cruel Surf ("Dakotas" solo)

TRAINS AND BOATS AND PLANES   US-Imperial LP 12291 / 1965

- Trains And Boats And Planes / Mad Mad World / Twilight Time / Under The

Boardwalk / When You Walk In The Room / Sneaking Around / To Take Her Place /

When You Ask About Love / I Live To Love You / Tennessee Waltz (Live) / Irresistible You (Live)

Unreleased tracks

In 1963, **Billy J. Kramer with the Dakotas** recorded a great version of "**I'm In Love**", which was also recorded, released and became a chart success for the **Fourmost**.

In 1964, the group recorded an alternative take of "**When You Walk In The Room**", which was much more powerful than the later take released on the album. This song, of course, was also recorded, released and became an international hit for the **Searchers**.

Another Paul McCartney song was recorded with "**One And One Is Two**" in 1965, but it was never released. However, the song was also recorded and released by a group called **The Strangers with Mike Shannon** (which was not the Liverpool group of the same name) but it did not have any great chart success.

THE KREW

This group originated from Birmingham where it was formed by **Ray Thomas** and **Mike Pinder**, who had previously played together in **El Riot & the Rebels**. Accordingly, it was a real Brumbeat group and this could lead to the conclusion that they should not be included here, but their story will prove to the contrary. Their name was often documented with a variety of different spellings – from the **Crew-Cuts**, the **Krew-Cats** and, sometimes, the **Krewkats.** The latter name is most probably the right one, judging by the records that were released. However, after some personnel changes, the **Krewkats,** in 1962, consisted of the Birmingham musicians, **John 'Brad' Bradley** (voc/bg), **Ted Tunnicliffe** (lg), **Rob Nicholls** (rg) and **Don Hawkins** (dr).

They went to France and were immediately signed by the big Parisian record company, 'Pathe Marconi'.

Initially, the group cut two EPs in their own right with 'Polaris' and 'Tonight' but still, in 1963, also backed the famous French Rock 'n' Roll singer, **Dick Rivers,** on three EPs and some album tracks.

Around that time, **Don Hawkins** left and was replaced by Liverpudlian (?), **Eddie Sparrow**.

The Krewkats toured Germany and, among other venues, they played an extended engagement at the 'New York City Club' in Duisburg. Toward the end of that engagement, the **Pawns** from Liverpool, who were due to take over, arrived. Sax player, **Howie Casey**, a member of the **Pawns**, played a gig with the **Krewkats** and joined them. This five-piece line-up returned to France where they again worked with **Dick Rivers.** They were joined by **Mann Hoaurie** as an additional sax player and they accepted a booking to play a club in Itzehoe, North Germany for a month. Unfortunately, the club burned down and most of the group's equipment was destroyed. **Peter Eckhorn** of the famous 'Top Ten' in Hamburg, helped out and offered them an engagement at his club. They were joined by **Johnny Phillips** (tr/sax), who had formerly played with the **Roadrunners** and the **Eyes**.

As the **Top Ten Allstars,** the group backed Scottish girl singer, **Isabella Bond,** on her records, "Bread And Butter" and "Everything's Alright", that were released on the German Decca label in 1964. They also recorded a solo single as the **Top Ten Allstars** with "I Feel Fine", and none other than **Tony Sheridan** played the guitar to the lead vocals of **John Bradley**. After that engagement ended, the **Krewkats** went to London where the line-up changed constantly until the group finally broke up.

John Bradley followed **Howie Casey** back to Liverpool where they both joined the **Big Three** for a short time. After that, **Howie Casey** had a short spell with the **Griff Parry Five**, while **John Bradley** played with the **Jam Buttees**. Then they both got together again with **Eddie Sparrow** and resurrected their former group under the shortened name of

ISABELLA BOND

The Krew, together with **Mike Hart** (g/sax/voc), formerly with the **Tenabeats** and the **Roadrunners**.

John Bradley did not stay for too long and disappeared from the scene. **Archie Leggett**, who came from the **Bobby Patrick Big Six**, joined as their bass guitarist. Their new singer was **Steve Aldo**, who formerly had sung with **Steve Aldo & the Challengers**, the **Nocturns** and, for a short time, with **King Size Taylor & the Dominoes** and the **Griff Parry Five**.

Steve Aldo did not stay for too long either, he left the **Krew** and joined the **Fyx**. He later sang with the **In Crowd** and then was backed by the **Fairies** from Colchester for a short time before he quit showbiz.

Mike Hart had left a little earlier and joined the **Richmond**. After that, he played with the **Kinsleys** and then formed a new group called **Henry's Handful**. He later appeared with **Mike Hart & the Moondogs** and **Liverpool Scene** before he started a successful solo career. The **Krew,** under the leadership of **Howie Casey** in 1965, decided to go back to France in a line-up with:

Owen Gray	(voc)
Tommy Murray	(g)
Howie Casey	(sax)
Archie Leggett	(bg)
Alan Reeves	(org)
Eddie Sparrow	(dr)

Tommy Murray, a great guitarist, had formerly played with the **Memphis Rhythm & Blues Combo** and the **Kinsleys**. Unfortunately, the former groups of **Owen Gray** and **Alan Reeves** are not known, but both hailed from the Mersey scene.

The **Krew** used France as their base and from there toured throughout Europe. It is said that, around that time, they also backed successful French girl singer, **Sylvie Vartan,** on various recordings but this could not be confirmed, as the group was never named on any of her singles or EP labels.

The huge Barclay recording company signed the **Krew** for its Riviera label and, in 1966, an EP was released with the songs, "Everything's Alright", "63-45789", "Somebody Stole My Girl" and "Sugar Pie". This record showed the **Krew** to be a great group and it apparently sold quite well. It was followed by a single coupled out from that same EP with the songs "Everything's Alright" and "Somebody Stole My Girl", but no new material. This lack of new material might have been due to the fact that the line-up kept changing continuously.

Eddie Sparrow left and was replaced by **Pete Clarke**, who had previously played with **Vince & the Volcanoes**, **Groups Inc.** and the **Escorts**. He did not stay for too long and joined **Them Grimbles** before he returned to the **Escorts**. Later he was a member of **Liverpool Scene**.

His replacement was **Chris Mutch** who came from Liverpool. Besides this, the group was joined on sax by **Ivan Roth** and the French sax player, **Gilbert D'Alanese**.

When **Owen Gray** left, his replacement was **Ernie Garrett Jr.** and later the **Krew** were also joined by songstress, **Barry St. John,** who formerly had various solo singles released on Decca and Columbia. Of those, the most popular was her great version of "Bread And Butter".

It was probably in 1968 that the group disbanded totally, when **Tommy Murray** joined a group called **Mumble** and, after that, became a member of the **Swinging Blue Jeans**, who, at that time, recorded under the name of **Music Motor**.

Archie Leggett re-appeared on the scene as a member of the **Kevin Ayers Band**, where he met up with **Owen Gray** again.

Chris Mutch also joined the **Swinging Blue Jeans** and, after that, disappeared from the scene.

Howie Casey got married to **Barry St. John**, who, from 1968 on, kept recording in her own right, while **Howie Casey** continued playing in various groups including the **Roy Young Band** and **Rigor Mortis**. Besides this, he became a very successful studio musician and, as such, he is credited on a number of records by well known artists, including **Paul McCartney** and the **Hollies**. Today he is married to **Sheila McKinley** of the **McKinleys** recording duo and still leads his own group, the **Howie Casey Band**.

The group name **Krew** existed on the scene until the early Seventies, but it is not known who the members were because of the steadily changing line-ups.

The Krew with Beryl Marsden

Discography :

The Krew :

EP Everything's Alright / 63-45789 / Somebody Stole My Girl / Sugar Pie	F – Riviera 231 214 / 1966
Everything's Alright / Somebody Stole My Girl	F – Riviera 121087 / 1966

The Top Ten Allstars :

I Feel Fine / Sha-la-la	G – Decca D 19651 / 1964

Isabella Bond & the Top Ten Allstars :

Bread And Butter / Downtown (both titles sung in English)	G – Decca D 19650 / 1964
Bread And Butter / Downtown (both titles sung in German)	G – Decca D 19657 / 1964
Everything's Alright / Thanks	G – Decca D 19668 / 1964

Tracks on compilation-albums :

Bread And Butter on 'Beat Party'	G – Decca ND 106 / 1965

Hurt on 'Beat Party' G – Decca ND 106 / 1965

The **Krewkats** :

EP Tonight / Tuxedo Twist / You Are My Sunshine / Diggedle Boing	F - Pathe Marconi / 1963
EP Polaris / The Ice Cream Man / Bleak House / For My Good Fortune	F – Pathe Marconi /1963

As backing-group for **Dick Rivers** :

EP **A Séville** / Pour Une Fille (Why Little Girl) / J'ai Choisi L'amour (For My Good Fortune) / Virginie

(please note that the **Krewkats** were only featured on the 2nd and 3rd title)   F – Pathe EG 630 / 1963

EP **Bien Trop Court** (Life's Too Short) **/ La Fille Qu'on A Tant Aimée / Au Coeur De La Nuit**

(A Picture Of You) **/ Je Suis Bien**   F – Pathe EG 639 / 1963

EP **L'effet Que Tu Mes Fais** (How Do You Do It) **/ Je Ne Peux Pas T'oublier** (Can't Get Used To Losing You) **/
Sarah Jane** (The Folk Singer) **/ T'as Seize Ans Demain** (Sweet Little Sixteen)   F – Pathe EG 650 / 1963

Album tracks :

T'as Seize Ans Demain (Sweet Little Sixteen)	on '100 % Rock'	F - MF 5602 / 196?
Tobacco Road	on '100 % Rock'	F – MFP 5602 / 196?
Whole Lotta Shakin' Goin' On	on '100 % Rock'	F – MFP 5602 / 196?

(Please note that all the French recordings as the **Krewkats** were obviously without the participation of the Liverpool musicians)

THE KRUZADS

This group was formed under the name of the **Crusaders** in Liverpool in 1962 by **Frank McTigue**, who formerly had played with the **Texans** together with **Ken 'Dixie' Dean**, a former member of **Gerry Marsden's Skiffle Group**, formerly known as the **Mars Bars**.

Shortly after their formation, **Frank McTigue** returned to his old group, which now were called the **Easybeats** and his replacement was **Eddie Hill** who came from the **Easybeats**.

The group probably, at that time, became the **Kruzads**, and very soon established themselves as one of the local attractions. In 1963, they accepted an offer to tour the military bases in France and Germany with the following line-up:

Ken 'Dixie' Dean	(voc/g)
Billy Roberts	(lg)
Eddie Hill	(bg/voc)
Danny Bell	(dr)

Billy Roberts and **Danny Bell** were both former members of the **City Beats**, a very interesting group that had recently won a recording contract in the national 'Frankie Vaughan Talent Competition', but that is another story.

The **Kruzads** signed with Liverpool's 'Merseysounds Agency' and their new manager, **Gordon Brown**, arranged for them to play the 'Star-Club' in Hamburg.

Ken 'Dixie' Dean claims that, during their stay in Germany, they were signed to the German Polydor label and recorded the **Mick Jagger/Keith Richard** composition, "Tell Me", as well as **Arthur Alexander**'s "You Better Move On" as a single, but nothing is known about such a release. Maybe it was released under another name, but this is only a possibility and not an absolute certainty, although German Polydor was known for confusing or simply changing the names of their artists.

However, back in Liverpool, **Gordon Brown** worked at building up a big name for the **Kruzads**, who were then trumpeted as 'Liverpool's answer to the Rolling Stones' and, obviously, there were similarities in their sounds. The **Kruzads** were one of Merseyside's really good 'hard' Beat and Rhythm & Blues bands. In spite of this, they were never able to achieve nationwide popularity.

For unknown reasons, **Dixie Dean** left the group and became a session musician down in London and, from 1972 until 1974, he played with **McGuinness Flint**. **Mal Jefferson** (voc/harp), who had previously played with **Buddy Dean & the Teachers** and the **Mastersounds** replaced him in the **Kruzads**.

Later, in 1964, **Eddie Hill** also left and disappeared from the scene. He was replaced by **Arthur Megginson**, who came from the **Clayton Squares**. **Arthur Megginson** did not stay for too long, his replacement on bass guitar was **Paul Eker**, who was also was a former member of the **City Beats** and, in the interim, had played with the **Profiles**.

Then, **Chris Finley,** who had previously played with the **Runaways**, was added on keyboards. This line-up lasted until the group broke up in early 1966.

Danny Bell and **Paul Eker** disappeared from the scene while **Chris Finley** joined the **Masterminds** and, after that, played with the **Fruit Eating Bears**. He then became a member of **Confucius**, a group that had evolved from the **Hideaways**. Later he played with the new **Merseybeats** and **Herman's Hermits**.

Initially, **Mal Jefferson** also disappeared from the scene but, in 1974, he played with the **Chesterfields** and, after that, ran the Mastersound Studios in Southport.

However, this was not the end of the **Kruzads.** Within a short time, still in 1966, they were re-formed by **Billy Roberts** with the following line-up:

Steve Barton	**(voc)**
Billy Roberts	**(g/voc)**
Joey Maher	**(org)**
Jimmy Ikonomides	**(bg)**
Pete Wiggins	**(dr)**

Jimmy Ikonomides was a former member of the **Knights**, the **Abstrax**, the **Mafia-Group** and **Them Calderstones**, while **Pete Wiggins** was also a former member of the **Mafia** and in the interim he had played with the **Profiles**.

Jimmy Ikonomides, John Thompson, Joey Maher, Paul Hitchmough
Front: Billy Roberts, Steve Barton

Pete Wiggins did not stay for too long, he was replaced by **Paul Hitchmough** on drums and **John Thompson** as an additional singer, both of these new members came from **Sounds plus One**. Before that, **Paul Hitchmough** had played with the **Hangmen**, the **Victims** and the **Corals**.

Their management was taken over by **Jean Vanloo** of the Unidans Agency in Belgium and accordingly the **Kruzads** often played in France and Belgium, where they became the resident group at the 'Twenty Club' in Mouscron. They became extremely popular in both countries and made various TV appearances. The Belgium Vogue label signed them up and it is said that a single was released with the live version of the **Billy Roberts** original "The promise". This line-up of the **Kruzads** also recorded an acetate with the **Kinks** numbers "Stop your sobbing" and "Till the end of the day".

It was probably in 1967 that this group broke up and this time the name **Kruzads** disappeared from the scene forever.

Paul Hitchmough joined the **Clayton Squares**, who a little later continued as the **T-Squares**, but toured Germany under the **Clayton Squares** name again. After that he was a member of **Curiosity Shoppe** and then he disappeared from the scene until 1990, when he toured Germany with the **Beryl Marsden Group**. After that he was a member of **Karl Terry & the Cruisers**, before continuing to play as a session drummer.

Of **Jimmy Ikonomides** it is known that he joined the **Detours**, who had returned to Liverpool after their stay in the south of England.

Billy Roberts formed a new group under the name of **Arnold Grenyar**, who toured France again and later changed their name into **Family Dog**. **Billy Roberts** is a very popular professional stage and television psychic/medium today and in the meantime he has written no less than 18 books.

Discography :

Tell me / You better move on (*)	G - Polydor unreleased / 1964
The promise (live) / Reason to believe	B – Vogue VB ??? / 1966
Stop your sobbing / Till the end of the day	UK - ? Acetate / 1966

(* please note, that it is not certain if the German record was actually released. It is a possibility that it was issued under another name (perhaps on a sampler album), as the German Polydor label was known for doing such things. However, **Dixie Dean** claims that it was released - any doubts?)

MR. LEE & CO.

In 1963, a trio was formed on the 'other' side of the river Mersey, in Leasowe on the Wirral under the name of the **Cuban Heels**, consisting of **Dennis Barton** (voc/g), **Alan Chesters** (bg/voc) and **Derek Cashin** (dr).

They mostly gigged in the areas of New Brighton, Wallasey and Birkenhead. In early 1964, they became friends with the singer, **William Carruthers**, better known as **Clay Ellis**, who, at that time, was the vocalist for **Clay Ellis & the Corsairs** and, before that, he had fronted the very popular **Clay Ellis & the Raiders**. Besides him, the tenor-saxophonist, **Mike Grannon,** joined, who at that time was playing with the **Pasadena Jazz Men.**

In the beginning, it was more of a loose association between those members, but they rehearsed together and, occasionally, they would play gigs under different names.

Amongst the venues they played was the 'Witch's Cauldron' in New Brighton and the owner of this club, **Freddy G. Scanes**, recognized their outstanding musical quality. He convinced them to stay together and took over their management.

Around that time, **Dennis Barton** left to join **Screaming Lord Sutch & the Savages** on a tour of Germany. That group remained in Germany for nine months but, during that time, the **Savages** separated from **Screaming Lord Sutch** and, after some personnel changes, had become the **Dodos**. **Dennis Barton** played with the **Dodos** until 1968, he then returned to Liverpool and joined the newly formed **Undertakers**. After that, he played with **Y-Kickamoocow** and then became a member of a Country-band called **Wild Country**. Later he went solo in the cabaret-scene under the name of **Alexander Scott**.

Derek Cashin also left and joined the **Graduates** (which may have been **Cole Young & the Graduates** previously), with whom he also went to Germany and there he teamed up again with **Dennis Barton** in the **Dodos**. When he returned to Liverpool, he played with **Paper Chase**, that, with him as a member, went on to become the new **Merseybeats** and, after that, he was a member of **Liverpool Express**.

But back to the other musicians who, in the meantime, had become a steady group under the name of **Mr. Lee & Co.** and appeared in a line-up with:

Mr. Lee	(voc)
Paul Wise	(lg/voc)
Alan Chesters	(bg/voc)
Mike Grannon	(sax)
Nigel Whinyates	(dr)

Nigel Whinyates came from the **Rockerfellers** that, in the early Sixties, had evolved from **Johnny Autumn & the Fall Guys** and still included the singer, **Johnny Autumn**, as well as **Doug Pond** on lead guitar. **Paul Wise** came from the **Matadors** and **Mr. Lee** was, of course, **Clay Ellis**.

'Mr. Lee' was a mythological Rock 'n' Roll character and, as the group was much more Rock 'n' Roll than most of their contemporaries, they thought it was a great idea to call their singer **Mr. Lee** and, from a calendar in a Chinese restaurant called Lee & Co., they ended up using the name of **Mr. Lee & Co.**

Their manager, **Freddy Scanes,** was a man with an eye for publicity and so he got the singer to dress up as a city-gent with a bowler hat and carrying an umbrella – really for promotional purposes but, occasionally he would do an entire gig rather than just open the show in that outfit.

Mr. Lee & Co. became the resident group at the 'Witch's Cauldron' but, besides this, played almost every night at the major venues throughout the region – sometimes even two or three gigs per night.

The group went into **Alan Cheetham's** AGC-studios in Stockport and recorded an acetate which, besides the **William Carruthers** original, "Cry A Little", also featured interesting covers of **Bobby Day's** "Rockin' Robin" and the **Ray Peterson** teeny-ballad, "Corinna, Corinna".

This acetate was sent to various record-companies in London but no contract was offered to the group. A little later they went into the Unicord-studios in Moorfields and recorded another EP acetate with "Peter Gunn", "All Night Worker", "Wooly Bully" and "Bright Lights Big City".

Mr. Lee & Co. were in huge demand on Merseyside throughout 1965 and, in the summer of that year, they won the 'Northern Sounds '65' competition. Their reward was new band-equipment and a record-contract.

They got the new equipment but the record-deal did not materialise, so the musicians decided to take matters into their own hands. They all turned professional and, in January 1966, left for London, where they met up with **Micky Most**, who was keen to arrange a recording-session with the group which, in the end, did not take place because the producer lost the telephone-number for the group.

Instead of this, **Mr. Lee & Co.** recorded a few originals and quite a few numbers from their play-list for **Joe Meek** at his Holloway Road studio.

Spring 1966 rolled around and nothing was happening on the **Joe Meek** front. No deals seemed to be on the horizon, so a certain disillusionment set in with both **William Carruthers** and **Mike Grannon**. They both went back to Merseyside, where **Mr. Lee** became **Clay Ellis** again and continued as a solo-act in the cabaret-circuit, while **Mike Grannon** most probably re-joined the local Jazz-scene.

Paul Wise, **Alan Chesters** and **Nigel Whinyates** remained in London and continued recording for **Joe Meek**, who then got them together with **Peter Meers** (voc), **Chris Hedger** (g) and **Jim Husband** (dr), who all came from the **Hotrods**, one of the producer's recording-groups, that had just disbanded.

This new line-up continued as **Peter, Chris & the Outcasts**. With their double-drum sound they became very popular in the London scene and soon were signed to Columbia.

In May 1966, a single was released with the **Peter Meers** original, "Over The Hill", which, in spite of good musical quality, did not become a chart-success.

Sometime in 1967, **Peter Meers** left the group and disappeared from the scene. This was followed by the departure of **Nigel Whinyates**, who became a member of the Polydor recording-group, the **Cortinas** from Hatfield. As there was already a Nigel in that line-up, **Nigel Whinyates** changed his name to **Gary Whinyates** and he was still with the group when, in 1968, it became **Octopus**, who then recorded for Penny Farthing.

OPEN EVERY NIGHT

WHISKY A' GO GO

THURSDAY, MAY 9th

THE CHANTERS

SUNDAY, MAY 12th

THE CORTINAS

33-37 WARDOUR STREET, W.1   01-437 7676

In 1969, **Nigel Whinyates** left the group and the music-business and, in the late Eighties, he emigrated to Switzerland, where he is still living in Basel and was last known as a member of the **Blues Priority**.

But back to the **Outcasts**, that, as a quartet, continued to play the London scene and to record for **Joe Meek**, although no further records were released.

The Outcasts - L to R:
Jim Husband, Chris Hedger, Paul Wise & Alan Chesters

When they finally broke up, **Paul Wise** returned to Merseyside, while **Alan Chesters** remained in the south of England and later played with the recording-groups, **Sale** (MCA) and the **Dyaks** (Elevator), before he played with the **Boogaloos** from Norfolk for almost 25 years. He then went into stage-design and formed his own company, who handled a plethora of mega-shows all over Europe.

In 2009, there was a re-union of the **Outcasts** that included **Chris Hedger**, **Paul Wise**, **Alan Chesters** and **Jim Husband** again but, unfortunately, it was only a one-off show.

Discography :

Mr. Lee & Co. :

Cry A Little / Rockin' Robin / Corinna, Corinna   UK - AGC acetate EP / 1965

Peter Gunn / Wooly Bully / All Night Worker / Bright Lights Big City   UK – Unicord acetate EP / 1965

Besides this **Mr. Lee & Co.** recorded quite a few songs for **Joe Meek** during their stay in London in 1965/1966. Unfortunately, the names of those songs are not known.

Peter, Chris & the Outcasts :

Over The Hill / The Right Girl For Me   UK- Columbia DB 7923 / 1966

This group as **Peter, Chris & the Outcasts** and later as the **Outcasts** also recorded many more songs for **Joe Meek** during 1966/1967. But again, it proved impossible to determine the names of those songs.

THE LIVERBIRDS

This band was most probably the first all female vocal and instrumental group in Liverpool when they came together in 1962. For sure, they were the first British female group that made a real impact on the male-dominated scene - something of an early act of emancipation.

The Liverbirds were named after the mythological birds of Liverpool's Atlantic coast that also became the emblem of the harbour city and can be seen as monuments on the top of the Liver Building.

Within a quite short time, the Liverbirds rocked themselves into the hearts of the Beat fans on Merseyside. The original line-up consisted of:

Irene Green	**(voc)**
Sheila McGlory	**(g)**
Valerie Gell	**(g/voc)**
Mary McGlory	**(bg)**
Sylvia Saunders	**(dr)**

Mary McGlory had played with the **Squaws** before she teamed up with her cousin, **Sheila McGlory**, **Valerie Gell** and **Sylvia Saunders** in an instrumental group called the **Debutones**. They were then joined by singer, **Irene Green,** and then their name was changed to the **Liverbirds**.

The Liverbirds at the Star Club

At a performance at the 'Whisky A-Go-Go' in Newcastle, **Irene Green** informed the other group members that she would be leaving and she then started a successful solo career under the name of '**Tiffany**'. Initially, she was backed by the **Four Dimensions** (as **Tiffany's Dimensions**) and later by the **Thoughts** (as **Tiffany & the Thoughts**).

With the latter group, she recorded the nice single, "Find Out What's Happening" but, before that, she had already released a solo single with the great, "Am I Dreaming". But that is a different story which can be followed under **Tiffany** in this book.

On the same evening **Irene Green** left the **Liverbirds,** she was replaced by a girl singer from Newcastle called **Heather**, who went back with the group to Liverpool. Unfortunately, it soon became obvious that she was not the right replacement. Besides this, she became homesick and so she left and returned to Newcastle.

When the **Liverbirds** received an offer to play the 'Star-Club' in Hamburg, **Sheila McGlory** also left because she wanted to stay in Liverpool, where she then joined the **Demoiselles**.

It was in London that **Ray Davies** of the **Kinks** introduced **Pamela Birch** (voc/g), the sister of **Dyan Birch** of the **Excelles**, to the **Liverbirds**. She had a very impressive stage personality and immediately joined them. With this line-up, the **Liverbirds** went to Hamburg for a long residency where they became a steady and significant part of the so-called 'Star-Club' scene.

Over time, the **Liverbirds** achieved popularity throughout Germany but, because they seldom returned to Liverpool, they never received the recognition they deserved in the Beat scene of their hometown.

Thus, they never released a record in England but were quite successful in Germany with their singles, "Diddley Daddy" (No. 1 in the Musicbox Hit Parade in 1965), "Shop Around", "Peanut Butter" and "Loop Di Loop", which were all released on the 'Star-Club' label. Besides this, the **Liverbirds** cut two albums for the same label with 'Star-Club Show 4' and 'More Of The Liverbirds'.

Both were quite interesting, and ballads such as "Love Hurts", "Leave All Your Old Loves In The Past", "He Hardly Ever Calls Me 'Honey' Anymore" and "Why Do You Hang Around Me", left an especially good impression, as did the rocking numbers like "It's So Exciting", "He's About A Mover" and so on.

Sometimes, it is stated that the **Liverbirds** had no outstanding musical quality but, for sure they had a good driving sound at the right time, so their success in Germany was not undeserved.

The Liverbirds in the back-yard of the Star Club

In 1967, **Sylvia Saunders** got married to **John Wiggins**, the former organist of the **Big Six,** and she returned to England with him.

She was replaced by German girl drummer, **Dixie Wassermeyer**, who had previously played with the **Rag Dolls** from Duisburg and, it was probably this change in the line-up that caused **Valerie Gell** to also leave the group a little bit later, when she got married in Munich.

Her replacement was **Christiane Schulz**, who hailed from Cologne. Unfortunately, her former group is not known. In this line-up, the **Liverbirds** went for a long tour of Japan, where they were very successful.

They may have also recorded again in Japan, but there is nothing known about any releases in the Far East other than those that had previously been released in Germany. In spite of the success of the Japan tour, the **Liverbirds** disbanded shortly after their return to Germany.

Mary McGlory got married to **Frank Dostal**, a German musician from the 'Star-Club' scene who had played with the **Faces**, the **Rattles** and **Wonderland**.

Chris Schulz returned to Cologne, where she probably continued to play but nothing was heard of her again. **Dixie Wassermeyer** went back to Duisburg and sadly, soon after, committed suicide at a very young age.

Pamela Birch, who also worked sporadically as a songwriter, settled down in Hamburg, where she continued playing on the local scene with a number of different session groups.

In 1977, she was featured, together with other former musicians, at a revival concert of the legendary 'Star-Club' scene at the Markthalle in Hamburg. At this concert, the group **Rock Circus** was formed and she became one of their members. But this group also had more of a session character and a steadily changing line-up. After that, **Pamela Birch** was a member of the very short-lived group, **Full O'Juice,** and then disappeared again from the scene for some time.

At the end of the Seventies, **Mary McGlory**, **Sylvia Saunders** and **Pamela Birch** got together again and, with the guitarist, **Tony Coates** from **Liverpool Express,** had one more appearance as the **Liverbirds**.

In 1999 and 2000 there were two other revival-shows in Hamburg and, for that, even **Valerie Gell** came from England and so completed the Sixties line-up of the **Liverbirds** again.

Unfortunately, these were one-off shows and the group did not continue on the scene.

Pamela Birch sadly died on the 28th of October 2009 in Hamburg and so she never got to see the complete recordings of the **Liverbirds** being re-released on a double-CD in 2010.

Single discography :

Shop Around / It's Got To Be You	**G- Star-Club 148508 / 1965**
Diddley Daddy / Leave All Your Old Loves In The Past	**G- Star-Club 148526 / 1965**
Peanut Butter / Why Do You Hang Around Me	**G- Star-Club 148528 / 1965**
Loop Di Loop / Bo Diddley Is A Lover	**G- Star-Club 148554 / 1966**

Different US release :

Why Do You Hang Around Me / Diddley Daddy	**US- Philips 40288 / 1965**

LP discography :

STAR-CLUB SHOW 4   **G- Star-Club 158003 / 1965**

- **Johnny B. Goode / Can't Judge A Book By Looking At The Cover / Love Hurts / Talking About You / Mona / Money / Too Much Monkey-Business / Roadrunner / Diddley Daddy / Hands Off / Before You Accuse Me / Leave All Your Old Loves In The Past / Got My Mojo-workin'**

MORE OF THE LIVERBIRDS   **G- Star-Club 158021 / 1965**

- **Peanut Butter / It's So Exciting / He Hardly Ever Calls Me 'Honey' Anymore / For Your Love / Oh No, Not My Baby / Around And Around / Down Home Girl / He's Something Else / Heatwave / Why Do You Hang Around Me / He's About A Mover / Long Tall Shorty**

Tracks on compilation albums :

Diddley Daddy	on 'Star-Club Parade'	**G- Philips 6558 / 1965**
It's So Exciting	on 'Beater's Hit parade'	**G- Philips 75-283 / 1967**
He Hardly Ever Calls Me 'Honey' Anymore	on 'Beater's Hit parade'	**G- Philips 75-283 / 1967**

Some people state that there was a connection between the **Liverbirds** and another all girl group called **Gilded Cage** that may possibly have included some of the former **Liverbirds**. This is definitely not true! **Gilded Cage** consisted of musicians from different countries, including the United States and Scandinavia, but none of the former **Liverbirds** members ever had any connection to that group.

THE LONG & THE SHORT

This group with the quite unusual name was formed in the area of St. Helens in the late Fifties as a Skiffle band under the name, **The L'Ringos**.

When the big Beat boom arrived, the group jumped on the train, they changed their music and their name - to the **Long & the Short**.

The band at that time consisted of the following musicians:

Bob McKinnley	(voc)
Les Saints	(g/voc)
Alan Grindley	(g/voc)
Bob Taylor	(bg/voc)
Gerry Watt	(dr)

The individual members had not participated in other groups previously, with the exception of **Les Saints** whose real name is **Les Stuart**. He was the former leader of the **Les Stuart Quartet** from Liverpool, he had also played with **Frank Knight & the Barons**, **Danny Havoc & the Ventures** and the **Kansas City Five**.

In 1964, the **Long & Short** were featured in the musical movie, 'Gonks Go Beat', and can be found on the corresponding soundtrack album with the song, "Take This Train", which probably was an original by the group.

They were signed to Decca and in the same year their first single, "The Letter", was released and climbed to No. 30 in the British charts. The mysterious thing about this was, that no one really took notice of this undoubtedly surprising success, not even the Liverpool 'Mersey Beat' or 'Combo' music papers. Maybe Liverpool was too spoilt by the success of many of the other local groups, but that should not have been reason enough to justify this ignorance, especially as it was unfair to the **Long**

& the Short. But much more mysterious is the fact that this group and their records were also ignored in discographies of Liverpool's Merseybeat scene printed later.

They had another top-50 hit with their second single "Choc Ice", which climbed up to No. 49, also in 1964.

After this release, the lead vocalist, **Bob McKinnley,** left the group to join the newly-formed **Epics,** which included some of the former members of the **Mojos**. This group was paid more attention by the press than the **Long & the Short**, although the **Epics** broke up without ever having performed in public! Unfortunately, what happened to **Bob McKinnley** afterwards is not known.

His departure from the **Long & Short** was probably the reason for the group disbanding, which is very hard to understand, as there were more potential vocalists in the group which, all in all, was very successful with their two hit singles. It should not have been too difficult for them to solve the vocalist problem, so there must have been another reason for the split, but no detailed information was obtainable.

However, it seems that even Decca did not care too much for this really good group and so the **Long & the Short** disappeared as if they had never existed and none of the members appeared again on the scene. What is left is just two really good singles worth seeking out!

Discography :

The Letter / Love Is A Funny Thing	**UK- Decca F.11959 / 1964**
Choc Ice / Here Comes The Fool	**UK- Decca F.12043 / 1964**

Tracks on compilation-albums :

Take This Train	**on 'Gonks Go Beat'**	**UK- Decca LK 4673 / 1964**

THE MARACCAS

It was in 1964 that three teenagers from Vauxhall, one from Norris Green and one from Anfield, decided to form a Beat group, the first band any of them had played in. They called themselves the **Maraccas** right from the start.

In this context, it should be mentioned that the spelling of the group's name is sometimes reported with a single 'c'. However, judging by their manager **Kim Pemberton's** business card and the logo on their drum kit, the spelling with a double 'c' has to be the right one.

The Maraccas - Original line-up 1964
L to R: Tommy Cunningham, Brian Donovan, Fred Seddon, Frank Baker & Dave Rhodes

Leaving that aside, they were considered a second generation Merseybeat group and the **Maraccas** started to play the pubs and social clubs around Liverpool before breaking into its circle of famous Beat clubs such as the 'Blue Angel', the 'Iron Door', the 'Cavern' and the 'Mardi Gras'.

Sometime in 1965, the original drummer, **Brian Donovan,** left and the **Maraccas**, who had developed a more bluesy sound, continued in a line-up with:

Dave Rhodes	(voc/harp)
Frank Baker	(lg/voc)
Tommy Cunningham	(rg/voc)
Fred Seddon	(bg/voc)
Ted Hesketh	(dr)

Ted Hesketh had formerly played in a school group called the **Impressions**.

The **Maraccas** very soon became quite popular and started to play clubs throughout the north of England such as the 'Bluesville' in Wigan, the 'Mandrake' in York, the 'Beachcomber' in Leigh and the 'Cubik' clubs in Birkenhead and Rochdale. In particular, they built up a great following in the latter one.

Clive Kelly, owner of the Cubik clubs, with the agreement of the musicians, came up with the term 'Bluestempomusik' to describe their unique blend of Poetry and Blues. In addition to lots of their own compositions, the group also played popular songs such as, **Arthur Alexander's** "You Better Move On", **Jimmy Reed's** "Shame, Shame, Shame" and **Chuck Berry's** "Around And Around". One of their favourites was **Bob Dylan's** "Blowin' In The Wind".

It was still in 1965 that **Clive Kelly** took the **Maraccas** into the Cavern Sound studios where they recorded an independent record with their original, "The Fiery Brand", under the wings of **Jimmy Powell**, leader of the established recording group, **Jimmy Powell & the Five Dimensions**. This group often appeared on the same bill with them in Rochdale.

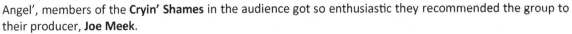

In early 1966, during a gig at the 'Blue Angel', members of the **Cryin' Shames** in the audience got so enthusiastic they recommended the group to their producer, **Joe Meek**.

The **Maraccas** did an audition for him at the David Lewis Theatre in Liverpool and were invited down to his studio in London where they recorded a song called "A Different Drummer", which was written by a friend of **Joe Meek**.

Unfortunately, this was only cut on an acetate and was not followed by an official release. The reason for that may have been the fact that **Joe Meek** committed suicide not long afterwards.

Although the **Maraccas** kept very busy playing on the scene, the original group split in 1967.

Frank Baker was later a member of the re-formed **Solomon's Mines**, while **Tommy Cunningham** disappeared from the scene.

Dave Rhodes and **Fred Seddon** joined **Paul Tennant** (g/voc) and **Paul Clarke** (dr) in the **Obsession**.

This was a short-lived group that disbanded very soon when **Dave Rhodes** and **Paul Tennant** teamed up with **Ted Hesketh** to form **Focal Point**.

In the same year, 1967, **Fred Seddon** and **Paul Clarke** re-formed the **Maraccas** with **John Dunne** (lg), formerly with the **Hungry I's** and the **Kegmen** and **Pete Duke** (bg) from the **Wishbones**, whereby **Fred Seddon** switched from bass to organ and took over the lead vocals.

The Maraccas (re-formed group)
L to R: Paul Clarke, Pete Duke, John Dunne & Fred Seddon

Musically, this new line-up now developed more in the direction of the **Animals** and **Procol Harum**.

Again, it was a good and interesting group who, unfortunately, disbanded again sometime in 1968 when **Fred Seddon** moved to Nantwich where he became the manager of 'Blutos' night club and also played with the resident trio there.

John Dunne and **Paul Clarke** disappeared from the band scene, while **Pete Duke** went down to London and, as a fulltime professional, played with various groups including **Dirty Work**, **Little Matthew & the Intentions** and **Mississippi John L. Watson & the Odyssey Blues Band**, among others.

The coloured singer, **John L. Watson,** was known, of course, from London's Sixties scene as the former leader of the recording groups, **John L. Watson & the Humelflugs** and the **Web**.

Pete Duke also had short stints with **John Mayall**, **Phil May** of the **Pretty Things** and **Screaming Lord Sutch**. More recently, he played with **Reuben Richards**.

Back to **Fred Seddon**, who among others, also booked his old mates, **Jimmy Powell & the Dimensions** to appear at 'Blutos'. He jammed with them and finally joined and remained as a member of the **Dimensions** right through the early Seventies.

After that, he took up his studies again at Keele University and was employed at the Padua University in Italy as a professor of music education for many years.

He returned to England in 2009 and, since then, has worked as an enterprise researcher at the Northampton Business School, which is part of the Northampton University.

Discography :

The Fiery Brand / ???	UK- Cavern Sound acetate (?) / 1964
A Different Drummer / ???	K- RGM acetate / 1965

(The **Maraccas** are also said to have made test recordings for PYE in London in 1965, but nothing was released and there are no further details or songs known from these sessions.)

THE MARKFOUR

Now every insider will know that the **Mark Four** later became the hit group, the **Creation**, but this was a totally different band. Giving consideration to the fact that the **Creation** guitarist, **Bob Garner,** was a former member of **Lee Curtis & the All Stars** and the **Merseybeats**, and that the **Creation** drummer, **Dave Preston,** also hailed from Liverpool where he had played with groups that included **Vince & the Volcanoes**, the **Harlems** and the **Secrets**, it is only natural to assume that the **Creation** came from Liverpool. Unfortunately, that is an error that has confused many people in the past. The **Creation,** and also the **Mark Four** (written in two words), hailed from Cheshunt in the south-east of England and there was absolutely no connection between them and the **Markfour** (written in one word), that hailed from the Prescot area of Liverpool.

To prevent more confusion, it should be pointed out that there was also no connection to the **Mark Five**, as that was another totally different group which hailed from Scotland but had a long residency in Liverpool. Now that all the confusion has been removed, we can concentrate on the story of another very interesting Merseybeat group, **The Markfour.** Formed as the **Sapphires** in the early Sixties, they were initially based at the 'B.I.C.C. Social Club'. When they joined the Musicians' Union, they were instructed to change the name, because another **Sapphires** already existed.

So they decided on the name, the **Markfour**, and, from the beginning, the group consisted of the following musicians:

Bill Rawlinson	**(voc/g)**
Derek Shaw	**(g/voc)**
Bev Brown	**(bg/voc)**
Gordon Harrison	**(dr)**

The group was managed by a certain **Ray Charles** (of course, not the Soul singer) and became quite popular on Merseyside, where they often played at the 'Cavern' and other major clubs and venues.

In early 1964, the **Markfour** were recorded by CBC (Canadian Broadcast Corporation) for the TV show 'Live At The Cavern', together with the **Merseybeats** and a German group, the **Rattles**.

A little later, the group was signed to Decca and recorded the **Everly Brothers** song, "Walk Right Back", and the group's original, "Karen", for a single release.

But shortly after the recording sessions, **Derek Shaw** decided to leave the group and go to college, so the **Markfour** broke up before the single was released.

Of **Gordon Harrison** it is known that he later joined a group named the **Colts**, who probably had no connection to **Johnny Ringo's** group of the same name.

Bill Rawlinson and **Bev Brown** stayed together as a duo under the name of **Mark & John**.

Despite the split, Decca released the single in December 1964, but decided to name the artists **Mark & John**, although it was recorded by the complete **Markfour**. This was probably to prepare for follow-ups if this record became a hit. But it did not, although it was a well-produced commercial record and showed the **Markfour** to be a really good group, especially on the B-side, "Karen", which was clearly the better song.

Mark & John continued as a duo, but they did not get any further recording chances from Decca. So they gigged around the local clubs, nothing being known of a backing group.

Bill Rawlinson (Mark) and **Bev Brown** (John) later simply disappeared from the scene.

Suddenly, in 1972, the name **Mark & John** appeared again when the record, "This One's For You", was released on the 'UK'-label in Germany, where it was distributed by the Decca group (DL 25 551).

This **Ken Howard/Alan Blaikley** song wasn't Merseybeat, but a catchy pop tune with orchestral backing.

This was really the last time that the name **Mark & John** appeared again and it is not known for certain if it really was **Bill Rawlinson** and **Bev Brown** behind the pseudonyms this time.

Discography :

as **Mark & John** :

Walk Right Back / Karen   UK- Decca F.12044 / 1964

(* please note that this single was recorded by the complete line-up of the **Markfour**, but, because of their split prior to the release, it was issued under the name of **Mark & John**, who had continued on the scene as a duo after the group had split up)

BERYL MARSDEN

Born **Beryl Hogg**, she started her singing career at a very young age and doubtless was the best female singer in the male dominated Merseybeat scene.

She had her first live appearance in 1961 at 'Picton Road Town Hall' when she sang "Boys" and was backed by **Karl Terry & the Cruisers**.

Under the stage name of **Beryl Marsden**, she began to sing regularly with the **Undertakers**, but also had appearances with the **Renegades** (from Liverpool), the **Kansas City Five** and probably also some other groups, but without becoming a steady member of any of those bands.

When **Joe Flannery** took over her management, she appeared mostly with Joe's brother, **Lee Curtis,** and his band, the **All Stars**.

Joe Flannery acquired a recording contract for her with Decca and soon after this, **Beryl Marsden** was featured on the legendary live compilation, 'At The Cavern', with the song, "Everybody Loves A Lover", and she did a really great job on it. This impressive debut was followed by the great single, "I Know", also in 1963. Unfortunately, this record was not paid the attention it deserved and so it failed to become a chart success although, these days, it is something of an evergreen song of the unique Liverpool Beat decade.

The **Supremes** number, "When The Lovelight Starts Shining Through His Eyes", was her next single in 1964. This was also well done but, again, failed to make the charts and did not help this great singer gain the breakthrough she deserved. **Beryl Marsden** was a real Beat singer and terribly underrated at the time, although she was already a star on the Liverpool scene.

In 1965, she was booked for her first appearance at the 'Star-Club' in Hamburg and, because she was only 17 years of age at the time, her manager, **Joe Flannery,** became her 'legal guardian' for that booking. Otherwise, she would not have been able to obtain the required 'artist' license. She did not stay too long in Hamburg, but appeared regularly at that famous club where she went down a bomb, mainly backed by the **All Stars**. As a result, **Beryl Marsden** became a big name in the so-called 'Star-Club' era.

In Liverpool, she appeared with the **Griff Parry Five,** as well as later with the **Krew**, and also occasionally as a guest singer with **Johnny Kidd & the Pirates** on the national circuit.

Probably around that time, she recorded **Little Eva**'s "He Is The Boy" and the songs, "I've Got To Find A Way" and "You're A User" as demos, as well as a version of "This Empty Place". These were to be her final recordings for Decca that, unfortunately, were never released.

She signed with Columbia and her first single for that new label was the great "Who You Gonna Hurt", which was coupled with another potential A-side, "Gonna Make Him My Baby".

The following single, "Music Talk", was coupled with a great version of the **Jackie DeShannon** composition "Break-a-Way", which had been a hit for coloured singer, **Irma Thomas,** and became an international success again for **Tracy Ullman** in 1983.

"Break-a-Way" should have also become a hit for **Beryl Marsden**, as her version was, at least, as good as the others, if it had not been chosen for the B-side.

However, in 1966, she recorded her final single for Columbia with "What's She Got (what I ain't got)" which, unfortunately, also failed to make any progress in the charts.

At the end of the Sixties, **Beryl Marsden** went down to London and, after a short spell with **She Trinity,** she joined **Shotgun Express**, a group that also included **Rod Stewart**, **Peter Bardens** and **Mick Fleetwood**.

Beryl Marsden - Shotgun Express

This was probably the time of **Beryl Marsden's** biggest international success when their single, "I Feel The Whole World Turn Around" entered the lower regions of the British charts.

When **Shotgun Express** broke up, she returned to Liverpool where she became a member of the group, **Sinbad**, a really great Soul band which, besides **Paddy Chambers** (g), also included **Pete Newton** (bg), **Bob Hardy** (sax), **Geoff Workman** (p/org) and **Dave Irving** (dr) – all former members of the **Terry Hines Sextet** which evolved into **Eddie Cave & the Fyx**.

She did some recordings with this band, of which the Soul influenced ballad, "Here We Go Again", sung by **Beryl Marsden** and **Paddy Chambers**, was a potential hit song but, unfortunately, it was never released on record, just like all the other recorded **Sinbad** material.

Sinbad was sometimes billed as the **Beryl Marsden Group**, but that association was only short lived.

Beryl Marsden later recorded solo again - as **Beryl Marsden**, but also under the name **Lynn Jackson**. In 1980, she returned to Hamburg for the re-opening of the 'Star-Club' and was featured on a corresponding live sampler with **Arthur Alexander**'s "Shot Of Rhythm & Blues" and, in 1990, she toured Germany again with her own band and, since then, appears regularly over there.

Today she is still a great 'looker' and a great singer with a fantastic stage presentation. If you ever get the chance to see her live, don't miss it!

I Know / I Only Care About You	UK- Decca F. 11707 / 1963
When The Lovelight Starts Shining Through His Eyes / Love Is Going To Happen To Me	
	UK- Decca F. 11819 / 1964
Who You Gonna Hurt / Gonna Make Him My Baby	UK- Columbia DB 7718 / 1965
Music Talk / Break-a-way	UK- Columbia DB 7797 / 1965
What's She Got (that I ain't got) / Let's Go Somewhere	UK- Columbia DB 7888 / 1966

Tracks on compilation albums :

Everybody Loves A Lover	on **At The Cavern**	UK- Decca LK 4597 / 1963

Unissued tracks :

The known unissued tracks are "**This Empty Place**", "**You're A User**", "**He Is The Boy**" and "**I've Got To Find A Way**", which were probably all recorded in the years 1965 and 1966. Of the first one, it is known that it was recorded for Decca, as it should have been the third single for **Beryl Marsden**. All the others were released as acetates.

Besides this, **Beryl Marsden** also recorded with the group, **Sinbad,** in 1968, but nothing was released on record. Of the various recordings, only the great ballad, "**Here We Go Again**", is known, which was a potential hit-record.

She Trinity (with **Beryl Marsden** ?) :

He Fought The Law / Union Station Blues	UK- Columbia DB 7874 / 1966
Have I Sinned / Wild Flower	UK- Columbia DB 7943 / 1966
Wild Flower / The Man Who Took The Valise Off The Floor	UK- Columbia DB 7959 / 1966
Yellow Submarine / Promise You'll Never Cry	UK- Columbia DB 7992 / 1966

Shotgun Express (with **Beryl Marsden**) :

I Could Feel The Whole World Turn Round / Curtains	UK- Columbia DB 8025 / 1966
Funny 'Cos Neither Could I / Indian Thing	UK- Columbia DB 8178 / 1967

EP "**I COULD FEEL THE WHOLE WORLD TURN ROUND**"	FR- Columbia ESRF 1864 / 1966

- **I Could Feel The Whole World Turn Round / Funny Cos Neither Could I / Curtains / Indian Thing**

JACKI MARTIN

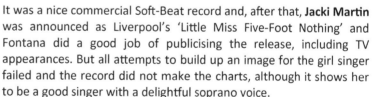

THE BLACK KNIGHTS

NORMAN HURST
LAR 5574

DOMINATORS
DOWNBEATS
STEREOS

ALSO AVAILABLE
SEPTEMBER ONWARDS **THE ROADRUNNERS**

Of course, this should be the story of **Jacki Martin & the Dominators** but, because of a lack of information about the **Dominators**, it concentrates on the girl singer, **Jacki Martin**.

She was born **Patricia Macken** in July 1947 in the Liverpool area of Clubmoor and started her singing career in 1963 with a group called **The Stormers**, who consisted of **David Rimmer**, **Michael Gavin**, **Michael Carroll** and **Roman Bomba**.

Michael Carroll most probably was the younger brother of singer, **Irene Carroll**, who, in the mid-Sixties, teamed up with her three brothers in the **Carrolls**, but that is another story that can be found in this book.

Jacki Martin also appeared with some other local groups until she teamed up with the **Dominators** but, unfortunately, none of the names of those groups, or their members, are known.

There may have been a connection with the **Four Dominators**, who came from Kirkby and later became the **Verbs**, but this is just a possibility.

In 1964, **Jacki Martin & the Dominators,** under the management of **Dr. Bernard Hart,** became quite a popular club act and, in July of that year, played the 'Cavern' for the first time, albeit in a lunchtime session.

They went down to London where they did lots of shows, and it was probably at one of these gigs when someone from Fontana became aware of the seventeen year old girl singer and signed her (but as it seems) without the group.

In July 1964, her first and only single was released with "Will You" on the A-side, backed by "Till He Tells Me".

'WILL YOU'

FONTANA
TF487

MEET
LIVERPOOL'S
LITTLE MISS
5 FOOT NOTHING

JACKI MARTIN

ON HER
FIRST RECORD
ON SALE
TO-MORROW

It was a nice commercial Soft-Beat record and, after that, **Jacki Martin** was announced as Liverpool's 'Little Miss Five-Foot Nothing' and Fontana did a good job of publicising the release, including TV appearances. But all attempts to build up an image for the girl singer failed and the record did not make the charts, although it shows her to be a good singer with a delightful soprano voice.

After the record, very little was heard of **Jacki Martin**, but it is known that she continued with the **Dominators** as her backing group on the club-circuit of the northwest.

Discography :

Will You / Till He Tells Me   **UK- Fontana TF 487 / 1964**

THE MASTERMINDS

The group had its origins in the formation of a school band at the 'Dingle Vale Secondary Modern School' in Liverpool by **Dougie Meakin** and **George Cassidy**, and some other schoolmates, under the name, **The Dingle Dices**, in 1961.

In 1962, **George Cassidy** left the school and also left the group to become a merchant seaman. He was replaced by **Tommy Meakin**, a cousin of **Dougie Meakin**.

A little later, the **Dingle Dices** changed their name to **Clay & the Classics**. In 1963, **George Cassidy** returned to the group, but they very soon disbanded because the singer, 'Clay', whose real name was **Frank Campbell**, left the group, as did as the rhythm guitarist, **Harry**.

Their drummer, **Bob Scott,** joined the **Clayton Squares**, while **Dougie Meakin** and **George Cassidy** formed the **Mindbenders**. The name of the new group was very soon changed to prevent any confusion with Manchester hit group, **Wayne Fontana & the Mindbenders**. So, the Liverpool **Mindbenders** became the **Masterminds** - with the following line-up:

Dougie Meakin	(voc/g)
Brian Slater	(g)
George Cassidy	(bg/voc)
Jay Rathbone	(dr)

They were featured in the German TV documentary, 'In den Kellern von Liverpool', playing at the 'Blue Angel', and this showed them to be a really good Beat group, .

Brian Slater left in October 1964 and was replaced by **Joey Molland**, who had formerly played with the **Assasins** and the **Profiles**.

In this line-up, the **Masterminds** established themselves on the Mersey scene within a very short time and, in August 1965, they had their first recording session in the Unicord studios, where they recorded the song, "She's About A Mover", which unfortunately, was not released on record.

It was **Bob Wooler** who then drew the attention of producer, **Andrew 'Loog' Oldham,** to the group and, later in 1965, he produced the single, "She Belongs To Me", with the **Masterminds** for the new 'Immediate' label. The B-side, "Taken My Love", was written by **Andrew Oldham** himself.

So the **Masterminds** were the first Liverpool group to record a **Bob Dylan** song and, accordingly, sounded more American than most of the other Merseybeat groups. The record was performed and produced well and had that slightly 'West Coast' touch, which was very popular at that time.

Shortly after the release of that single, which unfortunately failed to make the charts, the **Masterminds** were joined by **Chis Finley** on organ as an additional member, he had previously played with the **Runaways** and the **Kruzads**.

The group existed in this line-up until 1966 but did not have any more records released.

The split came when **Dougie Meakin** joined the **Denny Seyton Group**, that had just separated from their vocalist, **Denny Seyton**, who left show business at that time. The **Denny Seyton Group** then gigged around in Liverpool for a short time under the name of the **Lovin' Kind** but then they went to Italy as the **Motowns**, where they became very popular and released a string of great records, **Dougie Meakin** still lives in Italy.

John 'Jay' Rathbone (born Jaskett) joined the **Almost Blues** and was later a member of the newly-formed **Faron's Flamingos**. In the late Eighties and early Nineties, he was the drummer with **Karl Terry & the**

Cruisers and, after that, joined the new **Dimensions** before he disappeared from the scene.

The three remaining **Masterminds** members, **George Cassidy**, **Joey Molland** and **Chris Finley,** joined up with the two drummers, **Kenny Goodlass** from the **Escorts** and **Kenny Mundye**, who formerly had played with the **Santones** and the **Anzacs**.

This new line-up, under the name of the **Fruit Eating Bears,** became the backing-group for the **Merseys**. But that is a different story that can be found under the **Merseybeats** in this book.

After that, **Joey Molland** had a short spell with the **Cryin' Shames** in 1967 before he, together with **Paul Crane** of that group, joined **Gary Walker & Rain**.

In 1969, he became a member of the very successful hit group, **Badfinger,** that had evolved from the **Iveys** and which also included Liverpudlian, **Tom Evans** (bg), a former member of the **Inbeats** and the **Calderstones**, as well as **Pete Ham** (voc/g) and **Mike Gibbins** (dr), both from Wales.

Chris Finley later appeared in a number of different Merseyside groups, including **Confucius** (the former **Hideaways**) and the newly-formed **Merseybeats**, as well as **Herman's Hermits** from Manchester.

George Cassidy teamed up with former **Easybeats** members in the **Beechwoods** that later recorded as **Taste Of Honey**. After that, he most probably quit show business.

Discography :

She Belongs To Me / Taken My Love   UK- Immediate IM 005 / 1965

Unissued tracks :

In August 1965, the **Masterminds** recorded the song, "**She's About A Mover**", in a private session at the Unicord studios. Unfortunately, it was never released on record.

THE MASTERSOUNDS

This group was formed in Liverpool in early 1963 and, initially, not too much attention was paid to the **Mastersounds**, as they were named right from the start.

The original line-up of that really good band consisted of the following musicians:

Tony Kane	**(g/voc)**
Mal Jefferson	**(bg/voc)**
Frank Hopley	**(bg/voc)**
Mike Price	**(dr)**

Tony Kane's real name is **Anthony Cockayne**, while **Mike Price** was **Mike Neilson**'s pseudonym.

Mal Jefferson's real name is **Malcolm Andrew** and he was a former member of **Buddy Dean & the Teachers** and is, by the way, the brother of **Don Andrew** of the **Remo Four**.

In 1964, **Frank Hopley** left to join the **Pathfinders** and was replaced by **Gerry Stewart**, who had previously played with the **Black Cats**, one of Liverpool's very early Rock 'n' Roll groups, as well as with the **In Crowd**.

In addition, **Tony Ashton** (voc/org) was also added to the line-up. He had formerly played with the **College Boys** from Eton, the **Executives** from Liverpool (Preston?), the **Tony Ashton Trio**, the backing group for **Jimmy Justice** and the **John Barry Seven**. He eventually left the **Mastersounds** to join the **Remo Four**. After that, he was a member of the internationally successful trio, **Ashton, Gardner & Dyke**.

His replacement in the **Mastersounds,** in April 1964, was **Peter Cook** (org), a former member of Birmingham's **Gerry Levene & the Avengers,** but he didn't stay too long and probably returned to Birmingham.

The **Mastersounds** were joined by **Adrian Lord**, whose real name is **Adrian Wilkinson**. This singer and guitarist was a former member of the **Missouri Drifters**, the **Nomads**, as well as of their successors, the **Mojos**.

In this line-up, the **Mastersounds** were signed to RCA and, amongst others, recorded the songs, "Don't Leave Me" and "What Went Wrong", in 1964, on which the background vocals are said to have been sung by **Marvin Gaye** and **Dusty Springfield**. But none of these songs, all probably **Adrian Lord** originals, were ever released on record, although the songwriter maintained that there were singles released in the USA under the name **Adrian Lord & the Mastersounds**. This is not proven but, of course, this doesn't mean it is absolutely impossible.

Also in 1964, the group, which was managed by **Gordon Brown**, changed it's name to the **Bluesville Bats** but disbanded soon after that.

Adrian Lord and **Gerry Stewart**, together with other musicians, formed the **Faces**. This group was not very successful and soon disappeared from the scene.

Adrian Lord then went to Germany and, while there, joined the **Mersey Five**. He then returned home and became a member of Liverpool's **Easybeats**, before he joined **Them Grimbles**.

Gerry Stewart later emigrated to Canada, where he is still living today.

Adrian Lord (left) & the Mastersounds

Mal Jefferson became a member of the **Kruzads** and played with the **Chesterfields** in the Seventies. Today he owns the 'Mastersound Studios' in Southport.

Tony Kane later emigrated to the USA, where he quit the music business.

Mick Price (aka **Mike Neilson**) went to Germany, where he continued to play but, unfortunately, it is not known in which groups. After a time, he returned to England and often appeared with various scratch-bands at the charity-events of the 'Liverpool Rock & Roll Society'.

Discography :

It is not certain if the assertion of **Adrian Lord,** that some singles by the group were released in the USA under the name **Adrian Lord & the Mastersounds** is true, because there is really no information about these records.

But the **Mastersounds** recorded some songs for RCA in 1964 - including the **Adrian Lord** originals, "Don't Leave Me" and "What Went Wrong", which must have been released on acetate, at least.

THE MERSEYBEATS

Although this band never had a number one hit like the **Beatles**, the **Searchers** or **Gerry & the Pacemakers**, it was one of the most important and popular groups of the Liverpool scene and, therefore, their name became a legend in the music business.

The Mavericks - 1961
L to R: Dave Elias, Frank Slone, Tony Crane & Billy Kinsley

The story of the group goes back into the late Fifties when **Tony Crane** and **Billy Kinsley** formed a band under the name of the **Pacifics**, who later changed their name to the **Mavericks**. Then, following a suggestion by the famous 'Cavern' DJ, **Bob Wooler**, called themselves the **Merseybeats**.

In the very early days, **Billy Butler** also appeared with the group as a guest vocalist but he never was a steady member and later he amalgamated with the **Tuxedos**.

In 1962, drummer, **Frank Sloane**, left the **Merseybeats** to join the **Four Musketeers** and, a little later, was followed to that group by the original bass guitarist, **Dave Elias**. Both musicians after that were members of the newly-formed **Nocturns**, another story in this book.

Billy Kinsley switched to bass guitar and the most popular line-up of the **Merseybeats** had come together with:

Tony Crane	**(voc/g)**
Billy Kinsley	**(voc/bg)**
Aaron Williams	**(g/voc)**
John Banks	**(dr)**

Aaron Williams was apparently a newcomer to the scene but, for sure, he was already a member when that group was still playing as the **Mavericks**.

John Banks was a former member of the **Four Musketeers**, that simply had swapped drummers with the **Merseybeats**. A little later, the **Merseybeats** were featured on the Oriole compilation, 'This Is Merseybeat' Vol. 1, with an interesting version of the **Ruby & the Romantics** success, "Our Day Will Come", which was their first recording ever.

The group was immediately signed to Fontana and their first single, "It's Love That Really Counts", a great tune, brought the first chart success for the **Merseybeats** in 1963 when it climbed to No. 23.

The follow-up became their biggest success when, "I Think Of You" went to No. 5 in the British charts in 1964.

"Don't Turn Around" and "Wishin' And Hopin' " both stopped at no. 13 in 1964, while records such as, "Last Night" (Top 30), "Don't Let It Happen To Us", "I Love You, Yes I Do" (Top 20) and "I Stand Accused" (all in 1965) were not that successful and some only reached the lower regions of the charts, which still means that they sold very well. All of their singles were nice and catchy Beat ballads and are still very interesting within the colourful picture that was Merseybeat.

In the early spring of 1964, **Billy Kinsley** left the group to form his own band under the name, the **Kinsleys**.

His replacement in the **Merseybeats** was **Bob Garner**, who previously had played with the **Brokers** from Warrington. He didn't stay too long and then became a member of the **Ice Blues** before he went to Hamburg where he played with **Tony Sheridan & the Beat Brothers** prior to joining **Lee Curtis & the All Stars**. Following this, he was a member of the hit group, **Creation**.

The Merseybeats with Johnny Gustafson (right)

His place in the **Merseybeats** was taken by **Johnny Gustafson**, who was very popular on the scene as a former member of groups that included **Cass & the Casanovas**, the **Big Three** and the **Seniors**.

This means that **Johnny Gustafson** was featured on most of the above mentioned singles from 1964, as well as on the album, 'The Merseybeats', and the great rocking EP, 'The Merseybeats On Stage'.

At the end of 1964, **Billy Kinsley** returned to the **Merseybeats**. He remained with them until they disbanded in 1965.

After the **Merseybeats** had split up, **John Banks,** together with **Johnny Gustafson** (who in the meantime had led the **Johnny Gus Set**), formed a duo under the name **Johnny & John**, which were backed by the **Thoughts** from Liverpool. They released a quite unsuccessful single with "Bumper To Bumper". After that, they both went down to London where they joined the **Quotations**, with whom they recorded the great single, "Cool It", in 1968.

John Banks became a member of **Rupert's People** but then emigrated to Israel. He returned to Liverpool in the Eighties and sadly died much too young in 1988.

Johnny Gustafson later played in groups such as **Episode Six**, **Quartermass**, **Hard Stuff**, **Roxy Music**, the re-formed **Big Three** and finally with the internationally successful **Pirates**, who were the successors of **Johnny Kidd's** original backing group.

Aaron Williams left show business, while **Tony Crane** and **Billy Kinsley** continued as a duo under the name of **The Merseys** and had a No. 4 hit with their first single, "Sorrow", in early 1966.

On the initial recording, the **Merseys** were backed by a group that included **Jimmy Page** (g), **John Paul Jones** (g), **Jack Bruce** (bg) and **Clem Cattini** (dr). Unfortunately, this original version was never released, while on the released record, they were backed by the **Fruit Eating Bears** who also appeared with them 'live'.

The **Fruit Eating Bears**, in spite of this connection, were an independent group that consisted of:

Joey Molland	(g)	- ex **Profiles** and **Masterminds**
George Cassidy	(g)	- ex **Masterminds**
Chris Finley	(bg)	- ex **Kruzads** and **Masterminds**
Kenny Mundye	(dr)	- ex **Santones** and **Anzaks**
Kenny Goodlass	(dr)	- ex **Kirkbys**, **Escorts** and **Swinging Blue Jeans**

The Merseys & the Fruit Eating Bears

Kenny Goodlass was replaced by **Terry McCusker** in 1967 and, around the same time, **Dave 'Mushy' Cooper** took the place of **George Cassidy**, who joined the **Beechwoods**, who later recorded as **Taste Of Honey**. After that, **George Cassidy** disappeared from the scene.

Kenny Goodlass joined **23rd Turn-Off**, which was a continuation of his original group, the **Kirkbys**.

In the Seventies, he appeared again as a member of the newly-formed **Merseybeats** and, in the Nineties, was the drummer with the legendary **Karl Terry & the Cruisers**, before he joined the re-formed **Kirkbys**.

Terry McCusker was a former member of **Pete Demos & the Demons**, the **Four Dymonds**, **Rip Van Winkle & the Rip-It-Ups**, the **Valkyries** and the **Roadrunners**, while **Dave Cooper** had formerly played with the **Topspots**, the **Vegas Five**, **Faron's Flamingos** and the **Pawns**.

Joey Molland joined the **Cryin' Shames** and, from there, went on to play with **Gary Walker & Rain** before he later became a member of the hit group, **Badfinger**.

Chris Finley joined **Confucius**, which had evolved from the **Hideaways** and, in 1974, he played with **Herman's Hermits**, while **Terry McCusker** joined the **Cordes**, another story that can be followed in this book.

The singles released by the **Merseys** after that powerful debut, such as the fantastic "So Sad About Us" and "Rhythm Of Love" (both in 1966), as well as their version of "The Cat", coupled with the great "Change Of Heart" and the weak "Penny In My Pocket" (both from 1967) did not bring any additional chart honours for them. On their final single, "Lovely Loretta", which became a big hit in Holland in 1968, the **Merseys** were backed by the **Funky Bottom Congregation**, whoever that was.

After that, the duo released one more single as the **Crackers**, but "Honey Do" didn't make it either.

Billy Kinsley then joined the **Jackie Lomax Band** and, after that, he had a short spell with the **Swinging Blue Jeans** and **Gerry & the Pacemakers**.

Later, he and **Jimmy Campbell** (formerly with the **Kirkbys**) formed the group, **Rockin' Horse**, who released a real great Merseybeat tune with "The Biggest Gossip In Town", but this story can be followed under **The Kirkbys**.

After that, **Billy Kinsley** formed the international hit group, **Liverpool Express**.

The other members of **Liverpool Express, Roger Craig** (key), **Tony Coates** (bg) and **Derek Cashin** (dr), had formerly played with **Tony Crane** in the re-formed **Merseybeats**. And, under the name of **Crane,** had also recorded the singles, "American Dream/Julie" (UK-Buk BU 3003) and "I Just Ain't Good Enough For You" (Uk -Buk BU 3015), at the end of 1974.

Tony Crane, who had previously formed the <u>New</u> **Merseybeats** in 1970, re-formed the group using the same name but with different musicians. A little later, the 'New' was dropped from the name.

Since then, **Bobby Packham** (bg) has been a member of the 'new' **Merseybeats**, having played with the **Galvanisers** in the Sixties.

Kenny Goodlass and **Chris Finley** were included again in the 'new' **Merseybeats** until 1980, as well as **Kenny Barry** (key), **Steve Fleming** (org) and other musicians in a steadily changing line-up.

Steve 'Tiger' Fleming, a brother of **Mark Peters**, had previously played with bands that included **Mark Peters & the Cyclones**, **Mark Peters & the Silhouettes** and **Mark Peters & the Method** in the Sixties. After his time with the 'new' **Merseybeats** in the Eighties, he became a member of **Clouds**, a cabaret band which, besides him, consisted of former **Fourmost** members. After that, he was with the **Vince Earl Attraction**.

The **Merseybeats** released an album with the title 'Greatest Hits' in 1977, mainly including second takes of their big Sixties hits, as well as the new recordings, "I'll Be Home" and a great version of "American Dream", which seems to be one of **Tony Crane's** favourites. In addition, a single with the title, "This Is Merseybeat", was released, which was a medley of big Merseybeat hits with new arrangements.

In August 1978, **Tony Crane** recorded a live album as a tribute to **Elvis Presley** entitled 'Tony Crane sings Elvis Presley'. On this record he was backed by **Kenny Parry, Bobby Packham, Sammy Rothwell, Kenny Berry** and **Phil Chittick**, who were the complete **Merseybeats** line-up at that time, as well as by **Billy Kinsley** and **Tony Coates** of **Liverpool Express**.

In the sixties, **Phil Chittick** had played with **Johnny Ringo & the Colts** (among others) and, after his time with the **Merseybeats,** he became a member of **Cy Tucker & the Friars**.

The **Tony Crane** album on 'Downing Records' was most probably a private production by **Tony Crane**.

When **John Banks** died in 1988, the **Merseybeats**, in their successful Sixties' line-up with **Tony Crane, Billy Kinsley** and **Aaron Williams**, came together for a memorial concert. The place on drums was taken by none other than the former **Beatles** drummer, **Pete Best**. This concert led to the founding of the 'MerseyCats' organisation.

The **Merseybeats** continued successfully on the British club scene and, in 1992, **Billy Kinsley** also returned to the group, which then consisted of **Tony Crane** (voc/g), **Billy Kinsley** (voc/g), **Bobby Packham** (bg/voc), **Dave Goldberg** (key) and **Alan Cosgrove** (dr).

In 1993, they recorded a modern version of the **Beatles** song, "I'll Get You", as a single on vinyl and CD, but it flopped. **Alan Cosgrove** was later replaced by **Lou Rosenthal**.

The **Merseybeats** in that line-up are still a very successful and busy live act in England these days and **Tony Crane** proudly confirms that they now have as many bookings as they did during their heyday in the Sixties, which is easy to believe, as they are still a fantastic group.

Single discography :

The Merseybeats :

It's Love That Really Counts / Fortune Teller	UK- Fontana TF 412 / 1963
I Think Of You / Mr. Moonlight	UK- Fontana TF 431 / 1964
Don't Turn Around / Really Mystified	UK- Fontana TF 459 / 1964
Wishin' And Hopin' / Milkman	UK- Fontana TF 482 / 1964
Last Night / See Me Back	UK- Fontana TF 504 / 1965
Don't Let It Happen To Us / It'll Take A Long Time	UK- Fontana TF 568 / 1965
I Love You, Yes I Do / Good Good Lovin'	UK- Fontana TF 607 / 1965
I Stand Accused / All My Life	UK- Fontana TF 645 / 1965

Different German release :

Nur Unsere Liebe zählt / Nur Du Allein	G- Fontana 269310 / 1964

(the German versions of "**It's Love That Really Counts**" and "**I Think Of You**")

The Merseys :

Sorrow / Some Other Day	UK- Fontana TF 694 / 1966
So Sad About Us / Love Will Continue	UK- Fontana TF 732 / 1966
Rhythm Of Love / Is It Love	UK- Fontana TF 776 / 1966
The Cat / Change Of Heart	UK- Fontana TF 845 / 1967
Penny In My Pocket / I Hope You're Happy	UK- Fontana TF 916 / 1967
Lovely Loretta / Dreaming	UK- Fontana TF 955 / 1968

The Crackers :

Honey Do / It Happens All The Time	UK- Fontana TF 995 / 1969

Johnny & John :

Bumper To Bumper / Scrape My Boot	UK-Polydor BM 56087/ 1966

(on this record **Johnny Gustafson** & **John Banks** were backed by the **Thoughts** from Liverpool)

EP discography

The Merseybeats :

MERSEYBEATS ON STAGE	UK-Fontana TE 17422/ 1964

- Long Tall Sally / You Can't Judge A Book By It's Cover / I'm Gonna Sit Right Down And Cry / Shame

I THINK OF YOU   UK-Fontana TE 17423/ 1964

- I Think Of You / Mr. Moonlight / Fortune Teller / It's Love That Really Counts

WISHING AND HOPING   UK-Fontana TE 17432/ 1964

- Wishin' And Hopin' / Milkman / Jumping Jonah / Hello Young Lovers

Different French release of **The Merseys** :

RHYTHM OF LOVE   F- Fontana 465356 / 1966

- Rhythm Of Love / Is It Love / So Sad About Us / Sorrow

LP discography

THE MERSEYBEATS   UK-Fontana TL 5210/ 1964

- Milkman / Hello Young Lovers / He Will Break Your Heart / Funny Face / Really Mystified /

The Girl That I Marry / Fools Like Me / My Heart And I / Bring It On Home To Me /

Lavender Blue / Jumping Jonah / Don't Turn Around

Different German release :

THE MERSEYBEATS   G-Fontana 832 259-1/ 1964

- Wishin' And Hopin' / Milkman / Hello Young Lovers / Fortune Teller / He Will Break Your Heart /

Funny Face / Really Mystified / Nur Unsere Liebe Zählt / Mr. Moonlight / Fools Like Me /

My Heart And I / Bring It On Home To Me / Jumping Jonah / Don't Turn Around / Nur Du Allein

Tracks on compilation albums :

Our Day Will Come	on 'This Is Merseybeat' Vol.1	UK- Oriole PS 40047 / 1963
I Think Of You	on 'Liverpool Beat'	G- Fontana 681 557 TL / 1964
It's Love That Really Counts	on 'Liverpool Beat'	G- Fontana 681 557 TL / 1964

Unreleased tracks :

Unissued tracks by the **Merseybeats** are "Things I Want To Hear" (1962), "Soldier Of Love" and "Cry Me A River", probably from 1964, as well as the original version of "Sorrow" and "Nothing Can Change This Love" by the **Merseys**, and "Charly Noone" from 1966. The latter was recorded together with **Kiki Dee**.

THE MERSEY FIVE

There is an interesting story regarding the development of this group, formed in Liverpool by **Pete Campbell** and **Robert James Peter Montgomery** in 1964.

Pete Campbell was a former member of **Karl Terry & the Cruisers**, the **Beathovens**, the **Mersey Four** and Liverpool's **Fontanas**, while **Robert Montgomery** had played with **Derry Wilkie & the Others**.

They both teamed up with **Tony Nelson** (voc/g) and **Carl Riche** (dr) as the backing group for Oldham singer, **Tony Prince,** under the name of the **Tony Prince Combo**, which had a successful residency down in Bristol.

Tony Nelson, whose real name is **Anthony Gilbertson**, was a former member of **Gerry Savage & the Wildcats** that evolved into **Sonny Webb & the Cascades**. He had also played with the **Beathovens** and the **Mersey Four.**

Carl Riche, real name **Charles Richard Evans**, was a former member of the **Mustangs**, **Gerry Bach & the Beathovens** (that became the **Beathovens**) and the **Mersey Four.**

Beside these Liverpool musicians, the **Tony Prince Combo** was joined by the sax-player, **Gary Clampett,** from London.

When the **Tony Prince Combo** split up, obviously without having released a record, **Tony Prince** became a very popular radio DJ in London.

The group then continued as the **Mersey Five** and accepted a long engagement in Munich, Germany.

Gary Clampett was not happy with being away from England for such a long time and playing the long hours in Germany. He left and returned to London, while the others continued as a four piece, but could not go back to their old name of the **Mersey Four** as the former **Toledos** from Southport had taken over that name.

So the quartet decided to take an inflatable rubber puppet as the 'fifth member' and continued as the **Mersey Five** in the line-up with:

Pete Campbell	(voc/g)
Tony Nelson	(g/voc)
Robert Montgomery	(bg/voc)
Charlie Evans	(dr)

The **Mersey Five** continued to play in Germany, they had a long residency in the North where they became very popular and were signed to the independent Storz-label from Osterode.

While they were in Germany, the **Mersey Five** made every effort to obtain 'the dirtiest beat group in the world' image for themselves. These efforts were successful - so successful that, at one time, they were not allowed into a recording studio in Hamburg because of their (artificially created) untidy looks. When they were finally let in after their German record company exerted some pressure, the producer refused to work with such 'down-at-heel' types, until he was knocked out by the musical quality of the four Liverpool boys.

So, in the end, the **Mersey Five** recorded two singles for the German 'Storz' label with a great version of the **Larry Williams** song, "Slow Down" (very unusual without piano) and the original, "What's It All About", which was written by **Bob Montgomery**.

The Mersey Five (four) with their inflatable fifth member & German producer Erich Storz

Both records had that naturally unaffected Beat sound, which was typical of all the singles that were produced by the interesting 'Storz' label. In spite of this, the records of the **Mersey Five** were not too successful at that time, but today are highly desired and expensive collector's items.

"Slow Down" was coupled with a no less interesting version of "Ecstasy", while their version of **Chuck Berry**'s "Sweet Lil' Rock 'n' Roller" on the reverse side of "What's It All About" is not worth powder and shot.

The **Mersey Five** were really one of the hard and uncompromising beat groups out of Liverpool. Like their stage show, their image was quite wild, with their long hair brushed into their faces.

In Germany they had all the markings of a beat band and made appropriate headlines in the papers. Over there they were nicknamed 'the artistic beat machines' which was an accurate description.

Founding member, **Pete Campbell,** left the group while they were still in Germany and joined **John O'Hara & the Playboys**, a Scottish recording-group. After he joined them, both he and the group lived in Germany for quite some time. Upon his return to Liverpool, he played with the **Secrets** and then, together with his brother **Jimmy Campbell** of the **Kirkbys,** in a group called the **Clique**.

He was replaced by **Adrian Lord**, a former member of the **Nomads**, the **Mojos** and the **Mastersounds**. But he did not stay for too long and returned to Liverpool to become a member of **Them Grimbles** and after that he played with the **Easybeats**.

The rest of the group teamed up with **King Size Taylor** - and also appeared under the name of **King Size Taylor & the Dominoes**.

Then **Charlie Evans**, aka **Carl Riche**, decided to go back to Liverpool, where he played with **Rory Storm & the Hurricanes** and in later years was a member of the popular C&W group, **Western Union**.

The new drummer with the **Mersey Five** or **King Size Taylor & the Dominoes** was **Don Alcyd**, a former member of **Tommy & the Metronomes**, **Faron & the TTs** and the **Renegades**, who evolved into another **All-Stars** for **Lee Curtis**.

As the group spent most of its active time in Germany, it missed the boat in England where they did not become very popular and never released a record. It was probably in 1966, that the **Mersey Five** disbanded totally and all the members returned to England.

After playing in London for a while, **Don Alcyd**, a fantastic drummer, joined the **Delmonts** from Liverpool, who, around that time, were also associated with **Freddie Starr**.

Unfortunately, what happened to **Tony Nelson** and **Bob Montgomery** is not known.

Discography :

| **Slow Down / Ecstasy** | G- Storz SRI 45205 / 1964 |
| **What's It All About / Sweet Lil' Rock 'n' Roller** | G- Storz SRI 45206 / 1964 |

THE MERSEY MONSTERS

This is a case of two stories in one and could also have been entitled **J.J. & the Hi-Lites,** as that group was the starting point when it was formed by the singing twin brothers, **Alan** and **Brian Grundy,** most probably in January 1963 in Bootle.

The initials J.J. stood for the two brothers. There isn't too much information available about their early days but it seems they were one of the softer groups that played in a line-up with:

Alan Grundy	(voc)
Brian Grundy	(voc)
John Tarpey	(lg)
Gregg Murphy	(rg)
Ron Smith	(bg)
Geoff Lloyd	(dr)

Only **Geoff Lloyd** had appeared on the scene previously, when he was a member of **Tommy & the Satellites, Vic & the Spidermen** and after that with **Ken Dallas & the Silhouettes,** who shortly before his departure had become **Mark Peters & the Silhouettes.**

JJ & The HI-LITES

J.J. & the Hi-Lites became part of the 'Dave Forshaw Enterprises' stable which ensured them lots of gigs at all the Merseyside venues. Unfortunately, they were only marginally successful and, for some reason, **Brian Grundy** left and disappeared from the scene, while his brother then kept the 'J.J.' initials for himself.

The group hit the headlines of the music papers only once, when they cut a demo disc for Parlophone towards the end of 1963. However, in the end, nothing was released and so it is not known which songs were recorded at that time, but it is highly probable that one of the group's own compositions called "Saturday Morning" was included.

Gregg Murphy was the next to leave and he became a member of the **Jaguars** from Birkenhead in 1963. He was not replaced and the group continued as a four-piece.

For unknown reasons, **J.J. & the Hi-Lites** parted from **Dave Forshaw** and their management was taken over by a certain **Tony Reuben.** Much like **Brian Epstein,** he was also of Jewish descent and owned record shops where he mainly dealt with so-called 'ex jukebox' records. He had big plans for the group who were obviously the only one under his management at that time.

Following the example of **Screaming Lord Sutch**, he wanted something like a monster group and so, in early 1964, **J.J. & the Hi-Lites** became the **Mersey Monsters**.

It seems that their start-up was a bit difficult because they didn't just have to change their name but also their music, programme and stage presentation.

Ron Smith, who also used the stage name, **Chuck Vincent**, apparently did not think too much of the idea and left the group to join **Johnny Templer & the Hi-Cats**.

JJ & the Hi-Lites

He was replaced in the **Mersey Monsters** by **Kelvin Harrison**, who came from **Ricky Gleason & the Topspots** and, before that, he had also played with **Tommy & the Satellites**.

It was in May 1964 when the **Mersey Monsters** appeared on Merseyside for the first time, in the following line-up:

Alan Grundy	(voc)
John Tarpey	(g)
Kelvin Harrison	(bg)
Geoff Lloyd	(dr)

ARE THEY HUMAN? . . .
THOUSANDS OF YOUNGSTERS WILL BE WANTING TO KNOW.
WHAT ARE THEY LIKE?
THOUSANDS OF YOUNGSTERS WILL BE WANTING TO SEE THEM.
BE SMART . . . BOOK THEM NOW !!!

THE
MERSEY MONSTERS

AVAILABLE TO CHILL YOU FROM MARCH 8th.
Sole Booking Manager: TONY REUBEN.
POP RECORD INN ENTERPRISES. 361-3 STANLEY ROAD.
BOOTLE, LIVERPOOL 20. Tel.: BOOtle 3778.

They played at the 'Majestic Ballroom' and also backed the resident DJ and singer, **Barbara Dee**, at that gig. Later on **Barbara Dee** occasionally sang with the **Detours**.

This debut did not make headlines for the **Mersey Monsters** and this didn't suit **Tony Reuben's** plans, who had also taken **Paul Ryan & the Streaks** from Newcastle under his wing around that same time.

With regard to the **Mersey Monsters**, he decided to let them play outside Liverpool at first, so that the group could develop an exciting stage act. In June 1964, he sent them down to London for two weeks and then, from July until November 1964, the group played at the 'Casino Ballroom' in Blackpool every Friday night.

Meanwhile, **Tony Reuben** was busy generating clever publicity for the musicians, who always wore special make-up or masks that made them look like monsters and whose names were kept a secret, as the members were nicknamed as 'Igor', 'Morfo', 'Krom' and 'Orlak'. Do not ask, who was who!!

A myth developed around the group, who still did not play in Liverpool at that time. Advertisements and articles in the newspapers made sure that the audience's attention was steadily drawn to them by imaginative stories such as the **Mersey Monsters** had emerged from the depths of the river Mersey or had climbed from the graves behind the Anglican Cathedral.

It must have been around that same time that the group cut their first Deroy acetate. That EP included the **Johnny Ray** classic, "Yes Tonight Josephine", and the three **Don Gibson** songs, "Don't Tell Me Your Troubles", "Love Has Come My Way" and "Just One Time". These were rough and interesting recordings, but too much Country-influenced to be acceptable for a monster group.

The following single on acetate featured the two **Coasters'** numbers, "Wait A Minute" and "Wake Me, Shake Me", and this was a step in the right direction expected by their management and, of course, their audience. As the group always played away from its hometown, the musicians needed to become professionals, but **Geoff Lloyd** was unwilling and so he left the group.

His replacement was **Tommy Limb**, who came from the recently disbanded **Topspots**.

The **Mersey Monsters** now had gigs mainly down in Gloucestershire while their management kept the fire burning in Liverpool. **Tony Reuben** had good contacts with the Radio Luxembourg DJ, **Pat Campbell**, who, in turn, had good connections to the RCA Victor record company. **Pat Campbell** sent some of his own song material for the **Mersey Monsters** to record and, as it seems, RCA really became interested in signing the group. An ABC television team from the United States also filmed a clip about the group, a very mythological one, which was shown on American television.

After a very successful tour of Scotland, it was time for the 'monsters' to return to Merseyside, where their first appearance was at the 'Floral Hall' in Southport. The huge hall was absolutely packed and the **Mersey Monsters** went down a bomb with their new heavy Rock 'n' Roll sound, their frightening outfits and their wild stage act.

Now that they appeared regularly on Merseyside, the question was, how to keep a variation and freshness in their live act. This must have been a continuous strain, involving a lot of effort and work.

It was **Alan Grundy** who finally broke the chain. He was a good looking guy, who in the past was really admired by girls and he didn't want to continue disguised as a monster. **Tony Reuben**, on the other hand, only wanted a monster-group, and so the **Mersey Monsters** broke up not too long after their impressive and powerful return to Merseyside and before a contract with RCA was signed.

Alan Grundy and **Kelvin Harrison** joined the **Rebels**, formerly known as **Ian & the Rebels**, who had just parted from their singer, **Ricky Gleason**.

After that, **Alan Grundy** got married and emigrated to Australia, where he is still living.

Kelvin Harrison emigrated to Canada, where he possibly remained in the music business. A few years later, he returned to England where he settled down in Leeds.

Tommy Limb quit show business for a while but then returned to the scene as a freelance drummer in the Liverpool clubs and pubs, but he never joined a group again.

John Tarpey, a great guitarist by the way, became a sales manager for British Leyland and had an impressive career in the British motor industry.

In 1998, **Kelvin Harrison** and **Tommy Limb** teamed up again at a revival concert of their former group, **Ricky Gleason & the Topspots,** at the Orrell Park Ballroom and, around ten years later, both were members of the re-formed, **Ricky Gleason & the Topspots**, where they are still playing today.

Discography :

Yes Tonight Josephine / Don't Tell Me Your Troubles / Love Has Come My Way / Just One Time

UK- Deroy acetate EP / 1964

Wait A Minute / Wake Me, Shake Me   **UK- Deroy acetate   / 1964**

Unissued tracks :

At the end of 1963, **J.J. & the Hi-Lites** recorded a demo-disc for Parlophone, most probably with the group's own composition, "**Saturday Morning**". Unfortunately, the other songs are not known.

Sometime in late 1964 or early 1965, the **Mersey Monsters** recorded some songs for RCA-Victor, but disbanded before a contract was signed and so there are no details known about these recordings.

THE MOJOS

This group originated from a trio formed by **Keith Karlsson** (voc/g), real name **Keith Alcock**, **Roy Wood** (g) and **Bob Conrads** (aka **John Konrad**) (dr) in Liverpool in the early Sixties.

Keith Karlsson and **John Conrads** had already played together in other groups, two of them being **Dave Bell & the Bell Boys** and **Jet & the Valiants**.

Roy Wood left in 1962 to join **Johnny Templer & the Hi-Cats** and, after that, became the lead guitarist for **Sonny Webb & the Cascades**.

He was replaced in the trio by **Adrian Wilkinson** (voc/g), who also used the stage name, **Adrian Lord,** and who had formerly played with the **Missouri Drifters**. A little later this line-up was expanded by the addition of a pianist, **Stuart Slater**, who changed his name to **Stu James**.

This line-up of musicians called themselves the **Nomads** and in 1963 they were featured under that name on the Oriole compilation, 'This Is Merseybeat' Vol. 2, with the song, "My Whole Life Through".

The Nomads

Because there was also a London group called the **Nomads**, the Liverpool band changed its name to the **Mojos**.

Then **Terry O'Toole** (aka **Tim Stavely**), the former band roadie joined as pianist, resulting in **Stu James** taking over on lead vocals and lead guitar. **Adrian Lord,** was so angry that he left the group to join the **Mastersounds**, who later changed their name into the **Bluesville Bats**. After that, he formed the **Faces** and was later a member of the **Mersey Five**, **Them Grimbles** and Liverpool's **Easybeats**.

His place in the **Mojos** was taken by **Nicky Crouch**, a former member of **Robin & the Ravens** and the just disbanded, **Faron's Flamingos**. He became the new lead guitarist, while **Stu James** switched to rhythm.

The longest lasting and most popular line-up of the **Mojos** thus consisted of:

Stu James	**(voc/g/harp)**
Nicky Crouch	**(g/voc)**
Terry O'Toole	**(p/voc)**
Keith Karlsson	**(bg/voc)**
Bob Conrads	**(dr)**

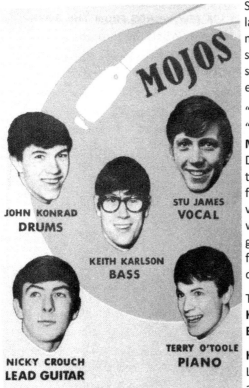

JOHN KONRAD
DRUMS

KEITH KARLSON
BASS

STU JAMES
VOCAL

NICKY CROUCH
LEAD GUITAR

TERRY O'TOOLE
PIANO

Still in 1963, the **Mojos** were signed to Decca and, a little later, had their first single released with "Forever", which was not extremely successful. However, in 1964, their second single, "Everything's Alright", an original by the group, went straight up to No. 9 in the British charts and helped the **Mojos** establish themselves on the national Beat scene.

"Why Not Tonight" reached No. 25 and their version of "Seven Golden Daffodils" stopped at No. 30, and so the **Mojos** had three top-30 hits in a row in 1964. "Seven Golden Daffodils" could have been more successful but, at the same time, Columbia had released the same song by the **Cherokees** from Leeds and their record climbed to No. 33. If the Mojos version had been the only version released at that time, it would certainly have become another Top 10 hit for the group. However, these three singles were the only chart hits for the Mojos, although their only EP, 'The Mojos', still sold quite well.

The **Mojos** almost disbanded at the end of 1964 when **Keith Karlsson**, **Terry O'Toole** and **Bob Conrads** left to form the **Epics** who, in the end, never made a public appearance.

Keith Karlsson emigrated to the USA but, in 1989, returned to Liverpool and joined **Faron's Flamingos**. **Terry O'Toole** joined a Jazz band and **Bob Conrads**, who also used the stage-name of **John Konrad**, later appeared with a group called **Nasty Pop**.

The remaining **Mojos** members, **Stu James** and **Nicky Crouch**, formed a new band under the old name with **Lewis Collins** (bg/voc) and **Aynsley Dunbar** (dr).

Lewis Collins had formerly played the drums for the **Renegades** from Liverpool and with the **Kansas City Five** before he had switched to bass guitar and played with the **Georgians** and the **Eyes**.

Aynsley Dunbar was a former member of the **Merseysippi Jazz Band**, **Derry Wilkie & the Pressmen**, the **Flamingoes**, **Freddie Starr & the Starr Boys** and the **Excheckers**. He left the **Mojos** in 1965 to join **John Mayall's Bluesbreakers**. Later, he formed his own group under the name **Aynsley Dunbar Retaliation** and then played with groups such as **Journey** and **Jefferson Airplane**.

His replacement in the Mojos was **Stan Bennett**, who came from the **Denims**.

It was probably this line-up that recorded the singles, "Comin' On To Cry" and "Wait A Minute" (the latter released as **Stu James & the Mojos**). Both records sold quite well but did not get near the charts.

Around that time, the **Mojos** became the backing group for **Paul & Barry Ryan**, but they also continued to perform in their own right.

Stu James and **Nicky Crouch** also worked together as a 'composer duo' and, amongst others, wrote the single, "I Come Smiling Through" for the **Le Roys**.

Stan Bennett left and was replaced by **Gordon 'Snowy' Fleet**, who came from the **Four Musketeers** but he did not stay very long. He then emigrated to Australia where he was a founding member of the **Easybeats**, who later became internationally famous with hits that included "Friday On My Mind" and "Hello, How Are You". He was replaced in the **Mojos** by **'Deakin' Vernon.**

Then **Lewis Collins** left to become a member of the **Robb Storme Group**, he was replaced by **Steve Snake**. **Lewis Collins** started quite a successful career as an actor and, in 1983, recorded a solo single.

Their final Decca single, "Goodbye Dolly Grey", was probably released with this line-up in 1967. The **Mojos** then switched to Liberty, where they released one more single with "Until My Baby Gets Home" in 1968. Both records failed to make the charts and, after that, the **Mojos** disbanded totally.

Stu James started a solo career but apparently this was not too successful. All that is known is that he released two solo singles with the titles, "I Only Wish

Stu James & the Mojos

I Had The Time" and "I'm In The Mood", on the Bradleys label in 1974 and 1976, respectively. Neither record sold any better than the last of the **Mojos** singles.

Stan Bennett was later a member of **Poacher**. Of the other former members of the **Mojos** or **Stu James & the Mojos**, only **Keith Karlsson** appeared again when he started a new, short-lived group under the name of the **Mojos** in the Nineties.

Nicky Crouch quit the music business but, in the early Nineties, was back on the scene with the newly formed **Cliff Roberts' Rockers**. After that, he appeared on quite a regular basis at the 'MerseyCats' events, where he played with various groups.

In 2005, he re-formed the **Mojos** with fellow Merseybeat musicians from the Sixties. This line-up consisted of **Les Williams** (rg/voc) of the **Dimensions**, **Eric London** (bg/voc) of **Faron's Flamingos** and **Group One**, **Tommy Hughes** (p/voc) of the **Kansas City Five** and **Brian Johnson** (dr) of the **Strangers**.

In July 2010, the **Mojos** played at the 'Beat-Club '66 ' in Bielefeld/Germany in their 'Merseybeat Open-Air' concert and this was the first time since the Sixties that **Stu James** played with the group again. Unfortunately, as he was living in London, he did not continue to perform with them.

<u>Single Discography :</u>

Forever / They Say	UK- Decca F.11732 / 1963
Everything's Alright / Give Your Lovin' To Me	UK- Decca F.11853 / 1964
Why Not Tonight / Don't Do It Anymore	UK- Decca F.11918 / 1964
Seven Daffodils / Nothing At All	UK- Decca F.11959 / 1964
Comin' On To Cry / That's The Way It Goes	UK- Decca F.12127 / 1965
Wait A Minute / Wonder If She Knows	UK- Decca F.12231 / 1965
Goodbye Dolly Grey / I Just Can't Let Her Go	UK- Decca F.12557 / 1967
Until My Baby Gets Home / Seven Park Avenue	UK- Liberty 15097 / 1968

(please note that "**Wait A Minute**" was released as **Stu James & the Mojos**)

EP **THE MOJOS**	UK-Decca DFE 8591 / 1964

- Everything's Alright / I've Got My Mojo Working / The One Who Really Loves You / Nobody But Me

as **The Nomads** :	
My Whole Life Through on 'This Is Merseybeat' Vol. 2	UK-Oriole PS 40048 / 1963

<u>Unreleased tracks :</u>

Unissued tracks by the **Mojos** include the songs, "**Spoonful**" and "**Drive It Home**", which were recorded for Decca, as well as "**Call My Name**" and "**To Know Her Is To Love Her**", which were recorded for PYE.

For collectors, it might be of interest that, in 1982, there was an album released on the Edsel label (ED110) with the title, 'The Mojos Working', on which all single titles from 1963 to 1965 that the **Mojos** recorded for Decca plus the songs from the EP can be found.

THE NASHPOOL FOUR

This group was formed in Liverpool in 1963 and very soon became one of the local attractions in the Beat city. They appeared regularly at the major clubs and venues but, in spite of their local success, they never achieved nationwide popularity.

The original **Nashpool Four** line-up consisted of:

Jan Ferguson	(voc/g)
Eric Savage	(g/voc)
Sid Edwards	(bg/harp/voc)
Eddie Edwards	(dr)

Sid Edwards was a former member of the **Flames**, the **Nutrockers** and he had also played with **Lee Shondell & the Capitols, Danny Havoc & the Ventures** and **Groups Inc.**, while his brother **Eddie Edwards** came from the **Del Renas** but, before that, he had also been a member of the **Flames**.

Jan Ferguson left the group quite soon and disappeared from the scene.

He was replaced by the sax player **Tommy Husky**, who came from the **Deejays**.

Eric Savage took over the lead vocals but then he also left to join the **St. Louis Checks**.

Sid Edwards switched to lead guitar and shared the lead vocals with the new bass guitarist, **Harry Scully**, who came from **Lee Shondell & the Boys**.

The group then became a five-piece when **Robb Deka** (org) joined as an additional member, having formerly played with the **Prestons**.

The Nashpool - L to R: Eddie Edwards, Tommy Husky, Sid Edwards Harry Scully & Rob Decca (on organ)

They shortened their name to **The Nashpool** and, around that time, **Joe Meek** became aware of this Liverpool outfit and produced the songs, "Shakin With Linda" and "Sweet Mary", with them for EMI in 1964, but for mysterious reasons these recording sessions were not followed by a release.

A little later, the **Nashpool** were booked for a long residency at the 'Star-Club' in Hamburg, which obviously helped the groups popularity.

Harry Scully left to join the **Trends** and then he became a member of the London-based **Brian Auger** group, the **Bootleggers**. After that, he returned to Liverpool and was a long time member of the very successful cabaret group, **Elliot**.

His replacement was **Reg Welch**, who had formerly played with the **Rebels** and the **Questions** from Preston, as well as with **Freddie Starr & the Midnighters**.

Shortly after that, when **Tommy Husky** left to join **Earl Preston's Realms** and later to play with the **Almost Blues** and the **Detours**, he was not replaced in the group, instead they continued to play as the **Nashpool Four** again.

Reg Welch left and became a member of the **Suspects** and his replacement was **Alan Burton**, who came from the **Valkyries**.

But very soon, the **Nashpool Four** disbanded totally and, by that time, the brothers **Sid** and **Eddie Edwards** were the only remaining members of the original line-up.

Robb Deka disappeared from the scene. However, in the Nineties, he had a comeback as a singer under the stage name of **Robb Shenton**.

Eddie Edwards joined **Rory Storm & the Hurricanes** and, after that, played with the **Beechwoods** while none of the other members appeared on the scene again.

Discography :

There were no records released by the **Nashpool Four** but, in May 1964, when the group was a five-piece under the name of **The Nashpool,** the well known producer, **Joe Meek,** recorded "Shakin With Linda" and "Sweet Mary" with them for EMI which, unfortunately, were never released.

THE NEWTOWNS

This interesting group was formed in late 1962 by the guitarists, **Glyn Harris** and **Jim Jones** in the Liverpool suburb of Kirkby. As Kirkby was a newly built town, they decided on the name of the **Newtowns** and recruited local vocalist, **Dennis Donafee,** to front the group.

They then recruited **Dave Pickstock** on bass guitar and a drummer, **Eric Lee,** to complete this melodic Beat group, who were sometimes advertised as **Dennis & the Newtowns**.

Ian Comish, at that time also the manager of the **Fontanas**, another Kirkby-based outfit, took the group under his wing and the **Newtowns** soon became a popular live act.

Then in 1963, **Dave Pickstock** and **Eric Lee** both left and apparently quit showbiz.

The **Newtowns** from that moment on appeared in the following line-up:

Dennis Donafee	(voc)
Glyn Harris	(g/voc)
Jimmy Jones	(g/bg/voc)
Bob Frazer	(bg/org/voc)
Bob Williams	(dr/voc)

Bob Williams was a former member of **Dino & the Wild Fires**, who had gone down to London and continued as the **Wackers**, but that is another story in this book.

The **Newtowns** appeared at the 'Cavern' but, apart from this, they seldom actually played in the Liverpool 'Beat centre'. They never obtained national popularity but were very busy in the north of England and especially in south Lancashire.

According to the May issue of the 'Combo' music paper, they were 'mobbed and chased by hordes of screaming girls' when they appeared for the 'Freedom From Hunger Campaign' in 1964.

It was in early 1966 that the **Newtowns** recorded two acetates in the Liverpool Unicord studios in Moorfields, with "Somewhere Over The Rainbow", the little known **Georgie Fame** number, "Something",

The original Newtowns

the original "Tomorrow" and an interesting version of "Please Stay" which, in a very similar arrangement, became a big hit for the **Cryin' Shames** in the same year.

Unfortunately, these recordings were not followed by an official release and so this really did not help the **Newtowns**.

The group continued to play the normal Merseyside gigs until 1966, then both **Dennis Donafee** and **Bob Frazer** left and the group disbanded. **Dennis Donafee** later was a member of a group called **Sandlewood**.

The remaining three teamed up with **Brian Jones** and **Geoff Nugent** to reform the **Undertakers** but, when they turned professional, **Glyn Harris** left and was replaced by the returning **Bob Frazer**.

The new **Undertakers** continued until 1968 and when they broke up. **Jimmy Jones** and **Bob Williams** teamed up again with **Glyn Harris** and, together with singer, **Ted Clucas,** re-formed the **Newtowns**.

They stayed on the cabaret circuit and when **Ted Clucas** left, sometime in the Seventies, the others continued as a trio with **Bob Williams** taking over the lead vocals. Later, the two founders **Glyn Harris** and **Jimmy Jones** continued on as a cabaret duo until 1976, when **Glyn Harris** decided to pursue a solo career as a singer and comedian. He occasionally teamed up again with **Bob Williams** in a trio called **Northern Lights**.

Bob Williams is still active in the music scene these days as a drummer for the **Prime Suspects**.

Discography :

Somewhere Over The Rainbow / Something	**UK- Unicord acetate / 1966**
Please Stay / Tomorrow	**UK- Unicord acetate / 1966**

(Please note that "**Somewhere Over The rainbow**", "**Tomorrow**" and "**Please Stay**" were released recently on the CD 'Unearthed Merseybeat' on the Viper label)

THE NOCTURNS

This typical Merseybeat group was formed in 1963 in Liverpool and, as all their members were experienced musicians who had played in other well-known groups previously, the **Nocturns** established themselves on the scene and became professionals within a very short time.

The group from the beginning consisted of:

Barry Elmsley	**(voc/p)**
Keith Draper	**(g/voc)**
Brian Cox	**(g)**
Dave Foley	**(bg)**
Frank Sloane	**(dr)**

Keith Draper, **Brian Cox** and **Dave Foley** were former members of the **Cadillacs** and the follow-on group, the **Sorrals** or **Alby & the Sorrals**, respectively.

Drummer, **Frank Sloane** came from the **Four Musketeers** and, before that, he had played with the **Merseybeats** as well as their forerunner groups, the **Pacifics** and the **Mavericks**.

Barry Elmsley did not want to become a professional and he did not stay for too long. He was replaced by **Steve Aldo**, who had formerly sung with **Steve Aldo & the Challengers** and, for a short time, with **King Size Taylor & the Dominoes**. But he also did not stay for too long and then he joined the **Griff Parry Five**, with whom he recorded under his name for Parlophone. After that he became a member of the **Krew** (better known as **The Crew**), the **Fyx** and the **In Crowd**, before he was backed by the **Fairies**.

His place in the **Nocturns** was taken by **Dave Wilcox**, whose real name is **David Christie,** and who had formerly sung with **Danny Royl & the Strollers**, the **Sensations**, the **Young Ones** and **Rikki Jansen & the Q-Kats** who, despite all the different names, were one and the same group.

Brian Cox left and was replaced by **Arthur McMahon**, who was also known as **Arthur Roy** and who had formerly played with **Arthur Roy & the Rockers**, the **Gerry Marsden Skiffle Group**, the **Gerry Marsden Trio** and **Gerry & the Pacemakers**. But he also did not stay too long and then disappeared from the scene.

His replacement was **Dave Elias**, who also came from the **Four Musketeers** and was a former member of the **Merseybeats** and the **Mavericks**.

In this line-up, the **Nocturns** secured a part in the **Lionel Bart** musical, 'Maggie May', and, a little later, their first single, "Carrying On", was released, which was their song from the musical.

On stage at the musical 'Maggie May'

This single, which was coupled with "Three Cool Cats", climbed up to No. 61 in the British charts.

So it was no surprise that, soon after, a second single was planned to be released on the Decca label and the songs, "Too Much Monkey Business" and "I'm Hurt", were recorded and announced in the 'Mersey Beat' newspaper but apparently never released. At least it is not listed in the Decca catalogue.

At this time, the **Nocturns** were appearing regularly at the well-known 'Blue Angel' club in Liverpool.

The group did not release any more records under their own name but, in 1964, backed the female vocal duo, **The Charmers,** on their single, "Are You Sure", although the **Nocturns** were not named on the label.

After that, little was heard of the **Nocturns**, who shouldn't be confused with the **Nocturnes** who probably came from Manchester and later released records on the Columbia label.

In 1965, the Liverpool **Nocturns** disbanded totally and it is only known that **Keith Draper** and **Dave Elias** continued in the music business. They first joined the **Beat-Chicks** (from London?) and then played in various groups before they ended up as a cabaret duo called the **Jade Brothers**.

Dave Wilcox continued solo and recorded one more single for CBS with "Just like him" in 1966 but, after that, he disappeared from the scene like all the other members of the **Nocturns**.

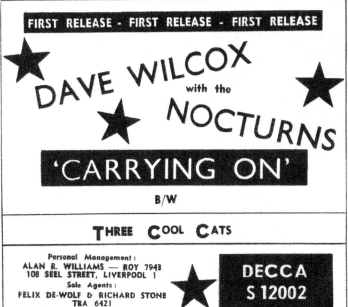

FIRST RELEASE - FIRST RELEASE - FIRST RELEASE

★ DAVE WILCOX
with the
★ NOCTURNS

'CARRYING ON'

B/W

THREE COOL CATS

Personal Management:
ALAN R. WILLIAMS — ROY 7943
108 SEEL STREET, LIVERPOOL 1
Sole Agents:
FELIX DE-WOLF & RICHARD STONE
TRA 6421
18 YORK BUILDINGS, LONDON, W.C.2

★ DECCA S 12002

Single discography :

Carrying On / Three Cool Cats   UK- Decca F.12002 / 1964

Also in 1964, the **Nocturns** were included in the EP 'Carryin On' that contained additional songs from 'Maggie May' (UK-Decca DFE 8602). However, it is very likely that only the two songs from their single were featured.

David Wilcox – solo :

Just Like Him / If You Believe In Love   UK – CBS 202 090 / 1966

as backing group for **The Charmers** :

Are You Sure / My Heart Has A Mind Of Its Own   UK- Decca F. ??? / 1964

Unreleased tracks :

In 1964, the **Nocturns** recorded the songs, "**Too Much Monkey Business**" and "**I'm Hurt**", for Decca as a follow-up single to their debut but, for mysterious reasons, this record was not released.

THE NOTIONS

When this group was formed in Liverpool in 1962, it initially appeared as a trio under the name, the **Phantoms**. In the first year of its existence, the group played only occasional gigs at local venues due to school and work commitments of the members, who were only 16 years old at the time.

The Phantoms
L to R:
Dave Delaney
Dave Armstrong
Keith Balcomb

Eventually, they discovered that there were already other groups that were using the same name so, when they were joined by a fourth member, they became the **Notions** and now appeared in the following line-up:

David Delaney	**(voc/lg)**
Keith Balcomb	**(rg/voc)**
Joe Short	**(bg/voc)**
Dave Armstrong	**(dr)**

The original line-up of the Notions at the Cavern (Feb 1964)
L to R: Keith Balcomb, Joe Short, Dave Armstrong & Dave Delaney

Once established on the scene, they played regularly at many of the well-known clubs and dance halls, such as the 'Iron Door', the 'CI Club', the 'Jacaranda', Litherland Town Hall and St. Luke's in Crosby. After their first appearances at the 'Cavern', the group's popularity grew rapidly and the **Notions** became something of a resident group at that famous club playing there over 100 times. Together with the **Hideaways**, they probably made the most appearances there of all the Liverpool groups. This certainly was an outstanding achievement and should be recognised as such.

Besides their evening performances, the **Notions** played on the first Saturday afternoon session at the 'Cavern' and they also recorded a 'Sunday Night At The Cavern' show, which was broadcast on Radio Luxembourg.

Not without good reason, **Bob Wooler** dubbed the group as the 'Cavern's choice for 1964'.

In 1964, it looked like they would make a national breakthrough when they recorded 14 songs live at the 'Cavern' for the mobile recording unit of Oriole. It is not known why these tracks were never issued, possibly due to changes within Oriole at the time, but a big chance for the Notions passed.

Keith Balcomb left the group in April 1964 and quit the music business. The **Notions** were then joined by **Dave McCarthy**, who had not played in a group previously.

Notions

WATerloo 6023

With Dave McCarthy (L) & Kevin Short (R)

Close harmony became the group's speciality and, a little later, the **Notions** recorded various demos at the 'Cavern Sounds' studio in Matthew Street. The recorded material, besides some covers, comprised of original numbers including "Another Time", "You'll See A Difference", "I'm In Love With You" and "Can You See A Way". As a result of the demos, a formal recording session followed a little later at the 'Advision Studios' in London.

Unfortunately, these recordings were not followed by a release on a national label and so, in this respect, the **Notions** were not the luckiest of groups.

However, despite not having a recording contract or turning professional, the **Notions** continued to be very popular and survived well on the music scene, being one of the busiest outfits in the area and playing at venues throughout Merseyside and various towns in the northwest, such as Manchester, Northwich, Chester, Bury, Blackpool and others.

In 1965, **Joe Short** left the group and quit the music business to become a Catholic priest.

He was replaced by his older brother, **Kevin Short**, a former member of the **Jokers** from Southport.

For a short time in early 1966, the **Notions** were also the backing group for the **Excelles**, a popular Liverpool vocal harmony group comprising both male and female singers.

In 1967, the **Notions** became a trio again when **Dave McCarthy** left to join the London group the **League Of Gentlemen**. He later emigrated to the USA and continued there in the music business.

It was sometime in 1968 that the **Notions** finally disbanded without having had the big breakthrough that they undoubtedly deserved.

Kevin Short subsequently joined the **Beechwoods**, a successor-group of the **Easybeats**, who, in 1969, recorded as **Taste Of Honey**, although it is not known whether he was still with the group at that time.

Dave Armstrong, some time later, joined the **Takers**, a group that included former members of the **Undertakers**.

Dave Delaney went into academia and industry, left Liverpool and, for the past ten years, has played regularly with the Derby-based band, **Flying Mallet**.

Final line up as a trio (1967)
Kevin Short, Dave Armstrong, Dave Delaney

Discography :

In 1964, the **Notions** recorded the following songs, that have mainly survived on reel to reel tape: **'Memories Are Made Of This'**, **'Nothing Shakin''**, **'Take Out Some Insurance'**, **'Just In Case'**, **'Maybelline'**, **'Sure To Fall'**, **'Go On Home'**, **'Lend Me You Comb'** and **'With All My Love'**.

In 1965 they recorded five original numbers **'Another Time'**, **'You'll See The Difference'**, **'I'm In Love With You'**, **'If She Knew'** and **'You've Been Looking'**, for the 'Cavern Sounds' label. All melodic songs with great vocal-harmonies, unfortunately, none of them were ever released.

Finally, in 1966, the group went down to the Advision Studios in London and in addition to a version of **'Hey Jude'** (sung by **Dave McCarthy**) they recorded the originals, **'Can You See A Way'** and **'I'll be Taking You Home'**. The last named track featured the lead-vocals of **Fred Lloyd**, the A&R man for the session. Unfortunately, once again, this was not followed by a record-release.

THE PATHFINDERS

It was sometime in 1960 that this group was formed at the Rock Ferry High School in Birkenhead by schoolmates, **Tom Earley** (voc/g) and **Roy Brockhurst** (voc/bg), together with Roy's younger brother, **Peter Brockhurst** (g/voc), **Dave Stephenson** (g) and the drummer, **Tony Berry**.

After the first appearances in local youth clubs, **Dave Stephenson** left and was replaced by **Mike Jones** (lg/voc).

Besides this, the **Pathfinders**, as they were named from the beginning, added the guitarist and singer, **Billy May,** to their line-up, who formerly had played with the **Beat Cats**.

The group soon established themselves on the local scene. They became regulars at the 'Kraal' in New Brighton but also played the Liverpool venues, including the 'Cavern'.

In early 1963, **Billy May** left to join the **Valkyries**, who just had accepted an offer to tour in France.

His departure was followed by founding member, **Tom Earley,** leaving. He amalgamated with the **Masqueraders** to form the **Kinsmen**, that later continued as **Steve Day & the Kinsmen**.

The **Pathfinders** continued as a four-piece for a few months but, in May 1963, when **Mike Jones** left, **Tom Earley** returned to the **Pathfinders**, who at that time did not have a real lead guitarist. When **Pete Brockhurst** left to concentrate on his job and then **Tony Berry** left to join the **Asteroids**, the group temporarily disbanded.

Tony Berry by the way is not the singer of the same name, who fronted the **Tempos**.

The Pathfinders

In late 1963, the founders **Tom Earley** and **Roy Brockhurst** re-formed the **Pathfinders** with the former **Pressmen** members, **Ritchie Prescott** (lg) and **Tommy Bennett** (dr). Besides this, **John Hinton,** a pianist, was added to the line-up.

But this only lasted until February 1964, when **Ritchie Prescott** was replaced by the returning **Billy May** and **Tommy Bennett** left to join the **Kinsmen**, that later carried on as the **New Pressmen**. The new drummer was **Tony Aldridge**, who had formerly played with the **Masqueraders** and the **Kinsmen**.

In July of that year, the **Pathfinders** had their first TV-appearance at the 'Ready Steady Win' show, which obviously resulted in the group being signed to Decca. Initially they recorded the originals, "It's Time" and "I Can't Wait", but these songs were not released.

At the same time Radio Caroline was to begin broadcasting, **Tom Earley** and **Billy May**, in an attempt to get air-play there, wrote the song, "I Love You Caroline", hoping to get it adopted as the station's signature-tune. Before the track was recorded, **John Hinton** left to join the **Four Sounds** that, together with **Gus Travis,** also appeared as **Gus Travis & the Midnighters** for a while. He later moved to London as a professional musician.

The **Pathfinders**, after all the personnel changes, now consisted of:

Tom Earley	(voc/rg)
Billy May	(lg / voc)
Roy Brockhurst	(bg / voc)
Frank Hopley	(p)
Tony Aldridge	(dr)

The new pianist, **Frank Hopley,** was a former member of the **Mastersounds**.

In this line-up, the **Pathfinders** recorded "I Love You Caroline" and another great **Billy May/Tom Earley** song, "Something I Can Always Do", for Decca.

Radio Caroline, in the end, decided to use the **Fortunes** record, "Caroline", as their signature-tune, but the **Pathfinders** record became a regularly played favourite at the station and apparently sold quite well, although the B-side, "Something I Can Always Do", was clearly the better Beat song. These numbers were really good enough for two singles but, unfortunately, the record did not enter the British charts and so did not contribute to a national breakthrough for the group.

Frank Hopley, for unknown reasons, left and disappeared from the scene. He was not replaced in the **Pathfinders** who successfully continued to play in the greater Liverpool area and appeared regularly at all the major venues in and around the city centre.

In the middle of 1965, organist **Kingsley Foster** joined the group. He had formerly played with the **Kingfishers** and **Steve Day & the Kinsmen**. A little later the **Pathfinders** turned professional

The American independent producer, **Shel Talmy**, became interested in the **Pathfinders** and recorded the songs, "In My Lonely Room" and "Love, Love, Love", with them. Unfortunately, for mysterious reasons, these tracks were never released. The **Pathfinders** also recorded the original, "I'm Ashamed Of You Baby", the **Marvin Gaye** success, "Can I Get A Witness" and **Ernie K. Doe's** "A Certain Girl", for Decca but, again, these were not followed by a release.

The **Pathfinders** secured a deal with EMI and, still in 1965, went into the famous 'Abbey Road' studios, where they recorded the originals, "Don't You Believe It" (written by **Billy May**, but credited to their manager **Barry Lloyd**) and "Castle Of Love", written by their road-manager, **Mike Rooms**, which was released as their second single – this time on Parlophone.

Although nowhere near as strong as their debut on Decca, it again was a remarkable record, that was often played on Radio Luxembourg and featured on 'Juke Box Jury'. Unfortunately, it never achieved the sales needed to elevate the group to the national success that they honestly deserved.

Kingsley Foster then left and the group continued as a quartet in the classic line-up with two guitars, bass and drums. In early 1966, they were called into the studio again and recorded the **Detroit Spinners** number, "I'll Always Love You", and **Roddie Joy's** "Come Back Baby" which most closely represented their live sound.

While waiting for the release, the **Pathfinders** went over to France where they mainly played in and around Paris. When they returned and found out that the single was not going to be released due to contractual difficulties over royalties, this was the beginning of the end of the **Pathfinders** who declined various offers to tour France again, kept on playing on Merseyside, but very soon split up.

Of **Billy May,** it is known that he continued in the music-business as a solo-performer and **Tony Aldridge** later was a member of the cabaret group, the **Trend**, while **Tom Earley** and **Roy Brockhurst** apparently quit showbiz. **Tom Early** later emigrated to Australia, where he is still living.

It was in 1989 that the **Pathfinders** re-formed for a MerseyCats charity-show in Tranmere in the line-up with **Tom Earley**, **Roy Brockhurst**, **Billy May**, **John Hinton** and **Tony Aldridge**.

But this was an exception, although later there were some repetitions at charity-events, but they were more jam-sessions with other musicians being involved, including **Ian Hunter** and **Allan Burton** of the **Valkyries**, **Tommy Hughes** of the **Kansas City Five**, **Brian Jones** of the **Undertakers** and **Barry Irlam**.

> **AUJOURD'HUI SAMEDI 16 AVRIL**
>
> *De retour au*
> *Club Pierre Charron*
>
> # THE PATHFINDERS
>
> *en matinée à 15 heures*
>
> après leur triomphal succès à Monte-Carlo

Single discography :

I Love You Caroline / Something I Can Always Do	UK- Decca F.12038 / 1964
Don't' You Believe It / Castle of love	UK – Parlophone R 5372 / 1965

Unreleased tracks :

The **Pathfinders** first recorded the originals, "**It's Time**" and "**I Can't Wait**", for Decca in 1964 which were never released. After their first single was released, they recorded the **Billy May** original, "**I'm Ashamed Of You Baby**", plus, "**Can I Get A Witness**" and "**A Certain Girl**" for Decca, as well as "**Love, Love, Love**" and "**In My Lonely Room**" for the independent producer, **Shel Talmy** (all in1964/65). None of these recordings ever saw the light of day in the record market.

Finally, in 1966, the **Pathfinders** recorded "**I'll Always Love You**" and "**Come Back Baby**" as a follow-up single for Parlophone, which also was never released.

THE PAWNS

This great Rhythm & Blues group was formed as a trio in Liverpool in 1963. Initially, they had somewhat limited success, which was probably due to the fact that they were just one of three or four hundred groups that were active at that time.

However, because the **Pawns**, as they were named from the beginning, had plenty of bookings on both sides of the River Mersey, their popularity continued to grow, not the least because of their good musical quality.

The original line-up of the **Pawns** consisted of:

Dave Percival	**(voc/g)**
Derek France	**(bg/voc)**
Sid Knapper	**(dr)**

Dave Percival and **Sid Knapper** were former members of the just disbanded **Climbers** and, while it could not be confirmed, **Dave Percival** was possibly identical with **Dave Percy**, who had also played with the **Roadrunners** for a time.

But this line-up of the **Pawns** only lasted until spring 1964 and then **Dave Percival** left to join the **Kinsleys**. He later became a member of the **Epics,** who mainly consisted of former members of the **Mojos**, but who never had a public performance together - a so-called 'stillborn child'.

He was replaced in the **Pawns** by **Dave Myers**, who formerly had played with **Cliff Roberts' Rockers**, the **Climbers** and the **Renegades** from Liverpool.

When **Derek France** also left shortly after that and disappeared from the scene, the **Pawns** became a quartet when they were joined by **George Peckham** (voc/g) and **Dave 'Mushy' Cooper** (bg/voc).

The Pawns at the Star Club, Bielefeld

George Peckham was also a former member of Liverpool's **Renegades** and, prior to joining the **Pawns**, he had played with **Lee Curtis & the All Stars** together with **'Mushy' Cooper**, who before that had been a member of the **Topspots**, **Bob Evans' Five Shillings**, the **Vegas Five** and **Faron's Flamingos**.

It was probably this line-up that toured Germany at the end of 1964 where, among other venues, they also appeared at the 'Star Club' in Bielefeld, where they created a really great impression.

They recorded "Casting My Spell" and "Who", for Decca which, unfortunately, were never released.

THE
IRON DOOR
CLUB

THURSDAY. 4 JUNE
The Pawns
SONNY KAY & THE REDS
FRIDAY, 5 JUNE
Liquorice Lockings Allsorts
THE EXCHECKERS
RICKY GLEASON & THE TOP SPOTS
SATURDAY, 6 JUNE
Freddy Starr and The Flamingoes
THE ST. LOUIS CHECKS
THE PILGRIMS
SUNDAY, 7 JUNE
The Pawns
MARK PETERS & THE SILHOUETTES
THE PATHFINDERS
SUNDAY AFTERNOON SESSION
THE RIOT SQUAD
THE PRINCIPALS
TUESDAY, 9 JUNE
Earl Royce & The Olympics
THE DELEMERES

TEMPLE ST., L'POOL

For a brief period of time, the **Pawns** were joined by sax player, **Howie Casey**, formerly with **Derry & the Seniors**, **Howie Casey & the Seniors** and with **King Size Taylor & the Dominoes**. He did not stay for very long and joined the Birmingham outfit, the **Krewkats**. After that, he played with the **Big Three** for a short time and briefly with the **Griff Parry Five** before re-forming the **Krew** – another story in this book. Later he was a member of the **Roy Young Band** and **Rigor Mortis**.

In late 1964, **George Peckham** left to join **Groups Inc.**, who very soon disbanded. He then joined the **Kinsleys** and, after that, played with **Earl Royce & the Olympics** and the **Fourmost**.

It is not known if the **Pawns** continued as a group or if they broke up at that time. Whatever happened, nothing was heard of them again in 1965.

In 1978, the band name, the **Pawns,** appeared again on the revival sampler, 'Mersey Survivors', on which the **Pawns** were featured with the songs, "Let's Dance" and "Tallahassee Lassie".

But this was more a session band that only came together to record these songs and **George Peckham** was probably the only featured member of the Sixties' line-up.

There will always be question marks about the **Pawns** as they weren't paid the attention they honestly deserved in the Sixties.

In the Nineties, **Dave Myers** suddenly appeared again on the scene, playing sessions with musicians of the 'New Brighton Rock' organisation. When the group **Johnny Sandon & the Specials** evolved from these sessions, he became a member and, after singer **Johnny Sandon** left, the band continued as the **Mersey Specials** for some time.

After that, **Dave Myers** was a member of **Persuader,** who later changed their name into **Rocket 88.** Nowadays, he plays in the group **Tempest**.

Discography :

Casting my spell / Who   UK – Decca test recording (acetate) / 1964

Tracks on compilation-albums :

| **Tallahassee Lassie** | on 'Mersey Survivors' | **UK-Raw RWLP 104 / 1978** |
| **Let's Dance** | on 'Mersey Survivors' | **UK-Raw RWLP 104 / 1978** |

(Please note that the songs on the compilation albums were most probably recorded by a group of session musicians and that **George Peckham** was likely the only participant from the Sixties' line-up of the **Pawns**)

MARK PETERS & THE SILHOUETTES

Peter Fleming (aka **Mark Peters**) started his singing career in the late Fifties with the group, **Dean Fleming & the Flamingos,** and, after that, he had a short spell with the **Teen Tones** and the **Hi-Spots** in Liverpool. When he changed his stage name to **Mark Peters**, he became the leader of **Mark Peters & the Cyclones**, quite a popular and important group on the Merseybeat scene.

In 1962, he left the **Cyclones,** who continued as a group on the scene and later recorded for Oriole. **Mark Peters** amalgamated with the **Silhouettes** who, until that time, had been the backing group for singer, **Ken Dallas**.

Under the name of **Mark Peters & the Silhouettes**, this new connection appeared in the following line-up:

Mark Peters	(voc)
Rod McClelland	(g/voc)
Malcolm Aston	(g/voc)
David May	(bg/voc)
Steve Fleming	(org)
Geoff Lloyd	(dr)

Steve Fleming, a brother of **Mark Peters**, was also a former member of **Mark Peters & the Cyclones**.

Geoff Lloyd, who was new in this line-up, had previously played with **Tommy & the Satellites** and **Vic & the Spidermen**. In January 1963, he left to join **J.J. & the Hi-Lites** and the original drummer, **Bob O'Hanlon,** returned to the **Silhouettes** after having played with the **Classics** from St. Helens, as well as with **Lee Castle & the Barons**.

In this line-up, **Mark Peters & the Silhouettes** were featured on the legendary Oriole sampler, 'This Is Merseybeat' Vol. 1, with a good version of "Someday (When I'm Dead And Gone)".

Because of their convincing debut, the group was signed to Oriole and, still in 1963, a nice single with the original, "Fragile", was released by **Mark Peters & the Silhouettes**. This song was also featured on the sampler, 'Group Beat' 63'.

But "Fragile" wasn't a big hit and so did not help this really good group achieve any sort of a breakthrough.

Bob O'Hanlon left and was replaced by **Brian Johnson**, a former member of **Jet & the Tornados**, the **Strangers** and **Rory Storm & the Hurricanes**.

MARK PETERS
ORIOLE RECORDING ARTIST

Probably in this line-up, the single, "Cindy's Gonna Cry", was recorded for Oriole, which was only credited to **Mark Peters**. Once again, it wasn't very successful and that might have been why **Rod McClelland** left and quit the music business.

He was replaced by **Arthur Ashton**, who came from **Chick Graham & the Coasters** and, before that, he had played with the **Confederates**. But he only stayed for a short time and then joined **Ian & the Zodiacs**.

Mark Peters & the Silhouettes at the Star Club

His replacement in **Mark Peters & the Silhouettes** was **Norman Scroggei**, who came from the recently disbanded **Lee Eddie Five**. This line-up accepted an engagement at the 'Star-Club' in Hamburg, where they went down really well and probably would have been re-booked.

However, after it looked like the line-up had become stable, **Mark Peters** left, followed by his brother, **Steve Fleming**.

Mark Peters initially recorded the solo single, "Don't Cry For Me", which was released on the Piccadilly label, a nice song but, unfortunately, it failed to achieve any great success.

After that release, **Mark Peters** and his brother, **Steve Fleming**, amalgamated with the **Squad**, formerly known as the **Riot Squad**, under the name **Mark Peters & the Method**.

Then, both **Mark Peters** and **Steve Fleming** teamed up with the **Rats** from Wigan, who shortly before had released two singles with "Parchment Farm" on Oriole and "Sack Of Woe" on CBS. But **Mark Peters & the Rats**, as they were called then, did not record together.

Steve Fleming left and formed the **Steve Alan Set** and shortly thereafter he was joined in that group by his brother. However, after a short spell with the **Steve Alan Set**, **Mark Peters** quit show business and emigrated to Sri Lanka, where he continued to live until his death a few years ago.

THE SILHOUETTES
Mickey Hayes 17. Poulton Rd. Bebington. Wirral. Ches
Phone 051~Bro 1925

But back to the **Silhouettes**, who, after **Mark Peters** and **Steve Fleming** had left, continued under their old name in a line-up with **Norman Scroggei** (voc/g), **Malcolm Aston** (g), **David May** (bg/voc) and **Brian Johnson** (dr).

Brian Johnson then left to join the **Tabs** and was replaced by **Tony Sounders**, who also was a former member of **Chick Graham & the Coasters**. As far as it is known, this line-up toured Germany again but did not make any more recordings and disbanded in late 1965 or early 1966.

David May joined **Rory Storm & the Hurricanes** but later teamed up again with **Norman Scroggei** and the drummer, **Jimmy Lacey** (formerly with the **Profiles**, **Johnny Templer & the Hi-Cats** and **Chick Graham & the**

Coasters), and formed a group under the name of the **Three Cheers**, who later became **Phase Three** and may have recorded for Polydor, although there is nothing known about such records.

David May later formed a duo together with **Ricky Gleason**, who formerly had led the groups, **Denny & the Escorts**, **Ricky Gleason & the Topspots**, **Ricky Gleason & the Nighthawks** and the **Rebels**.

After that, **David May** was a member of the cabaret band, **The Maddisons**.

Malcolm Aston left show business after the **Silhouettes** had disbanded, while **Tony Sounders** became a member of **Mark Peters & the Method** and later also of the **Steve Alan Set**.

In the Eighties, **Steve Fleming** was a member of the **Merseybeats** but then joined the **Clouds**, a cabaret group that mainly consisted of former **Fourmost** members. After that, he joined the **Vince Earl Attraction**.

THE THREE CHEERS

In conclusion, it can be said that although they were only short-lived and not too successful on the national scene, **Mark Peters & the Silhouettes** were one of the more interesting groups of the first Merseybeat wave and it is a shame that more records were not released by them.

Discography :

Mark Peters & the Silhouettes :

Fragile (Handle With Care) / Janie   UK- Oriole CB 1836 / 1963

as **Mark Peters :**

Cindy's Gonna Cry / Show Her   UK- Oriole CB 1909 / 1964

Don't Cry For Me / I Told You So   UK- Piccadilly 7N 35207 / 1964

(Please note that "**Cindy's Gonna Cry**" was most probably recorded together with the **Silhouettes**, although the group was not named on the label, while the second one clearly was a solo release by **Mark Peters**.)

Tracks on compilation albums :

Someday (When I'm Dead and Gone)   on 'This Is Merseybeat' Vol. 1   UK- Oriole PS 40047 / 1963

Fragile (Handle With Care)   on 'Group Beat '63'   UK- Realm RM 149 / 1963

Unissued tracks :

The songs, "**I Love You**" and "**It Wasn't Meant To Be**", were recorded by Oriole at the "**Cindy's Gonna Cry**" session in 1963. These could have been solo recordings by **Mark Peters**, but its also possible the **Silhouettes** were featured on them.

THE PREMIERS

This band originated from the Skiffle group, **Tony Goldby & the Goldminers**, formed by **Tony Lane** in Liverpool in the late Fifties. The members at that time were **Tony Lane** (voc/g), **Dennis Conroy** (g/voc), **Alan Walton** (bass) and **Arthur Gilbert** (dr).

In the early Sixties, the group changed their musical style and, of course, their name - and the result was a Rhythm & Blues band called **The Premiers**. Changes in the line-up followed and when **Dave Forshaw** took over their management, the **Premiers** consisted of the following musicians:

Tony Lane	(voc/g)
Dennis Conroy	(g/voc)
Paul Lofthouse	(bg)
Ronnie Barker	(dr)

The former bass guitarist, **Alan Walton,** had become a member of the **Soul Seekers**, while **Arthur Gilbert** probably had quit show business.

Within a short time, the **Premiers** became popular on the local scene and they were something of a resident group at 'St. Johns Hall' in Bootle, where the **Beatles** also appeared a few times.

In 1964, this line-up of the **Premiers** recorded an EP on acetate with the songs, "Beautiful Deliliah" and "Skinny Minnie", as well as their own compositions, "I'm Blue" and "Honest I Do", the latter being a very nice and melodic Beat number, which would have been great on record. But, of course, an acetate did not help the group's popularity and neither did it contribute to any sort of a breakthrough for the **Premiers**.

In 1965, **Tony Lane** left and became a member of the **Inbeats**, who later became the **Phoenix Sound. Paul Lofthouse** and **Ronnie Barker** also left and most probably quit show business.

The remaining lead guitarist, **Dennis Conroy**, re-formed the group with former member, **Alan Walton** (bg), who returned from the recently disbanded **Soul Seekers**.

The other new members were **Peter Wheelen** on drums and a singer and rhythm guitarist with the name **Gary**, whose surname is not known, but it is known that he had also been a member of the **Soul Seekers**. This new line-up only continued for a short time as the **Premiers** and then they followed the stupid fashion (at that time) of naming a group after popular TV dolls or puppets.

So in 1965, the **Premiers** became the **Gonks**, but when the musicians found out that there was already a group of the same name in the south of England, the Liverpool outfit changed into the **Mersey Gonks**. But the musicians quickly found out that this new name did not help in making any sort of a breakthrough, so then the group became the **Pityful**, another unfortunate choice of names!

Regardless, under the leadership of **Dennis Conroy**, the group only continued until the end of 1966.

During that time, they did not make any more recordings and nothing is known about any other outstanding success they may have had but, obviously, there were some more personnel changes in the group, as for a short time, an organ and a saxophone was added to the line-up. Unfortunately, the names of the musicians are not known. After they split up, all members disappeared from the scene.

It is only known that the former leader, **Tony Lane,** later played in **Barney Rubble's Boosband**, a seven-piece group that had some appearances on BBC Radio One.

Discography :

as **The Premiers** :

Beautiful Delilah / Skinny Minnie/ I'm Blue / Honest I Do   **UK- Deroy acetate / 1964**

EARL PRESTON'S REALMS

This band was formed by **George Spruce** (aka **Earl Preston**) in Liverpool in 1964. Before that he had sung with **Gene Day & the Django Beats**, the **Comets** and the **TT's** (under the name **Earl Preston & the TT's**). As a singer, **Earl Preston** had outstanding success on the scene at the time and today he is considered to be one of the real Merseybeat legends.

Earl Preston's Realms, in their original line-up, consisted of the following musicians:

Earl Preston	**(voc)**
Tony Priestly	**(lg/voc)**
John Caulfield	**(bg/voc)**
Dave Tynan	**(org)**
Tommy Husky	**(sax)**
Tommy Kelly	**(dr)**

Tony Priestly was a former member of **Mike & the Merseymen** and the **Beatcombers**, while **Tommy Kelly** had previously played with **Danny Royl & the Strollers**, the **Sensations**, the **Young Ones** and **Rikki Janson & the Q-Kats**, which were one and the same group under different names.

Tommy Husky had previously played with **John Paul & the Deejays** and the **Nashpool**.

In 1964, **Earl Preston's Realms** were signed to Fontana and in the same year, their first single was released with an interesting version of the **Dee Clark** classic, "Raindrops".

In spite of its quality, this record was not successful, but it is a desired collector's item today.

John Caulfield left to join the new band of the former **Roadrunners** member **Mike Hart**, which probably was **Henry's Handful** at that time.

Earl Preston's Realms

He was replaced by **Brian Norris**. Unfortunately, his former group is not known.

After the recordings "I'll Be Doggone", "Blue Monday", "Missing You", "Nobody But You" and "Daddy Rolling Stone" for the live compilation 'Liverpool Today', which was released on Ember in 1965, **Brian Norris** left and joined the **Cryin' Shames**. He later played with the **Dimensions** who, at that time, were a trio. The **Dimensions** ultimately became **Jet** and after that **Pendulum**. In the Seventies, he was a member of the newly formed **Tiffany's Dimensions**.

His replacement in **Earl Preston's Realms** was **Charlie Smullan** who came from **Cy Tucker & the Friars**. Before that, he had played with **Wayne Calvert & the Cimarrons**.

In August 1965, the band had a recording test with Decca where the song, "Memory Of Our Love", was recorded but, unfortunately, never released. The group was then signed to CBS and with "Hard Time Loving You", another great single was released in 1966 - but only under the name of the **Realm**, even though **Earl Preston** was still their singer.

This record was not too successful and did not help the band achieve any sort of a breakthrough.

> **FIRST EVER FABULOUSLY EXCITING**
>
> ## ALL NITE BEAT BOAT
>
> *Starring these Top Groups*
>
> ★ THE CLAYTON SQUARES ★ EARL PRESTON'S REALMS
> ★ THE HIDEAWAYS ★ ST. LOUIS CHECKS
> ★ THE ROAD RUNNERS ★ AMOS BONNEY & THE TTs
>
> *and Special Guest Stars*
>
> ### THE SENSATIONAL MEASLES
>
> ---
>
> MIDNIGHT EASTER SUNDAY, 18th APRIL, 1965
> **IMPORTANT!** SEE OVERLEAF   N⁰ 1648

After that, **Tommy Kelly** left to join the **Escorts** and he was replaced by **Ritchie Galvin**, a former member of the **Galvanisers** and **Earl Preston & the TT's**, but he soon went on to join **Gerry De Ville & the City Kings** and was replaced in the **Realm** by **Tommy Hart**, another former member of **Cy Tucker & the Friars** and **Wayne Calvert & the Cimarrons**.

There were probably some more changes in the line-up before the group disbanded in 1968.

Even though **Earl Preston's Realms** or the **Realm**, as they were named later, did not achieve international stardom, they were one of the very good and significant Liverpool groups, which are still remembered today.

Tony Priestly later emigrated to Canada and **Tommy Husky** joined the **Detours**, before he became a session musician in the British Rockabilly scene of the Nineties and also recorded some solo albums.

Earl Preston joined the quite popular **Reflections**, where he sang until 1979. After that, he, together with **John Lloyd**, a former member of the **Kirkbys**, formed a cabaret duo under the name, the **Raffels**, before he quit show business for years and went back to a normal day job.

In 1987, **Earl Preston** re-appeared on the scene, playing the Liverpool clubs as a solo act under the name **Joey Preston** and he still proves that he is an excellent vocalist.

<u>Discography :</u>

as **Earl Preston's Realms** :

Raindrops / That's For Sure	**UK-Fontana TF 481 / 1964**

as **The Realm** :

Hard Time Loving You / A Certain Kind Of Girl	**UK- CBS 202044 / 1966**

<u>tracks on compilation albums :</u>

as **Earl Preston's Realms**:

I'll Be Doggone	on **'Liverpool Today'**	**UK- Ember 5028 / 1965**
Blue Monday	on **'Liverpool Today'**	**UK- Ember 5028 / 1965**
Missing You	on **'Liverpool Today'**	**UK- Ember 5028 / 1965**
Nobody But You	on **'Liverpool Today'**	**UK- Ember 5028 / 1965**
Daddy Rolling Stone	on **'Liverpool Today'**	**UK- Ember 5028 / 1965**

<u>Unreleased tracks :</u>

In 1965, **Earl Preston's Realms** had a recording test with Decca but, unfortunately, the song, "Memory Of Our Love", was never released.

EARL PRESTON & THE T.T.s

In the beginning, they were **Johnny Tempest & the Tornadoes**, formed in Liverpool in 1958, in a line-up with **Johnny Tempest** (voc), **Lance Railton** (lg), **Dave Gore** (rg), **Wally Sheppard** (bg) and **Rod Cameron** (dr). They were one of the early Liverpool Rock 'n' Roll groups that became very popular within a short period of time. Because of an illness, **Johnny Tempest** had to leave at the beginning of the Sixties and, a little later, he sadly died at a very young age.

Johnny Tempest & the Tornadoes

His place in the group was taken by **Billy 'Faron' Ruffley** and the band continued as **Faron & the Tempest Tornadoes**, but then they shortened their name to **Faron & the T.T.s**.

Rod Cameron left to join **Karl Terry & the Cruisers** and was replaced by **Donald Singleton**, who had adopted the stage-name of **Don Alcyd**, he came from **Tommy & the Metronomes**.

In this line-up **Faron & the T.T.s** recorded an acetate in the Kensington studios of **Percy Phillips** with the songs 'Wedding Bells', 'Red Sails In The Sunset', 'Wooden Heart' and 'Cheatin' Heart'.

When '**Faron**' left to join the newly formed **Flamingos**, that group changed their name to **Faron's Flamingos** and wrote Merseybeat history.

Faron's replacement in the **T.T.s** was **George Spruce**, who had formerly led the groups, **Gene Day & the Django-Beats** and the **Comets**.

George Spruce, who was formerly known as **Gene Day**, changed his stage name to **Earl Preston** and the band continued under the name of **Earl Preston & the T.T.s**.

Around this time, drummer, **Don Alcyd**, left to join the **Renegades** from Liverpool and later, among others, he also played with **Lee Curtis & the All Stars** and the **Delmont Four** for a time.

He was replaced by **Richard Hughes**, who had chosen the stage name **Ritchie Galvin**, as he was a former member of the **Galvanisers**.

In 1961, the group was joined by **Cy Tucker** as an additional member, who played guitar and became the second lead singer. **Cy Tucker**, whose real name is **Thomas Thornton**, was the former leader of the **Cimarrons**.

As a result of all these changes, **Earl Preston & the T.T.s**, in 1962, appeared in the following line-up:

Earl Preston	(voc)
Cy Tucker	(voc/g)
Lance Railton	(lg)
Dave Gore	(rg)
Wally Sheppard	(bg)
Ritchie Galvin	(dr)

In June 1963, **Dave Gore** left the group and quit show business. One month later, **Earl Preston & the T.T.s** were featured on the Oriole compilations, 'This Is Merseybeat' Vol. 1 and Vol. 2, with the songs, "Thumbin' A Ride" (sung by **Earl Preston**), as well as with "Hurt" and "All Around The World", which were both sung by **Cy Tucker**.

Because these songs had such a great quality, the group was immediately signed to Fontana. A few weeks later, their first single was released, but "I Know Something", an original by the group, did not make it, although it was a good song. It was coupled with a great version of "Watch Your Step". Both songs featured the lead vocals of **Earl Preston**.

In September 1963, the band backed **Eden Kane** on his single "Like I Love You", which was not too successful but, when the **T.T.s** backed the same singer four months later on "Boys Cry", it became a Top 10 hit. Unfortunately, the group was not given any credit on the label and so this success did not help the band in any way.

Earl Preston & the T.T.s then cut a great version of "Beautiful Delilah" for Fontana but, for mysterious reasons, this was not released. Their next single was released under the name of **Cy Tucker with Earl Preston's T.T.s**, but the great ballad, "My Prayer", also failed to make the charts.

In 1964, **Earl Preston** left the group to form **Earl Preston's Realms** who, after their first single release, changed their name to the **Realm**, which is another story in this book.

The **T.T.s** continued under the name, **Cy Tucker & the T.T.s,** but did not make any more recordings.

Cy Tucker also left very soon after to form **Cy Tucker & the Friars**, that mainly consisted of former members of the **Cimarrons** or **Wayne Calvert & the Cimarrons**, as they were named after **Cy Tucker** had left them.

Eden Kane

He was replaced in the **T.T.s** by **Vic Wright**, who had formerly led the groups, **Pete Picasso & the Rock-Sculptors** and **Vic & the Spidermen**, the latter being very popular on the Liverpool music scene.

Vic & The T.T.s then recorded the originals, "Miss You Baby", "If You Would" and "Somewhere, Somehow, Sometime", for Decca. The latter one was written by **Earl Preston** and **Lance Railton**, while the other two were solo compositions by **Lance Railton**. For unknown reasons these songs were never released.

Still in 1964, **Vic Wright** left to form the group, **Vic Takes Four**. This new group had their debut at the 'Cavern' on August 9th, 1964. They became quite popular on the local scene but they split up after a very short time together. According to the 'Mersey Beat' newspaper, in October 1965, **Vic Wright** was a member of **The Script**, but this is not absolutely certain. He later emigrated to Australia where he is still living.

The new singer with the **T.T.s** was a newcomer on the scene. His real name was **Ronnie Cotton**, but he adopted the stage name, **Amos Bonny**, and so the group continued as **Amos Bonny & the T.T.s**.

But this also did not last too long and no records were ever released, which is very hard to understand because it was a really good group with a talented songwriter in **Lance Railton**.

Amos Bony & the TT's

Regardless, **Amos Bonny** left the group to join the **Defenders**, after that, he sang with the Liverpool **Easybeats**, and, in 1968, with a group called **Mumble**.

Around the same time, **Wally Sheppard** also left and quit show business. The new members of the **T.T.s** were the 'Sheik of Shake', **Karl Terry** (voc/g) and **Gordon Evans** (bg), whose real name is **Gordon Loughlin**.

Karl Terry, under his real name **Terence Connor**, was a former member of the **Gamblers Skiffle Group**, **Terry Connor & the Teen Aces**, **Karl Terry & the Cruisers**, **Group One** and the **Delemeres**.

Karl Terry & the T.T.s, as the group was now named, continued until 1966 and broke up when **Lance Railton** left and joined the **Clayton Squares**.

Initially, it was planned to add **Neil Ford** as a new guitarist to the line-up who, at that time, was a member of the **Vaaveros**, but he decided to join **Johnny Ringo & the Colts** instead.

L to R: Karl Terry, Ritchie Galvin, Amos Bonny (aka Ronnie Cotton), Gordon Loughlin & Lance Railton

Karl Terry and Gordon Evans joined the Talismen who had just parted from Vince Earl. But then the two of them re-formed the T.T.s again, as a trio, together with Ritchie Galvin.

This only lasted for a very short time and then Karl Terry and Gordon Evans teamed up again with Lance Railton and the remaining members of the just disbanded, Clayton Squares, under the name of the T-Squares. This group, who then sometimes appeared as the Clayton Squares again, did not exist too long and, after some personnel changes and two Germany tours in 1967 and 1968, faded away.

Karl Terry became the bass guitarist with Rory Storm & the Hurricanes. After that, he played with a group called Capricorn and then he re-formed Karl Terry & the Cruisers, who are still going strong on the scene.

Gordon Evans (aka Gordon Loughlin) disappeared from the scene for years but, in 1990, he was a member of Johnny Guitar & his Hurricanes.

After the T-Squares, Lance Railton was a member of the re-formed Karl Terry & the Cruisers. Sadly, he died on Christmas eve 1989 at the very young age of 46.

Ritchie Galvin initially joined Earl Preston's Realms, but he did not stay for too long and then he joined Gerry De Ville & the City Kings. After that, he became a member of Liverpool's Country scene and played with groups that included the Kentuckians, Phil Brady & the Ranchers and later with a Country & Western band called Western Union.

When Lance Railton died, Earl Preston & the T.T.s came together again for a charity concert in a line-up with Earl Preston, Karl Terry, Dave Gore, Wally Sheppard and Ritchie Galvin. They later did a few concerts for 'MerseyCats' and then split up again.

Earl Preston & the TT's

But the formerly retired Wally Sheppard and Dave Gore remained in the music business. After they had played for a short time with Karl Terry & the Cruisers, both joined the newly formed Cliff Roberts' Rockers, who did not last for too long, but occasionally played for the 'MerseyCats' organisation.

After that, both musicians formed the group, Persuader, which later became Rocket 88. Then Dave Gore left and became the roadie for Cy Tucker, before he retired again.

Wally Sheppard today plays with a group called **Tempest**.

Earl Preston is also active again and, under the name of **Joey Preston,** he sings to backing tapes in the Liverpool clubs. **Ritchie Galvin** sadly died in July 2001.

In spite of the fact that **Earl Preston & the T.T.s** never achieved international stardom or had any chart success in their own right, they are one of the Merseybeat legends that will certainly never be forgotten.

Single discography :

as **Faron & the T.T. s** :

Wedding Bells / Red Sails In The Sunset / Wooden Heart/ Cheatin' Heart	UK-Phillips acetate EP / 1961

as **Earl Preston & the T.T.s** :

I Know Something / Watch Your Step	UK- Fontana TF 406 / 1963

as **Cy Tucker with Earl Preston's T.T.s** :

My Prayer / High School Dance	UK- Fontana TF 424 / 1963

as backing-group for **Eden Kane** :

Like I Love You / Come Back	UK- Fontana TF 413 / 1963
Boys Cry / Don't Come Crying To Me	UK- Fontana TF 438 / 1964

Tracks on compilation albums : (all as **Earl Preston & the T.T.s**)

Thumbin' A Ride	on 'This Is Merseybeat' Vol. 1	UK- Oriole PS 40047 / 1963
Hurt	on 'This Is Merseybeat' Vol. 1	UK- Oriole PS 40047 / 1963
All Around The World	on 'This Is Merseybeat' Vol. 2	UK- Oriole PS 40048 / 1963

Unissued tracks :

As unreleased tracks, the following **Earl Preston & the T.T.s** songs are known: "**Too Much Monkey-Business**", "**Betty Jean**", "**Please Believe Me**", "**Why Did It Have To Be You**", "**Back Again To Me**" and "**Beautiful Delilah**" ;

As **Cy Tucker & the T.T.s** the songs, "**Bonie Moronie**" (great version!!!) and "**I Apologize**" ;

As **Eden Kane with Earl Preston & the T.T.s** the tunes, "**Gonna Make A Comeback**" and "**Do You Love Me**".

All the above mentioned songs were recorded for Fontana in the years 1963 and 1964.

In addition, **Vic Wright & the T.T.s** recorded the songs, "**Miss You Baby**", "**If You Would**" and "**Somewhere, Somehow, Sometime**" for Decca in 1964.

THE PRESTONS

This group remained relatively unknown on the national music scene during its lifetime, but on Merseyside, and especially in its hometown, Preston, it was popular, even if only briefly.

History tells us that they originated from the **Downbeats**, that were formed in 1962. Some people say that it was this group who backed **Eden Kane** on "I Won't Believe Them", the B-side of his 1963 single, "Tomorrow Night". This was definitely a completely different group and there is also nothing else known about any recordings by this Preston group.

The **Downbeats** from Preston changed their name into the **Prestons** in 1963 and, at this time, the group consisted of the following musicians:

Robb Deka	**(voc/p)**
Roger James	**(g/voc)**
Andy Leigh	**(bg)**
Gene Richie	**(dr)**

Robb Deka, whose real name is **Robert Eccles**, had already played with the Preston groups, the **Crusaders**, the **Strangers**, the **Falcons** and with **David John & the Mood**. After that, he had made a test recording for **Joe Meek** in London on which he was backed by the **Puppets**, who also hailed from Preston. It is known that all the recorded songs were originals by **Robb Deka**, but there was never anything released.

Roger James formerly was a member of **Danny Storm & the Strollers**. He was also with **Robby Hood & the Merrymen** in Germany, **Eddie King & the Chequers** and the **Johnny Woolaston Band** when they came to Preston as the resident band at the 'Top Rank Ballroom'.

Andy Leigh was a former member of the **Corries**, while **Gene Richie**, whose real name is **Gene Carberry**, formerly played with the **Crusaders**, the **Questions** and had toured Poland with the **Atoms**.

The **Prestons** were very active songwriters and, by 1964, they had already written 70 of their own compositions!

That could have been why **Joe Meek** became interested and arranged a contract with Columbia for them. They recorded the songs, "I Love You", "That's What We're Going To Do", "I'll Get Over You" and "Good To You". In the music paper, 'Combo', in April 1964, there was a notice that their first single was to be released very soon, but this was not followed by a release - at least not from the **Prestons** in their own right.

In 1964, however, there was the single, "Hear You Talking", released on the Parlophone label by **Beverly Jones & the Prestons** and it is almost certain that these were the **Prestons** from Preston.

This record is the only known release by the group who eventually disbanded in 1964.

Gene Richie

Andy Leigh

Robb Deka went to Liverpool and became a member of the **Nashpool Four**, who then shortened their name to **The Nashpool**. From there, he went down to London and joined **Flip & the Dateliners** as their organist for a tour of Germany. When they returned, **Flip** parted from the group and **Rob Deka** took over the lead vocals and the group continued on as the **Dateliners**.

He remained in the business as a vocalist. In 1976, he changed his name to **Robb Shenton** and, in 1980, he recorded the Meek tribute, "Lonely Joe", co-produced by **Clem Cattini**, who also played drums on it. After a long break, he recently started an impressive recording comeback as **Robb Shenton & the Western All Stars**.

Roger James, who had caused the group's split-up due to his leaving them after a gig in London, became the leader of the **Roger James Four**, who cut two great Beat singles for Columbia with "Letter From Kathy" (with its terrific B-side "Leave Me Alone") and "Better Than Here". He then was a member of **Hobbyshop** and, after that, led the **Roger James Group**, that also recorded.

Gene Richie joined the **Executives** of "March Of The Mods" fame and, after that, played with the **Wheels** from Belfast, with whom he recorded some great records in 1965 and 1966.

Andy Leigh became a member of **Matthews Southern Comfort**, with whom he appeared at the legendary Woodstock Festival.

Discography :

As far as it is known, there was never a record release credited to the **Prestons** only, although there was an advance notice in the 'Combo' newspaper in April 1964 suggesting an upcoming release.

In 1964, there was a single released by **Beverly Jones & the Prestons** and it can be assumed that this at least was associated with the Merseybeat group from Preston.

The **Prestons** recorded the originals, **"I Love You"**, **"That's What We're Going To Do"**, **"I'll Get Over You"** and **"Good To You"** – produced by **Joe Meek** for Columbia in 1964, but these songs were never released.

as **Beverly Jones & the Prestons** :

Hear You Talking / Heat Wave   **UK- Parlophone R 5189 / 1964**

as **The Roger James Four** :

Letter From Kathy / Leave Me Alone   **UK- Columbia DB 7556 / 1965**

Better Than Here / You're Gonna Come Home Cryin'

UK- Columbia DB 7813 / 1966

THE PROFILES

This typical Merseybeat group was formed by **Peter Feldman** in Liverpool in August 1963. By the beginning of 1964, the **Profiles** had established themselves as one of the leading and busiest groups on the local scene, although **Peter Feldman** had to struggle with changes in the line-up from the start. This might have been the main reason that they did not make any sort of a breakthrough.

The original line-up of the **Profiles** consisted of:

Peter Feldman	(voc)
Dave Williams	(g/voc)
Carl Stevenson	(g)
Paul Eker	(bg)
Jimmy Lacey	(dr)

Paul Eker came from the recently disbanded **City Beats**, while **Dave Williams** was a former member of a group called the **Pacifics**, who most probably were not the forerunner group of the **Merseybeats**. While the possible association with the **Merseybeats** is not known for certain - it is known for certain that **Dave Williams** was not the guitarist of the same name who played with **Dale Roberts & the Jaywalkers**, **Group One** and the **Four Originals**.

It was probably this line-up of the **Profiles** that went into the Eroica studios in Eccles and recorded their first acetate with the songs, "My Heart Is Broken", "Sensation", "I Can Tell" and the somewhat Skiffle sounding,

"If You Love Me", all apparently written by **Peter Feldman**.

In August 1964, **Jimmy Lacey** left to join **Johnny Templer & the Hi-Cats** and, after that, he played with **Chick Graham & the Coasters** and the **Three Cheers**, who later changed their name to **Phase Three**. His replacement in the **Profiles** was **Pete Wiggins**, who came from the recently disbanded **Mafia Group**.

Dave Williams also left and was replaced by **Eddie Gaye**

The Profiles

and, when a little later, **Paul Eker** left to join the **Kruzads**, the new bass-guitarist for the **Profiles** was **John Owen**.

Then **Carl Stevenson**, the last remaining original member besides **Peter Feldman,** left in 1964 and was not replaced.

Peter Feldman took over the guitar and the group continued as a quartet, probably under the name of the **Profiles Four**.

Eddie Gaye then left and the guitarists, **Joey Molland** and **Alan Stock,** arrived as new members. **Joey Molland** had formerly played with the **Assasins.**

The group changed its name again - this time into **Peter & the Profiles.** Obviously, **Peter Feldman** wanted to point out that, in spite of all the changes in the line-up, he was still with the group.

In October 1964, **Joey Molland** left to join the **Masterminds** and later became a member of the **Fruit Eating Bears.** He had a short spell with the **Cryin' Shames** down in London and, in 1967, joined **Gary Walker & Rain.** 1969 saw him as a member of the hit group, **Badfinger,** who still appear sporadically on the scene under his leadership, mainly in the USA.

His replacement was **Carl Stevenson** who returned to the **Profiles** (they had reverted to using their original name again).

It is probable that this line-up recorded the demos, "My Baby Kissed Me" and "You Know She's Mine", both written by **Peter Feldman** once again. He was obviously a talented songwriter and it is hard to understand why the group was never signed to a recording company.

Sometime in the mid-Sixties, the **Profiles** disbanded totally. Of **Pete Wiggins,** it is known that he joined the **Kruzads.** All the other members disappeared from the scene.

It can be assumed that there had been some more personnel changes in the interim and that **Peter Feldman** continued with his efforts to find a consistent line-up for his group.

That the name of the **Profiles** is still well remembered these days is doubtless credit to **Peter Feldman** and to him alone.

Discography :

The Profiles never released a record but recorded the following demos on acetate that featured the exceptional original numbers of **Peter Feldman**:

My Heart Is Broken / If You Love Me / I Can't Tell / Sensation	**UK- Eroica - acetate / 1963**
My Baby Kissed Me / You Know She's Mine	**UK- Eroica - acetate / 1964**

THE PUPPETS

In retrospect, it can be stated that this group, in some way, originated from **Bob Johnson & the Bobcats**, a local pioneer-group in Preston, Lancashire that disbanded in late 1962.

Their drummer **Des O'Reilly**, who formerly had played with the **Rebels**, had a short stint with **Rory Storm & the Hurricanes**. He then met up again with his former guitarist from the **Bobcats** and, together with the bassist from the **Thunderbeats,** they re-formed the **Bobcats** as a trio, which was quickly recruited by local singer, **Robb Deka,** to back him on some test recordings for **Joe Meek**.

The legendary producer was impressed with the trio, took them under his management and christened them the **Puppets** – in the line-up with:

Dave Millen	(g/voc)
Jim Whittle	(bg/voc)
Des O'Reilly	(voc/dr)

After some recording sessions which included "Little Bitty Pretty One", "Zip-A-Dee-Doo-Da", "Roll Over Beethoven" and "Money", in September 1963, the first single by the **Puppets** was released on PYE with the original, "Everybody's Talking", and a great version of "Poison Ivy".

Unfortunately, the record did not make it but PYE kept the contract and their next single, another original with the title, "Three Boys Lookin' For Love", was recorded but withdrawn for unknown reasons.

In May 1964, "Baby Don't Cry" was released but, again, it failed to make the charts.

Maybe that was the reason for PYE to drop the **Puppets**, but they kept very busy on the scene and established a good name for themselves.

In 1965, they were joined by **Don Parfitt** (org/p/voc) from the **Keys** as an additional member.

The **Puppets**, beside having their own career, backed lots of well known singing stars such as, Liverpudlians **Billy Fury** and **Michael Cox**. They also supported many top American acts, including **Brenda Lee,** the **Ronettes** and **Gene Vincent** on their British tours.

Still in 1965, they went on tour with **Gene Vincent** in Scotland and then Germany, where they mainly played the 'Star-Club' circuit.

1966 was another good year for the **Puppets**, as they became the backing group for **Crispian St. Peters** who had just had a big hit with "You Were On My Mind". They toured all over England with him, where amongst other venues, they played the 'Cavern' in Liverpool, and they very likely also accompanied him on his European tour.

For the BBC radio show, 'Saturday Club', the **Puppets** and **Crispian St. Peters** recorded "You Were On My Mind", "Peggy Sue Got Married", "Darlin'", "That's The Way I Feel" and "Lonely". The **Puppets** also recorded two solo numbers, "My Name Is Mud" and a great version of "My Girl", for that same show. Unfortunately, none of these songs were ever released on a record.

The **Puppets** disbanded in 1967 and **Des O'Reilly** and **Dave Millen**, together with **Dave 'Daz' Smith** formed another trio under the name of **Three-D**, who were sometimes joined by **David John** as an additional singer.

Des O'Reilly left **Three-D** and went solo on the cabaret circuit. In 1979, he emigrated to Australia where he is still living and active in show business.

Three-D with **Fred Kelly** as their new drummer, together with **David John**, evolved into the recording group, **Thundermother**.

Dave Millen went to London and, among others, played with a group called the **Hi-Guys**.

Don Parfitt later was a member of the groups, **Stax Of Soul** and **Soul Review**. Of **Jim Whittle**, it is said that, in the Seventies, he was a member of the **Four Just Men** but then retired from playing.

Discography :

Everybody's Talking / Poison Ivy	UK - PYE 7N 15558 / 1963
Baby Don't Cry / Shake With Me	UK - PYE 7N 15634 / 1964

(besides this, the single, "**Three Boys Lookin' For Love / Shake With Me**" (**PYE 7N 15625**), was recorded but withdrawn in 1964)

Unreleased tracks :

From the **Joe Meek** recording sessions the following numbers are known:

"**Zip-A-Dee-Doo-Da**", "**Roll Over Beethoven**", "**Money**" and "**Little Bitty Pretty One**" - all from 1963.

In 1966, the **Puppets** recorded the numbers, "**My Name Is Mud**" and "**My Girl**", for the popular BBC radio show, 'Saturday Club', and, besides this, for that same show they backed **Crispian St. Peters** on "**You Were On My Mind**", "**Peggy Sue Got Married**", "**Darlin'** ", "**That's The Way I Feel**" and "**Lonely**".

The details of their very first recordings with **Robb Deka** for **Joe Meek** are not known with the exception that they all were originals by the group.

THE RAINCHECKS

To describe the complete development of this interesting band, it is necessary to start with the stories of two other groups, as there were some very important connections and interchanges.

The first group is **Wump & his Werbles**, formed on the Wirral in the late Fifties and consisting of **Rod 'Wump' Pont** (voc), **Dave Georgeson** (g), **Neville Humphries** (g), **Jim Mellor** (bg) and **John Cochran** (dr).

John Cochran was a former member of **Gus & the Thundercaps** and **Gus Travis & the Midnighters**.

Wump & his Werbles, in spite of being quite popular, disbanded very early on.

Neville Humphries and **Jim Mellor** quit show business, while **Dave Georgeson** and **John Cochran**, together with **Ian McQuair**, also a former member of **Gus & the Thundercaps** and **Gus Travis & the Midnighters**, formed a new group under the name, **The Lil' Three**, that later changed their name into the **Chuckles**. **Rod Pont** became a popular Merseybeat singer under the name, **Steve Day**.

The second group is **Johnny Rocco & the Jets** from Wallasey, one of the pioneering groups of the Merseybeat scene. They consisted of **Johnny Rocco** (voc/g), whose real name is **Graham Hodgson**, **Mike Nicholson** (g), **Spike Jones** (g), **Derek Bond** (bg) and **Phil Duggan** (dr). Because **Johnny Rocco** had a bad throat, he had to give up singing and left the group to join **Frank Knight & the Barons** as their drummer. Later, he was active for a long time as a guitarist in the clubs of Tenerife/Spain.

His place in the **Jets** was taken by **Rod Pont** and during the early sixties the band continued under the name, **Steve Day & the Jets,** but then changed to **Steve Day & the Drifters**.

Mike Nicholson left and was replaced by **Barry Ezzra**, who came from **Vince Earl & the Zeros** and, before that, he was a member of the **Firecrests**.

Steve Day & the Drifters became very popular on the scene until **Steve Day** left the band in May 1963 to join the **Black Jays** from London. Back in Liverpool, he first appeared with the **Kingfishers** but then formed **Steve Day & the Kinsmen**, but that is another story in this book.

The remaining **Drifters** became the backing group for **Gus Travis**, the former leader of **Gus & the Thundercaps** and **Gus Travis & the Midnighters**.

This new co-operation continued under the name of **Gus Travis & the Rainchecks** but then, **Gus Travis** left the group.

Around the same time, **Spike Jones** and **Derek Bond** left the band. **Spike Jones** is most probably the musician of the same name who later played the organ with both the **Griff Parry Five** and the **Steve Aldo Quintet** that evolved from it.

The Rainchecks

Midlands Office
K. D. S. Enterprises
Sutton Coldfield 3070
Warwickshire

Sole Representation

Northern Office
Darville Entertainments
Wallasey 1421
Cheshire

Derek Bond became the new bass guitarist with **Derry Wilkie & the Others**, that later evolved into the recording group, **This 'n' That**, or their shorter name, **TNT**.

The **Rainchecks** continued in their own right with the following line-up:

Barry Ezzra	(voc/g)
Graham Nugent	(g/voc)
Colin Briscoe	(bg/voc)
Phil Duggan	(dr)

Colin Briscoe and **Graham Nugent** both were former members of the **Scorpions** from Wallasey.

This new line-up very soon earned a good name in the north of England music scene and was signed to the new record label, 'Solar'. Their first single was released towards the end of 1964 with "Something About You", coupled with the nice Beat ballad, "My Angel".

Both numbers were **Barry Ezzra** compositions. This was a very good Beat record which was highly praised by a number of critics and sold very well on the local scene. Much of the credit being due to the extensive publicity it received. But Solar was not able to publicize the record on the international market, probably because the distribution system of that new label had not matured enough yet.

Keep the Liverpool light burning by sending your latest Recording Group up the Charts!!

THE DYNAMIC

RAINCHECKS

"Something About You"

Available from your local Record Shop on Solar Records S.R.P.104

Management: Darville Entertainments

WALLASEY 1421 & 2484

Also, at the same session, a version of **Chris Kenner**'s "Something You Got" may have been recorded, but this was never released.

"Something About You" did not become a hit, but the **Rainchecks** toured Europe shortly after its release. The tour was successful, particularly in Germany where, amongst others, they played the 'Star-Palast' in Kiel, the 'Savoy' in Hannover and another big club in Braunschweig.

They were one of the hopeful 'new' groups in Liverpool. Unfortunately, they were a little bit too late to make any sort of a breakthrough because, by this time, Merseybeat had already started to lose ground on the international music scene. Later, little was heard of the **Rainchecks** even though they had successfully established themselves among the leading groups on Merseyside, where they regularly appeared at all the major venues.

If the **Rainchecks** had come together earlier in this line-up and, if they had found the right manager, they probably would have had greater success, perhaps even internationally, because they were one of the really good groups from Merseyside.

But they had 'missed the boat' and no further records were released, as Solar very soon faded from the scene and there was no contract signed with any other record company.

It was probably still in 1965 when the **Rainchecks** disbanded and, apart from **Graham Nugent**, who joined the re-formed **Pilgrims**, none of the individual members appeared on the scene again until a type of revival took place in the early Nineties, when the **Rainchecks** appeared again at the 'MerseyCats' and the 'New Brighton Rock' organisations' charity concerts.

The **Rainchecks**, who only appeared occasionally, always included **Phil Duggan** and **Graham Nugent** and sometimes **Barry Ezzra** and **Colin Briscoe**.

<u>Single discography :</u>

Something About You / My Angel   **UK- Solar SRP 104 / 1964**

<u>Unreleased tracks :</u>

It is said that at the session for the above single, the **Rainchecks** also recorded a version of **Chris Kenner**'s "**Something You Got**", which was never released, maybe due to the failure of 'Solar' records.

(Please note that the single, "How Are You Boy", which was released on the 'R&B' label by a group called the **Rainchecks** in 1965, was definitely not by this Liverpool/Wallasey outfit)

THE RATS

This real Rhythm & Blues group hailed from Wigan near Liverpool, where it was formed in 1963.

With **Jimmy Jenkins**, they had a manager from the Beat capital. So the group, besides playing throughout Lancashire and the greater Manchester area, became a steady part of Liverpool's Merseybeat scene, where they first appeared in the following line-up:

Allan Parkinson	(voc/harp)
Malcolm Grundy	(g/voc)
Gerry Kenny	(bg)
Bill Geldard	(dr)

In a way, this group was something of an offshoot of the legendary Wigan group, **The Beat Boys**, as **Allan Parkinson** and **Malcolm Grundy** came directly from them and **Gerry Kenny** had also been a short-term member of that same band in 1962.

Prior to their membership in the **Beat Boys, Allan Parkinson** and **Gerry Kenny** were former members of the Martinis. Unfortunately, what **Gerry Kenny** had done prior to joining the Rats and, in which group **Bill Geldard** had previously played, is not known.

IT'S THE
AMAZING
RATS
SINGING
'PARCHMAN FARM'
ORIOLE CB1967

CATCH THEM
NOW 'COS IT'S
IN THE SHOPS

Sole management:
RACHEL ENTERPRISES
Sefton Park 7207

The **Rats** became very popular within a short time, especially in Liverpool, and soon were signed to Oriole who, at that time, had a great interest in Merseybeat groups and were responsible for so many of them taking their first steps into the recording business.

Still, in 1964, the first single of the **Rats** was released with their version of "Parchment Farm", which was also released in Scandinavia.

The song, "Parchment Farm", since the late Fifties, had become something of a Rhythm & Blues classic and, because of that, there were already too many versions on the market. That is probably the reason why this single didn't become a bestseller, though it was a great single in every respect.

Around that time, Oriole was taken over by CBS and the **Rats** released their second single on that label. Once again, "Sack Of Woe" was a pure Rhythm & Blues number and a great recording that showed the outstanding quality of the group. It got some very good critical acclaim but, in the end, it was not a great success.

There were also two singles, "Gotta See My Baby" and "Spoonful", released by a group called the **Rats** on the Columbia label in 1965, but this definitely was not the group from Wigan.

After the CBS-release, **Allan Parkinson**, who in the meantime had adopted the stage name **Dave Allen**, left the **Rats** and formed a new group under the name of **Dave Allen & the Exotics** who had a long and successful residency in Italy, but that is another story in this book.

★ THE RATS C B S RECORDING ARTISTS ★ RACHEL ENTERPRISES Sefton Park 7202

For quite some time, little was heard of the **Rats**, but they stepped back into the limelight when, sometime in 1966, they became the backing group for the very popular Liverpool singer, **Mark Peters**, whose real name was **Peter Fleming** and who had previously sung with the groups, **Dean Fleming & the Flamingos**, the **Teen Tones**, the **Hi-Spots**, **Mark Peters & the Cyclones**, **Mark Peters & the Silhouettes** and **Mark Peters & the Method**.

Mark Peters & the Rats, as they were called now, became quite successful on the scene but did not release any records. In 1967, **Mark Peters** separated from the group and later emigrated to Sri Lanka, where he lived until he died a few years ago.

The **Rats** disbanded totally in 1967 and only of **Malcolm Grundy** is it known that he later went to Italy to join **The Bigs**, which was the new name adopted by the **Exotics** after **Dave Allen** had left to start a solo career. It should be noted that **Dave Allen** also recorded as **Al Torino** and later as **Guy Challenger**.

Single discography :

Parchment Farm / Every Day I Have The Blues   UK- Oriole CB 1967 / 1964

Sack Of Woe / Gimme That Wine   UK- CBS 201 740 / 1965

(Please note that the two singles by the **Rats** on the Columbia label were certainly not by this Wigan band)

THE REMO FOUR

This story could, of course, have been featured in this book under the name **Johnny Sandon & the Remo Four** or **Tommy Quickly & the Remo Four** but, as one name had to be selected, the **Remo Four** is probably the best solution. While the **Remo Four** obviously played and recorded in their own right, their story also includes the various singers that were backed by them for a certain period of time.

But let's start at the beginning, when the group was formed in the late Fifties by **Colin Manley** in Liverpool under the name, the **Remo Quartet**, but soon changed their name to **The Remo Four**.

The original line-up consisted of **Colin Manley** (g/voc), **Don Andrew** (g), **Keith Stokes** (bg) and **Harry Prytherch** (dr). They very soon became one of the most popular groups on Merseyside but, in 1962, **Keith Stokes** and **Harry Prytherch** left to form **Group One**, which is another story in this book.

ROCK! ROCK! ROCK!

This Saturday and Sunday to
- DUKE DUVAL'S ROCKERS
  - REMO QUARTET
    - DERRY AND THE SENIORS
      - METRONOMES

AT

HOLYOAKE JIVE HALL

(Smithdown Road—Near Penny Lane) 7-30

The new members of the **Remo Four** were **Phil Rodgers** (bg) and **Billy Buck** (dr), who both came from the recently disbanded **Dale Roberts & the Jaywalkers**.

When, in 1963, the **Searchers** separated from their singer, **Johnny Sandon**, he joined forces with the **Remo Four** under the name **Johnny Sandon & the Remo Four**.

This development meant the musicians had to become professionals, which was the reason for **Billy Buck** leaving and joining a Liverpool dance band. However, before he left, he suggested his successor be the young **Roy Dyke** who, at that time, was a member of **Karl Terry & the Cruisers**. **Roy Dyke** agreed to join them and, from then on, **Johnny Sandon & the Remo Four** appeared in the following line-up:

Johnny Sandon	(voc)
Colin Manley	(g/voc)
Don Andrew	(g)
Phil Rodgers	(bg)
Roy Dyke	(dr)

JOHNNY SANDON & THE REMO FOUR
(PHIL, ROY, JOHNNY, DON & COLIN)
TEL ROYAL 7749

Still in 1963, the group was signed to PYE and the singles, "Lies" and "Yes", were released, gaining only local success. "Lies" was an original by the group and written by lead guitarist, **Colin Manley**.

354

After these two singles failed to make it, **Johnny Sandon** separated from the group and went solo. He recorded three further singles with "Sixteen Tons", "Donna Means Heartbreak" and "The Blizzard". The last of these was initially released as the B-side of "Sixteen Tons" and then again as an A-side, coupled with "I'd Be A Legend In My Time". These singles showed **Johnny Sandon** to be more of a Country singer than a Beat vocalist. After these releases, none of which were very successful, little was heard of **Johnny Sandon**, who then disappeared from the scene for years. In the mid Nineties he was back with a new group under the name **Johnny Sandon & the Specials**. Then **Johnny Sandon** quit showbiz again and committed suicide in December 1997.

When **Johnny Sandon** left, the **Remo Four** first backed **Gene Pitney** and **Gene Chandler** on their UK tours, but then they got together with the singer, **Tommy Quickly**, who had formerly sung with the **Challengers**. He was the latest signing of **Brian Epstein** and had already released the solo single, "Tip Of My Tongue". **Brian Epstein** was also responsible for his co-operation with the **Remo Four**.

The individual members of the **Remo Four**, as well as playing in their own group, also had a number of sessions, short spells and stand-ins with other Merseyside groups. **Colin Manley** stood in for **Nicky Crouch** with the **Mojos** at one time and **Roy Dyke** for **Tony Mansfield** with **Billy J. Kramer & the Dakotas** at another time, which certainly says something about their musical abilities.

Tommy Quickly & the Remo Four kept their contract with Piccadilly and, in 1964, released a string of records including "Kiss Me Now", "Prove It", the interesting "You Might As Well Forget Him" and the great "Wild Side Of Life", as well as the quite weak "Humpty Dumpty", which at least had a good flip-side with "I'll Go Crazy". From these singles, only "Wild Side Of Life" became successful when it climbed up to no. 33 in the British charts in 1964. It was also released on the European continent and in the USA, where it sold well.

Tommy Quickly

Tommy Quickly and the group separated in 1964, after the **Remo Four** had recorded the singles. "I Wish I Could Shimmy Like My Sister Kate", which was coupled with an incredible version of the instrumental, "Peter Gun", and "Sally Go Round The Roses"/"I Know A Girl". Unfortunately, neither record had any success, but that terrific version of "Peter Gun" was a milestone in the history of Liverpool's Merseybeat.

In addition, the **Remo Four** also backed singer, **Gregory Phillips,** on his single, "Everybody Knows", in 1964, while they were still backing **Tommy Quickly**.

Gregory Phillips, who was not from Liverpool, had previously had a nice single released with "Angie" in 1963. It is also more than probable that the **Remo Four** backed him on his next single, the **George Harrison** composition, "Don't Bother Me". Although they were not named on the label, the backing sound is identical to "Everybody Knows" and one member of the **Remo Four** once stated that they had backed **Gregory Phillips** on two singles. After that, **Gregory Phillips** recorded his version of the **Joe South** composition, "Down In The Boondocks", for Immediate in 1965, which became a big hit for **Billy Joe Royal** in the same year.

Don Andrew left the **Remo Four** to join the **Blue Mountain Showband**, an offshoot of the recording Liverpool Country band, **The Blue Mountain Boys**, which were also quite popular at that time. The **Blue Mountain Showband** later changed their name to the **Quintones**.

He was replaced in the **Remo Four** by **Tony Ashton** (voc/org), who had formerly played with the **College Boys** (from Eton), the **Executives**, the **Tony Ashton Trio**, and also in the backing group of **Jimmy Justice**, the **John Barry Seven**, the **Mastersounds** and **Mike Hurst & the Method**.

In 1965, the **Remo Four** went to Hamburg, where they became a very successful part of the 'Star-Club' scene, but they also appeared at all the other significant clubs in Germany.

Because of their many appearances on the very popular German TV music show, 'Beat-Club', they became well-known all over Germany, and so they re-recorded a version of "Peter Gun", which seemed a little bit harmless in comparison to their Piccadilly recording. In spite of this, and probably because the Germans were unaware of the other version, the German release became something like a hymn of the legendary 'Star-Club' era. The following single, "Live Like A Lady", with a superb version of "Sing Hallelujah" on its reverse side, was not that successful, although it was another masterpiece.

At this time, the sound of the **Remo Four** was already totally different as compared to that of other groups. In retrospect, it can be said that musically they were way ahead of their time and maybe this was the reason that they did not have any great commercial success with their recordings.

This is also valid for their only album, 'Smile', on which the influences of Soul, Blues and Jazz can be found. The full organ and 'rusty' voice of **Tony Ashton** gave their sound a distinctive tone but it was simply not commercial enough for that time.

The attention they deserved was only paid to the **Remo Four** after they had disbanded in 1967.

Of **Phil Rodgers** it is said, that he later went to London and joined a Country band.

Tony Ashton and **Roy Dyke**, together with **Kim Gardner** (ex **Birds** and **Creation**), formed the trio, **Ashton, Gardner & Dyke,** who had a big international hit with "Resurrection Shuffle" and were very successful in the European music scene for years. In 1972, that trio disbanded and **Tony Ashton** joined **Family**, while **Roy Dyke** and **Kim Gardner** formed the band, **Badger**, together with **Brian Parrish** (ex **Londoners** and **Knack**), **Paul Pilnick** (ex **Vince & the Volcanoes**, **Lee Curtis & the All Stars**, **Big Three**, etc.) and **Jackie Lomax** (ex **Undertakers**).

Some time later, **Roy Dyke** returned to Hamburg and appeared again on the scene, where he played a lot of sessions in Hamburg and was also a member of the trio, **Bauer, Garn & Dyke**, who played a sort of modern Rock 'n' Roll and sang in German. He later became a member of the **Shamrocks** and is still living in Hamburg.

After the **Remo Four** split up, **Colin Manley**, certainly one of the best guitarists to come out of England, played in the backing groups of **Clodagh Rodgers** and **Freddie Starr**. He then joined the **Swinging Blue Jeans** in the mid-Seventies, where he played until he sadly died in April 1999 from cancer. **Tony Ashton** also died from cancer in May 2001.

Single discography :

as **Johnny Sandon & the Remo Four** :

Lies / On The Horizon	UK- PYE 7N 15542 / 1963
Yes / Magic Potion	UK- PYE 7N 15559 / 1963

as **Tommy Quickly & the Remo Four** :

Kiss Me Now / No Other Love	UK-Piccadilly 7N 35151 / 1964
Prove It / Haven't You Noticed	UK-Piccadilly 7N 35167 / 1964
You Might As Well Forget Him / It's As Simple As That	UK-Piccadilly 7N 35183 / 1964
Wild Side Of Life / Forget The Other Guy	UK- PYE 7N 15708 / 1964
Humpty Dumpty / I Go Crazy	UK- PYE 7N 15748 / 1964

Unissued tracks :

Tommy Quickly & the Remo Four recorded the **Beatles** song, "**No Reply**", for PYE in 1964. Unfortunately, it was not released.

as **Gregory Phillips & the Remo Four** :

Everybody Knows / Closer To Me	UK- PYE 7N 15593 / 1964

as **The Remo Four** :

I Wish I Could Shimmy Like My Sister Kate / Peter Gun	UK-Piccadilly 7N 35175 / 1964
Sally Go Round The Roses / I Know A Girl	UK-Piccadilly 7N 35186 / 1964

Different German releases :

Peter Gun / Mickey's Monkey	G- Star-Club 14855 STF / 1966
Live Like A Lady / Sing Hallelujah	G- Star-Club 14857 STF / 1967

<u>Unissued tracks :</u>

The **Remo Four** recorded the song, "**The Honeymoon Song**", for PYE in 1964, but it was never released.

<u>Johnny Sandon</u> – solo :

Sixteen Tons / The Blizzard	UK- PYE 7N 15602 / 1964
Donna Means Heartbreak / Some Kinda Wonderful	UK- PYE 7N 15665 / 1964
The Blizzard / I'd Be A Legend In My Time	UK- PYE 7N 15717 / 1964

(Please note that the songs, "**Donna Means Heartbreak**" and "**I'd Be A Legend In My Time**", were most probably still recorded with the **Remo Four,** as these songs can also be found on two acetates that were coupled with the songs, "**Magic Potion**" and "**On The Horizon**", that were both released as the B-sides of the two singles of **Johnny Sandon & the Remo Four**)

<u>Tommy Quickly</u> – solo :

Tip Of My Tongue / Heaven Only Knows	UK-Piccadilly 7N 35137 / 1963

<u>Gregory Phillips</u> – solo :

Angie / Please Believe Me	UK- PYE 7N 15546 / 1963
Don't Bother Me / Make Sure That You're Mine	UK- PYE 7N 15633 / 1964
Down In The Boondocks / That's The One	UK- Immediate IM 004 / 1965

(Please note that the single, "**Don't Bother Me**", was most probably recorded together with the **Remo Four**, as it was stated that the **Remo Four** recorded two singles with **Gregory Phillips** and the sound on the record is absolutely identical with the single of **Gregory Phillips & the Remo Four**)

<u>LP discography (as **The Remo Four**)</u>

SMILE	G-Star-Club 158.034 STY/ 1967

-Peter Gunn / Mickey's Monkey / Heart Beat / The Skate / No Money Down / Rock Candy / The Seventh Son / Roadrunner / Brother Where Are You / Jive Samba / Nothing's Too Good For My Baby / Live Like A Lady / Sing Hallelujah

THE RENEGADES

This group was formed by drummer **Bob Evans** in the Wallasey/Birkenhead area on the west side of the river Mersey in early 1962, after leading both **Bob Evans & the Five Shillings** and the **Vegas Five**, who ultimately evolved into the **Undertakers**.

The **Renegades**, who should not be confused with the 'Cadillac' hit group from Birmingham, were a real Rock 'n' Roll group and very soon developed a good name and a large following on the Liverpool scene. In their original line-up, the group consisted of:

George Peckham	(voc/rg)
Dave Myers	(lg)
Derek Peckham	(bg)
Bob Evans	(dr)

George Peckham was a former member of the **Skylarks** and **Dave Myers** came from the recently disbanded **Climbers**. Before that, he had played with **Cliff Roberts' Rockers**.

In the same year, **Bob Evans** left and later played with **Dixie & the Dare Devils**, **Combo Six**, the **Dawnbreakers** and the **Dresdens**.

His replacement was **Lewis Collins**, a newcomer on the scene who did not stay for too long. He joined the **Kansas City Five** and later played bass guitar with the **Georgians**, the **Eyes** and the **Mojos**, before he settled on a career as an actor and was 'Bodie' of 'The Professionals', a UK TV series.

His replacement in the **Renegades** was **Don Alcyd**, who had formerly played with **Tommy & the Metronomes** and **Faron & the Tempest Tornadoes**, as well as a short spell with its follow-on group, **Earl Preston & the T.T.s**.

The RENEGADES

Jimmy McManus joined the **Renegades** as an additional vocalist. He had formerly sung with **Bob Evans' Five Shillings** and the **Vegas Five**.

When **Derek Peckham** left to join the **New Avengers**, his replacement was **Dave 'Mushy' Cooper**, who had played with the **Vegas Five**, the **Undertakers** and **Faron's Flamingos**.

Dave Myers left to join the **Pawns** and was replaced by **Pete Jones**, who came from the **Crosbys** and besides this, sax player, **Jack Curtis,** joined the **Renegades** as an additional member.

So, **George Peckham** was the only remaining member of the original line-up and, because all these changes happened within a very short time, it was not possible for the **Renegades** to achieve any sort of a breakthrough.

In spite of this, they were chosen to be featured on the planned Oriole sampler, 'Cavern Alive', and were recorded by **John Schroeder**. Unfortunately, this record was never released, so it is not known which songs were recorded by the **Renegades**.

A little later, they completely split up when **George Peckham**, **Dave Cooper** and **Don Alcyd** teamed up with **Paul Pilnick** of **Vince & the Volcanoes** in **Lee Curtis & the All Stars**.

However, when **Lee Curtis & the All Stars** disbanded after a successful residency in Germany, **Dave Cooper** joined the **Pawns**, and **George Peckham** became a member of **Groups Inc.**, before he also joined the **Pawns**. **Dave Cooper** then played with the **Vauxhalls** and the **Fruit Eating Bears**, while **George Peckham** was later a member of the **Kinsleys**, **Earl Royce & the Olympics** and the **Fourmost**.

Don Alcyd remained in Germany, where he became a member of the **Mersey Five**, that also backed **King Size Taylor** for some time. After a short spell on the London scene, **Don Alcyd** appeared again in Liverpool as a member of the **Delmont Four**.

Initially, **Pete Jones** also joined **Groups Inc.** but, after that, he teamed up again with **Derek Peckham** in the **New Avengers**.

Vocalist, **Jimmy McManus,** disappeared from the scene for a short time but, in 1965, he was back as a member of the **Blackwells**, while **Jack Curtis** joined the **Secrets** and later also played with the **Dresdens**.

That was the Sixties' story of the **Renegades** but, in 1978, their name appeared again – on the revival compilation, 'Mersey Survivors', where they were featured with the songs, "Hippy Hippy Shake" and "My Babe". In the end, this was more of a recording session group than a real band and, of the **Renegades** from the Sixties, only **George Peckham** and **Pete Jones** were included. However, at least there were two recordings made under the name of the **Renegades**, unfortunately, they were the only ones.

Despite the many changes in the line-up and the short time that the **Renegades** were on the scene in the Sixties, they were a really impressive group and they left behind a name that is still fondly remembered.

Discography :

Nothing was ever released by the **Renegades** in the Sixties, but it is known that they were recorded in early 1964 (?) by **John Schroeder** for the planned 'Oriole' sampler 'Cavern Alive', which in the end was never released and, accordingly, it is not known which songs were recorded.

Tracks on compilations

Hippy Hippy Shake	on **'Mersey Survivors'**	**UK- Raw RWLP 104 / 1978**
My Babe	on **'Mersey Survivors'**	**UK- Raw RWLP 104 / 1978**

RHYTHM & BLUES INC.

It all started when a Beat group was formed by some pupils at a Catholic school in Southport in the early Sixties. Among the members were **Pete Kelly** on vocals, **John McCaffrey** on bass and **Pete 'Ollie' Halsall** on drums. This band did not last for too long and, while **Pete Halsall** later switched to guitar and went on to play with such famous recording groups as **Timebox** and **Patto**, the other two members formed a new group, in 1963, under the name of **Rhythm & Blues Incorporated**.

The first line-up did not stay together for too long and the original guitarist, **Mike Foden,** and the drummer, **Barry Tweedale,** were very soon replaced.

After these changes, the group consisted of:

Pete Kelly	(voc)
George Eccles	(lg)
Mike McKay	(rg)
John McCaffrey	(bg)
Alan Menzies	(dr)

George Eccles and **Alan Menzies** came from the **Gems**, formerly known as **Chris & the Quiet Ones**, a group already established on the local scene. Prior to that, **Alan Menzies** had been a member of the Liverpool school band, **The Kestrels,** and also **Jan & the Vendettas** from Southport. **Mike McKay** had formerly played with the **Fireflys**.

When **George Eccles,** left he was replaced by **Barry Womersley** (lg/voc), who came from the **Diplomats**, who were a very popular group on the local scene.

Rhythm & Blues Inc. soon became the No. 1 group in Southport and, at the same time, became a steady and important part of Liverpool's Merseybeat scene.

Fontana signed the group in 1964 and, in the same year, their first single was released with a great version of the **Kingsmen** hit, "Louie, Louie", which was a real knockout! It was coupled with an interesting version of the **Carl Perkins'** standard, "Honey Don't". This record really deserved to become a big hit but, unfortunately, it failed to make the charts. This may have been because the group's music, and thus the record, was not as catchy as the fans at large liked it.

R & B Inc. on their way to appear on 'Ready, Steady Go!' TV show

However, "Louie, Louie" really had everything needed to make a good Beat record and, therefore, it is very hard to understand why it was ignored.

In 1965, there were some more changes in the line-up and the first to leave was **Barry Womersley**, who joined the **Big Three** and, after that, played with the **Clayton Squares**. He was replaced by **Bill Lovelady**, a former member of the **Music Students**.

Next to leave was **Alan Menzies**, who became a member of the **Tabs** and later played with the **Expressions** from Liverpool. His replacement in **Rhythm & Blues Inc.** was **Ian Magee**, who came from **Mike Dee & the Detours**.

Around that same time, two additional members were added to the group, **John Surguy** (sax) from the **Alibis** and **Colin Ashton** (tr).

For mysterious reasons, **Rhythm & Blues Inc.** did not get a second chance to record and it was probably in 1966 when the group changed its name to **Pete Kelly's Solution** and continued successfully on the scene.

They were signed to Decca and, in 1968, released a great single with the **Grass Roots** song, "Midnight Confessions", which was coupled with the group's original ,"If Your Love Don't Swing".

The record sold quite well but again failed to make the charts. Despite this, it was re-released towards the end of the year, this time coupled with "The House That Jack Built", which was played by **Bernie & the Buzz Band** from Liverpool.

At this point, we have to come back to the former **Rhythm & Blues Inc.** members, **Barry Womersley**, **George Eccles** and **Alan Menzies**, who, in 1967, had teamed up again in a group called **Wall Street Diversion** together with **Brent Pickthall** (bg) from the **Principles** and a Scot named 'Tam' as sax player.

In 1968, **Wall Street Diversion** broke up and **Barry Womersley**, together with **John McCaffrey** and **John Surguy** from **Pete Kelly's Solution,** plus the original **Rhythm & Blues Inc.** drummer **Barry Tweedale** and **Alan Solomon** (key/sax) formed the group, **Jasmin-T**. A little later, **Barry Tweedale** was replaced by **Alan Menzies**.

Brent Pickthall replaced **John McCaffrey** on bass guitar in **Pete Kelly's Solution**, who apparently broke up in the very early Seventies.

Ian Magee appeared again on the scene in the Eighties as a drummer with the **Swinging Blue Jeans** and Pete Kelly went solo on the cabaret circuit.

In early 1969, **Jasmin-T** cut a single with a musically up-dated version of "Some Other Guy", which was coupled with the bluesy **Barry Womersley** original, "Evening". This interesting record was also released on the Metronome label in Germany and sold quite well over there but failed to become a chart success.

In June 1969, the group played the famous 'Top Ten' in Hamburg for one month and from there went on tour in Denmark where **Barry Womersley**, for some reason, became unnerved, sold his guitar and returned to Southport. The others kept playing in Denmark but, in 1970, they also returned to Southport where they disbanded.

In 1975, **Barry Womersley** and **John Surguy** were members of the group, **Inner Sleeve**, which probably also included **John McCaffrey**.

This group released a single for EMI with the **John Surguy** original, "Here We Go", as well as two further acetates with **Barry Womersley** compositions and then they disappeared from the scene.

Barry Womersley went solo and cut the single, "Standing On The Corner", in 1977 which was produced by none other than **Bruce Welch** of the **Shadows**.

After that, **Barry Womersley** kept playing the solo scene for several years and, in 1983, he was back with another single, but "You're My Wife" did not have any real success.

Alan Menzies, together with **George Eccles** and **Brent Pickthall**, formed a trio in 1970. For a while they played without a name at the 'Westend Club' in Southport but then carried on as **Jasmin-T** again. At the instigation of **Lally Stott** and together with the girl singer, **Sharon Day**, they went to Italy, where they were meant to appear as a replacement for **Middle Of The Road** in the **Lally Stott** productions. Somehow, this did not work out and **Sharon Day** returned to England while the group had a long residency in the sunny south and were signed to RCA Italiano. In 1972, they released the single, "Sands Of Sahara". In 1974, **George Eccles** left the group and was replaced by **Terry Walters**.

In this line-up, **Jasmin-T** cut the album, 'Direct from Liverpool', which was most probably a private release, sold at gigs.

The lead guitarist position changed quite often and, after one more single, "Wait A Minute" for the Danish CBS label in 1979, **Jasmin-T** became a **Beatles** tribute band under the name of the **Bootles**, with **Brent Pickthall** and **Alan Menzies** as members. In the beginning of the Eighties, the group cut a nice album with **Beatles** numbers on the Bulgarian 'Balkanton' label.

The **Bootles** settled down in Denmark and for many years they were going strong throughout all of Scandinavia with band leader, **Alan Menzies,** being the only surviving original member.

It was also him who disbanded the **Bootles**, when he returned to live in England in 2009.

In November 1994, **Rhythm & Blues Inc.** gave a very successful revival concert in Southport but all that is known about the line-up is that **Barry Womersley** and **Pete Kelly** were part of it.

Single discography :

Louie Louie / Honey Don't	UK- Fontana TF 524 / 1964

as Pete Kelly's Solution :

Midnight Confessions / If Your Love Don't Swing	UK- Decca F.12755 / 1968
Midnight confessions / (Bernie & the Buzz Band: The House That Jack Built)	UK- Decca F.22829 / 1968

Jasmin-T :

Some Other Guy / Evening	G- Metronome 25158 / 1969

(for further releases of **Jasmin-T, Inner Sleeve, Barry Womersley** and **The Bootles** – please see story)

THE RICHMOND GROUP

This group was formed in Liverpool under the name, the **Poets,** in 1964. Much too late for an international breakthrough as Merseybeat had already started to lose its leading role in the worldwide music scene.

As there was a recording group from Glasgow with the same name, following a suggestion by **Bob Wooler,** the Liverpool band became **The Richmond Group.**

Around the same time, one of their two vocalists, **Arthur Alcock,** left the group and was replaced by **Dave Kerrigan,** who came from **Ricardo & the Toreadors.**

Accordingly, the **Richmond** ('**Group**' was later dropped from the name) consisted of the following musicians:

Eddie Cave	**(voc)**
Dave Kerrigan	**(voc)**
Barry David	**(g/voc)**
Barry Wheldon	**(g)**
Howie Jones	**(bg)**
Peter Taylor	**(dr)**

At that time, it was quite unusual to have two vocalists in the line-up of a Beat group, and the **Richmond** didn't just have two, they had two great ones.

In 1965, the **Richmond** were chosen to be featured on the Ember live compilation, 'Liverpool Today', which was recorded at the 'Cavern'. Besides **Earl Preston's Realms** and the **Michael Allen Group**, the **Richmond** were featured with the songs, "That's All Right", "I Shall Not Be Moved", "Cops And Robbers", "I'm Alright" and the great folksy "I Won't Let You Down", which was an original by the group.

Their music was a bit of a mixture of Folk and Rhythm & Blues, which was interesting and attractive. The **Richmond** on that album were deemed to be 'one of the youngest and most exciting new groups from Liverpool' by **Bob Wooler**, which was a justified comment, based on the record.

Although the group created a good impression on this compilation, this was not followed by a contract with a record company and this could have been the reason why **Eddie Cave** decided to leave.

He teamed up with the **Sextet**, that recently had parted from their singer, **Terry Hines,** and this new group then continued as **Eddie Cave & the Fix** - another story in this book.

Mike Hart (voc/g/sax) joined the **Richmond** after having previously played with the **Roadrunners**, **Henry's Handful**, the **Kinsleys** and the **Krew**.

Bob Wooler arranged a meeting for the group with the well known record producer, **Andrew 'Loog' Oldham,** and, still in 1965, he recorded some songs with the **Richmond** for the new Immediate label, but nothing was released as the **Richmond** disbanded at Christmas 1965.

It is rumoured that shortly before the split up, **Howie Jones** was replaced by **Dennis Swale**, who formerly had played with the **Dimensions** and the **Croupiers**, but this is not absolutely known for sure.

However, **Howie Jones**, **Barry David**, **Barry Wheldon** and **Peter Taylor** disappeared from the scene while **Mike Hart,** at first, teamed up with a new group under the name, **Mike Hart & the Moon Dogs,** and then became a member of **Liverpool Scene**, which also included the poet, **Adrian Henry**.

Mike Hart then started a solo career and released three albums and, on one of those, the artists were named as **Mike Hart & the Comrads**, although this certainly was not a steady band.

Dave Kerrigan formed a vocal trio under the name, the **Signs**, who were always backed by the **Times** and recorded for Decca, but that is another story that can be followed in this book.

Discography :

Tracks on compilations :

That's All Right	on **'Liverpool Today - Live At the Cavern'**	**UK-Ember NR 5028 / 1965**
I Shall Not Be Moved	on **'Liverpool Today - Live At the Cavern'**	**UK-Ember NR 5028 / 1965**
Cops 'n' Robbers	on **'Liverpool Today - Live At the Cavern'**	**UK-Ember NR 5028 / 1965**
I'm Alright	on **'Liverpool Today - Live At the Cavern'**	**UK-Ember NR 5028 / 1965**
I Won't Let You Down	on **'Liverpool Today - Live At the Cavern'**	**UK-Ember NR 5028 / 1965**

Unreleased tracks :

The **Richmond Group** were signed to the 'Immediate' label in 1965, and **Andrew 'Loog' Oldham** produced some songs with them. Unfortunately, they were not released as the group broke up shortly after these recordings, so it is not known which songs were recorded.

JOHNNY RINGO & THE COLTS

From this group's name, it may be concluded that this was a Country & Western outfit but, on the contrary, it was a real Beat group that was formed in Liverpool's Anfield area by **Fred Fargher** (aka **Johnny Ringo**) and **Les Holt** in the very early sixties.

It was undoubtedly one of the first Beat groups on Merseyside, but also one of the unlucky ones who never made a breakthrough on the national scene.

Johnny Ringo & the Colts, as they were named right from the beginning, originally consisted of:

Johnny Ringo	(voc/g)
Les Holt	(g)
John Smith	(bg)
Derek Kay	(dr)

According to an article in the 'Mersey Beat' newspaper, **Derek Kay** for a very short time was possibly replaced by **John Weathers** but then **Derek Kay** returned to the group. A little later, the mysterious **John Weathers**, who nobody seems to remember, moved to South Wales where he possibly played with the **Raiders** and **Peter Shane & the Vikings**.

This information seems to be doubtful but, as it was documented in the 'Mersey Beat', it should be mentioned here.

Johnny Ringo & the Colts were without a manager for a long time and maybe this was the reason that the group did not have much success and did not obtain a recording contract. But they had a lot of engagements in the leading clubs on Merseyside so they must have had really good musical ability.

In 1963, **Johnny Ringo & the Colts** went into Percy Phillips' studio in Kensington and recorded an acetate with the songs, "Mean Woman" and "Baby You Make Me Cry". Unfortunately, this was not followed by a record release.

It was probably in 1964 that **Gerry Jackson**, the brother of **Searchers** vocalist **Tony Jackson**, who also managed the **Easybeats** from Liverpool, took over their management and things started to go better for **Johnny Ringo & the Colts**.

Les Holt had to leave for business reasons, he was replaced by **Neil Ford** (voc/g/harp), who came from the **Vaaveros** and who, around that same time, was also asked to join the **T.T.s**.

He played with the group for a couple of months but then decided to go to London to work as a professional musician. He later returned to Liverpool and, in 1968, he joined **Bernie & the Buzz Band**.

His replacement in **Johnny Ringo & the Colts** was **Peter Anyon**, who came from the **Cave Dwellers**, but he soon went back to his old group and **Les Holt** returned and took up his original place again.

Unfortunately, it was too late for **Johnny Ringo & the Colts** to ride the 'Merseybeat wave' of National or International stardom and, as far as it is known, there was nothing more recorded by the group.

John Smith left the group and quit the music scene.

He was replaced by **Dave Hughes** who, most probably, was the musician of the same name who had previously played with the **Vampires** from Wallasey. He also did not stay for too long and **Graham Ball** became the new bass-guitarist with **Johnny Ringo & the Colts** in 1965.

Once the changes in the line-up started, the cohesion of the group was disrupted. The next to leave was drummer, **Derek Kay**, who apparently also gave up playing at that time.

Initially, he was replaced by **Bob Rowland**, but then **Phil Chittick** took over his place on drums.

Towards the end of 1966 or in early 1967, **Johnny Ringo & the Colts** changed their name into the **Dominoes** and then **Phil Chittick** left to join the great Liverpool Soul and R&B group, **Sinbad**.

Fred Fargher (aka **Johnny Ringo**), **Les Holt** and **Graham Ball** then changed the name of the group into the **Fortune Brothers** and continued on the cabaret-scene, always using the clubs' resident drummer.

When **Graham Ball** left, probably in the late Sixties, **Fred Fargher** and **Les Holt** continued under the same name as a duo until they both left show business in the mid seventies.

Fred Fargher sadly died much too young in 1982.

Of **Phil Chittick** it is known that, after **Sinbad,** he became a member of the new **Merseybeats**, then played with **Alby Donnelly's Supercharge**, returned to the **Merseybeats** and, for the last 20 years, has been playing with **Cy Tucker & the Friars** or the **Cy Tucker Band**, as it is sometimes named.

So what was left of **Johnny Ringo & the Colts,** besides a good name, is a very interesting acetate worth seeking.

Discography :

Johnny Ringo & the Colts never released a record, but recorded the following acetate, which were both original numbers by the group:

Mean Woman / Baby You Make Me Cry   **UK- Phillips acetate / 1963**

THE ROADRUNNERS

Formed in 1963 on the Wirral, the west side of the River Mersey, it did not take too long until the **Roadrunners** had established themselves as one of the leading Rhythm & Blues groups of the Beat city and, at the same time, they also managed to achieve nationwide popularity.

In an interview, **George Harrison** of the **Beatles** once described the **Rolling Stones** as 'being almost as good as the **Roadrunners**'. This certainly overshot the mark a bit, but it also shows what kind of importance and acceptance the **Roadrunners** had in Liverpool at that time.

In their original line-up, the group consisted of the following musicians:

Mike Hart	(voc/g/sax)
Dave Percy	(g/voc)
Pete MacKay	(bg)
John Peacock	(p)
Dave Boyce	(dr)

Pete MacKay was a former member of the **Tremeloes** (not to be confused with **Brian Poole's** group) and he had also played with the **Tenabeats**, where he had met up with **Mike Hart**.

The **Roadrunners** soon went to Hamburg where they had a long residency at the famous 'Star-Club'. They became a steady part of the so-called 'Star-Club' scene and, with one exception, all their records were recorded 'live' at the European 'Mecca of Beat' and originally released in Germany.

In 1964, **Dave Percy** left and he was perhaps identical with **Dave Percival**, who played in the **Climbers**, the **Pawns**, the **Kinsleys** and the **Epics**. But this is an assumption and not proven.

Mike Hart took over on lead guitar and two new members were added, **Nick Carver** (sax/fl) and an American, **John Phillips** (sax), who allegedly had formerly played with **Danny & the Juniors**.

It could have been this line-up that **John Schroeder** recorded for the planned Oriole compilation, 'Cavern Alive', which, unfortunately, was never released.

In 1965, the only studio recording of the **Roadrunners** was released with the EP, 'In Pantomania', which was recorded by 'Cavern Sound' as a special edition for Liverpool University. But, the only typical **Roadrunners** song on this EP is the title, "Cry, Cry, Cry", while the instrumental, "Fun At Twenty-one", as well as the jokey rewrite of "Leaving Of Liverpool", seem to have been more studio foolings from which the real quality of the **Roadrunners** cannot be recognised. Of course, the whole record was more a joke than a serious one and the fourth title on that EP, "If You Want To Know The Time", is a spoken sketch by students **Chris**

THE ROADRUNNERS

Edwards and **Clive Wood**. 5,000 copies of the EP were pressed, and 10 of them were special copies that featured a sketch about the Royal Family with the title, "My Husband And I", but this of course was banned by the Lord Chamberlain. This EP is both hard-to-find and a very expensive collectors item today.

While they were In Germany the **Roadrunners** released a great album on the Ariola label with 'Twist Time Im Star-Club Hamburg - Nr. 4', which, amongst others, featured Rhythm & Blues standards including "You Can Make It If You Try", "Hoochie Koochie Man", **Arthur Alexander's** "You'd Better Move On" and a great version of "Slow Down" - all live recordings from the Star-Club, of course.

From this album the songs, "Little Ruby/Beautiful Delilah" and "Slow Down/Roadrunner", were coupled out on singles.

The **Roadrunners** also shared one album with Newcastle's **Shorty & Them** on the 'Star-Club' label. This was also a live recording from the 'Star-Club' with the title 'Star-Club Show 2' and featured the **Roadrunners** with the songs, "Mary Ann", "Have You Ever Had The Blues", "My Baby Left Me", 'Hitchhike", "Cry, Cry, Cry" and "Got My Mojo Working".

It is interesting that, probably in 1965, a single was released in France with "Mary Ann" from this Philips album and "You Can Make It If You Try" from the Ariola long player.

In March 1965, **Bob Harrison** (tr) joined the **Roadrunners**, who were about to face a number of personnel changes that would ultimately lead to the group disbanding.

In August of the same year, **Mike Hart** became a member of the **Kinsleys** and later played with **Henry's Handful**, the **Krew**, the **Richmond Group**, **Mike Hart & the Moon Dogs** and **Liverpool Scene** before he recorded some solo albums.

He was replaced in the **Roadrunners** by **Mike Byrne** (voc), a former member of **Mike Byrne & the Thunderbirds** and **Them Grimbles**, while the lead guitar was taken over by **Mike Kontzle,** who came from **Chick Graham & the Coasters** and, before that, he had played with the **Beatwoods** and the **Gibsons**.

In September 1965, **John Phillips**, **Dave Boyce** and **Nick Carver** left and, while **John Phillips** became a member of the **Krew**, the others disappeared from the scene. It is known that **Nick Carver**, then using the name **Nick La Grec,** tried to form another group that, among others, may have included the drummer, **Pete Clarke**, but nothing was ever heard of that group.

Drummer, **Terry McCusker** from the **Valkyries** then joined the **Roadrunners**.

Sax player, **Dennis Overton**, who had formerly played with **John O'Hara & the Playboys**, is also said to have been a member, but this information is very doubtful.

At the end of 1965, the **Roadrunners** disbanded totally. At that time, **Pete MacKay** and **John Peacock** were the only remaining original members.

Mike Byrne got married and quit show business but, in 1966, he became a member of the **Cordes**, who later became **Fringe Benefit** and then **Colonel Bagshot's Incredible Bucket Band**, which also included **Terry McCusker**.

After that, **Mike Byrne** became a solo performer on the cabaret scene but, in 1995, he joined a group called **Persuader**, that later changed its name into **Rocket 88** but then broke up. **Mike Byrne** joined the **Juke Box Eddies** and today is the leader of **Mike Byrne & the Sun Rockers**.

It was **Mike Kontzle** who formed a new group under the name of the **Roadrunners** in late 1966 which, besides himself on lead guitar, included **Bruce McCaskill** (voc/rg), a former member of the **Bluegenes** and the **Kansas City Five**, **Stuart McPherson** (bg) and **Kenny Mundye** on drums, who formerly had played with the **Santones**, the **Anzaks** and the **Fruit Eating Bears**.

Probably because they anticipated problems about re-using the name, this line-up of the **Roadrunners** did not attempt to participate in the Liverpool scene at all. Instead, they toured Europe for approximately two years, playing the American military bases in France and Germany, ending up in Gstaad in Switzerland, where, for a long time, they entertained the Swiss high society.

When they returned to Liverpool, this final line-up of the **Roadrunners** disbanded and **Mike Kontzle** became a member of **Colonel Bagshot's Incredible Bucket Band**, while **Kenny Mundye** joined **Tony Crane** and **Billy Kinsley** in a trio line-up of the **Merseybeats**.

==

To avoid confusion, it should be pointed out that in 1962 there was another Liverpool Beat group with the name the **Roadrunners**, but this was a completely different and short lived band that had no connection with the recording group. They are Identified elsewhere in this book as **Roadrunners (II)** Those **Roadrunners** consisted of:

Brian ???	**(voc)**	- ex Carribeans
Pete Cooke	**(g/voc)**	- ex Topspots and Dee & the Dynamites
Ken Colly	**(bg)**	- ex Columbians
John Bedson	**(dr)**	- ex Four Clefs

This group never recorded and, because it was so short-lived, they never had any outstanding success and the only members that appeared again on the scene were **John Bedson**, who became a member of the **Challengers** and then played with the **Harlems** and the **Myths**, and **Peter Cooke**, who later played with the **Kansas City Five**, **Groups Inc.**, **Earl Royce & the Olympics**, the **Trend**, as well as with the newly-formed **Faron's Flamingos** in the seventies.

Single discography :

Little Ruby / Beautiful Delilah (Live)	G- Ariola 10794 AT / 1964
Roadrunner / Slow Down	G- Ariola 18078 AT / 1964

Different French release :

You Can Make It If You Try / Mary Ann (Live)	F- Byg 529.705 / 1965

EP discography

IN PANTOMANIA	UK- Pantomania (Cavern Sounds) 2.BSN.L7 / 1965

- Cry, Cry, Cry / Fun At Twenty-one / If You Want To Know The Time / The Leaving Of Liverpool

(Please note that only "**Cry, Cry, Cry**" and the jokey re-writing of "**The Leaving Of Liverpool**" were played by the **Roadunners**, while "**Fun At Twenty-one**" was an instrumental (by the **Roadrunners**?) and the other track was a spoken sketch by **Chris Edwards** and **Clive Wood**)

LP discography

STAR-CLUB SHOW 2	G- Star-Club 158.001 / 1964

- Mary Ann / Have You Ever Had The Blues / My Baby Left Me / Hitchhike / Cry, Cry, Cry / Got My Mojo Working——— plus 5 tracks by **Shorty & Them** from Newcastle

TWIST-TIME IM 'STAR-CLUB' HAMBURG - 4	G- Ariola 71224 IT / 1965

- Rip It Up / You Can Make It If You Try / Little Ruby / Baby You Don't Have To Go / Slow Down / That's

All Right / Beautiful Delilah / Long Tall Sally / Hoochie Koochie Man / You'd Better Move On / Roadrunner

Tracks on compilations

Have You Ever Had The Blues	on '**Star-Club Informationsplatte**'	G- Star-Club 111.371 / 1964
Beautiful Delilah	on '**Rock and Beat im Star-Club**'	G- Ariola 70982 IT / 1965

(Please note that all German and French releases were live recordings from the 'Star-Club', Hamburg)

Unreleased tracks :

The **Roadrunners,** in 1964, recorded under the wings of **John Schroeder** for the Oriole sampler, 'Cavern Alive', which was not released and therefore it is not known which songs were recorded.

CLIFF ROBERTS' ROCKERS

Well, this was one of the real pioneering groups on the Liverpool music scene, which was formed by singer/ guitarist **Cliff Roberts** on the west side of the River Mersey in the late fifties. Before that, he was a member of the **Sinners**.

Besides lots of US Rock 'n' Roll numbers, the band mainly played **Cliff Richard** material and, within a short time, became very popular throughout Merseyside.

In their original line-up, the group consisted of the following musicians:

Cliff Roberts	**(voc)**
Frank Bowen	**(lg)**
Dave Myers	**(g)**
Malcolm Linnell	**(bg)**
Alan Schroeder	**(dr)**

It is known that lead guitarist, **Frank Bowen,** had formerly played with a group called the **Teenbeats**, while the other members were probably newcomers to the scene.

Cliff Roberts' Rockers played all the major venues of that time and were the top-of-the-bill at many events, while other groups who, later became well known, were still their supporting acts, amongst them the **Beatles**.

Live at the Cavern

Unfortunately, the status of this really good group began to suffer as Beat music became more and more popular. So **Cliff Roberts' Rockers** broke up in the early sixties, without having released a record.

At that time, **Cliff Roberts** continued as a solo performer but then apparently quit the music business.

Malcolm Linnell joined the **Blue Diamond Combo** that later continued simply as the **Blue Diamonds**.

Frank Bowen, one of the most talented guitarists on the Merseybeat scene, first joined the **Blue Stars**, a Glaswegian group, who had a long residency in Liverpool at that time.

After that, **Frank Bowen** played with the **Lonely Ones** and then became a member of **Howie Casey & the Seniors**. When that band split, he joined **Lee Curtis & the All Stars** and was still a member when this group evolved into **Pete Best & the Original All Stars**. He then joined the **Pathfinders**, had a short spell with **Rory Storm & the Hurricanes** and then became a member of **Mike & the Merseymen**, who changed their name to the **Trends** and went down to London. When the **Trends** broke up, **Frank Bowen** remained in London and became a member of the **Bootleggers**, led by **Brian Auger**. Then he returned to Liverpool where he joined **Earl Royce & the Olympics**. He sadly died much too young in the Sixties.

Dave Myers initially played with the **Climbers** and then he became a founding member of the **Renegades** from Liverpool. In 1963, he joined the **Pawns,** with whom he toured Germany. He remained with them until the group disbanded.

After that, **Dave Myers** disappeared from the scene but, in the mid Nineties, was back as a member of the newly formed **Johnny Sandon & the Specials**. After **Johnny Sandon** left, the band continued under the name, the **Mersey Specials,** on the club circuit in Liverpool. He is still active today as a member of a group called **Tempest**.

Alan Schroeder joined the **Black Knights**, a trio that was also featured in the motion picture, 'Ferry Cross The Mersey', in 1964. After the band released a single, **Alan Schroeder** left and became a freelance drummer on the scene and, as such, he was a member of **Admiral Street** for a short time. In the mid nineties, he was a member of **Johnny Sandon & the Specials** and also played with the follow-on band, the **Mersey Specials**. In addition to him and **Dave Myers**, this group included **Mike Swift** (voc/rg) and **Colin Roberts** (a brother of **Cliff Roberts**) on bass guitar.

After that, **Alan Schroeder** re-formed the **Black Knights** who are still active on the scene.

In the early Nineties, **Cliff Roberts** stepped back into show business and formed a new group under the name, **Cliff Roberts' Rockers**, sometimes introduced as the **Cliff Roberts Band**. Besides him, this group initially consisted of the following well-known musicians:

Nicky Crouch	**(lg)**	-Who in the Sixties was with **Faron's Flamingos** and the **Mojos**
Dave Gore	**(rg)**	-Ex **Johnny Tempest & the Tornadoes** and **Earl Preston & the T.T.s**
Wally Sheppard	**(bg)**	-Ex **Johnny Tempest & the Tornadoes**, **Earl Preston & the T.T.s**,
Sam Hardie	**(p/voc)**	-The legendary founder and pianist of **King Size Taylor & the Dominoes**
Brian Johnson	**(dr)**	-Who, in the Sixties, played with groups including the **Strangers**, **Rory Storm and the Hurricanes**, **Mark Peters & the Silhouettes** and the **Tabs**.

Later, band leader **Cliff Roberts** younger brother **Steve Roberts**, a really good guitarist who had previously played with the re-formed **Faron's Flamingos**, replaced **Nicky Crouch**.

This group played the Rock 'n' Roll songs of the fifties again, as well as **Cliff Richard** material, which suited the voice of **Cliff Roberts** just like in the 'good old days'.

But the group almost exclusively played benefit concerts for the 'MerseyCats' or 'New Brighton Rock' organisations until they disbanded again.

Cliff Roberts stepped back from the music business again, while **Dave Gore** and **Wally Sheppard**, after a short time with **Karl Terry & the Cruisers**, formed **Persuader**, who later changed their name to **Rocket 88** and then broke up. **Dave Gore** stopped playing while **Wally Sheppard,** today, is still a member of a group called **Tempest** which, by the way, also includes **Dave Myers**.

Sam Hardie re-formed the original **Dominoes,** who occasionally also appeared with their old singer as **King Size Taylor & the Dominoes**, while **Brian Johnson** joined the re-formed **Mojos** under the leadership of **Nicky Crouch**.

Not too long ago, the **Cliff Roberts' Rockers** were re-formed again, even if their appearances are only occasionally. Steady members besides **Cliff Roberts** are **Steven Roberts** (lg), **Alan Schroeder** (dr) and **Les Williams** (bg), who, in the Sixties, played with the **Dimensions**. This line-up sometimes includes other guitarists and, on some shows, they are even joined by their original bass-guitarist **Malcolm Linnell**.

DALE ROBERTS & THE JAYWALKERS

It was hard to determine the true starting point of this group from Ellesmere Port on the Wirral. Most probably, it was the Skiffle group, the **Del Rio Mountain Boys**, that only played occasionally and included **Dale Roberts** and **Dave Williams**.

Dave Williams was a very active musician, at the same time being a member of the **Firecrests** and a Rockabilly trio without a name, which had **Ian Goyle** on bass.

In 1959, when the **Firecrests** disbanded, he formed the **Jetblacks**, that, besides his friends from the Rockabilly trio, also included **Phil Rodgers** on rhythm-guitar and a singer called **Ken Price**.

Ken Price did not stay very long and he was replaced by **George Roberts**, also known as **Dale Roberts** of the **Del Rio Mountain Boys**.

After a further change on drums, the **Jetblacks** changed their name into **Dale Roberts & the Jaywalkers** and now appeared in the following line-up:

Dale Roberts	(voc)
Dave Williams	(lg/voc)
Phil Rodgers	(rg)
Ian Goyle	(bg)
Billy Buck	(dr)

Insiders predicted a bright future for this band and, in fact, **Dale Roberts & the Jaywalkers** had a large following in the Liverpool area in the early Sixties. Rock 'n' Roll and a driving Beat was the hallmark of the band that for sure was one of the first 'rocking' groups that appeared at the 'Cavern' in February 1960.

Here, it should be pointed out that **Dale Roberts & the Jaywalkers** had nothing in common with **Peter Jay & the Jaywalkers**.

In spite of the fact that they were amateurs, they now appeared regularly at the 'Cavern', as well as at all the other major clubs in Liverpool and on the Wirral.

When **Ian Goyle** left the group, **Phil Rodgers** switched to bass guitar, while **Terry Willet** joined as the new rhythm guitarist.

He did not stay for too long and, when he left, **Dale Roberts** himself took over on rhythm guitar and the group continued as a quartet. Neither **Ian Goyle** or **Terry Willet** appeared on the scene again.

In January 1962, **Dale Roberts & the Jaywalkers** were voted No. 20 in the popularity poll of 'Mersey Beat' newspaper, which was a big success, as it has to be taken into account that there were already a few hundred groups on the scene at that time. Probably because of that placing, the group was offered a recording contract.

However, before the contract was signed, **Dale Roberts & the Jaywalkers** disbanded in April 1962, because their leader **Dale Roberts** was getting married in May and wanted to quit show business.

Phil Rodgers and **Billy Buck** joined the **Remo Four**, but **Billy Buck** did not stay for too long, he left and joined a Liverpool dance band.

When the **Remo Four** split in the late Sixties, **Phil Rodgers** went down to London, where he joined a Country band.

Dave Williams initially became a member of **Group One** and, in 1964, was a founding member of the **Four Originals,** that, a little later, were joined by **Dale Roberts**, returning to the music business two and a half years after having left it.

This new group, without exception, consisted of experienced musicians that had been on the scene right from the beginning and were all Merseybeat 'originals'. For a very long time they played in the same line-up and, only in the Seventies, had their first personnel changes.

On occasions, they also appeared as **Dale Roberts & the Jaywalkers** again, especially at charity-events for the 'MerseyCats' organisation in the Nineties.

Under the leadership of **Dave Williams,** the **Four Originals** are still going and apparently still have a lot of bookings – more than 45 years after their formation, which is a success story of its own.

George Roberts was a member of that group until, after a lengthy illness, he sadly died in January 2007.

NOTE: The complete story of the **Four Originals** can be found in the book 'Some Other Guys' (ISBN 9781588502025 or ISBN 1588502023).

EARL ROYCE & THE OLYMPICS

The forerunner of this group could have been the band **Tommy & the Olympics** that was already playing on the Liverpool scene in 1961.

This is only a supposition and not proven, but it is known for a fact that, in early 1963, **Billy Kelly** (aka **Earl Royce**) was a member of the **Olympics** who, from that time on, appeared as **Earl Royce & the Olympics** in the following line-up:

Earl Royce	**(voc)**
Peter Cooke	**(g/voc)**
Derek Nodwell	**(g)**
Stu Hazzard	**(bg/voc)**
Jimmy Jordan	**(dr)**

Peter Cooke had just joined and was a former member of the **Topspots**, **Dee & the Dynamites**, the short-lived **Roadrunners (II)**, the **Kansas City Five** and **Groups Inc**.

Earl Royce & The Olympics
Manager B. Robinson
9 Layford Close Huyton Liverpool. STO 1704

With the latter group he had just returned from a tour in France, where they had backed **Freddie Starr**.

For a time, he changed his name to **Pete Melody**, while **Jimmy Jordan** sometimes called himself **Jimmy Young**. **Stu Hazzard**, in the same fashion, was also named **Kenny Lazzard** occasionally and so it is possible that he was the former bass guitarist of the **Five Stars**, the forerunners to the **Midnighters**, that backed **Gus Travis** and **Freddie Starr**.

Derek Nodwell did not stay for too long and he was replaced by **Brian Myers**, who used the stage name **Brian Dee** and was (the second) 'Dee' of **Dee & the Dynamites**, one of the groups who preceded the legendary **Undertakers**.

George Blood took the group under the wings of his Peppermint Promotions and **Earl Royce & the Olympics** quickly became a top act on the Liverpool scene. Of course, they very often played in their manager's club, the well remembered 'Peppermint Lounge' which, formerly was known as the 'Cassanova Club'. In addition, the group also had plenty of engagements throughout the north of England.

In 1964, **Earl Royce & the Olympics** were chosen to take part in the motion picture, 'Ferry Cross The Mersey', where they were featured with an up-tempo version of "Shake A Tail Feather", which was included on the US release of the corresponding soundtrack.

This was their very first recording but, it was soon followed by their first single, a nice, catchy version of **Doris Day**'s "Que Sera Sera", which for sure was one of the outstanding records of that time and became a real Merseybeat classic. Of course, this record helped with the group's popularity but, for incomprehensible reasons, it failed to make the charts.

During 1964, **Earl Royce & the Olympics** sometimes backed female singer, **Rita Hughes**, better known on the scene as '**Jeannie**' and who already had two singles released with her old group **Jeannie & the Big Guys**, but that is a story of its own which can also be followed in this book.

In 1965, **Brian Dee** put aside his guitar and stepped in front as the group's second singer.

Then **Peter Cooke** left a little later to form a new group under the name, the **Trend** (without the 's') and, in the Seventies, he was a member of the newly formed **Faron's Flamingos**, before he continued on as a solo-performer.

In 1965, **George Peckham** became the new lead guitarist with **Earl Royce & the Olympics**. He had formerly played with groups that included the **Skylarks**, the **Renegades** from Liverpool, **Lee Curtis & the All Stars**, **Groups Inc.**, the **Pawns** and the **Kinsleys**.

This was most probably the line-up that cut the second single, "Guess Things Happen That Way".

This release, once again, showed the musical ability of the group and was an interesting Merseybeat record. However, it was not as strong as its predecessor and so, it was no real surprise that it also did not make it.

Earl Royce & the Olympics toured Germany quite often where they mainly appeared in the various 'Star-Clubs' where they established a good name for themselves.

George Peckham only stayed with them until December 1965, he then joined the **Fourmost**.

He was replaced in **Earl Royce & the Olympics** by **Frank Bowen**, an excellent guitarist, who was a former member of various groups such as **Cliff Roberts' Rockers**, **Howie Casey & the Seniors**, **Lee Curtis & the All Stars**, the **Pathfinders**, **Rory Storm & the Hurricanes**, the **Trends**, as well as some others. He sadly died much too young in October 1967, which was a real loss for the scene. This sad fact most probably caused **Earl Royce & the Olympics** to disband.

Billy Kelly, aka **Earl Royce**, left show business and went back to a normal day job, and **Jimmy Jordan** became a member of the **Vince Earl Attraction,** until he also quit the music business in 1973.

None of the other members of **Earl Royce & the Olympics** appeared on the scene again after that.

So what's left of this great group, who were popular in both north and central England, and also in Scotland, where they were one of the most successful live acts for a long time, is a good name that is still remembered these days - and, of course, their records which are worth looking out for.

Single discography :

Que Sera Sera / I Really Do   UK- Columbia DB 7433 / 1964

Guess Things Happen That Way / Sure To Fall   UK- Parlophone R 5261 / 1965

Tracks on compilations :

Shake A Tail Feather   on '**Ferry Cross The Mersey**'   US-United Artists UAS 6387/ 1964

(Please note that this compilation is the US release of the original soundtrack album from the legendary film)

THE RUNAWAYS

This group was formed in the Wavertree area of Liverpool by **Dave Potter** (voc/rg) and **Chris Finley** (org/g/voc), most probably in mid 1963.

As the Liverpool music press did not pay too much attention to the group, it was very difficult to recreate their story but, it is known that **Chris Finley** left the **Runaways** as early as 1964 to become a member of the **Kruzads**. After that, he played with the **Masterminds** and then joined the **Fruit Eating Bears**. He later appeared again as a member of **Confucius**, who had evolved from the **Hideaways** and, after that, he played with the re-formed **Merseybeats** and **Herman's Hermits**.

After he had left in 1964, the line-up of the **Runaways** consisted of:

Dave Potter	**(voc/rg)**
Tony Webster	**(lg/voc)**
Marion Hill	**(org/voc)**
David Cato	**(bg)**
Roy Smith	**(dr)**

The female keyboard player **Marion Hill** was the direct replacement for **Chris Finley** and, before that, she had played with the **Memphis Rhythm & Blues Combo**.

Tony Webster had only just joined the **Runaways**, he had formerly played with **Tommy & the Metronomes**, **Mark Peters & the Cyclones**, that became the **Cyclones,** and then evolved into a trio named **The Few**, who disbanded in January 1964.

The original guitarist with the group was most probably **Dave Davis**.

David Cato and **Roy Smith** were obviously the other remaining original members of the **Runaways** who went into the studio in late 1964, or early 1965, to cut an acetate with the songs, "Back Again" and "I Remember So Well", which were both originals by the group.

Unfortunately, this interesting acetate did not lead to a record contract and so it did not result in any sort of a breakthrough for the **Runaways**, who continued to play the usual Merseyside gigs.

It was probably in early 1966 that the group was joined by **Bill Kenwright** as an additional lead vocalist. Liverpool-born **Bill Kenwright** had started his music career in the early Sixties as a member of the **Chevrolets**, who did not achieve any major significance on the scene.

Besides his main profession as an actor, **Bill Kenwright** also doubled as a singer on the local music scene. In 1964, he recorded an acetate with the songs, "I'll Find A Way" and "Karen", though it is not known whether he was backed by the **Chevrolets** on that record.

The disc-jockey **Carl Gresham** took over their management and somehow obtained a recording contract with Columbia for **Bill Kenwright & the Runaways**.

In 1967, the single, "I Want To Go Back There Again", was released – a nice medium-paced Beat song with a dominating organ, played in the typical commercial way of that time.

This record did not make the charts and, it seems, **Bill Kenwright** then separated from the **Runaways** who continued as a group until the end of the Sixties. At some point during that time, **Tony Webster** was replaced by **Bob Wolem** on lead guitar.

After the **Runaways** disbanded, **Marion Hill** joined the London based international female recording group **She Trinity**, who also recorded under the name **Gilded Cage**. After that, not much information is known, but It's probable that at some later date, she played the clubs in Germany.

Dave Potter later appeared again as the vocalist for the **B-Jays** from Widnes. All the other members disappeared from the scene.

Bill Kenwright remained on the music scene and, in 1968, was signed to MGM and had his second single released with the nice ballad, "Love's Black And White".

On this record, which he also produced, he was accompanied by the **Lew Warbeton** orchestra.

This record no longer had anything in common with Beat but sounded much more American with the full orchestral arrangement. It did not have much success, although it was also introduced in the UK 'Coronation Street' TV series.

After that, only one more record by **Bill Kenwright** was released –"Tiggy" in 1969, which had the same orchestral backing as the preceding one and was equally unsuccessful.

Bill Kenwright concentrated on acting again and later established and operated a production company.

Today he is by far the biggest producer of musicals in England and, besides this, he is the chairman of the internationally successful Everton F.C. football club - what a career . . .!

Discography :

The Runaways :

Back again / I Remember So Well	**UK – Phillips acetate / 1964**

Bill Kenwright & the Runaways :

I Want To Go Back There Again / A Walk Through Dreams	**UK- Columbia DB 8239 / 1967**

Bill Kenwright – solo :

I'll Find A Way / Karen	**UK - ? ? ? acetate / 1964**
Love's Black And White / Giving Up	**UK - MGM MGM 1430 / 1968**
Tiggy / House That Fell On Its Face	**UK - MGM MGM 1463 / 1969**

PHIL RYAN & THE CRESCENTS

Crewe born **Philip Rylance** started to play guitar as a teenager together with his friend, **Keith Haynes**, who was already playing in a group called the **Rebels**. Once Phillip had improved enough on his instrument, he also joined this group in 1959.

One year later, the two friends started a new group – the **Echoes** which also included **'Skiff' Becket** (voc), **Bob Sant** (rg), **Malcolm Steele** (bg) and **Alan Betts** (dr).

Besides playing the local clubs with this group, in 1961, **Philip Rylance** and **Keith 'Ted' Haynes** also started to play as a vocal/guitar duo in the style of the **Allisons** or **Everly Brothers**.

As such, they called themselves the **Diamonds** and, after taking part in a talent contest, they were auditioned by BBC Radio producer, **Billy Scott-Coomber** and contracted to record for the 'Here We Go' BBC radio show.

They recorded the **Ricky Nelson** song, "Lonesome Town", and their original number, "After Thinking It Over", at the 'Hippodrome Theatre' in Hulme. For these recordings, the **Diamonds** were supported by **Harry Archer** (bg) and **Bobby Turner** (dr) from the **N.D.O.** (Northern Dance Orchestra). They went down a bomb on the radio show and were invited back a little later, at which time they recorded another original. Unfortunately, the title is not known.

The Diamonds

In early 1962, **Ted Haynes** was asked to join another local group – **Gary B. Goode & the Hot Rods**, all apprentices from the Rolls Royce works in Crewe who had started off as the **Bentleys Skiffle Group** and originally consisted of **Gary Burgess** aka. **Gary B. Goode** (voc), **Bob Steele** (lg), **Mick Machin** (rg), **Howard Lynch** (bg) and **Dennis Berry** (dr).

Ted Haynes replaced **Mick Machin** and, when the group's drummer left, **Phil Rylance**, who, in the meantime had disbanded the **Echoes**, joined them.

With this line-up, **Gary B. Goode** became quite popular on the scene and also appeared in Liverpool, mainly at the 'Iron Door', where they once shared the bill with the **Beatles**.

Bob Steele left and **Ted Haynes** took over on lead guitar, while **Phil Rylance** switched to rhythm guitar and a new drummer, **Dave Heaps**, came in.

This line-up was recruited by the management of Rock 'n' Roll singer **Tommy Bruce** to become his backing group, the **Bruisers**, for all his appearances in northern England.

Gary B. Goode & the Hot Rods at the Iron Door (1961)
L to R: Howard Lynch, Phil Rylance, Gary B. Goode
Ted Haynes & Bob Steele

Tommy Bruce, at that time, was very popular as his record, "Ain't Misbehavin'", had recently reached No. 3 in the UK charts. Accordingly, the group became very busy backing him as the **Bruisers,** in addition to doing gigs in their own right as **Gary B. Goode & the Hot Rods.**

Phil Rylance left to replace **Pat Withers** in another Crewe group, the **Crescents,** who then consisted of **Phil Rylance** (voc/rg), **Bernard Hibbert** (lg), **Steve Jenks** (bg) and **Keith Billington** (dr).

Bernard Hibbert and **Keith Billington** had formerly played with the **Zephyrs** and the **Zodiacs** and, before that, **Bernard Hibbert** was a member of **Tom Keay & the Keynotes.**

Steve Jenks was replaced by **Ken Lockwood** and this line-up was contracted to back London songstress, **Susan Singer,** on her three-week tour. She, by the way, was a cousin of **Helen Shapiro.**

Tommy Bruce

Following that tour, **Bernard Hibbert** switched to piano and the lead guitar was taken over by **Ken Lockwood,** while **Steve Jenks** returned to the **Crescents** as a bass guitarist and they continued to be very active on the scene until they disbanded in May of 1963.

In September 1963, **Bernard Hibbert** re-formed the group as a trio, they were joined by **Phil Rylance,** again, and continued as **Phil Ryan & the Crescents** in the following line-up:

The Zodiacs (Crewe)

Phil Ryan	(voc/rg)
Bernard Hibbert	(lg/voc)
Dave Birkenhead	(bg/voc)
Roger Keay	(dr)

MARY DON'T YOU WEEP
C/W **YES I WILL**   COLUMBIA DB 7406
PHIL RYAN AND THE CRESCENTS
★   A MUST for YOUR Record Collection   ★
PHIL RYAN AND THE CRESCENTS Now on Nation Wide Tour
Fan Club: Shirley & Elaine, 43 Longfield Avenue, Timperley, Cheshire
Management & Agency: 79 NORTHBROOK RD., WALLASEY 1421
DARVILLE ENTERTAINMENTS . WALLASEY   WALLASEY 2484
PHIL RYAN

Dave Birkenhead was a newcomer to the scene, while **Roger Keay** had formerly played the saxophone in his father's band, **Tom Keay & the Keynotes,** and the **Lincoln Lee Showband.**

Phil Ryan & the Crescents won a talent competition at the 'Blue Ball' in Liverpool and were signed by **Ken Smith** of Darville Entertainments, Wallasey.

Soon they were playing all the major clubs in Liverpool, such as the 'Iron Door', the 'Cavern', the 'Grafton', the 'Locarno', the 'Peppermint Lounge' and the Rialto Ballroom, as well as the 'Majestic' in Birkenhead and the 'Tower' in New Brighton and, of course, other venues in Ellesmere Port, Runcorn, Widnes, Chester and Crewe.

Their new management organised an audition with **Norrie Paramor** at EMI and, in June 1964, they recorded "Mary Don't You Weep", a great Beat ballad in the style of the **Merseybeats,** which was arranged by **Phil Ryan** himself. The flipside of this Columbia record was "Yes I Will", written by **Bernard Hibbert** and **Dave Birkenhead** – and this would have been good enough to become another A-side. The record sold very well but, in the end, failed to become a chart success.

In spite of this, **Phil Ryan & the Crescents** got a further recording contract for two more releases but, before their next record was issued, they went to Germany for two months together with **Freddie Starr & the Delmonts,** playing at **Manfred Woitalla's** 'Star Palast' chain in Kiel, Lüneburg, Eckernförde and Buchholz, as well as the 'Savoy' in Hannover and a big club in Braunschweig (Brunswick). They went down extremely well in all these places.

Mid 1965 saw the next single by **Phil Ryan & the Crescents** with a good version of **Curtis Mayfield's** "Gypsy Woman" but, unfortunately, the sales were not as good as those of its predecessor.

Maybe that was the reason Columbia didn't release "It Could Well Be", which had already been recorded, another original by **Bernard Hibbert** and **Dave Birkenhead**.

Despite that decision by the record company, **Phil Ryan & the Crescents** made a good living as professionals and, in August or September 1965, they went back to Germany again.

After touring Germany continuously for one more year, they were all tired of being on the road and disbanded sometime in 1966.

Bernard Hibbert formed a duo with **Valerie Hayes**, who had been a member of the **Zodiacs** with him and, under the name, **Avocardo Pair,** they appeared on 'Opportunity Knocks', a talent show on ITV television, for three shows of the series.

Roger Keay joined **Hedgehoppers Anonymous** and, after that, became a member of **Sandy Shaw's** backing group, the **Streamliners,** who came from Stoke and were formerly known as the **Shandykins Four**.

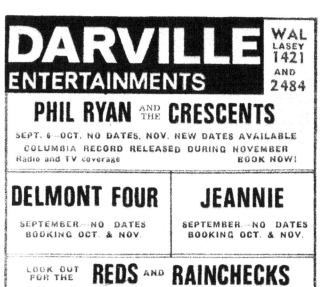

Initially, **Dave Birkenhead** played with the **Scorpions** and, after that, with the **Times,** before playing keyboards with **Hedgehoppers Anonymous**. He then followed **Roger Keay** to **Sandy Shaw's** group.

Phil Ryan quit professional showbiz and went to university to study drama. He became a teacher in Crewe in 1969 but then taught for the British Army in Germany for almost 20 years.

During that time, he started to sing and play again in a duo with **Laurie Lewin** and under the name **Phil & Laurie** they entertained at the British military bases in Germany.

Sometime in the Nineties he teamed up again with his old mates, **Dave Birkenhead** (key) and **Roger Keay** (sax), in the **Phil Rylance Rock & Roll Band,** which is still going strong on the scene and also includes **Neil Winfield** (bg) and Phil's son **Paul Rylance** on drums.

PHIL RYAN and the CRESCENTS

Discography :

Mary Don't You Weep / Yes I Will	**UK - Columbia DB 7406 / 1964**
Gypsy Woman / Be Honest With Yourself	**UK - Columbia DB 7574 / 1965**

Unreleased tracks:

In 1965, **Phil Ryan & the Crescents** recorded the **Bernard Hibbert/Dave Birkenhead** original, **"It Could Well Be"** as a third single for Columbia, but this was not released.

Also, in 1962, **Phil Rylance** and **Keith Haynes**, under the name of the **Diamonds**, had recorded **Ricky Nelson**'s **"Lonesome Town"**, the original **"After Thinking It Over"** as well as another original for the BBC 'Here We Go' broadcast.

CHRIS SANDFORD & THE CORONETS

The first group of Wallasey born **Chris Sandford** was named the **Tennessee Disciples**, but then he quit the music business to become an actor. After some minor roles, he had his breakthrough when he became the aspiring pop singer, 'Walter Potts', in the successful British TV saga, 'Coronation Street'.

The song he performed in the saga was "Not Too Little, Not Too Much" which became very popular with the TV audience. Decca issued this song as a single in 1963 and it is almost certain that, on the record, **Chris Sandford** was already backed by the musicians, whom he later performed with under the name of **Chris Sandford & the Coronets** - in the line up were:

Chris Sandford	(voc)
Tony Cartwright	(p/voc)
Norman Hale	(g/voc)
Jim Kent	(bg)
Mitch Mitchell	(dr)

"Not Too Little, Not Too Much", a catchy up-tempo song, climbed to No. 17 in the British charts and remained in the hit parade for nine weeks. It also climbed to No. 27 in the charts of the national music paper, 'New Musical Express'. This record was only credited to **Chris Sandford** as probably, at that time, his backing group did not have a name.

However, it was a real Beat group that mainly consisted of Liverpool musicians.

In 1964, the second single was released with "You're Gonna Be My Girl" and, this time, it was credited to **Chris Sandford & the Coronets**, but it was not as successful as the debut, although it was more interesting in its arrangement. The record sold quite well but did not enter the charts.

Shortly after that release, the group disbanded when **Chris Sandford** left. He released one more solo single in 1965, with the strange but interesting "I Wish They Wouldn't Always Say I Sound Like The Guy From USA", which had quite a nice B-side with the folksy "Little Man, Nobody Cares".

This record was not successful and **Chris Sandford** quit the music business to concentrate on his acting.

In 1972, he sang again with a new group under the name **Chris Sandford's Friendship**, who released the single, "Listen To The Music", on Decca. He didn't have much success with this and nothing was heard of him or his group again in the music business.

But now, back to the **Coronets**, who in 1965 recorded a solo-single with "I Wonder Why" on the obscure Stresa label. However, they apparently disbanded shortly after this release.

Mitch Mitchell became a member of the London recording group, the **Riot Squad**, not to be confused with the Liverpool group of the same name, which did not record. At the end of 1965, he was a member of **Georgie Fame & the Blue Flames** and then he joined the **Jimi Hendrix Experience**. The rest of course is history.

The three Liverpool musicians, **Tony Cartwright**, **Norman Hale** and **Jim Kent,** remained in London and formed the **Lively Set** in 1965, together with drummer, **Eric Dillon,** from Swindon and a lead guitarist from Southampton, whose name is not known.

Tony Cartwright took over the lead vocals in the new band who were signed to PYE in 1965 and, in July of that year, released the single, "Don't Call My Name", probably an original by the group but, unfortunately, it was not too successful.

It seems that for some time, the **Lively Set** were quite popular and kept busy on the London scene.

The 1966 single, "Let The Trumpets Sound", by a group called the **Lively Set** on Capitol was definitely not the group that had evolved from **Chris Sandford & the Coronets**, as they had already disbanded in the second half of 1965.

Norman Hale and **Eric Dillon**, at that time, joined **Neil Landon & the Burnettes** and, after that, **Norman Hale** became a member of **Brain Police**, while **Eric Dillon** went on to play with **Fat Mattress**.

Unfortunately, what happened to **Tony Cartwright** after the **Lively Set** disbanded, is not known, but he most probably returned to Liverpool.

Single discography :

Chris Sandford & the Coronets :

Not Too Little, Not Too Much / I'm Looking	UK- Decca F.11778 / 1963
You're Gonna Be My Girl / Don't Leave Me Now	UK- Decca F.11842 / 1964

(Please note that the first single was only credited to **Chris Sandford**, although it was obviously recorded with the **Coronets**)

The Coronets – solo :

I Wonder Why / You're Leaving Tomorrow	UK – Stresa L 5881 / 1965

Chris Sandford – solo :

I Wish They Wouldn't Always Say I Sound Like The Guy From USA / Little Man, Nobody Cares

UK-Fontana TF 633 / 1965

Chris Sandford's Friendship :

Listen To The Music / The Man Who Lost His Smile	UK- Decca F.13348 / 1972

The Lively Set :

Don't Call My Name / What Kind Of Love	UK- PYE 7N 15880 / 1965

(Please note that the single, "Let The Trumpets Sound", by the **Lively Set** on the Capitol label was not by the Liverpool group – see text).

THE SEARCHERS

This story begins with three separate Liverpool Skiffle groups formed sometime in or around 1957-1958. There were the **Wreckers** from Kirkdale, with guitarist, **Mike Pendergast**, who, a little later, moved to the **Confederates,** who played more Rock 'n' Roll orientated music.

Then there were the **Martinis** from the Sefton Park area, who, in addition to **Bernie Devey** (wb) and **Jimmy Moran** (g), also included the singer and guitarist, **Tony Jackson** and drummer, **Norman McGarry**.

And last, but not least, there was another Skiffle group from Kirkdale (probably without a name) which was led by guitarist, **John McNally,** that, besides him, included a singer called **'Big Ron' Woodbridge**, **Brian Dolan** (g), **Tony West** (bass) and **Joe Kennedy** (dr).

John McNally and **Mike Pendergast** knew each other from school and, in 1959, they decided to form a guitar/vocal duo in style of the **Everly Brothers**.

Around the same time, the **Martinis** broke up and their singer, **Tony Jackson,** continued as solo performer in the Liverpool clubs, singing and playing Rock 'n' Roll songs under the name of **Clint Reno**.

One night he met up with **John McNally** and **Mike Pendergast** who had come to one of his performances. They had a chat about music and decided to form a group together.

Of course, they were in need of a drummer and **Tony Jackson** remembered **Norman McGarry**, his friend from the **Martinis**.

These four then formed the first line-up of the **Searchers** at the beginning of 1960. The group's name was adopted from a **John Wayne** western.

Norman McGarry had to leave, as he got a job in a bakery, where he also had to work the nightshift. Later, he was a member of the **Sassenachs**, who cut a nice single with "That Don't Worry Me" for Fontana.

John McNally and **Mike Pender**, as he now called himself, contacted an old friend from school, **Chris Crummey**, who then joined as their drummer under the name of **Chris Curtis**.

Through his parents, **John McNally** knew **Billy Beck** who, at that time, was singing Country songs in the clubs where he was backed by John's father on accordion.

John McNally offered **Billy Beck** the job as lead singer in the new group, as **Tony Jackson** at that time was concentrating on learning the bass guitar. **Billy Beck** agreed and changed his name to **Johnny Sandon**.

Johnny Sandon & the Searchers

389

So the group was called **Johnny Sandon & the Searchers** and, within a very short time, became highly popular on the scene. In December 1961, they were placed fifth in the 'Mersey Beat' newspaper popularity poll. In spite of that success, **Johnny Sandon** and the group separated in 1962.

Initially, the **Remo Four** backed **Johnny Sandon** before he became a solo performer again.

The **Searchers** continued as a quartet in the following line-up:

Tony Jackson	**(voc/bg)**
Mike Pender	**(g/voc)**
John McNally	**(g/voc)**
Chris Curtis	**(dr/voc)**

Les Ackerley, the owner of the famous 'Iron Door' club, became their manager, and it was probably in 1962 when he arranged an acetate LP to be cut of one of their live performances at that club. This acetate included a version of "Sweets For My Sweet".

In 1963, the **Searchers** were signed to PYE and produced by **Tony Hatch**.

Their debut single, "Sweets For My Sweet", didn't sell too well at first and really looked like a 'miss' but, when the Searchers returned from the 'Star-Club' in Hamburg, where they had been playing for quite a long time, this single had become a giant hit, holding the 'pole position' in the British charts for some weeks and, from there, it became a hit almost all over the world.

The follow-up, "Sugar And Spice", was not as successful as their debut but climbed to No. 2 in the charts and became another international best seller.

The Philips recording company also wanted their piece of the success and the next single released in England was a live version of "Sweet Nothings", taken from the recently released German album, 'Sweets For My Sweet' (Live at the 'Star-Club'), just like it's flip-side, "What'd I Say", but this single did not make it.

The following PYE release, "Needles And Pins", became the biggest hit for the **Searchers** when it climbed to No. 1 in 1964 in all the important charts. This outstanding success placed the **Searchers** alongside the **Beatles** on the international scene.

On this record, the lead vocals, for the first time, came from **Mike Pender**, while **Tony Jackson** had sung the previous two.

The follow-up, "Don't Throw Your Love Away", another No. 1 hit, was also sung by **Mike Pender**.

He then became the band's lead singer, which must have been frustrating and disappointing for **Tony Jackson** and might have been the reason for him leaving the **Searchers** in 1964.

He then formed his own group under the name of **Tony Jackson & the Vibrations**, who later became the **Tony Jackson Group**, but that is another story which can be followed in this book.

His replacement in the **Searchers** was **Francis McNiece**, who came from London and used the stage name, **Frank Allen**. Originally, he had led his own group under the name, **Frank Allen & the Skyways,** after that he was a member of **Cliff Bennett & the Rebel Rousers**.

The **Searchers** had met him during their stay in Hamburg, when **Cliff Bennett & the Rebel Rousers** also played at the 'Star-Club'. **Frank Allen** was a good singer and bass guitarist and was a very good fit with the rest of the group.

They continued to have chart successes with records such as "Someday We're Gonna Love Again", the great "When You Walk In The Room" and a superb "What Have They Done To The Rain" in 1964, as well as the tremendous "Goodbye My Love". Their own composition, "When I Get Home", another superb "Take Me For What I'm Worth" and a relatively unsuccessful, "Take It Or Leave It", were released in 1965. In the same year, the **Searchers** also topped the US Billboard with their version of "Love Potion No. 9", which was belatedly coupled out from their first album.

In Germany, a great version of **Fats Domino's** "I'm Ready" was released on single and, in the Netherlands, "Where Have All The Flowers Gone" together with the 1964 release, "What Have They Done To The Rain", confirmed the **Searchers** as the first folk rock group with international stardom. They were later followed by groups that included the **Byrds**, the **Turtles,** the **Leaves**, all with their own individual musical styles, but all influenced by the Liverpool quartet.

Chris Curtis, who in the meantime, had also produced groups including **Eddie Cave & the Fyx** and the **Five A.M. Event** (formerly **The Crescendoes**) for PYE, left the group in early 1966 when the Beat boom was slowly coming to an end.

He initially recorded the solo single, "Aggravation", with the nice flip-side, "Have I Done Something Wrong", and, after that, formed the group, **Roundabout**, where he was the drummer and lead vocalist. This band, which included the musicians, **Jon Lord** (org) and **Ritchie Blackmore** (g), later evolved into the super group **Deep Purple** but, at that time, **Chris Curtis** had already quit show business - too early. **Chris Curtis** sadly died in February 2005.

John Blunt was his successor in the **Searchers**. He had formerly played with the **Tree** and his big idol was **Keith Moon** of the **Who**. He also looked a little bit like him.

In this line-up, the **Searchers** had their last chart entry with "Have You Ever Loved Somebody" in 1966. Further PYE releases were the nice "Popcorn Double Feature", a great version of "Western Union" with the nice flip-side, "I'll Cry Tomorrow".

There was also the slightly boring "Second Hand Dealer" as the final single on PYE, while in Denmark only the up-tempo "Everybody Come And Clap

The Searchers with John Blunt

Your Hands" was released which, in its arrangement, was a little bit out-dated by 1967, not really surprising as this song was taken from the EP, 'Four By Four', from 1965.

The **Searchers** switched to Liberty, where they had a great debut with "Umbrella Man" which, at least, brought them back onto the TV music shows in England and Germany. This was followed by a good version of the **Andy Kim** song, "Shoot 'Em Up Baby". However, in spite of their quality, both records failed to make the charts, as did the follow-up, "Kinky Kathy Abernathy", which was not as good as the other two and which was the last release for Liberty in 1969.

Interestingly, in 1968, "Somebody Shot The Lollipop-man" was another single released by the **Searchers** on Liberty, but under the name of **Pasha**. This record was a real flop, and it deserved to be, as it was a really awful record - the A-side as well as the B-side, "Pussy Willow Dragon".

In 1970, **John Blunt** left to join **Orange Seaweed** and later became a member of the **Love Affair** before he joined the revival band, **The Reflections**.

He was replaced in the **Searchers** by the Scot, **Billy Adamson**, who hailed from Glasgow and had formerly played in the backing groups of **Emile Ford**, Lulu, and **P.P. Arnold**. In addition, with his own group the **Blues Council**, he had played the London scene and it was there that he joined **This 'N' That**, often shortened to **TNT**, which had evolved from **Derry Wilkie & the Others**, but that is also another story in this book.

Back to the **Searchers**, that were now signed to RCA and, with their first release, "Desdemona", had a minor hit in the USA again. It is worth mentioning that the flip-side, the great "The World Is Waiting For Tomorrow", would have been good enough to be another A-side.

However, chart success remained an exception although, in 1973, a well-arranged version of the **Bee Gees** classic, "Spicks And Specks", was released. This was coupled with an even better version of **Neil Sedaka's** "Solitaire", which clearly showed the quality vocals of lead singer, **Mike Pender**.

The following album, 'Second Take', which was also released in 1973, was not that good and mainly included the second takes of the big **Searchers** hits, but the arrangements were quite thin and unimaginative. The only exceptions were their single success, "Desdemona", and the song, "Come On Back To Me", which became the B-side of their next single, "Sing Singer Sing". That record had a popular Reggae influenced sound and turned out very well, but was also unsuccessful.

The follow-up, "Love Is Everywhere", was also a great tune, while the final single for RCA, "Vahevala", lost out again by comparison to its predecessor.

In spite of this, the **Searchers** had no problems existing as professionals in show business, mainly in Germany where they became a very popular live act.

In 1979, the **Searchers** (still in the same line-up) seriously tried a comeback for the first time when the album, 'Searchers', was released on the Sire label. This had some very good reviews and it was honestly a great album which included some outstanding songs such as "Hearts In Her Eyes" (in the very best **Searchers** sound) and "Too Late". A correct decision was made to couple both songs out as singles and they sold quite well.

The following long player, 'Love's Melodies', again was a good one but the outstanding songs were missing. It is interesting to note that this album was initially intended to be released under the title, 'Play For Today', but it was only released as a promotional copy. On that 'promo', "Love's Melodies", which became the **Searchers** next single, was not featured but, in its place, there was a terrific version of "Sick And Tired". This was a real knockout, missing on the official release and just for this song alone, it is worth looking for a promo-copy of 'Play For Today'.

The **Searchers** were suddenly a group of topical interest again and very close to a real comeback, which for incomprehensible reasons did not happen.

It should be mentioned here that, on the first Sire album, **Bob Jackson** was featured as keyboard player, but he was never a steady member of the group, while the second Sire album featured **Mick Weaver** on keyboards.

In 1986, the group was close to disbanding when lead vocalist **Mike Pender** left to form his own group under the name of **Mike Pender's Searchers**. Initially, it was rumoured that the former original member **Tony Jackson** would be included in the line-up. However, for unknown reasons, it never happened, possibly because he re-formed **Tony Jackson & the Vibrations** around that time. **Tony Jackson** died in 2004.

Besides **Mike Pender**, the group included **Chris Black** (g), **Barry Howell** (bg) and **Steve Carlyle** (dr) and, at the beginning of the Nineties, released a CD, of course, with the old **Searchers** hits again.

Previously, also in 1986, **Mike Pender** had released the solo single, "It's Over", which had a modern sound but it was no great success, and quite honestly, not very exciting.

The other **Searchers**, which these days only include one original member with **John McNally**, (if **Frank Allen** was not considered as such), were joined by **Spencer James** as both a lead singer and guitarist. He was formerly a member of **First Class**, **Nightfly** and **Heyday**.

On the German bootleg album, 'Live In Germany', it is obvious that **Spencer James** is a very good singer, but it is also a fact that the voice of **Mike Pender** was the characteristic sound of the **Searchers**' and difficult to replace no matter how good the singer.

Billy Adamson also left the group, probably after that bootleg.

Single discography ;

Sweets For My Sweet / It's All Been A Dream	UK- PYE 7N 15533 / 1963
Sugar And Spice / Saints And Searchers	UK- PYE 7N 15566 / 1963
Sweet Nothin's / What'd I Say	UK-Philips BF 1274 / 1963
Needles And Pins / Saturday Night Out	UK- PYE 7N 15594 / 1964
Don't Throw Your Love Away / I Pretend I'm With You	UK- PYE 7N 15630 / 1964
Someday We're Gonna Love Again / No one Else Could Love You	UK- PYE 7N 15670 / 1964
When You Walk In The Room / I'll Be Missing You	UK- PYE 7N 15694 / 1964
What Have They Done To The Rain / This Feeling Inside	UK- PYE 7N 15739 / 1964
Goodbye My Love / Till I Met You	UK- PYE 7N 15794 / 1965
He's Got No Love / So Far Away	UK- PYE 7N 15878 / 1965
When I Get Home / I'm Never Coming Back	UK- PYE 7N 15950 / 1965
Take Me For What I'm Worth / Too Many Miles	UK- PYE 7N 15992 / 1965
Take It Or Leave It / Don't Hide It Away	UK- PYE 7N 17094 / 1965
Have You Ever Loved Somebody / It's Just The Way	UK- PYE 7N 17170 / 1966
Popcorn Double Feature / Lovers	UK- PYE 7N 17225 / 1967
Western Union / I'll Cry Tomorrow	UK- PYE 7N 17308 / 1967
Second Hand Dealer / Crazy Dreams	UK- PYE 7N 17424 / 1967
Umbrella Man / Over The Weekend	UK- Liberty LBF 15202 / 1968
Kinky Kathy Abernathy / Suzanna	UK- Liberty LBF 15240 / 1969

as **Pasha** :

Somebody Shot The Lollipop-man / Pussy Willow Dragon	UK-Liberty LBF 15199 / 1968

Chris Curtis – solo :

Aggravation / Have I Done Something Wrong	UK- PYE 7N 17132 / 1966

Different German releases :

Sweets For My Sweet / Listen To Me (Live)	G- Philips 345.606 / 1963
Sick And Tired / Led In The Game (Live)	G- Philips 345.621 / 1963
Money / Hungry For Love	G- Dt.Vogue DV 14111 / 1963
Süß ist sie / Liebe	G- Dt.Vogue DV 14116 / 1963
Tausend Nadelstiche / Farmer John	G- Dt.Vogue DV 14130 / 1964
I Sure Know A Lot About Love / Don't You Know	G-Star-Club 158500 STF/ 1964
Someday We're Gonna Love Again / Alright	G- Dt.Vogue DV 14176 / 1964
Love Potion No. 9 / What Have They Done To The Rain	G- Dt.Vogue DV 14277 / 1964
Verzeih' My Love / Wenn ich Dich seh	G- Dt.Vogue DV 14338 / 1965
Farmer John / Tricky Dicky	G- Dt.Vogue DV 14365 / 1965
I'm Ready / Don't You Know Why	G- Dt.Vogue DV 14458 / 1965
Bumble Bee / If I Could Find Someone	G- Dt.Vogue DV 15206 / 1965

(Please note that all the other singles released in Germany by the group were identical with the British releases. "**Süß ist sie**" was the German version of "**Sweets For My Sweet**", "**Liebe**" the German version of "**Money**", "**Tausend Nadelstiche**" was "**Needles And Pins**" in German and "**Farmer John**" was also sung in German. "**Verzeih My Love**", of course, was "**Goodbye My Love**" and "**Wenn ich Dich seh**" was the German version of "**When You Walk In The Room**")

Different Dutch releases :

Twist And Shout / Farmer John	NL- PYE 7N H 102 / 1963
Bumble Bee / Let The Good Times Roll	NL - PYE 7N H 108 / 1965
I Don't Want To Go On Without You / A Tear Fell	NL - PYE 7N H 109 / 1965
Where Have All The Flowers Gone / Money	NL - PYE 7N H 113 / 1965

Different Danish releases :

Sugar And Spice / Sweets For My Sweet	DK - PYE 7N 15566 / 1963
Sea Of Heartbreak / Love Potion Number 9	DK – PYE 7N 15751 / 1965

Different US releases :

Ain't Gonna Kiss Ya / Ain't that Just Like Me	US – Kapp K 584 / 1964
Love Potion Number Nine / Hi-Heel Sneakers	US – Kapp KJB 27 / 1964
Bumble Bee / Everything You Do	US – Kapp KJB 49 / 1965

Everybody Come And Clap Your Hands / Till You Say You'll Be Mine   S – PYE 7N 312 / 1967

EP discography

AIN'T GONNA KISS YA   UK-PYE NEP 24177 / 1963

- Ain't Gonna Kiss Ya / Farmer John / Alright / Love Potion No. 9

SWEETS FOR MY SWEET   UK-PYE NEP 24183 / 1963

- Sweets For My Sweet / It's All Been A Dream / Since You Broke My Heart / Money

HUNGRY FOR LOVE   UK-PYE NEP 24184 / 1964

- Hungry For Love / Don't Cha Know / Oh, My Lover / Ain't That Just Like Me

PLAY THE SYSTEM   UK-PYE NEP 24201 / 1964

- The System / This Empty Place / Sea Of Heartbreak / Can't Help Forgiving You

WHEN YOU WALK IN THE ROOM   UK-PYE NEP 24204 / 1964

- When You Walk In The Room / I'll Be Missing You / Someday We're Gonna Love Again /

No One Else Could Love You

BUMBLE BEE   UK-PYE NEP 24218 / 1965

- Bumble Bee / Everything You Do / Magic Potion / If I Could Find Someone

SEARCHERS '65   UK-PYE NEP 24222 / 1965

- What Have They Done To The Rain / This Feeling Inside / Goodbye My Love / Till I Met You

FOUR BY FOUR   UK-PYE NEP 24228 / 1965

- Till You Say You'll Be Mine / I Don't Want To Go On Without You /

Everybody Come And Clap Your Hands / You Wanna Make Her Happy

TAKE ME FOR WHAT I'M WORTH   UK-PYE NEP 24263 / 1966

- Take Me For What I'm Worth / Too Many Miles / Take It Or Leave It / Don't Hide It Away

Different German releases :

HULLY GULLY   G-Philips PE 423469 / 1963

- Hully Gully / Listen To Me / Sweets For My Sweet / Sweet Nothin's

SUGAR AND SPICE   G- Dt.Vogue PNV 24112 / 1964

- Sugar And Spice / Saints And Searchers / Unhappy Girls / Ain't That Just Like Me

SOME OTHER GUY   G- Dt.Vogue PNV 24114 / 1964

- Some Other Guy / Since You Broke My Heart / Don't You Know / Hungry For Love

NEEDLES AND PINS   G- Dt.Vogue PNV 24116 / 1964

- Needles And Pins / One Of These Days / Saturday Night Out / Ain't Gonna Kiss Ya

Different French releases :

SWEETS FOR MY SWEET   F- Vogue PNV 24108 / 1963

- Sweets For My Sweet / Alright / Tricky Dicky / Farmer John

DON'T THROW YOUR LOVE AWAY   F- Vogue PNV 24120 / 1964

- Don't Throw Your Love Away / I Pretend I'm With You / It's All Been A Dream / Love Potion No. 9

C'EST ARRIVE COMME CA   F- Vogue PNV 24121 / 1964

- C'est Arrivé Comme Ca / C'est De Notre Age / Mais C'était Un Réve / Ils La Chantaient Il y aLongtemps

(these are the French versions of "Don't Throw Your Love Away", "Sugar And Spice", "It's All Been A Dream" and "Saints And Searchers")

BUMBLE BEE   F- Vogue PNV 24137 / 1965

- Bumble Bee / Till I Met You / Goodbye My Love / If I Could Find Someone

Different Spanish release :

Take It Or Leave It / He's Got No Love / When I Get Home / Four Strong Winds

                                   ES – Hispavox HPY 337-30 / 1965

Different Japanese release :

Love Potion No. 9 / It's In Her Kiss / Bumble Bee / What Have They Done To The Rain

                                   J – PYE LSS 302-Y / 1965

MEET THE SEARCHERS

UK- PYE NPL 18086 / 1963

- Sweets For My Sweet / Alright / Love Potion No. 9 / Farmer John / Stand By Me / Money / Da-Doo-Ron-Ron / Ain't Gonna Kiss Ya / Since You Broke My Heart / Tricky Dicky / Where Have All The Flowers Gone / Twist And Shout

SUGAR & SPICE

UK- PYE NPL 18089 / 1963

- Sugar And Spice / Don't You Know / Some Other Guy / One Of These Days / Listen To Me / Unhappy Girls / Ain't That Just Like Me / Oh My Lover / Saints And Searchers / Cherry Stones / All My Sorrows / Hungry For Love

IT'S THE SEARCHERS

UK- PYE NPL 18092 / 1964

- It's In Her Kiss / Glad All Over / Sea Of Heartbreak / Livin' Lovin' Wreck Where Have You Been / Shimmy Shimmy / Needles And Pins / This Empty Place / Gonna Send You Back To Georgia / I Count The Tears / Hi-Heel Sneakers / Can't Help Forgiving You / Sure Know A Lot About Love / Don't Throw Your Love Away

SOUNDS LIKE SEARCHERS

UK- PYE NPL 18111 / 1965

- Everybody Come And Clap Your Hands / If I Could Find Someone / Magic Potion / I Don't Want To Go On Without You / Bumble Bee / Something You Got / Let The Good Times Roll / A Tear Fell / Till You Say You'll Be Mine / You Wanna Make Her Happy / Everything You Do / Goodnight Baby

TAKE ME FOR WHAT I'M WORTH

UK- PYE NPL 18120 / 1965

- I'm Ready / I'll Be Doggone / Does She Really Care For Me / It's Time / Too Many Miles / You Can't Lie To A Liar / Don't You Know Why / I'm Your Loving Man / Each Time / Be My Baby / Four Strong Winds / Take Me For What I'm Worth

THE SEARCHERS' SMASH HITS Vol.1

UK-Marble Arch 673 / 1966

THE SEARCHERS' SMASH HITS Vol.2

UK-Marble Arch 689 / 1967

THE SEARCHERS' SMASH HITS Vol.3

UK-Marble Arch 704 / 1968

(All three above-named Marble Arch albums were compiled from the former albums and so were not originals)

SWEETS FOR MY SWEET (Live At The Star-Club)

G- Philips P 48052 / 1963

- Sweets For My Sweet / Ain't That Just Like Me / Listen To Me / I Can Tell / Sick And Tired / Mashed Potatoes / I Sure Know A Lot About Love / Rosalie / Led In The Game / Hey Joe / Always It's You / Hully Gully / What 'D I Say

- Needles And Pins / I Want To Hold Your Hand / Sweets For My Sweet / She Loves You / Sugar And Spice / Roll Over Beethoven / Hungry For Love / Please Please Me / Saturday Night Out / Twist And Shout / Farmer John / From Me To You

(It is often said that the **Beatles** cover versions, included on the above album, were not recorded by the **Searchers** but by **Ian & the Zodiacs**. But, fact is, the recordings were neither by the **Searchers**, nor by **Ian & the Zodiacs**. These numbers were taken from an album on the German Tempo-label, called 'Beatlemania'. This label was a so called 'cheapo' which worked closely with 'Top Six' in England who, at the same time, also provided Dt. Vogue with cover versions for their 'Original Beat aus England' series on the sub-label 'Pop'. So the artists on those songs were most probably the **Beat Kings**, which cannot be said for sure, as it seems that 'Top Six' used various imaginative names for mainly one and the same group or groups for various recording sessions)

Tracks on compilations :

Beautiful Dreamer	on **'Twist im Star-Club'**	G- Philips P 48036 / 1963
Sweet Nothin's	on **'Twist im Star-Club'**	G- Philips P 48036 / 1963
Shakin' All Over	on **'Twist im Star-Club'**	G- Philips P 48036 / 1963

(These three live tracks from the 'Star-Club' were the very first recordings of the **Searchers**, a little later they were also released on the British Philips label - BL 7578 / 1963)

Unissued tracks :

From the **Searchers** the following Sixties' unissued tracks are known:

"**Bye Bye Johnny**" (sung by **John McNally** !), "**Goodbye So Long**" - probably both from 1963,

"**Somewhere In The Night**" (written and released by **Jacki Trent**), "**I Who Have Nothing**", "**Shame, Shame, Shame**" - all from 1964, "**Once Upon A Time**" from 1965, as well as various live tracks that were recorded for the BBC 'Saturday Club', such as "**I'll Be Loving You**" (a group's original), "**See See Rider/Jenny Take A Ride**", "**I Don't Believe**", "**Goodbye So Long**", "**Blowin' In The Wind**" and "**Sweet Little Sixteen**".

For the independent producer, **Bill Landies**, they recorded the song, "**The Great Train Robbery**", in 1968, as well as "**For What It's Worth**" and "**Don't Shut Me Out**" for Liberty in 1969.

THE SECRETS

This group originated from the **Hi-Cats**, one of the first Beat groups in Liverpool, formed by **Vic Grace** after he had left **Mark Peters & the Cyclones** in the very early Sixties.

Danny Havoc (voc) and **Dave Collins** (bg/voc) of the **Hi-Cats** formed the **Ventures** in early 1963, together with **Les Stuart** (g), who had formerly played with the **Les Stuart Quartet** and **Frank Knight & the Barons**.

This trio was joined by drummer **Pete Orr**, also a former member of the **Hi-Cats** who had then played with **Groups Inc.** in France and **Sid Edwards** (g/voc), who had also played with **Groups Inc.** in France. **Sid Edwards** had previously played with the **Flames**, **Nutrockers** and **Lee Shondell & the Capitols**.

The **Ventures** soon became the backing group for **Freddie Starr** (aka **Freddie Fowell**), formerly of **Howie Casey & the Seniors**, the **Kansas City Five** and **Groups Inc.**, on the above-mentioned French tour. But **Freddie Starr & the Ventures** only existed until the middle of 1963 and then the singer left to lead **Freddie Starr & the Midnighters** and, later, **Freddie Starr & the Starr Boys** (sometimes also appearing as **Freddie Starr & the Flamingoes**) and **Freddie Starr & the Delmonts**.

The **Ventures** continued as a group and were joined by songstress, **Barbara Harrison**, also a former member of the **Hi-Cats** who, prior to joining the **Ventures,** had sung with **Faron's Flamingos**.

The group then changed their name to **Danny Havoc & the Ventures** and when **Vic Grace** replaced **Les Stuart** a little later, the **Hi-Cats** line-up was almost complete again. **Les Stuart** became a member of the **Kansas City Five** and, after that, played with **The Long & The Short**.

When **Barbara Harrison** left a short time later to join the **Kansas City Five**, the band name was changed again—this time to **Danny Havoc & the Secrets**. The group, at that time, consisted of the following musicians:

Danny Havoc	(voc)
Vic Grace	(g/voc)
Sid Edwards	(g/voc)
Dave Collins	(bg/voc)
Pete Orr	(dr)

But the changes in the line-up did not end there and the next to leave was **Danny Havoc**, who disappeared from the scene and was not replaced in the group, who now continued as the **Secrets**. **Sid Edwards** left to join the **Nashpool Four**, who later became the **Nashpool**. **Pete Orr** also decided to leave the group and joined the **Easybeats** from Liverpool.

These changes, in late 1963, probably resulted in the best known and most successful line-up of the **Secrets** with:

Vic Grace	(voc/g)
Denny Alexander	(g/voc)
Dave Collins	(bg/voc)
Dave Preston	(dr)

Denny Alexander was a former member of the **Aarons**, while **Dave Preston** came from the **Harlems**, the backing group for the Liverpool vocal group, the **Chants**. Before that, he had been a member of **Vince & the Volcanoes**.

It was most probably this line-up that was signed to Oriole, but it seems there was never a record released by the **Secrets**. The reason may have been that, soon after they were signed, Oriole was taken over by CBS.

Another reason may also have been due to the continually changing line-up at that time.

In April 1964, **Dave Preston** left to join the newly formed **Kinsleys** and, a little later, **Denny Alexander** also followed him to the **Kinsleys**. After that, **Dave Preston** was a member of the hit group, **Creation**, who had evolved from the **Mark Four** (not the Liverpool group), while **Denny Alexander** joined the **Clayton Squares**.

The new members of the **Secrets** were **Austin Brown** (g) and **Peter Hall** (dr). **Austin Brown** was a former member of **Johnny Templer & the Hi-Cats**, a successor group of the previously-named original **Hi-Cats**. **Peter Hall** only stayed for a few weeks and then joined the **Memphis Rhythm & Blues Combo**. He was replaced by **Johnny Gee**, from Liverpool's **Tokens**.

Vic Grace & the Secrets

The **Secrets** also expanded their line-up with the addition of a sax player, **Jack Curtis,** who had formerly played with the **Renegades** from Liverpool.

It was probably this line-up that recorded the song "Mojo", which was meant to be featured on the live compilation album, 'Cavern Alive', but, for unknown reasons, the album was cancelled.

Dave Collins left the group to join the **Hideaways,** he was replaced in the **Secrets** by **Harold Williams,** who came from **The Mafia**. At the beginning of 1965, **Johnny Gee** joined the **Delmonts** and was later a member of the **Pikkins**. **Jack Curtis** also left and later played with various groups.

Colin Woodruff from the **Fontanas** joined the **Secrets** as their new drummer and they continued on as a four piece.

When **Austin Brown** left in April 1965, he was replaced by **Pete Campbell**, a former member of the **Beathovens**, **Karl Terry & the Cruisers**, the **Fontanas**, the **Tony Prince Combo** and the **Mersey Five**. This line-up of the **Secrets** lasted until September 1965 when **Pete Campbell** left to join the Scottish group **John**

O'Hara & his Playboys in Germany. The remaining **Vic Grace**, **Harold Williams** and **Colin Woodruff** continued as a trio together until 1967. Then **Colin Woodruff** became a member of the **Times**, who, for a while, backed the Liverpool vocal trio the **Signs**. The new drummer for the **Secrets** was **Roy Hesketh**.

As **Vic Grace & the Secrets,** the group went to Italy where they met up and amalgamated with two sax-players, **Alan Gaskell** and **John Chisholm,** and organist **Iain Bradshaw**, who had just departed from the **Valkyries**, who had already been performing in Italy for a few months.

Vic Grace & the Secrets toured quite successfully in Italy and then joined forces with the coloured Jamaican singer, **Nevil Cameron,** to become **Nevil Cameron & the Groove**.

Under that name, the group signed a recording contract and it was probably in 1968 that the Italian 50's-star, **Marino Marini,** produced the single, "L'ultima Partite", from the western movie, 'Sentenza di Morte', with **Nevil Cameron & the Groove** for the Tiffany label. It did not become a big hit, but the group continued touring in Italy for two more years. During this time, **Alan Gaskell** was featured on the original version of "Chirpy Chirpy Cheep Cheep", which was recorded by the composer, **Lally Stott**, a former member of the **Denny Seyton Group** and the **Motowns**, who had settled down in Rome.

NEVIL CAMERON And The GROOVE

It was in the very early Seventies that **Nevil Cameron & the Groove** disbanded and the individual members mostly disappeared from the scene.

Alan Gaskell kept playing with various Liverpool groups and, in the late Seventies, formed **Gaz & the Groovers,** who became really successful and they are still a popular act on the Merseyside scene.

Vic Grace also remained in the music business, returned to England and it is said he was a real virtuoso on guitar. Sadly, both he and **Harold Williams**, who had settled down in Italy, died a few years ago.

In retrospect, it can be said that the **Secrets** were one of the really good and very interesting groups on Liverpool's music scene. This, in spite of the countless personnel changes, which were in the end, the reason that this legendary and fondly remembered group never made a major breakthrough.

Discography :

A lot has been written about connections between the **Secrets** and Oriole and for this label, the group recorded the song "**Mojo**" in 1964, which was meant to be for the sampler, 'Cavern Alive'. In the end, the record was not released. A group with the name of the **Secrets** also released some singles on the CBS label, but that was not the Liverpool group.

as **Nevil Cameron & the Groove** :

L' ultima Partite / Preghiera Negra	**IT- Tiffany TIF 538 / 1968**
Black Prayer / The Last Game	**IT-Tiffany TIF 543 / 1968**

Unreleased tracks :

In 1969, the **Secrets** recorded a number of tracks in Livorno, Italy including **"Dark Dark", "Dead For Your Love", "O Mio Dio", Ed Ora Vai"** and **"Lasciami Solo",** none of these were ever released.

THE SEFTONS

This group was formed in Liverpool in 1966 and, because one of their members came from Sefton Park, the musicians decided on the name, the **Seftons**.

Initially, the band was influenced by the music of the **Beatles** but, as pure Beat was already starting to become somewhat outdated, the **Seftons** later began to play a sort of Rhythm & Blues style of music.

From the beginning, the group consisted of the following musicians:

David Stephenson	(voc/org/sax)
Yanny Tsamplacos	(g/voc)
David Edwards	(bg/voc)
Michael Barron	(dr/voc)

All the musicians were newcomers on the scene and the **Seftons** was the first group for all of them. **Yanny Tsamplacos** was of Greek origin, just like **Dee Christopholus** of the **Four Just Men, Jimmy Iknomides** of the **Mafia** and **Savva Hercules** of **Savva & the Democrats**.

Within a short time, the **Seftons** became popular in Merseyside and had appearances at all the well known venues such as, the 'Mardi Gras', the 'Downbeat' (then known as the 'Victoriana') and of course, the 'Cavern'.

But one of their most important appearances was one night at the 'Blue Angel' where they met **Alan Williams**, who was enthusiastic about the group and its music. It was probably him who organised a gig at the 'Cavern' for the group and arranged some clever publicity for it when he managed (in some way) to have a lot of girls present, as well as some magazine reporters. He introduced the **Seftons** as 'Merseyside's new number one band', and those exact words were written on the front page of a magazine a little later. Because of that, CBS became aware of the **Seftons** and signed them.

The group went down to London in 1967 and recorded the single, "I Can See Through You", which was produced by **Des Champ**, while the A+R man was none other than **Arthur Greenslade**. The single sold quite well but didn't have much success in the charts.

The **Seftons** musical style was increasingly influenced by the upcoming Tamla Motown sound from the USA, but they did not eliminate the 'Beat' from their programme and, so, they had an interesting mixture in their music.

They continued to be very busy on the northern club scene but then decided to move down to London. However, **David Edwards** did not want to become a professional musician, and instead, he decided to continue on with college. He was replaced by **Norman Bellis**, who had formerly played bass guitar for the **Inbeats** and the **Calderstones**.

In 1968, the **Seftons** changed their name to **The Perishers** and, in July of that year, the group cut their first single under that new name.

Fontana released the great "How Does It Feel", which was coupled with "Bye Bye Baby". However, this record, which was also released in Europe, did not get into the charts.

In December 1968, the **Perishers** recorded the group's original, "Living In The Land Of The Broken Hearted", but, unfortunately, it was not released. In spite of this, they were kept very busy on the live scene in London and had no problems making a living.

In July 1969, **Norman Bellis** left for the USA, where he remained for nine months, playing sessions with such well-known artists as **Jr. Walker & the All Stars**, the **Four Tops** and the **Walker Brothers**.

After he had left, the **Perishers** disbanded totally, but all the musicians continued to perform on London's music scene. When **Norman Bellis** returned to England, he initially joined the group, **Rusty Harness**, who had a big hit in Scandinavia, at that time, with the song, "Ain't Gonna Get Married". (Ember EMB-S 283).

Norman Bellis then met up with his old friends from the **Perishers** again and they decided to re-form the group, this time under the name of **Worth**. It did not take too long before **Worth** was signed to CBS and, in 1970, a nice version of the **Andy Kim** number, "Shoot 'em Up Baby", was released. This single did not become a chart success but sold quite well and so it was followed by four more singles from **Worth**. Unfortunately, none of them brought any chart honours for the group, but all their singles, some of which were also released in Europe, sold quite well.

In 1975, **Worth** broke up but **Yanny Tsamplacos**, **Norman Bellis** and **Mike Barron** continued together as a 'Hard Rock' band under the name, **Tiger,** and, in the same year, released one more single with the song, "Heavy Animal", before they also disbanded.

As far as it is known, **Norman Bellis**, who in the Seventies returned to Liverpool and joined **Perfumed Garden**, later owned a recording studio in Devonshire.

Yanny Tsamplacos kept on playing and is still active today in a group called the **Merseybeat Legends**.

Unfortunately, what happened to the other former members of the **Seftons**, **Perishers**, **Worth** or **Tiger** is not known.

Single discography :

as **The Seftons** :

I Can See Through You / Here Today   UK - CBS 202491 / 1967

as **The Perishers** :

How Does It Feel / Bye Bye Baby   UK- Fontana TF 965 / 1968

Living In The Land Of The Broken-Hearted (unreleased)   UK- Fontana acetate / 1968

as **The Worth** :

Shoot 'em Up Baby / Take The World In Your Hands   UK- CBS 5309 / 1970

Let's Go Back To Yesterday / Let Me Be   UK- CBS 7460 / 1971

Don't Say You Don't / Polecat Alley   UK- CBS 7728 / 1972

I Ain't Backing Down / I'm Not Fooling   UK- CBS 1589 / 1973

Keep It In The Family / Hey Mr. Lonely   UK- Epic EPC S 1009 / 1973

as **Tiger** :

Heavy Animal /   UK- Epic EP S 35848 / 1975

THE SELOFANE

After seeing the great London Soul group **Geno Washington & the Ram Jam Band** live, the Liverpool bass-guitarist **Benny Higginson** from Sefton Park was so enthusiastic that he became obsessed by the idea of forming such a group in Liverpool.

The Washington Soul Band

So, together with his friend, **Alan Davies** (lg), both of whom had previously played together in a group whose name is not known, they formed the **Washington Soul Band** sometime in 1966.

They recruited the drummer, **Geoff Hulme,** and Benny's old school mate, **Arnie Arnold,** on saxophone.

In addition, they were joined by **Barry Cohen** (key), a former member of the **Wild Things**, and two singers, one of which (whose name is not known) left before the first appearance of the **Washington Soul Band**. The other vocalist was **Bob Robertson**.

This line-up was joined by **Richard 'Spider' Cuthrell** on trumpet, who was the real 'musician' in the group, being able to read music and play several different instruments.

The **Washington Soul Band** picked up speed at a fast pace and, from their very first gig, proved to be very popular and, accordingly, became really busy on the scene.

After a couple of months, **Bob Robertson** was replaced by **John Gobin**, who originally was with the **Aztecs** and, prior to joining the **Washington Soul Band,** he had sung with **Clockwork Orange**.

Then **Alan Davies** left to get married and **Ray Kelly** became their new lead guitarist.

In spite of all the success this new group had on the scene, the changes in the line-up continued and it was probably when **Barry Cohen** left to join **Perfumed Garden**, that the **Washington Soul Band** split up in 1967.

Four members, namely **John Gobin, Arnie Arnold, Richard Cuthrell** and **Geoff Hulme** decided to continue together and formed a new group called the **Selofane**, that in early 1968 appeared in the following line-up:

John Gobin	(voc/g)
Judd Lander	(harp)
Les Martin	(bg/voc)
Alex Galvin	(org/voc)
Arnie Arnold	(sax)
Richard Cuthrell	(tr)
Geoff Hulme	(dr)

Judd Lander came from the **Hideaways**, while **Les Martin** and **Alex Galvin** both had previously played with the **Expressions**. **Les Martin** was a former member of the **Tabs**, who had been popular on the Liverpool scene for quite a while.

Of course it might be debated whether the music of the **Selofane** was still Merseybeat or not, but who can really judge that. The simple fact is, all the members of the group hailed from Merseyside and from the Beat days and their music was in the fashion of the time, but still with a Beat.

The **Selofane** did not play on the Liverpool circuit for too long as they soon moved down to London in search of international fame. Things went well for the group and soon the London based 'emigrated Liverpudlians' were signed to CBS.

A little later, their first single was released with the superb "Girl Called Fantasy", written by **Tony Waddington** (see **Pete Best Four**), **Judd Lander** and a certain **Marchant**. This record, meant to be the theme music for the 'Musica '68' pop festival in Palma, Spain, was produced by the American **Albert Hammond**, later of "It Never Rains In Southern California" fame, who, together with **Lee Hazlewood,** also wrote the B-side "Happiness Is Love".

"Girl Called Fantasy", in its music, melody and arrangement, was similar to the big hit success, "From The Underworld", by the **Herd**.

It was a huge disappointment for the musicians, the producer and the record company when the 'Musica '68' festival was cancelled, as it could have been a major breakthrough for the **Selofane** with their very first record. Fortunately, the cancellation of the pop festival in no way affected the amount of 'plugs' the record got, and the group was not only featured on almost every radio show, but also appeared a few times on the British television, including the 'Tony Blackburn Show'.

The single was also released in Europe and did especially well in Spain, as well as in Germany and Holland. "Girl Called Fantasy" did not make the charts but what it did do was help in getting the **Selofane** truly established on the scene.

This played a big part in CBS releasing a second single by the group, also in 1968. "Shingle I-A-O" was also written by Hammond/Hazlewood and was again produced by **Albert Hammond**. A nice commercial song with a great musical arrangement but, it did not compare to their debut single, and so it also failed to become a chart success.

After that release, **Judd Lander** left the group and became a very successful session musician in London. As such, his harmonica can be heard on the "Karma Chameleon" hit success of **Boy George**.

Ray Hall then joined the **Selofane** as their new lead guitarist and, while many of the insiders on the music scene saw a bright future for the group in 1969, it disbanded in 1970. The musicians returned to their hometown of Liverpool, where they disappeared from the scene.

Only of **John Gobin** is it known, that he went back to London, where, in 1972, he was a member of the recording-group, **Panhandle**, that also included the famous musicians, **Chris Spedding** and **Herbie Flowers**.

What is left of the short-lived but very impressive career of the **Selofane** are two great singles, worth looking out for.

Discography :

Girl Called Fantasy / Happiness Is Love   UK - CBS 3413 / 1968

Shingle I-A-O / Chase The Face   UK - CBS 3700 / 1968

DENNY SEYTON & THE SABRES

Brian Tarr (aka **Denny Seyton**) formed this very interesting group in 1961 in Liverpool and, until the end of 1962, they toured as a relatively popular band on the Northern scene.

They took part in the nationwide 'Frankie Vaughan Beat Group Contest' and won. Because of this success, **Denny Seyton & the Sabres** were taken over by **Frankie Vaughan's** manager and immediately signed to Mercury.

In 1963, their first single, "Tricky Dicky", was released and sold very well but it did not become a chart hit. "Tricky Dicky" later became the most popular number for the group and was also covered by the **Searchers**, **Wayne Fontana & the Mindbenders** and many others. However, it was not the most successful record by

DENNY SEYTON & THE SABRES

MERCURY RECORD   MF 800   **TRICKY DICKY**

C W Baby what you want me to do

Denny Seyton & the Sabres who, in the meantime, had become professionals. In their original line-up the group consisted of:

Denny Seyton	**(voc)**
Dave Maher	**(g/voc)**
John Francis	**(g/voc)**
John Boyle	**(bg/voc)**
Tommy Walker	**(dr)**

At the time the record was released, **Tommy Walker** had already left the group and quit show business. He was replaced by **Bernie Rogers**, who had previously played with the **Moon Rockers**, the **Travellers**, that sometimes also appeared as **Johnny Saint & the Travellers**, and with **Lee Curtis & the All Stars**.

DENNY SEYTON and the SABRES

The second single by **Denny Seyton & the Sabres**, "Short Fat Fanny", also became very popular and sold quite well but, once again, was only 'almost' a chart success.

'All good things come in threes' is an old truism and, so, it was in the case for **Denny Seyton & the Sabres**. Their third release, a moody ballad with the title, "The Way You Look Tonight", brought their first chart success in 1964, when this record climbed up to No. 48 in the British charts.

This became the group's best selling record in England but, for mysterious reasons, this song did not make as strong an impression over the years as did "Tricky Dicky", although, "The Way You Look Tonight" was also covered by **Gerry & the Pacemakers**.

Denny Seyton & the Sabres had engagements all over the UK and especially in Scotland, where they were a top attraction. They also went to Germany where they established an excellent name for themselves and, at that time, they had the most appearances on German TV of any of the Liverpool groups.

In 1964, an album was released by **Denny Seyton & the Sabres** with the title, 'It's The Gear', which featured cover versions of the big Beat hits of that time but, unfortunately, no original material. This album, which did not sell too badly, was the final record by the group under the name, **Denny Seyton & the Sabres**.

A little later, with the exception of leader, **Denny Seyton**, all the group members were replaced, one after another.

John Francis emigrated to Vancouver, Canada and was replaced by **Eddie Murphy**, who had formerly played with **Dean Stacey & the Detonators**.

The next to leave was **Dave Maher**, who quit show business, his replacement on keyboards was **Mike Logan**, who came from **Lee Eddie & the Chevrons**.

Bernie Rogers left and his place on drums was taken over by **Dave Saxon**, a former member of the **Eden Kane Group**. In 1989, **Bernie Rogers** appeared again with **Johnny Guitar & his Hurricanes** and then, in 1992, he joined **Faron's Flamingos**.

Then, when **John Boyle,** the last of the original **Sabres** left, he was replaced by **Danny Dring**, who was a former member of **Mister X & the Masks** and **John Paul & the Deejays**. Then **Bernie Rogers** also left, and his place on drums was taken by **Dave Saxon**, who came from the **Eden Kane Group**.

The group now changed their name into the **Denny Seyton Group**.

Denny Seyton Group

Eddie Murphy then left the group and his replacement, from Prescot, was **Harold 'Lally' Stott,** who was originally a member of the **Vaqueros** and, prior to joining the **Denny Seyton Group,** he had played with the **Four Just Men**.

A little later, the group went to Germany again - accordingly with all the changes most probably in the following line-up:

Denny Seyton	**(voc)**
Lally Stott	**(g/voc)**
Danny Dring	**(bg)**
Mike Logan	**(org/voc)**
Dave Saxon	**(dr)**

In Germany, the **Denny Seyton Group** was signed to Decca and, in 1965, the singles, "Do The Jerk", "Hushabye" and "It's Alright" with its German flip-side, "Du Bist Meine Wahre Liebe", were released.

Of these records, the German version of "Hushabye", a real masterpiece and one of the loveliest Merseybeat ballads ever, was released under the name of **Denny Seyton's Showgroup**, it became their most successful single and entered the German hit parade.

In the meantime, there were some more changes in the line-up. **Danny Dring** had left and initially joined the **Dodos** and, after that, he played with **Cy Tucker & the Friars**, where he remained until 1988, before teaming up in a duo with his brother.

He was replaced in the **Denny Seyton Group** by **Rob Little**, whose real name is **Robert Burns** and who formerly had played with **Them Grimbles**.

Dave Saxon also left to form a new group with former member, **Eddie Murphy,** and he was replaced by **Tony Crawley**, who also came from the just disbanded, **Them Grimbles**.

Dave Saxon continued in the music business and today is still active as a drummer on Merseyside.

George Martin took this new line-up under his wing and produced an album with them for Parlophone, which is said to have exclusively featured originals written by **Harold 'Lally' Stott**.

But in the end, only the single, "Just A Kiss", with its flip-side, "In The Flowers By The Trees", was released. Unfortunately, it had no success in the charts and so all the other recorded songs remained unissued.

Maybe because of the constant changes, **Denny Seyton** decided to leave and he quit show business in 1966.

The group was then joined by **Dougie Meakin**, who came from the **Masterminds** and it is said that this line-up gigged around Liverpool for a short time under the name of the **Lovin' Kind**, but this information is doubtful. However, it is a fact that the group changed its name to **The Motowns** and, soon after, went to Italy in a line-up with:

Dougie Meakin	(voc/rg)
Lally Stott	(lg/voc)
Rob Little	(bg)
Mike Logan	(org/voc)
Tony Crawley	(dr)

The **Motowns** became very popular in Italy within a very short time and were signed to RCA Italiana in 1967. In the same year, their first single, "Prendi La Chitarra E Vai", was released, which was the Italian version of

the **David & Jonathan** success, "Lovers Of The World Unite".

This became very successful and the **Motowns** released two more singles in 1967, which included the Italian versions of "Iko Iko" and "New York Mining Disaster 1941".

An album entitled 'Si, Proprio I Motowns' was released, which, among others, included the Italian versions of "See See Rider" and "Summer In The City".

Probably around that time the Italian **Piero Pintucci** replaced **Rob Little**.

The group had really settled down in Italy, signed a new recording contract with Durium and, by 1970, had cut six more singles, which included the Italian versions of **Arthur Brown's** "Fire", the **Lemon Pipers** success, "Blueberry Blue" and the **Steam** bestseller, "Na Na Hey Hey, Kiss Him Goodbye". Most of them entered the Italian hit parade and the **Motowns** had developed into a real top act.

The final single by the group was "Lassu", which was released on the Carosello label in 1970 but, by that time, there had obviously been more changes in the line-up, although it can be taken for granted that **Dougie Meakin** was still with them.

In the meantime, **Lally Stott** had left and formed a new group under the name of **Lally Pop** that, for a time, also included the Liverpool musician, **Francis Galloway**, a former member of **King Size Taylor & the Dominoes**, the **Griff Parry Five** and the **Freddie Kelly Combo**. A little later **Francis Galloway** went on to play with **I Baronetti** who were the backing-group for the female Italian pop-star, **Nada,** and then with the **Four Kents**, all in Italy, before he returned to Liverpool. He then joined the **In Crowd** and, after that, he became a session-musician and, as such, he backed various American Blues artists on their British tours.

Back to the **Motowns** that had split up in the early Seventies. Because of his popularity, **Dougie Meakin** remained in Italy and continued to be successful on the scene, he is still living there.

Lally Stott also decided to stay in Italy, where he recorded the solo singles, "Jacaranda" and "Sweet Meeny". He also continued on as songwriter and, amongst others, wrote the big hit, "Chirpy Chirpy Cheep Cheep", for **Middle Of The Road**, which he himself also released as a single and which, by the way, featured Liverpudlian, **Alan 'Gaz' Gaskell** on saxophone.

In 1971, a solo album was released under the title 'Chirpy, Chirpy, Cheep, Cheep' which consisted exclusively of his own compositions. After that, he formed the **Lovebirds**, with whom he was very successful on the Italian music scene. The **Lovebirds** also included his wife, **Cathy Stott,** and he later continued recording as a duo with her. In 1977, on the day of the Queen's Silver Jubilee, **Lally Stott** was killed in a motorbike accident in Italy.

What happened to **Mike Logan** and **Tony Crawley** after the **Motowns** had disbanded is not known, but they probably returned to England.

Now back to **Denny Seyton**, who later returned to show business, but under his real name of **Brian Tarr**. Together, with his former group member, **John Boyle**, as well as with **Ron Burns**, he formed a cabaret trio under the name of the **Ron Hamilton Group**, which lasted until 1988 and then split up.

After that, **Brian Tarr** and **John Boyle** formed the duo, **Old Gold**, which kept going for some years and on occasions they were joined by **Paul Stewart**, who was normally the drummer with **Julian Lennon's** group.

On the 2nd December, 1990 at a 'MerseyCats' concert at the 'New Montrose' club in Liverpool, **Denny Seyton & the Sabres** stepped back into the limelight with a really great performance. Besides **Denny Seyton**, this line-up featured **Dave Maher** and **John Boyle** again, as well as **Paul Stewart** on drums. They did a few gigs for the 'MerseyCats' and then broke up again, but this, of course, may not be forever as the musicians proved at those gigs that they still had great musical ability - so let's wait, hope and see ....

Single discography :

as **Denny Seyton & the Sabres** :

Tricky Dicky / Baby What You Want Me To Do	**UK- Mercury MF 800 / 1963**
Short Fat Fanny / Give Me Back Your Heart	**UK- Mercury MF 814 / 1964**
The Way You Look Tonight / Hands Off	**UK- Mercury MF 824 / 1964**

as **The Denny Seyton Group** :

Just A Kiss / In The Flowers By The Trees	**UK-Parlophone R 5363 / 1965**

as **Denny Seyton's Showgroup** :

Do The Jerk / Along Came Jones	**G- Decca D 19674 / 1965**
Hushabye / Mir Geht Es Wieder Besser	**G- Decca D 19681 / 1965**
It's Alright / Du Bis Meine Wahre Liebe	**G- Decca D 19682 / 1965**

The Motowns :

Prendi La Chitarra E Vai / Per Quanto Io Ci Provi	**IT- RCA PM 45-3374 / 1966**
Una come lei / Prendi la chitarra e vai	**IT- RCA PM 45-3414 / 1967**
Sagamafina / Mister Jones	**IT- RCA PM 45-3420 / 1967**
Dentro La Fontana / In Un Villaggio	**IT- Durium LDA 7585 / 1968**

Fuoco / In The Morning	IT- Durium LDA 7594 / 1968
Dai Vieni Giu' / (B-side by **Los Marcellos Ferial**)	IT- Durium LDA 7616 / 1969
Sogno, Sogno, Sogno / Hello To Mary	IT- Durium LDA 7629 / 1969
Na-Na-Hey-Hey Kiss Him Goodbye (in Italian) / In The Morning	IT- Durium LDA 7667 / 1970
Lassu / Sai Forse T'amero	IT- Carosello CI 20254/ 1970

LP discography

Denny Seyton & the Sabres :

| IT'S THE GEAR | UK- Wing WL 1032 / 1964 |

- Hippy Hippy Shake / Needles And Pins / Candy Man / All My Loving / Good Golly Miss Molly /

Little Children / I Want To Hold Your Hand / Bits And Pieces / I Think Of You / Can't Buy Me Love /

Just One Look / Not Fade Away / I'm The One / Glad All Over

The Motowns :

| SI, PROPRIO I MOTOWNS | IT- RCA S 14 / 1967 |

Se la va, la va / Si, Si, Silvana / L'uomo in cenere / Don't fight It / Everybody Loves A Lover /

Per quanto io ci provi / Prendi la chitara e vai / Um, Um, Um, Um, Um / Cuore facile /

Last Train To Clarksville / Something You've Got / Una verita

Tracks on compilation-albums :

as **Denny Seyton's Showgroup** :

Along Came Jones	on 'Beat Party'	G- Telefunken ND 106 / 1965
Hush-A-Bye	on 'Beat Party'	G- Telefunken ND 106 / 1965
Mir Geht es Wieder Besser	on '16 Teen Tops'	G-Telefunken SHZT 525 / 1965
Along Came Jones	on '16 Teen Tops'	G-Telefunken SHZT 525 / 1965

Unissued tracks :

The known unissued tracks by **Denny Seyton & the Sabres** are the songs, "**House of Bamboo**", "**That's What Love Will Do**", "**Karen**", "**Hello Josephine**" (on acetate) and "**I'm Gonna Love You Too**" - all from 1963— 1964.

The **Denny Seyton Group** recorded a complete album for Parlophone in 1965, under the wing of **George Martin**. Unfortunately, in the end, only the single, **"Just A Kiss",** and its flip-side was released.

SIGNS (& TIMES)

This was probably the first Liverpool group which had no 'The' in its name; something that only later became popular with band names. Of course, this is not important but it was unusual.

The second unusual thing about the **Signs** is it was a purely vocal trio, formed at the beginning of 1966 and consisting of:

Dave Kerrigan	(voc)
Pete O'Connell	(voc)
Tony Burns	(voc)

All members were experienced musicians from the Merseybeat scene. **Dave Kerrigan** had sung with the **Toreardors** and the **Richmond Group** previously, while **Pete O'Connell** was a former member of **September** and **Tony Burns** came from the **Kwans**.

SIGNS at The Cavern
During a colour film session for N.B.C. Television — America

Of course, (and thank God) at that time, playback was unknown in the music clubs and, because the **Signs** did not want to work with continually changing bands, they had a steady backing group with the **Times**. These two names suited each other - **Signs & Times** - and so did the musicians and that is why it became quite a successful co-operation.

The **Times** were the former **Dions Sole Band** that had evolved from the **Dions**, or **Roy & the Dions**, as they were initially named. This meant that they also consisted of experienced musicians from the scene and their line-up was as follows:

Stan Alexander	(g)
Andy O'Hagan	(sax/harp)
Alan Currie	(org)
Derek Marl	(sax)
Ian Collier	(bg)
Bill Geeleher	(dr)

Prior to joining the **Dions**, **Stan Alexander** had played with the **Black Velvets**, while **Derek Marl** was a former member of the **Michael Allen Group** and the **Secrets**.

Bill Geeleher originally had played with the **Modes** and then was a member of **Them Calderstones**.

Bill Geeleher did not stay with the **Times** for too long, he left to join the **Curiosity Shoppe.**

He was replaced by **Paul Comerford**, who formerly had played with the **Pulsators, Tiffany & the Thoughts**, the **Cryin' Shames** and the **Escorts**.

Alan Currie later was replaced by **Dave O'Hagan** who, like his brother, **Andy O'Hagan,** played the saxophone and, then, **Paul Eick** came in as their new bass guitarist when **Ian Collier** left.

The **Signs,** together with the **Times**, often appeared at the 'Cavern', where they became very popular.

The famous songwriter **Les Reed** wrote a number especially for the **Signs** which was recorded for Decca. This song was "There's A Kind Of Hush" which, for incomprehensible reasons, was not released but, a little later, became a million seller for **Herman's Hermits** on Columbia.

This must have been hugely annoying for the **Signs** as a release

The Times (Both photos)

of their record would most probably have meant an international breakthrough for them. Once again, Decca had missed the boat and they tried to patch things up with another release. The Murray/Callander song, "Ain't You Got A Heart", was released on a single in 1966 with the Leiber/Stoller composition, "My Baby Comes To Me", on the flip-side.

"Ain't You Got A Heart" had **Tony Burns** as lead singer, while "My Baby Comes To Me" featured the lead vocals of **Dave Kerrigan**. Both songs, in no way comparable to "There's A Kind Of Hush", had a full orchestra backing and it is not known if the **Times** were included in this **Ivor Raymonde** production or not.

It was one of the typical pop records of that time, common in melody and arrangement, and it showed the **Signs** to be really good singers. This record, also released in Europe, didn't make the charts. Maybe in the end the frustration and disillusionment caused by the missed chance with "There's A Kind Of Hush" led to the **Signs** splitting in late 1967 or early 1968. All three singers disappeared from the scene.

The **Times**, who, in the meantime, had also appeared on their own, continued as a group on the Merseyside scene but they had a number of changes in their line-up.

Dave O'Hagan left and was replaced by **Allen 'Gaz' Gaskell**, a great sax-player, who had previously played with the **Young Ones** from Birkenhead (not to be confused with the Decca recording group of the same name), the **Tiyms**, the **K-Ds** and also with **Combo Six**.

The next to leave was **Andy O'Hagan**, who followed his brother to **Bernie & the Buzz Band** and **Derek Marl** also parted from the **Times** and joined the **Almost Blues**. In the Seventies, he was a member of the successful recording group, **Champagne**.

Alan Gaskell later joined the **Robby Gray Soul Band** before he became a member of **Ian Hunter & the Valkyries**, with whom he went to Italy. In Rome, he teamed up with **Vic Grace & the Secrets**, who had a long residency down there and, with the Jamaican singer, **Nevil Cameron**, appeared and recorded as **Nevil Cameron & the Groove**. In 1978, **Alan Gaskell** was a member of **Karl Terry & the Cruisers**, which evolved into the first line-up of the legendary **Gaz & the Groovers**, that also appeared in Germany as **Juke** and then as **Supercharge '84'**.

When **Paul Comerford** left, the new drummer for the **Times** was **Colin Woodruff**, who had formerly played with the **Fontanas** and the **Secrets**.

It is not clear how long the **Times** continued on the scene but, of **Stan Alexander**, it is known that later on he was a member of the Rock 'n' Roll band, **Darts**, who had some international hits in the Seventies.

Sometime in the Seventies, the **Signs** were 'back' as a cabaret-group that included **Tony Burns** and his wife, as well as **Dave Kerrigan** again. Therefore, it is also possible that the **Signs**, with a short break after their split in 1967, continued on the scene but nothing was heard of them.

In the Seventies, **Kenny Baker** also played with them, he was a former member of the **Defenders** and the **Myths**.

Dave Kerrigan appeared again on the scene in the Nineties, but only as a committee member of the 'MerseyCats" and not as a singer for a band - yet!

Single discography :

Ain't You Got A Heart / My Baby Comes To Me   UK- Decca F.12522 / 1966

Besides this, the **Signs** recorded the original of "**There's A Kind Of Hush**" for Decca in 1966, but this version was never released. One year later it became a million seller for Manchester's **Herman's Hermits**.

SOME PEOPLE

This Chester-based group originated from the **Musketeers**, a college band formed by **Keith Muscott** and **Terry Ord** in 1961.

When this band split up in mid 1962, the two friends decided to stay together in the music business and to form a new group - **Some People**. This new combo featured the following musicians:

Terry Ord	(voc)
Keith Muscott	(g/voc)
Nick Cowap	(g)
Dave Meredith	(bg)
Colin Harris	(dr)

Some People played a mix of Beat and Rhythm & Blues music and **Dennis Critchley** took over the management of the group. He was the owner of the 'Royalty Theatre' in Chester and also managed the **Black Abbots**, who later became very famous in the English cabaret scene. Under the wing of Mr. Critchley, **Some People** were soon on their way up.

Obviously, the group frequently played at the 'Royalty Theatre' and also Quantways', the other important live venue in Chester. Because Chester is not far from Liverpool, **Some People** also had regular appearances in the Beat metropolis, where they played gigs at 'St. George's Hall', as well as the well known clubs such as the 'Cavern' and the 'Iron Door'. Consequently, they also became a popular act on the Merseyside scene.

In 1964, **Some People** went down to London where a recording session was held for Oriole.

At that time, they were joined by **Nick Bennett** as an additional guitarist. He had formerly played with **Clay Ellis & the Corsairs**. But he only came into the group for the recording sessions and, after that, he disappeared from the scene.

The band recorded four songs, which, in addition to the **Terry Ord** original, "This Is The Night", included "Sure Know A Lot About Love", "Jeremiah Peabody" and "Just One More Dance".

"Sure Know A Lot About Love", which was also recorded by the **Searchers** and "This Is The Night" were meant to be released on single but, for unknown reasons, this did not happen.

This unlucky development, added to the fact that **Dennis Critchley** resigned as their manager to concentrate on the career of the **Black Abbots**, as well as the fact that a planned tour of Europe did not happen, were probably the reasons why **Some People** split up in late 1964.

Keith Muscott and **Colin Harris** later played in various dance combos before they also quit show business, as the other members had done before them.

Discography :

Some People never released a record but recorded an EP with the following songs for Oriole :

This Is The Night / Jeremiah Peabody /
Just One More Dance / Sure Know A Lot About Love   UK- Oriole demo- EP / 1964

SOUNDS PLUS ONE

It was somewhat of an adventure obtaining any information about this group, formed in the Tuebrook area of Liverpool, most probably sometime in 1964.

It was a four-piece group, at least for some time, which included the following musicians:

John Thompson	**(voc)**
Len Bowers	**(lg/voc)**
Alan McDonald	**(bg)**
Paul Hitchmough	**(dr)**

For vocalist, **John Thompson,** it was his first group, while **Len Bowers** had previously played with the **Statesmen** and the **Four Musketeers**.

Paul Hitchmough was not the original drummer and, during late 1964 and early 1965, he had previously played with the **Hangmen**, the **Victims** and the **Corals** prior to joining **Sounds Plus One**

Sounds Plus One played the normal club circuit throughout Merseyside where they had a large following, especially in the area of West Derby, but they never really made the headlines.

It was most probably in early 1965 when they cut an interesting acetate on Unicord.

The group's original, "Girl Of My Dreams", is a very nice Merseybeat ballad. It was coupled with a re-arranged and slowed-down version of the **Jessie Hill** success, "Ooh-Poo-Pah-Doo".

Unfortunately, in spite of its quality, this acetate was not followed by a record release and so it did not help the group's popularity, which might have been the reason for **Sounds Plus One** disbanding in 1965.

Of **Len Bowers** it is known that he joined Liverpool's successful Country scene, playing first with the **Don West Trio** and, after that, with the **Kentuckians** and the **Topics**.

Alan McDonald also joined the Country scene but it is not known with which group.

John Thompson and **Paul Hitchmough** joined the **Kruzads** where they were featured on the acetate release of "Stop Your Sobbing".

After that, **John Thompson** quit the music business and never returned to it, while **Paul Hitchmough** kept playing drums and later was a member of a number of popular groups that included the **Clayton Squares** and **Curiosity Shoppe**.

In the Nineties, he appeared again as a member of **Beryl Marsden's** group and, after that, he played with **Karl Terry & the Cruisers**.

What is left of the short career of the **Sounds Plus One** is a great acetate, worth seeking out.

Discography :

Girl Of My Dreams / Ooh-Poo-Pah-Doo   UK- Unicord acetate / 1965

THE SPORTSMEN

Sometime in 1958, the two guitarists/singers, **George Chamberlain** and **Ian Watts,** formed a duo at Wigan Grammar School under the name of the **Rocking Vampires**.

Through the addition of **Maurice Myers** (t-bass) and **Roy Ellison** (dr), the **Rocking Vampires** became a real Rockabilly group, however, **Roy Ellison** was soon replaced by **Dave Rylance**.

Ian Watts left due to family problems and **Keith Wright** took over on lead guitar.

This line-up then changed their name into **Danny Lee & the Stalkers** and started to play outside Wigan, mainly gigs in Liverpool, Southport and, a little later, in Manchester. The group received an offer to play four nights a week at the 'Domino' club in Manchester and this meant that the musicians would have to become professionals but only **George Chamberlain** was prepared for that step, so the group disbanded.

George Chamberlain recruited **Jimmy Martin** (g) and **Keith Battersby** (bg) from the **Avalons**, as well as drummer, **John Boffey,** from the Wigan-based **Dominoes**. This new line-up of **Danny Lee & the Stalkers** accepted the 'Domino' club offer but this adventure was short lived.

After that, **George Chamberlain** continued in the Manchester scene, where he had brief spells with **Pete & the Rebels** and the **Boydells**, while **Jimmy Martin,** together with **Dave Rylance** and others, formed the **Martinis**.

When **George Chamberlain** returned to Wigan, he was contacted by his old comrade, **Maurice Myers**, who, at that time, was playing with the resident band at the new 'Sportsman' club in Wigan.

They wanted to expand the group and **George Chamberlain** was asked to join, which he did. A little later, the **Sportsmen** were born, in the line-up with:

George Chamberlain	(voc)
Derek Taylor	(voc/perc)
Keith Wright	(lg)
Reg Parker	(rg)
George Twist	(org/p)
Maurice Myers	(bg)
Dave Rylance	(dr)

Accordingly, the basis of that new group was the complete first line-up of the former **Danny Lee & the Stalkers**.

George Twist was a former member of the **Blues Set**, a name that the **Beat Boys** used for some time. The **Sportsmen** recorded some demos at **Alan Cheetham's** studio in Stockport and sent them off to various record companies. It was the **George Chamberlain** number titled "And It Shows", that attracted the interest of **Ted Taylor**, the former leader of the **Ted Taylor Four**, who was now working as producer for CBS. The **Sportsmen** were invited down to London for test recordings, which resulted in them being signed by CBS.

It was in 1966 that the single with the **Buddy Buie** song, "I Miss You (When I Kiss You)", was released by the **Sportsmen,** coupled with "If It's Love". Both numbers were not Beat but nice ballads, zapped up with a full orchestral backing by **Les Reed**. In its presentation and sound, the record reminded one a little bit of the style of the **Fortunes**, which means that great vocals were also featured on it. The record just got into the Top-50 and it seems that this was not satisfactory for CBS, as they did not extend the contract with the **Sportsmen**, but were interested in keeping **George Chamberlain** as a solo artist. This was not well received by the musicians and, after a number of arguments, the group broke up in 1966.

George Chamberlain signed with CBS, adopted the name of **Paul Craig** and, still in the same year (1966), his first solo single, "Midnight Girl", was released. This record became quite popular around London and **Paul Craig** had some radio and TV appearances but, in the end, it did not sell well enough to make the charts.

To promote the record, **Paul Craig** had formed another band under the name of **Paul Craig & the Theme** which, besides him, included **Keith Wright** and **George Twist** again, as well as **Ken Fillingham** (g) and **Johnny Hutchinson** (dr).

Kenny Fillingham was a former member of the **Beat Boys** and **Johnny Hutchinson**, of course, came from Liverpool's **Big Three**.

Paul Craig

This group was short-lived and the former **Sportsmen** members, **Paul Craig** (aka **George Chamberlain**), **Keith Wright** and **George Twist**, formed a new group called **The New City Showband** which, after **Keith Wright** had left for Germany, included **Kenny Fillingham** again, as well as **Ronnie Carr** (bg), formerly with the **Beat Boys**, plus **John Kelly** (dr) and a brass section with **Steve McMahon** (trombone), **Tony Morgan** (trumpet) and 'Roz' Rosbottom** (saxophone).

This group specifically played the cabaret-circuit, which had become big business by that time. The **New City Showband** became very successful on the scene and played all the major venues for a couple of years. When they split up, **George Chamberlain**, together with **Ronnie Carr,** went on to form a group called **Major Minor**, which also included **Barry Ascroft** (key), **Dave Brown** (lg) and another former **Beat Boys** member, **Eric Eastham** on drums.

After that, **George Chamberlain** retired from showbiz, as probably all the others did, as nothing was heard of them again .

Discography :

I Miss You (When I Kiss You) / If It's Love   UK- CBS 202043 / 1966

George Chamberlain solo as Paul Craig :

Midnight Girl / Autumn   UK-CBS 202406 / 1966

Unreleased tracks :

The **Sportsmen** recorded a number of tracks as demos to send out to the record companies in 1965. Of them, only the **George Chamberlain** original, "**And It Shows**", is known.

THE ST. LOUIS CHECKS

This real Rhythm & Blues band was formed by **Eric Savage** in Liverpool in 1964 after he had previously sung with the **Nashpool Four**.

In addition to the **Roadrunners**, the **Clayton Squares**, the **Hideaways** and the **Almost Blues**, the **St. Louis Checks** were soon considered to be one of the leading bands of that sound in Liverpool.

In their original line-up, the group consisted of the following musicians:

Eric Savage	(voc/harp)
Terry Kenna	(g/voc)
Lawrence Swerdlow	(org/p)
Alan Collins	(bg/voc)
Johnny Sze	(dr)

Johnny Sze, who came from the **Satanists**, did not stay for too long, he left to join the re-formed **Harlems**, which, as a backing group for **Beryl Marsden**, went to Germany and played at the 'Star-Club' where the **Harlems** were sometimes billed as the **Blue Boys**.

After that, he became a member of the **Cherry Stones** in Stockholm, that later evolved into the **Kinetic**, who settled down in Paris and released a string of records there, but that is another story.

The new drummer with the **St. Louis Checks** was **Roy 'Triff' David**. It is not known where he had played previously, but it might have been with the **Smokestack Blues Band**.

In the middle of 1964, after a really promising start, **Lawrence Swerdlow** and **Alan Collins** left the group. **Alan Collins** became a member of the **Memphis Rhythm & Blues Combo**, while **Lawrence Swerdlow** disappeared from the scene.

The **St. Louis Checks** were joined by **Julius David** (bg), who was possibly the brother of the new drummer, as well as by **Dave Carr** (p/sax), who both came from the **Smokestack Blues Band**, who apparently had just disbanded.

This line-up lasted until the end of the year, at which time the **St. Louis Checks** disbanded totally before they were signed to a recording company and, as far as it is known, there was never anything recorded by this really good group.

In spite of the fact that the **St. Louis Checks** were quite short-lived and had constant changes in their line-up, they left behind a lasting impression on the Liverpool music scene of the Sixties.

Of the individual members, **Terry Kenna** later appeared again as a member of the **Terry Hines Sextet** and then he joined the **Blues System**, a Scottish group that had settled down in Liverpool and became the resident group at the 'Blue Angel'.

It is known that **Roy David** joined the **Rebels**, formerly known as **Ian & the Rebels** who, after singer, **Ian Gregson** left, had become the backing group for **Ricky Gleason** for some time.

Then **Roy David** joined the **Richmond** where his brother (?), **Barry David,** was already playing.

Unfortunately, what happened to the other musicians is not known.

FREDDIE STARR & THE MIDNIGHTERS

The story of this group from the Wirral reaches back to the Skiffle days and starts with the formation of the **Five Stars**, most probably by the great guitarist, **John Kelman**, who had previously played with the **Dons**. One of the original members was **Kenny Lazzard** (t-bass), who is probably the musician, **Stu Hazzard**, who later played bass guitar with **Earl Royce & the Olympics**.

The **Five Stars** broke up when their other guitarist, **Dave Carden**, joined **Gus & the Thundercaps**, one of the very early and very good Rock 'n' Roll groups on Merseyside that soon changed their name into **Gus Travis & the Midnighters**. At that time, **John Kelman** became a member of **Dee Fenton & the Silhouettes**.

It was in May 1963, that **Gus Travis & the Midnighters** were booked to play at the opening of the 'Streatham Ice-Rink' in London and **Gus Travis** refused to go down there.

The **Midnighters** then teamed up with the singer, **Freddie Fowell**, from the disbanded **Howie Casey & the Seniors** who, prior to joining the **Midnighters,** had also sung with the **Kansas City Five**, **Groups Inc.** and with **Freddie Starr & the Ventures**.

They played the ice-rink gig and decided to continue together as **Freddie Starr & the Midnighters**.

Both the guitarist, **Ian McQuair,** and the drummer, **John Cochran,** left very soon after and, together with **Dave Georgeson** (g) of **Wump & His Werbles,** formed the **Lil' Three**. This group later added former members of the **Pressmen** and evolved into the **Chuckles**.

When **Alan Watts**, the pianist of the **Midnighters,** made the decision to concentrate on the management of the group, **Freddie Starr & the Midnighters** continued in the following line-up:

Freddie Starr	(voc)
John Kelman	(lg/voc)
Dave Carden	(rg/voc)
Brian Woods	(bg/voc)
Ian Broad	(dr)

John Kelman had returned from **Dee Fenton & the Silhouettes**. **Brian Woods** had played with the **Morockans** before he teamed up with **Dave Carden** in **Gus Travis & the Midnighters**.

Ian Broad was also a former member of the **Five Stars** and, prior to joining **Freddie Starr & the Midnighters,** he had played with the short-lived **Seniors**.

Freddie Starr himself had occasionally been backed by the **Five Stars** in the Fifties when he still appeared as '**Freddy the Teddy**'.

Joe Meek became aware of the band and took them under his wing as his first group from Liverpool.

In 1963, he produced the single, "Who Told You", with **Freddie Starr & the Midnighters** for the Decca label, which was coupled with the interesting "Peter Gunn Locomotion" but, unfortunately, it was unsuccessful. The group was joined by **Roger James** on piano.

FREDDIE STARR & THE MIDNIGHTERS

Their second single, "Baby Blue", was a very nice ballad but was too harmless to cause a sensation or to become a chart success. Both records are desired collectors' items today.

Shortly after this single, **John Kelman** left to re-join **Dee Fenton & the Silhouettes** who, in the meantime, had settled down in Manchester under the name of **The Four Just Men**, another story in this book.

Within a matter of weeks, the complete line-up of the **Midnighters** changed. **Ian Broad** went down to London to join **Heinz & the Wild Boys**. When he later returned to Liverpool, he played with **Rory Storm & the Hurricanes** and then with **Dave Allen & the Exotics**.

Freddie Starr & the Midnighters were joined by **Keef Hartley**, the former drummer with the **Thunderbeats** from Preston.

Around the same time, **Dave Carden** left to join the **Pressmen** (that evolved into the **Flamingoes**) and, a little later, **Brian Woods** followed **Ian Broad** to **Heinz & the Wild Boys** in London.

Their replacements in **Freddie Starr & The Midnighters** were **Reg Welch** (lg) and **John Brierley** (bg), who both came from the just disbanded **Questions**. Both musicians hailed from Preston where **Reg Welch** had previously played with the **Rebels** and the **Questions** and **John Brierley** with the **Thunderbeats**.

Heinz & the Wild Boys - with former members of the Midnighters & Ritchie Blackmore

Maybe because of all these changes, **Freddie Starr** separated from the group in 1964.

Initially, he had a role in the Lionel Bart musical, 'Maggie May', and then he teamed up with the **Flamingoes** (formerly **The Pressmen**) under the name of **Freddie Starr & the Starr Boys**, which is another story. After that, he was backed by the **Delmont Four** (also another story) under the name of **Freddie Starr & the Delmonts**. He later started a solo career on the cabaret scene and today is still a very popular TV star in England and he also records from time to time. In 1964, after **Freddie Starr** left the group, the **Midnighters** split up.

John Brierley returned to Preston where he joined **David John & the Mood** and **Reg Welch** became a member of the **Nashpool** (formerly the **Nashpool Four**) and then went back to Preston and joined the **Suspects**.

Keef Hartley and **Roger James**, together with **Bob Garner** from the **Merseybeats** and the sax-player, **Dave McShane**, formed **The Ice Blues**.

This group was only short-lived and, afterward, **Keef Hartley** became a member of **Rory Storm & the Hurricanes** and later played with the **Artwoods** from London and **John Mayall's Bluesbreakers**, before he formed his own group under the name of the **Keef Hartley Band**. In the mid-Seventies, he played with the **Michael Chapman Group** and today he is still regarded as one of the best drummers in England.

Roger James, who by the way is not the guitarist of the same name who played in the **Prestons** and the **Roger James Four**, disappeared from the scene, while **Bob Garner** and **Dave McShane** joined a new line-up of **Lee Curtis & the All Stars**.

Discography :

Who Told You / Peter Gunn Locomotion	**UK- Decca F.11663 / 1963**
Baby Blue / It's Shaking Time	**UK- Decca F.11786 / 1963**

(Note: for further records by **Freddie Starr,** see the story of **Freddie Starr & the Starr Boys**)

FREDDIE STARR & THE STARR BOYS

This group originated from the **Pressmen**, that were formed in Wallasey on the Wirral in 1961.

The **Pressmen** were initially an independent band but then became the backing group for coloured singer **Derry Wilkie**, who had previously sung with **Derry & the Seniors** and **Howie Casey & the Seniors** and was also backed by **Geoff Stacey & the Wanderers** for a short while.

The Flamingoes

When **Derry Wilkie** separated from them to form **Derry Wilkie & the Others**, the **Pressmen** were joined by **Dave Carden** (g/voc), who replaced the original guitarist, **Ritchie Prescott**.

Dave Carden was a former member of the **Five Stars** and **Gus & the Thundercaps** that evolved into **Gus Travis & the Midnighters** and then into **Freddie Starr & the Midnighters**

Shortly after **Faron's Flamingos** disbanded in 1964, they received an offer to tour Germany - instead, the **Pressmen** adopted the **Flamingoes** name (with an 'e') and went to Germany, where they became quite popular and recorded a single for the Dt.Vogue label with the songs, "Mein Beatle Baby", the German version of "Roll over Beethoven" and "Glücklich Wie Noch Nie", the German version of "I'll Get You". Unfortunately, it was not very successful, although it was a really good Beat record and today it is a most desirable and expensive collector's item.

During their stay in Hamburg, the group, under the name of the **Liverpool Triumphs**, also backed coloured singer, **Tony Cavanaugh,** on his poorly produced album, 'Rock 'n Twist, Slop, Hully Gully' on the Somerset label. **Tony Cavanaugh** was the former drummer with **Tony Sheridan's** band and it should be pointed out very clearly that the poor production of the record was certainly not the fault of the **Liverpool Triumphs (Flamingoes)**.

The group kept the **Flamingoes** name until it teamed up with singer, **Freddie Starr**, under the name **Freddie Starr & the Starr Boys** - also in 1964.

Freddie Starr, whose real name is **Freddie Fowell**, had previously sung with the Liverpool groups, **Howie Casey & the Seniors**, the **Kansas City Five**, **Groups Inc.**, **Freddie Starr & the Ventures** and **Freddie Starr & the Midnighters**.

Freddie Starr & the Starr Boys also appeared as **Freddie Starr & the Flamingoes** in the following line-up:

Freddie Starr	**(voc)**
Dave Carden	**(g/voc)**
Bob Pears	**(bg)**
Dave Roberts	**(sax)**
Aynsley Dunbar	**(dr)**

With the exception of **Dave Carden** and **Freddie Starr**, all musicians were former members of the **Pressmen**.

Freddie Starr & the Starr Boys were signed to Decca and, in September 1964, released the single, "Never Cry (On Someone's Shoulder)", which was not too successful and so it remains as the only single recorded by the group. But, because of the connection the **Flamingoes** had to Dt. Vogue, an album was released in the same year by **Freddie Starr & the Starr-Boys** on that label in Germany with the title, 'This Is Liverpool Beat'. This great live recording from the 'Iron Door' club in Liverpool captured the real excitement of the music of that time and today is a highly desirable collector's item.

During their tour of Germany, **Aynsley Dunbar** became homesick and desperately wanted to return to Liverpool. Therefore, he swapped places with **George Roberts**, the drummer of the **Excheckers**, who were also on tour in Germany at the same time but were about to return to Liverpool.

After playing with the **Excheckers** for a time, **Anysley Dunbar** joined the **Mojos** and, after that, played with such well known groups as **John Mayall's Bluesbreakers**, **Journey**, the **Aynsley Dunbar Retaliation**, **Aynsley Dunbar & Blue Whale**, **Frank Zappa**'s **Mothers Of Invention** and **Jefferson Starship**. He is based in Los Angeles today and is still a world class drummer.

Freddie Starr & the Starr Boys

As early as 1965, **Freddie Starr** left the group and a little later was backed by the **Delmont Four** under the name of **Freddie Starr & the Delmonts**.

He later started a solo career as one of the most popular TV stars in England but he also kept on recording. In the Seventies, he had his biggest record success when his single, "It's You", climbed to No. 9 in the British charts in 1974 and the 1975 follow-up, "White Christmas", reached No. 41.

But back to the **Starr Boys** who, in 1965, changed their name back to the **Flamingoes** and for a short time were very successful on the Merseybeat scene but then disbanded without having released any more records.

Unfortunately, what happened to **Dave Carden** after the **Flamingoes** broke up, is not known, but it can be taken for granted that he remained in the music business.

George Roberts became a member of the **Delmont Four**, that also backed **Freddie Starr**. He then had a short spell with **Amen Corner** before he joined the **Mindbenders** from Manchester.

Bob Pears went on to play with the **Chuckles** and in the Seventies, teamed up with original **Pressmen** drummer, **Nick Arnott,** in a cabaret duo that appeared under various names. **Nick Arnott** later played with the groups **Persuader** and **Rocket 88** before he met up again with **Ritchie Precott** in the **Juke Box Eddies**. **Bob Pears** sadly died in 1995.

Dave Roberts formed the **Dave Anthony Three** together with **Tony Crofts** (dr) and **Robin Thomas** (keys). In this trio, **Dave Roberts** played bass guitar again, the instrument that he originally started with in the **Pressmen**. Sometime later **Tony Crofts** was replaced by **Pete James** and **Robin Thomas** by **Dave Saltrese**. In this line-up, the **Dave Anthony Three** were featured on the EP, 'Four For You', by a duo called **Dual Control** (UK-Riga HP 49/1976), which consisted of the original **Pressmen** lead guitarist, **Ritchie Prescott,** and a certain **Gary Nicholls**.

When the **Dave Anthony Three** finally split up in 1978, **Dave Roberts** left show business.

Single discography :

as **Freddie Starr & the Starr Boys** :

Never Cry (On Someone's Shoulder) / Just Keep On Dreaming   UK- Decca F. 12009 / 1964

as **The Flamingoes** - without **Freddie Starr** :

Glücklich Wie Noch Nie / Mein Beatle Baby

G- Dt.Vogue DV 14158 / 1964

Dave Anthony Three

LP discography

as **Freddie Starr & the Starr Boys** :

THIS IS LIVERPOOL BEAT   G-Dt.Vogue LDV 17006 / 1964

- Tutti Frutti / Lucille / Peter Gunn / One Mint Julep / Rip It Up / Mean Woman Blues / Skinny Minny /

You Are My Sunshine / Shop Around / Another Saturday Night / Oh Baby / Will You Love Me Tomorrow

(This album is said to be a live recording from the famous 'Iron Door' club in Liverpool)

as **Tony Cavanaugh & die Liverpool Triumphs** :

ROCK'N TWIST, SLOP, HULLY GULLY   G- Somerset 583 / 1964

- My Babe / Mashed Potatoes / I'm Talking About You / What Did I Say / Hummel-Twist / Money /

Jezebel / Hully Gully / We Are Slopping / Twiullyop / Tell Me Baby

(This album, recorded with **Tony Sheridan's** former drummer on vocals, was released before the group teamed up with **Freddie Starr**)

Tracks on compilation – albums :

Lucille	on 'Original Beat aus England'	G- Pop Z 10006 / 1965
Tutti Frutti	on 'Original Beat aus England'	G- Pop Z 10006 / 1965
Rip It Up	on 'Original Beat aus England'	G- Pop Z 10006 / 1965
Mean Woman Blues	on 'Original Beat aus England'	G- Pop Z 10006 / 1965

(Please note that the songs on the above compilation were released under the name of **The Liverpool Beats**, a name that the **Excheckers** used in Germany, but these tracks are definitely by **Freddie Starr & the Starr Boys** as they were taken from their live album.)

Unreleased tracks :

In 1964 **Freddie Starr & the Starr-Boys** also recorded a version of "**You'll Never Walk Alone**", sung in German as "**Du Wirst Niemals Einsam Sein**" for the Dt. Vogue label, which was not released at that time. However, in 2007 it was featured on the German CD-compilation '1000 Nadelstiche'

STEVE & THE SYNDICATE
(THE BOBBY BELL ROCKERS)

The origin of this very interesting group begins with the formation of the **Bobby Bell Rockers**, another group that claims to have been the first Merseyside Rock 'n' Roll group - and, with a certain entitlement, as this story will show. The **Bobby Bell Rockers** were formed in the northern part of Liverpool in late 1956. Their name was inspired by the classic **Bill Haley** musical film, "Rock Around The Clock", which also co-starred the American group, **Freddie Bell & the Bell Boys**.

The **Bobby Bell Rockers** were probably from the Seaforth or Litherland area and their programme was filled with real Rock 'n' Roll songs, popular at that time, such as "Giddy up a ding dong" and "Hound dog".

As they were one of the very early groups, it has proved impossible to re-create their complete story, but it is known that the **Bobby Bell Rockers,** in their original line-up, consisted of the following musicians:

Bobby Crawford	**(voc)**
Charlie Flynn	**(lg/voc)**
George Watson	**(g/voc)**
Billy Gough	**(rg)**
Joe Healan	**(acc)**
'The Baron'	**(dr)**

Of the individual members, only **George Watson** had previously appeared on the scene as a member of the **Sinners** Skiffle group.

From 1957 until the middle of 1959, the line-up of the **Bobby Bell Rockers** changed constantly. **Charlie Flynn** and **George Watson** left and joined in with initiator, **Keith 'Sam' Hardy,** to form the very first **Dominoes** line-up, way before the arrival of **Ted 'Kingsize' Taylor**. After that, **George Watson** joined the **Blackhawks** and **Charlie Flynn** had a short stint with the **Memphis Three**. He then became a long-time member of **Ian & the Zodiacs** and, after that, played with the **Connoisseurs** before he joined the **Vince Earl Attraction**. Their replacements, at some point, were **Dave Moore** (lg) and **Charlie Mac** (g).

By the middle of 1959, only **Bobby Crawford** had survived from the original line-up, he was joined by **Wayne Bickerton** (rg/voc) and **Charlie Mitchell** on drums.

As well as the normal club circuit, the **Bobby Bell Rockers** also played quite regularly at the 'Aintree Institute', the 'Orrell Park Ballroom', 'St. John's Hall' in Bootle and, of course, the 'Jive Hive' in Crosby, from where they were also booked to appear at the 'Ivamar Club' in Skelmersdale.

THIS
SATURDAY
DANCE
WILL BE HELD IN
Cambridge Hall
LORD STREET
SOUTHPORT
JANUARY 23RD
FEATURING
Rory Storm and his Hurricanes
Bobby Bell Rockers
The Black Cats
7.30 to 11 p.m.
ADMISSION 4/-

In mid 1961, the **Bobby Bell Rockers** were joined by **Owen Clayton** (bg), a former member of the **Gerry Owen Four** and the recently disbanded **Creoles**.

Then **Bobby Crawford** left and a little later it is believed that he most probably joined the **Set-Up**, a group consisting of musicians from both Liverpool and London but based in Liverpool.

His replacement was **Gordon Cummings**, who had adopted the stage name **Steve Bennett**. This line-up continued for a short while as the **Bobby Bell Rockers** but, when **Charlie Mitchell** was replaced by **Brian McNally** on drums, they changed their name to **Steve Bennett & the Syndicate**.

The next to leave was **Dave Moore**, who became a member of the **Black Cats** and then **Charlie Mac**, who disappeared from the scene, also left. As a result of all these changes, in October 1961, **Steve Bennett & the Syndicate** consisted of:

Steve Bennett	**(voc)**
Paddy Chambers	**(lg)**
Wayne Bickerton	**(rg/voc)**
Owen Clayton	**(bg)**
Brian McNally	**(dr)**

The new lead guitarist, **Paddy Chambers,** was a former member of the **Creoles**.

Apparently, it was this line-up that went down to London a month later and recorded **Fats Domino's** "Red Sails In The Sunset" and "Milk Cow Blues" for PYE. Unfortunately, this was not followed by a release as, in the end, PYE rejected the group as 'too scruffy', what a shame!

Steve Bennett & the Syndicate

Around this time, **Owen Clayton** left and joined the **Sundowners** from Liverpool, who should not be confused with the later Piccadilly recording group.

He was with the **Sundowners** for many years but then disappeared from the scene for a very long time. In the Eighties, he was a member of **Karl Terry & the Cruisers** before he formed his own group under the name of the **Blues Syndicate**. After that, he played with the **Juke Box Eddies**.

Initially, **Steve Bennett** took over the bass-guitar and, as a quartet, they gigged around in London and South Wales for a while but then returned to Liverpool, at which point **Wayne Bickerton** took over on bass-guitar.

In January 1962, **Steve & the Syndicate** were voted No. 17 in the popularity poll by the readers of 'Mersey Beat' newspaper. Undoubtedly, a big success if it's taken into account that, around that time, the Liverpool scene started to explode and there were already hundreds of groups on Merseyside.

Paddy Chambers joined **Faron's Flamingos** and, after that, played with the **Big Three**, the **Eyes**, which evolved into **Paddy, Klaus & Gibson** and the **Escorts**. He was later a member of **Big John's Rock' n 'Roll Circus** and the great Liverpool Blues group, **Sindbad**. Finally, he was the leader of **Paddy Chambers & the Java Jive** but sadly died much too young in 2000.

His replacement in **Steve & the Syndicate** was **Tony Waddington**, a former member of the **Zephyrs** from St. Helens. He had also played with **Gene Day & the Django Beats** and the **Comets**.

The group shortened it's name to the **Syndicate** but only continued for a few more months and broke up in late 1962 or very early 1963.

Steve Bennett did not appear on the scene again and later went to live in the United States.

Brian McNally also disappeared from the scene, while **Wayne Bickerton** and **Tony Waddington** joined **Lee Curtis & the All Stars** and played with the follow-up groups, the **Pete Best All Stars**, the **Pete Best Four** and the **Pete Best Combo**, before they became very successful songwriters and producers for groups such as **World Of OZ**, the **Rubettes** and the **Flirtations**.

Discography :

as "**Steve Bennett & the Syndicate**":

Red Sails In The Sunset / Milk Cow Blues   UK- PYE unreleased / 1961

RORY STORM & THE HURRICANES

This legendary group evolved from the **Alan Caldwell Skiffle group**, which was formed in the Liverpool area of Broadgreen in the mid-Fifties and consisted of **Alan Caldwell** (voc), **John Byrne** (g/voc), **Paul Murphy** (g/voc), **Jeff Truman** (t-bass) and **Reg Hales** (wb).

In 1958, **Jeff Truman** was replaced by **Spud Ward**, who came from the **Bluegenes**, the forerunner of the group, the **Swinging Blue Jeans**, who, at that time, still played a sort of Trad-Jazz.

Before that, **John Byrne** and **Paul Murphy** had recorded the private metal single, "She's Got It/Butterfly", at the **Percy Phillips** studio in Kensington in 1957.

In 1959, the **Alan Caldwell Skiffle Group** split and **Paul Murphy** later played with the **Galvanisers** and **Eddie Dean & the Onlookers** before he recorded as a solo artist and then became quite a successful producer for Polydor in Germany and later, also in England.

All the other musicians disappeared from the scene - with exception of **Alan Caldwell** and **John Byrne**, who formed the group, the **Raving Texans**, that, a little later, changed their name to **Al Storm & the Hurricanes**. For a short time, they also appeared as **Rory Storm & the Wild Ones**, but then they ultimately became **Rory Storm & the Hurricanes**, that consisted of the following musicians:

Rory Storm	**(voc)**
Johnny Guitar	**(g/voc)**
Ty Brian	**(g)**
Lu Walters	**(bg/voc)**
Ringo Starr	**(dr)**

With the exception of **Lu Walters**, all the other musicians used stage names and so **Rory Storm,** of course, was **Alan Caldwell** and **Johnny Guitar** was **John Byrne**.

Ringo Starr's real name is of course **Richard Starkey** and **Ty Brian**'s real name was **Tony O'Brian**. **Ringo Starr** had previously played with the **Eddie Clayton Group** and the **Darktown Skiffle Group**.

Within a short time **Rory Storm & the Hurricanes** became one of the top groups on Merseyside and then a top attraction in the entire north of England and the Midlands. They were also one of the very first Liverpool groups that went to Hamburg, where they appeared regularly at the 'Kaiserkeller'.

The Hurricanes at the 'Kaiserkeller' Hamburg

It is interesting that, in 1960, **Lu Walters** recorded in Hamburg with the **Beatles** as his backing group, with **Ringo Starr** on drums, having stood in for **Pete Best**.

In this private session, the songs, "Fever", "Summertime" and "September Song", were recorded with the lead vocals of **Lu Walters** but, unfortunately, they were never released although the 'Mersey Beat' newspaper announced they would be.

Rory Storm was certainly one of the most interesting and impressive personalities of the whole Merseybeat movement. He had a speech impediment but this, in a wondrous way, disappeared when he sang. He had a very good knack for publicity, coupled with a good sense of humour and, with lots of little escapades, he knew how to draw the public's attention to himself and his group. One night at a gig at the 'Majestic Ballroom' he presented himself to the fans on the balcony and then jumped down to the stage where his band was already playing and broke his leg. The press photographer, whom **Rory Storm** had specifically instructed to  take a photograph of his jump, was laughing so hard that he wasn't able to take the photo! Another incident occurred when a porter at Bootle train station caught a young guy writing 'I love Rory' on the walls, and this young guy was Rory himself.

He also directed a real show when he and his **Hurricanes** were engaged to play the legendary Mersey ferry boat, the 'Royal Iris'. The boat was docked at the Pier Head and Rory stood on the dock combing his blonde hair with a giant comb until the ship cast off. His fans were certain that he had missed the boat, but then he made a big jump and caught a rope hanging from the ship and pulled himself on board, hand over hand. It seemed like a clip from an adventure movie but, of course, the rope was not hanging down by chance, everything having been pre-arranged in advance by **Rory Storm**.

It would be worth writing a book about him, his life and his group, which certainly would be a very interesting read.

Rory Storm was 'Mr. Showmanship' of the British Beat scene and lots of other stars of that time paled in comparison to him.

In 1962, **Ringo Starr** left to join the **Beatles** after there were rumours that he would become a member of **Howie Casey & the Seniors**.

His place on drums with **Rory Storm & the Hurricanes** was taken by **Gibson Kemp**, a very talented drummer who formerly had played with the **Night People** and the **Memphis Three**.

Then **Lu Walters** left to join **Howie Casey & the Seniors**, where he sang the lead vocals on the recordings "Gone, Gone, Gone" and "Nashville Blues" which, once again, were not released, probably because this group broke up shortly after these recordings for Fontana.

His replacement in the **Hurricanes** was **Bobby Thompson**, who came from **King Size Taylor & the Dominoes** and who was also a great singer. In 1962, he returned to his old group and **Lu Walters** came back to **Rory Storm & the Hurricanes**.

A little later, **Gibson Kemp** also joined **King Size Taylor & the Dominoes** and he was replaced by **Brian Johnson**, a former member of the **Strangers** and the backing group of French Rock 'n' Roll star, **Dick Rivers**.

In this line-up, **Rory Storm & the Hurricanes** were featured on the Oriole compilations, 'This Is Merseybeat' Vol. 1 and Vol. 2, with the songs, "Beautiful Dreamer" (sung by **Lu Walters**), "Dr. Feelgood" and "I Can Tell", both sung by **Rory Storm**. The latter two were also released as the first single by the group.

Before that, songs including "Green Onions" and "Lend Me Your Comb" were recorded in private sessions - perhaps with **Ringo Starr** still on drums - but never released.

In 1963, the song, "Peepin' And Hidin'", was recorded live and was meant to be featured on a Decca live sampler from the 'Cavern' but, once again, nothing was released in the end.

Brian Johnson left to join **Mark Peters & the Silhouettes** and later played with the **Tabs**.

His replacement was **Trevor Morais**, the former drummer with the **Cadillacs**, the **Ravens**, **Faron's Flamingos**, and the short-lived **Trevor Morais Combo** who backed Manchester songstress, **Lorraine Gray**. He also played with the Manchester group, **Ian Crawford & the Boomerangs,** and later became a member of the **Peddlers**, a kind of Jazz/Blues group who a little later had nationwide success with their single, "Let The Sun Shine In".

After **Trevor Morais** left, **Ian Broad** joined as the new drummer for **Rory Storm & the Hurricanes.** He had previously played with the **Five Stars**, **Gus Travis & the Midnighters**, **Freddie Starr & the Midnighters**, **Heinz & the Wild Boys** and with the short-lived **Seniors**, who were not connected to the group of **Howie Casey**.

It was probably this line-up that cut the second **Rory Storm & the Hurricanes** single, a version of "America" from 'West Side Story'. Produced by none other than **Brian Epstein** and released by EMI on the Parlophone label - the only record ever produced by him that was actually <u>released</u>.

"America" was coupled with an interesting version of the **Everly Brothers** ballad, "Since You Broke My Heart", sung by **Lu Walters** and **Johnny Guitar**. The record had no great success, which was not too surprising, as it was a poor idea to record the song, "America", because it was not timely and absolutely untypical for the music of **Rory Storm & the Hurricanes**. Consequently, it did not help their career, though they were very popular in most parts of England and also on the European continent, especially in Germany, at that time.

Brian Epstein also produced the songs, "I'll Be There" and "Ubangi Stomp", with **Rory Storm & the Hurricanes** which, in the end, were never released.

Then **Lu Walters** left again, and this time, he apparently quit show business. He was replaced by **David May**, a former member of **Mark Peters & the Silhouettes**.

The drummer carousel also kept on turning and, after **Ian Broad** left to join **Dave Allen & the Exotics**, he was replaced by **Keef Hartley**, who had played with the **Thunderbeats** and **Freddie Starr & the Midnighters** previously. But he also didn't stay too long and then became a member of the **Artwoods** from London and **John Mayall's Bluesbreakers**, before he formed his own group, the **Keef Hartley Band**. In the mid-Seventies, he was a member of the **Michael Chapman Group**.

The new drummer with **Rory Storm & the Hurricanes** was **Eddie Edwards**, who had formerly played with the **Flames**, the **Del Renas** and the **Nashpool Four**. But he left to join the **Beechwoods** and was replaced by **Jimmy Tushingham**, a former member of the **Four Clefs**.

Then **David May** left to return to the **Silhouettes** and, after that, he was a member of the **Three Cheers**, who later changed their name to **Phase Three**.

The new bass guitarist was **Vince Earl**, the former leader of **Vince Earl & the Zeros** and **Vince Earl & the Talismen**. He was also a good singer but did not stay too long and then he joined the **Connoisseurs** and, a little later, **Jimmy Tushingham** followed him to this band, which has a separate story in this book.

The new drummer for **Rory Storm & the Hurricanes** was **Carl Riche** (real name **Charlie Evans**), a former member of the **Mustangs**, **Gerry Bach & the Beathovens** and the **Tony Prince Combo**, who had just returned from Germany where he had a long residency with the **Mersey Five**.

Besides him, the legendary 'Sheik Of Shake', **Karl Terry** joined as bass guitarist, who formerly had led the **Gamblers Skiffle Group**, **Terry Connor & the Teen Aces** and **Karl Terry & the Cruisers** and, prior to joining **Rory Storm & the Hurricanes,** he had played with the **Delemeres**, **Group One**, **Karl Terry & the T.T.s**, the **Talismen** and the **Clayton Squares**.

When **Ty Brian** died in early 1967, the group almost disbanded but it was re-formed by **Rory Storm**, **Johnny Guitar** and **Carl Riche** together with **Adrian Lord** (voc/g), a former member of the **Nomads**, the **Mojos**, the **Mastersounds**, the **Bluesville Bats**, the Liverpool **Faces**, the **Easybeats** from Liverpool and **Them Grimbles**, as well as with **Keith Karlsson** (bg), who had also previously played with the **Nomads** and the **Mojos**.

But this line-up only lasted for a very short time and then **Rory Storm & the Hurricanes** split forever. **Rory Storm** himself continued in show business as a disc-jockey and, as such, had a long residency in the Netherlands.

On September 28, 1972 **Rory Storm** died from an overdose of sleeping pills. Some people say that it was an accident and some others talk about suicide, but Rory took that secret with him to his grave.

Because of this tragedy, his old mate **Johnny 'Guitar' Byrne** decided to hang up his guitar. He went back to a normal day job and became an ambulance driver.

Rory Storm & the Hurricanes always were, still are, and will always be a legend of this great and unique Merseybeat era, although they never had any great success with their records.

That is why they will always be featured in every good Merseybeat biography.

At the end of the Eighties and the beginning of the Nineties, two plays about **Rory Storm & the Hurricanes** with the titles, 'Need For A Hero' and 'King Of Liverpool', toured quite successfully in England and, because of the influence of the 'MerseyCats' organisation, **Johnny Guitar** formed a new group in memory of **Rory Storm & the Hurricanes**.

This group was named **Johnny Guitar & his Hurricanes** and mainly played the old **Rory Storm** songs. Besides **Johnny Guitar**, the band, in 1990, consisted of **Dave Blackstone** (g/voc), **Gordon Loughlin** (bg) and **Bernie Rogers** (dr) - all experienced musicians from the Sixties.

Dave Blackstone was a former member of the **Tabs**, while **Gordon Loughlin** once was with **Karl Terry & the T.T.s** and the **Clayton Squares**. **Bernie Rogers** had played in a string of groups in the Sixties, including **Lee Curtis & the All Stars** and **Denny Seyton & the Sabres**.

Dave Blackstone later was replaced by **Billy Wright**, who came from the group **Y-Kickamoocow**.

Johnny Guitar & his Hurricanes proved to be a real Rock 'n' Roll band - with that individual Mersey touch - simply the best way to remember a significant Merseybeat group with a really great showman as their leader - **Rory Storm & the Hurricanes**!

Johnny Guitar sadly died on August 18, 1999 and, with his tragic death, the last chapter of this group was closed for eternity.

Single discography :

Dr. Feelgood / I Can Tell	**UK- Oriole 45-CB 1858 / 1963**
I Can Tell / <u>Faron's Flamingos</u> : Let's Stomp	**UK- Columbia 43018 / 1964**
America / Since You Broke My Heart	**UK-Parlophone R 5197 / 1964**

<u>**Johnny Guitar** & **Paul Murphy**</u> :

She's Got It / Butterfly	**UK-Phillips acetate (private) / 1957**

<u>Tracks on compilation albums :</u>

Dr. Feelgood	on 'This Is Merseybeat' Vol.1	**UK- Oriole PS 40047 / 1963**
Beautiful dreamer	on 'This Is Merseybeat' Vol.1	**UK- Oriole PS 40047 / 1963**
I Can Tell	on 'This Is Merseybeat' Vol.2	**UK- Oriole PS 40048 / 1963**

<u>Unissued tracks :</u>

The unissued tracks by **Rory Storm & the Hurricanes** are **"Green Onions"** and **"Lend Me Your Comb"** (both from 1962), **"Peepin' And Hidin'"** (live) from 1963 and **"I'll Be There"** and **"Ubangi Stomp"** from 1964. The latter two were produced by **Brian Epstein** for Parlophone.

Lu Walters recorded the following songs which remained unissued: **"Fever"**, **"Summertime"** and **"September Song"** in 1961 – on which he was backed by the **Beatles**. In 1962 he also recorded **"Gone, Gone, Gone"** and **"Nashville Blues"** - backed by **Howie Casey & the Seniors**.

THE STRANGERS

This was not only one of the first, but also one of the most important Beat groups in Liverpool, where it was originally formed as **Jet & the Tornados** at the end of the Fifties.

The **Strangers** are a legend of Liverpool's early beat days. They will never be forgotten on Merseyside, even though they failed to achieve international success. The fact that, in October 1961, they were voted No. 5 in the popularity poll of 'Mersey Beat' newspaper proves how popular they already were at that time.

The original line-up of the **Strangers** consisted of the following musicians:

Joe Feegan	**(voc/g)**
Harry Hutchings	**(g/voc)**
George Harper	**(bg/voc)**
Brian Johnson	**(dr)**

The group played all the major Liverpool venues in its hometown and built up a really big following. In addition, the **Strangers** were also one of the first Liverpool groups to play the 'Star-Club' in Hamburg, where they were very successful. Because of that success the group decided to stay in Germany for an extended period of time. Unfortunately, the **Strangers** never recorded in their own right and, in 1963, while in Germany, they disbanded for unknown reasons.

The Strangers at the Star Club, Hamburg with Adrian Barber

Harry Hutchings returned to Liverpool and disappeared from the scene, while **Joe Feegan**, **George Harper** and **Brian Johnson** went to France, where they became the backing group for famous French Rock 'n' Roll singer, **Dick Rivers**. Amongst others, they recorded the French version of "Bo Diddley" with him, which became extremely popular in France. Unfortunately, there is no information available regarding all the recordings **The Strangers** made with **Dick Rivers**.

After that, **George Harper** and **Brian Johnson** returned to Liverpool, where **George Harper** most probably quit show business, as nothing was heard of him later.

Brian Johnson became a member of **Rory Storm & the Hurricanes**, **Mark Peters & the Silhouettes** and finally the **Tabs**, before he went back to a normal day job.

The Strangers

In the early Nineties, he returned to the music scene when he became a member of the newly formed **Cliff Roberts' Rockers**. Today he is the drummer with the newly formed **Mojos**, under the leadership of **Nicky Crouch**.

Joe Feegan remained in France and became a member of the legendary rockers, **Vince Taylor & The Playboys**. After **Vince Taylor** had separated from the group, **Les Play-Boys** continued solo but also backed **Johnny Hallyday** for a time and recorded with him.

In the early Eighties, **Joe Feegan** went solo under the name of **Joe Fagin** and released some brilliant singles, including "Why Don't We Spend The Night". He had a chart success in England with "That's Living Alright" and released four great albums which brought him international stardom.

His smoky voice suited his handmade Blues influenced rock music but, unfortunately, in spite of all his success, **Joe Fagin** still remains a very underrated musician.

Les Play-Boys - Joe Feegan (2nd from L)

Discography :

The **Strangers** never recorded in their own right, but three of them backed the French Rock 'n' Roll singer, **Dick Rivers,** on his hit version of "**Bo Diddley**" in 1964, as well as on some other recordings. Unfortunately, no details are known.

THE SWINGING BLUE JEANS

Ray Ennis and **Norman Kuhlke** had played together since 1956 in various Skiffle groups in Liverpool before they joined a Skiffle/Trad-Jazz band which was formed by **Bruce McCaskill** in 1957 under the name, the **Bluegenes,** which also included **Tommy Hughes** (bj), a former member of the **Pinetop Skifflegroup**, as well as **Spud Ward** (t-bass).

The **Bluegenes** became something of a resident band at the 'Cavern' where, over time, they introduced lots of other Liverpool groups on their so-called 'guest night' - amongst them the very young **Beatles.**

Bandleader, **Bruce McCaskill** split from the group and was replaced by **Ralph Ellis** (g) and **Johnny Carter** (voc), who had formerly led **Johnny Carter & the Hi-Cats.**

It was probably this line-up of the **Bluegenes** that made their first recordings with the songs, "I'm Shy Mary Allen, I'm Shy", "Yes Sir That's My Baby", "Bonaparte's Retreat" and a nice and interesting version of "Isle Of Capri", but they were only released on acetate.

Tommy Hughes had to join the Army and his replacement was **Paul Moss** who, not only took the place of **Tommy Hughes,** but also his banjo!

Bruce McCaskill and **Tommy Hughes** later formed the **Kansas City Five** and then **Bruce McCaskill** formed **Groups Inc.** before he joined the **Escorts.** After that, he was a member of the **Roadrunners.** In later years, he managed the **Average White Band** and was the road manager for **Eric Clapton**. He sadly died on 24th December 1993.

When **Spud Ward** joined the **Raving Texans** (the forerunner group of **Rory Storm & the Hurricanes**), he was replaced by **Les Braid**, who also came from **Johnny Carter & the Hi-Cats** and, before that, he had played with the **Gamblers Skiffle Group**, the first band of the 'Sheik Of Shake', **Karl Terry**.

Johnny Carter emigrated to Canada where he formed a Beat group whose name, unfortunately, is not known.

At the beginning of the Sixties, the **Bluegenes** went to play the 'Star-Club' in Hamburg where they flopped as their sound was totally 'out-of-date' in Germany at that time. After their return to Liverpool, **Paul Moss** left and became the bass guitarist with **Johnny Goode & the Kinfolk.**

The **Bluegenes** changed their sound to Rock 'n' Roll and their name into **Swinging Bluegenes**, which, a little later, became **The Swinging Blue Jeans**.

Their second trip to Hamburg was much more successful because they had become a real Beat group now, in a line-up with:

Ray Ennis	(voc/g)
Ralph Ellis	(g/voc/g)
Les Braid	(bg/voc)
Norman Kuhlke	(dr/voc)

The **Swinging Blue Jeans** were signed to EMI and their first single, in 1963, was the original, "It's Too Late Now", a nice, but not very exciting Beat record which had no great success, just like the follow-up, "Do You Know".

Their third release, a wild version of **Chan Romero**'s "Hippy Hippy Shake" had the required excitement and climbed to No. 2 in the British charts in 1963 and from there it became an international hit success. Their next single, also a wild version of "Good Golly Miss Molly" climbed to No. 11, while the follow-up "You're No Good" hit the top 10 again when it stopped at No. 3.

The **Swinging Blue Jeans** suddenly seemed to be potential hit makers, but no further chart success followed, although singles, such as "Promise You'll Tell Her", "It Isn't There", "Crazy 'bout My Baby", "Sandy", "Tremblin' " and "Don't Go Out In The Rain", at least sold quite well, but only their great version of "Don't Make Me Over" became a minor hit.

At the beginning of 1968, **Ralph Ellis** and **Norman Kuhlke** left the group for unknown reasons and apparently quit show business. They were replaced by **Terry Sylvester** (g/voc) and **Kenny Goodlass** (dr), who both came from the **Escorts**.

Before that, **Kenny Goodlass** had played with the **Panthers** and the **Kirkbys**, as well as with the **Fruit Eating Bears** and also with **23rd Turn-Off**.

For their next single, "What Have They Done To Hazel", the group's name was changed to **Ray Ennis & the Blue Jeans**, and the follow-up, "Sandfly", was released as the **Blue Jeans**, both on the Columbia label.

In 1968, **Terry Sylvester** left to join the **Hollies**, where he played until the Eighties and then went solo. At one time, it was rumoured that he formed a new group under the name of the **New Escorts**, but nothing was ever heard of them. So it probably was no more than a rumour.

Mike Gregory, also a former member of the **Escorts**, joined as their new singer. Prior to joining the **Swinging Blue Jeans** he had done a short spell with the **Hollies**.

In addition, **Tommy Murray** (g/voc), who came from the **Krew,** was added to the line-up. Before the **Krew,** he had played with the **Memphis Rhythm & Blues Combo** and the **Kinsleys.**

In 1970, the group was signed to Deram and, under the name **Music Motor,** released one more single with the songs, "Happy" and "Where Am I Going", which, unfortunately, also had no success, so the group went back to its old name, the **Swinging Blue Jeans.**

In the meantime, **Kenny Goodlass** had left and, in the late Seventies, was a member of the newly formed **Merseybeats**, where he played until the early Eighties. In 1992, he played with **Karl Terry & the Cruisers** who, at that time, often toured in Germany, where they recorded a great Rock 'n' Roll album in 1994.

His replacement in the **Swinging Blue Jeans** was **Chris Mutch**, also a former member of the **Krew**. **Tommy Murray** left and later on he appeared again as a member of a group called **Mumble**.

Mike Gregory left and became a member of **Big John's Rock & Roll-Circus** and, for a short time, **Billy Kinsley** joined the **Swinging Blue Jeans**, having played with the **Merseybeats**, **Kinsleys**, the **Merseys** and **Rockin' Horse**. He later formed **Liverpool Express** and also became a member of the **Merseybeats** again.

His replacement in the **Swinging Blue Jeans** was the Canadian, **Mike Pynn**, and, around the same time, **John Lawrence** joined the group in place of **Chris Mutch**.

This line-up recorded the single, "Ring Ring", which became a minor hit for the group in the early Seventies. In addition, they also released two albums.

In the meantime, **John Lawrence** was replaced by **Ian Magee** who, in the Sixties, had played with **Mike Dee & the Detours** and **Rhythm & Blues Inc.** from Southport.

In 1975, **Mike Pynn** left and was replaced by **Garth Elliott** (g) who soon left to join **Herman's Hermits**.

His replacement was none other than **Colin Manley** who, in the Sixties, was the lead guitarist with the legendary **Remo Four**. Prior to joining the **Swinging Blue Jeans,** he had played in the backing groups of **Clodagh Rodgers** and **Freddie Starr.**

This line-up released some more records and toured Germany and Scandinavia.

In 1984, **Ian Magee** got married in Sweden and left the group, he was replaced by **Phil Thompson**. The group continued releasing records on a sporadic basis. Some still had that typical driving Merseybeat sound, while others were more Pop. This was not really the characteristic music of the **Swinging Blue Jeans**, as unlike many other groups they never became a cabaret band.

Colin Manley sadly died from cancer in April 1999 and, after that, the group had various lead-guitarists. When **Les Braid** also died in July 2005, it looked like that was the end of the **Swinging Blue Jeans**, but **Ray Ennis** found other members with whom he continued until 2010 and then retired.

Single discography :

It's Too Late Now / Think Of Me	UK- HMV POP 1170 / 1963
Do You Know / Angie	UK- HMV POP 1206 / 1963
Hippy Hippy Shake / Now I Must Go	UK- HMV POP 1242 / 1963
Good Golly Miss Molly / Shaking Feeling	UK- HMV POP 1273 / 1964
You're No Good / Don't You Worry About Me	UK- HMV POP 1304 / 1964
Promise You'll Tell Her / It's So Right	UK- HMV POP 1327 / 1964
It Isn't There / One Of These Days	UK- HMV POP 1375 / 1964
Make Me Know You're Mine / I've Got A Girl	UK- HMV POP 1409 / 1965
Crazy 'Bout My Baby / Good Lovin'	UK- HMV POP 1477 / 1965
Don't Make Me Over / What Can I Do Today	UK- HMV POP 1501 / 1966
Sandy / I'm Gonna Have You	UK- HMV POP 1533 / 1966
Rumors, Gossips, Words Untrue / Now The Summer's Gone	UK- HMV POP 1564 / 1966
Tremblin' / Something Coming Along	UK- HMV POP 1596 / 1967
Don't Go Out Into The Rain / One Woman Man	UK- HMV POP 1605 / 1967

as **Ray Ennis & the Blue Jeans** :

What Have They Done To Hazel / Now That You've Got Me	UK-Columbia DB 8431/ 1968

as **The Blue Jeans** :

Sandfly / Hey Mrs Housewife	UK-Columbia DB 8555/ 1969

as **The Music Motor** :

Happy I Am / Where Going	UK- Deram DM 282 / 1970

Different German releases as **The Swinging Blue Jeans** :

Das Ist Prima / Good Golly Miss Molly (sung in German)	G - Elektrola 22734 / 1964
Tutti Frutti (in English) / Lawdy Miss Clawdy	G - Elektrola 22831 / 1964
Tutti Frutti (in German) / Das Ist Vorbei	G - Elektrola 22870 / 1964
Hippy Hippy Shake / Lawdy Miss Clawdy	G - Elektrola 23607 / 1968

("**Das Ist Prima**" and "**Das Ist Vorbei**" are the German versions of "**Shaking Feeling**" and "**You're No Good**")

Shakin' All Over / Shake, Rattle And Roll   DK – HMV X 8647 / 1964

Ol' Man Mose / It Isn't There   DK – HMV X 8655 / 1965

EP discography

SHAKE   UK- HMV EG 8850 / 1963

- Hippy Hippy Shake / Shaking All Over / Shake, Rattle And Roll / Shaking Feeling

YOU'RE NO GOOD MISS MOLLY   UK- HMV EG 8868 / 1964

- You're No Good / Don't You Worry About Me / Good Golly Miss Molly / Angie

Different French releases :

HIPPY HIPPY SHAKE   F- HMV EGF 707 / 1963

- Hippy Hippy Shake / Do You Know / Too Late Now / Now I Must Go

GOOD GOLLY MISS MOLLY   F- HMV EGF 736 / 1964

- Good Golly Miss Molly / Don't You Worry About Me / You're No Good / Shaking Feeling

IT'S SO RIGHT   F- HMV EGF 782 / 1964

- It's So Right / It Isn't There / Promise You'll Tell Her / Shake, Rattle and Roll

RUMORS, GOSSIP, WORDS UNTRUE   F- HMV EGF 950 / 1966

- Rumors, Gossip, Words Untrue / Now The Summer's Gone / Don't Make Me Over /

  I'm Gonna Have You

Different Foreign release :

Around And Around / Long Tall Sally / It's So Right / Tutti Frutti   Asian (??) HMV ??? / 1964

LP discography

BLUE JEANS A' SWINGING   UK - HMV CLP 1802 / 1964

- Ol' Man Mose / Save The Last Dance For Me / That's The Way It Goes / Around And Around /

It's All Over Now / Long Tall Sally / Lawdy Miss Clawdy / Some Sweet Day / It's So Right /

Don't It Make You Feel Good / All I Want Is You / Tutti Frutti

Re-released in 1964 with the title **THE SWINGING BLUE JEANS**   UK - MFP 1163 / 1964

Different US – release :

THE SWINGING BLUE JEANS   US-Imperial LP 9261 / 1964

- Good Golly Miss Molly / Angie / It's Too Late Now / Think Of Me / Do You Know /

Hippy Hippy Shake / Shaking Feeling / Shake, Rattle and Roll / Shakin' All Over /

Now I Must Go / Wasting Time / Save The Last Dance For Me

Different German releases :

SHAKING TIME   G- Elektrola E 83716 / 1964

- Hippy Hippy Shake / Now I Must Go / Shaking Feeling / You're No Good /

Good Golly Miss Molly / Don't You Worry About Me / Shake, Rattle And Roll /

Too Late Now / Think Of Me / Shaking All Over / Do You Know / Angie

HEY HEY HEY HEY (Live aus dem 'Cascade-Club', Köln)   G-Elektrola SME 83927 / 1965

Kansas City / Johnny B. Goode / Tutti Frutti / Eight Days A Week / Chug-A-Lug / I've Got A Girl /

King Of The Road / Long Tall Sally / Good Golly Miss Molly (in German) / In The Mood / Das Ist Prima

Tracks on compilation-albums :

It's So Right	on 'Liverpool'	G-Columbia C 83777 / 1964
Promise You'll Tell Her	on 'Liverpool'	G-Columbia C 83777 / 1964
One Of These Days	on 'Liverpool '65'	G-Columbia SMC 83980 / 1965
It's So Right	on 'Liverpool '65'	G-Columbia SMC 83980 / 1965

Unreleased tracks :

The group as Skiffle/Trad-Jazz band under the name of the **Bluegenes** recorded the songs, **"I'm Shy Mary Allen I'm Shy"**, **"Yes Sir That's My Baby"**, **"Bonaparte's Retreat"** and **"Isle Of Capri"**, on acetate in 1957 or 1958. Unissued tracks by the **Swinging Blue Jeans** are **"Dizzy Chimes"**, **"Keep Me Warm 'til The Sun Shines"**, **"We're Here Again"**, **"Reddy Teddy"** and **"You Got Love"** from various years.

THE TABS

This group was formed in Liverpool in 1964, which was obviously too late to make an international break through as by that time the 'Merseybeat wave' had crested.

In spite of this, within a very short period of time, the **Tabs** became one of the hopes of a new generation of bands on Merseyside. They entered various Beat contests in which they were very successful, but this was more or less limited to the local scene.

The original line-up of the **Tabs** consisted of:

Dave Crosby	(voc/p)
David Blackstone	(g/voc)
Les Martin	(bg/voc)
Ray Aubrey	(dr)

Dave Crosby was the former leader of **Dave & the Rave-Ons**, which was one of Liverpool's early groups. None of the other members had previously appeared on the scene.

In 1964, the **Tabs** recorded a private EP which was handed out to fans at their performances. So, of course, it is very rare these days. The record included the songs, "Fever", "I Still Remember", "Caroline Caroline" and "Hurt", very probably the middle two were originals by the band.

At the beginning of 1965, the first change in the line-up occurred when **Brian Johnson** replaced **Ray Aubrey** on drums, who disappeared from the scene.

Brian Johnson was a well known drummer on the scene as he had previously played with such popular groups as the **The Strangers**, **Rory Storm & the Hurricanes** and **Mark Peters & the Silhouettes**.

The **Tabs** were also joined by **Steve McGhee** (sax) and **Terry Sterling** (tr) and so their music became more influenced by Rhythm & Blues and Soul, which can be clearly heard on their Unicord acetate with the songs, "Finger Poppin' " and "Don't You Hear Me Calling".

In August 1965, the **Tabs** won the big 'Northern Sounds '65' contest and, a little later, were signed to PYE. This recording contract with PYE may have been the prize for the winners of this contest but that is not certain.

The band went down to London and recorded the **John D. Laudermilk** classic, "Tobacco Road", and probably some other songs, but nothing was ever released.

As these recording sessions were not followed by a release, still in 1965, **Brian Johnson** left the **Tabs** and quit show business for many years. At the beginning of the Nineties, he was back on the scene as a member of the newly formed **Cliff Roberts' Rockers** and today he is with the re-formed **Mojos**.

Brian Johnson's replacement in the **Tabs** was **Alan Menzies**, the former drummer with the **Chris & the Quiet Ones**, **Rhythm & Blues Inc.** and others.

In addition, they were also joined by a new trumpet player, **Terry Hedley**.

Unfortunately, the **Tabs** did not get a second chance to record and so they disbanded, probably in early 1967, without ever having released a 'commercial' recording.

Alan Menzies later appeared with the **Expressions**, **Jasmin-T** and then as a member of the **Bootles**, that he led until 2010.

Les Martin also joined the **Expressions** but, at the end of 1967, he became a member of **The Selofane**, who cut two great singles for CBS in 1968.

Dave Crosby became a member of the **Reaction,** he later owned some record shops on the Wirral. In the Seventies, he started to produce records with local artists on his own Rox label, including the only single by **Karl Terry & the Cruisers**.

In the Nineties, **Dave Blackstone** was a member of **Johnny Guitar & his Hurricanes** and then he joined **Karl Terry & the Cruisers**. He was with them for some time before he formed his own group under the name of **Mayday**. He kept on playing on the scene until he sadly died in 2008.

Discography :

Fever / I Still Remember / Caroline Caroline / Hurt	UK - Unicord EP / 1964
Finger Poppin' / Don't You Hear Me Calling	UK - Unicord acetate / 1964

Unreleased tracks :

After the **Tabs** won the big 'Northern Sounds '65' contest in August 1965, they were signed by PYE and went down to London for a recording session where the song, "**Tobacco Road**", was recorded, as well as some others but, in the end, nothing was released.

KING SIZE TAYLOR & THE DOMINOES

This band story is probably one of the most complicated but, also, one of the most interesting in the world of Merseybeat.

The best way to start might be with the very first line-up that ever appeared under the name of **King Size Taylor & the Dominoes**, whose forerunner groups were the **James Boys** and the **Dominoes**, both of which were formed in Liverpool in the mid-Fifties. In 1960, **King Size Taylor & the Dominoes,** in the first line-up under that name, consisted of:

Ted 'King Size' Taylor (voc/g)	- Former member of the **James Boys** and the **Dominoes**
Charlie Flynn (g/voc)	- Former member of the **Bobby Bell Rockers** and the **Dominoes**
John Kennedy (voc/g)	- Former member of the **Zodiacs** and the **Dominoes**
Bobby Thompson (bg/voc)	- Former member of the **James Boys** and **Dominoes**
Geoff Bethel (org)	- Former member of the **Deltones** and the **Dominoes**
Sam Hardie (p)	- The founding member of the **Dominoes**
Cliff Roberts (dr)	- Former member of the **Dominoes**

In 1961, **Charlie Flynn**, **Geoff Bethel** and **Cliff Roberts**, who shouldn't be confused with the leader of **Cliff Roberts' Rockers**, left together to join **Ian & the Zodiacs**. **Johnny Kennedy** teamed up with the **Rayurn Four**, but he is not the musician of the same name who played with **Carl Vincent & the Counts**.

The 3 remaining members of the group were joined by two new musicians and accordingly the line-up was:

King Size Taylor	(voc/g)
Bobby Thompson	(bg/voc)
John Frankland	(g)
Sam Hardie	(p/voc)
Dave Lovelady	(dr)

Dave Lovelady was a former member of the **Zodiacs** and **Ian & the Zodiacs**, while **John Frankland** came from the **Legends**.

Dave Lovelady did not stay for too long, he left to join the **Four Mosts** who, a little later, became **The Fourmost**. **Brian Redman**, the drummer with the **Four Mosts**, formerly known as the **Four Jays**, then joined **King Size Taylor & the Dominoes**, and this was probably the line-up that played Hamburg the first time.

They were a real Rock 'n' Roll group and, doubtless, one of the very best that ever came out of Liverpool, if not England. So it was no surprise that **King Size Taylor & the Dominoes** went down a bomb in Germany and especially in Hamburg.

In 1962, **Bobby Thompson** played for a short time with **Rory Storm & the Hurricanes** and, during that time, he was initially replaced by **Ken Shalliker**, formerly of the **Blackhawks**, who then went on to join **Deke Rivers & the Big Sound** from Manchester and, after that, played with the Liverpool Country group, **The Foggy Mountain Ramblers**. **Ken Shalliker** was replaced by **Francis Galloway** (bg) who, when **Bobby Thompson** returned, switched to saxophone.

When **Francis Galloway** left to go back to Liverpool, **King Size Taylor & the Dominoes** were joined by sax player, **Howie Casey**, who had just disbanded his group, **Howie Casey & the Seniors** who, under the name of **Derry & the Seniors,** were the first Liverpool band to go to Hamburg.

This was the line-up of **King Size Taylor & the Dominoes** that backed German girl singer, **Audrey Arno** on her single, "Bitte Bleib Doch Bei Mir", which was released as **Audrey Arno & die Tony Taylor Band.**

Brian Redman then left and returned to Liverpool where he became a member of **Sonny Webb & the Cascades.**

His replacement was **Gibson Kemp**, a terrific drummer who had formerly played with **Night People**, the **Memphis Three** and **Rory Storm & the Hurricanes**.

In 1963, **King Size Taylor & the Dominoes** recorded the great album, 'Let's Do The Slop, Twist, Maddison, Hully Gully', for the German Polydor label under the name of the **Shakers.**

From that, the singles, "Hippy Hippy Shake", "Whole Lotta Lovin' " and "Memphis Tennessee", were coupled out for the German market, as well as "Dr. Feelgood" for the English market.

Around the same time, the group - as **King Size Taylor & the Dominoes** - recorded the single, "Fortune Teller", with the tremendous B-side, "Never In A Hundred Years", for Philips.

After that, they switched to Ariola where, in 1964, they recorded one album and two half albums. The other side of the half albums featured the **Bobby Patrick Big Six** from Scotland. From these really great albums recorded live at the 'Star-Club' in Hamburg, a string of singles were coupled out for the German market of which "Stupidity" was also released on Decca in England.

Despite fantastic records by **King Size Taylor & the Dominoes**, they never made the charts, although all the singles, EPs and albums sold quite well in Germany where **King Size Taylor & the Dominoes** were really one of the absolute top groups on the entire Beat scene.

In 1964, **Steve Aldo,** who had previously been with the **Challengers,** joined the group as an additional singer. The former Liverpudlian musician, **Paul Murphy** (ex **Alan Caldwell Skiffle Group, Galvanisers,** etc.), recorded this line-up for German Polydor - under the pseudonym of **Boots Wellington & his Rubber Band.** They recorded songs for a complete album but, in the end, only some of these songs were released on different German compilation albums – mainly featuring the lead vocals of **Steve Aldo.**

It is also interesting that the first album by Scottish musician, **Alex Harvey** (voc/g) (also on Polydor), featured **King Size Taylor** (g), **Bobby Thompson** (bg), **Gibson Kemp** (dr) and probably also **Howie Casey** of the **Dominoes** as backing musicians, although this album was credited to **Alex Harvey & his Soul Band.**

In 1964, **Sam Hardie** left to join **Tony Sheridan & the Beat Brothers** and, after that, became a member of the Hamburg group, **The Tramps**, who recorded an interesting Beat single with "Eene-Meene-Ming-Mang-Mo" on the German Telefunken label.

He was replaced by **Dave Woods**, another sax player, who is said to have previously played with the **Sons Of The Piltdown Men**.

Paddy Chambers, formerly of the **Creoles**, **Steve & the Syndicate**, **Faron's Flamingos** and the **Big Three** joined the group as an additional guitarist.

A little later, still in 1964, **King Size Taylor & the Dominoes**, one of the everlasting legends of Liverpool's Merseybeat and the German 'Star-Club' scene, disbanded totally.

Bobby Thompson joined **Cliff Bennett & the Rebel Rousers** and was later a member of the **Rockin' Berries** from Birmingham.

Steve Aldo became a member of the **Griff Parry Five** where he met up with **Francis Galloway** again.

Howie Casey played with the **Pawns** and the **Krewkats**. After short spells with the **Big Three** and the **Griff Parry Five**, he re-formed the **Krew** and later played with the **Roy Young Band** and **Rigor Mortis**, while **Steve Aldo** sang with the **Krew**, the **Fyx**, the **In Crowd** and later was backed by the **Fairies** from Colchester.

John Frankland, **Paddy Chambers** and **Gibson Kemp** remained in Hamburg where they, together with **Lewis Collins** (bg), formed the **Eyes**.

Lewis Collins also came from Liverpool and was a former member of the **Renegades**, the **Kansas City Five** and the **Georgians**.

John Frankland then left the **Eyes** to get married to a German girl, while **Lewis Collins** went back to Liverpool, where he joined the **Mojos**. **Klaus Voormann** from Hamburg was their (single) replacement, and the recording trio, **Paddy, Klaus & Gibson,** was born. More Information about that is featured in the story of the **Eyes**.

Paddy Chambers later joined the **Escorts**, while **Gibson Kemp** remained in Hamburg where he played with the 'Star-Club' band, the **Giants,** and later in the backing group for the **Les Humphries Singers**.

King Size Taylor, who had disbanded the group, also returned to Liverpool where he formed a new backing group, with no special name, that featured **Barry 'Baz' Davies** (g) who came from the **Connoisseurs**, **Kenny Rees** (bg), a former member of the **Black Velvets** and the **Topspots**, as well as **Cliff Roberts** from the original **King Size Taylor & the Dominoes** line-up on drums.

Whether or not this group backed **King Size Taylor** on his Decca single, "Somebody's Always Trying", is not certain, but very possible.

Kenny Rees left and was replaced by another former 'Domino' – **Francis Galloway** of the **Griff Parry Five**.

In this line-up, **King Size Taylor & his Band** existed until 1965, toured Germany with two additional sax players, **Rolf Roger Reich**, formerly of the **Black Devils** from Brunswick, and **Mahmoud Hoaurie**, a French musician of Moroccan origin.

In early 1965, this group split again and **Barry Davis** joined **Mike Warner & the New Stars** from Bielefeld.

On another Germany tour, **King Size Taylor** was backed by the **Tramps** and at gigs in England by the **Griff Parry Five**. Around this time, the single, "Let Me Love You", was released by **King Size Taylor** on the British Polydor label - his final record.

The King Size Taylor Band

King Size Taylor was then backed by the **Mersey Five**, a Liverpool group that had a long residency in Germany and they again were billed as **King Size Taylor & the Dominoes**. But this did not last for too long and probably, still in 1966, **King Size Taylor** quit show business.

In spite of countless attempts by musicians and promoters, he did not return to the stage for many years. In October 1990, on a memorial night for **Rory Storm** planned by **Bob Wooler** and organised by 'MerseyCats', the **Dominoes** were also on the bill - sadly without **Ted Taylor**, who had taken over his parents' butchers shop in Southport in the Sixties.

The **Dominoes** appeared in a line-up with **Charlie Flynn** (g/voc), **Bobby Thompson** (bg/voc), **Sam Hardie** (p/voc), **John Kennedy** (g/voc), **Howie Casey** (sax) and **Dave Lovelady** (dr) and, in an impressive manner, made it clear that they were still great musicians.

Sam Hardie joined the re-formed **Cliff Roberts' Rockers**, where he played until the mid-Nineties.

When **King Size Taylor** started to appear again at the 'MerseyCats' events in 2002, he was occasionally backed by the **Dominoes** again. Initially, the line-up included **Sam Hardie**, **Barry Davis**, **John Frankland** and **Mesh Stephenson** as drummer who, in the Sixties, had played with the **Deltones** and **St. Paul & the Angels**, who were both connected to **Ian & the Zodiacs**.

Later, for various gigs in Hamburg, the group appeared in the full line-up of the Sixties again– with **King Size Taylor** (voc/g), **Bobby Thompson** (voc/bg), **John Frankland** (g/voc), **Sam Hardie** (p/voc), **Howie Casey** (sax) and **Gibson Kemp** on drums.

In 2006, **King Size Taylor** moved to live in Hamburg and occasionally appears on the scene again, where he is backed by various musicians and, from time to time, by the original **Dominoes**, who meanwhile also perform in their own right without their former singer.

Single discography :

as **Audrey Arno & die Tony Taylor Band** :

Bitte Bleib Doch Bei Mir / Limbo Italiano	G- Polydor NH 52-098 / 1962

(the A-side is the German version of "**Please Stay With Me**")

as **The Shakers** :

Hippy Hippy Shake / Money	G- Polydor NH 52-158 / 1963
Whole Lotta Lovin' / I Can Tell	G- Polydor NH 52-272 / 1963
Memphis Tennessee / Dizzy Miss Lizzy	G- Polydor NH 52-928 / 1964
Memphis Tennessee / Money	K-Polydor NH 66-990 / 1964
Dr. Feelgood / Hippy Hippy Shake	UK-Polydor NH 66-991 / 1964

as **King Size Taylor & the Dominoes** :

The Fortune Teller / Never In A Hundred Years	G- Philips 345.618 PF / 1963
Hello Josephine / Stupidity	G- Ariola 10.578 AT / 1964
I'm Late / I've Been Watching You	G- Ariola 10.728 AT / 1964
Skye Boat Song / Down In The Valley	G- Ariola 10.730 AT / 1964
Lipstick, Powder And Paint / Heebie Jeebies	G- Ariola 18.074 AT / 1964
Stupidity / Bad Boy	UK- Decca F.11874 / 1964

King Size Taylor – solo :

Somebody's Always Trying / Looking For My Baby	UK- Decca F.11935 / 1965
Let Me Love You / Thinkin'	UK- Polydor N 56152 / 1966

EP discography as **The Shakers** :

TWIST & SHAKE	G- Polydor 21628 / 1963

- Mashed Potatoes And Hot Pastrami / Green Onions / Hello Josephine / Long Tall Sally

(this EP was re-released as '**King Size Taylor & the Dominoes**' in 1964 on the red Polydor label with the same catalogue number)

Different French release :

LES SHAKERS   **F- Polydor 50035 / 1963**

- Memphis Tennessee / Money / Twist And Shout / Mashed Potatoes And Hot Pastrami

King Size Taylor & the Dominoes :

KING SIZE TAYLOR & THE DOMINOES - (TEENBEAT 2)   **G- Ariola 41168 CT / 1964**

- I've Been Watching You / Shake, Shake, Shake / Clarabella / I'm Late

TEENBEAT 2   **UK- Decca DFE 8569 / 1964**

- All Around The World / Slippin' And Slidin' / You Can't Sit Down / Hello Josephine

Different Spanish release :

SHOW EN STAR-CLUB   **E – Vergara 117 – XC / 1964**

- Unchain My Heart / Hello Josephine / Stupidity / All Around The World

LP discography as **The Shakers** :

LET'S DO THE SLOP, TWIST, MADDISON, HULLY GULLY   **G- Polydor 46639 / 1963**

- Twist And Shout / Hippy Hippy Shake / Money / Hello Josephine / Memphis Tennessee /

Whole Lot Of Lovin' / Domino Twist / I Can Tell / Mashed Potatoes / Ruby Ann / Long Tall Sally /

Dr. Feelgood / Sweet Little Sixteen / Country Music / Dizzy Miss Lizzy / Green Onions

(Please note that this album was re-released in Germany in 1964 with the title, '**Shaker's Twist Club with King Size Taylor & the Dominoes**' (**G-Polydor 46639**). It was also released in England with the title, '**The Shakers**' in 1964 (**UK-Polydor LPHM 46639**) and in the USA as '**Real Gonk Man**' (**US-Midnight HLP 2101**). On the US release the songs, "**Whole Lot Of Lovin'** ", "**Domino Twist**", "**Mashed Potatoes**" and "**Country Music**", are missing.)

as **King Size Taylor & the Dominoes** :

TWIST-TIME IM STAR-CLUB HAMBURG - Folge 2   **G- Ariola 70952 IT / 1964**

- All Around The World / Stupidity / Slippin' And Slidin' / Unchain My Heart / Bad Boy /

Short On Love / Hello Josephine / You Can't Sit Down- - - the other side of this album featured the **Bobby Patrick Big Six** - - -

STAR-CLUB TIME MIT KING SIZE TAYLOR & THE DOMINOES G- Ariola 71430 IT / 1964

- I've Been Watching You / All Around The World / Down In The Valley / She Said Yeah /

You Make Me Happy / Sherry Baby / Shake, Shake, Shake / Skye Boat Song / Golly Golly What /

Bad Boy / Clarabella

KING SIZE TAYLOR & THE DOMINOES / BOBBY PATRICK BIG SIX G- Ariola 71764 IT / 1964

- Heebie Jeebies / Oo Papa Doo / Wa-Watussi / Let's Dance / Broken Arrow /

Lipstick, Powder And Paint- - - the other side of this album featured **the Bobby Patrick Big Six** - - -

Tracks on compilation albums :

as **King Size Taylor & the Dominoes** :

Slow Down	on 'Liverpool Beat'	G- Fontana 681557 TL / 1964
Fortune Teller	on 'Liverpool Beat'	G- Fontana 681557 TL / 1964
Fortune Teller	on '11 Stars At The Star-Club'	G- Star Club 148005 STL / 1964

as **Boots Wellington & his Rubber Band** :

What'd I Say	on '16 Beat Groups From the Hamburg-Scene'	G Polydor LPHM 46.439 / 1964
What'd I Say	on 'Beat City'	G-Polydor SLPHM 237.660 / 1965
Summertime	on 'Beat City'	G-Polydor SLPHM 237.660 / 1965
Baby Face	on 'Beat City'	G-Polydor SLPHM 237.660 / 1965
Unchain My Heart	on 'Go, Go, Go'	G-Polydor Intern. 623.001 / 1965
Feel So Bad	on 'Go, Go, Go'	G-Polydor Intern. 623.001 / 1965

Unreleased tracks :

In 1957/58, **The Dominoes** (feat. **King Size Taylor**) recorded the songs, "**Shortnin' Bread**", "**Matchbox**" and "**Roll Over Beethoven**", in private sessions which were probably the first Merseybeat recordings ever.

Further songs by the group that were recorded and at least partially featured on acetates are "**Whole Lotta Shakin' Goin' On**", "**Baby**", "**Great Balls Of Fire**", "**Guitar Boogie**", "**So Long**", "**I Want You To Know**", "**Mean Woman Blues**", "**Autumn Leaves**", "**Lend Me Your Comb**", "**Good Golly Miss Molly**", "**Hey, Hey, Hey, Hey**", "**Your True Love**", "**Sad And Blue**", "**My Soul**", "**Saw My Baby With Another Boy**", as well as some instrumentals.

JOHNNY TEMPLER & THE HI-CATS

The **Hi-Cats** originally were formed by **Vic Grace** in Liverpool in 1961 after he had previously played with **Mark Peters & the Cyclones**.

Under the name of **Vic & the Hi-Cats**, the group, in its original line-up, consisted of **Vic Grace** (g/voc), **Austin 'Aussie' Brown** (g/voc), **Tony Gaskell** (bg) and **Brian Cochen** (dr).

Except for **Vic Grace**, all the musicians adopted stage names. So **Austin Brown** became **Johnny Sanchez**, while **Tony Gaskell** called himself **Tony Tarson** and **Brian Cochen's** stage name was **Chick Broderick**.

In the beginning, **Vic & the Hi-Cats** mainly played instrumentals in the style of the **Shadows** but realised that they needed a real lead vocalist.

They found one in **Wally Staines**, who had adopted the name of **Danny Havoc**, he had previously sung with **Danny Havoc & the Dakotas**.

The group continued as **Danny Havoc & the Hi-Cats**, now mainly playing the topical hits and **Cliff Richard** numbers, from which it can be concluded that it was not one of the harder Beat groups.

Between **Danny Havoc** and the other members, some personal problems arose and, during that time, **Tony Tarson** temporarily was replaced by **Dave Collins** on the bass guitar.

Danny Havoc and **Dave Collins** then left to form the **Ventures**, who later became the **Secrets**, but that is another story in this book.

Once again, the **Hi-Cats** were looking for a lead singer and recruited **John Dempsey** from the just disbanded **G-Men**, who then became **Johnny Templer** and the group accordingly, **Johnny Templer & the Hi-Cats**.

When **Chick Broderick** left and quit showbiz, he was replaced by **Pete Orr**, who left quite soon to join **Groups Inc.** and then he also became a member of the **Ventures**.

Johnny Templer
Lead Singer

Accordingly, after all these changes, **Johnny Templer & the Hi-Cats** then appeared in the following line-up:

Johnny Templer	(voc)
Vic Grace	(lg/voc)
Tony Gaskell	(rg)
Austin Brown	(bg)
Mal Thory	(dr)

Tony Gaskell had returned and the new drummer, **Mal Thory**, was a former member of the **Black Cats**.

Johnny Templer & the Hi-Cats quickly became popular on the scene and were recorded for the BBC radio show, 'Here We Go'. They played two songs. Of them, only the **Tommy Roe** number, "Sheila", is known. A little later, the group recorded an acetate - not in one of Liverpool's studios but in a church hall somewhere on Rose Lane in Allerton. Besides the **Johnny Templer** original, "Tonight Will Be The Night", they recorded three more cover versions, probably all **Cliff Richard** songs.

As only **Vic Grace** kept his copy and he died a few years ago in London, nobody can remember the other songs. **Johnny Templer** believes that they were all **Cliff Richard** numbers, but could not recall the titles.

Because of disagreements about their musical direction, founder, **Vic Grace**, left to join **Danny Havoc & the Ventures** who, a little later under his leadership, became the **Secrets**.

From then on, the music of the group was influenced by American Rock 'n' Roll.

The new lead guitarist with **Johnny Templer & the Hi-Cats** was **Roy Wood**, who had formerly played with the **Nomads**, that a little later evolved into the **Mojos**.

He did not stay for too long and went on to join **Sonny Webb & the Cascades**. A few months later, he sadly committed suicide.

Then young **Stan Smith**, a newcomer on the scene, was selected as their new guitarist. The group was also joined by girl singer, **Barbara Harrison**, who had previously toured with **Faron's Flamingos** in France.

In November 1962, **Johnny Templer & the Hi-Cats** were voted No. 20 in the popularity poll of the 'Mersey Beat' newspaper but, in spite of that success, **Barbara Harrison** soon went on to join **Danny Havoc & the Ventures** and, a little later, was followed by **Austin Brown** to this group which, by then, had already changed their name into the **Secrets**.

Johnny Templer & the Hi-Cats were joined by **Ron Smith** as their new bass guitarist, he had previously played with **J.J. & the Hi-Lites** and the **Mersey Monsters**.

The next to leave was **Mal Thory** and his replacement was **Jimmy Lacey**, who came from the **Profiles**. These continuing changes in the line-up resulted in **Johnny Templer & the Hi-Cats** disbanding in 1964.

Johnny Templer, together with his brother, **Mike Dempsey,** and drummer, **Frank Stewart,** then formed the **Borderliners**. They were joined by **Tony Gaskell** as fourth member.

Tony Gaskell later played with **Screaming Lord Sutch & the Savages** and then joined a group called **Hartford West**, where he met up again with **Austin Brown**. He is still active in the music business and today plays in the Country & Rock trio **Bojangles**.

Jimmy Lacey appeared on the scene again as a member of **Chick Graham & the Coasters** and the **Three Cheers**, who had evolved from **Mark Peters & the Silhouettes** and later changed their name to **Phase Three**.

Barbara Harrison

Stan Smith joined the **Country Five** and later was a long time member of the **Everglades**. He sadly died in 2008.

Discography :

Johnny Templer & the Hi-Cats never released an official record but were recorded for BBC's 'Here We Go Show" in 1962 with two songs. Of them, only the **Tommy Roe** number, "**Sheila**", is known. Besides this, the group, in that same year, recorded an acetate EP which, unfortunately, has not survived the years. Therefore, it is only known that the **Johnny Templer** original, "**Tonight Will Be The Night**", was one of the songs.

KARL TERRY & THE CRUISERS

This began with the **Gamblers Skiffle Group**, formed in Liverpool by **Terry Connor** (voc/g) in 1956, together with brothers, **Les Braid** (bass) and **Gordon Braid** (g).

The Gamblers Skiffle Group

Les Braid became a member of **Johnny Carter & the Hi-Cats** in 1957 and then joined the **Bluegenes**, who later became the **Swinging Blue Jeans**, where he played until he sadly died in July 2005.

Gordon Braid apparently quit the music business, while **Terry Connor** formed **Terry Connor & the Teen-Aces**, who were more Rock 'n' Roll orientated.

This group existed until the early Sixties and then disbanded without having achieved anything more than local popularity. **Terry Connor** changed his stage name to **Karl Terry** and formed **Karl Terry & the Cruisers** that, in the original line-up, consisted of:

Karl Terry	**(voc/g)**
David Hamilton	**(g/voc)**
Gerry Clayton	**(g/voc)**
Don McCormack	**(bg)**
Gordon Templeton	**(dr)**

Gordon Templeton was a former member of **Terry Connor & the Teen-Aces** and, prior to joining **Karl Terry & the Cruisers,** he had played with **Cy & the Cimarrons**.

The Cruisers (including Larry 'Jet' Clarke - 2nd from right)

This was a real Rock 'n' Roll group and the line-up was joined by **Larry Clarke** as an additional member who, a little later, took over on lead guitar when **David Hamilton** left the group.

Larry 'Jet' Clarke was the former leader of **Jet & the Valiants**.

Karl Terry who, in the meantime, had put his guitar aside, was given the epithet, 'Lover Boy', by his fans. A little later he was christened the 'Sheik Of Shake' by famous Cavern DJ, **Bob Wooler**.

In October 1961, **Karl Terry & the Cruisers** were voted No. 7 in the 'Mersey Beat' newspaper popularity poll, clearly showing how popular this band had become within a very short time.

In 1962, **Gordon Templeton** left the group and was replaced by **Roy Dyke**, who did not stay for too long, he then joined the **Remo Four**.

Gordon Templeton returned to **Karl Terry & the Cruisers**, who, very soon after, disbanded as not all the musicians wanted to become professionals.

Larry 'Jet' Clarke became the leader of the Liverpool group, **Jet & the Centrebeats,** and **Gerry Clayton** went on to play with **Hobo Rick & the City Slickers** but later joined the Jazz-scene, where he is still playing today.

'The Sheik Of Shake', **Karl Terry,** and **Gordon Templeton** then re-formed the band under the old name, together with **Freddie Ennis** (bg/voc) and **John Kirkpatrick** (g), who both came from **Johnny Saint & the Travellers**. Before that, **John Kirkpatrick** had played with the **Moon Rockers**. The group was also joined by songstress, **Nicolette Moran**.

Karl Terry & the Cruisers L to R: Karl Terry, Freddie Ennis, John Kirkpatrick & Gordon Templeton

But still in 1963, **Karl Terry & the Cruisers** split up again when **Karl Terry** first joined **Group One** and then became a member of the **Delemeres**, a Newcastle group that had settled down in Liverpool. With them **Karl Terry** recorded an interesting acetate with "See you On Saturday Night" at the Eroica studios in Eccles.

Freddie Ennis joined **Mark Peters & the Cyclones**, who later, without the singer, recorded as the **Cyclones** and then evolved into the **Few**.

John Kirkpatrick played with **Lee Shondell & the Boys** before he became a member of **Jason Eddie & the Centermen**. The drummer, **Gordon Templeton,** joined the **Valkyries** from Birkenhead.

When the **Delemeres** moved back to Newcastle, **Karl Terry** became a member of **Amos Bonny & the**

The Delemeres with Karl Terry - Live at the Cavern

T.T.s. After **Amos Bonny** left, they continued as **Karl Terry & the T.T.s** and later there was an amalgamation between the remaining members of this group and the remaining members of the **Clayton Squares**, under the name of **The T-Squares**. This group also included **Karl Terry** again, after he had played for a short time with the **Talismen**, who had separated from **Vince Earl**.

The **T-Squares** toured Germany twice with different line-ups under the name of the **Clayton Squares** before their final break up.

Karl Terry then became a member of **Rory Storm & the Hurricanes** for a short time and, after that, played with **Capricorn.** Then he re-formed **Karl Terry & the Cruisers** sometime in 1967 - 1968.

Since that time, **Karl Terry & the Cruisers** have been an original Rock 'n' Roll band and, in 1978, they were featured on the revival sampler, 'Mersey Survivors', with their version of "I'm Gonna Be A Wheel Someday", which was the first official release ever by 'The Sheik Of Shake', **Karl Terry.**

It was not a very exciting recording as it was played much too fast, but this was obviously a decision by the producer. There was a rumour that an album was released by the group with the title, 'Cruisin', that included songs from the 'Mersey Survivors' recording session. This has never been verified and even **Karl Terry** is not sure if it really was released. No one can really swear that it does exist, although it is improbable.

A little later, their first single, "Haunted House", was released on **Dave Crosby's** 'Rox' label and, this time, it sounded like **Karl Terry & the Cruisers**, which is not really a surprise as the group had a great line-up that consisted of **Bob Hardy** (lg), **Allen 'Gaz' Gaskell** (sax), **Mike Kearns** (sax), **Dennis Swale** (bg) and **Tommy Maguire** (dr). **Dennis Swale** left and got married and was replaced by **Tony Dunmore** but, shortly after this, the complete group parted from **Karl Terry** and became the original **Gaz & the Groovers**, a legend of its own that had a long residency in Germany under the name of **Juke.** At one point, together with **Alby Donnelly,** they also appeared as **Supercharge.**

The constantly changing line-ups of **Karl Terry & the Cruisers,** over the years, involved lots of well-known Merseybeat musicians from the Sixties scene. They included, for example, **Vinnie Ismail** (g), who in the good old days, was a member of **Vince & the Volcanoes** and the **Harlems, Chris Wilson** (g), a former member of the **Galvanisers, John Rathbone** (dr), who had played with the **Masterminds** and the **Almost Blues, Billy Conroy** (dr), who was once a member of **Jason Eddie & the Centermen, Pete Newton** and **Kenny Guy** from the **Detours,** and saxophonist **Brian Jones** from the **Undertakers. Lance Railton** (g), **Wally Shepard** (bg) and **Dave Gore** (g), all three ex-members of the legendary **Earl Preston & the T.T.s.** These are just a few of the names, as it would take a complete book about **Karl Terry & the Cruisers** if all the different line-ups were considered. In 1993, the 'Sheik Of Shake' found quite a steady line-up for his group that included:

Kenny Goodlass (dr)	- A former member of the **Kirkbys,** the **Fruit Eating Bears,** the **Escorts,** the **Swinging Blue Jeans** and the **Merseybeats.**
Ritchie Prescott (g)	- Who in the Sixties played with **Derry Wilkie & the Pressmen.**
Alan Stratton (bass)	- A former member of the **Black Cats** and the **Kansas City Five.**
Andy Bourne (sax)	- A former member of **Faron's Flamingos.**

With this line-up, in the summer of 1994 **Karl Terry & the Cruisers** recorded the great album, 'Rock 'n' Roll - That's All', on the small German collectors label, 'Merseyside Records'.

This long player was recorded live at the studio and, accordingly, captured the real sound of **Karl Terry & the Cruisers**, especially songs such as "Sea Cruise", "Twenty Flight Rock", "Queen Of The Hop", "Shake Rattle & Roll", "Mess Of Blues", the fantastic rocking "High School Confidential" and the **Karl Terry** original "What's Wrong With Me".

After that, the line-up changed again numerous times but **Karl Terry** is still going strong on the scene and of course his music is still good old Rock' n 'Roll.

<u>Discography :</u>

It is hard to understand that there was no record released by this first class Rock 'n' Roll band in the Sixties, although it was one of Liverpool's pioneering groups. But in 1978, the band had its first release on the revival sampler, '**Mersey Survivors**' (**UK-Raw RWLP 104**), with the song, "**I'm Gonna Be A Wheel Someday**". From the same recording session, an album by **Karl Terry & the Cruisers** may have been released with the title **Cruisin'**, but this information is very doubtful as nobody has ever seen this long player, not even any of the musicians that would have been involved.

Shortly after the revival sampler recording, **Karl Terry & the Cruisers** released the following single:

Haunted house / Stick It In Your Pipe And Smoke It   **UK- Rox 008 / 1978**

LP **'Rock 'n' Roll – That's all'**   **G- Merseyside ME 00.102 / 1994**

- **Sea Cruise / Mess Of Blues / Blueberry Hill / What's Wrong With Me / High School Confidential /**

   Ain't That A Shame / Twenty Flight Rock / My Blue Heaven / Queen Of The Hop / Will You Still

   Love Me Tomorrow / Pretend / Shake, Rattle & Roll / They Say

<u>Karl Terry</u> with <u>the Delemeres</u> :

See You On Saturday Night / Summertime   **UK – Eroica acetate / 1963**

THE THOUGHTS

It proved to be very difficult to find anything out about the genesis of this group but, from the information available, the following scenario is the most probable :

The **Thoughts** were formed some time in 1964 by **Phil Boardman**, a former member of the **Corsairs** from Huyton, and drummer, **Paul Comerford**, who had previously played with the **Pulsators** from Aintree.

According to an article in the 'Mersey Beat' newspaper, these two were joined by the female organist **Marion Hill** from the **Memphis Rhythm & Blues Combo** and **Alan Hornby**, who was a former member of **Danny & the Asteroids**.

It is not absolutely sure, but highly probably, that this was the original line-up of the **Thoughts**.

After playing some gigs on the scene, the 'Liverpool Echo' and 'Mersey Beat' newspaper columnist, **Geoff Leack,** became aware of the group and signed them to his management stable.

At that time, **Geoff Leack** was also the manager of **Tiffany's Dimensions** and, when the songstress parted from that group in 1965, **Geoff Leack** arranged for **Tiffany**, whose real name was **Irene Green** and who originally had sung with the **Liverbirds**, to team up with the **Thoughts**.

In the meantime, **Marion Hill** had left to join the **Runaways** and **Paul Comerford** had joined the **Cryin' Shames** or **Paul and Ritchie & the Cryin' Shames**, as they were called at that time. He later played with the **Escorts** and the **Times**.

Still in 1965, **Tiffany with the Thoughts**, as they were called now, had a great record released with "Find Out What's Happening" on Parlophone, which was also released on the German Odeon label.

After that record, which unfortunately did not become a chart success, **Tiffany** parted from the **Thoughts** and recorded for Decca with the **Robbie Gray Soul Band**. After that, she appeared as a solo-act in the cabaret-scene. In 1966, she teamed up with the **Defenders**. Her career can be followed in a separate story in this book.

The **Thoughts** continued in their own right with the following line-up:

Pete Beckett	(voc/rg)
Phil Boardman	(lg/voc)
Alan Hornby	(bg)
Dave Croft	(dr/voc)

Pete Beckett came from the **Modes**, while the new drummer, **Dave Croft,** had previously played with the **Cliftons**, the **Blues System** and the **Aztecs**.

The **Thoughts** toured Germany, where they mainly appeared in the Frankfurt area.

In 1966, **Dave Croft** also played with the **Fruit Eating Bears** for a short time, but then he returned to the **Thoughts** who teamed up with the duo, **Johnny & John**, consisting of the former **Merseybeats** members, **Johnny Gustafson** and **John Banks**.

With this duo, the **Thoughts** recorded some songs for Polydor, of which "Bumper To Bumper" coupled with "Scrape My Boot" were released on single in 1966, but only credited to **Johnny & John**.

Johnny & John

The **Thoughts** frequently played down in London and, still in 1966, through their connection with **Johnny & John,** they were introduced to American record-producer, **Shel Talmy**, who signed the group for the new label, 'Planet'.

In September 1966, the **Ray Davies** song, "All Night Stand", was released on a single coupled with the group's original, "Memory Of Your Love", written by **Pete Beckett** and **Phil Boardman**.

Two different versions of "All Night Stand" were released, a slower version in England and a more upbeat version in the United States.

The single received great reviews from the critics but just barely made the charts.

Dave Croft left the group again for another three weeks and, during this time, played with the Australian **Easybeats**, who recorded a follow-up single to their big international hit, "Friday On My Mind", with the title, "Heaven And Hell", on which **Dave Croft** was featured on drums.

Dave Croft then returned to the **Thoughts**, who had now settled down in London.

When **Pete Beckett** left to form **Beckett's Kin** in Liverpool, together with saxophonist, **Keith Wilson** from the **Doug Barry Sound** and guitarist, **Alan Hanson**, he was replaced in the **Thoughts** by **Denny Alexander** who came from Liverpool's **Clayton Squares** and, before that, he had played with the **Aarons**, the **Secrets** and the **Kinsleys**.

It was probably this line-up of the **Thoughts** that also made a topical film for Paramount, called

The Thoughts

'Girls In Short Short Dresses' about 'Swinging London'. In this film, two of their unreleased songs, "Pretty Girl" and "Call Me Girl", from the recording session with **Shel Talmy** were featured. Both songs were probably originals by the group.

It was some time in late 1968 or early 1969 that the group broke up totally and all the members went separate ways.

Denny Alexander disappeared from the scene and, of **Alan Hornby,** it is known that he later worked for an insurance company in Formby, while **Dave Croft** became the owner of a pub in Liverpool.

Phil **Boardman** joined the Army but, in the early Seventies, went back to London and formed a duo with **Trevor Davies**, who is better known under the name of '**Dozy**' of **Dave Dee, Dozy, Beaky, Mick & Tich** fame. They called themselves **Woodsmoke** and recorded the song, "Slow Dancer", for Parlophone, which was not released - as a version of the same song was released in the USA by **Sam & Dave** at the same time.

In spite of that bad luck, the duo obviously had a good time and also toured in Germany, until '**Dozy**' returned to the re-formed **Dave Dee, Dozy, Beaky, Mick & Tich**.

Phil **Boardman** then formed **Big Combo** and, with this group, began to work in Norway, where he has been living since the early Eighties, still successfully playing, writing and recording.

Pete **Beckett** went back to London and, in 1967, joined the group, **Winston G. & the Wicked**, that later changed their name into the **Winston G. Set**, then into **Fox** and later into **Whip**.

In 1969, Pete **Beckett** had a short stint with **World Of OZ** but then, together with **Lou Stonebridge** and **Derek Foley** of Manchester's **Grisby Dyke,** formed the group **Paladin**. When they split in 1973, Pete **Beckett** worked with **Tin Tin** and, after that, emigrated to Los Angeles. There he kept on playing with a group called **Friends** that, in 1974, became the **Skyband**. After that, he played with **Riff Raff** and **Bandana** before he joined the great west coast group, **Player**, with whom he had the chart-topper, "Baby Come Back", in 1978, for which the group was awarded a gold record.

In the early Nineties, Pete **Beckett** joined the internationally successful **Little River Band** and played with them for eight years. After that, he started a highly successful solo career as singer/songwriter. Amongst others, he wrote songs for **Olivia Newton-John, Kenny Rogers** and the **Temptations**.

Pete **Beckett** is still living and playing in Los Angeles.

Finally, it should be pointed out, that the Liverpool **Thoughts** had absolutely no connection to the recording group, **Paul Dean & the Thoughts**, which was the group of singer, **Paul Nicholas,** and hailed from London .

Discography :

as **Tiffany with the Thoughts** :

Find Out What's Happening / Baby Don't Look Down   **UK- Parlophone R 5439 / 1965**

as backing-group for **Johnny & John** :

Bumper To Bumper / Scrape My Boot   **UK- Polydor BM 56087 / 1966**

The **Thoughts** – solo :

All Night Stand / Memory Of Your Love   **UK- Planet PLF 118 / 1966**

Unreleased tracks :

During their session for the Planet single, the **Thoughts** also recorded the songs, "**Pretty Girl**" and "**Call Me Girl**", for producer, **Shel Talmy**, which later were featured in the Paramount film-clip, 'Girls In Short Short Dresses', of 1966. Both numbers most probably were originals, written by **Phil Boardman** and **Pete Beckett**.

'TIFFANY'

Irene Green was born in Liverpool and grew up in the Wavertree area of the city. She started singing at a very young age and, as she matured, she decided that she wanted to become a professional singer.

It was sometime in 1962 that she replied to a newspaper advert for a group that was looking for a female vocalist. That group turned out to be the all female **Liverbirds** that, until then, had only played instrumentals. They rehearsed together and **Irene Green** got the job.

She had great stage presentation and an extremely powerful voice, singing songs of the **Shirelles**, **Jackie De Shannon** and similar numbers.

The **Liverbirds** became very popular and played throughout the north of England.

One night, after a gig at the 'Whiskey-A-Go-Go' in Newcastle, **Irene Green** decided to pursue a solo-career and left the **Liverbirds**. Shortly after this, they went over to Germany where they became stars of the so called 'Star-Club' era. They have a separate story in this book.

Irene Green remained in Liverpool, adopted the stage-name of '**Tiffany**' and teamed up with the **Four Dimensions**, formerly known as **J.C. & the Strollers**.

As **Tiffany's Dimensions**, the group soon became very popular on the Merseybeat scene and also toured Scotland. Beside her solo numbers, **Tiffany** also sang duet with **Jimmy Clarke**, the lead vocalist of the **Dimensions**, in the style of the **Everly Brothers** but also doing real Soul numbers, such as the songs of **Charlie & Ines Foxx**, that suited both of their strong voices.

The 'Liverpool Echo' and 'Mersey Beat' newspaper columnist, **Geoff Leack** from Childwall, took over their management and somehow organised a recording test for **Tiffany's Dimensions** with **George Martin** in 1964.

It is told that the famous producer liked the singer and the group so much that he signed them but wanted to make two recording acts out of them.

So it happened that the **Dimensions**, who had dropped the 'Four' from their name, had a single released with their great "Tears On My Pillow", while **Tiffany's** release of the **Jackie De Shannon** song, "Am I dreaming", on which she was backed by studio-musicians, followed very soon after.

It was a good record with a great version of **Barbara George's** "I Know" on the flipside, that identified **Tiffany** as being a really tremendous Beat singer.

Irene Green aka 'Tiffany'

For more information about the **Dimensions**, please see their story in this book.

Tiffany, besides occasionally still appearing with the **Dimensions,** also began accepting cabaret style bookings.

Unfortunately, her record only entered the lower regions of the charts and so it did not create a breakthrough. **Tiffany** apparently did not feel too comfortable in the cabaret scene as she really was more of a 'rocking' Soul singer.

Still in 1965, **Geoff Leack** arranged for her to team up with the **Thoughts**, a relatively new Liverpool outfit, that was also part of his management stable.

As **Tiffany & the Thoughts,** the next single was released with a great "Find Out What's Happening" coupled with the **Irma Thomas** original, "Baby Don't Look Down'.

If her first record was great, this was just fantastic and it was also released in Germany on the Odeon label.

Tiffany's Dimensions at the Cavern

In spite of this, it did not result in a breakthrough for **Tiffany** who, in 1966, parted from the **Thoughts. The Thoughts,** as a group, continued solo but also backed the duo, **Johnny & John**, which consisted of the former **Merseybeats** members, **Johnny Gustafson** and **John Banks**.

With **Johnny & John,** they recorded their only Polydor single and, after that, the **Thoughts** kept recording, in their own right, for producer, **Shel Talmy,** on Planet, but this, again, is another story in this book.

Tiffany with the Dimensions

Tiffany, for a short time, was backed by the **Robbie Gray Soul Band** and, with them, recorded the songs, "Hallelujah, I Love Him So" and "All Night Worker", for Decca in 1966. Unfortunately, they were never released. She then went back into the cabaret circuit for some time and used the resident club musicians as backing.

Still in 1966, she amalgamated with the **Defenders** and, as **Tiffany & the Defenders,** they had regular appearances at venues such as the 'Orrell Park Ballroom', 'Blair Hall', the 'Mardi Gras', the 'Downbeat' and the 'Holyoake', as well as at the 'Queens Hall' in Widnes. Besides these local venues, they were kept busy playing all over Lancashire and Cheshire and touring Scotland again.

Due to problems with their management, after approximately 6 months, the **Defenders** parted from the songstress and continued in their own right, as can be followed in their separate story.

Tiffany then worked with various groups but also got back into the cabaret-scene until she lost her heart for singing and got married to her manager, **Geoff Leack,** sometime in the early Seventies.

The last that was heard of her was that she was working in the reception department of a big Liverpool hotel on Mount Pleasant but, sadly, died some time ago without ever having returned to showbiz.

Discography :

'Tiffany' - solo :

Am I Dreaming / I Know	UK – Parlophone R 5311 / 1964

as **Tiffany & the Thoughts** :

Find Out What's Happening / Baby Don't Look Down	UK – Parlophone R 5439 / 1965

Unreleased tracks :

Hallelujah, I Love Him So / All Night Worker	UK – Decca unreleased / 1966

(On this Decca-recording, **Tiffany** was backed by the **Robbie Gray Soul Band** from Birkenhead, formerly known as the **Tributes**)

T.L.'s BLUESICIANS

A real Blues group (as the name suggests) originally called **T.L.'s Groundhogs.** They were formed in the Old Swan area of Liverpool during the Autumn of 1963.

When this quintet was booked to play the 'Cavern' for the first time in April 1964, they were on the same bill as the American Blues legend, **John Lee Hooker**, who, that night, was backed by a London group also named **The Groundhogs. Bob Wooler**, resident DJ and also programme manager of the 'Cavern', insisted that the Liverpool group change their name if they wanted the gig, which is how **T.L.'s Bluesicians** were born.

However, as this unexpected name change was requested at such short notice, the boys found themselves advertised in the Liverpool Echo to appear on the 'Peppermint Lounge' before midnight as **T.L.'s Groundhogs**, and, after midnight, on the 'Cavern All-Night Session' as **T.L.'s Bluesicians**.

From that moment on they continued with that name in a line-up with:

Tony Leeuwangh	(voc/harp)
Bob Hardy	(lg/voc)
Chris Lawson	(rg)
Pete Newton	(bg/voc)
Phil Perry	(p)
Vic Brunskill	(dr)

It is said that **Vic Brunskill** formerly had played guitar in the **Statesmen** - that could not be confirmed, but that does not mean that it is impossible.

The group played material by artists such as **Sonny Boy Williamson**, **T-Bone Walker** and **Chuck Berry** and soon became popular on the local scene.

Still in 1964, **T.L.'s Bluesicians** went into the CAM studio in Moorfields and recorded **T-Bone Walker's** "The Hustle's On (T-Bone Blues)", as well as the **Chuck Berry** version

T. L⁵. Groundhogs

Jack Ross Enterprises • Tel. GRE 5993

of the **Amos Milburn** hit, "Down The Road A Piece", which were kept on acetate. In 2002, these great and very interesting recordings were released on the compilation CD, 'This Is Merseybeat Vol. 3', which was put out by BBC radio presenter, **Mike Brocken**.

In 1965, some members of the group wanted to turn professional and some did not - with the result that **Tony Leeuwangh**, **Chris Lawson** and **Vic Brunskill** quit playing. At least there is no record of them having joined any other bands after that.

Bob Hardy then organized **Phil Perry**, **Pete Newton**, former **Clayton Squares** frontman **Terry Hines** and two other Liverpool musicians into the **Terry Hines Sextet**, but that is another story that can be followed in this book.

Discography

Down The Road A Piece / The Hustle Is On (T-Bone Blues)   **UK- CAM acetate / 1964**

(The two songs mentioned above were released on the Mayfield CD 'This Is Merseybeat Vol 3' in 2002).

THE TRAVELLERS

This group was formed under the name of **Johnny Saint & the Travellers** by **Johnny Laffin** in Liverpool in 1960 and, accordingly, was one of the pioneering groups of the Merseybeat scene.

In 1962, the group's name was shortened to **The Travellers** but, even after the name change, it was sometimes still announced under the original name. Of course, **Johnny Saint** was none other than **Johnny Laffin,** who was the founding member of the group.

Right from the beginning, the **Travellers** consisted of the following musicians:

Johnny Saint	**(voc/g)**
John Kirkpatrick	**(g/p/voc)**
Freddie Ennis	**(bg/voc)**
Roy Cresswell	**(dr)**

John Kirkpatrick's name sometimes was shortened to **John Kirk** and he was a former member of the **Moon Rockers**.

In April 1962, the **Travellers** went down to London to make test recordings for PYE and, among others, the songs, "Let's Twist Again" and "Dream Baby", were recorded but, unfortunately, nothing was ever released.

A little later, **Roy Cresswell** left the group to join **Mark Peters & the Cyclones** who, after **Mark Peters** had left, continued on as the **Cyclones** and later evolved into **The Few**.

The **Travellers** were joined by **Bernie Rogers** as their new drummer. This line-up only existed until October 1962 and then the **Travellers** disbanded totally, which is quite hard to understand as they were one of the most popular groups on the Merseybeat scene at that time.

Freddie Ennis

However, **John Kirkpatrick** and **Freddie Ennis** became members of **Karl Terry & the Cruisers** and, after that, **Freddie Ennis** also joined the **Cyclones**, where he met up with **Roy Cresswell** again.

John Kirkpatrick became a member of **Lee Shondell & the Boys** and, after that, played with **Jason Eddie & the Centermen**. In the Seventies, he was a member of the very successful **Albion Dance Band**.

Bernie Rogers joined **Lee Curtis & the All Stars** and, after that, was a member of **Denny Seyton & the Sabres**. Later, he continued on as a freelance drummer. In the early Nineties, he played with **Johnny Guitar & his Hurricanes** and, after that, he joined **Faron's Flamingos**.

What happened to **Johnny Saint** is not known exactly but, in 1964, a group with the name the **Travellers** appeared again on the Liverpool scene. As it is impossible that the old band was re-formed in its original line-up, it might have been the case that the 'new' **Travellers** were led by **Johnny Saint** again and included different musicians. But this is not proven at all and this is only one of many possibilities.

However, the 'new' **Travellers** had no great success on the scene and disappeared again a little later.

Discography :

There were never any records released under either the **Johnny Saint & the Travellers** or the **Travellers** name. However, in 1962, the **Travellers** recorded the songs, "**Let's Twist Again**" and "**Dream Baby**", for PYE and these are probably still sleeping in the archives of the record company - if they were actually kept at all.

GUS TRAVIS & (various groups)

It was most probably the music of **Gene Vincent** that encouraged the young **Graham Bull** from Heswall on the Wirral to start on a Rock 'n' Roll career.

Specifically for a local 'Church Harvest Festival' in 1957, he, together with some friends, formed a group called the **Rockin' Six**, kicking off a set with the **Crickets'** "That'll Be The Day", which was currently climbing up the Pop-charts. **Graham Bull** still insists that this was the first and the last time he learned and performed a new song that was in the charts at the time.

Graham Bull (aka - Gus Travis)

Anyway, the **Rockin' Six** consisted of the following musicians:

Graham Bull	(voc)
Steve Laigne	(lg)
Ian McQuair	(rg)
Alan Watts	(p)
Clive Watkin	(t-bass)
Ian Douglas	(dr)

Although this was meant to be a one-off appearance, the musicians kept in touch and, a few months later, **Graham Bull** gave it another go with the same line-up.

He changed his name into **Gus Travis** and inspired by **Gene Vincent's** group, the **Bluecaps**, he renamed his group **Gus & the Thundercaps**. The group's repertoire mainly consisted of songs by **Gene Vincent, Carl Perkins, Jerry Lee Lewis, Buddy Holly, Johnny Burnette, Buddy Knox** and **Roy Orbison**.

With that, **Gus & the Thundercaps** were, for sure, one of the first Rock 'n' Roll groups on Merseyside.

In 1958, **Steve Laigne** left the group and was replaced by **Dave Carden**, who came from the **Five Stars**.

When **Clive Watkin** also left, he was not immediately replaced and the **Thundercaps** continued as a five-piece. But, in 1960, when **Alan Watts** left and went down to London, **Billy Bingham** was added to the line-up as a bass guitarist.

Then **Ian Douglas** moved to Scotland and the new drummer was **Pete Williams**, who soon left to join the **Morockans**. Accordingly, after all those changes, the final line-up that appeared as **Gus & the Thundercaps** consisted of:

Gus Travis	(voc)
Dave Carden	(lg/voc)
Ian McQuair	(rg)
Billy Bingham	(bg)
John Cochran	(dr)

The new drummer, **John Cochran**, was a former member of **Wump & his Werbles**.

During 1961, **Gus Travis** wanted to change the name of the group, mainly because the musicians refused to wear their caps and the group consistently was billed as *Gus & the Thunderclaps*, which he did not like at all. As their opening-number at that time was the **Hank Ballard & the Midnighters** number, "Let's Go, Let's Go, Let's Go", the above line-up became **Gus Travis & the Midnighters**.

Billy Bingham soon left for London and, when he returned to the Wirral, his place in the **Midnighters** had already been given to **Dave Woods** from the **Morockans**, so **Billy Bingham** joined the **Four Sounds**.

Then **Alan Watts** returned from London and, besides playing in the group, also took over the management of **Gus Travis & the Midnighters**, now appearing with:

Gus Travis	**(voc)**
Dave Carden	**(lg/voc)**
Ian McQuair	**(rg)**
Alan Watts	**(p)**
Dave Woods	**(bg/voc)**
John Cochran	**(dr)**

This was probably the most successful line-up of **Gus Travis & the Midnighters**, who had become very popular and had a large following on both sides of the River Mersey but, for incomprehensible reasons, they never signed a recording-contract.

It was some time in early 1963 that **Alan Watts** accepted a booking for the group to appear at the opening of the 'Streatham Ice Rink' in London.

Gus Travis did not want to go there and, in a dispute over this booking, he left the group, who then teamed up with **Freddie Fowell** as their singer. He came from the disbanded **Howie Casey & the Seniors** and had adopted the stage-name of **Freddie Starr**.

They stayed together and later also recorded, but the continuation of

Gus Travis & the Midnighters
L to R: John Cochran, Alan Watts, Dave Woods, Gus Travis, Ian McQuair & Dave Carden

The Four Sounds

that group and the ways of the individual musicians can be followed under **Freddie Starr & the Midnighters** in this book.

Gus Travis who, because of his stage 'show', was nicknamed **Gus 'Crazy Legs' Travis**, contacted his old bass-guitarist, **Billy Bingham,** and teamed up with his group, the **Four Sounds**, who adopted the name of **Gus Travis & the Midnighters** for their appearances with **Gus Travis**. This co-operation was only a temporary arrangement and the **Four Sounds** also carried on in their own right in a line-up with **Dave Keighly** (voc/lg), **John Hinton** (p), **Billy Bingham** (bg/voc) and **Alan Denton** (dr) until they split up in 1964.

Dave Keighly and **Alan Denton** then joined the **Exiles,** but **Dave Keighly** did not stay for too long, he left to join the **Pilgrims**. In 1965, the **Pilgrims** broke up but then they re-formed with both **Dave Keighly** and **Alan Denton** as members. **John Hinton** became a successful professional musician in London and **Billy Bingham** later became popular as a TV and late night radio announcer.

The Four Dymonds

Gus Travis then amalgamated with the **Four Dymonds** from Birkenhead – of course under the name of **Gus Travis & the Dymonds** in a line-up with:

Gus Travis	**(voc)**
Geoff Brown	**(g)**
Jim Percival	**(g)**
John Holford	**(bg)**
Terry McCusker	**(dr)**

Of **Terry McCusker,** it is known that he was a former member of **Pete Demos & the Demons**, who also hailed from Birkenhead.

Again, **Gus Travis & the Dymonds** became popular on the scene but, as with all the previous groups, **Gus Travis** did not stay with them for too long.

In 1964, he left the group, which apparently disbanded at that time. Of the individual members, only **Terry McCusker** appeared again on the scene as a member of **Rip Van Winkle & the Rip-It-Ups**. After that, he played with the successful **Valkyries** and the legendary **Roadrunners** before he joined **Fringe Benefit**, who very soon changed their name to **Colonel Bagshot & the Incredible Bucket Band**.

The new backing group for **Gus Travis** was the **Drifters**, who originated from **Johnny Rocco & the Jets** which had evolved into **Steve Day & the Drifters**. This new co-operation continued under the name of **Gus Travis & the Rainchecks**.

It was a really great group that again had lots of success on the local scene but, as with previous bands, the amalgamation with **Gus Travis** did not last too long. Apparently, the reason for this was due to the fact that **Gus Travis** never wanted to leave Merseyside, where he had a good job and, accordingly, always refused to turn professional.

The Rainchecks

The **Rainchecks** continued on without him and not only remained one of the top acts on the scene, but also recorded a single in their own right - a different story that is also featured in this book.

After he left the **Rainchecks, Gus Travis** continued on as a singer on the scene but, as far as it is known, he no longer had a steady backing group.

Throughout the years, his name was always popular, first on the Rock 'n' Roll scene and, after that, on the cabaret circuit of Liverpool and the surrounding area.

It was in the early Eighties that **Gus Travis & the Midnighters** were re-formed again for a few performances. The line-up was constantly changing but the members included **Brian Woods** again on lead-guitar, as well as the former **Morockans** members, **Pete Watson** (g) **Robin Cartwright** (bg) and **Derek Cooper** (dr), who was replaced by **Dave Jones.** At times, the line-up also included **Ritchie Prescott** who, in the Sixties, was the lead guitarist for the **Pressmen.**

In 1992, at a memorial concert for **Rory Storm** (an idea of **Bob Wooler** and realised by the 'MerseyCats' organisation) the name **Gus Travis & the Midnighters** appeared on the bill once again. This line-up also included the original members, **John Cochran** and **Ian McQuair.**

After that gig, the group sporadically appeared on the scene and, at one time, were also joined by drummer, **Alan Denton,** from the **Four Sounds.**

But in the end, this never became a steady group and **Gus Travis,** who is still a great stage personality, continued as solo singer in the Liverpool pubs and clubs.

Discography :

Throughout his long career, **Gus Travis** never made a record, although he appeared with a few really good groups. Only an early Seventies concert was professionally recorded, which was solid Rock 'n' Roll with **"Crazy Legs"** and **"Love Me"** as outstanding numbers. At that concert, he was not backed by any one of the above named groups and, as far as it is known, not even one of the musicians who played with him in his various groups of the Sixties was included.

THE TRENDS

At the beginning of the Sixties, **The Beatcombers** were formed in Liverpool and, in 1963, they changed their name to **Mike & the Merseymen**. They toured Germany the same year and, amongst other venues, appeared at the famous 'Star-Club' in Hamburg. Back in England, the band mainly worked in London, where their name was changed again, this time to the **Trends**.

This might have been a little confusing as there was a Liverpool group with the name the **Trents**, and the only difference in the name was one letter, but they were two totally different groups that had no connection to each other. However, the **Trends** of this story consisted of:

Mike Kelly	(voc/bg)
Frank Bowen	(g/voc)
John Hayes	(g/voc)
Freddie Self	(dr/voc)

Until 1963, before they changed their name from **Mike & the Merseymen** into the **Trends**, **Tony Priestly** (g/voc) was a member of the group, but he then joined **Earl Preston's Realms** and was replaced by **Frank Bowen**, something of a Beat globetrotter, who had previously played with the **Teenbeats, Cliff Roberts' Rockers, Howie Casey & the Seniors** and **Lee Curtis & the All Stars**.

Tammy St. John & the Trends

In 1964, **Mike Kelly** left the group and returned to Liverpool where he disappeared from the scene. He was replaced in the **Trends** by **Harry Scully** from Liverpool, who had previously played with the **Nashpool Four**. The lead vocals were then most probably taken over by **Freddie Self**.

This line-up was signed to PYE and very soon their first single was released on the Piccadilly label, a cover-version of the **Beatles** song, "All My Loving". This single wasn't successful in the charts but it sold quite well. The follow up, "You're A Wonderful One", was released on the PYE label and was a great record, with an interesting version of "The Way You Do The Things You Do" on the flip-side but, in spite of good sales, it did not make the charts.

On their next release, also in 1964, the **Trends** backed girl singer, **Tammy St. John,** on her PYE single, "Hey, Hey, Hey, Hey", an up-tempo number which was coupled with the **Shirelles** classic, "Boys".

The group most probably also backed **Tammy St. John** in her live appearances for a time but, towards the end of 1964, the **Trends** disbanded totally.

Frank Bowen and Harry Scully remained in London and became members of the **Bootleggers**, led by **Brian Auger**. After that, both musicians returned to Liverpool where **Harry Scully** later became a long time member of the cabaret-group, **Elliot**, while **Frank Bowen** joined **Earl Royce & the Olympics**. He sadly died in 1966 at a very young age.

John Hayes disappeared from the scene but **Freddie Self** started a solo career as a singer and, in 1964, the single, "Don't Cry", was released on Mercury under his name.

After that release, he continued recording as **Freddie Ryder** and, as such, in 1965 had three singles out with "To Get Your Love Back", "Some Kind Of Wonderful" and "Man Of The Moment" which showed him to be a really good singer but, in spite of this, he did not make a breakthrough.

The Trends

Nothing was heard of him for a long time but, in 1968, **Freddie Ryder** was back with a new recording contract and he cut the singles, "Shadows (I Can't See You)" and "The Worst That Could Happen", for the Columbia label. Unfortunately, none of his records made it into the charts and, at the end of the Sixties, he disappeared from the scene, which could mean that he quit show business and went back to his hometown of Liverpool. This, at least, was rumoured but it is not certain.

Single discography :

as **The Trends** :

All My Loving / Sweet Little Miss Love	UK- Piccadilly 7N 35171 / 1963
You're A Wonderful One / The Way You Do The Things You Do	UK- PYE 7N 15644 / 1964

as backing-group for **Tammy St. John** :

Hey, Hey, Hey, Hey / Boys	UK- PYE 7N 15682 / 1964

Freddie Self – solo :

Don't Cry / Why Should I	UK- Mercury MF 839 / 1964

Freddie Self as **Freddie Ryder** – solo :

To Get Your Love Back / A Little Thing Called Love	UK- Mercury MF 864 / 1965
Some Kind Of Wonderful / Slow Down	UK- Mercury MF 879 / 1965
Man Of The Moment / My Block	UK- Mercury MF 935 / 1965
Shadows / Airport	UK- Columbia DB 8335 / 1968
The Worst That Could Happen / World Of My Own	UK- Columbia DB 8427 / 1968

CY TUCKER & THE FRIARS

Thomas Thornton was a singing postman from Liverpool who had adopted the stage-name, **Cy Tucker,** and, in the very early Sixties, started his musical career as a member of the **Cimarrons**, sometimes also named **Cy & the Cimarrons**.

The group came from somewhere in the Kensington/Old Swan area of Liverpool and soon became quite popular locally.

It was sometime in late 1961 or early 1962 that **Cy Tucker** went on to become a member of **Earl Preston & the T.T.s** as an additional guitarist and, sometimes, also as a second lead-singer.

His old group, at that time, was joined by **Alan Greer** from **Mister X & the Masks** as the new singer/ guitarist, who adopted the stage-name of **Wayne Calvert** and, accordingly, the group continued on as **Wayne Calvert & the Cimarrons**.

Earl Preston & the T.T.s, without a doubt, were counted as one of the stars of Liverpool's early Merseybeat scene and were chosen to be featured on the legendary Oriole-compilations, 'This Is Merseybeat' Vol. 1 and Vol. 2. On these albums **Earl Preston** sang "Thumbin' A Ride", while the distinctive lead-vocals of **Cy Tucker** can be heard on the songs, "All Around The World" and "Hurt".

After that recording-debut, the group was signed to Fontana and, still in 1963, the single, "High-School Dance", was released by **Cy Tucker with Earl Preston's T.T.s** which, unfortunately, did not become a major success, although it sold quite well.

After **Wayne Calvert** parted from the **Cimarrons** in late 1963, **Cy Tucker** teamed up with his old group again. However, by that time, the guitarist, **Paul Doyle,** was the only remaining member of the original line-up. In 1964, as **Cy Tucker & the Friars,** the group recorded the single, "Let Me Call You Sweetheart". Soon after that, **Charly Smullan** (bg) and **Tommy Hart** (dr) left and joined the newly-formed **Earl Preston's Realms**.

Cy Tucker and **Paul Doyle** recruited new musicians and continued on as **Cy Tucker & the Friars** in a line-up with:

Cy Tucker	(voc/rg)
Paul Doyle	(lg/voc)
Danny Dring	(bg/voc)
Les Cave	(dr)

Danny Dring formerly had played with **Mister X & the Masks** that evolved into the **Renegades**, he had also played with **John Paul & the Deejays** and the **Denny Seyton Group**.

Les Cave was also a former member of **Mister X & the Masks** and the **Renegades**, and he had previously played with **Steampacket**.

In 1965, Fontana released another single with "My friend", which was coupled with a re-recorded version of "Hurt", which, obviously, was a solo-recording of **Cy Tucker** as the **Friars** were not credited on the label. Again a great record, showing the outstanding quality of **Cy Tucker** as a singer but, once again, no big success.

This may have been the reason for Fontana to drop **Cy Tucker & the Friars**. However, in spite of such bad luck, they continued in the same line-up until 1969. Then **Les Cave** left and his place in **Cy Tucker & the Friars** was taken over by **Len Brady**, who came from the **Top-C Three**.

In 1975, **Paul Doyle** left and was replaced by **Terry Barrat**, who came from the **Silver Set**. Between 1975 and

1978, this line-up recorded the songs, "Once In a While", "Sweet City Woman" and "Funny Face", for a live album with comedian, **Al Dean** (Stag-Music SG 1009/1975). Allegedly, they also recorded a single with a cover version of the **Status Quo** hit, "Rockin' All Over The World", as well as four nice EPs with the songs :

"Something About You Baby I Like", "Don't Play That Song", "Sweet City Woman" and "What's The Matter Baby" (Amazon Records AR 7001 S / 1975) ;

"Leaving On Your Mind", "Gifts", "Long Tall Sally" and "Funny Face" (Amazon AR 70012 S / 1976) ;

"Pearl's A Singer", "My Prayer", "Southern Nights" and "Hurt" (Amazon AR 70016 S / 1977) ;

"If We're Not Back In Love On Monday", "Higher And Higher", "It's So Easy" and "I Don't Wanna Talk About It" (Jungle-Records JR 7029 S / 1978).

All these records were only sold at gigs and are really worth looking out for.

In 1980, **Terry Barrat** left and was replaced by **Alan Greer**, formerly also known as **Wayne Calvert** who, after leaving the **Cimarrons,** had played with the **Plainsmen**, the **Ryles Brothers** (backing-group of **Solomon King**), **Me & Them** (who had backed **Chris Andrews** for some time) and with the **Lettermen** from Birkenhead.

In the same year, **Len Brady** left and **Cy Tucker & the Friars** were joined by **Vince Cadmore**, who stayed until 1982 and then he was replaced by the returning **Les Cave**.

Alan Greer quit showbiz and he was replaced by **Arthur Kerrivan** as their new lead guitarist, he had formerly played with **Staxx** and a group called **Pepperbox**.

In this line-up, **Cy Tucker & the Friars** existed until 1988 and were very successful on the Liverpool club scene. Then **Danny Dring** left and a little later teamed up with his brother in a cabaret duo.

He was replaced by **Dave Dover**, who in the Sixties amongst others, had been a member of the **Cordes** and, after that, he had played with **Colonel Bagshot & his Incredible Bucket Band**.

A little later, **Les Cave** also left and joined **Geoff Nugent's Undertakers**. After that, he quit the music scene.

The new drummer with **Cy Tucker & the Friars**, or the **Cy Tucker Band** as it was now sometimes named, was **Phil Chittick** who, in the Sixties, had played with **Johnny Ringo & the Colts** and **Sinbad**. He had also been a member of the **Merseybeats** and **Supercharge**.

Cy Tucker is still going strong on Merseyside but today, very often, only as a duo together with **Arthur Kerrivan**.

Single discography :

as Cy Tucker with Earl Preston's T.T.s :

My Prayer / High-School Dance   UK- Fontana TF 424 / 1963

as Cy Tucker & the Friars :

Let Me Call You Sweetheart / I Apologize   UK- Fontana TF 470 / 1964

Cy Tucker – solo :

My Friend / Hurt   UK- Fontana TF 534 / 1965

Please note that the group also recorded under the name of **Cy Tucker & the Friars** on different labels in the Seventies. For detailed information, please see the story.

TYME & MOTION

This was another Liverpool harmony group in the style of the **Everly Brothers** and the **Beach Boys**, which had its origin in the formation of **Rita & the Rebs** in the Crosby area of Merseyside in 1963/1964.

The group consisted of two vocalists, **Rita Jacobson** and **Roy Ennis**, guitarist and singer **Ray Bright**, singing bass guitarist **John Ross**, and **Ritchie Conner** on drums.

They played the usual local gigs but did not make the headlines and, when **Rita Jacobson** left in early 1966, the group almost broke up but then continued as **Tyme & Motion** in the line-up with:

Roy Ennis	(voc)
Ray Bright	(voc)
Tony Petches	(lg)
Alan Lucket	(rg)
John Ross	(bg/voc)
Robert Ninnim	(dr)

Robert Ninnim came from the great Liverpool harmony group, the **Easybeats,** while the former groups of **Tony Petches** and **Alan Lucket** are not known.

When **Robert Ninnim** sadly died in early 1967, his place was taken over by **Robert Milne** who came from the **Admins**.

Still in 1967, **Tyme & Motion** cut an interesting acetate with the song, "September In The Rain", which had been released as a single shortly before by **Paul and Ritchie & the Cryin' Shames**. This song, as well as the B-side, a version of **Del Shannon**'s "Kelly", showed the great singing ability of the group but, unfortunately, the acetate did not help to obtain a deal with a record company.

Tyme & Motion
L to R: Roy Ennis, Robert Ninnim & Ray Bright

Tony Petches left and **Alan Lucket** took over on lead guitar, while **Ray Bright,** for a short time, played guitar again.

With the arrival of **Eric Woolley** as their new rhythm guitarist, **Ray Bright** stepped in front again as a second singer but soon decided to leave. From then onwards, the lead vocals were shared by **Roy Ennis** and **John Ross** who, at that time, were the only remaining original members of **Rita & the Rebs**.

In this line-up, **Tyme & Motion** went down to London and did some test recordings for an agency that was looking for groups to tour Europe. The group did not get to tour Europe but, from these recordings, another acetate was cut with the **Drifters** song, "I'll Take You Where The Music's Playing", and the **Ronettes** classic, "Be My Baby".

Tyme & Motion returned to Liverpool and kept on playing the normal club circuit but split up totally in early 1969.

Robert Milne and **Eric Woolley** joined the **Almost Young**, who later toured Germany.

All the other members disappeared from the scene for years until **Ray Bright** re-formed **Tyme & Motion** in the mid Eighties, together with his old comrades, **Alan Lucket** and **John Ross**. Two new members were **Dave Smith** on lead guitar and the drummer, **Chris Mutch**, who, in the Sixties, had played with the **Krew** and, after that, had been a member of the **Swinging Blue Jeans**.

They played the cabaret circuit, but the revival of **Tyme & Motion** did not last too long and, afterwards, none of the members appeared again on the scene.

Discography :

September In The Rain / Kelly   UK - Deroy (?) – acetate / 1967

I'll Take You Where The Music's Playing / Be My Baby   UK - private acetate / 1968

THE UNDERTAKERS

It was very difficult to find out how this legendary Liverpool group developed and thus quite complicated to document. It is not easy to follow, but here is the real story:

In the late Fifties, there was a Birkenhead-based group called **Bob Evans & the Five Shillings** consisting of **Bob Evans** (voc), **Geoff Nugent** (g/voc), **Mike Millward** (g/voc), a certain **Ike** (bg) and **Billy Evans** (dr).

At live appearances, this group sometimes mixed with the musicians of another Birkenhead/Wallasey group the **Topspots**, consisting of **Robbie Hickson** (voc), **Peter Cooke** (g/voc), **Jimmy Sloan** (g), **Dave Cooper** (bg) and **Tommy Bennett** (dr).

The Topspots

So, **Bob Evans & the Five Shillings** sometimes became a sort of 'Bob Evans & the Nine Shillings', which was disliked by some of the musicians who left the group because of this. They were, **Geoff Nugent**, **Billy Evans**, the band leader's brother, and **Mike Millward**, who later became a member of the **Fourmost**.

Bob Evans & the Five Shillings were then joined by **Chris Huston** as a new guitarist, while **Bob Evans** himself took over the drums. When the line-up had stabilized again as a five piece, **Bob Evans & the Five Shillings** changed their name to **The Vegas Five**, which consisted of **Jimmy McManus** (voc) the returning **Geoff Nugent** (g/voc), **Chris Huston** (g/voc), former **Topspots** member, **Dave 'Mush' Cooper** (bg) and **Bob Evans** (dr).

In the meantime, the **Topspots** had changed their name to **Dee & the Dynamites** and, after the original 'Dee' **Robbie Hickson** had left to join the **Kansas City Five**, and drummer **Tommy Bennett** had become a member of the **Pressmen**, **Dee & the Dynamites** consisted of **Brian Myers**, who adopted the name 'Dee' and called himself **Brian Dee** (voc/g), **Peter Cooke** (g/voc), **Jimmy Sloan** (g), **Jackie Lomax** (bg/voc) and **Bugs Pemberton** (dr).

Back to the **Vegas Five**, who changed its name again - to the **Undertakers**. They then became a six-piece when sax-player, **Les Maguire**, was added. Also, due to illness, **Bob Evans** was replaced by **Bugs Pemberton** from **Dee & the Dynamites**.

Dave Cooper left the **Undertakers** to join **Faron's Flamingos** and, after that, he played with the **Renegades**, **Lee Curtis & the All Stars**, the **Pawns** and the **Fruit Eating Bears**. The new bass guitarist with the **Undertakers** was **Jackie Lomax** from **Dee & the Dynamites**, who apparently had split up at that time.

When **Dee & the Dynamites** split up, **Jimmy Sloan** disappeared from the scene while **Peter Cooke** and **Brian Dee** later teamed up again in **Earl Royce & the Olympics**. **Peter Cooke** had also played with the **Kansas City Five** and **Groups Inc.** and **Brian Dee** had spent some time with the **Dawnbreakers**, where he had met up with **Bob Evans** again.

Les Maguire left the **Undertakers** to become the pianist with **Gerry & the Pacemakers** and he was replaced by **Brian Jones** as the new sax player, who came from the Wallasey group, the **Rebels**.

Then **Jimmy McManus** left to join the **Renegades** who, at that time, were led by **Bob Evans** and where he met up again with former bass guitarist, **Dave Cooper**. **Bob Evans** later became a member of **Dixie & the Dare Devils** and the **Combo Six**. **Jimmy McManus** was not replaced in the **Undertakers**, who continued as a five-piece with:

Jackie Lomax	(voc/bg)
Geoff Nugent	(g/voc)
Chris Huston	(g/voc)
Brian Jones	(sax)
Bugs Pemberton	(dr)

The story that led to the name change from the **Vegas Five** to the **Undertakers** is also interesting: When the group was booked to play a gig at the 'Litherland Town Hall', there was a misprint in the newspaper and the **Vegas Five** were listed in the 'deaths' column instead of under 'concerts'. **Bob Wooler**, who was the resident disc-jockey at 'Litherland Town Hall', made the best out of that mistake and that evening played the "Death March" and introduced the band as the **Undertakers**, which was a tremendous success. The musicians liked it, adopted the name and so the legendary **Undertakers** were born.

In 1963, the group was signed to PYE and, in July of the same year, released the single, "Everybody Loves A Lover" (sung by **Geoff Nugent**), which was coupled with "Mashed Potatoes", sung by **Jackie Lomax**. This record did not make it, although "Mashed Potatoes" became a standard for lots of bands after that, most probably because of the **Undertakers** release, which was really great.

The follow-up, a good recording of the **Coasters** number, "What About Us", coupled with a great version of "Money" also failed to become a chart success for incomprehensible reasons.

The **Undertakers** had their first chart hit in 1964 with the fantastic, "Just A Little Bit", climbing to No. 38, although it was really good enough to have made it into the Top 10.

Unfortunately, this was also the last chart entry for the **Undertakers** who, in spite of the misfortune with their records, were one of the most important Liverpool groups and also influenced a lot of other European bands with their music - especially in Hamburg, where they often played at the 'Star-Club'.

In 1964, the **Undertakers** decided to change their image and so changed their outfits and also shortened their name to **The Takers.**

But this did not bring them any additional luck or success and the first record under their new name, the great rocking "If You Don't Come Back" was probably the least successful of their singles.

At the beginning of 1965, the group started to split when first **Chris Huston** and, a little later, **Geoff Nugent** left. But in the same year, **Jackie Lomax**, **Brian Jones** and **Bugs Pemberton** went to USA on a tour as a three-piece where they met up again with **Chris Huston**, who had emigrated there a little earlier.

In the United States, the attention of independent producer, **Bob Gallo,** was drawn to the group and he recorded the songs, "If I Fell In Love" and "Throw Your Love Away", with them as a single and probably more songs for a complete album but, in the end, none of them were released.

Historically, it is said that the group then changed their name twice, first to the **Lost Souls** and then to the **Mersey Lads**, but this is incorrect and the connection here is as follows:

In late 1965, because of an illness, **Brian Jones** had to return to Liverpool so the group broke up and **Chris Huston** quit show business, remained in the U.S.A. and later became a Sheriff.

However, **Bugs Pemberton** also remained in the U.S.A. and joined the **Mersey Lads**, which was a sort of **Beatles** band and, after that, he teamed up with **Jackie Lomax** in a Rhythm & Blues group called the **Lost Souls**. But this was only for a very short time and then they both, together with **Tom Gacetta** (bg) and **John Cannon** (lg) from the **Lost Souls**, formed the **Lomax Alliance** that was signed to CBS and did some recording sessions.

When the group returned to England, **John Cannon** remained in the U.S.A. so the **Lomax Alliance** in the UK and Europe continued as a trio, with **Jackie Lomax** on lead vocals and rhythm guitar.

As the **Lomax Alliance**, the group also played the 'Star-Club' in Hamburg again, but they were unable to achieve the same level of popularity as the original **Undertakers**. In 1967, this group recorded two good singles for CBS in England with "Try As You May" and "Genuine Imitation Life", of which only the first one was released as **The Lomax Alliance**, while the second one was only credited to **Jackie Lomax**, although it was recorded by the entire group. Neither record sold very well, and the **Lomax Alliance** returned to the U.S.A., where they were joined again by **John Cannon**.

A little later, **Jackie Lomax** parted from the group and went back to England, while the others continued on in the U.S.A. They released one more single with the songs, "Hey Taxi" and "Enter Into My World". Of those two songs, the first was from the initial recording session with CBS and, as **Jackie Lomax** was no longer with the group, the record was credited to **The One**.

After that release, the group broke up and **Bugs Pemberton** remained in the U.S.A., where he later was a member of **Aim Of Blue Thumb**.

Jackie Lomax started a solo career, was managed by **Brian Epstein** and recorded for the Apple label. He released three solo albums and four singles before he became a member of **Badger**. Then he joined the Birmingham group, **Balls,** and, after that, went solo again and emigrated to the USA.

But back to the **Undertakers,** as their story continued when the group was re-formed in Liverpool in 1966, under their old name, by **Geoff Nugent** and the returning **Brian Jones**, together with **Bob Frazer** (org), **Jimmy Jones** (bg) and **Bobby Williams** (dr), who all came from the just disbanded **Newtowns**. Before that, **Bobby Williams** had played with **Dino & the Wild Fires** who, in the interim, had evolved into the **Wackers**.

In 1966, this line-up recorded a great version of the **Sam & Dave** success **Hold On I'm Coming** which, unfortunately, was not released. They played together until 1968 when **Geoff Nugent** quit show business for years. Later, he returned to the cabaret circuit scene as a solo artist under the name of **Vern Gordon**. He was replaced in the new **Undertakers** by **Dennis Barton**, but the group did not survive for too long.

Brian Jones became a session musician and, amongst others, was featured on the B-side of the **Beatles** hit single, "Let It Be". In 1975, he appeared on the 'Sold Out' album by the **Scaffold** and, shortly after that, became a member of **Karl Terry & the Cruisers**. He then joined the **Glitter Band** but, in the Eighties, played with the newly formed **Faron's Flamingos** before returning to the **Glitter Band**. After that, he was a member of the great Liverpool Soul group, **Y-Kickamoocow**, which also included former **Undertakers** vocalist, **Dennis Barton** again.

In the early Eighties, **Geoff Nugent** formed a new band under the name, the **Undertakers**, but he was the only member who had previously played under that legendary name. In 1987, the 'new' **Undertakers** recorded a nice EP with the songs, "Just A Little Bit", "Will You Still Love Me Tomorrow", "Barefootin'" and "Ferry Across The Mersey" (SYNC 001), most probably a private record, produced to sell at gigs - it is already a collector's item.

Because of quarrels with the musicians, **Geoff Nugent** left the group in 1988 and formed another band which also included **Les Cave**, the former drummer with **Mister X & the Masks** and **Cy Tucker & the Friars** and also **Billy Good** (bg) who, in the Sixties, was a member of the **Shufflers Sound** and **Lee Curtis & the All Stars**.

This new band appeared under the name of **Geoff Nugent's Undertakers** for some time because the former band kept the name, the **Undertakers,** and was also still performing but more of a kind of dance band, while **Geoff Nugent's Undertakers** was a really good 'rough' band.

Ultimately, they reverted back to the original name of the **Undertakers**, but the line-up had also changed again. Besides **Geoff Nugent** and **Billy Good**, the group now included drummer, **Jimmy O'Brien**, who came from **New Image** and had also played with the **Soul Survivors**, the **Morockans** and the **Dark Ages**. **Barry 'Baz' Davis** was the replacement for lead guitarist, **Chris Evens**, who had to leave due to health reasons. In the Sixties, **Barry 'Baz' Davis** had played with the **Connoisseurs**, the **King Size Taylor** band and the German group, **Mike Warner & his New Stars**. After that, he had been a member of such well known groups as the **New Vaudeville Band** and **Jimmy James & the Vagabonds**.

On special occasions, this line-up of the **Undertakers** is also joined by original sax-player, **Brian Jones**, who nowadays sporadically plays with the **Kirkbys** and a Soul band called **Nighttrain**.

Single discography :

as **The Undertakers** :

Everybody Loves A Lover / Mashed Potatoes	**UK- PYE 7N 15543 / 1963**
What About Us / Money	**UK- PYE 7N 15562 / 1963**
Just A Little Bit / Stupidity	**UK- PYE 7N 15607 / 1964**

as **The Takers** :

If You Don't Come Back / Think	**UK- PYE 7N 15690 / 1964**

The Lomax Alliance :

Try As You May / See The People	**UK- CBS 2729 / 1967**

Jackie Lomax – solo :

Genuine Imitation Life / One Minute Woman	**UK- CBS 2554 / 1967**
Sour Milk Sea / The Eagle Laughs At You	**UK-Apple APPLE 3 / 1968**
New Day / Fall Inside Your Eyes	**UK-Apple APPLE 11/ 1969**
How The Web Was Woven / Thumbln' A Ride	**UK-Apple APPLE 23/ 1970**

(Please note that the single "**Genuine Imitation Life**" for CBS was recorded by the **Lomax Alliance** although it was only credited to **Jackie Lomax**)

LP **IS THIS WHAT YOU WANT**   UK-Apple ST 3354 / 1969

- Speak To Me / Is This What You Want / New Day / Sunset / Sour Milk Sea / Fall Inside Your Eyes /

Little Yellow Pills / Take My Word / The Eagle Laughs At You / Baby You're A Lover /

You've Got Me Thinking / I Just Don't Know

as **The One** (see story) :

Hey Taxi / Enter Into My World   US- CBS / 1967

Tracks on compilation albums :

as **The Undertakers** :

Mashed Potatoes   on **'Package Tour"**   US-Golden Guinea GGL 0268 / 1964

Unissued tracks :

It is known that the **Undertakers** recorded the songs, "**Peaches And Cream**", "**Tricky Dicky**", "**Nothing Can Stop Me**", "**Watch Your Step**", "**What's So Good About Goodbye**" and "**Hey, Hey, Hey, Hey**" - all great numbers that, unfortunately, remained unreleased at that time. The group under the name of **The Takers** recorded the songs, "**If I Fell In Love**" and "**Throw Your Love Away Girl**", for the independent US producer, **Bob Gallo**, which were never released. It is also rumoured that they recorded songs for a complete album in the United States, but this is not absolutely certain. Besides this, in 1966, the new **Undertakers** recorded **Hold On I'm Coming** which also remained unreleased.

THE VALKYRIES

This group had it's origin in the formation of a school band in Birkenhead in 1960. They did not have a name and consisted of **Allen Burton** (g), **John Martin** (g), **Adrian Campbell-Kelly** (bg) and **John Adams** (dr). A little later, the group was joined by another school-mate, **John 'Tony' Conway** on saxophone.

In the same area, there was also a vocal/guitar duo comprising of **Ian Hunter** and **Billy May** that had already been together for some years. It was in 1960 that **Billy May** split and formed a group called the **Beat Cats** and, after that, he became a member of the **Pathfinders**.

Ian Hunter then joined the above mentioned school band that still did not have a name.

This group was re-organised in 1962 when **John Martin** left to go to university and **Adrian Campbell-Kelly** concentrated on the group's management. **Allen Burton** then switched to bass-guitar and **Ian Hunter** played lead.

They decided on the name the **Valkyries**, taken from a US jet-bomber, not knowing at that time that 'Valkyries' were actually Norse goddesses that were empowered to decide who died on the battlefield!

However, the career of the group was interrupted when **Allen Burton** had to concentrate on his exams and was not able to play for quite some time.

So the rest of the group, with **Adrian Campbell-Kelly** on bass, joined up with **Robbie Dee** (real name **Robbie Hickson**) and **Peter Cooke** in a second-take of **Dee & the Dynamites**. But this was only for a short time and then **Ian Hunter** and **Tony Conway** went on to play with **Pharoh & the Exiles**, that had evolved from **Tony & the Quandros**.

Pharoh & the Exiles - with Ian Hunter & Tony Conway

1963 saw the **Valkyries** re-united in a line-up with:

Ian Hunter	(voc/lg)
Allan Burton	(voc/bg)
Tony Conway	(sax)
John Adams	(dr)

Adrian Campbell-Kelly had gone back to managing the **Valkyries** and he got them a booking to tour the American military bases in France, which required that the **Valkyries** turn professional. Specifically for that 1963 tour, the group was joined by Ian's old partner, **Billy May,** as an additional singer and guitarist. Also, for the summer of that same year, they had secured a month-long engagement at the 'Star-Club' in Hamburg,

But when they signed to the agency of **Jim Ireland**, who already had the **Swinging Blue Jeans** and the **Escorts** under his wing, the new manager for mysterious reasons cancelled all the already existing bookings of the **Valkyries**, including the 'Star-Club'.

The group then played regularly at all the normal Merseyside venues but they were not happy with the management and, in the end, signed with Londoner, **Eric Easton** who, at that time, was the manager of the **Rolling Stones**.

He got the **Valkyries** into the Decca studios where they recorded "What's Your Name", "Rock 'n' Roll Music", "Rip It Up" and "Talkin' 'Bout You" which, unfortunately, remained on acetates and did not result in a recording contract. Finally they were signed to Parlophone and, in 1964, their single, "Rip It Up", was released, coupled with the great and much more interesting group's original, "What's your name".

Although it really was a good Beat record, it wasn't too successful and so the first record by the **Valkyries** was also their last one. The group was featured on the German compilation, 'Great Beat From Great Britain', with both songs but, of course, this was not sufficient to achieve any sort of a breakthrough for them.

The **Valkyries** parted from **Eric Easton** and continued to play the clubs in the northwest, but then **Ian Hunter** became seriously ill and had to leave for extended hospital treatment.

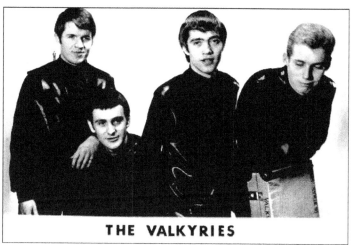

THE VALKYRIES

That was the reason for **John Adams** to also part from the group. He quit the music business at that time.

That left **Allen Burton** and **Tony Conway** who recruited the former **Pressmen** members, **Ritchie Prescott** (lg) and **Tommy Bennett** (dr), but this did not last too long and then the **Valkyries** broke up.

Tony Conway went to university and **Allen Burton** joined the **Nashpool** with whom he went to play the 'Star -Club'.

After **Allen Burton** returned from Germany, he teamed up again with the recovered **Ian Hunter** and, together with drummer, **Terry McCusker,** they toured France again as the **Valkyries**.

Terry McCusker formerly had played with **Pete Demos & the Demons**, the **Four Dymonds** and **Rip Van Winkle & the Rip-It-Ups**.

Back from France, they got **Pete MacKay** from the **Roadrunners** to join them on bass-guitar and recorded a Phillips-acetate with the **Ian Hunter** originals, "I Feel This Way" and "Keep A Hold On What You've Got".

Pete MacKay only stood in for that recording but continued to play with the **Roadrunners** that, a little later, were also joined by **Terry McCusker**.

The **Valkyries** were joined by **Gordon Templeton** as their new drummer, who formerly had played with **Terry Connor & the Teen-Aces**, the **Cimarrons** and **Karl Terry & the Cruisers**.

Besides this, sax-player, **Tony Conway,** then returned to the **Valkyries**.

In this line-up, with **Billy May** as an additional guitarist, the **Valkyries** recorded another acetate in the

Cam-studios in 1966 with the cover-versions of "Summertime" and "Day Tripper", as well as the originals, "Don't Take Your Heart From Me" and "Give Me A Helping Hand".

After that, and without **Billy May**, who had joined the **Pathfinders**, the **Valkyries** played the summer season at the Casino in St. Jean-de-Lux in France, where they met the Cuban impresario, **Ramiro Arango**, who, with his International connections, took over the management of the group.

Gordon Templeton then left, as did **Tony Conway** , both of them disappeared from the scene.

Tony Williams became the new drummer and the **Valkyries** were also joined by two sax players, **John Chisholm** from the **In Crowd** and **Allen 'Gaz' Gaskell**, who came from the **Times**, who were backing the vocal trio, the **Signs,** at that time. Before that, **Allen Gaskell** had played with the **Young Ones** from Wallasey, the **Tiyms**, the **K-Ds** and **Combo Six**.

In addition, **Iain Bradshaw,** who came from a group called **Speed**, was added as a keyboard player.

In April 1967, this line-up set out for Madrid, Spain but the destination was changed mid-journey to Rome, Italy. After they had been in Italy for three months and continuously experiencing problems with the tour-promoter, **Iain Bradshaw**, **John Chisholm** and **Allen Gaskell** left and joined another trio – the remaining members of **Vic Grace & the Secrets**, who were also in Italy for a long residency at that time.

The remaining **Valkyries**, namely **Ian Hunter**, **Allan Burton** and **Tony Williams** also remained in Italy and they were joined by Liverpudlian, **Dick Hanson** (tr), from the **Fix** and the two Londoners, **Rob Pratchett** and **Mike Lye**, both playing saxophone.

The brass section kept changing while the **Valkyries** continued to play in Italy and recorded the songs, "Watch Your Step", "Senza Luce" and "A Chi", the Italian version of "I'm Hurt", probably for Ariston in Rome which, for unknown reasons, were not released.

Towards the end of their stay in Italy, **Gordon Templeton** had taken over on drums again from **Tony Williams**. The **Valkyries** were also joined by the Liverpool sax-players, **Keith Wilson**, who formerly had played with the **Doug Barry Sound** and **Beckett's Kin**, and **Ken Newton**, a former member of the **Robbie Gray Soul Band**. On their return to Liverpool in late 1967, the two sax players, together with other members of the **Robbie Gray Soul Band,** formed the group, **Kasper's Engine**.

Next **Ramiro Arango** got the **Valkyries** a year's engagement in Tunisia, where they played one month at a vineyard and the rest in beach hotels. During this time, they had quite a few brass musicians coming and going again.

At the end of the stint in Tunisia, besides **Ian Hunter** and **Allen Burton,** the group now included **Ray Jewell** (dr), a certain **Peter** (sax/flute) and **Joe Bartlett** (tr/flugle).

Ian Hunter & the Valkyries at the Copacabana Tokyo

During their stay in Italy, the three wives of the 'core' **Valkyries** members, namely **Sheila Hunter**, **Barbara Burton** and **Gwynne Williams** had dances choreographed for them and had become a steady part of the show, calling themselves *The Go Go Girls di Liverpool*.

The band, now as a nine-piece, called **Ian Hunter & his Valkyries** accepted a six-month engagement at the 'Copacabana' in Tokyo, where they also backed many major stars.

After that, they went on to Singapore and they were the first Merseyside group to play in Taiwan.

From there, they played for an extended period at the 'Cesar Key Club' in Bangkok and then travelled to Teheran, where, among others, they played for Shah's sister and the prime-minister.

This monumental tour ended with three months at the famous 'Caves De Roy' in Beirut, Lebanon, where they also had a 13-week show on local television. Lebanon was the final chapter of the **Valkyries**' story, as the group disbanded totally when they returned to Liverpool.

Ian Hunter continued to work with **Ramiro Arango** and, with a different group, went back to Tunisia over the following years but then **Ramiro Arango** left for America to manage the 'Eden Roc' hotel in Miami. Following that, **Ian Hunter** played with **John O'Hara's Playboys** before he joined the **Carl Simmons** band. In the early Seventies, he once again went abroad with the group, **Casino**, when they toured Finland and Germany. Since then, he has played with various groups on Merseyside, including **Karl Terry & the Cruisers**.

Discography :

| **Rip It Up / What's Your Name** | UK- Parlophone R 5123 / 1964 |

Tracks on compilation albums :

| **Rip It Up** on **'Great Beat From Great Britain'** | G- Odeon O 83680 / 1965 |
| **What's Your Name** on **'Great Beat From Great Britain'** | G- Odeon O 83680 / 1965 |

Unreleased tracks :

In 1964, before the single was released, the **Valkyries** recorded the following songs for Decca, which were not released : "**What's Your Name**", "**Rip It Up**" (probably alternative versions), "**Talkin' 'Bout You**" and "**Rock 'n' Roll Music**".

In 1967, during their stay in Italy, they recorded "**Watch Your Step**", "**A Chi**" (the Italian version of "**I'm Hurt**") and "**Senza Luce**" - probably for Ariston, none of which were ever released.

In addition, the **Valkyries** cut the following acetates :

I Feel This Way / Keep A Hold On What You've Got	UK – Phillips acetate / 1965
Summertime / Day Tripper / Don't Take Your Heart From Me / Give Me A Helping Hand	
	UK – CAM acetate EP / 1966

VIC & THE SPIDERMEN

This real Merseybeat group was formed as **The Spidermen** in Liverpool in early 1962. However, when their singer, **Norman Dunn,** left in the same year, he was replaced by **Vic Wright**, who was formerly known as **Pete Picasso** and had led the group **Pete Picasso & the Rock Sculptors.**

Because of that change, the group changed its name to **Vic & the Spidermen** and soon became very popular on the Liverpool scene.

In December 1963, they were voted No. 11 in the 'popularity poll' by the readers of the 'Mersey Beat' newspaper. This means that not only had they established themselves amongst the leading Liverpool groups, but they were also more popular than many of them.

Vic & the Spidermen, in their original line-up, consisted of:

Vic Wright	**(voc)**
Pete Molly	**(g/voc)**
Phil Roberts	**(bg/voc)**
Ray Binnion	**(dr)**

The group was also joined by guitarist, **Glynn Jones,** as a fifth member, in 1962.

In June of that same year, **Geoff Lloyd** from **Tommy & the Satellites** replaced **Ray Binnion,** who had to go to London on business matters for a month. But he returned to **Vic & the Spidermen** and **Geoff Lloyd** joined **Ken Dallas & the Silhouettes** who, a little later, became **Mark Peters & the Silhouettes.** After that, he played with **J.J. & the Hi-Lites** and the **Mersey Monsters,** who evolved from that group.

In 1963, **Glynn Jones** left and most probably formed his own group whose name, unfortunately, is not known. However, it should be clearly pointed out that he was <u>not</u> the recording vocalist, **Glyn Johns.**

He was not replaced in **Vic & the Spidermen,** who, also in 1963, went into the studio to record the originals, "Cruel To You", "Helpless One", "Teenage Love" and "Don't Set Me Free".

SPIDERMEN
LIVER
ENTERTAINMENTS
2 RICHMOND WAY
HESWALL

HESWALL 4638
BIR 7442 (day)

SPIDERMEN

But these were only test recordings, not followed by a recording contract or a record release.

Vic Wright left the **Spidermen** in 1964 to take the place of **Earl Preston** as lead vocalist with the **T.T.s**. Obviously, from then on, the group appeared as **Vic & the T.T.s**.

For unknown reasons, he did not stay for too long with them, he then teamed up with musicians from Widnes under the quite unusual name, **Vic Takes Four**.

The group was quite successful on the scene for a short time but then disappeared. In 1965, according to an article in the 'Mersey Beat' newspaper, **Vic Wright** was the singer for a group called **The Script**. He later emigrated to Australia where he is still living today.

But back to the **Spidermen**, who initially continued on as a trio, and when **Ray Binnion** left and quit show business in August 1965, he was replaced by none other than **Johnny Hutchinson**, who came from the recently disbanded, **Big Three**. But, he only stayed for one month and then he re-formed the **Big Three** with other musicians. However, the re-formation only lasted for a short time and then **Johnny Hutchinson** joined **Paul Craig & the Theme**, before he quit show business forever.

This fact led to the **Spidermen** splitting up in September 1965, and all the members disappeared from the scene and most probably concentrated on their normal day jobs that they had kept all the time, never becoming professional musicians.

Discography :

A commercial record was never released by the group but, in July 1963, **Vic & the Spidermen** recorded the originals, **"Cruel To You"**, **"Helpless One"**, **"Teenage Love"** and **"Don't Set Me Free"**, as test recordings that were probably done on an acetate.

THE VICTIMS

This trio was formed in the Wavertree area of Liverpool in late 1962, inspired by the American Rock 'n' Roll sound.

They soon became quite popular and started to play the usual Merseyside gigs in a line-up with:

Edward Gale	**(voc/bg)**
Peter Francis Barton	**(g/voc)**
Paul Hitchmough	**(dr)**

Eddie Gale and **Paul Hitchmough** were both former members of the **Hangmen** and, before that, **Eddie Gale** had played with the **Saints** from Liverpool. **Pete Barton** apparently was a newcomer on the group scene.

The **Victims**, as they were named right from the beginning, had a very tight sound in spite of the fact that they were only a three-piece group. However, they never made the headlines, did not have any outstanding success and most probably did not even play outside Merseyside.

Therefore, it is quite surprising that, in 1963, they went to the studio of **P. F. Phillips** in Kensington and cut an acetate with the **Carl Perkins** classic, "Blue Suede Shoes", sung by **Eddie Gale** and the nice Merseybeat ballad, "I'd Never Find Another You", an original by the group, sung by **Pete Barton**. Unfortunately, this interesting acetate did not help the group to obtain a recording contract. So the **Victims** disbanded as early as the middle of 1964.

Paul Hitchmough became a member of the **Corals** and then joined a group called **Sounds Plus One** and, with them, he recorded a nice Unicord acetate before he went on to join the **Kruzads**.

After that, he was a member of the **Clayton Squares**, who also toured Germany under the name of the **T-Squares**. He then had a spell with the Deram recording group, **Curiosity Shoppe**, before he disappeared for years from the scene. He returned as a member of **Beryl Marsden's** backing group in the Nineties. He then played with **Karl Terry & the Cruisers** and, after that, withdrew from the scene once again.

Unfortunately, what happened to **Eddie Gale** is not known but, after the **Victims** had split up, **Pete Barton** formed a new group under the name of the **Locations** who, in addition to him, included **'Dosi' Jones** (voc), **Billy Fidler** (bg) and **Tommy Longman** (dr). They were also joined by **Dave Keegan** as an additional guitarist, who apparently came from the final line-up of the recently disbanded **Talismen**, formerly known as **Vince Earl & the Talismen**.

At his instigation, the **Locations** adopted the name of the **Talismen** and, as such, existed very well on the scene and even toured Germany and France. When they split up, all the musicians disappeared from the scene, though it is known that **Pete Barton** carried on playing until he seriously injured his left hand in an accident in 1989.

Discography :

Blue Suede Shoes / I'd Never Find Another You   **UK- Kensington acetate / 1963**

THE WACKERS

This group originated from the Liverpool band, **Dino & the Wild Fires**, formed in 1961 in the southwest of the Beat metropolis. After playing the clubs and pubs for a few years, the group decided that it was time to turn professional. The one exception was their original drummer, **Bobby Williams**, who left because he wanted to keep his job, as the future of a professional musician was too uncertain for him. He joined the **Newtowns** and, in 1966, he was a member of the newly formed **Undertakers**, where he played until 1968 and then returned to the **Newtowns**. Today he is still active as a drummer on the scene.

Dino Grant, (whose real name is **Gwylim Philips**), **Bernard Lee** and **Julian Johnson** turned professional and went down to London where they formed **The Wackers,** together with two London musicians, they then appeared in the following line-up:

Terry Anton	**(voc)**
Dino Grant	**(voc/g)**
Bernard Lee	**(g)**
Julian Johnson	**(bg)**
John Foster	**(dr)**

John Foster shouldn't be confused with the drummer of the same name who played in Liverpool with the **Dions** and the **Escorts** and used the stage name **John Sticks**.

The **Wackers** did not actively take part in the Liverpool scene and only had a few gigs in their hometown, but they established themselves as a typical Merseybeat group on the London scene, where they became quite successful.

In early 1964, the group was signed to Oriole and, a little later, recorded their first single, "I Wonder Why", which was not the **Dion & the Belmonts** number, but a composition by **Bernard Lee** and a really nice Beat record which, unfortunately, did not achieve the success it deserved.

In the same year, the **Wackers** were featured in the musical film, 'Swinging U.K.', which was followed by a recording contract with PYE.

For their first single, they recorded "Love Or Money", a song that was described as Merseybeat in the above film. It really had the typical marks of Merseybeat but, unfortunately, it failed to enter the charts, although, for sure, it sold quite well. This record and their collaboration in 'Swinging U.K.', of course, helped the group's popularity throughout the UK.

In 1965, another single was released on the Piccadilly label and "The Girl Who Wanted Fame" was undoubtedly the best record by the **Wackers**. A very nice Folk orientated Beat song with good arrangement and excellent vocals but, again, it was not successful in the charts.

After that release, little was heard of the group and they probably disbanded totally in 1965.

Terry Anton started a solo career after the split and, in the same year, released the single, "Leave A Little Love", on the PYE label but then disappeared from the scene just like **Dino Grant**, **Bernard Lee**, **Julian Johnson** and **John Foster** before him. They probably all quit the music business.

In the end, it can be said that the **Wackers** were a really good group and perhaps they would have had more success on the scene if they had stayed in Liverpool because, at that time, the Mersey scene was still getting more attention than the London scene. This, of course, is only speculation, but who knows ?

Single discography :

I Wonder Why / Why Can It Happen To Me	UK- Oriole CB 1902 / 1964
Love Or Money / Hooka Tooka	UK- Piccadilly 7N 35195 / 1964
The Girl Who Wanted Fame / You're Forgetting Me	UK- Piccadilly 7N 35210 / 1965

Terry Anton – solo :

Leave A Little Love / Don't Say Goodbye	UK- PYE 7N 15871 / 1965

THE WASHINGTON D.C.s

Writing about this group in this book may mean that a non Liverpool group is being featured but, the quality of the band, their somewhat fantastic records and their interesting story justify that risk. It was really hard to get information about the **Washington D.C.s** who, at least, on their German tours claimed to be from Liverpool and most probably some of their members were from Merseyside.

Supporting this assumption is the fact that the group played the 'Cavern' at an evening session together with three other Liverpool outfits **Group One**, the **Beatcombers** and the **Easybeats** on 5th October 1963. Of course, this fact alone does not prove anything but, according to **Bob Wooler**, non Liverpool groups mostly played an evening session and the next day, a lunchtime session, but the **Washington D.C.s** did not play the next day's lunchtime session! However, it seems that the band left the Liverpool area quite soon to try their luck elsewhere, most probably down in London and maybe that fact caused some personnel changes in the line-up.

Consequently, in 1964, the **Washington D.C.s** consisted of the following musicians:

Barry Fitzgerald	**(voc)**
Roger Saunders	**(g/voc)**
Gary Lee Illingworth	**(org/voc)**
Bernie Trott	**(bg)**
Glen Duke	**(dr)**

Around this time, the group was signed to the Ember label and, for their debut, almost a complete album was released. On this LP, the **Washington D.C.s** were featured with eight songs, while the other group on that long player, the **Dave Clark Five**, contributed just two songs.

In spite of this, only a photo of the **Dave Clark Five** was featured on the front cover and their name was written in large print, while the **Washington D.C.s** received almost no mention by comparison - clearly a case of sales politics! The back cover of the album did not provide any information about the artists.

With 'Merseybeat-ish' songs such as "Where Did You Go", "Little One", "Is It Me", "Have You Seen My Baby" and a great version of the **Coasters** classic, "Yakety Yak", the **Washington D.C.s** created a great impression, while their other cover versions of "Shimmy Shimmy", "Sweet Little Rock 'n' Roller" and "Carol" were also not too bad. This album did not become a big seller and accordingly it is a desired collectors' item today. This, of course, did not help the **Washington D.C.s** popularity at that time. Still in 1964, with a great version of "Kisses Sweeter Than Wine", the group's first single was released on Ember in England and also on the obscure Flip label in the United States. In spite of the fact that this release had everything that a good Beat record needed at that time, it did not sell too well. In France, a nice EP with "Kisses Sweeter Than Wine" plus the three album tracks, "Where Did You Go", "Shimmy Shimmy" and "Yakety Yak", was also released.

Their next single was coupled out from the above mentioned album and featured the songs, "Have You Seen My Baby" and "Is It Me". This record was again released on Flip in the U.S.A. and, of course, on Ember in England but, once again, it did not contribute to a breakthrough for the group.

After that, the **Washington D.C.s** regularly appeared in Germany where they became quite popular and also backed singer, **Paul Jones,** of **Manfred Mann** fame. With him, they were also featured on the very successful German TV series, "Beat-Club".

In 1966, an excellent single was released with "32nd Floor" on CBS in England, France, Germany and Denmark, as well as on 'Date' in the U.S.A. This was a potential hit-record with a really great instrumental arrangement and it also showed the impressive vocal ability of the group which, judging by the picture on the German and Danish sleeve at that time, was still a five-piece.

"32nd Floor", as well as the flip-side, "A Whole Lot More", were written by Whittingham/Bradley and obviously were original recordings. It is absolutely incomprehensible that this record did not make the charts as it was one of the best singles of that particular year.

In 1967, the follow-up, "Seek And Find", was again a great single, written and produced by none other than **Paul Samwell-Smith** and co-written by **Barry Mason**. Again, it failed to achieve a breakthrough for the group although it was released in England and Germany and possibly elsewhere.

After that, things were quiet for the **Washington D.C.s** for a time and it appears that they had left CBS by then. The reason for this might have been the personnel changes that took place at that time.

Bernie Trott and **Glen Duke** left the group and disappeared from the scene. They were replaced by **Walt Monaghan** (bg) and **Brian Hillman** (dr.).

Furthermore, **Gary Lee Illingworth** also left the group, they then continued as a four-piece.

In 1969, the **Washington D.C.s** were back with a new single, released on Hit-Ton in Germany and on the obscure Domain label in England. "Anytime", as well as the flip-side, "I've Done It All Wrong", was written by Fitzgerald, Hillman, Monaghan and Saunders but, in all honesty, was weak compared to the previous records, especially "32nd Floor". This time it was no surprise that it was not successful for the **Washington D.C.s**, who then disappeared from the scene and probably broke up in 1969.

Roger Saunders joined the group **Freedom** and, after that, became a member of **Medicine Head**, who had a big international hit with "One And One Is One". In the Seventies, **Roger Saunders** appeared again in **Gary Glitter's** band.

Nothing was heard of the other former members of the **Washington D.C.s** after that.

<u>Discography</u>

Kisses Sweeter Than Wine / Where Did You Go	UK- Ember EMB S 190 / 1964
Have You Seen My Baby / Is It Me?	UK- Ember EMB S ??? / 1964
32nd Floor / A Whole Lot More	UK- CBS 202226 / 1966
Seek And Find / I Love Gerald Chevin The Great	UK- CBS 202464 / 1967
Anytime / I've Done It All Wrong	UK- Domain DOM 9 / 1969

<u>EPs :</u>

TEEN SCENE '64   UK-Ember EMB EP 4540 / 1964

- **The Washington D.C.s : Where Did You Go**- compilation EP plus 2 songs by **Dave Clark Five**

   and one by **Ray Singer**

KISSES SWEETER THAN WINE   FR- Pathé EGF 761 /1964

- **Kisses Sweeter Than Wine / Where Did You Go / Shimmy Shimmy / Yakety Yak**

LP

DAVE CLARK FIVE and the **WASHINGTON D.C.s**   UK- Ember FA 2003 / 1964

<u>Songs by the **Washington D.C.'s** :</u>

- **Where Did You Go / Shimmy Shimmy / Sweet Little Rock 'n' Roller / Yakety Yak /**

Little One / Is It Me / Where Have You Been / Carole

<u>Songs by the **Dave Clark Five** :</u> - **Chaquita / In Your Heart**

<u>Tracks on compilation-albums :</u>

Yakety Yak	on '**Live At The Pink Flamingo**'	FR- Albatros 2001 / 1965
Where Did You Go	on '**Live At The Pink Flamingo**'	FR- Albatros 2001 / 1965
Kisses Sweeter Than Wine	on '**Live At The Pink Flamingo**'	FR- Albatros 2001 / 1965

(These were obviously real live-recordings from the 'Pink Flamingo' in London. Other artists featured on this interesting album were **Paul's Troubles**, the **Clockwork Oranges**, **Russ Hamilton**, **Ray Singer** and **Bobby Johnson & the Atoms**.)

<u>Unreleased tracks :</u>

In 1965, the **Washington D.Cs** recorded the song, "**Return To Me**", and an alternate version of "**Have You Seen My Baby**" for Ember. Unfortunately, they were not released at that time.

To prevent any confusion, it should be pointed out that there was absolutely no connection between the **Washington D.Cs** of this story and **Tony Washington & his D.Cs**, an American group, who in 1964/1965, cut four singles for the British 'Sue', 'Fontana' and 'Black Swan' labels.

SONNY WEBB & THE CASCADES

The origin of this group, belonging to the 'pre-Beatles era', leads back to the beginning of 1960, when **Kenny Johnson** and **Joe Butler** formed the band, **Kenny Johnson & the Country Four,** in Liverpool. This Country band consisted of **Kenny Johnson** (voc/g), **Joe Butler** (g/voc), **Tony Evans** (p), **Dave Stevens** (bg), who came from the **Vigilantes**, and **Freddie Cain** (dr).

When **Kenny Johnson** had to leave Liverpool for professional reasons, he was replaced by **Brian Newman**, a former member of **Ron McKay's Skiffle-Group**. Because of that, the band changed its name to **The Country Four & Brian Newman**.

When **Joe Butler** also left the group, there were two more name changes - first to **The Topics**, and later to **The Kentuckians**. Under the latter name, the group released some singles, an EP and an album in the late Sixties but, in the meantime, the line-up had changed again - of course.

In 1962, **Kenny Johnson** returned to Liverpool and joined **Mike Savage & the Wild Cats**, taking the place of **Mike Savage**, who had left the group together with rhythm guitarist, **Jerry Gilbertson**.

Jerry Gilbertson, better known as **Tony Nelson,** later became a member of the **Beathovens**, then played with the **Tony Prince Combo** that evolved into the **Mersey Five**.

The group continued with **Kenny Johnson** as **The Wild Cats** and, when the bass guitarist, **Bill Duncan,** also left, he was replaced by **Kenny Johnson's** former partner, **Joe Butler**. Very soon the group's name was changed from the **Wild Cats** to **Sonny Webb & the Cascades**.

Sonny Webb, of course, was none other than **Kenny Johnson**, who had chosen this name because he was a fan of the Country singers, **Sonny James** and **Webb Pierce**.

Guitarist, **John State**, who was a former member of the **Connoughts**, and drummer, **Roger Wilcox**, who had formerly played with the **Gerry Owen Four**, both left the group. **Roger Wilcox** became a member of the **Topics** and then played with the **Blue Mountain Showband**, while **John State** joined **Phil Brady & the Ranchers**.

The new members of **Sonny Webb & the Cascades** were **Roy Wood** (g), who had formerly played with the **Nomads** and **Johnny Templer & the Hi-Cats** and **Dave Preston** (dr) from **Vince & the Volcanoes**. However, they both left after a short time, **Dave Preston** joined the **Harlems** and later played with groups such as the **Secrets**, the **Kinsleys** and the **Creation**. **Roy Wood** apparently quit the music-scene and, a few months later, committed suicide - a really sad story.

Sonny Webb and **Joe Butler** very soon found new members for their group and then appeared with the following line-up:

Sonny Webb	(voc/rg)
Frankie Wan	(lg)
Joe Butler	(bg/voc)
Brian Redman	(dr)

The new drummer, **Brian Redman** was a former member of the **Four Jays**, the **Four Mosts** and **King Size Taylor & the Dominoes**. It was probably him who brought the Beat 'drive' into the group's music, which had a strong Rockabilly influence.

Frankie Wan had formerly played with the **Zephyrs**, **Gene Day & the Django Beats** and the **Comets**.

In this line-up, **Sonny Webb & the Cascades** were featured on the Oriole albums, 'This Is Merseybeat' Vol. 1 and Vol. 2, with "You've Got Everything", "Border Of The Blues", "Excuse Me" and "Who Shot Sam".

Their music was a very attractive mixture of Beat and Nashville sound which was accepted by both scenes.

The great "You've Got Everything" and "Border Of The Blues" were also released on single - unfortunately, without any chart success. In spite of this, **Sonny Webb & the Cascades** were very successful throughout the north of England.

In 1964, **Brian Hilton** (g/harp/perc) joined the group as an additional member, having formerly played with **Vince Earl & the Zeros** and with **Group One**.

Sonny Webb & the Cascades then changed their name to the **Hillsiders** and it is a very interesting fact that this line-up released an album in Germany with 'Western Songs' but still under the old and better sounding name of **Sonny Webb & the Cascades**.

The **Hillsiders** developed into a real Country & Western group and became one of the most popular, if not the leading band of this sound in England, for many, many years. They were also the first English Country band ever to appear at the 'Grand Ole Opry' in Nashville, a success in its own right.

For Beat fans, the first two singles released as the **Hillsiders** are also very interesting. They were the **Everly Brothers** song, "I Wonder If I Care As Much", and the really great "Please Be My Love", both released on Decca in 1964 and 1965, respectively.

The **Hillsiders** existed in this line-up until the late Sixties and, during that time, cut two albums with the titles, 'The Hillsiders Play Their Country Hits' (Decca-Rex) and 'Leaving Of Liverpool' (RCA), as well as some more singles. They were also featured on the legendary 'Liverpool Goes Country' sampler.

Frankie Wan left the group and later was a member of the **Everglades**. His replacement, in 1969, was **Ron Bennett**, who played the pedal steel guitar. This line-up cut the albums, 'The Hillsiders' (1970) and 'Our Country' (UK-Polydor 2460-203/1973), of which the latter is very nice and, with one exception, only included compositions of **Kenny Johnson** and **Joe Butler**.

In the interim, in 1971, the **Hillsiders** had recorded the album, 'Heritage' (RCA), together with US Country star **George Hamilton IV** and also backed this singer on his British and European tour where, among other places, they appeared at the 'Royal Albert Hall' and 'Wembley Stadium' in London. Their follow up album, 'To Please You' (Stile-Records2001/1975), was a little boring as it was missing the necessary outstanding songs.

In 1975, **Kenny Johnson** left to form his own group under the name of **Kenny Johnson & Northwind**, but more about this later in the story.

He was replaced in the **Hillsiders** by **Kevin McGarry** and, with this line-up, the album, 'A Day In The Country' (LP-Records SRTX/LP004 / 1979), was released. After that, **Ronnie Bennett** left and was replaced by **Dave Rowlands**. Two further albums were released with 'Hillsiders' (LP-Records LP 005/1980) and 'Only One You' (Suitbag-Records HS 36001/1984).

The **Hillsiders** remained one of the most popular and successful Country bands in England, alongside **Kenny Johnson & Northwind**, **Phil Brady & the Ranchers** from Liverpool and the **Raymond Froggatt Band** from Birmingham, until they split in 1994 when **Joe Butler** left and quit show business.

Kenny Johnson & Northwind first consisted of **Kenny Johnson** (voc/g), **John Ferrington** (bg/voc), **Bobby Peters** (dr) and **John Hodgson** (lg) who, in the Sixties, was a member of the **Heartbeats**, that evolved into the **Excerts**, **Georgie's Germs** and the **George King Group**. He also had a short stint with the **Almost Blues**. In 1976, the group cut an excellent album with 'Lakeside Highway' (North West Gramophone76103). Their follow-up albums, 'Let Me Love You Once' (OBM-Records OBM 1001/1980) and 'A Tree In The Meadow' (OBM-Records OBM 1002/1981), were only released under the name of **Kenny Johnson**, although they were obviously recorded by the whole group. Unfortunately, it is not known which line-up accompanied him at that time.

In 1990, the group consisted of **Kenny Johnson** (voc/g), **Bobby Arnold** (lg) who, in the Sixties, was a member of the **Kentuckians**. **Pete Newton** (bg), a former member of the Sixties bands, **T.L.'s Bluesicians**, the **Terry Hines Sextet**, **Eddie Cave & the Fyx** and **Karl Terry & the Cruisers**, as well as **Kenny Guy** (dr), who had previously played with the **Detours** and **Karl Terry & the Cruisers**. This fantastic and musically brilliant line-up from time to time also appeared again as **Sonny Webb & the Cascades** and were going strong on the scene until the great guitarist, **Bobby Arnold,** sadly died a few years ago which led to a split-up.

Kenny Johnson became a DJ at Radio Merseyside and continued to perform as a solo singer.

Single discography

as **Sonny Webb & the Cascades** :

You've Got Everything / Border Of The Blues	UK- Oriole 45-CB 1873 / 1963

as **The Hillsiders** :

I Wonder If I Care As Much / Cotton Fields	UK- Decca F.12026 / 1964
Please Be My Love / The Children's Song	UK- Decca F.12161 / 1965
Almost Persuaded / Wastin' My Time	UK- Strike JH 322 / 1966
Kentucky Woman / Days	UK- RCA RCA 1804 / 1969

as **Sonny Webb & the Cascades** :

WESTERN SONGS / HILLBILLY JAMBOREE   G- Dt.Vogue Pop ZS 10124 P / 1964

- I'll Take A Chance On Loving You / Is It Wrong / Love's Gonna Live Here / I'm Tired / I'll Never Have To Be Alone / I've Got My Fingers Crossed / The Picture At St. Helene / High As The Mountain / Riders In The Sky / 500 Miles / Raining On The Mountain / There's More Pretty Girls Than One / I Ain't Never / Faded Bible / One Is A Lonely Number / I've Got Some

as **The Hillsiders** :

THE HILLSIDERS PLAY THEIR COUNTRY HITS   UK- Rex (Decca) LPR 1003 / 1965

- Act Naturally / You're The Reason / Release Me / Cotton Fields / Every Minute, Every Hour, Every Day / Just One Time / Please Be My Love / Hello Trouble / Abilene / Diggy Liggy Lo / I Wonder If I Care As Much / What Am I Gonna Do / Hillsliding / The Window Up Above

THE LEAVING OF LIVERPOOL   UK- RCA-Victor SF 8002 / 1968

- The Leaving Of Liverpool / One Time And One Time Only / I Will Miss You When You Go / One Mile More / Someday, Someone, Somewhere / Don't Waste Your Time / (I'm A) Travelling Man / Doesn't Anybody Know My Name / Coming Home / If You Really Want Me To, I'll Go / The Road / Old Memories Never Die

THE HILLSIDERS   UK- Lucky LUS 3002 / 1970

- Dear Heart / Tiger Woman / It Takes A Lot Of Money / You Just Can't Quit / Black Cloud / He's A Jolly Good Fellow / Sincere Best Wishes / Take Me / Big Job / We Don't Know / I Don't Love You Anymore / Isn't It About Time

Tracks on compilation albums :

as **Sonny Webb & the Cascades** :

You've Got Everything	on 'This Is Merseybeat' Vol.1	UK- Oriole PS 40047 / 1963
Border Of The Blues	on 'This Is Merseybeat' Vol.2	UK- Oriole PS 40048 / 1963
Who Shot Sam	on 'This Is Merseybeat' Vol.2	UK- Oriole PS 40048 / 1963
Excuse Me	on 'This Is Merseybeat' Vol.2	UK- Oriole PS 40048 / 1963

as **The Hillsiders** :

Hello Trouble	on 'Liverpool Goes Country'	UK- Rex LPR 1002 / 1965
Above And Beyond	on 'Liverpool Goes Country'	UK- Rex LPR 1002 / 1965

Release Me	on 'Liverpool Goes Country'	UK- Rex LPR 1002 / 1965
Please Be My Love	on 'Liverpool Goes Country'	UK- Rex LPR 1002 / 1965
You're The Reason	on 'Liverpool Goes Country'	UK- Rex LPR 1002 / 1965
Diggy Liggy Lo	on 'Liverpool Goes Country'	UK- Rex LPR 1002 / 1965
Abilene	on 'Liverpool Goes Country'	UK- Rex LPR 1002 / 1965

The **Hillsiders** as backing group for **Tom O'Connor** :

For The Life Of Me	on 'Liverpool Goes Country'	UK- Rex LPR 1002 / 1965
Pretty Pictures	on 'Liverpool Goes Country'	UK- Rex LPR 1002 / 1965

DERRY WILKIE & THE OTHERS

This group was formed in Liverpool in early 1964 (as far as it is known) by **Derry Wilkie**, **Phil Kenzie** and drummer, **Tommy Bennett**, all former members of the **Pressmen**.

In the interim, **Tommy Bennett** also had a short spell with **Johnny Autumn & the Fall-Guys**. He did not stay for too long and became a member of the **Pathfinders**, before he formed the **New Pressmen**.

Derry Wilkie had started his career as a singer with **Derry & the Seniors**, the first Liverpool group to play in Hamburg and who then evolved into **Howie Casey & the Seniors**, featuring **Derry Wilkie** and **Freddie Starr** as lead vocalists.

After that, **Derry Wilkie,** for a short time, was backed by **Geoff Stacey & the Wanderers** and then teamed up with the **Pressmen** as **Derry Wilkie & the Pressmen**, but that is another story.

Derry Wilkie & the Others initially consisted of the following musicians:

Derry Wilkie	(voc)
Ernie Hayes	(lg)
Bob Montgomery	(bg)
Phil Kenzie	(sax)
Mike Holmes	(dr)

Ernie Hayes came from Widnes, where he had previously played with **Geoff Stacey & the Wanderers**.

Bob Montgomery soon left the group to join the **Tony Prince Combo**. After that, he played with the **Mersey Five**.

Derek Bond took his place in **Derry Wilkie & the Others**, he was a former member of **Johnny Rocco & the Jets**, **Steve Day & the Drifters** and the **Rainchecks**, who were one group under different names with different lead singers and slightly different line-ups. Besides this, **Derek Bond** also had a short stint with the **Pressmen**.

In this line-up, **Derry Wilkie & the Others** became really popular in Liverpool and also toured Germany quite successfully, the popularity of the coloured singer from his previous German trips with **Derry & the Seniors** certainly being very helpful.

After their return to England, **Mike Jeffries** from Newcastle took over their management. He was also the manager of the **Animals**.

A little later, **Derry Wilkie & the Others** recorded the song, "Sweet Tasting Wine", for a single on Fontana. This was apparently coupled with "Can You Think Of Another", a composition by **Ernie Hayes** and **Phil Kenzie** which was also recorded, but for mysterious reasons neither of them were ever released. As far as it is known, this was not followed by any further recordings, although there was occasionally mention of recording sessions by the group in the 'Mersey Beat' newspaper.

In the meantime, the group had moved down to London and, after they returned from another German tour, **Mike Holmes** did not want to stay in London, so he went back to Liverpool.

Derry Wilkie & The Others

He was replaced by the Scottish drummer, **Billy Adamson**, who had gone to London as a member of **Lulu's** backing-group. After that, he had played with **Emile Ford** before he settled down with the London-based group called the **Blues Council**.

In addition, the group was joined by two sax-players, **Noel McManus** and **Tony Tootell**, who came from the just disbanded **Savages** of **Screaming Lord Sutch**.

With this line-up, **Derry Wilkie & the Others** became the backing-group for **Screaming Lord Sutch** for his European tour. This tour included Sweden, which is where they recorded the single, "One Eyed Purple People Eater", for the Hep House label in 1966 - of course as **Screaming Lord Sutch & the Savages**.

Interesting, but not proven, is the rumour that **Nicky Hopkins** played the piano for this recording .

At that time, **Derry Wilkie** was still with the group and, when he was not singing as a supporting act, he mimed the victim in the show of **Screaming Lord Sutch**.

After their return to London, the group parted from **Screaming Lord Sutch** and **Noel McManus** also left.

Still in 1966, the group changed their name to **This 'N' That** and recorded the single, "Someday", for Mercury.

After that recording, **Billy Adamson** likely left the group and became a member of the backing group of **P.P. Arnold**. Later, he joined the **Searchers**, where he played for a long time but then disappeared from the scene. Unfortunately, it is not known who his successor was in **This 'N' That** who then teamed up with the US singers, **Cleo Sylvester** and **Ronald Bertram Greaves**, who had adopted the stage-name of **Sony Childe**. The group name was shortened to **TNT** and, still in 1966, the single, "Heartbreak", was released on Polydor as **Sony Childe & TNT**.

It is not known if the group was also featured on the single, "Two Lovers", that had previously been recorded and was only credited to **Sony Childe**. The same is valid for the Polydor album, "To Be Continued", by **Sony Childe** that was also released in 1966.

In the meantime, **Derry Wilkie** had left the group as he was not given equal status with **Sony Childe**. He initially went solo but then he joined the **Mack Sound** from London before he returned to Liverpool. He later went to live (and sing) in Italy for a long time.

This 'N' That then parted from **Sony Childe** (aka **Ronald Bertram Greaves**) who continued solo as **R.B. Greaves** and, in 1969, had a worldwide hit with his own great composition, "Take A Letter Maria".

In 1967, **This 'N' That** were signed to the Strike label and released one more single with "Get Down With It". The vocals on this record were most probably done by **Cleo Sylvester**.

After that, nothing further was heard of the group and it is only known that **Phil Kenzie** became a member of **Tuesday's Children** and later was a very successful session musician and, as such, appeared with many big names in showbiz.

Derry Wilkie returned from Italy to Liverpool and, in 1980, he appeared again on the Hamburg-scene, when the 'Star-Club' was re-opened. On a corresponding live-sampler, he was featured with the songs, "Hallelujah, I Love Her So" and "I Am Going Home".

In the Nineties, he went down to London again, where he continued as a singer, working with various groups and often appearing under the name of **Derry Wilkie & the Pressmen**.

These groups, at certain times, also included **Archie Leggett** of the **Kevin Ayers Band** on bass-guitar who, in the Sixties, was a member of the **Bobby Patrick Big Six** and the **Krew. Tony Ashton** (key), of **Ashton, Gardner & Dyke** fame who, in the Sixties, among others, had played with the **Remo Four**, the **Mastersounds** and **Mike Hurst & the Method**. Other known members were **Ron Magness** on keyboards and the guitarist **Michael Wynne**, also first-class musicians.

Derry Wilkie sadly died on 22nd December 2001.

Discography :

In May 1965, **Derry Wilkie & the Others** recorded the songs, "Sweet Tasting Wine" and "Can You Think Of Another", for Fontana, but the planned single was never released.

It is not certain if there were further recordings made around that time which, in the end, were also not issued. But the fact is, there was never an official record released by **Derry Wilkie & the Others**.

as **This 'N' That** :

Someday / Loving You	UK – Mercury MF 938 / 1966
Get Down With It / I Care About You	UK – Strike JH 310 / 1967

backing **Screaming Lord Sutch** as the **Savages** :

One Eyed Purple People Eater / You Don't Care	SW – Hep House HS 04 / 1966

as **Sony Childe & TNT** :

Heartbreak / I Still Love You	UK – Polydor 56141 / 1966

(please note, that it is also probable that **This 'N' That** as TNT also backed **Sony Childe** on his other Polydor single, "**Two Lovers/Ain't That Good News**" (56108), and the album, "**To Be Continued**" (Polydor 582 003) from 1966, although these were only credited to **Sony Childe**)

DERRY WILKIE & THE PRESSMEN

The **Pressmen** were originally formed as an instrumental/vocal group in the New Brighton area on the west side of the River Mersey in 1959 by **Dave Anthony Roberts** (voc/g), **Ritchie Prescott** (g), **Bob Pears** (bg) and **Nick Arnott** (dr).

Shortly after its formation, the group disbanded but was immediately re-formed by the original members, **Dave Roberts**, who now played saxophone, **Ritchie Prescott** and **Bob Pears.** Their new drummer, **Tommy Bennett**, had previously played with **Dave Roberts** in the **Casuals** and, after that, he was a member of the **Topspots**, as well as the follow-on band, **Dee & the Dynamites**. A little later, **Phil Kenzie** was added to the line-up as a second saxophonist.

Girl singer, **'Mickey' Rooney,** of the **Vernon's Girls** sometimes appeared with the **Pressmen**, but she was never a steady member of the group.

In 1962, the coloured singer **Derek Davis**, who had adopted the stage name **Derry Wilkie**, teamed up with the band, who then changed its name to **Derry Wilkie & the Pressmen**.

The original Pressmen

Derry Wilkie had previously sung with **Derry & the Seniors** and the follow-on group, **Howie Casey & the Seniors.** After that, he was backed by **Geoff Stacey & the Wanderers** for a short time.

In 1963, **Derry Wilkie & the Pressmen** appeared in the following line-up:

Derry Wilkie	(voc)
Ritchie Prescott	(g)
Bob Pears	(bg)
Dave Roberts	(sax)
Phil Kenzie	(sax)
Tommy Bennett	(dr)

With two sax players the group was able to produce a completely different sound to most of the other Merseybeat bands. This can best be heard in the song, "Hallelujah, I Love Her So", by **Derry Wilkie & the Pressmen** which was featured on the Oriole sampler, 'This Is Merseybeat' Vol. 1, in 1963. This Soul influenced song was one of the outstanding tracks on that legendary **John Schroeder** produced album, but it did not help the group obtain a recording contract.

In December 1963, **Derry Wilkie & the Pressmen** were voted No. 20 in the popularity poll of the music newspaper, 'Mersey Beat' - undoubtedly a big success. In addition, the group also won a big Beat contest in that same year and the prize was a recording contract with Decca.

Derry Wilkie & the Pressmen went down to London and made some test recordings. Among others, the **Isley Brothers** classic, "Twist And Shout", was recorded which, a little later, became an international success for **Brian Poole & the Tremeloes** (on Decca!!!), while the version by **Derry Wilkie & the Pressmen** remained unreleased.

Tommy Bennett left the group in early 1964. He had a short spell with **Johnny Autumn & the Fall-Guys** and later joined the **Pathfinders**. His replacement was none other than **Aynsley Dunbar**, who came from the **Allan De Aldo Quintet** and, before that, he had played with the **Merseysippi Jazz Band**.

Because no record was released and a planned Germany tour was cancelled, **Derry Wilkie** and **Phil Kenzie** split from the group and formed **Derry Wilkie & the Others** - another story in this book. **Ritchie Prescott** also left the **Pressmen**. A single new member, **Dave Carden** (voc/g), was then added to the **Pressmen** line-up. He had formerly played with the **Five Stars, Gus & the Thundercaps, Gus Travis & the Midnighters** and **Freddie Starr & the Midnighters**.

When **Faron's Flamingos** were offered a Germany tour shortly after they had split up, the offer was passed on to the **Pressmen**, who adopted the **Flamingoes** name (with an 'e') and went in their place. In Germany, they were signed to Dt. Vogue and recorded the single, "Glücklich Wie Noch Nie", which was the German version of the **Beatles** song, "I'll Get You".

Although this **Flamingoes** single is a desired collectors' item nowadays, it flopped in the Sixties.

The **Flamingoes** then recorded a very poorly produced album with coloured singer, **Tony Cavanaugh,** for the German 'Somerset' label under the name, **Tony Cavanaugh & the Liverpool Triumphs.** They then returned to Liverpool, where they amalgamated with singer, **Freddie Starr,** under the name of **Freddie Starr & the Starr Boys**— sometimes, also appearing as **Freddie Starr & the Flamingoes**.

For the continuation of this story, please see the story of **Freddie Starr & the Starr Boys**.

But this was not the end of the **Pressmen** story, because the former drummer, **Tommy Bennett,** separated from the **Pathfinders** at the end of 1964 and formed the **New Pressmen** together with **Howard Morris** (g), **Willie van Geffen** (voc/g) and **Adrian Flowerday** (bg).

Howard Morris was a former member of **Rip Van Winkle & the Rip-It-Ups**, while **Willie van Geffen** had formerly played with the **Alley Cats, Rhythm Amalgamated** and the **Outcasts**.

Adrian Flowerday had previously played with **Dave & the Rave-Ons**, and also with **Steve Day & the Kinsmen**. For a short time, the **New Pressmen** were quite successful on the scene but then disappeared without ever having released a record.

Howard Morris joined the **Chuckles** and **Tommy Bennett** became a member of the **Three Dees**.

In the early Nineties, **Tommy Bennett** and founding member, **Ritchie Prescott,** re-formed the **Pressmen,** but this band only played at 'MerseyCats' events and broke up again quite soon afterwards.

Tommy Bennett then formed the **Dees,** together with bass guitarist, **Mike Rudzinsky,** who, in the Sixties, had played with the **Avengers** and **Johnny Kidd & the Pirates** - amongst others.

Ritchie Prescott became a member of **Karl Terry & the Cruisers**, with whom he also toured Germany and, in 1994, they recorded a great Rock 'n' Roll album over there. After that, he joined the **Juke Box Eddies** where he met up again with original **Pressmen** drummer, **Nick Arnott**, who today plays with a Soul group called **Nighttrain**. **Ritchie Prescott** then returned to **Karl Terry & the Cruisers** for a short time, but then he quit the group-scene.

Discography :

Hallelujah, I Love Her So	on 'This Is Merseybeat' Vol. 1	UK- Oriole PS 40047 / 1963

Derry Wilkie & the Pressmen also won a recording contract with Decca in 1963 and recorded some songs for that label, of which only "**Twist And Shout**" is known, but none of them were ever released.

For more record releases by the group as the **Starr Boys** and the **Flamingoes,** please see the story of **Freddie Starr & the Starr Boys**.

THE YOUNG ONES

This group was formed in Liverpool under the name of **Danny Royl & the Strollers** in 1961.

One year later, the band changed their name to **The Sensations** and, then again, to **The Young Ones**. In the original line-up, this group consisted of the following musicians:

Dave Wilcox	(voc)
Wilma York	(voc)
Ricky Coburn	(g)
Alan Moorhouse	(g)
George Varcas	(bg)
Tommy Kelly	(dr)

Dave Wilcox, whose real name is **David Christie** was, in fact, **Danny Royl** from the original group.

In 1962, the **Young Ones** won a Beat contest at Liverpool's 'Broadway' club, followed by **Faron's Flamingos** in second place. The prize for the winners was a record release and a TV appearance. So, in 1963, the **Young**

Ones released their first single with "Baby That's It" on the Decca label. This song, written by Liverpudlian **Jimmy Stevens**, was a classic Merseybeat number with a catchy melody, a really good drive and great vocals by **Dave Wilcox**, while the B-side, "How Do I Tell You", was a sentimental ballad about the permanent problem of how to say Goodbye. This was sung by **Wilma York**, who proved that she was also a good singer. It was one of the better Merseybeat records with two totally different and very interesting sides that sold quite well. But it did not make the charts, although it really had everything that was needed.

It is also interesting that, in the interim, the group had changed its name again to **Rikki Janson & the Q-Kats** and sometimes also appeared as **The Q-Kats with Wilma**, but had then changed it back to the **Young Ones** when the record was released.

This single was the first and only release by the **Young Ones** who almost disbanded in late 1963 when **Dave Wilcox** left to join the newly formed **Nocturns**, who became quite successful on the scene, secured a part in the **Lionel Bart** musical, 'Maggie May', and recorded for Decca. A little later, **Dave Wilcox** recorded the solo single, "Just Like Him", for CBS in 1966, but then disappeared from the scene.

Wilma York had also gone solo and she became one of the city's leading female singers but, in spite of this, did not release any more records.

Alan Moorhouse also left and disappeared from the scene. His replacement was **Rod Long**, a former member of **Gerry Bach & the Beethovens** and **Alby & the Sorrals**.

In 1964, **Tommy Kelly** left and joined **Earl Preston's Realms** and, after that, he was a member of the **Escorts** with whom he also toured in Germany. His replacement in the **Young Ones** was **Maurice Daniels**, another former member of **Alby & the Sorrals** who had also played a few gigs with **Denny Seyton & the Sabres** and **Danny Havoc & the Ventures**.

The Young Ones with Wilma York

At that time, the group changed their name to the **Coins** and, when **Rod Long** left, he was initially replaced by **Pete Corcoran** who came from the **Pilgrims**. But he did not stay for too long and then the lead-guitar was taken over by **John O'Reilly**.

This line-up of the **Coins** continued successfully to play the scene until 1966 at which time, **Ricky Coburn** emigrated to Australia and the group broke up. Only of **Maurice Daniels** it is known that he continued in the music-business and later became a member of **Gerry De Ville & the**

THE COINS

City Kings. After that, he played with cabaret-groups including **Total Sound**, **Patchwork Dream** and later with **Sandlewood.**

So, what is left of that really good group with the name **The Young Ones** is a great Beat single, worth looking out for!

Single discography :

Baby That's It / How Do I Tell You   UK- Decca F.11705 / 1963

Dave Wilcox – solo :

Just Like Him / If You Believe In Love   UK– CBS 202 090 / 1966

YOUNG ONES
Sole Management Doug Martin, Stuart Enterprises
Phone WAT 7554

"BABY THAT'S IT"
c/w "HOW DO I TELL YOU?"
released Friday, 23rd August

SOME OTHER MERSEYSIDE GROUPS

While we are almost at the end of this book, here is a list of an additional 100 Merseyside groups and their line-ups. However, only one line-up of each group is identified and changes in personnel have not been taken into account. None of these groups are featured elsewhere in this book.

Comparing this list to a similar list in the book, "The Sound With The Pound", there have been changes. Some groups have been omitted because their individual stories are featured in the follow-on book, "Some Other Guys", (ISBN 9781588502025 or ISBN 1588502023) and some additional groups have been included.

A

THE ADVALS

from Speke (1965)

Donald Stewart (voc)

John Harrison (lg/voc)

Phil Arons (rg)

Tony Porter (bg)

Barry Guy (dr)

THE ALPHAS

from Allerton (1964)

Paul McLean (lg/voc)

Robert Baillie (rg/voc)

Brian Eccles (bg)

Derek Burnham (sax)

David Wamp (dr)

THE AMBASSADORS

from Childwall (1962)

Deke Wade (voc)

Dave Dover (lg)

Dave Dickinson (rg)

Gene McCulloch (bg)

Stan Booth (dr)

THE ASTEROIDS

from Broadgreen (1963)

L to R: Keith Williams, Alan Hornby, Mike Cove & Tony Berry

Keith Williams (lg/voc)

Mike Cove (rg/voc)

Alan Hornby (bg)

Tony Berry (dr)

(until 1962 as **Danny & the Asteroids**)

B

THE BEAT CATS

from the Wirral - ? (1961)

Billy Hatton (voc)

Billy May (lg/voc)

Eddie Malley (rg)

Ken Robinson (bg)

Harry Hughes (dr)

THE BLACK JACKS

from West Derby (1960)

Ken Brown (voc/g)

Bill Barlow (g)

Chas Newby (bg)

Peter Best (dr)

THE BLACK VELVETS

from Waterloo (1962)

Kenny Rees (voc/bg)

Leo Edwards (voc/rg)

Maurice Loughlin (lg)

Gerry Winstanly (dr)

THE BLUE CHIPS

from Ormskirk (1964)

The Blue Chips

Arthur Hughes (voc/rg)

Jim Fox (lg/voc)

John Cheetham (bg/voc)

Lenny Chantry (org/p/voc)

Brian Anderton (dr)

BOBBY & THE BACHELORS

from West Kirby (1964)

Bobby Dalton (voc)

Mike Godwin

Mike Barrie

Ian Gordon

Pete Davies

PHIL BRADY & THE RANCHERS

(Country) from Liverpool (1964)

Phil Brady (voc/g)

Ray Owen (g)

Frank Peters (steel-g)

Tommy Bowness (bg)

Eddy Waff (dr)

C

THE CAVE DWELLERS

from Liverpool (1964)

Ray Hudson (voc)

Peter Anyon (lg)

John D. Procter (rg)

Brian Atkinson (bg)

Peter G. Penter (dr)

THE CAVERNERS

from Bromborough (1964)

Ken Smith (g)

Mark Farrell (g)

Steven Roberts (bg)

Colin Roberts (dr)

THE CHEQUERS

from Liverpool (1964)

Harry Emmett (g)

Tony Kendall (g)

Doug Woollie (bg)

Pete Hodge (dr)

THE CHESSMEN

from Litherland (1963)

Tony Christian (voc)

Barry Brooks (lg)

Roy Backhouse (rg)

Graham Dooley (bg)

Bob Ramsey (dr)

THE CITADELS

from Litherland (1964)

RICKY
LEAD GUITAR

JOHN
BASS & VOCAL

TONY
RHYTHM

JOHN
DRUMS

TONY
LEAD VOCAL

MANAGEMENT:
ROB MARSHALL
GREAT CROSBY 1765

THE CITADELS

ALSO
ENQUIRIES TO.
WATERLOO 5432

Anthony Mathieson (voc)

Ricky O'Neill (lg/voc)

Tony Sefton (rg)

John Jenkins (bg)

John Swift (dr)

THE CITROENS

from Liverpool (1964)

Willy Tomlinson (voc)

Bob Simpson

Charles Gorton

Arthur Torres

George Guile

COMBO SIX

from Wallasey (1964)

Kenny Smith (voc/lg)

Billy Burrows (bg/voc)

Allen 'Gaz' Gaskell (sax)

Allan Halliday (sax)

Bob Evans (dr)

THE COMMANCHEROS

from Speke (1963)

Billy Quirk (lg)

Patrick Horne (rg)

John Morley (bg)

Kenny Williams (dr)

THE CORDAYS

from Huyton (1964)

Gerry A. Downes (voc/g)

Peter Glasby (g)

Norman Bellis (bg)

James Hughes (sax)

Richard Sillitoe (dr)

THE CRACKSMEN

from Bootle (1964)

Steve Abernethy (voc/rg)

Jimmy Coleman (lg)

Andy Harris (bg/voc)

Terry Garvin (dr)

LEE CROMBIE & THE SUNDOWNERS

from Rock Ferry (1962)

Lee Crombie (voc)

Pete Goodall (g)

Gary Hughes (g)

Dave Calvely (bg)

Dave Crombie (dr)

THE CROUPIERS

from Liverpool (1963)

L to R: Vincent Thomas, Dennis Swale,
Arthur Hurst, Geoff Barrow & Bobby Roberts

Arthur Hurst (voc)

Vincent Thomas (g/voc)

Dennis Swale (g/voc)

Geoff Barrow (bg)

Bobby Roberts (dr)

D

THE DARK AGES

from Liverpool (1967 - ?)

Mersey Scene Promotions Present :

BEAT CITY '66

at THE GRAFTON, WEST DERBY ROAD
on THURSDAY 24th MARCH 1966

Starring . . . **The Realm** Hard Time Lovin' You Baby (CBS.)

**The Hideaways · The Dark Ages
The Defenders · The Excerts**

Introducing . **The Keez**   Compere . *Billy Butler*

Dancing 7.30 - 12.30   Admission 6/-   Bars 7.30 - Midnight

Kenny Gilmore (voc)

Charlie Newport (g/voc)

Stan Metcalfe (bg/voc)

Brian Gilmore (dr/voc)

DAVE & THE RAVE-ONS

from Wallasey (1963)

Harold Dickinson (g/voc)

Adrian Flowerday (bg/voc)

Dave Crosby (voc/dr)

EDDIE DEAN & THE ONLOOKERS

from Liverpool (1962)

Eddie Dean (voc)

Tony Randall (g)

Johnny Stephens (g)

Paul Murphy (bg)

William Brooks (dr)

MIKE DEE & THE DETOURS

from Southport (1963)

Mike Pierce (voc)

Dave Mason (g)

Ray Borsey (g)

Gary Barton (bg)

Ian Magee (dr)

THE DEERSTALKERS

from Liverpool (1964)

Peter Minnis (voc)

Mike Fletcher (lg)

John Martin (rg)

Al Stone (bg)

Dave Marcroft (dr)

THE DELACARDOS

from Toxteth (1962)

Peter John Day (voc/g)

Charles 'Cy' Richmond (bg/voc)

Neil Foster (sax)

Rodney Day (dr)

THE DEMOISELLES

from Liverpool (1964)

Sheila McGlory (voc/g)

Sheila Lewis (g/voc)

Susan Henderson (bg/voc)

Linda Turner (dr)

THE DEMONSTRATORS

from Litherland (1963)

John Almond

Alan Jones

Tony Cunningham

Brendon Jones

THE DETONATORS

from Stoneycroft (1963)

Dean Stacey (voc)

Eddie Murphy (g)

Doug Eaton (g/p)

Roger Eaton (bg)

John Morris (dr)

THE DIALS

from Liverpool (1966)

Jose (Joe) McLaughlin

Jose McLaughlin (voc/p/org)

Paul Booth (lg/voc)

Frank Comber (rg/voc)

Kevin Gerrard (bg)

Ronnie Swainbank (dr)

E

DAVE EAGER & THE BEAVERS

from Wrexham (1962)

Dave Eager (voc)

Roy McMahon (g)

Ron Nicholson (g)

Noddy Crewe (bg)

Jim Nobel (dr)

THE ELEKTRONS

from Huyton (1964)

Colin Bellingham (g/voc)

Syd Rimmer (bg/voc)

Alan Moss (dr/voc)

THE ELEMENTS

from Maghull (1964)

David E. Russel

Roger Asplin

Brian Clarke

William Wilson

F

THE FEDERAL FIVE

from St. Helens (1963)

Martin O'Brian (voc)

Phil Ganson (g)

Shirt Clayton (g)

Mike O'Brian (bg)

John Gwilliam (dr)

THE FONTANAS

from Kirkby (1963)

Pete Campbell (voc/g)

Les Coates (g)

Pete Dunn (bg/voc)

Colin Woodruff (dr)

THE FORTUNES

from Ormskirk (1964)

Dennis Pickering (voc)

Jim Fox (lg/voc)

Arthur Hughes (rg/voc)

Ken Renfry (bg)

Brian Anderton (dr)

G

THE G-MEN

from Liverpool (1962)

The G Men

John Dempsey (voc/rg)

Dave Watson (lg)

John Davis (bg)

Bob Newport (dr)

THE GALVANISERS

from Liverpool (1962)

Roy Morton (voc/rg)

Chris Wilson (lg)

Robert Packham (bg)

Derek Cumberledge (dr)

(formerly known as "**The Tigers**")

THE GEORGIANS

from Liverpool (1962)

Tim Dougdale (voc/g)

Lawrence Ashley (g)

Geoff Jones (bg/voc)

Roger Lewis (sax)

Mike Sloan (dr)

THE GHOST RIDERS

from Anfield (1964)

Howard Blackburn (lg/voc)

Pat Hughes (voc/rg)

Robert O'Hare (bg)

Brian McGarry (dr)

THE GIBSONS

from Liverpool (1963)

Ted Graham (voc)

Mike Kontzle (lg/voc)

Ray Fowlis (sax)

Jan Coyler (bg)

Colin ? (dr)

COUNT GRENVILLE & THE KRINKS

from Crewe (1963)

Grenville Lyons (voc/rg)

Keith Barber (lg/voc)

Christopher Dunn (bg)

David Nixon (dr)

H

THE HAWKS

from Huyton (1964)

David S. Masters

Ken Roberts

Jim Woodcock

Rick Malmsteen

HENRY'S HANDFUL

from Liverpool (1965)

Mike Hart (voc/sax/g)

Vinnie Ismael (lg)

Rob Eccles (bg)

Chris Hatfield (org)

Peter Taylor (dr)

THE HUSTLERS

from Tuebrook (1964)

John Yeatrohmo

Austin O'Dowd

Frank Norton

Ron Payne

I

THE INTERNS

from Wallasey (1964)

Charles Wood

Victor Rose

Andrew Wylie

Richard Bainbridge

THE INVADERS

from Liverpool (1963)

Dave Fowler (voc)

Kevin O'Brian (g)

John Kirwin (g)

Ronnie Woods (bg)

Mike Campbell (dr)

J

THE JAGUARS

from Birkenhead (1963)

Dave Scarratt (voc/bg)

Greg Murphy (g)

Alan Swindles (g)

Ken Hughes (dr)

JENNY & THE TALL BOYS

from the Wirral - ? (1963)

Jenny Ellison (voc)

John Ellison (g)

Ray Hughes (g)

Pete Byrom (bg)

Keith Murray (dr)

JOAN & THE DEMONS

from Bromborough /Birkenhead (1964)

Joan Woolton (voc)

Geoffrey Jones (g)

Dave Rushton (g)

Michael Daly (bg)

Paul Liddy (dr)

K

THE K-Ds

from Wallasey (1963)

Allen 'Gaz' Gaskell (lg/voc)

Harry Thomas (bg/voc)

Norman Smith (dr)

THE KOP

from Liverpool (1966)

Eddie Kennedy (voc)

Joey Youds (voc/harp)

Terry Cummins (lg)

Tommy ? (org/p)

John Brothers (bg)

Barry Robinson (dr)

L

THE LAVELLS

from Aintree (1964)

Mauro Meadows (voc)

Roy Jenkinson (lg)

Robert Tracey (rg)

Tommy Pauline (bg)

John Allen (dr)

THE LEGENDS

from Bootle (1960)

John Frankland (voc/rg)

John Gallagher (lg)

Edward McMonnies (bg)

Kenny Baker (dr)

M

THE MAJORITY PLUS

from Liverpool (1965)

John Howson (voc/rg)

Alan Artwood (lg/voc)

Colin Fitzgibbon (org)

Aaron Maher (bg)

Les O'Neill (dr)

JOHNNY MARLOWE & THE WHIP-CHORDS

from Kensington -? (1963)

Johnny Marlowe (voc)

Chris Scutt (g)

Bob Caddock (g)

Colin Owen (bg)

Mike Donald (dr)

THE MEMPHIS THREE

from Liverpool (1963)

The Memphis Three.

Brendon McCormack (g/voc)

John Bancroft (bg)

Gibson Kemp (dr)

THE MINITS

from Seacombe (1964)

HOLE IN THE FLOOR
OPENS FRIDAY 26th JUNE
featuring
THE MINITS
7-0 till 11-45 p.m.
106 BRIGHTON ST., SEACOMBE, WALLASEY

Trevor Thomas (voc)

Ian Heath (g)

John Duggan (g)

Barry Henry (bg)

Philip Dyer (dr)

THE MODES

from Liverpool (1963)

Derek Arfield (lg/voc)

Pete Beckett (rg/voc)

Stuart Lynch (bg)

Billy Geeleher (dr)

THE MOON ROCKERS

from Liverpool (1960)

John Kirkpatrick (lg)

Geoff Hughes (rg)

Kevin Kennedy (bass)

Bernie Rogers (dr)

THE MUSTANGS

from West Derby (1961)

Brian Carroll (voc)

Mike Frost (lg)

Brian Bennett (rg)

Russ Parry (bg)

Charlie Evans (dr)

N

THE NIGHTGUYS

from Seaforth (1964)

Tony Deller

Terence Maguire

Derek Devine

Brian Dodson

THE NIGHT WALKERS

from Wallasey (1964)

THE **TOWER**
BALLROOM
(New Brighton Tower Co.)
PRESENTS
MERSEY SOUNDS No.1
Friday, 17th July
7-30 to Midnight
THE NIGHTWALKERS
THE TRIBUTES
THE EXECUTIONERS
THE KIWIS
Compere: GERRY NORTON
Admission: 4/-

Dave Jones (voc/rg)

John Piggot (lg)

Billy Burrows(bg/voc)

Robert W. Dennis (dr)

O

THE OUTCASTS

from Birkenhead (1963)

Paul Christo (voc)

Willie van Geffen (g)

John Loy (g)

William Clare (bg)

John Clare (dr)

P

THE PRINCIPLES

from Southport -? (1963)

Brent Pickthall (voc)

Trevor Wilkinson (g)

Maurice Wallbridge (g)

Malcolm Peart (bg)

Pete Cockhill (dr)

R

THE REBELS

from Wallasey (1960)

Malcolm Kinnea (lg)

Victor Rose (rg)

Kenny Edwards (bg)

Brian Jones (sax)

Stuart Jones (dr)

RICK & THE DELMONTS

from Liverpool (1963)

Ricky Yates (voc)

John Hare (g)

Peter Howe (g)

Frank Howard (bg)

Barry Coonbe (dr)

RIKKI & THE RED STREAKS

from Waterloo (1961)

Pat 'Rikki' Clusky (voc)

Brendan McCormack (lg/voc)

Billy Loane (rg/voc)

Dave O'Neill (bg)

Geoff Bamford (dr)

THE RIVERMEN

from the Wirral (1961)

Tony Hughes (voc)

Harry Rimmer (lg)

Bob Atherton (rg)

Ray Whitehead (bg)

Mike Oldham (dr)

RORY & THE GLENEAGLES

from Wrexham (1963)

John 'Rory' Marubbi (voc)

David Johnston (g/voc)

Derick Pawis (g/voc)

Allan Bramwell (bg)

Fred Baker (dr)

S

THE SATANISTS

from Liverpool (1963)

Bill Rooney (voc/rg)

Garth Hennie (lg)

Alan Collins (bg)

Johnny Sze (dr)

SAVVA & THE DEMOCRATS

from Wallasey (1962)

SAVVA WITH THE DEMOCRATS

PETE GOODALL   ROC 6279

Savva Hercules (voc)

Ted Thompson (g/voc)

Roger Parrott (p)

Malcolm Shelbourne (bg)

Billy Robinson (dr)

THE SCHATZ

from Kirkby (1965)

Kevin McCormack (lg/voc)

Jack Gordon (rg)

John Cushion (bg)

Pete Ward (dr)

(until '64 as "**The Warriors**")

THE SET UP

from London /Liverpool (1963)

Stan Ferguson (voc/g)

Robbie Crawford (voc/bg)

Ron Southall (g)

Steve Davis (dr)

LEE SHONDELL & THE BOYS

from Liverpool (1963)

Lee Shondell (voc)

John Kirkpatrick (g)

Edward Houlihan (g)

Harry Scully (bg)

Les Watkinson (dr)

LEE SHONDELL & THE CAPITOLS

from Aigburth (1962)

Lee Shondell (voc)

Leonhard Kehoe (g)

John McGregor (g)

Jack Hughes (bg)

Martin Duncan (dr)

THE SINNERS

from Liverpool (1957)

Malcolm Smith (voc/perc)

George Watson (voc/g)

Cliff Roberts (g)Brian Hall (g)

Eddie Rowlands (t-bass)

THE SKELETONS

from Broadgreen (1964)

John Brownrigg (voc/rg)

Peter Hornby (bg/voc)

David Worthington (harp)

Jeffrey McCormick (lg)

Dennis McNeely (dr)

THE STEREOS

from Liverpool (1961)

Frank Evers (voc/rg)

Irvin Banks (lg/voc)

Kenny Harper (bg/voc)

Mike Needham (dr)

THE STORMERS

from Prescot -? (1964)

David Rimmer

Michael Gavis

Michael Carroll (g/voc)

Roman Bomba

THE STRETTONS

from Liverpool (1964)

Billy Pinto (voc)

Colin Lomas (g)

Freddie Hulse (g)

Eric Anderson (bg)

Jack Clarke (dr)

(formerly known as "**The Everests**")

THE SUBTERRANES

from Birkenhead (1964)

Bill Fernley (voc)

Chris Blades (g)

Ron Bird (g)

John Kenney (bg)

Nicki Huggins (dr)

T

THE TEENAGE REBELS

from the Wirral (1959)

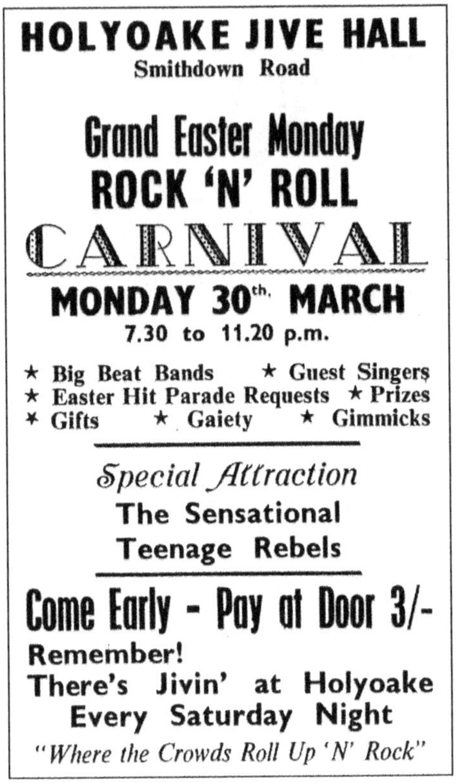

HOLYOAKE JIVE HALL
Smithdown Road

Grand Easter Monday
ROCK 'N' ROLL
CARNIVAL
MONDAY 30th MARCH
7.30 to 11.20 p.m.

★ Big Beat Bands   ★ Guest Singers
★ Easter Hit Parade Requests ★ Prizes
★ Gifts   ★ Gaiety   ★ Gimmicks

Special Attraction
The Sensational
Teenage Rebels

Come Early - Pay at Door 3/-
Remember!
There's Jivin' at Holyoake
Every Saturday Night
"Where the Crowds Roll Up 'N' Rock"

Vince Earl (voc/bg)

Pete Wright (lg)

Joey Aptor (rg)

Dave Pears (g)

John Cruice (dr)

THE TIYMS

from Wallasey (1964)

Pete Clarke (voc)

Allen 'Gaz' Gaskell (lg/voc)

Stan Ellison (rg)

Mike White (bg)

Mike Cooper (dr)

THE TOKENS

from Liverpool (1964)

Terry McAdam (voc/g)

Richard Quilliam (g)

Stan Davis (g)

Charlie King (bg)

Derek Aveton (dr)

THE TRAVELLERS

from Wallasey/Birkenhead (1962)

Bill Knaggs (lg)

Mike Rudzinsky (rg)

Tony McDonough (bg)

Ron Smith (dr)

THE TRIUMPHS

from Toxteth (1964)

Kenneth Davies

Raymond Pratt

Haydn Kirkwood

Ronald Wilson

Part-time also with

Raymond Wilson (voc)

Edward Ankrah (voc)

Bernie Wenton (voc)

THE TROLLS

from Old Swan (1963)

John Wishart (g/voc)

Paul Cronin (g)

Steve Watson (bg)

Jimmy Lunt (dr)

V

THE VAAVEROS

from Tuebrook (1964)

Neil Ford (lg/voc)

David Tubb

Mike Espie

David Ray Stinger

THE VABERS

from Liverpool (1964)

Jim McNaught (voc)

Steve Carey (g)

Bob Rowland (g)

Jim Carr (bg)

Stuart Henderson (dr)

THE VAQUEROS

from Old Swan (1964)

Eric Holding

Steve Lennett

James Atherton

Norman Downs

THE VERBS

from Kirkby (1965)

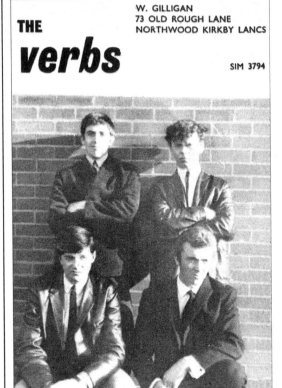

Bill Dunn (voc/g)

Tommy Perks (g)

Ron Duffy (bg)

Barney Curry (dr)

('til the end of '64 as "**The Four Dominators**")

THE VIGILANTES

(Country) from Liverpool (1962)

Ray Shaw (voc)

Arthur Quinn (g)

Mike Whitehead (g)

Alan Whitehead (bg)

Mike Donald (dr)

(from 1963 as **The Aristocrats**)

THE VOID

from Aintree (1965)

John Thompson (voc/lg)

Steve Faulkner (rg/voc)

David Scutts (bg)

Dave Crilley (dr)

W

THE WHIRLWINDS

from St. Helens (1964)

Glyn Hourihan

Scott Morris

Ray Stockton

John Roberts

RIP VAN WINKLE & THE RIP-IT-UPS

from Birkenhead (1964)

Jimmy 'Ginger' Geary (voc)

Keith Nixon (g)

Geoff Brown (g)

Howard Morris (bg)

Terry McCusker (dr)

Y

THE YOUNG ONES

from Wallasey (1963)

Allen Gaskell (g/voc)

Dennis Jeffcoate (g)

Alan Webster (g)

Les McFarlane (bg)

Kenny Webster (dr)

Z

THE ZEROS

from Kirkdale (1964)

John Parry

David Skinner

John Kitson

David Brown

Kenny Webster (dr)

FINALLY

This is a list of an additional 344 groups from Merseyside not previously named in this book. However, these groups were active in the Liverpool area from the late 1950's to the late 1960's. Some names may be confusing because there were also other local groups and groups from outside the area with identical names. However, this list includes exceptional (non-recording) bands from Merseyside. Stories for the groups marked with ** and line-ups for those marked with * can be found in the book, "Some Other Guys" ISBN 9781588502025 or ISBN 1588502023.

A big THANK YOU to them all for having been there at that time . . . .

A

The Abstracts**

The Abstracts *Tel.* Wat 5609

The Abstract Minds

The Accoustics

The Ads

The Admins

The Advocats

Ahab & his Lot

The Aintree Four

The Alamos*

The Albany Four

The Alibis*

The Alligators

Annette & the Riverdales

The Apaches

The Approachers*

Arrow & the Archers

The Astronaughts

The Atlantics

The Avalons

B

The Bachelor Boys

The Backbeats

The Banshees**

The Belltones

Bennie & the Jumping Beans

Bernadette & the Four Gents

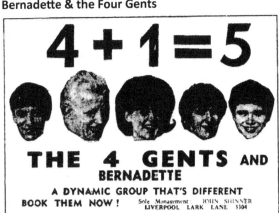

Bernie & the Tornados

J.B. Bishop & the Curates

The Black Diamonds*

The Blue Notes

The Blue Streaks

The Blues Giants

Bobby & the Be-Bops

Bobby & the Halers

The Boleros

The Boot Hill Billys

The Boys

The Breakdowns*

The Broadways

Bruce & the Spiders

The Buccaneers

The Buffaloes*

Johnny Burns & the Renegades

C

Cal's Combo

Carol & the Corvettes

Cash & the Cashmen

The Catalinas

The Cavaliers

The Cavels

The Cavemen*

The Censors

The Centurians

The Champions

The Chandels

The Chee Sydney Group

The Chequers

The Chicades

Chris & the Autocrats

The Cirques

The Clearways

The Climaks*

The Clive Lord Five

The Cobblestones

The Cockroaches

The Collegians

The Conquerors

The Conspiratiors

The Contenders

The Corvettes*

The Crackerjacks

The Mal Craig Trio

The Crestas

The Cross Rocks

D

The Daleks**

Danny & the Strollers

Eddie Danton & the Medics

The Dateliners

Dave & the Crusaders

The Daybreakers

The Dealers

Dean & the Capitols

The Decibels

Deek's Bohemians

The Defiants

The Dekkas

The Dell Stars

The Delta Combo

The Deltics

The Demons

Dene & the Citizens

The Deputies

The Detroits

Dean Devlin & the Dynamites

The Diablos*

The Doug Barry Sound

The Doug Barry Sound 1967

The Downbeats**

The Dresdens

The Drone Tones

The Druids

The Drumbeats*

The Dynachords

The Dynamics

The Dynamites

The Dynamos

E

The Earthlings

Eddie & the Phantoms

Eddie & the Razers

The El Diablos

The Elks

The Billy Ellis Trio

F

The Fabz

The Factotums

The Falcons

The FBI

The Feelgoods

The Fenton Weill Five

The Fire Flites

The Firebrands

The Flyaways

The Flyovers

The Forgers

The Four Quarters

The Fractions

The Steve Francis Four

Freddie & the Fireballs

Freddie & the Rousers

G

The Gay Tones

The Globetrotters

The Les Graham Five

The Group Five

H

The Hailers

The Hammers

Hank's Hoppers

The Harlequins

The Harpos

The Hellions

Roy Hepworth & the Hep Cats

The Heralds

The Hispanos

The Hoboes

The Hornets

The Hot Rocks

The Hungry I's*

Roy Hunter & the Falcons

The Huntsmen

I

The Illusions

The Impacts

The Informers

The Inner Circle

The Interludes

J

The Jacobeats**

Al James & the Tornados

Jay & the Juniors

The J-Beats

The Jensons*

The Jesters

Jimmy & the Teenbeats

The J.L.'s

Joey & the Kodaks

Johnny & the Semitones

The Jokers*

Kenny Jordan & the Rousers

K

The Kandies

The Karacters*

The Katz

The Keenbeats

Prince Khan & the Babes

The King Bee's

The Kingpins*

The Kingstrums

The Kiwis

The Klaxons

The Ko-Dels

The Kobras*

The Kommotions

The Konkers

The Kreeps

L

The Landslides

The Lawmen

The Lectrons

The Leemen

Liam & the White Brothers

The Liberators

The Lidos

The Lincolns

Count Linsey & the Skeletons

The Little Boys Blue

The Live Jive Five

The Lonesome Travellers

The Lonesome Travellers

M

The Madcaps

The Mad Monks

The Mailmen

The Majestics

The Mal Craig Trio

The Managers

A Great Sound . . .
A Great Group
* * * THE * * *
MANAGERS
DAVE – JIMMY – PHIL – DAVE
Telephone: WAT 3517

The Manhattans

The Marawacks

The Marlins

The Matchbox Five

MATCHBOX 5

The Medallions*

The Megatones

The Meteors

Johnny Mike & the Shades

Mike & the Creoles

Mike & the Explorers

The Minutes

The Mission Men

The Mistake

The Mohawks

Roy Molloy & the Teenbeats

The Monarchs

The Moonrakers

The Mosquitos

The Music Students

The Musicians

The Mustangs*

The Mysteries

The Mystics

N

The Chris Nava Combo

The Night Boppers

O

The 1-2-3-4-5

The Opals

P

The Page Boys

Paul & the Diamonds

The Pegasus Four

The Peppermint Twisters

Peter & the Sceptres

The Phantom Five

The Photons

The Plebs

The Plims

The Presidents

The Pretenders

The Problems

The Protests

The Prowlers**

The Pyramids*

Q

The Quiet Three

R

The Rainmakers

The Ramblers

The Ramrods

The Rawhides

The Reason Why

The Reasons

The Red Diamonds

The Red Mountain Boys

The Red River Boys

The Regents

The Rembrants

The Renicks**

Vince Reno & the Sabres

Ricky & the Vibrators

The Rigg*

Rita & the Renegades

The Robettes

The Rockerfellers

The Rockin' Clippers

Dave Roman & the Chariots

The Rontons

The Bob Ross Group

Roy & the Falcons

S

The Sad Saks

Remo Sand & the Spinning Tops

The Sandgrounders*

The Saracens

THE SARACENS

Satan & the Hellcats

Russ Saunders & the V-Tones

The Screaming Sculls

The Sentinals

The Sepias

The Shakespears

The Sheriffs

The Shimmy Shakers

The Shondells

THE SHONDELLS

The Silverstones

The Sinisters

The Skyliners

The Sleepwalkers

The Sneakers

Solomon's Mines**

The Soundsmen

The Spades

The Spectres

The Spekeasys*

The Spitfires

The Sputnicks

Wayne Stephens & the Vikings

Paul Stevens & the Emperors

Al Stone & the Earthquakes

The Sunnysides

The Swaydes

T

The Tagg

J. Taylor & the Top Spots

The Team-Mates

The T-Beats

The Teddybears

The Teentones

Terry & the Zodiacs

The Three Deuces

Three Dots & A Dash

The Thrillers

The Thundermen

The Tigers

The Tomboys

Tommy & the Teenbeats

Tony & the Black Shadows

Tony & the Quandros

Tony & the Triads

Tony & the Tuxedos

The Traders

The Trakkers

The Travelons

The Trebletones

The Tremas

The Tremolos

The Tremors

The Trend-Setts

The Tributes**

The Tudors*

Mel Turner & the Souvenirs

U

The Unicorns

The US-Limited

V

The Vaders

The Vanguards

The Varasounds*

The Vermont Quartet

The Vibrators*

The Vibros

The Viceroys

The Victors

The Vikings

Vikki & the Moonlighters

Vince & the Hot Rods

The Vocals

The Vocanics

W

The Wayfarers

The Waysiders

The Wild Ones

The Wranglers

The Wyverns

X

The X-L's

Y

Cole Young & the Graduates

Dale Young & the Seminoles

Z

The Zef Four

The Zeniths*

The Zwinging Coronets

. . . and any other group that was around and is not included in this list!

INDEX

CLAYTON SQUARES: 7, 16, 32, 47, 55, 71, 91, 92, **97-99**, 115, 146, 153, 213, 219, 221, 222, 252, 273, 275, 294, 340, 341, 362, 400, 418, 421, 435, 436, 457, 458, 461, 467, 495

CONCORDS: 100

CONNOISSEURS: 77, **101-103**, 153, (154), 187, 193, 225, 226, 227, 429, 435, 449, 486

CORDES: 104-107, 300, 370, 478

CROSSBEATS: 108-109

CRYIN' SHAMES: 70, 71, **110-113**, 147, 167, 220, 286, 295, 300, 317, 336, 346, 415, 460, 480

CURIOSITY SHOPPE: 72, 99, **114-115**, 275, 415, 418, 495

LEE CURTIS & THE ALL STARS: 14, 16, 41, 48, 49, 55, 82, **116-120**, 131, 139, 181, 185, 193, 214, 215, 226, 235, 252, 288, 290, 299, 306, 328, 338, 356, 360, 373, 378, 408, 425, 431, 436, 469, 475, 483

CYCLONES: 9, 50, **121-122**, 194, 301, 330, 353, 380, 399, 454, 457, 468, 469

RICK E. DARNE & THE TOPLINS: 123-124, 235

STEVE DAY & THE KINSMEN: 125-126, 325, 326, 349, (473), (506), 510

DEFENDERS: 127-130, 156, 163, 340, 416, 460, 465

DELMONT FOUR: 131-132, 139, 176, 236, 338, 360, 425, 427

DEL RENAS: 14, 19, 89, **133-135**, 157, 166, 315, 435

DENNISONS: 14, 32, (36), **136-138**

DETOURS: 33, 116, **139-141**, 275, 308, 316, 336, 458, 503

GERRY DE VILLE & THE CITY KINGS: 25, **142-144**, 165, 174, 336, 341, 513

DIMENSIONS: 18, 61, 70, 92, 112, 129, **145-147**, 185, 213, 280, (295), 313, 336, 365, 374, 460, 463, 464

DIONS: 47, 93, **148-151**, 166, 414, 496

VINCE EARL & THE TALISMEN: 18, 102, (103), **152-154**, (194), (212), (226), (301), (332), 341, (349), (378), (429), 435, 457, 495, (502)

EASYBEATS: 129, **155-157**, 167, 173, 174, 273, 295, 297, 305, 311, 313, 324, 340, 366, 399, 435, 480, 498

JASON EDDIE & THE CENTERMEN: 158-159, 457, 458, 469

LEE EDDIE & THE CHEVRONS: 160-161, 163, 409

LEE EDDIE FIVE: 82, 128, 160, **162-163**, 331

CLAY ELLIS & THE RAIDERS: 142, **164-165**, 169, 260, 276, (277), (417)

ESCORTS: 16, 55, 92, 112, 133, 148, 156, **166-168**, 181, 184, 210, 215, 243, 254, 270, 295, 300, 336, 415, 431, 439, 440, 449, 458, 460, 488, 496, 513

EXCELLES: 165, **169-172**, 260, 280, 323

EXCERTS: 33, 156, **173-174**, 503

EXCHECKERS: 14, 17, 131, **175-177**, 235, 312, 427, 428

EXECUTIONERS: 178-179

EYES: 55, 167, **180-182**, 184, 243, 269, 312, 359, 431, 449

FARON'S FLAMINGOS: 14, 15, 18, 22, 55, 67, (98), 117, (131), 146, 167, 180, **183-185**, 212, 214, 236, 243, 295, 300, (306), 312, 313, 328, 338, (342), (359), 360, 370, 374, 378, 399, 409, 426, 431, 434, 436, 449, 455, 458, 469, 483, 485, 510, 512

FOUR CLEFS: 26, 94, 102, 130, 178, **186-187**, 207, 370, 435

FOUR JUST MEN: 188-191, 348, 403, 409, 424

FOURMOST: 10, 13, 16, 41, 102, 103, 154, 185, **192-195**, 196, 197, 201, 215, 226, 252, (268), 301, 329, 332, 360, 378, 447, 482

GERRY & THE PACEMAKERS: 3, 4, 7, 10, 13, 16, 18, 58, (62), 67, 148, 175, (192), **196-202**, 227, 235, 240, 252, 260, (273), 298, 300, 320, 409, 483

RICKY GLEASON & THE TOPSPOTS: 129, **203-205**, 308, 309, 310, 332, (422), (449)

CHICK GRAHAM & THE COASTERS: 106, 187, **206-208**, 226, 263, 331, 345, 369, 455,

GRIFF PARRY FIVE: 81, 82, 92, **209-211**, 217, 269, 270, 290, 319, 329, 349, 411, 449, 450

GROUP ONE: 70, 145, 183, **212-213**, 313, 340, 345, 354, 376, 435, 457, 498, 502

GROUPS INC.: 18, 35, 88, 117, 132, 156, 166, 167, 193, **214-216**, 243, 252, 270, 315, 329, 360, 370, 377, 378, 399, 423, 426, 439, 454, 483
JOHNNY GUS SET: 55, 82, 210, **217-218**, 299

HIDEAWAYS: 18, 70, 98, 112, **219-221**, 273, 295, 300, 323, 380, 400, 406, 421
TERRY HINES SEXTET: 47, 91, 92, 97, 98, **222-223**, 291, (365), 422, 467, 503

IAN & THE ZODIACS: 3, 14, 16, 101, 102, 103, 119, 154, 180, 192, 193, 198, 208, **224-229**, 331, 397, 429, 447, 450
INCAS: 230-231

TONY JACKSON & THE VIBRATIONS: (155), **232-234**, (366), (389), 390, 392
JEANNIE & THE BIG GUYS: 131, 175, **235-237**, 378
DAVID JOHN & THE MOOD: 238-239, 343, (348), 425
JYNX: 240-241

KANSAS CITY FIVE: 18, 61, 62, 81, 88, 89, 132, 167, 180, 183, 214, **242-244**, 283, 290, 312, 313, 327, 359, 370, 377, 399, 423, 426, 439, 449, 458, 482, 483
SONNY KAYE & THE REDS: 245-247
KINETIC: 96, **248-250**, 421
KINSLEYS: 94, 97, 193, 215, **251-252**, 254, 270, 299, 328, 329, 360, 365, 368, 369, 378, 400, 441, 461, 502
KIRKBYS: 8, 89, 167, 168, 184, 251, **253-256**, 300, 301, 305, 336, 440, 458, 486
KLUBS: 257-259
KOOBAS: 13, 165, 197, **260-262**
BILLY J. KRAMER WITH THE DAKOTAS: 3, 10, 16, 41, (189), 206, (207), (208), (226), 245, **263-268**, 355
KREW: 55, 81, 167, 180, 210, 215, 252, **269-272**, 290, 319, 329, 365, 369, 441, 449, 481, 508
KRUZADS: 71, 97, 99, 115, 141, 155, 196, 220, 244, **273-275**, 297, 300, 345, 346, 380, 418, 495

MR. LEE & CO.: 276-279
LIVERBIRDS: 17, 145, 169, 180, **280-282**, 460, 463
LONG & THE SHORT: 88, **283-284**, 399

MARACCAS: 285-287
MARKFOUR: 288-289
BERYL MARSDEN: 3, 14, 16, 58, 92, 96, 99, 115, 168, 243, 248, 271, 275, **290-292**, 418, 421, 495
JACKI MARTIN: 76, **293**
MASTERMINDS: 16, 33, 156, 220, 273, **294-295**, 300, 346, 380, 411, 458
MASTERSOUNDS: 61, 156, 244, 273, **296-297**, 305, 311, 326, 355, 435, 508
MERSEYBEATS: 3, 10, 14, 15, 16, 17, 18, 19, 35, 51, 55, 56, 69, 70, 107, 112, 115, 118, 126, 166, 168, 194, 217, 220, 221, 226, 251, 252, 254, 255, 273, 276, 288, 289, 295, **298-303**, 319, 320, 332, 345, 367, 370, 380, 384, 425, 441, 458, 461, 464, 478
MERSEY FIVE: 17, 156, 254, 297, **304-306**, 311, 360, 401, 435, 450, 501, 506
MERSEY MONSTERS: 17, 129, 139, 204, **307-310**, 455, 492
MOJOS: 16, 18, 19, 70, 127, 147, 155, 156, 176, 180, 184, 212, 213, 243, 244, 284, 296, 305, **311-314**, 328, 355, 359, 374, 427, 435, 438, 446, 449, 455

NASHPOOL FOUR: 33, 133, 140, 157, **315-316**, 335, 344, 399, 421, 425, 435, 475, 489
NEWTOWNS: 317-318, 485, 496
NOCTURNS: 27, 92, 196, 209, 270, 298, **319-321**, 512
NOTIONS: 157, 169, **322-324**

PATHFINDERS: 82, 117, 125, 126, 179, 296, **325-327**, 373, 378, 488, 490, 506, 510

PAWNS: 18, 81, 117, 183, 193, 215, 251, 252, 269, 300. **328-329**, 360, 368, 373, 378, 449, 483

MARK PETERS & THE SILHOUETTES: (9), 14, 15, 88, 121, (147), 154, 162, 194, 204, 208, 226, 301, 307, **330-332**, 353, 374, (380), (399), 434, 438, 445, (454), 455, (457), (468), 492

PREMIERS: 24, **333-334**

EARL PRESTON'S REALMS: 14, 30, 33, 111, 140, 143, 146, 147, 167, 316, **335-337**, 339, 341, 364, 475, 477, 513

EARL PRESTON & THE T.T.s: 14, 92, 143, (153), (156), 335, 336, **338-342**, 359, (366), 374, (435), (436), (457), 458, 477, 479, (493)

PRESTONS: 238, 316, **343-344**, 425

PROFILES: 208, 273, 274, 294, 300, 331, **345-346**, 455

PUPPETS: 238, 239, 343, **347-348**

RAINCHECKS: 125, **349-351**, 473, 474, 506

RATS: 28, 29, 37, 331, **352-353**

REMO FOUR: 3, 16, 26, 212, 264, 265, 296, **354-358**, 376, 390, 441, 457, 508

RENEGADES: 18, 35, 67, 117, 131, 180, 193, 214, 243, 252, 290, 306, 312, 328, 338, **359-360**, 373, 378, 400, 449, 477, 483

RHYTHM & BLUES INC.: 55, 98, **361-363**, 441, 446

RICHMOND GROUP: 14, 30, 91, 222, 252, 270, **364-365**, 369, 414, 422

JOHNNY RINGO & THE COLTS: 47, (289), 301, 340, **366-367**, 478

ROADRUNNERS: 14, (26), (94), 97, 105, 106, 180, (186), 208, 210, (214), (242), 251, 252, 269, 300, 328, 335, 365, **368-371**, (377), 421, 439, 473, 489

CLIFF ROBERTS' ROCKERS: 9, 19, 65, 80, 116, 184, 185, 313, 328, 341, 359, **372-374**, 378, 438, 446, 450, 475

DALE ROBERTS & THE JAYWALKERS: 135, 162, 212, 243, 345, 354, **375-376**

EARL ROYCE & THE OLYMPICS: 3, 13, 82, 117, 153, 193, 197, 201, 214, 215, 236, 243, 252, 329, 360, 370, 373, **377-379**, 423, 476, 483

RUNAWAYS: 122, 220, 273, 295, **380-382**, 460

PHIL RYAN & THE CRESCENTS: 383-386

CHRIS SANDFORD & THE CORONETS: 387-388

SEARCHERS: 3, 4, 10, 14, 16, 18, 70, 92, 155, 167, 175, 186, 198, 207, 213, 221, 232, 233, 234, 268, (298), 354, 366, **389-398**, 408, 417, 507

SECRETS: 30, 33, 94, 97, 121, 131, 149, 156, 183, 219, 251, 288, 305, 360, **399-402**, 414, 416, 454, 455, 461, 490, 502

SEFTONS: 72, **403-405**

SELOFANE: 220, **406-407**, 446

DENNY SEYTON & THE SABRES: 3, 16, 18, 24, 116, (161), 185, 188, (295), 401, **408-413**, 436, 469, (477), 513

SIGNS (& TIMES): 30, (33), 47, 130, 149, (167), 365, (385), 401, **414-416**, (460), 490,

SOME PEOPLE: 417

SOUNDS PLUS ONE: 99, 115, 274, **418**, 495

SPORTSMEN: 38, **419-420**

ST. LOUIS CHECKS: 92, 96, 222, 248, 315, **421-422**

FREDDIE STARR & THE MIDNIGHTERS: 18, 28, 54, (61), 81, 82, (88), 90, 132, (139), (156), 166, 188, (214), (215), (219), 238, 242, (243), (306), 316, (325), (349), (357), (377), (385), 399, **423-425**, 426, 434, (441), (471), (472), (474), (506), 510,

FREDDIE STARR & THE STARR BOYS: 14, 81, 131, 132, 176, 242, 312, 399, 425, **426-428**, 510, 511

STEVE & THE SYNDICATE (THE BOBBY BELL ROCKERS): 9, 49, 61, 116, 183, (224), **429-431**, (447), 449

RORY STORM & THE HURRICANES: 2, 7, 9, 14, 22, 27, 28, 39, 41, 54, 57, 80, 82, 90, 99, 102, 117, 133, 146, 153, 157, 180, 184, 185, 187, 204, 306, 316, 330, 331, 341, 347, 373, 374, 378, 424, 425, **432-436**, 438, 439, 445, 447, 448, (450), 458, (474)

STRANGERS: 9, 198, 313, 330, 343, 374, 433, **437-438**, 445

SWINGING BLUE JEANS: 3, 7, 10, 14, 16, 18, 112, 167, 168, 214, 220, 242, 251, 254, 270, 271, 300, 357, 362, 370, 432, **439-444**, 456, 458, 481, 488

TABS: 143, 331, 362, 374, 406, 434, 436, 438, **445-446**

KING SIZE TAYLOR & THE DOMINOES: 8, 14, 16, (19), 27, 55, 63, 64, (77), 81, 92, (101), (103), (154), 180, 192, (204) 209, (210), 224, (225), (227), 270, 305, 306, 319, 329, (360), 374, 411, 429, 433, **447-453**, (486), 502

JOHNNY TEMPLER & THE HI-CATS: 61, (121), (156), 183, 208, (214), (219), (243), 308, 311, 331, 345, (399), 400, **454-455**, 502

KARL TERRY & THE CRUISERS: 3, (6), 9, 18, 33, 36, 48, 51, 61, 71, (91), 93, 98, 99, 112, 115, 121, 122, 141, 143, 145, 146, (153), 158, 159, 168, 213, 244, 248, 254, 255, 275, 290, 295, 300, 304, 338, 340, 341, 354, 374, 401, 416, 418, 430, 435, (436), (439), 441, 446, **456-459**, 469, 485, 489, 491, 495, 503, 511

THOUGHTS: 98, 111, 129, 146, 167, 217, 218, 280, 299, 302, 415, **460-462**, 464, 465

TIFFANY: 70, 111, 129, 145, 146, 147, 213, 280, 336, 415, 460, 462, **463-465**

T.L.'s BLUESICIANS: 91, 222, **466-467**, 503

TRAVELLERS: 9, 116, 121, 158, 408, 457, **468-469**

GUS TRAVIS & (various groups): 8, 28, 54, 82, 90, 125, 325, 349, 377, 423, 426, 434, **470-474**, 510

TRENDS: 82, 117, 316, 373, 378, **475-476**

CY TUCKER & THE FRIARS: (98), 107, 159, 220, 301, 336, 339, (341), (342), 367, 410, **477-479**, 486

TYME & MOTION: 156, **480-481**

UNDERTAKERS: 3, 9, 16, 18, 48, 67, 103, 117, 119, 183, 184, 185, 196, 203, 205, 213, 227, 242, 255, 276, 290, 318, 324, 327, 356, 359, 360, 377, 458, 478, **482-487**, 496

VALKYRIES: 105, 300, 316, 325, 327, 369, 401, 416, 457, 473, **488-491**

VIC & THE SPIDERMEN: 55, 307, 330, 339, **492-493**

VICTIMS: 494

WACKERS: 317, 485, **496-497**

WASHINGTON D.C.s: **498-500**

SONNY WEBB & THE CASCADES: 12, 14, 94, 192, 213, 304, 311, 448, 455, **501-505**

DERRY WILKIE & THE OTHERS: 81, 304, 350, 392, 426, **506-510**

DERRY WILKIE & THE PRESSMEN: 14, 81, 176, 312, 458, 506, 508, **509-511**

YOUNG ONES: 23, 24, (34), (134), 167, 319, 335, (416), (490), **512-513**

Publishers Note: For all those readers interested in statistics, the book includes a total of 607 groups that were active in Merseyside in the 1960's. At that time, the population of the City was approximately 650,000.

NOW THAT YOU HAVE READ THE BOOK ~ WOULD YOU LIKE TO HEAR THE MUSIC?

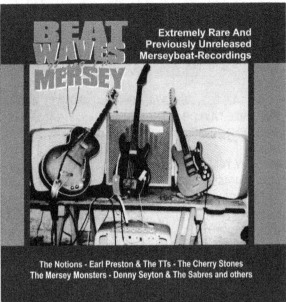

CD Insert (rear)   CD Insert (front)

A series of CD's that compliment the stories in this book. All original recordings from the 1960's, many of them never previously released.
Plus some live recordings from the famous Liverpool clubs, all digitally re-mastered.

For additional details, pricing and online purchasing information please visit our web-site:
www.velocepress.com/books/arts/

As a 'thank you' to everyone that purchased a copy of this book please enter the code MBWSOG in the coupon box in order to receive your special discounted pricing.

Here's just a sample of the groups (and the songs) that you will find on these CD's:

The Undertakers - Hold On I'm Coming; the Notions - Another Time; Gus Travis - My Babe; the Prowlers - I'm A King Bee; the Rebels - Little Queenie; the Black Knights - That Feeling; the Defenders - Mr. Soul; Alby & the Sorrals - Why; Johnny Ringo & the Colts - Mean Woman; Clay Ellis & the Raiders - Put The Blame On Me; J.J. & the Hi-Lites - Yes Tonight Josephine; Mike Mulloy & the Mountwoods - Parchment Farm; the Kirkbys - Friends And Relations; L.S.D. - Oh Carol; the Mersey Monsters - Wait A Minute; the Original All-Stars - Hide And Seek; Them Calderstones - Children And Flowers; the Profiles - I Can Tell; the Victims - I'd Never Find Another You; the Tabs - Don't You Hear Me Calling; Sounds Plus One - Girl Of My Dreams; the Runaways - Back Again

ALSO NUMBERS BY: Ricky Gleason & the Topspots; the Topspots; the Premiers; the Blackhawks; the Newtowns; a 1966 live-tape of the Kruzads; the Cordes; the Panthers; the Motifs; the Deans; two recordings of Perfumed Garden; the complete Connoisseurs recordings; a terrific live-recording of Ogi & the Flintstones; as well as Earl Preston & the TTs; Denny Seyton & the Sabres; the Clayton Squares; Cy Tucker; Almost Blues; Terry Hines Sextet; T.L.s Bluesicians

COMING SOON ~ THE EAGERLY AWAITED FOLLOW-UP TO 'BEAT WAVES 'CROSS THE MERSEY'

Featuring the complete stories of another 65 Merseyside groups of the 1960's.
NONE of these stories are included in "Beat Waves 'Cross The Mersey" - they are all 'new'.
Also includes an additional 104 line-ups ~ for a total of 169 groups!

So here we go again . . . ., it's completely unexpected that you are looking at an advertisement for my third Merseybeat book!

Once my first book, "The Sound With The Pound", was published, I began to receive communications from many of the musicians mentioned in the book that, for one reason or another, I had previously been unable to contact. Some of them had lost touch with their fellow group members and some no longer lived in Liverpool or even in the UK. These new contacts were able to provide me with additional information such that I felt a revised version of "The Sound With The Pound" was necessary. Ultimately, this resulted in the publication of a completely updated edition titled, "Beat Waves 'Cross The Mersey", which contains significant additions to my original publication.

The information I received through these new, direct contacts with the musicians, finally led me to make the decision to write this follow-up book. Leaving all those interesting stories and line-ups behind, or ignoring them because they were not included in "Beat Waves 'Cross The Mersey" would, in my opinion, have been a historical sin. And then all these wonderful photos, these alone were worth a book . . . .

All the groups featured were part of that incredible movement and all had their place in it and should not be forgotten! "Some Other Guys" was the best title I could think of for this book, as it hits the 'nail on the head' in various respects. From the point of view of my first book, the musicians and groups named are 'Some Other Guys' who helped to push the Merseysound out into the world.

Publication date: Autumn 2012 ~ ISBN 9781588502025 or ISBN 1588502023
For additional details, pricing and online purchasing information please visit our web-site:
www.velocepress.com/books/arts/

ANOTHER 'MERSEYBEAT' BOOK FROM: www.VelocePress.com

THIS BOOK MAY BE PURCHASED ONLINE AT www.velocepress.com/books/arts/ PAYMENT BY PAYPAL
AND SHIPPED DIRECTLY TO YOU, FROM OUR DISTRIBUTION CENTERS IN THE USA, UK & AUSTRALIA

Rear Cover   Front Cover

148 pages, 162 illustrations, size 8.5 x 11 inches. The 1960's were a time of change and uncertainty. In 1961 the Berlin wall was built, in 1962 the Cuban Missile Crisis erupted, in 1963 JFK was assassinated, and on February 7, 1964 the Beatles arrived in New York to be welcomed by 10,000 screaming fans and music, as the world knew it, would never be the same again.

While the Beatles are by far the most famous Liverpool group of the era, they did not create the 'Mersey Sound', it created them. Unfortunately, it's sad that a great era of musical history will only be documented for future generations by the multitude of books that have been written about them. Liverpool in the 60's was a wondrous place, it was alive with music and the sheer number of local musicians and the depth of the talent pool was mind numbing.

Depending on your method of research, you will find that there were between 750 to 950 Liverpool based groups performing at any one time during the early to mid 1960's. So here's a story of one of the not-so-famous groups that's part of that total. While their story will always be overshadowed by those that made the 'big time', it is an honest and down to earth tale and a fairly typical representation of the many hundreds of other groups that created the 'Mersey Sound' and the real Merseybeat era.

Colour Edition: ISBN 9781588501615 or 1588501612
Black & White Edition: ISBN 9781588501646 or ISBN 1588501647

MERSEY BEAT

The only official Mersey Beat site on the internet is:

www.mersey-beat.com

The only official Mersey Beat section on Facebook is

Mersey Beat

The only official Mersey Beat Twitter is:

Mersey Beat

You can contact Bill Harry via the Mersey Beat website or messages on Facebook

ADDITIONAL COPIES OF THIS BOOK (and other VelocePress books) MAY BE PURCHASED ONLINE AT

www.VelocePress.com

PAYMENT BY PayPal AND SHIPPED DIRECTLY TO YOU, FROM OUR DISTRIBUTION CENTERS IN THE USA, UK & AUSTRALIA

ALSO AVAILABLE THROUGH THE FOLLOWING UK, USA & AUSTRALIAN SUPPLIERS:

Available in the UK from:

Adlibris.com

Amazon.co.uk

Bertrams

Blackwell

Book Depository

Coutts

Gardners

Mallory International

Paperback Shop

Eden Interactive Ltd.

Aphrohead

I.B.S – STL U.K

Available in the USA from:

Ingram

Amazon.com

Baker & Taylor

Barnes & Noble

NACSCORP

Espresso Book Machine

Available in Australia from:

TheNile.com.au

RainbowBooks.com.au

DA Information Services

ALS Library Services

Dennis Jones & Associates

Emporium Books Online

James Bennett

PeterPal.com.au

If for any reason you are experiencing difficulty in purchasing a copy of this book, please contact us by email at: info@VelocePress.com and we will be happy to assist you.

© 2012 Veloce Enterprises Inc., San Antonio, TX 78230, USA

All rights reserved. This work may not be reproduced or transmitted in any form without the express written consent of the publisher.

Lightning Source UK Ltd.
Milton Keynes UK
UKOW07f0712231117

313214UK00008B/618/P

9 781588 502018